John Miers

On the Apocynaceae of South America

With some preliminary remarks on the whole family

John Miers

On the Apocynaceae of South America
With some preliminary remarks on the whole family

ISBN/EAN: 9783337315160

Printed in Europe, USA, Canada, Australia, Japan

Cover: Foto ©ninafisch / pixelio.de

More available books at **www.hansebooks.com**

ON

THE APOCYNACEÆ

OF

SOUTH AMERICA,

WITH SOME

PRELIMINARY REMARKS ON THE WHOLE FAMILY.

WITH THIRTY-FIVE PLATES, TO ILLUSTRATE THE STRUCTURE OF THE GENERA.

BY

JOHN MIERS, F.R.S., F.L.S.,

DIGNIT. ET COMMEND. ORD. IMPER. BRAS. ROSÆ, ACAD. CÆS. NAT. CUR. ET REG. SOC. BOT. RATISB, SOCIUS.

WILLIAMS AND NORGATE:
14 HENRIETTA STREET, COVENT GARDEN, LONDON,
AND
20 SOUTH FREDERICK STREET, EDINBURGH.
1878.

PRINTED BY TAYLOR AND FRANCIS,
RED LION COURT, FLEET STREET.

MEMOIR ON THE APOCYNACEÆ.

PRELIMINARY REMARKS.

During my residence in Brazil, now many years ago, I had numerous opportunities for studying many points of structure peculiar to this family, and of examining many plants in detail, intending at a future time to describe several Brazilian species.

This design, however, was superseded by the publication of Dr. Müller's admirable monograph in the 'Flora Brasiliensis,' in 1860. But as many curious facts relative to the organs of fertilization, and others concerning the structure of the seeds, were observed by me, which do not appear to have come under the cognizance of that botanist, I have been induced, at this late period, to take up the subject again, and to embody my observations in this volume.

The order, in the time of Jussieu, was little understood, when, in his 'Genera' (1789), he comprised in it all Asclepiadaceous plants. The celebrated Robert Brown, in 1811, first separated them into two well-characterized distinct families [*]; this memoir furnished the materials for Endlicher's enumeration of the genera (1838). But we cannot appreciate too highly the admirable monograph of this interesting family by Prof. A. De Candolle, in his 'Prodromus' (1844). We must bear in mind that the task of elaborating the features of all the species in full detail was then too vast; and we must regard the enumeration of the host of heterogeneous species under the heads of *Tabernæmontana* and *Echites* as an instalment of high value, as it furnished materials for work to be afterwards completed. Dr. Müller followed this example, in describing under the same heads a mass of Brazilian species; but he did little to enable us to distinguish one species from another.

In order to promote this object, it appears to me necessary to classify and subdivide the whole of them into uniform groups, each marked by peculiar and easily recognized characters. In aid of this design the present memoir is offered; but it is limited in its range.

[*] Mem. Wern. Soc. i. p. 12.

PRELIMINARY REMARKS.

As a preliminary step towards the proposed classification, the family may be divided into two principal sections, distinguished by the characters of the anthers. Thus we have:—1st, *Haplanthereæ*, where the anther-cells are simply adnate, without connective, or with a soft one scarcely longer than they. 2nd, *Symphyantheræ*, where the cells, usually much shorter, are collaterally agglutinated upon the face of a large horny connective, generally bifid at its base, and furnished at the apex with a soft pointed appendage; these anthers conniving in a cone, their apical appendages bend inwards, closing together by their margins, so as to form a complete covering over the stigmata, at the same time that the ten anther-cells, thus brought into juxtaposition, become placed opposite to as many nectariferous glands belonging to the *clavuncle*, and thus become agglutinated to them: we shall have occasion to refer again to this singular disposition.

The above plan evidently occurred to Prof. De Candolle in his arrangement of the family; but he did not follow it as a means of classification. Dr. Müller only adopted it to a partial extent. But there are other equally important points of structure, which serve to form the limits of the proposed subdivisions; among these are the direction of the convolution of the segments of the corolla, the relative position of the stamens, the differences in their form, the shape and the divisions of the disk, and especially the nature of the fruit and the development of the seeds. This latter much neglected feature is here employed as far as possible, because it ought to form an important element in every system of classification. It includes the situation of the hilum on the seed, and the direction of the embryo in regard to it. De Candolle and Müller rarely give any indication on this point; and Endlicher, usually precise, is equally silent about it; but it is here employed to the full extent that my own observations allow. In those cases where no information is recorded, analogy has been the guide until more certain data are observed.

In the second class of this family we find many points of extreme interest, in regard to structure and function, which have not received the attention they deserve, and which call for especial notice. Among these is the part here called the *clavuncle*, which is a fleshy cylindrical process, attached to the summit of the style, and which has generally been regarded as a part of the stigma; but as the two stigmata, placed upon its summit, are fully developed, this idea cannot be maintained: it must be regarded as a distinct indusiate process, adapted to a peculiar function. Upon the exterior surface of the clavuncle we find five or ten parallel longitudinal glands, exuding a nectariferous juice.

The singular juxtaposition of the anther-cells has been above alluded to—leaving a hollow space in the centre, closed at the summit by the *stegium* formed by the conniving apexes of the connectives, at the same time that the ten basal forks of the connectives, tending downwards, allow a free ingress from below into this hollow space. By the growth of the style the clavuncle is carried upwards, being guided into the cavity by the forks; but it cannot go further and break through the valves of the stegium, as it is stopped by the broad basal peltate indusium, which, acting as a buffer, prevents its progress beyond the precise point required, so that the nectariferous glands now stand opposite to, and in contact with the ten anther-cells. The glands begin to exude their juice at the same time that the anthers emit their grains of pollen; and these, mingling together, form a magma, soon charged with pollen-tubes, all pervading the central space and confined within it: this magma now flowing over the stigmata, the pollen-tubes penetrate their papillæ, and pass down the stigmatic channels of the style, eventually impinging upon the ovules; and thus the work of fertilization is effected without the aid, or even the possibility of insect agency. This mechanism, tending to the exact apposition of the several parts towards one another, and their appliance to functional purposes, appears so wonderful, and so very like the most ingenious design, that it cannot fail to excite our admiration.

There is a considerable degree of analogy in the development and fertilization of the *Apòcynaceæ* and *Asclepiadaceæ*, more so than is generally supposed. In the latter family the prevailing floral structure is different. The corolla is much smaller, its tube very short, its segments equilateral and expanded: within these segments is a corona of five, ten, or fifteen petaloid lobes, in one, two, or three series; but their use is not manifest. The five conspicuous stamens, alternate with the border segments of the corolla, are peculiar in their construction: they are fixed to the short tube of the corolla by broad filaments united into a short funnel, each continued into a free broad connective, and terminated by an expanded membrane, all connivent in the centre over the stigma, thus forming what may be called a *stegium*. Each connective bears inside two adnate anther-cells, sometimes divided into four; each cell consists of two distinct laminæ, the outer one (*exothecium*) being part of the soft connective, the inner one (*endothecium*) being separable, forming a polliniferous lobule of an oblong form, terminating at one end in a thread. Here we find a singular arrangement: the thread of one of the lobules of one anther is conjoined at its apex with the thread of one of the lobules of the adjacent anther, and geminately united to a small corpuscle (*retinaculum*) which is agglutinated to one of the angles of the clavuncle, leaving them generally pendulous, but sometimes erect. Each endothecium is thick in substance, and is pitted all over with numerous minute hexagonal recesses, severally containing a granule of pollen, according to the analyses of Bauer and Brown[*]. The style is short, and surmounted in most of the genera by a very large, flattened, peltate, pentagonal *clavuncle*, its angles being furnished with nectarial glands, somewhat as in the *Apocynaceæ*, exhibiting in the centre, at the summit, two distinctly developed stigmata, often very short, which are studded all over with the usual papillæ. The nectarial juice of the glands is now conveyed by the agency of capillary attraction along the threads of the lobules, and is diffused over their polliniferous surface; and under this stimulus the pollen granules expand into long tubes or boyaux, which spread in all directions, a sufficient number reaching and penetrating the papillæ of the stigmata, thence passing down the ordinary stigmatic channels to arrive at the ovules. As the stegium is contrived so that nothing can enter that hollow space, it follows that the work of fertilization (as in the *Apocynaceæ*) is here effected without the aid of insect agency.

The apparent similarity in the mode of suspension of the pollen-masses in *Orchidaceæ* has suggested an affinity between that family and *Asclepiadaceæ*; but such an approxi-

---

[*] Linn. Trans. xvi. p. 734, tab. 34. figs. 4–6, tab. 35. figs. 7–11.

mation is negatived by every other point of structure. There can be no doubt, however, that fertilization in the *Orchidaceæ* is really accomplished by the agency of insects. The correctness of the foregoing résumé, as to the structure and relative positions of the sexual parts of the flower in the *Asclepiadaceæ*, is well confirmed by the admirable analytical figures drawn by Rio Creux, under the auspices of Prof. De Candolle, in thirty-seven genera of the family: here the clavuncle is constant, generally peltate and pentagonal, sometimes club-shaped or subcylindrical; but in all cases the five angles of that process are glandiferous, exuding a peculiar juice: the development during growth appears to me to show that self-fertilization follows as a necessary consequence, without the aid of external agency.

On the other hand, we cannot pass over the different view entertained by the celebrated Robert Brown, who states unequivocally that, in all the *Asclepiadaceæ* " that have been hitherto examined, the absolute necessity for the assistance of insects is manifest "[*]; and in proof of this he " considered the evidence complete."

But neither in this memoir, nor in any other work of that celebrated botanist, as far as I can remember, is any evidence produced to show how this agency is employed, or why it is necessary; on the contrary, the phenomena so minutely described by him, showing how the pollen tubes are generated, how they force their way through zigzag obstacles (*l. c.* p. 725) till they reach the stigma, whence they pass down the stigmatic channels of the style (" mucous tubes ") until they reach the ovules, are all effected through self-agency and natural development, without any external influence.

An explanation may be offered in regard to the *coma* of the seeds. This term is here confined to that process at the apex of the seed, formed by the strophiolar enlargement of the testa around the micropyle, which bears a number of long erect hairs in several series: this peculiar process is found only in the *true Echiteæ* and in the *Asclepiadaceæ*. The term *coma* is excluded from those instances where it has been employed to denote the excurrent mass of hairs which emanate from the *surface* of the testa.

Returning to our subject, I may here remark that the numerous observations made by me in many former years, the careful analyses obtained in Brazil and since my return, the plants I collected there, still preserved, those in the herbarium of the British Museum, including many original types, the care taken in the analyses of these, have afforded useful results, novel in great measure, all here interpolated with the recorded descriptions of botanists, and all arranged in consecutive order. I have also been able to identify with specimens in our herbaria the thirty species figured by Velloz under *Tabernæmontana* and *Echites*. The evidence thus obtained, copious as it is, is not sufficient to form a complete monograph of all the South-American species. To my extreme regret, illness and other causes have prevented my examination of the rich materials in the herbarium of Kew; I have not even attempted to examine the plants of this family belonging to the Old World; so that much more is required to be done, to form a complete arrangement.

[*] Linn. Trans. xvi. p. 732.

Following the views before suggested, I proceed to offer, in the first place, the proposed classification of the entire family, based on the principles already explained. To this arrangement will be prefixed, in each tribe, a review of most of the South-American genera thus eliminated, noting the peculiar characters by which they are distinguished, and followed in each case by a careful enumeration of the several species and their synonyms: we thus dispose of the great mass of recorded species of hitherto doubtful or wrongly assigned position. Whenever I have had access to the specimen described, and have been able to analyze a flower, a complete enumeration of all its characters is given in regular and continuous sequence. These may seem to many unnecessarily long; but, in my estimation, no diagnosis can be too long when it is confined to a simple narrative of facts: it is by such a method alone that we can with confidence assign any plant to a particular group, and distinguish it from other cognate species. But in those instances where the plant described by others has not been seen, its diagnosis has been remodelled, by arranging its given features in the same order of sequence as in the former case, thus avoiding the disruptions usually effected by authors—such breaks making it more difficult to compare one species with another, and to decide upon their identity or difference.

In order to render the details of the genera more intelligible, and the differences between the several groups more apparent, I propose to illustrate by analytical drawings the leading characters of their floral or carpological structure.

DISTRIBUTION OF THE GENERA.

Class I. HAPLANTHEREÆ: stamens each with two anther-cells, parallel, adnate, or often dorsally attached to a soft connective.

A. Ovule and seed anatropous.

    Tribe 1. OPHIOXYLEÆ: fruit drupiform and indehiscent, either single or double; cells monospermous: seed without pulp, erect, with a basal hilum and inferior radicle, or suspended with a superior radicle. All albuminous.

Ophioxylon,	*Rauwolfia,*	*Vallesia,*	*Bicorona.*

B. Ovule and seed heterotropous, when the hilum is on the middle of one of the faces, equidistant from the radicular and cotyledonary extremities.

    Tribe 2. CARISSEÆ: fruit drupaceous, indehiscent, 2-locular, or 1-celled by abortion: seeds imbedded in pulp, peltate, subcompressed; embryo straight, in albumen, with a basal radicle. *Acokanthera, Ceratites,* and *Pomphidea* are placed here on account of their stamens, though their fruit is unknown.

Carissa,	*Ambellania,*	*Carpodinus,*	*Clitandra,*
Macoubea,	*Lacmellia,*	*Otopetalum,*	*Cupirana,*
Pacouria,	*Lycimnia,*	*Vahea,*	*Ceratites,*
Couma,	*Zschokkia,*	*Chilocarpus,*	*Pomphidea,*
Hancornia,	*Winchia,*	*Landolphia,*	*Acokanthera,*
Melodinus,			

    Tribe 3. WILLUGHBEIEÆ: fruit drupaceous, indehiscent, 1-2-celled; seeds compressed, imbedded in pulp; embryo straight, without albumen, with a very short radicle: thus differing from the preceding in the absence of albumen.

        Willughbeia.

    Tribe 4. THEVETIEÆ: 1 or 2 indehiscent drupes, 1- or 2-celled, cells or pseudo-cells monospermous: seeds without pulp, oval, fleshy, peltately affixed, exalbuminous; embryo with a short radicle.

Thevetia,	*Ochrosia,*	*Chætosus,*	*Kopsia,*
Tanghinia,	*Pseudochrosia,*	*Leuconotus,*	*Vinca.*
Cerbera,	*Neubergia,*		

    Tribe 5. HUNTERIEÆ: 1 to 5 oval dry indehiscent drupes, monospermous: seed compressed, without pulp, laterally attached by a central hilum; embryo in copious albumen, with a superior radicle.

Hunteria,	*Lepimia,*	*Noterium,*	*Pleiocarpa.*
Amblyocalyx,			

Tribe 6. ASPIDOSPERMEÆ: 2 follicles, rarely combined into a 2-locular fruit, or generally only 1 by abortion, oblong or semi-oblong, compressed or quite flat, subligneous or coriaceous, without pulp, dehiscing along the marginal ventral suture into two gaping semivalves conjoined along the dorsal margin, with a narrow placenta on the suture: seeds large, parallelly adjacent, extremely compressed, broadly winged all round a central embryoniferous scutcheon, which has a small hilum in its centre on the side averse from its corresponding valve; or the scutcheon is truncated at one end, broadly winged at the other, or exalate; each suspended at the hilum by a slender funicle, either vertically from the summit, or horizontally emanating from the lateral margin of the suture: embryo filling the scutcheon, in a thin tegminiform albumen, extremely compressed, with a terete radicle pointing to the summit or obliquely to the margin, with large, thin, foliaceous, oval cotyledons more or less deeply cordate.

Aspidosperma,   *Strempeliopsis,*   *Conopharyngia,*   *Plectaneia.*
Thyroma,

Tribe 7. ALLAMANDEÆ: a single orbicular subcompressed, dry capsule, unilocular, with a thin pericarp, densely and coarsely echinated, furnished within the peripherial margin with a placentiferous replum, and divisible into two hemispherical valves, smooth inside; seeds not very numerous, suspended from the replum in two single series by filiform funicles; testa oval, with a broad thick callous margin (instead of a wing) surrounding a flat embryoniferous scutcheon, in the middle of which, on one face, is a central hilum, from which it is suspended as in *Aspidosperma*: embryo in thin tegminiform albumen, with a superior terete radicle and oval foliaceous cotyledons.

Allamanda.

Tribe 8. PLUMERIEÆ: 2 large, divaricated, thick, linear-oblong follicles, opening along their ventral suture, which expands internally into 2 flat septiform placentæ: seeds many, subcompressed, furnished below with a lacerated wing, and affixed peltately and imbricatively upon each semiseptum: embryo in corneous albumen, with foliaceous cotyledons and an inferior radicle.

Plumeria,   *Cameraria.*

Tribe 9. ALYXIEÆ: 2 lomentaceous flat indehiscent follicles, transversely articulated into several dry, monospermous cells, with a longitudinal placenta projecting along one of the internal faces, round which the seeds are longitudinally conduplicated, and peltately affixed by a central hilum on the ventral face: embryo in corneous albumen, with oval or oblong foliaceous cotyledons, and superior (or inferior?) radicle.

Alyxia,   *Condylocarpon.*

Tribe 10. CRASPIDOSPERMEÆ: an elongated subcompressed, 2-locular capsule, resolvable into 2 follicles by the splitting of its bilamellar dissepiment, whose edges are inflected at the axis, and there placentiform, bearing many imbricated seeds peltately attached by a central hilum on one face, oblong, much compressed, covered all over by numerous long hairs or scales, often extending far beyond the apex or beyond the margins, or sometimes lacerately winged: embryo in albumen, with a superior radicle.

Craspidospermum,   *Manothrix,*   *Tayotum,*   *Rheitrophyllum.*

CLASS II. SYMPHYANTHEREÆ: stamens connivent, each with 2 parallel anther-cells introrsely fixed upon a much longer horny connective, usually membranaceous or cuspidate at the apex, and terminating below in 2 longer or shorter forks, the pollen-cells adhering to the clavuncle of the style, all thus held together in a cone.

Tribe 11. TABERNÆMONTANEÆ: 2 follicles, ovoid or oblong, often pointed, dehiscing along their ventral suture, whose introflexed margins are seminiferous: pericarp thick, fleshy or coriaceous: seeds many, attached or suspended each by a more or less elongated fleshy funicle resembling pulp; seeds ovate, dorsally convex and striated, channelled on the ventral face, with a callous hilum in the middle, and there affixed to near the end of the funicle, the other end of which is suspended from the suture; testa coriaceous: embryo heterotropous, in corneous albumen, with foliaceous cotyledons and a superior terete radicle.

Peschiera,	Anacampta,	Stemmadenia,	Rejoua,
Bonafousia,	Rhigospira,	Merizadenia,	Orchipeda,
Tabernæmontana,	Phrissocarpus,	Anartia,	Voacanga.
Taberna,	Codonemma,	Geissospermum,	

Tribe 12. MALOUETIEÆ: 2 follicles, linear, oblong, or terete, dehiscing along their ventral suture, the margins of which are thickened introrsely into a solid resilient placenta, seminigerous on both sides: seeds many, compressed or cylindrical, oblong, imbricated, sub-winged at the extremities with the lateral margins incurved, peltately affixed by a median hilum: embryo heterotropous, linear or oblong, in thin albumen, with a superior radicle: seeds quite glabrous.

Malouetia,	Amsonia,	Hostmannia,	Blaberopus,
Thyrsanthus,	Rhazya,	Ellertonia,	Dissuraspermum.
Gonioma,	Lepimia,	Alstonia,	

C. Seeds anatropous without an apical coma.

Tribe 13. ROBBIEÆ: 2 long follicles dehiscing along their ventral suture, the margins of which expand internally into 2 septiform membranaceous placentas bearing many imbricated seeds, which are oblong, compressed, suspended from the ventral face, marked by a longitudinal median hilum; generally clothed with many long, soft hairs, some extending far beyond the summit, which is often prolonged into a slender rostrum, sometimes very long and covered plumosely with many fine setaceous hairs, often mistaken for a coma: embryo in thin albumen, with a superior radicle.

Robbia,	Chariomma,	Rhabdadenia,	Urechites,
Elytropus,	Adenium,	Laubertia,	Epigynum.
Skytanthus,	Eriadenia,		

Tribe 14. ODONTADENIEÆ: 2 elongated follicles (or 1 by abortion) dehiscing along their ventral suture, the margins of which are invariably expanded into 2 broad septiform placentæ studded extrorsely with numerous nodules in longitudinal series, each supporting a seed: seed long, terete, erect, narrow at its two extremities, everywhere bare; embryo terete, in albumen, with a basal radicle.

Odontadenia.

D. Seeds anatropous with an apical coma.

CLASS III. ECHITEÆ: seeds linear oblong compressed or terete, often with an elongated rostrum terminated by the micropyle, which is surrounded by a cup-shaped ring, bearing a crown of 1 or 2 series of long hairs, usually called a COMA.

Tribe 15. MACROSIPHONIEÆ: 2 very long subturulose follicles, dehiscing along the ventral suture, the narrow margins of which are inflected and seminiferous: seeds linear oblong compressed, with an apical coma. Low erect, or prostrate plants, with a few axillary handsome flowers, having an extremely long narrow tube with a broad rotate border.

Macrosiphonia.

Tribe 16. STIPECOMEÆ: 2 follicles with very thick pericarp, sometimes very long, rugous or verrucose, dehiscing along the ventral suture, either with 2 placentas conjoined by a keel attached to the suture and then detaching itself, or else narrower remaining separately attached to the suture: seeds elongated, terete, often with a long rostrum, suspended by a longer or shorter funicle, with an expanded apical coma: embryo in albumen, with a superior radicle.

Stipecoma,	*Rhynchodia,*	*Roupellia,*	*Retinocladus,*
Chonemorpha,	*Strophyanthus,*	*Rhodocalyx,*	*Haplophytum.*

Tribe 17. WRIGHTIEÆ: an oblong 2-celled capsule, splitting septicidally through a thick bilamellar dissepiment (becoming like 2 follicles), each cell gaping in the line of the axis, its introflected margins being seminigerous: seeds inverted, the coma pointing downwards: embryo without albumen, the cotyledons convoluted.

Wrightia,   *Kicksia.*

Tribe 18. PRESTONIEÆ: an oblong 2-celled capsule, splitting septicidally, as in the preceding tribe, the sutural margins being inflected, subseptiform and seminigerous: seeds many, imbricated, oblong, furnished at the apex with a long coma, near which they are suspended; the radicle of the embryo points to the coma.

Prestonia,	*Aptotheca,*	*Baifouria,*	*Aganosma,*
Nerium,	*Rhaptocarpus,*	*Lyonsia,*	*Heligme.*
Parsonsia,	*Beaumontia,*	*Villaris,*	

Tribe 19. DIPLADENIEÆ: 2 long terete follicles dehiscing along the ventral suture, which is inflected into 2 parallel placentæ, bearing many oblong seeds suspended from a point near the long apical silky coma: embryo in albumen, with a superior radicle. The chief peculiarity consists in a disk of 2 flat opposite lobes alternating with the ovaries.

Dipladenia,	*Homaladenia,*	*Prestoniopsis,*	*Carruthersia.*
Micradenia,			

Tribe 20. PROSECHITEÆ: 2 oblong or terete follicles, dehiscing along the ventral suture, which is inflected into 2 parallel or 1 combined placenta, bearing many sublinear seeds suspended from a point where the longitudinal raphe terminates, and which are crowned with a long silky coma: embryo in albumen, with a superior radicle: disk urceolate, entire, or more often partly cleft into 5 or 10 lobes.

Flowers often large and subcampanulate with broad segments; rarely much smaller, thus approaching those of the following tribe: sepals sometimes large, generally imbricated.

Anisolobus,	*Mandevilla,*	*Echites,*	*Secondatia,*
Angadenia,	*Amblyanthera,*	*Temnadenia,*	*Haplophytum.*
Perictenia,	*Mascarenhasia,*	*Mitozus,*	

Tribe 21. MESECHITEÆ: 2 long, terete or torulose follicles, dehiscing along the ventral suture, the inflected margins of which are seminiferous. Seeds many, crowded, linear or fusiform, with an apical coma, suspended as in the preceding tribe.

Corolla small, or of moderate size, with a short tube, and rotate segments simply convoluted: stamens included, or often more or less exserted: disk rarely obsolete, or very short and crenulated, or generally consisting of 5 erect, more or less free, fleshy lobes.

Mesechites,	*Isonema,*	*Holarhena,*	*Ichnocarpus,*
Anechites,	*Laseguea,*	*Alana,*	*Anodendron,*
Exothostemon,	*Hæmadictyon,*	*Motandra,*	*Cleghornia,*
Thenardia,	*Cycladenia,*	*Pachypodium,*	*Ecsydanthera,*
Forsteronia,	*Heterothrix,*	*Baissæa,*	*Micrechites,*
Zygodia,	*Oncinotis,*	*Rhynchodia,*	*Parameria,*
Pottsia,	*Apocynum,*	*Trachelospermum,*	*Pycnobotrys.*
Alafia,	*Urceola (Chavanesia),*	*Aganosma,*	

ON SOUTH-AMERICAN APOCYNACEÆ.

MACOUBEA.

This genus of Aublet, established upon a tall tree in Guiana, has been placed by most botanists in *Clusiaceæ*, though Cambassèdes expressed a contrary opinion. Its floral structure is unknown; but in its other characters it appears to belong to the *Apocynaceæ*, because all parts of the plant yield a lactescent juice: its leaves are opposite, with straight divergent nerves arcuately conjoined near the margin, and upon petioles somewhat embracing the branch. The fruit, supported upon a short pedicel, is drupaceous, globular, as large as an orange, much resembles that of *Cupirana*, borne upon the persistent calyx; it is indehiscent, with a rough, brown, thick pericarp, apparently unilocular, but only by abortion, as Jussieu observed, for the dissepiment of the ovary is here thrust on one side: it contains several oblong curving seeds, with a hilum in the middle of a ventral furrow; they are covered by a pulpy covering, which when dry is thick and spongy; each contains, within albumen, an embryo with two fleshy cotyledons and a small radicle. These characters show a close approach to *Ambellania*; and Aublet must have been aware of this affinity, as he figures the two genera in juxtaposition. Only one species is known, and that imperfectly. The following character is partly formed after the examination of Aublet's typical plant, now in the herbarium of the British Museum.

1. MACOUBEA GUIANENSIS, Aubl. Pl. Guian. ii. suppl. p. 18, tab. 378; Juss. Gen. p. 257; Juss. Ann. Mus. xx. p. 466; Cambass. Mém. Mus. xvi. p. 396; DC. Prodr. i. 364; Benth. & Hook. Gen. i. 169: arbor lactescens, foliis oppositis, ellipticis, utrinque subacutis, integris, glaberrimis, supra glaucoviridibus, nervis paullo divergentibus arcuatim nexis, reticulatis; petiolis semiteretibus, in nodum transversim fere junctis, limbo 8plo brevioribus: racemis oppositis, terminalibus, petiolo fere duplo longioribus, crebre plurifloris, floribus brevissime pedicellatis; sepalis minoribus, rotundatis, convexis, imo gibbosis, et in cupulam brevem coalitis, carnosis, valde imbricatis: pedunculo fructifero brevi; drupa majuscula, subsphærica subcompressa, vel obsolete trisulcata, punctis griseis notata, abortu 1-loculari; seminibus plurimis, obtuse oblongis, ad raphen longitudinaliter sulcatis, in carne fungosa nidulantibus; embryone intra albumen, oblongo, cotyledonibus 2, plano-convexis, radicula minima nexis. In Guiana: *v. pl. s. in herb. Mus. Brit.* Cayenne, in sylvis (Aublet); *fruct. non vidi.*

A tree 40 feet high, with a trunk 18 in. in diameter; its hard wood, of a greenish yellow colour, emits a fetid odour, all parts of the plant yielding a lactescent juice. The nodes of its branches are 1–2 in. apart; the leaves are 4 in. long, 2 in. broad, on petioles ¼ in. long, conjoined across the node. The fruit is suspended by a pedicel 2 lines long, is about 3 in. in diameter, the pericarp being hard and 1 line thick; the seeds are ¾ in. long, ¼ in. broad, slightly curved and sulcated along one side, by the middle of which they seem to be attached.

HANCORNIA.

The description of the fruit and seeds of this genus given, in a few words, by Endlicher, DeCandolle, and Müller is copied from that of Gomez; but it is incomplete. Aware of this, I lately procured from Pernambuco several fruits preserved in spirit; and I now give the results of their examination. The globular epicarp is a thin coriaceous skin, covering a paler yellowish fleshy mass, which exudes a milky juice, is sweet and of a pleasant flavour: it contains several white seeds somewhat sparsely imbedded in it, which are oval, compressed, consisting only of an albumen and enclosed embryo, the testa not having been noticed by any previous observer; this, however, exists, appearing like a smooth hollow cyst, in which the albuminous body reposes; this albumen shows on the ventral side, a little below the summit, a hollow with a mamillary point which has been mistaken for the hilum; but it is only the end of the radicle, which almost protrudes. The testa or cyst is of an orange colour, is covered externally with numerous papillose scales, between which the fleshy matter is insinuated, and thus holds it so fast that it is impossible to extricate it. Intermixed with the fertile seeds we find in the soft mass many sterile ones, where the nature of the testa is clearly seen; these are free from the mass, or at least easily separated. This is an empty sac, compressed, showing the true hilum in the centre of one face, all the rest of the surface being papillose as abovementioned.

Müller has united the different species as mere varieties of a single one; but I make out three distinct species:—1. HANCORNIA SPECIOSA, Gomez; well figured by Müller in his pl. viii. fig. 3; it is the *Ribeira sorbilis* of Arruda (in Cent. Pl. Pernam.), and flourishes in the sertãos or flat arid plains in the province of Pernambuco: its leaves are smaller, oblong, narrowing to the summit, quite glabrous, on a slender petiole ¼ their length: the peduncle of the inflorescence is 3 lines long, bears 2 or 3 flowers on pedicels 6 lines long, each flower 1½ in. long. 2. H. PUBESCENS, Nees & Mart., is found on the high tablelands in the province of Minas Geraës, is arborescent, with leaves covered beneath with fine ferruginous tomentum, which in my specimen (Claussen, 222) are 2-2¼ in. long, 10-12 lines broad, more gradually acute at both extremities than in the preceding species, and on a pubescent petiole 3 lines long; they differ especially in having few, remote, ascending nerves: its corymbose flowers are larger, with a shorter tube, and are more numerous. 3. H. GARDNERI is a tree about 12 feet high, from the province of Goyaz, has much larger and broader leaves, rounded towards the summit, where they are suddenly narrowed into a short linear acumen, with closely parallel patent nerves, quite glabrous, 2-3 in. long, 1½-1¾ in. broad, on petioles 1-1¼ line long; the terminal corymb has a very short peduncle bearing 6 or 8 erect flowers on pedicels 2 lines long; the flowers are 2 in. long, including the linear segments (9 lines); the fruit is more than double the size of that of the two preceding species, and is equal in size to a large peach. The differences are sufficiently great to constitute three valid species.

The typical species has long been cultivated near Pernambuco, and was first described by Gomez. The milky juice yielded by all of them, as well as by the fruits known by the name of *Mangaba*, affords a material like india-rubber, which is likely to become an article of commerce.

The *Hancornia floribunda*, figured by Pöppig, is a species of *Zschokkea*; and the *Hancornia laxa*, A. DC., belongs to *Ambellania*.

The analysis of the fruit and seed of *Hancornia speciosa* is shown in Plate 1 A.

AMBELLANIA.

A genus well described and figured by Aublet upon a single Guiana species: to this Dr. Müller added five others from Brazil, two of which must be excluded, as indicated below. The genus is easily distinguished from *Couma*, *Hancornia*, and *Zschokkea* by the segments of the corolla, which are linear-oblong, obtuse, membranaceous, simply convoluted sinistrorsely in æstivation, afterwards expanded, and by other characters. The fruit differs from those of the above genera in its fleshy envelope divided into 2 cells by a very thick fleshy placentiferous dissepiment, in which numerous small seeds are half imbedded; these seeds are oval, subcompressed, and peltately attached by a ventral hilum.

7. AMBELLANIA CUCUMERINA, Spruce in Hook. Kew Journ. v. 185 et 243: arborescens, undique lactescens: foliis ovato-oblongis, imo rotundatis, apice sensim apiculatis, integris, marginibus subrevolutis, tenuiter chartaceis, supra viridibus, opacis, subtus pallidioribus, valde opacis, sub lente minute granulatis, nervis numerosis tenuibus crebre parallelis recte divergentibus prope marginem arcuatis, venis vix ullis, costa supra sulcata, subtus prominula; petiolo tenui, canaliculato, limbo 40plo breviore; racemo brevi, axillari, pedunculo petiolum æquante, floribus subcongestis; pedicellis brevissimis; sepalis brevibus, ovatis; corollæ tubo cylindrico, glabro, superne sensim latiore, calyce quadruplo longiore, intus lineis 5 lanato-piloso, segmentis subæquilongis, lineari-oblongis, obtusulis, æstivatione simpliciter sinistrorsum convolutis, demum expansis; staminibus infra medium tubi insertis, filamentis brevissimis, antheris acuminatis, imo emarginatis; stylo brevi, valido, apice indusiatim concavo; stigmatibus 2, globosis, indusio nidulantibus: drupa ovato-oblonga utrinque obtusa, costatim pentagona, pericarpio crassissimo, carnoso, extus (modo *cucumeri*) muricato-tuberculato, 2-loculari, dissepimento crasso carnoso seminigero; seminibus plurimis, ovatis, planoconvexis; testa tenui, dura, hilo parvo supra medium peltatim affixa; embryone in albumine subcorneo subæquilongo incluso, cotyledonibus anguste semiteretibus radicula ad imum spectante triplo longioribus. In Brasilia: *v. pl. sicc. in hb. Hook., fructus in Mus. Kew.*, Panurè, Rio Negro (Spruce 2413).

A slender branching tree, 15–30 feet high, yielding an abundant milky juice; its opposite leaves are 4½–5½ in. long, 1¾–2¼ in. broad, on petioles about 1½ line long, having about 30 pairs of parallel nerves, with others shorter and intermediate; the small black dots mentioned by Spruce are merely superficial, and in no way resemble the pellucid dots of the *Myrtaceæ*; the imbricated pruinose sepals are 3 lines long; the tube of the corolla 5 lines long, its segments 4 lines long. The fruit, called "Pepino do matto" (wild cucumber), is 3¼ in. long, 1¾ in. broad, the angles alternate with the sepals; the pericarp, of firm texture, is edible, sweet-tasted, with the odour of a ripe apple, and 4–5 lines thick, the dissepiment between the 2 narrow cells being 3 lines thick, bearing about 60 oval compressed fleshy seeds 3 lines long, 2 lines broad, covered by a hard greenish scabrid testa, marked by a small hilum in the middle, by which it is attached to the dissepiment; the albumen is 2¾ lines long, ½ line thick; radicle superior, 3 times as long as the short obtuse linear cotyledons.

A figure of the inflorescence of this species, and of its fruit and seeds, are exhibited in Plate 1 B.

The *Tabernæmontana lucida*, H. B. K. (Gen. vii. 209), appears to belong to *Lacmellia*, as shown below.

To be excluded :—

Ambellania quadrangularis, Müll. = Rhigospira quadrangularis, nob.
Ambellania macrophylla, Müll. = Rhigospira venulosa, nob.

LACMELLIA.

This genus was established in 1856, by Karsten, upon a New-Granada plant, naming it after its vernacular title, "Leche e miel" (milk and honey). It has been acknowledged by Messrs. Bentham and Hooker (Gen. ii. 694), but only by absorbing into it Müller's genus *Zschokkea*: the latter appears to me, however, a valid genus, as will presently be shown. Only one species has been hitherto known; but a second and closely allied species is here added, from one of Bonpland's plants.

1. LACMELLIA EDULIS, Karst. Linn. xxviii. 450. Rio Meta, in littoribus (*non vidi*).

A middle-sized tree, growing on the banks of the river Meta (flowing from the New-Granada Andes), at a spot about 70° 40′ W. long. and 60° 20′ N. lat.: its trunk yields a lactescent juice, made into a cooling drink; it is crowned by a branching head; its opposite leaves are shining above, and on short petioles. The inflorescence is an axillary cyme of small yellow flowers, on bibracteolated pedicels; the calyx consists of 5 small, concave, imbricated, persistent sepals; the corolla is tubular, with a border of 5 linear lanceolate segments, twisted in æstivation and deciduous; the stamens, on very short filaments, are inserted in a pilose ring above the base of the tube of the corolla; the ovary is single, bilocular, with many hemianatropous ovules in longitudinal series in the axis; the style is conical, 10-costate; stigmata 2, lanceolate. The fruit is yellow, oval, baccate, as large as a hazel nut, crowned by the persistent style; by abortion it is 1-celled and contains a single, good-tasted seed enveloped in a mucilaginous covering; the albumen, as long as it, encloses the heterotropous embryo, of 2 oval foliaceous cotyledons conjoined by a superior fusiform radicle.

2. LACMELLIA LUCIDA, nob.: *Tabernæmontana? lucida*, H. B. K. vii. 209; *Psychotria lucida*, R. & Sch. (non H. B. K.), Syst. iv. 189. In Nova Granada ad Rio Atabapo (*non vidi*).

A closely allied species, collected by Bonpland at the Missiones of S. Francisco, in the same longitude, and about 50 miles southward of the locality of the preceding species. It forms a lactescent tree 50 feet high, growing on the border of the river, with fuscous branches 2-edged, compressed, smooth and incrassate, the axils by a transverse ridge conjoining the petioles; leaves opposite, oblong lanceolate, obtuse or rounded, rarely emarginated at the apex, narrowly cuneated at the base and running into the petioles, subcoriaceous, glabrous, thickened and entire on the margins, with many approximated parallel faint nerves, nitid above, concolorous beneath, with a prominent midrib, 3–3¼ in.

long, 10–11 lines broad, on channelled fossated petioles 4–5 lines long: panicle terminal, subtrichotomous, bracteated, glabrous; bracts small, ovate; flowers white, having the smell of jasmine; pedicels 1¼ line long: sepals small, ovate, imbricated, somewhat unequal; tube of corolla funnel-shaped, 8 times as long as the calyx, segments oblong, revolute at the apex, imbricated at the base: stamens acute, sessile, inserted within the tube: ovary subbilocular, ovules attached to a thickened placenta in the axis; style short, subulate; stigma simple: drupes ovate-oblong, fleshy, edible, 1 in. long, 2-locular, filled with a lactescent, glutinous pulp, each cell containing one plano-convex seed.

From these descriptions, *Lacmellia* is shown to differ from *Ambellania* in its more membranaceous corolla, with lanceolate segments revolute at the apex, in its much longer anthers, the filaments inserted in a pilose ring near the base of the tube, a conical 10-costate style, a much smaller fruit, of thinner consistence, with a single plano-convex seed in each cell, clothed in a mucilaginous envelope. Although it approaches *Zschokkea* in its fruit, it differs in its corolla with much longer and lanceolate segments and a shorter tube.

ZSCHOKKEA.

A valid genus, established by Müller in 1860 upon several species from Brazil and Guiana, besides another from the Upper Amazonas river. It has been united with *Lacmellia* by the authors of the Gen. Plant. (ii. 694); but it appears to me it should be kept distinct, as it differs from that genus in the extremely short rounded segments of the corolla, in its very long slender anthers bidentate at their base and enclosed within the upper part of the tube of the corolla, in its simple style, in the densely barbate stigmata, in its smaller, dry, capsular fruit, and contains a single plano-convex dry seed, in which respect it approaches *Rauwolfia*.

The following are its known species:—

1. ZSCHOKKEA GRACILIS, Müll. *l. c.* p. 21, tab. 6. fig. 1. River Amazonas, near Barra do Rio Negro (Spruce 1000).
2. —— RAMOSISSIMA, Müll. *l. c.* p. 21, tab. 7. River Uhaupes (Spruce 2628).
3. —— ARBORESCENS, Müll. *l. c.* p. 22, tab. 6. fig. 3. Rio Negro (Spruce 1001-1922).
4. —— MONOSPERMA, Müll. *l. c.* p. 22, tab. 6. fig. 2. Santarem (Spruce 679).
5. —— MICROCARPA, Müll. *l. c.* p. 23. Rio Negro (Spruce 3537).
6. —— FLORIBUNDA, Müll. *l. c.* p. 23 : *Hancornia floribunda*, Pöpp. Gen. iii. 70, tab. 279. River Amazonas, near Ega (Pöppig, 2723).
7. —— GUIANENSIS, Müll. Linn. xxx. 391. French Guiana (Poiteau).

CUPIRANA.

This genus is the *Coupoui* of Aublet, who figured the plant and unripe fruit only, which is represented as if crowned with a superior calyx—a mistake originating in the inversion of the detached drupe: hence the genus has been referred by most botanists to the *Myrtaceæ*, De Candolle placing it among the doubtful members of that family. Endlicher and Lindley ranged it among the *Barringtonieæ*, while Hooker and Bentham referred it to *Pentagonia* among *Rubiaceæ*. Its true place, however, is unquestionably in *Apocynaceæ*, as I have ascertained by flowering specimens of the same plant collected in Cayenne by Martin, preserved in the British Museum. I have not adopted Aublet's generic name, as it might be confounded with his genus *Couepia*, with his *Goupia*, and with DeCandolle's *Cupia*, but have given its vernacular, *Cupi-rana* (wild Cupi), a name given to it to distinguish it from the true Cupi (*Couepia guianensis*, Aubl.). The floral characters in the following diagnosis are derived from my own analysis of Martin's plants, which show two very distinct species; those of the fruit are derived wholly from Aublet's description and drawing, with the necessary correction.

CUPIRANA, nob. *Coupoui*, Aubl.; *Calyx* tubulosus, margine truncato obsolete 5-denticulato, crassiusculus, 5-nervis, e laminis 2 separabilibus coustans, *interiore* tenuiter membranacea, enervi, margine breviter ciliato, *exeriore* breviter 5-dentata, demum in lacinias 5 rupta, persistens. *Corollæ tubus* calyce paullo longior, crassus; *limbi segmenta* 5, lanceolata, acuta, tubo duplo longiora, imo brevissime auriculata, crasse carnosa, opaca, erecto-expansa, æstivatione valde imbricata et sinistrorsum simpliciter convoluta. *Stamina* 5, inclusa, laciniis alterna, imo tubo inserta; *filamenta* brevissima, lineari-membranacea; *antheræ* biloculares, imo cordatæ, sinu dorsali affixæ, loculis anguste linearibus ad connectivum tenue apice cuspidatim excurrens dorso adnatis, utrinque rima longitudinali introrsum dehiscentibus; *pollen* subtrigonum, e granulis cohærentibus. *Discus* parvus, breviter urceolatus, margine crenatus, glaber. *Ovarium* depresse globosum, bisulcatum, glabrum, disco insitum, eodem dimidio brevius, liberum, biloculare; *ovula* pauca, axi affixa. *Stylus* corollæ tubo dimidio brevior, tenuis, sub-4-angulatus, angulis hispidulis, imo pilosus, apice incrassatus; clavuncula cylindrica, simplex, aut glandulis 2 linearibus oppositis rigide hispidulis signata: *stigmata* 2, acute linearia, membranacea, adpressa, glabra, glandulis alterna et æquilonga. *Drupa* majuscula, ovata, calyce persistente rupto suffulta, abortu unilocularis, monosperma; *semen* magnum, amygdalinum. Arbores *in Cayenna vigentes, frondosæ*; folia magna, oblongo-lanceolata, nervosa; flores plurimi, *singulatim pedicellati, summis ramis congesti*; pedicelli *longi aut breves, imo bracteati*; drupæ *magnæ, indehiscentes*.

1. CUPIRANA AUBLETIANA, nob.: *Coupoui aquatica*, Aubl. Pl. Guian. ii. Suppl. p. 17, tab. 377 : procera, trunci cortice lævi, viridi; ramis crassiusculis, nudis; ramulis angulato-striatis, fistulosis, medulla repletis: foliis circa 6, alternis, ad apicem ramulorum congestis, magnis, lanceolato-oblongis, infra medium subangustioribus, imo cordatis, auriculis rotundatis et imbricantibus, sursum gradatim angustatis, apice repente acuminatis, glaberrimis, supra pallide viridibus, undique opacis, in costa nervisque sulcatis, venis reticulatis, subtus costa nervisque prominentibus; petiolo angulato, glabro, imo crassiore, limbo 4–5plo breviore: floribus circa 18, in apice ramulorum congestis; pedicellis teretibus, calyce 4plo longioribus, imo bracteatis; bracteæ oblongæ rubræ, iutus dense ramentaceæ et rufo-tomentosa: calyce tubuloso, adpresse velutino; corolla calyce 3plo longiore, opaca, segmentis vix explicatis: drupa oblonga, immatura ejus *Citri medicæ* magnitudine, viridi, imo calyce suffulta. In Guiana: *v. pl. s. in herb. Mus. Brit.* Cayenne (Martin); *fructus non vidi*.

Aublet's specific name is not adopted, as it presupposes a small aquatic plant, instead of a very tall tree. The trunk is smooth and greenish, with a soft white wood; its branchlets are filled with a soft pith. The leaves, aggregated at the summit of its bare branchlets, are, in the specimen quoted, 17–20 in. long, 7–8½ in. broad, on petioles 4–4¼ in. long; according to Aublet they are 22 in. long, 9 in. broad: they are prettily marked with about 24 pairs of divergent nerves, arcuately conjoined within the margin. About 18 flowers are aggregated on the summit of the branchlet, each on a pedicel somewhat thickened above, nearly 2 in. long, and furnished at its base with an oblong sessile reddish bract 1 in. long and ½ in. broad: the calyx is 6 lines long, 3½ lines in diam.;

the tube of the corolla is 7 lines long, 2½ lines in diam.; the border-segments 11 lines long, 3 lines broad, thick, fleshy, distinctly auriculated at the base, and so firmly convoluted sinistrorsely that they are with difficulty unrolled: the stamens are 4 lines long; the urceolate disk is 1 line high, 2 lines broad; the globular ovary is 1½ line in diam.; the slender style is 4 lines long; the clavuncle, with its glands, is 2 lines long; the 2 stigmata 1 line long, ½ line broad. The fruit, according to Aublet, is about the size of a citron, of a greenish colour when not quite ripe; it contains a single seed, as in *Zschokkea* and *Lacmellia*, the structure of which is unknown.

A drawing of the above species, explaining its floral structure, with a figure of the fruit, are given in Plate II.

2. CUPIRANA MARTINIANA, nob.: ramulis crassiusculis, nudis, angulato-striatis, apice foliiferis, cicatricibus foliorum caducorum crebre signatis; foliis hinc paucis, alternis, magnis, elongato-oblongis, a medio utrinque sensim angustioribus, imo cuneatis, et in petiolo subbrevi decurrentibus, apice acutis, supra pallide viridibus, subnitidis, sparsim pilosis, in costa nervisque sulcatis, nervis venisque transversim reticulatis immersis, subtus pallidioribus, costa, nervis venisque prominentibus et paullo pilosis; petiolo dense piloso, limbo 30plo breviore: floribus plurimis in apice ramulorum dense congestis, pedicellis duplo, et calyce 4plo brevioribus; calyce ore integro, extus dense flavide et adpresse villoso, intus tenuiter sericeo; corolla calyce duplo longiore, intus glabra, extus pilis densis flavidis adpressis retrorsis villosa, tubo calycis longitudine, limbi laciniis 6, tubo æquilongis, carnosis, oblongo-acutis, imo subcordatis, valde convolutis: staminibus præcedentis, cum filamentis paullo longioribus; disco brevi, campanulato, crenulato, glabro; ovario minimo, depresse globoso, glabro, 2-loculari; stylo tenui stamina attingente, imo dense piloso, superne glabro; stigmate ei æquilongo, bifisso, lobis lineari-acutis, adpresse erectis. In Guiana: *v. s. in herb. Mus. Brit. in flore* Cayenne (Martin).

A species very similar in habit to the preceding, but different in many characters. Its aggregated leaves are 15· in. long, 6½ in. broad, on a thick villous petiole only ½ in. long: it has about 12 densely aggregated terminal flowers, upon short villous pedicels, 1 line long, growing out of a cluster of very short acute bracts: the calyx is 6 lines long, 3 lines broad, somewhat gibbous at base; the tube of the corolla is 5 lines long, its border-segments 5 lines long; the aciculated anthers 4 lines long, on filaments 1½ line long, fixed to the bottom of the tube, and dorsally attached to the anther ½ line above its cordate base; the style, rising from a tuft of hairs on the summit of the ovary, is 3¼ lines long, is thickened above by a clavuncle 1 line long; the stigmata, 1½ line long, are lanceolate and erect: disk 1 line high, 2 lines broad; ovary depressed-globose, ½ line in diam., its 2 cells too minute to ascertain the number of ovules: several spiral threads were observed in the fleshy substance of the segments of the corolla.

CERATITES.

This genus, well elaborated by Dr. Solander, has escaped the notice of botanists, owing to the knowledge being only possessed by few of the rare books in the Banksian library, where the scarce work of Solander is deposited—a volume which minutely describes many rare Brazilian plants, well illustrated by several beautiful coloured drawings. *Ceratites* was founded on a single species, collected by him in Rio de Janeiro in 1768, the typical plant being still extant in the herbarium of the British Museum. It is curious that, in the interval of 110 years, this rare plant has not again been met with, although that neighbourhood has been since industriously searched by many scores of collectors. The genus is near *Couma*, differing in the singular form of its corolla (which suggested its generic name), in the shape of its stamens, the structure of its disk, and other features, as the following diagnosis will show.

CERATITES, Soland.—Char. emend.: *Sepala* 5, acute oblonga, membranacea, subreflexa. *Corolla* tubulosa, flavide tomentosa, *tubo* cylindrico, calyce triplo longiore, supra medium constricto, et hinc intus infra piloso, limbi *segmentis* 5 obtuse lanceolatis, tubo æquilongis, subdextrorsum contortis, extus cum appendicibus subulatis sub apicem cornutis tomentosis, intus concavis et glabris. *Stamina* 5, inclusa, ad constrictionem tubi inserta: *filamenta* subbrevia, tenuia, extus pilosula; *antheræ* liberæ, erectæ, lineares, 2-lobæ, sub medium divaricatim fissæ, in sinu affixæ, lobis utrinque obtusis, longitudinaliter dehiscentibus. *Discus* breviter tubulosus, liber, margine integro minute glanduloso. *Ovaria* 2, subglobosa, pilosa, disco æquilonga; *stylus* glaber, filiformis, stamina attingens, apice fusiformi-incrassatus; *stigmata* 2, parva, acuta, pilosa, subdivaricata. *Fructus* ignotus. Frutex *Brasiliana*; folia *opposita, elliptica, petiolata*; paniculæ *axillares folio dimidio breviores, bis trichotoma, floribus circ.* 9 *in dichotomiis, fere sessilibus, dense tomentosæ*.

1. CERATITES AMŒNA, Soland. MS. in sched. 1083; in Prim. Fl. Bras. p. 68, tab. pict. 26: ramulis teretibus cinereo-opacis, axillis nodulosis: foliis oppositis, elliptico-oblongis, imo acutis, apice sensim subacutis calloso-mucronatis, chartaceis, marginibus integris subrevolutis, supra pallide et læte viridibus, subnitidis, nervis tenuissimis vix prominulis, subtus flavide opacis, brevissime puberulis, costa nervisque prominulis; petiolo tenui, semitereti, glabro, tubo 20plo breviore: paniculis axillaribus, flavide puberulis, circa 9-floris; pedunculo 3-ramoso, ramis dichotome divaricatis, cum flore fere sessili in dichotomiis; pedicellis brevissimis; sepalis lanceolatis, membranaceis, reflexis, puberulis; corolla flavide tomentosa; cæt. ut in char. gener. In Brasilia: *v. s. in hb. Mus. Brit.* Rio de Janeiro (Solander, anno 1768).

I have stated that this genus approaches *Couma* in structure: the latter is described and figured by Müller, who alleges that it has no disk; but I have found in *C. dulcis* and *C. oblongifolia* a decided disk, concealing 2 pilose ovaries as in *Ceratites*. In the present species the branchlets are 1 line thick, the axils being ¾–1 in. apart; the leaves are 3¼–3½ in. long, 1¼–1¾ in. broad, on petioles 1½–2 lines long; the peduncle is 6 lines long, the 3 branches 4 lines long, each dichotomously divided, with a flower in each dichotomy, on pedicels ¾ line long; sepals 1 line long; tube of corolla 4 lines long, segments 3 lines long, with cornute appendages 2 lines long, placed below the apex: stamens seated in the contraction of the tube; filaments slender, 1½ line long; anthers 1 line long: style 4½ lines long.

A figure of this species, with an analysis of its peculiar floral structure, is exhibited in Plate I. c.

POMPHIDEA.

This genus[*] is proposed for a Jamaica plant collected by Swartz, and hitherto undescribed. Its floral structure, in many points, approaches that of *Ambellania*. It has

---

[*] So named from πομφός (*cutis tumide vesicata*) and ἰδέα (*facies*).

opposite leaves, a short axillary raceme with few flowers of rather small size, a calyx of 5 unequal oblong sepals, of which 2 are exterior, broader and twice the length of the others, all imbricated; within, at the base, are numerous minute scales, so united as to appear like a ring denticulated on its margin; the corolla has a short tube, with a border of 4 or 5 oblong fleshy suberect segments, dextrorsely convoluted in æstivation, the whole marked by many pustular elevations; stamens alternate with the segments, fixed in the base of the tube,—the filaments being also pustular, the anther-cells parallel placed upon a connective bearing on its apex a large gland; a disk of 5 free erect lobes, surrounding the base of an oblong 2-celled ovary crowned by a short thick style indusiate at its apex and enclosing 2 rounded stigmata as in *Ambellania*.

POMPHIDEA, nob.: *Flores* 5-, rarius 4-meri: *sepala* 5 (raro 4), lineari-oblonga, inæqualia, quorum 2 exteriora duplo longiora et latiora, imbricata, erecta, crassiuscula, intus squamulis numerosis membranaceis parvis acutis in annulum confluentibus: *corolla* tubo sepala majora æquante, cylindrico, *segmentis* tubo vix æquilongis, oblongis, subacutis, æqualibus, crassis, rigidis, glabris, suberectis, æstivatione paullo dextrorsum convolutis, cum tubo utrinque pellucide pustulatis. *Stamina* segmentis alterna, imo tubi inserta; *filamenta* tubo æquilonga, linearia, late complanata, utrinque pustulata, marginibus dense ciliato-pilosis; *antheræ* parallele 2-lobæ, *lobis* lineari-oblongis, dorso affixis, introrsis, rima longitudinali dehiscentibus; *connectivum* filamento continuum, excurrens, pustulatum, apice subito constrictum et in glandula majuscula pellucida terminatum. *Discus* 5-lobus, *lobis* liberis, erectis, lineari-oblongis, carnosis, apice crenulato-truncatis, ovario duplo longiori circumpositis. *Ovarium* oblongum, tubo corollæ brevius, angulatum, striatum, profunde 2-sulcatum, 2-loculare. *Stylus* subteres, ovario paullulo angustior et æquilongus, apice indusiatus excavatus et incrassatus, truncatus; *stigma* 2-glandulosum, cavitati semiimmersum. *Fructus* ignotus. Arbor *Jamaicensis*: foliis *opposita, oblongo-ovata, breviter petiolata*; racemus *axillaris, brevis, pedunculatus, pauciflorus*; flores *subparvi, pedicellati*.

1. POMPHIDEA SWARTZIANA, nob.: foliis oppositis oblongis, imo obtusis, apice in acumen subacutum constrictis, integris, glabris, chartaceis, utriuque opacis, minutissime pellucido-punctulatis, et granulato-rugulosis, supra flavide viridibus, nervis arcuatim nexis subimmersis, subtus ochraceo-ferrugineis; petiolo tenui, limbo 30plo breviore: racemo axillari, pedunculato, abortione 2-floro; floribus subparvis, pedicellatis, fuscis; sepalis extus pilosis et pustulatis, squamulis internis basalibus albis. In Antilles: *v. s. in herb. Mus. Brit.* Jamaica (Swartz).

No particulars are given by Swartz: the branchlet is slender, rugulose, with axils 1 in. apart, it is exstipulate: the leaves are 2¾–3¾ in. long, 1¼–1½ in. broad, on a very slender petiole 1 line long; the axillary peduncle is 4 lines long, on the summit of which only 2 flowers remain on pedicels, each 1½ line long: the 2 outer sepals are 2½ lines long, 1 line broad, the 3 inner ones being 1½ line long, ¾ line broad; the tube of the corolla is 2½ lines long, 1 line broad, its segments 2½ lines long, ¾ line broad: lobes of disk ¼ line long; ovary superior, ¾ line long; style ¾ line long.

A note in pencil upon the specimen states, "Sepals 4–5; petals 4–5; fruit a 4–5-locular capsule:" the former are probably as much in error as the latter, which cannot be a true statement; for I found the ovary to be 2-celled, and this is confirmed by the 2-lobed stigma.

A drawing to illustrate this species and its floral analysis is given, Plate I. D.

Thevetia.

A new species, from Venezuela, is here added to this genus, which nearly approaches the handsome plant described and figured by Mr. Bentham in the Botany of the 'Sulphur,' p. 124, tab. 43. I will first, however, explain my view of the carpological structure of the genus, which is not quite exactly described by Prof. DeCandolle in his 'Prodromus;' and it is difficult to understand the long description of Dr. Müller in Mart. ' Fl. Bras.,' which is not correct.

My analysis was made from a plant of *T. ahouai*, cultivated in Rio de Janeiro. This species is well figured in Lamarck's 'Illustr.' tab. 170: the compressed globular ovary is pseudo-4-locular, the true dissepiment being across the shorter diameter, having on each side a very broad placentary expansion extending nearly to the wall of the cells in the direction of the longer diameter, thus appearing pseudo-4-celled, a single ovule being peltately attached upon each side of each branch of the placenta. This structure is maintained in the ripe fruit; within the pericarp is a heart-shaped compressed osseous nut, shown in a reversed position in Lamarck's plate: along the emarginated apex of this nut is a suture, which extends nearly to the base along each edge, into which a knife easily penetrates; but it requires some force to cut through its more solid base: we thus divide the nut into two plano-convex portions, the division being through the bilamellar placentæ: upon the surfaces of the division, on each face a cord of spiral vessels rises from the base, diverges upwards, and is lost at a spot opposite to each seed, and therefore opposite to the hilum of each: around this spot, within the cell, is a deep hollow in the placenta, formed by the pressure of the rounded peltate hilum: the 4 seeds, which fill the spaces of the 4 pseudo-cells, are irregularly globose, flattened on one side around the large convex hilum: the testa is stoutly chartaceous, of a brownish colour, and so firmly attached to the hilum, that it cannot be there detached without rupture; this integument is lined within by a network of snow-white branching threads of the raphe; the inner integument is free, membranaceous, and of a darkish colour, closely investing an embryo, without any trace of albumen, which consists of 2 roundish plano-convex fleshy cotyledons united by a short obtusely conical radicle, projecting horizontally and centrifugally to the outer edge of the cell: this embryo is therefore heterotropous; *i. e.* the hilum is laterally placed between the two extremities of the embryo. The new species before mentioned is defined in the following manner:—

Thevetia calophylla, nob.: ramulis teretibus brunneo-opacis: foliis alternis, lanceolato-oblongia, imo cuneatis, apice acute acuminatis, chartaceis, marginibus subrevolutis, supra viridibus, opacis, corrugulatis, ad nervos semiimmersos sulcatulis, subtus opacis, brunnescentibus, corrugulatis, nervis omnino immersis; petiolo semitereti, limbo 11–12plo breviore: racemo brevi, terminali, paucifloro; pedicellis subvalidis, calyce 3plo longioribus; sepalis oblongis, acutis, membranaceis, parallele nervosis; corollæ tubo cylindrico, supra medium ampliore, limbi segmentis 5, tubo dimidio brevioribus, dolabriformibus, dextrorsum contortis, cum appendicibus 5 subacutis intra faucem alternis; staminibus 5, sub squamas insitis, inclusis, ex annulo piloso ortis; filamentis brevibus; antheris sine connectivo profunde 2-lobis, lobis imo divaricatis; disco annulari, carnoso; ovario paullo longiore, glabro, 2-loculari; stylo longo, filiformi, apice in clavunculam cylindricam 10-sulcatam imo fimbriatim 10-lobam incrassato; stigmatibus 2, acutis, terminalibus. In Venezuela: *v. s. in herb. Mus. Brit.* Valle la Cura (Moritz 1158).

The axils of the branchlets are $\frac{1}{2}$ in. apart; the leaves are $5\frac{1}{4}$–6 in. long, $1\frac{1}{8}$–$1\frac{3}{8}$ in. broad, on a petiole $\frac{1}{2}$ in. long: the peduncle of the raceme is shorter than the petiole, 3–4-flowered; the pedicels 5 lines long; the sepals 2 lines long; the tube of the corolla is 10 lines long, its segments 5 lines long, $2\frac{1}{2}$ lines broad.

The particulars of the floral structure of this plant, and a copious analysis of the fruit and seed of the Linnean species, are given in Plate IV. A.

Müller, in Linn. xxx. 392, describes another new species from Paraguay (Weddell 3112), under the name of *Thevetia cornuta*.

ASPIDOSPERMA.

This genus, established by Martius in 1824, consists of numerous species, 19 of which were enumerated by Prof. DeCandolle in 1854, and 30 others, soon after, described by Dr. Müller. They are generally trees of considerable size, yielding valuable hard white woods, known in Brazil as "marfim" (ivory), "peroba," and "piquiá;" they have generally alternate or crowded leaves, and an inflorescence of extremely small flowers, in the structure of which there is nothing that calls for remark, except that the æstivation was stated by DeCandolle, in error, to be of dextrorse convolution, instead of sinistrorse as more correctly shown by Müller, and that the disk, small, annular, and adhering to the ovaries, is sometimes evanescent. The structure of the fruit and seeds is very peculiar, and has hardly been correctly described. I have added here an analytical drawing of that of *A. Gomezianum*, A. DC., which I gathered and examined in 1835, in Rio de Janeiro, which will serve as an illustration of the carpological features of the genus.

The fruit, normally, should consist of 2 follicles; but I do not remember an instance where both are perfected; and it is certain that generally one is abortive. In *A. Gomezianum* this follicle, about 2 in. long, is of an obovoid form, much compressed, somewhat convex on both faces, the pericarp being hard, almost ligneous, much rounder along the ventral edge, in the line of which the dehiscence takes place by a suture which occupies $\frac{2}{3}$ of the whole periphery; and on the external faces a curved ridge is seen extending from one end of the suture to the other: hence it happens that, as the suture gapes open, the pericarp assumes the form of 2 valves, remaining united along the dorsal edge, when within each valve are seen 4 seeds (8 in all) extremely flat, closely applied to each other, of an oval form, filling the internal cavity, each having a flattened oval embryoniferous scutcheon surrounded by a broad membranaceous wing; in the centre, on one side of this scutcheon, is seen a small hilum, attached to one end of a long slender funicle, the other end of which emanates from the inner margin of the suture at the summit, and each seed is thus suspended; but as the hilum is invariably placed on the side furthest from its corresponding valve, the funicles of the 4th and 5th seeds touch one another, and all have an aspect towards the axis: the scutcheon, which is thinly chartaceous and indehiscent, is filled by a free, compressed body of thin pergamineous texture, which appears to me a thin albumen, as it bears no indication of a chalaza, which it should do if it were the inner integument: this albumen contains an embryo of equal length and breadth, consisting of 2 fleshy foliaceous oval cotyledons, deeply cordate at their summit, and furnished in the sinus with a superior terete radicle about $\frac{1}{3}$ of their length.

It has been hitherto considered that the seeds in this genus have no albumen; but I think its presence is here manifested.

Species excluded and otherwise referred:—

ASPIDOSPERMA RAMIFLORUM, Müll. *l. c.* p. 55 : referred to *Geissospermum*.
—— NITIDUM, Müll. p. 59   „   *Thyroma*.
—— POLYNEURUM, Müll. p. 57   „   „
—— PARVIFOLIUM, Müll. p. 57   „   „
—— CONDYLOCARPUM, Müll. p. 55   „   „
—— SELLOWI, Müll. p. 56   „   „
—— RIEDELII, Müll. p. 56   „   „
—— BICOLOR, A. DC. p. 397   „   „
—— LHOTZKIANUM, Müll. p. 60   „   „
—— ANOMALUM, Müll. p. 61   „   „
—— SESSIFLORUM, Müll. Linnæa, xxx. p. 399   „   „
—— CYLINDROCARPUM, Müll. p. 54 : probably belonging to *Strempeliopsis*.

A drawing of ASPIDOSPERMA GOMEZIANUM, its inflorescence, its floral analysis, its follicle, and details of its carpological structure are shown in Plate III. A.

THYROMA.

When examining the *Hippocrateaceæ* in the Hookerian herbarium in 1865, I observed a specimen from the island of Trinidad, named, in the handwriting of Dr. Grisebach, "*Hippocratea neurocarpa* Griseb.;" but this name was not included among the species of that genus in his 'Flora Br. W. Ind.' (1864). In that work, however (p. 411), I found the same plant described by him as *Aspidosperma sessiflora*, Müll. On referring to Müller's description of the same in Linn. xxx. 399 (1860), I was satisfied that it corresponded well with Grisebach's plant, also from Trinidad, from Sieber's collection. I found in the same herbarium another specimen, from the island of S. Vincente, under the handwriting of Grisebach, of *Hippocratea neurocarpa*, also in fruit. The examination of the flowers and fruits convinced me that they belonged to a new genus, near *Aspidosperma*, and then named by me *Thyroma**, the characters of which were at that time fully described.

THYROMA, nob.: *Aspidosperma* (in parte), Müll.; *Hippocrateæ* sp., Griseb.: *Flores* parvi, breviter pedicellati; *sepala* 5, imo in cupulam crassam connata, oblonga, acuta, crassiuscula, imbricata, quorum 2 exteriora, intus squamula ciliolata, sæpe obsoleta munita, immutata persistentia. *Corolla* calyce 2–3plo longior, *tubo* subcylindrico, crassiusculo, intus sub medium piloso, fauce squamulis 5 carnosulis segmentis oppositis apice conniventibus munito, *segmentis* 5 tubo 3–4plo brevioribus, ovatis aut oblongis, carnosis, glabris, vix expansis, valde imbricatis et simpliciter sinistrorsum convolutis.

* From θύρα (*janua*), ὅμοιος (*similis*), from the resemblance of its follicular capsule to two adjoining doors hinged and folded together.

Stamina 5, supra medium ad annulum pilosum inserta; *filamenta* brevissima, tenuia, glabra; *antheræ* faucem attingentes, subulatæ, imo cordatæ, connectivo excurrente apiculatæ, conniventes. *Discus* brevis, tenuiter cylindraceus, glaber, ovariis dimidio brevior. *Ovaria* 2, vix cohærentia, minima, imo disco adglutinata, superne valde pilosa: *ovula* pauca, superposita, funiculo brevi affixa: stylus tenuis, glaber; *clavuncula* stamina attingens, majuscula, globosa, carnosa, sæpe colorata, glabra: *stigmata* 2, terminalia, setosa, patentia, pilis patentibus basalibus munita. *Folliculus* solitarius (an semper?), calycis fundo stipitatus, unilateraliter oblonge subquadratus, compressissimus, utrinque planus, margine dorsali recto et mucronato, coriaceus, pro ¾ peripherii ad marginem ventralem replum simulans subtumidus, et hinc modo siliquæ hians, 1-locularis (hoc modo schedas 2 dorso cardinatas fingens). *Semina* 4, interdum plura, compressissima, oblonga, una extremitate acuto embryonifero truncata, altera pro dimidia parte ala membranacea signata, per paria inter schedas posita, quorum unum est cum scuto supero, alterum inverse infero, omnibus, in facie acuti ad axem spectante hilo centrali donatis, hinc funiculis totidem horizontalibus appensis, alternatim inversis et a replo marginali ortis: *scuta* hoc modo alternatim inversa, oblique ovata subchartacea, singula embryonifera. *Albumen* (integumentum simulans) subpergamineum, ad scutum semiadhærens; *embryo* inclusus, æquilongus, e cotyledonibus ovatis foliaceis profundius oblique cordatis, radicula in sinu æquilonga tereti, alternatim infera aut supera 5plo breviore, semper ad medium suturæ oblique spectante. Frutices *Antillani et Brasilienses* ramis *subscandentibus:* folia *opposita aut subalterna, oblonga, integra, glabra, breviter petiolata:* paniculæ *subbreves, axillares, ramose corymbosæ, multifloræ.*

1. **Thyroma sessiliflora**, nob.: *Aspidosperma sessiliflorum*, Müll. Linn. xxx. 399; Griseb. W. Ind. Fl. p. 411: *Hippocratea neurocarpa*, Griseb. MS. In Antilles: *v. s. in hb. Hook.* in ins. Trinidad (Sieber 53, in flore); ejusd. loco, sine nom. in fructu, sub *Hippocratea neurocarpa*, Griseb.; in ins. S. Vincente (Guilding, in fructu).

I have not changed Dr. Müller's specific name, although each flower of its panicle is supported on a pedicel longer than the calyx: the axils of its lenticellated branchlets are ¾–1 in. apart: the oblong obtuse opposite leaves, sometimes alternate, shining green above, yellowish opake below, are 2¼–3 in. long, 12–16 lines broad, on a petiole 2–3 lines long: the axillary panicle is 1¼–2 in. long, its alternate branches, closely approximated, have still more closely ramified branchlets bearing few subagglomerated flowers, on stout 5-grooved short pedicels with 3 approximated minute bracteoles: the erect ciliolated sepals are 1¼ line long: the tube of the corolla is 1½ line long, the segments of the border ½ line long, concave, obtusely oblong, thickish, with the left margin convoluted; the roundish fleshy scales in the mouth of the corolla are distinct, opposite the segments, above and alternate with the anthers, whose apiculated summits are scarcely exserted, and which are ½ line long; the style is terminated by a globose gland and 2 minute stigmata. The fructiferous rachis is 1 in. long; its pedicels 2–3 lines long; the flat follicle is 14 lines long, 7 lines broad: the seeds are 13 lines long, 5 lines broad, attached to the marginal replum as before described, 2 on each valve, one with a superior, the other with an inferior scutcheon 8 lines long, 5 lines broad, the embryo filling its space; the oval cotyledons, cleft at their base obliquely, have a narrow sinus 2 lines deep, in which the terete radicle is seen, always pointing to the middle of the external margin of the follicle.

A drawing of this species in flower and in fruit, showing its floral analysis, with explanatory figures of its peculiar carpological structure, are given in Plate III. B.

2. **THYROMA DECIPIENS**, nob.: *Aspidosperma decipiens*, Müll. *l. c.* p. 398. In Venezuela; *v. s. in herb. meo et aliorum* Rio Maypure, Rio Orinoco (Spruce 3657).

A species near the preceding, with slender verruculose branches, having opposite, or by abortion alternate axils, 3–4 lines apart: the oblong-ovate leaves, with rounded or emarginated summits, are 2 in. long, 1 in. broad, on a slender petiole 3 lines long; they are shining and glabrous above, with about 15 pairs of nerves, yellowish opake beneath, obsoletely tomentous under a lens, with prominent midrib and nerves: the panicle is 6 lines long, with about 4 alternate branches 3 lines long, bearing few flowers on very short pedicels; the structure of the flower as in the foregoing species.

3. **THYROMA NITIDA**, nob.: *Aspidosperma nitidum*, Benth. MS.; Müller in Mart. Fl. Bras. fasc. 26. p. 59. In Amazonas: *v. s. in hb. meo et alior*. Barra do Rio Negro (Spruce 1657).

A species, compared with the two former, inaptly called *nitida*: the axils of the subangular verruculose branchlets are $\frac{1}{2}$–$\frac{3}{4}$ in. apart: the opposite leaves, often alternate, are oblong, obtuse, subcoriaceous, with somewhat revolute margins, are 2$\frac{1}{2}$–3 in. long, 1$\frac{1}{4}$–1$\frac{3}{4}$ in. broad, on a petiole 3$\frac{1}{4}$–4 lines long, they are green, subopake above, closely impressed-punctate, and with about 16 pairs of nerves, of a yellowish dirty white beneath, with an impressed scrobiculate surface, with prominent midrib and sulcated nerves: the axillary panicle, densely corymbose, on a bifurcated peduncle 4 lines long, bearing 2 capitate heads of small flowers, 4–5 lines in diameter; the pedicels are $\frac{3}{4}$ line long, with 3 short ciliated bracts at base: the oval subacute sepals, puberulous outside, are $\frac{3}{4}$ line long; the corolla, 2 lines long, has a tube half that length, with bordersegments lanceolate-oblong, nearly erect, subfleshy and sinistrorsely convoluted; disk, ovary, style, and stigma as in the typical species.

4. **THYROMA POLYNEURA**, nob.: *Aspidosperma polyneurum*, Müll. in Mart. Fl. Bras. *l. c.* p. 57. In Brasilia, prov. Rio de Janeiro: *v. s. in hb. Hook*. (Sellow 632), Corcovado (Gardn. 5363).

A tree 80 feet high, giving a useful timber called "peroba," with a bitter bark: the specific name was applied because of its numerous fine parallel nerves, about 60 pairs, united by a common line within the revolute margin, and with fine reticulations between them: the leaves, sometimes subopposite, more often alternate, are glabrous, submembranaceous, elliptic, obtuse at the summit, gradually acute below, 2$\frac{1}{2}$–3$\frac{1}{2}$ in. long, $\frac{2}{3}$–1 in. broad, on petioles 4–5 lines long: the panicle is 9–10 lines long, with few branches and few flowers; the pedicel is 1 line long, the calyx $\frac{3}{4}$ line, corolla 3 lines long, tube narrowed gradually below, puberulous outside, retrorsely pilose inside, with 5 oblong obtuse erect segments, sinistrorsely convoluted, pilose within, $\frac{1}{3}$ length of tube; 5 small scales within the mouth of the tube opposite the segments; 5 short stamens beneath and alternate with the scales, anthers cordate at the base, on very short filaments: follicle single, very much flattened, straight on the dorsal side, semioblong on the other, both ends acute, 15–21 lines long, 4$\frac{1}{2}$–5 lines broad; seeds scutellate and tomentellous at the upper moiety, broadly winged and glabrous below.

5. **THYROMA SELLOWII**, nob.: *Aspidosperma Sellowii*, Müll. ibid. p. 56. In Brasilia meridionali: *v. s. in hb. Hook*. (Sellow 1204).

The leaves are like those of the preceding, but with only 10 pairs of immersed nerves,

2 in. long, 9 lines broad, on petioles 4 lines long: the panicle is 5 lines long, the peduncle 1 line, the pedicels ¼ line, the lanceolate sepals ½ line, the corolla 2 lines long, its obtuse oblong segments ⅓ length of tube, all cano-tomentose; buccal scales and anthers as in the preceding species; style terminated by a large oblong gland and 2 small stigmata: the follicle very much flattened, acute at the summit, narrowing below, is 1½ in. long, 5 lines broad, ½ line thick; the seeds, subtomentose, slightly imbricating, with the winged moiety pointing downwards, are 12 lines long, 3½ lines broad; the superior embryoniferous scutcheon, 4 lines long, has the funicle attached in its centre, in a horizontal direction, 2 lines long, emanating from the placentiferous margins of the follicle, as in the preceding; owing to the abortion of the lower ovules, all the seeds have a superior scutcheon.

6. THYROMA BICOLOR, nob.: *Aspidosperma bicolor*, Mart. Nov. Gen. i. p. 60; A. DC. *l. c.* p. 397; Müll. *l. c.* p. 54. In Piauhy (*non vidi*).

A species with squarrose branches and a solid bark; leaves obovate, roundly obtuse at the summit, rather acute at the base, glabrous above, cinereo-tomentose beneath, with about 10 pairs of nerves, with others shorter and intermediate, subreticulate; cymes short, sparsely cano-pubescent, sepals ovate, subacute, pubescent; follicles obliquely oblong, obtuse at the apex, with the dorsal margin in the axis straight and mucronulated, 1⅜ in. long, 6¼–7 lines broad; seeds ovoid oblong, with an eccentric scutcheon wherein the hilum is placed at ¼ the length of the seed from the scutal extremity, with a narrow wing,—characters answering to *Thyroma*.

7. THYROMA LHOTSKIANA, nob.: *Aspidosperma Lhotskianum*, Müll. *l. c.* p. 60. In prov. Minas Geraës (*non vidi*).

A species noted for its very minute flowers, forming a shrub 6–8 feet high; and Müller remarks that it resembles no other species of *Aspidosperma*; its spreading branches are extremely slender, subflexuous, cinereous; leaves elliptic, obtuse, or obtusely rounded at the summit, subacute at the base, glabrous above, with about 12 pairs of slender nerves, with others short and intermediate, very reticulated, glaucous below and obsoletely puberulous, 2¼–4 in. long, 1⅝–3½ in. broad, on adpressedly puberulous petioles 2¼ lines long; cymes lateral, umbelliform, laxly and divaricately branched, puberulous, many-flowered; pedicels twice as long as the calyx; sepals obtusely ovate, puberulous, ciliated, ¾ line long; corolla less than 2 lines long, yellowish green, its tube 1½ line long, segments broadly ovate, obtuse, the margins inflected; ovaries glabrous.

8. THYROMA PARVIFOLIA, nob.: *Aspidosperma parvifolium*, A. DC. *l. c.* p. 398; Müll. *l. c.* p. 57, tab. 17. In prov. S. Paulo (*non vidi*).

A tall tree, much branched, young branchlets covered with a deep-red tomentum; leaves lanceolate, spathulate, obtuse, gradually narrowed towards the petiole, fuscous above, glabrous, or very tomentous beneath in the younger ones, with 8–10 pairs of horizontally spreading red nerves, 2¾ in. long, 6–7½ lines broad, on petioles 1 line long; cyme lateral, about as long as the leaves, on a peduncle 3–4 lines long, shortly and bifidly branched, each branchlet bearing about 4 red flowers $3\frac{1}{2}$ lines long; pedicels $\frac{3}{4}$ line long; sepals $\frac{3}{4}$ line long, acutely ovate, ferruginously hirsutulous; tube of corolla $2\frac{1}{2}$ lines long, ovate segments $\frac{3}{4}$ line long, $\frac{1}{2}$ line broad; no apparent disk; ovaries semiglobular, pubescent at the apex; style short, with an oblong clavuncle.

9. THYROMA RIEDELII, nob.: *Aspidosperma Riedelii*, Müll. *l. c.* p. 56. In prov. S. Paulo, prope Ypanéma (Riedel 119 et 2771): *non vidi*.

A shrub 4–6 feet high, with widely spreading branches; leaves lanceolate, roundly obtuse, spathulately narrowed towards the petiole, shining and glabrous above, of a dark olive colour, with 7–10 pairs of straight diverging nerves, reticulated, paler beneath, $1-1\frac{3}{8}$ in. long, $2\frac{3}{4}-5$ lines broad, on petioles 5 lines long; cyme terminal, short, obsoletely puberulous, formed of numerous aggregated pedicels $3\frac{1}{4}$ lines long; sepals linear, obtusely liguliform, reflexed at the apex, $1\frac{3}{4}$ line long; flower $2\frac{1}{4}$ lines long; tube of corolla broadly cylindrical, angular above, cinereo-puberulous, segments obtusely ovate with inflexed margins, glabrous outside, half as long as the tube; follicles obliquely ovoid, obtuse, suddenly narrowed towards the base, 1 in. long, 7 lines broad; seeds ovate, narrowly winged, 8 lines long, with an embryo enclosed in the scutcheon. A species said to approach *T. Sellowi* and *T. parvifolia*.

STREMPELIOPSIS.

A genus established in 1876 by Messrs. Bentham and Hooker, its characters being little known: only one species is noticed.

1. STREMPELIOPSIS CUBENSIS, Benth. & Hook. Gen. ii. 702: *Rauwolfia strempelioides*, Griseb. Cat. Pl. Cub. 170: *in herb. Hook.* (*non vidi*).

All that is said regarding this is, that it is an erect, branching, glabrous shrub, with 2 minute stipules at the axils, opposite penninerved leaves, terminal cymes with numerous small flowers; sepals 5, ovate, biauriculate at the base, eglandulous; corolla salvershaped; tube cylindrical, without buccal scales, pilose within; segments short, obtuse, sinistrorsely convoluted, suberect; stamens included in the tube, on very short filaments, anthers free, acutely lanceolate, emarginated at the base; disk none; ovaries 2; style short, with an ovoidly globose clavuncle terminated by 2 short obtuse stigmata; ovules many in each carpel, biserial; follicles 2, erect or diverging, linear, subterete; seeds in 2 series, elongated, very compressed, with a very narrow acute wing at each extremity, with a central hilum to which they are affixed by a long filiform funicle.

PLUMERIA.

This handsome genus requires little notice, as its species have been fully described, and many of them well illustrated. They are all of Peruvian, Mexican, or Brazilian origin, 30 of them being enumerated by DeCandolle, and 15 others by Müller. They are mostly lofty trees or tall erect shrubs, much branched, the trunks affording a solid wood, the branchlets stout and fistulous, all yielding an abundant milky juice; they have alternate imbricated leaves, generally large, upon petioles articulated at the base, which soon fall off from the branchlets, leaving them closely studded with cicatrices; this disposition to disjunction of the parts is so marked, that we seldom find an entire specimen in herbaria. The inflorescence is terminal upon a long peduncle, having several alternate branchlets, dichotomously divided, and bearing many handsome pedicellated flowers, which are generally scarlet or rose-coloured; the tube of the corolla is slender; the segments, nearly its length, are spathulately and dextrorsely convoluted in æstivation. The fruit consists of 2 horizontally divaricated follicles nearly the shape and size of the pods of the common broad bean, and they open by a ventral suture, the margins of which are introflexed to form a single lamellar plate, which bears on both sides many imbricated seeds; these are oblong, flat, thickened, and truncated at one end into an embryoniferous scutcheon, and expanded at the opposite extremity into a long coriaceous lacerated wing, which points to the base of the follicle: they are furnished in the middle of the scutcheon on one face with a hilum, by which it is peltately attached to the placental lamina in 2 or 3 closely imbricated rows, without the intervention of any funicles. A thin corneous albumen fills the cell of each scutcheon, enclosing a heterotropous embryo, of 2 foliaceous cotyledons and a terete radicle many times shorter, which points to the summit of the follicle.

Some of the species furnish a large, solid, durable timber; the "sucuuba" for instance, from the Amazons, is of a reddish-brown colour, hard and close-grained, and used in shipbuilding, the timber sometimes 60 feet long and 4 feet in diameter; others give a smaller timber, useful for cabinet work.

CAMERARIA.

A genus established by Plumier in 1703, and adopted by Linnæus 50 years afterwards. It must not be confounded with the *Cameraria* of Aublet, now belonging to *Malouetia*. Although very different from it, this is nearly allied to *Plumeria*. It consists of only 2 species, both natives of the West Indies, one of which is a tall tree with many dichotomous branches, bearing opposite leaves and yielding a milky juice; the leaves are smallish, horizontally spreading, ovate-oblong, acuminated, entire, with numerous extremely close horizontally parallel nerves, and petiolated. It has axillary racemes on a peduncle 4 in. long, dichotomously branched above, bearing few pubescent flowers on long pedicels: the tube of the corolla is slender; its segments, somewhat longer than it, are oblong acute with dextrorse convolution: follicles 2, horizontally divaricated, oblong and broadly auriculated at the base; they open by a ventral suture, the margins of which are introflexed and placentiferous, as in *Plumeria*, and in like manner bearing several peltate seeds closely attached imbricately in a single series, winged at one extremity, which points to the summit of the funicle, contrary to the direction in *Plumeria*.

I cannot see where Müller (in Linn. xxx. 401) confounded *Cameraria* with *Skytanthus hancorniæfolia*, as Bentham and Hooker imply (Gen. ii. 701); this mistake is repeated in page 704, under *Skytanthus*.

CONDYLOCARPON.

The following new species may be added to nine others enumerated by Dr. Müller, which will afford a few more particulars regarding the peculiar structure of the genus:—

CONDYLOCARPON GRACILE, nob.: scandens, ramulis tenuibus teretibus, fuscis, striolatis, lenticellato-verruculosis, ad axillas vaginula crassissima prominente nodosis: foliis oppositis, ovatis, imo obtusis, apice in acumen subbreve recurvatum subito constrictis, marginibus revolutis, subcoriaceis, supra profunde viridibus, opacis, nervis recte divergentibus et arcuatim nexis semi-immersis, subtus pallidis, opacis, punctulis albis leprosis minute granulatis, costa nervisque prominulis; petiolis tenuibus, profunde canaliculatis, limbo 5–7plo brevioribus, ad nodum prominentem insitis, sæpius recurvatis: paniculis axillaribus, folio 2–3plo longioribus, late, laxe, iterumque divisis; pedunculo tenui, folio æquilongo, vel breviore, apice verticillatim ramoso; ramis 2–5, longissimis, gracillimis, divaricatis, iterumque pluridivisis; ramulis subcapillaribus, ultimis alternatim 5–6-floris; bracteolis minutis, membranaceis, ciliatis; pedicellis tenuissimis, calyce 5–6plo longioribus; floribus parvis: fructu pendulo, lomentis geminis, longissimis, 6–8-lobis, lobis isthmis anguste interceptis, acute ellipticis, valde compressis mono-dispermis. In Brasilia, prov. Rio de Janeiro: *v. v. et sicc. in herb. meo in flore* (n. 8086) *et fructu* (n. 4019), ad Magé, Freixal, et Iguassú.

A species easily distinguished by its nodose axils, its very laxly spreading inflorescence, with almost capillary ramifications. The branchlets are ¾ line thick, with axils 3–5 in. apart, swollen by a thickened interpetiolar cup, upon the margin of which the petioles are seated: the leaves are 1¾–3½ in. long, ¾–1¼ in. broad, on a petiole 4–6 lines long: the panicles are opposite, 5–6 in. long, 6–8 in. broad; peduncle slender, 1–2 in. long, the very slender primary branches 1½ in. long, the secondary and tertiary branchlets gradually shorter; pedicels 1 line long; sepals ¼ line long, membranaceous, ciliate; tube of corolla 1 line long, segments of border twice as long as the tube, spathulately orbicular, mucronated, expanded horizontally on the sinister margin, which is membranaceous, tranalucent, closely spotted with red dots; stamens seated at the base of the short tube; disk, none visible; ovaries ovate, collateral; style extremely short and thick, with a globose clavuncle; 2 stigmata, small, acute, pilose. Loments 6–8 in. long, strangulated into 6 or 8 flattened, elliptic, indehiscent lobes ⅜ in. broad, costately nerved on the dorsal face, 1-sulcated on the ventral side along the line of the intruding placenta; pericarp hard, thickly pithy on the edges: seed fusiform, 6 lines long, 1½ line broad, deeply sulcated for the reception of the placenta; testa black, corrugulated, with a white linear hilum 2 lines long, in the middle of the furrow.

A drawing of this species, showing its floral and carpological analyses, is given in Plate IV. B.

MANOTHRIX.

This genus is proposed for two Brazilian plants which I collected in the Organ Mountains in 1827; it approaches *Craspidospermum* in its fruit and ecomose seeds. A single flower was found upon one of them; and the other was simply fructiferous. The genus is remarkable for the peculiar structure of the hairs, of a reddish colour, which cover the seeds, and which, seen under the microscope, exhibit a capillary thread in the axis, from which, at irregular alternate intervals, a thick short line extends horizontally, terminating in an external hook; between these intervals are a number of very fine cross parallel lines, somewhat slanting, seeming like a long continuous spiral transparent cell, winding round the axis, giving it a somewhat ladder-like appearance, a structure almost unique*. These hairs do not emanate from an apical coronal ring, as in the *Echiteæ*, but from numerous scabrid points all over the surface of the testa, which bear the hairs, the lower ones being very short, gradually lengthening upwards, the upper hairs exceeding the length of the seed. The floral characters are founded on the examination of the single flower above-mentioned.

MANOTHRIX, nob.: *Flores* subparvi: *calyx* parvus, imo cupularis, margine in lacinias acutas 5-fidus: *corolla* tubularis, extus glabra, *tubo* imo paullo angustiore, ad medium constricto, intus infra constrictionem annulo lato densissime piloso, imo glabro, superne ventricoso, utrinque glabro, parallele nervoso, subplicato, *segmentis* 5, paullo brevioribus, obtuse oblongis, dextrorsum convolutis : *stamina* ex annulo piloso orta, segmentis alterna ; *filamenta* compressa, linearia, retrorsum pilosa, erecto-conniventia, longitudine antherarum; *antheræ* angustatæ, subexsertæ, in conum cohærentes, corneæ, acuminatæ, dorso pruinosæ, antice paullo sub medium et infra locellos polliniferos glandula puberula munitæ, et hinc ad filamenta affixæ, imo in furcas 2 breves obtusas vix fissæ: *ovarium* parvum, conice oblongum, pilosum, calyce suffultum, 2-loculare: *stylus* tenuis, stamina attingens, apice valde incrassatus, et viscosus, staminibus adhærens; *stigmata* 2, breviter setacea, terminalia. *Fructus* capsularis, 2-locularis, conice cylindricus, 2-sulcatus, in sulcis septicidus, valvis ad axin centralem dehiscentibus, marginibus introrsum inflexis et placentiferis: *semina* numerosa, *hilo* ventrali ad placentas affixa, imbricata ; *testa* fusiformis, scabrida, pilis forma peculiari vestita, inferioribus brevibus, gradatim longioribus, sub apicem longissimis, erecte sparsis : *embryo* in *albumine* copioso, parvus, *cotyledonibus* ovatis, *radicula* 4plo breviore, superne spectante.

Frutices Brasilienses, ramulis *fistulosis, ad axillas plus minusve transversim nodosis* : folia opposita, elliptica, petiolata: racemi brevissimè pedunculati ; pedunculo paucifloro, pedicellis tenuibus brevibus.

1. MANOTHRIX VALIDA, nob.: ramulis crassiusculis, fistulosis, opace brunneis, interrupte striatis, glabris, lenticellatis, axillis oppositis, vix nodosis, linea transversali sulcata nexis: foliis ellipticis, imo canaliculatim recurvis et acutis, apice in acumen acutum subito constrictis, marginibus subrevolutis, glaberrimis, rigidule chartaceis, supra fusco-viridibus, opacis, minutissime granulatis, nervis omnino immersis, subtus pallide opacis, rugulosis, enerviis, costa striolata vix prominula; petiolo fusco, canaliculato, imo crassiore, limbo 14plo breviore: racemis fructiferis et terminalibus brevibus, pedunculo cicatricibus 3–4 notato, unico fructifero persistente: capsula subsessili, subcylindrica, 2-sulcata, apice attenuata, 2-nodosa; pericarpio sublignoso, opace granuloso, glabro, imo calyce aucto suffulto; cæteris ut in char. gen. In Brasilia : *v. v. et sicc. in hb. meo* (n. 2052) in montibus Organensibus.

I found this species later in the same year than the following one, without flowers: its branches are 2–3 lines thick, with axils ¾–1 in. apart; the leaves are 3½ in. long, 1¾ in. broad, on petioles 3 lines long. The capsule is terminal on short lateral branchlets, or on the main stem, upon a short thickened peduncle 4 lines long, marked by 3 or 4 crowded cicatrices of others that have fallen, perhaps prematurely: this capsule is 2½ in.

* Whence the generic name, μανός (*rarus*), θρίξ (*capilla*).

long, 8 lines broad in the wider, 4 lines broad in the narrower direction, being somewhat compressed and 2-grooved; it is seated on the persistent calyx, and terminates in 2 small rounded lobes; when ripe, it splits along the grooves, and through the dissepiment, into two follicle-like moieties, each again dehiscing along the median line of the much thinner dissepiment, where its margins are inflected within the cell, to form 2 linear placentæ, to which the numerous seeds are attached by a linear ventral hilum; these placentæ, 2 in each moiety, are 2½ in. long, 1 line broad, submembranous, studded with the points of attachment of the seeds, which are linear, compressed, acute and setaceous at the base, 1½ line long, ¼ line broad, flat, red, covered with scabrid points, each supporting a reddish rigid hair of peculiar structure, the lower shorter hairs ½ line long, gradually longer upwards; the upper longer hairs are very numerous, 6 lines long, and extending 5 lines beyond the apex; the albumen is small, oblong in shape, enclosing an embryo with 2 oval fleshy cotyledons, with a small terete superior radicle ¼ of their length.

From the different habit of the two plants here described, we might infer that they are the types of two distinct new genera; but as they were found within the same region, and agree in their veinless opposite leaves seated below the level of the transverse line that crosses the nodes, and in their fistulose branches, I have ventured to regard them as two species of the same genus, one furnishing the elements of the floral structure, the other presenting the characters of the fruit and seeds; this, however, remains to be confirmed.

A drawing of this species, with a carpological analysis, is given in Plate V. A.

2. MANOTHRIX NODOSA, nob.: volubilis, ramulis tenuiter virgatis, subangulatis, striolatis, fistulosis, glabris; axillis remotis, transversim incrassatis et nodosis: foliis oppositis, infra nodos insertis, ellipticis, imo obtuse acutis, apice in acumen cuspidatum attenuatis, integris, submembranaceis, supra viridibus, opacis, costa tenui nervisque tenuissimis immersis, venis nullis, subtus flavide pallidioribus, opacis, costa rubescente nervisque immersis, petiolum versus minute 2-glandulosis; petiolo tenui, recurvato, limbo 9plo breviore: racemo axillari; pedunculo subbrevi, crassiusculo crebre bracteolato, bracteolis imbricatis, ovatis, glabris, mox deciduis, paucifloro; pedicello tenui brevissimo; floris structura ut in char. gen. In Brasilia: *v. v. et sicc. in hb. meo* (n. 2044), in montibus Organensibus.

The flexuose branchlets are ¾ line thick, with axils 5 in. apart and 2 lines thick across the nodes: the leaves are 3-8½ in. long, 1¼-1½ in. broad, on recurving petioles 4-5 lines long: the pedicel is 1 line long; the calyx 2 lines long; the tube of the corolla is 5½ lines long, its obtuse segments 3½ lines long, 2 lines broad; the filaments are 1 line long; the anthers 3 lines long, anteriorly fixed above the sinus of the basal lobes.

A drawing of this species, giving the floral analysis, is seen in Plate V. B.

TRIBE TABERNÆMONTANEÆ.

This tribe is here restricted within more precise limits than those employed by De Candolle. Its chief character resides in its 2 broad spreading follicles dehiscing along the ventral suture, which is bent inwards and placentiferous on both margins; the seeds all present similar characters to those explained under *Peschiera*, being half-immersed in a soft fleshy substance shown to be a funicle—a fact of great importance, a structure, as far as we yet know, peculiar to this tribe. Its numerous species are incoherently classified by Müller, being confounded by him in the single genus *Tabernæmontana*, and placed in his tribe *Plumerieæ*. The following clavis shows the differential features of the genera into which the South-American and Mexican species are here divided.

A. Estivation of corolla sinistrorse : leaves opposite.
  a. Disk, none.
    1. Tube of corolla very slender, cylindrical, swollen at the base, and there staminigerous, segments shorter than the tube, and simply contorted; follicles subovoid and muricated . . . . *Peschiera*.
  b. Disk cylindrical, often short, wholly adnate to the lower portions of the ovaries.
    2. Tube of corolla cylindrical, swollen below the contracted mouth, and there staminigerous, segments long and narrow with a peculiar introflexed æstivation, and descending into the mouth of the tube; follicles oblong, gibbously curved, smooth . . . . *Bonafousia*.
    3. Tube of corolla slender, cylindrical, a little swollen in the mouth, segments dolabriform simply convoluted; stamens slender, of a bluish tinge, always more or less exserted in the apex; follicles smooth, arcuated . . . . . *Tabernæmontana*.
    4. Tube of corolla stouter, cylindrical, swollen in the middle and there staminigerous; anthers subcoherent in a cone; follicles oblong, arcuate, smooth . *Taberna*.
    5. Calyx long, tubular, with a 5-toothed margin; tube of corolla stoutish, cylindrical, constricted in the middle and there staminigerous; anthers slender, free; disk half length of ovaries, with a denticulated margin; follicles ovate, apiculated, smooth . . . . *Codonemma*.
  c. Disk cupshaped, half length of ovaries.
    6. Tube of corolla cylindrical, stoutish, fleshy, constricted in the middle, above which it is staminigerous; anthers free, slender; follicles ovate and muricated as in *Peschiera* . . . . *Phrissocarpus*.
  d. Disk cylindrical, truncated, fleshy, wholly or partially concealing the ovaries.
    7. Tube of corolla gradually swelling from below the mouth, segments oblong, obtuse, nearly as long as the tube, inflected at $\frac{1}{3}$ of their height, and descending within the mouth of the tube; follicles gibbously oblong, compressed, smooth . . . . *Anacampta*.
    8. Tube of corolla short, suddenly and shortly swollen at the base, segments

nearly as long, obtusely linear, oblong erect, simply convoluted in æstivation, in the form of a spire; branches fistulous; leaves large, rigid, with a peculiar petiole . . . . *Rhigospira*.

e. Disk of 5 free erect emarginated lobes partly adhering by their margins.

9. Calyx of 5 large, oblong, membranaceous sepals, having within at their base a corona of many series of scales; corolla large, with a broad funnel-shaped tube; stamens inserted in the middle of the tube . . . . *Stemmadenia*.

f. Disk of 5 very small free lobes.

10. Tube of corolla cylindrical, stoutish, slightly constricted below the middle, segments spathulately oblong, nearly as long as the tube, quite deflected, half introflected in æstivation; follicles subglobose, stipitated, and more or less retrorsely apiculated . . . . *Merizadenia*.

B. Æstivation of corolla dextrorse.

g. Disk none, or subobsolete; leaves opposite.

11. Tube of corolla slender, cylindrical, a little swollen below the constricted mouth, segments oblong, gibbous, elongated, with the æstivation of *Bonafousia*; stamens included in the swollen portion of the tube . . . . . *Anartia*.

h. Disk pilose, concealing the ovaries; leaves alternate.

12. Tube of corolla cylindrical, swollen below the mouth; stamens inserted in the middle of the tube; follicles oblong, pointed, spreading, smooth, subindehiscent . . . . *Geissospermum*.

To this tribe may be referred the following genera belonging to the Old World:—

Piptolæna, A. DC. Prodr. viii. p. 357, S. Africa.
Orchipeda, „ „ p. 358, Java.
Voacanga, „ „ p. 357, Madagascar.
Urceola, „ „ p. 358, Sumatra.
Roupelia, Hook. Niger Flora, p. 449, Africa.

PESCHIERA.

This valid genus, established by Prof. De Candolle in 1844, was reduced, in 1860, to a mere section of *Tabernæmontana* by Dr. Müller, who did not rightly observe its chief and constant peculiarities. It is readily distinguished from *Tabernæmontana*, *Taberna*, and *Bonafousia* by the slender tube of the corolla, always broader at its base, and there staminigerous, by the absence of a disk, by its ovaries free to their base, by its short style, and especially by its muricated or granular follicles. There is another peculiarity first noticed by me in 1836, when I was fortunately able to examine the fruit in a living state: the densely echinated follicle bursts along the convex ventral suture, gaping widely to allow the escape of its several seeds, which fall out suspended from the sutural placentæ by a thick, soft, coloured funicle of more than double their length, which at its lower end is attached to the hilum of the seed, placed in the middle of its deeply channelled ventral face, by which means the seeds remain suspended in the air. This significant fact determines the nature of the pulpy substance that partially envelops the seeds in all the *Tabernæmontaneæ*, and which has been erroneously regarded as an arillus.

PESCHIERA, A. DC.: *Tabernæmontana* (in parte) auct.: Sepala 5, subimbricata, subparva, sæpius lanceolata, submembranacea, intus squamula basali plurilacinulata munitis: *corolla* hypocrateriformis; *tubus* anguste cylindricus, imo paullo inflatus et staminigerus; *segmenta* dolabriformia tubo triplo breviora, æstivatione simpliciter sinistrorsum convoluta. *Stamina* gracillime elongata; *filamenta* tenuia, circa basin tubi inserta; *antheræ* conniventes, fere liberæ, apice cuspidatæ, imo tenuiter biaristatæ. *Discus* nullus. *Ovaria* 2, oblonga, usque ad basin libera. *Stylus* brevis, filiformis: *clavuncula* incrassata, cylindrice 5-angulata, apice breviter 5-dentata, glandulis 10 linearibus signata, basi membrana lacerata suffulta. *Stigmata* 2, terminalia, breviter subulata. *Folliculi* 2, divaricati, ovati vel oblongi, rarius rostrati, undique crebre muricati, vel aspere granosi, sutura ventrali late hiantes, sutura utrinque inflexa et placentifera. *Semina* plurima, compresse obovata, dorso parallele costata, ventre profunde canaliculata, marginibus elevatis sensim evanescentibus, et medium versus *hilo* oblongo signato, superne planata et *chalaza* parva fusca notata: *testa* pergaminea: *integumentum internum* tenuissimum, coalitum. *Albumen* conforme, carnoso-corneum. *Embryo* heterotropus, æquilongus: *cotyledones* 2, ovati, tenuissime foliacei, adpressi; *radicula* supera, æquilonga, teres, obtusa. *Funiculus* crassus, molliter carnosus, coloratus, testa duplo longior, hinc ad placentam ligatus, illinc ad hilum affixus, et hoc modo semina laxata; mox in aëre biserialiter suspensa.

Suffrutices *Americæ intertropicæ, debiles, ramosi*; ramuli *teretes, dichotomi, ad nodos annulati*: folia *elliptica vel lanceolata, breviter petiolata*; paniculæ *subaxillares, sæpius multidivisæ, rarius depauperatæ*; flores *submediocres, albi, aut sæpius flavi*.

1. PESCHIERA ECHINATA, A. DC. viii. 360: *Tabernæmontana echinata*, Aubl. Pl. Guian. i. 263, tab. 103. In Guiana (*non vidi*).

A small lactescent tree, with several erect stems 4-5 feet long, with slender dichotomous branches, annulated where the leaves have fallen off; opposite elliptic leaves, acute at the base, subacuminated, with undulated margins, green above, glabrous, with about 16 pairs of approximated ascending nerves, below covered with a slight white tomentum, 6½ in. long, 2½ in. broad, on petioles 2 lines long, conjoined across the node by a transverse ridge; panicles in the terminal axils, ¾ in. long; peduncles as long as the petioles, bearing about 6 flowers on bracteolated pedicels 2-3 lines long; sepals acute, 2 lines long; tube of corolla 4 lines long, with shorter segments, all spotted with red; stamens inserted near the base of the tube on a pubescent ring; 2 small divaricated subreniform follicles densely muricated, ¾ in. long, ⅜ in. broad.

2. PESCHIERA HYSTRIX, A. DC. Prodr. viii. 360: *Tabernæmontana hystrix*, Steud. Nom. p. 658: *Tabernæmontana echinata*, Vell. (non Aubl.) Fl. Flum. p. 105; Ic. iii. tab. 17: *Tabernæmontana bracteolaris*, Müll. Fl. Bras. fasc. 26, p. 83; *op. cit.* fasc. 40, p. 184, tab. 54. fig. 3. In prov. Rio de Janeiro: *v. v. et sicc. in hb. meo* (n. 2971), *in flore* ad Engenho d'agua, circa Lago de Jacarepaguá.

This specimen corresponds with the drawing of Velloz, who found the plant in about the same locality, near the southern shore of the metropolitan province. The branchlets are thick, fistulous, rugously striated, pale and opake, the lower portions, where the leaves have fallen off, being annulated at the axils, which are about ½ in. apart: the leaves are elliptic-oblong, somewhat acute at the base, obtuse towards the summit, with a blunted acumen, thinly chartaceous, the subundulated margins somewhat revolute, pale opake green above, sulcated on the midrib, with rather distant fine nerves, below pallid and yellowish, opake, spotted by many small elevated dots; they are 3–4½ in. long, 1¾–2 in. broad, on slender petioles broadly fossulated at the base, where they are conjoined by a transverse elevated ring, and vary in length from 3 to 5 lines. The axillary peduncles are 4–6 lines long, forked, the branches 3 lines long, each 4-flowered, with slender pedicels 5 lines long: sepals acute, erect, ¼ line long; tube of corolla 4 lines long, swollen below the middle, narrow above, its dolabriform segments 2½ lines long; stamens enclosed in the swollen part of the tube, and inserted a little above the base: no visible disk. The 2 follicles (which I have not seen) are widely divaricated, 2 in. long, 1 in. rod, reniform band adensely covered with subadpressed very acute spines. In Velloz's drawing they appear by mistake dehiscent on the dorsal side. They contain many ovate seeds, half immersed in scarlet fleshy funicles.

It is a small tree, lactescent, with a soft white wood, often carved into spoons and other utensils for domestic use, and is called "páo de culher" (spoonwood).

The characters given by Müller of *T. Salzmanni* accord with this species, as he expressly indicates, and differ in few particulars.

3. PESCHIERA MURICATA, A. DC. *l. c.* p. 361: *Tabernæmontana muricata*, R. & Sch. (non A. DC.) Syst. iv. 431, 797. In Brasilia (*non vidi*).

Its branches are glabrous and striated; its leaves are ovate-oblong, acuminated, repand on the margins, with elevated granular dots above, which are impressed beneath, more than 7 in. long, on very short petioles; the peduncle of the inflorescence is ½–1 in. long; pedicels less than 1 line long; sepals 1¼ line long; tube of corolla nearly 1 in. long; fruit muricated. It is a species near the following. Müller has confounded it with *P. ochracea*, a very different plant, as shown in the description of the latter (page 42).

4. PESCHIERA FUCHSIÆFOLIA, nob.: *Tabernæmontana fuchsiæfolia*, A. DC. *l. c.* 365 et 676; Müll. *l. c.* p. 83: *Tabernæmontana collina*, Gardn. Lond. Journ. Bot. i. 178. In prov. Rio de Janeiro: *v. v. et sicc. in herb. meo* (n. 3013), *in fl. et fr.* ad Morro Flamengo; *v. s. in flore in hb. Mus. Brit.* ex eodem loco (Gardn. 74, sub *T. collina*).

Prof. De Candolle recognized the identity of Gardner's plant with his *T. fuchsiæfolia*. The species is noted for its rubescent nerves and leaves. I was fortunate in finding its fruit in a living state, which enabled me to ascertain the funicular nature of the pulpy covering which half involves the seeds throughout the whole tribe of the *Tabernæmontaneæ*. This species is a small tree, from 6 to 20 feet high, much branched, the branches pale brown, rugosely striated, the branchlets rather slender and dichotomously divided; the leaves are heterophyllous in each node, elliptic, acute at the base, and terminated by a short obtuse acumen, margins subrevolute, chartaceously flaccid, pale green and opake above, granulo-punctulate on both sides, with immersed nerves, below somewhat paler, opake, yellowish, with prominulent reddish nerves; they are 2¼ and 3¼ in. long at each node, 1⅓ and 1⅔ in. broad, on slender petioles 2½ and 4 lines long, the upper pairs somewhat smaller; the petioles are conjoined across the nodes by a prominent arched ridge: raceme short, opposite at the nodes, on peduncles 4 lines long, its branches of the same length, each bearing about 2 flowers on bracteolated pedicels 6 lines long; sepals lanceolate, deflected at the apex, 2 lines long, with a pluridentate scale inside at the base; tube of corolla narrowly cylindrical above, swollen near the base, 5 lines long, dolabriform segments 3 lines long, simply contorted sinistrorsely in æstivation; stamens inserted in the basal portion of the tube; 2 oblong pointed ovaries, without any apparent disk; style very short, clavuncle incrassated and deeply 5-grooved; 2 oblong subreniform follicles, densely muricated, 1 in. long, 7 lines broad, each containing 16 seeds suspended from the two sutural placentæ by as many very thick orange-coloured fleshy funicles 9 lines long, nearly 2 lines thick; seeds oval, compressed, convex and striated on the dorsal side, longitudinally channelled to near the base on the ventral side, the hilum placed on the hollow below the centre, where they are attached to the funicle; they are 5 lines long, 3 lines broad; albumen corneous, of the same shape, containing an embryo of near its length, 3 lines long, with a slender terete superior radicle, as long as the oval flat cotyledons.

The granular elevations on the leaves are opake when dry; but in the living state they are pellucid.

This plant, its inflorescence, its follicles, and the peculiar manner of the suspension of its seeds are represented in Plate VI. A.

5. PESCHIERA LÆTA, nob.: *Tabernæmontana læta*, Mart. in Hb. Pl. Bras. p. 104; A. DC. *l. c.* p. 364 (excl. syn.); Gardn. in Lond. Journ. Bot. i. 179; Müll. in Flor. Bras. fasc. 26, p. 79; Mart. *op. cit.* fasc. 40, p. 183, tab. 54. fig. 1. In prov. Rio de Janeiro: *v. v. et sicc. hb. meo* (n. 3014), *in flore* in ascensu Monte Corcovado; *v. s. in hb. Mus. Brit.* ex eod. loc. (Gardn. 75).

I found this species in flower, in September 1837, in company with Gardner; it has been found also at Itagoahy in the same province; and in 1864 Dr. Peckholt sent to Von Martius a specimen of the same in flower and in fruit, the structure of which is shown in the plate above cited. This structure is quite similar to that I witnessed and figured in *P. fuchsiæfolia*; but Martius has drawn the funicle, seed, and embryo in an inverted position: he calls the funicle an *arillus*; but this cannot be, as one end of it is attached to the hilum, the other end to the placenta.

This is a small tree, with pale, angulo-sulcated, lenticellated, stoutish, dichotomous branchlets; the opposite leaves, somewhat heterophyllous in each node, are oblong or lanceolate-oblong, acute at both ends, somewhat inæquilateral at the base, sub membranaceous, entire or subrepand along the margin, palish green above, and sulcated along the midrib, yellowish opake below, with reddish immersed nerves on both sides, as in *P. fuchsiæfolia*; they are 3¼ and 4½ in. long, 1¾ and 1 in. broad, on petioles 5 and 8 lines long, conjoined across the node by an arching ridge in the upper superior axils. The subterminal panicle is 2½ in. long; the peduncle, 4 lines long, has three branches 6 lines long, each bearing 6 or 8 flowers on bracteolated pedicels 3–4 lines long; sepals scarcely 1 line long, acute, each with an internal pluridentate scale at its base; tube of corolla cylindrical, swollen at the base, 5 lines long, segments obliquely oblong, 4 lines long; stamens, as usual, inserted near the base; 2 free oblong ovaries without any disk; style short, clavuncle and stigmata as usual; follicles 2, much divaricated, greatly resembling those of the preceding species, but somewhat larger, 1½ in. long, 1 in. broad, each containing about 20 seeds 4-6 lines long, 2-3 lines broad, suspended by scarlet fleshy funicles; structure of the seeds as in the preceding species, and as depicted by Müller.

6. PESCHIERA LUNDII, nob.: *Tabernæmontana Lundii*, A. DC. *l. c.* p. 365; Müll. *l. c.* p. 81. Rio de Janeiro ad Botafogo: *v. v. et sicc. in flore et fructu in herb. meo* (n. 3965); *v. s. in herb. Mus. Brit.* Monte Corcovado (Gardn. 5546).

A species differing from *T. Gaudichaudii* in its more slender, more dichotomous, rugously striated branchlets, the younger ones smooth and closely lenticellated, its much darker leaves, less acute and more inæquilateral at the base, obtuse at the summit, with a short rounded excurrent point, subundulated margins, with a rougher surface above, with slender prominulent yellow nerves, yellowish opake below, with a pale interruptedly striated midrib and prominent yellow fine nerves, and on longer petioles: it has a more slender panicle with smaller flowers. The leaves are ovate, darkish and opake above, 3¼-4¾ in. long, 1¾-2 in. broad, on slender channelled petioles, fossulate at the base, 5-7 lines long; axillary panicles 1½ in. long, 10-12-flowered, with many slender, divided branches and deciduous bracteoles; peduncle 6 lines long, its alternate branchlets 2-4 lines long; pedicels 2 lines long; sepals acutely ovate, pruinose, with membranaceous ciliolate margins, ¾ line long; tube of corolla 2¼ lines long, yellow and subtomentose, rather swollen at the base, pilose within below the middle, glabrous above, segments shorter than the tube, dolabriform, subpuberulous within at the base; stamens inserted near the base of the tube, anthers 2-lobed at the base; disk none; 2 ovate ovaries, reddishly tomentose; style short, with an incrassated clavuncle; 2 reniformly ovate follicles 1¼ in. long, ¼ in. thick, obtuse at both ends, marked by several transverse interrupted ridges muricated on their acute edges, each containing 18 seeds, 4 lines long, 2½ lines broad, suspended from the sutural placentæ by stout pale yellow funicles.

7. PESCHIERA SPIXIANA, nob.: *Tabernæmontana Spixiana*, Mart.; Müll. *l. c.* p. 78. In prov. Rio de Janeiro: *v. s. in hb. Mus. Brit. in flore* Itagoahy (Bowie et Cunningham).

A shrub 10-12 feet high; branches terete, dichotomous, densely foliaceous; leaves but little heterophyllous, elliptic-lanceolate, narrowed and gradually acute at both ends, dark green above, sulcate along the midrib, with semi-immersed nerves, below of a darkish yellow colour, opake, with prominulent reddish nerves, 5 and 5½ in. long, 1¼ and 1⅜ in. broad, on slender petioles 4¾ lines long; upper pairs of leaves 4¼ and 3¾ in. long, 13 and 15 lines broad, on petioles 4 lines long; axillary panicles 2-3, fasciculated, 1¼ in. long; peduncles 6 lines long, bearing 5-6 branchlets 1 in. long, each supporting about 3 flowers, on pedicels 2 lines long, with small acutely oval bracteoles; sepals triangular ovate, subobtuse, with membranaceous margins, ¾ line long, each with an inner basal 4-6-laciniulate scale; tube of corolla cylindrical, broader at the base, segments broadly obovate, gibbous, pubescent within at their base and in the mouth of the tube; stamens inserted near the base of the tube, out of a pilose ring; disk none; ovaries 2, ovoid; follicles 2, spreading, broadly obovoid, obtuse, densely muricated, 1¼-1½ in. long; seeds ovoid, channelled on one side, scabridly granular on the other, 4–4¾ lines long, half enveloped in scarlet fleshy funicles.

8. PESCHIERA GRANULOSA, nob.: ramis validiusculis, dichotomis, rugulosis; ramulis tenuioribus, pallidis, striatis, ad nodos compressis; foliis lanceolato-oblongis, imo cuneatis, apice in acumen subbreve obtusulum constrictis, marginibus subretuse undulatis, tenuiter chartaceis, supra viridibus, costa sulcata, nervis patule divaricatis, sensim arcuatis et subimmersis, subtus paullo pallidioribus, opacis, granulatim subpruinosis, costa nervisque flavidis, prominulis; petiolis longiuscule tenuibus, canaliculatis, linea transversa nexis: racemis axillaribus, sæpius valde depauperatis, pedunculo (seu ramulo novello) tenui, ter opposite bracteolatis; bracteis linearibus, subfoliaceis, 1–7-floris; pedicellis in axillis bractearum sæpius abortivis aut in sinu ultimarum, 1-floris; pedicello bracteis calyciquc æquilongo; sepalis lanccolatis, pallide marginatis, erecto-patulis, intus squamula basali 4–5 laciniulata munitis; corollæ tubo anguste cylindrico, imo latiore, glaberrimo, segmentis oblique ovatis, tubo ter brevioribus, sinistrorsum convolutis; staminibus inclusis, filamentis complanatis, circa basin tubi insertis; disco nullo; ovariis 2, ovatis, obtusis, sepalis dimidio brevioribus; stylo paullulo longiore; clavuncula et stigmatibus præcedentium; pedunculis fructiferis valde incrassatis, acute angulatis, stramineis: folliculis 2, oblongis, divaricatis, vix compressis, exiguе granulatis, imo obtusis, dorso rectis, apice subreflexim breviter rostratis, ventre orbicularibus et sutura dehiscentibus; seminibus compressis ovatis, ventre canaliculatis, et hinc in medio ab hilo funiculis crassis pulposis rubris suspensis. In prov. Rio de Janeiro: *v. v. et sicc. in herb. meo* (n. 2065, 4028), *in flore et in fructu* montibus Organensibus, *in fructu immaturo* (n. 4654) Monte Corcovado.

A well-marked species, peculiar in the appearance of its leaves, which resemble those of *Tabernæmontana amygdalæfolia*: the axils of its branchlets are 1–1½ in. apart; the leaves are somewhat heterophyllous, 3½–4 in. long, 1–1½ in. broad, on petioles 7–9 lines long. In the Organ-Mountain plant the peduncle of the depauperated raceme is 1 in. long, bearing 3 pairs of bracts 4 lines apart, which are flowerless, and only a single flower is seen at the extremity between the last pair of bracts on a pedicel 2 lines long; sepals 2 lines long; the tube of the corolla 6 lines long, the segments 2 lines long and broad; follicles 1½ in. long, including the rostrum, ½ in. broad; seeds 5½ lines long, 3½ lines broad, suspended by thick red coloured funicles.

9. PESCHIERA CUSPIDATA, nob.: ramis dichotomis, teretibus, ramulisque pallidis, striatis, subfistulosis: foliis majusculis, in paribus altero opposito multo minore, ovato-oblongis, imo subito acutis, apice in acumine longe lineari repente cuspidatis, membranaceis, retuse undulatis, supra profunde viridibus, opacis, sub lente sparsim pilosulis, nervis tenuissimis semiimmersis, subtus pallide opacis, flavescentibus, in nervis fulvidis prominulis patentim hirsutulis, reticulatis; petiolis tenuibus sulcatis, pilosis, limbo 24plo brevioribus: racemis ad nodos supremos solitariis, folio dimidio brevioribus, puberulis; pedunculo elongato infra medium nudo, superne ramoso, ramis brevissimis subcrebris, bracteolatis, apice 2-floris,·pedicellis æquilongis bracteolatis; sepalis lanceolatis, recurvulis; corollæ tubo longo, angustissime cylindrico, imo latiore, intus pilosulo, segmentis oblique oblongis, tubo triplo brevioribus; staminibus supra basin insertis; disco nullo apparente: folliculis 2, divaricatis. oblongis, sensim augustioribus, creberrime hamato-muricatis. In Nova Granada: *v. s. in flore et fructu in hb. meo* (n. 22029) Rio Magdalena (Weir 76).

A species peculiar in its pilose branches, very cuspidate subpilose leaves, and in its inflorescence: each pair of leaves measure 4 and 7½ in. long (including the acumen of 9 lines), 2½–3½ in. broad, on petioles 2–4 lines long; in some of the axils they are somewhat more than half that size; the peduncle of the inflorescence is 2–2½ in. long, its superior branches 1½ line long; pedicels of the same length; sepals 1½ line long; tube of corolla 5 lines long, segments 3 lines long; follicles 15 lines long, 5 lines broad, on a thickened pedicel 5 lines long.

10. PESCHIERA STENOLOBA, nob.: *Tabernæmontana stenoloba*, Müll. in Linn. xxx. 407. In Peruvia, circa Cuchero, Yurimanguas et circa Guayaquil (*non vidi*).

A species near *P. heterophylla*, with slender branches, with opposite leaves in unequal pairs, ovate elliptic, acuminated, submembranaceous, 4 and 6 in. long, 2 in. broad, on petioles 3–3¾ lines long; cymes sublateral in the dichotomy of the branches, 6–8-flowered; peduncle 2 lines long, densely covered with imbricated ovate bracts 1 line long; sepals lanceolate, with an internal 4–5-dentate scale at the base; corolla in bud 1 in. long, with a slender tube broader at the base, densely pilose within, segments oblong obovate; stamens inserted a little above the base of the tube; 2 free acutely obovate ovaries, without a disk; style short; 2 obovate follicles, echinated.

11. PESCHIERA TENUIFLORA, Pöpp. Gen. iii. p. 70, tab. 280: *Tabernæmontana tenuiflora*, Müll. *l. c.* p. 76. In alta Amazonas ad Rio Japuré, circa Coary (*non vidi*).

A species with much the habit of *P. heterophylla*. It is a shrub 5–6 feet high, much branched, its branches pallidly fuscous, slender, terete, compressed at the nodes, divaricately dichotomous; leaves heterophyllous, spreading, the larger one elliptic, acute, and almost obsoletely petiolated at the base, 5½ in. long, 2½ in. broad, the opposite one ovate or roundish, sessile and subcordate at the base, 2½ in. long, 1⅞ in. broad, glabrous, concolorous; peduncle very slender, erect in the dichotomy of the branchlets, 1–1½ in. long, bearing near its apex 4 approximated flowers, on pedicels 3 lines long, the lower ones caducous; sepals lanceolate, 1 line long; tube of corolla very slender, 7 lines long, slightly swollen near the base, subpilose within, segments 3 lines long, 1 line broad; stamens inserted near the base of the tube, anthers slender, sagittate, subcoherent; ovaries 2, slightly tuberculated; no apparent disk; follicles 2, divaricated, one often abortive, obovate, or obtusely elliptic, subcompressed, verrucously muricated, orange-coloured, 1¾ in. long, 1¼ in. broad.

12. PESCHIERA HETEROPHYLLA, nob.: *Tabernæmontana heterophylla*, Vahl, Ecl. ii. p. 22, Icon. tab. 14 (non A. DC. nec Bth.); Müll. *l. c.* p. 76 (in parte). In Guiana et Amazonas: *v. s. in hb. Mus. Brit.* (*pl. typica*) Cayenne (Van Rohr), Guiana (Sagot 390); *in hb. meo* (n. 17796), San Gabriel, Rio Negro (Spruce 2106).

A species often confounded with the following. Its branchlets are slender at the extremity, dichotomous, terete, and slightly 4-angular, swollen at the axils; lower down, where the leaves have fallen off, they are marked by annular ridges at the nodes. The opposite leaves are unequal in size at each axil, are thinly chartaceous, oval, obtuse, or shortly acute at the base and subinæquilateral, suddenly attenuated at the summit into a sublanceolate acumen; they have about 10 pairs of patently divaricated slender nerves; at each node they are respectively 4¾–3 in. long, 2½–1½ in. broad, on channelled petioles 2–3 lines long, their margins conjoined across the node by an elevated ridge; the leaves towards the extremity are 2½ in. in length, and 1 in. in breadth. The raceme, simply spicated, rises in the dichotomy of the branches; the peduncle is ½–¾ in. long, very closely marked by the cicatrices of the abortive flowers, seldom leaving more than 2 flowers at the apex, on slender pedicels 6–8 lines long; the ovate sepals are 1 line long; the tube of the corolla is 5 lines long, narrowly cylindrical above, ventricose below the middle; the segments are inæquilateral and oblong, 3 lines long, 2 lines broad, of a reddish colour, simply convoluted sinistrorsely in æstivation. The stamens are seated in the swollen part of the tube; the filaments arise out of 5 pilose lines, a little above the base of the tube; the anthers, twice the length of the filaments, are 2-lobed at their base, acuminated by a lanceolated membrane. No disk. Ovaries 2, pointed oblong.

13. PESCHIERA DIVERSIFOLIA, Mig. Stirp. Surin. p. 164, tab. 47: *Tabernæmontana heterophylla*, Benth. (non Vahl), Journ. Bot. iii. 243; A. DC. (in parte) Prodr. viii. 361; Müll. (in parte) *l. c.* p. 76. In Guiana: *v. s. in hb. meo* (n. 9241) Guiana (Schomb. 3).

A species well distinguished from the former by its more slender branchlets, not thickened at the nodes, by its smaller, more lanceolate, very membranaceous leaves, almost sessile; branchlets striolated, dichotomous; leaves narrowly oblong, gradually cuneate and inæquilateral at the base, with a long narrow acute acumen, very slender arcuately ascending nerves, very unequal at each node, 3½–2½ in. long, 1–¾ in. broad, on petioles scarcely more than ¼ line long, or sessile. The peduncle, as in the preceding, is seated in the dichotomy, ½–1 in. long, densely crowded with cicatrices, rarely more than 3- or 4-flowered at the summit, on pedicels 6–8 lines long; sepals 1 line long; tube of corolla equally cylindrical, a little swollen above its base, very slender, 5 lines long, segments unequally linear, 2 lines long, ¼ line broad, of a pale yellow or whitish colour, convoluted sinistrorsely in æstivation; stamens as in the preceding species, enclosed in the swollen inferior portion of the tube; no disk; 2 conical oblong ovaries.

14. PESCHIERA ALBIDIFLORA, uob.: ramulis dichotomis, tenuissimis, teretibus, striolatis, pallidissimis; foliis paullo heterophyllis, lanceolato-oblongis, imo longe cuneatis et in petiolo decurrentibus, apice sensim acutis, membranaceis, marginibus recurvulis, utrinque opacis et obsolete corrugulatis, supra pallide viridibus, nervis utrinque 10 arcuatim divaricatis semiimmersis, subtus pallidioribus, nervis tenuissimis stramineis paullo prominulis, eveniis; petiolis tenuibus, semiteretibus, linea transversali nexis, limbo 7plo brevioribus: paniculis axillaribus, ramosis, pedunculo compresso, ramis tenuibus, imo bracteola parva lanceolata munitis; pedicellis tenuibus; floribus albis; sepalis acute lanceolatis, apice reflexis; corollæ tubo anguste cylindrico, basin versus ampliore, segmentis oblique oblongis, dimidio brevioribus, sinistrorsum convolutis; staminibus inclusis, filamentis tenuibus prope basin tubi insertis; disco nullo; ovariis 2, oblongis, liberis, cæteris ut in precedentibus. In prov. Rio de Janeiro: *v. s. in hb. Mus. Brit.* Itagoahy (Bowie and Cunningham).

A species near *P. diversifolia*: branchlets very slender, with annular nodes 1–1½ in. apart; lower leaves in subinequal pairs, 3 and 3¼ in. long, 1–1¼ in. broad, on petioles 5–6 lines long; the upper pairs of leaves half that size; axillary panicles on slender peduncles 9 lines long, bearing about 4 alternate flowers on pedicels 3 lines long; sepals 1¼ line long; tube of corolla 6 lines long, segments 2½ lines long.

15. **PESCHIERA GAUDICHAUDII**, nob.: *Tabernæmontana Gaudichaudii*, A. DC. *l. c.* p. 365; Müll. *l. c.* p. 79. In prov. Rio de Janeiro: *v. v. et sicc. in hb. meo* (n. 2830) Monte Corcovado; *v. s. in hb. Mus. Brit.* Corcovado (Gardn. 5546).

A species near *P. fuchsiæfolia*, differing in its branches, scarcely dichotomous, annulated at distances of ½–1 in. where the leaves have fallen off, in its ovate, less-acuminated leaves, scarcely unequal at the nodes, less acute at the base, rugously opake above, with yellowish slender immersed nerves and stouter panicles. It is a shrub 8 feet high; leaves ovate or elliptic, submembranaceous, subobtuse or acute at the base, suddenly and shortly acuminated at the summit, pruinosely granulated above, yellowish opake below, with prominent midrib and reddish fine prominulent nerves, veins scarcely visible, 4¾–3¼ in. long, 2–1¾ in. broad, on slender petioles 5–6 lines long; the more superior leaves are smaller; axillary panicles much branched, many-flowered, 1½ in. long; bracts very deciduous; peduncle 6 lines long, with three closely alternate branches 5 lines long, each again branched; pedicels approximated, 2–3 lines long; sepals acutely ovate, swollen at their base, ¾ line long; tube of corolla 3½ lines long, segments 2¼ lines long; stamens inserted near the base of the tube; anthers elongated, acutely 2-aristate at the base; style very short, with a thickened clavuncle; no disk; 2 conical oblong ovaries.

16. **PESCHIERA SALZMANNI**, nob.: *Tabernæmontana Salzmanni*, A. DC. *l. c.* p. 362; Müll. *l. c.* p. 78: *Tabernæmontana Rauwolfia*, A. DC. *l. c.* p. 364. In prov. Bahia (Salzm. 13, et Blanchet 713): *non vidi*.

A small tree, 10 feet high, with stiff branches, densely covered with leaves, which falling off leave the branches marked by annular ridges; leaves obovate, 2–3½ in. long, 1¾ in. broad, on petioles 2½–3¾ lines long; panicle trichotomously divided, many-flowered. This closely resembles *Peschiera hystrix*.

17. **PESCHIERA AFFINIS**, nob.: *Tabernæmontana affinis*, Müll. *l. c.* p. 83, tab. 26. fig. 1. Brasiliæ prov. centralibus: *v. s. in hb. Mus. Brit.* Minas Geraës, ad Arrayal das Mercês (Gardn. 5010).

A slender species, much resembling the two preceding, with dichotomous branchlets, their axils about ½ in. apart; leaves lanceolate, acute at both ends, thinly chartaceous, glabrous above, reddishly opake below, and shortly puberulous on the nerves, 3½–4½ in. long, ¾–1 in. broad, on petioles 2–3 lines long; cymes lateral, bi-trichotomously divided, 1¾ in. long, 5–10-flowered; peduncle 6 lines long, its branches 2–3 lines long, bracts shortly linear; pedicels 3 lines long; sepals 2 lines long, lanceolate, spreading, scabridulous; tube of corolla cylindrical, a little thicker below, puberulous inside, 5½ lines long, its segments oblong, 2¼ lines long; stamens inserted near the base of the tube, upon rather long slender filaments, anthers cuspidate and biaristate; disk none; ovaries acutely oblong, style slender, with a thickened clavuncle.

Gardner's specimen corresponds well with Müller's drawing.

18. **PESCHIERA FALLAX**, nob.: *Tabernæmontana fallax*, Müll. *l. c.* p. 84. In prov. Minas Geraës (St.-Hilaire 944): *non vidi*.

A species with small, obovate lanceolate leaves, 1⅝ in. long, 5¼–7 lines broad, on stout petioles 1¼ line broad; cymes terminal, with about 10 closely approximated flowers; peduncle many times longer than the calyx; pedicels a little longer than the calyx; bracts small, lanceolate; sepals lanceolate, subpatent, half the length of the tube of the corolla, which is swollen below the middle, with a pilose ring near its base, from which the stamens originate; it is pubescent in the throat.

19. PESCHIERA GRACILLIMA, nob.: *Tabernæmontana gracilis*, Müll. (non Bth.) *l. c.* p. 82. In prov. Rio de Janeiro, Sierra d'Estrella: *non vidi*.

The specific name is changed, that it may not be confounded with *T. gracilis*, Bth. It resembles the preceding in the small size of its linear lanceolate leaves, which are 1⅜–2 in. long, ¼ in. broad, on short petioles; cyme subterminal, 2–3 times shorter than the leaf; peduncle as short as the petiole; pedicels twice the length of the calyx; peduncle depauperated, bearing 2–3 bracteoles, often by abortion 1-flowered; sepals 2 lines long; tube of corolla slender, 5 lines long, narrow above, broader below, pubescent within, segments obliquely ovate, puberulous within,—all being the characters of *Peschiera*. It is a small tree, 12–15 feet high.

20. PESCHIERA HILARIANA, nob.: *Tabernæmontana Hilariana*, Müll. *l. c.* p. 85. In prov. S. Paulo: *non vidi*.

The leaves sublanceolate, suddenly acuminated at the apex, membranaceous, 3⅛–4 in. long (including the petiole), 8½–11¼ lines broad. The inflorescence is a terminal corymb, with about 20 crowded flowers; peduncle length of calyx; pedicels bracteolated, of the same length; sepals lanceolate, nearly as long as the tube of the corolla, which is narrow above, pubescent within; stamens inserted below the middle of the tube; ovaries ovate, length of style.

21. PESCHIERA CATHERINENSIS, nob.: *Tabernæmontana Catherinensis*, Müll. *l. c.* p. 85: A. DC. Prodr. viii. 365. In prov. S. Paulo: *non vidi*.

It has slender, spreading, dichotomous branches: leaves oblong elliptic, obtusely acuminated at both ends, 2–2½ in. long, including the puberulous petiole (2–2¾ lines long), 1–1½ in. broad; corymb as in *P. fuchsiæfolia*, but more densely flowered.

22. PESCHIERA FLORIDA, nob.: *Tabernæmontana læta*, var. *puberiflora*, Müll. *l. c.* p. 79. In Brasilia: *v. s. in hb. meo* prov. Minas Geraës (Gardn. 5011).

A species very proximate to *P. multiflora*, and with little resemblance to *P. læta*. It has stoutish, subdichotomous, pallid, rugously striated branches, the younger ones dark and very compressed; the leaves are elliptic oblong, subacute at the base, little constricted towards the shortish obtuse acumen, thinly chartaceous, with undulated or interruptedly revolute margins, darkish green and opake above, with sulcated midrib and semi-immersed fine nerves, yellowish opake below, subpruinose, with prominulent midrib and reddish fine nerves, 4–5 in. long, 1⅜–1¾ in. broad, on stoutish channelled petioles 5–6 lines long, fossulated at the base, and conjoined across the node by an arching, raised ridge; cymes 2 or 4, fasciculated at the end of the young branchlets; peduncles 9–12 lines long, their branches 2 lines long, minutely bracteolated; pedicels slender, 3 lines long; sepals acutely ovate, imbricated, with membranaceous margins, 1 line long, each with an internal 4–5-laciniated scale; tube of corolla narrowed above the middle, swelling to the base, pubescent above within, 4½ lines long, with dolabriform segments 2¼ lines long, densely pubescent within at their base; stamens inserted near the base of the tube; disk none; 2 pointed oblong free ovaries; style, clavuncle, and stigmata as usual.

23. PESCHIERA OCHRACEA, nob.: *Tabernæmontana ochracea*, Spruce MS.: *Tabernæmontana muricata*, Müll. (non R. & Sch.) *l. c.* pp. 80 et 114, tab. 54. fig. 2. In Amazonas: *v. s. in hb. Mus. Brit.* Santarem (Spruce 234).

This species is very distinct from *T. muricata*, R. & Sch., differing in its much smaller leaves, which are elliptic, canaliculately recurved at both ends, acute at the base, with a long narrow acumen at the apex, margins revolute, pale green above, opake, with numerous obsolete parallel corrugated lines, nerves immersed, opake and yellow below, with prominulent midrib and nerves, without the slightest indication of the peculiar dots, elevated above, impressed below, which characterize the species described by Römer and Schulz. In the present instance the leaves are only 3¼–4 in. long, 1¼–1½ in. broad, on petioles 3–4 lines long (in *T. muricata* they are above 7 in. long, on very short petioles); corymb terminal and many-flowered, half or a third the length of the leaf; peduncle very short, primary and secondary branches elongated; pedicels twice as long as the calyx, with a small basal bracteole; calyx barely 1 line long; the very slender tube of the corolla is 1 in. long, a little swollen at the base, segments oblong, curving, 5 lines long, sinistrorsely convoluted in æstivation; stamens inserted a little above the base of the tube; disk none; 2 free ovaries, with a very short style incrassated at its summit by a long 5-angular clavuncle and 2 small terminal stigmata.

24. PESCHIERA PSYCHOTRIÆFOLIA, nob.: *Tabernæmontana psychotriæfolia*, H. B. K. iii. 227: A. DC. *l. c.* p. 366. In Venezuela et Nova Granada: *v. s. in hb. meo* (n. 22019) Rio Magdalena (Weir 37).

This plant accords with Kunth's description. Its dichotomous, pallid, stout branchlets are rugously striated, marked by annular rings 4–6 lines apart where the leaves have fallen off; in the upper part they are sub-4-angular; the leaves, rarely quite equal in each node, are oblong, or subovate, subacute and inæquilateral at the base, rather obtusely acute, and mucronated at the apex, margins subrevolute, submembranaceous, pale green above, yellowish opake below, nerves rather patent and prominulent on both sides, 4–5¼ in. long, 2–2½ in. broad, on channelled petioles 3–5 lines long, conjoined across the node by an arched ridge; some of the upper leaves often smaller; axillary opposite corymbs 2 in. long and broad, very dichotomously branched, many-flowered, on bracteolated pedicels 2 lines long; sepals acute, reflected at the apex, 1 line long; tube of corolla cylindrical, broader at the base, 5 lines long, segments 4 lines long, 2 lines broad, sinistrorsely convoluted, very pubescent within at the base; stamens 2½ lines long, seated near the base of the tube; 2 ovaries oblong, free, without any disk; clavuncle, style, and stigmata as usual.

25. PESCHIERA LINGULATA, nob.: ramulis dichotomis opace brunneis, interrupte striatis, ad nodos (foliis

lapsis) annulatis: foliis heterophyllis, ellipticis, imo acutis, apice in acumen breve acutulum reflexum subito constrictis, chartaceis, supra opace viridibus, obsolete corrugulatis, ad nervos immersos sulcatulis, subtus flavide opacis, costa prominente, nervis sæpe rufulis prominulis; petiolis subtenuibus, canaliculatis, linea arcuata transversa conjunctis: panicula axillari, brevi, pauciflora; pedunculo bifurcato, ramis alternatim bracteolatis, 2-floris; pedicellis ramos æquantibus; sepalis parvis, ovatis, mucronatis, ciliatis, intus squamula plurilacinulata munitis; corollæ tubo anguste cylindrico, imo latiore, segmentis brevioribus, dolabriformibus, sinistrorsum convolutis; staminibus gracilibus, 2-aristatis, cum filamentis circa basin tubi insertis; disco nullo; ovariis oblongis; stylo brevi. In Peruvia: *v. s. in hb. meo* (Matthews 1542).

The stoutish branchlets, at their leafless nodes, 3–5 lines apart, are annulated by a curved ridge; the leaves, unequal at each node, are 4 and 2 in. long, $1\frac{5}{8}$ and $1\frac{1}{4}$ in. broad, on petioles 4 and 3 lines long; peduncle 6 lines long, 2 branches, each 4 lines long; pedicels 4 lines long, 2–3-bracteolated in the middle; sepals 2 lines long; tube of corolla 9 lines long; segments 5 lines long.

26. PESCHIERA ACUMINATA, nob.: *Tabernæmontana acuminata*, Müll. in Linn. xxx. 406. In Bolivia (Cuming 121): *non vidi*.

A species said to be near *P. Gaudichaudii*, *P. Lundii*, *P. fuchsiæfolia*, and *P. affinis*. It has smooth branches, with internodes three times as long as the leaves, and dichotomous, compressed, glaucous-green branchlets; leaves oblong lanceolate, acute at both ends, membranaceous, with about 12 pairs of divergent nerves, $2-3\frac{5}{8}$ in. long, $9\frac{1}{2}$–12 lines broad, on petioles 2–3 lines long, scarcely conjoined across the nodes; corymbs in the dichotomies of the branchlets, 3-fasciculate, each branch twice trichotomously and densely divided, 18–25-flowered, glabrous, $1-1\frac{1}{2}$ in. long; peduncles short; flowers in bud $6\frac{1}{4}$ lines long; bracts large, 2–3 lines long, $\frac{1}{2}$ line broad; sepals erect, linear lanceolate, blunt at the point, with a recurving margin, each with an inner basal 4–5-lacinulated scale; tube of corolla in bud twice the length of the calyx, distinctly swollen near the base, and there staminigerous on a pilose ring; disk none; ovaries 2, obtusely ovoid, about as long as the style. All these characters are obviously those of *Peschiera*.

27. PESCHIERA PUBERIFLORA, nob.: ramulis crassiusculis, 4-angulatis, sulcatis, axillis subcrebris et annulatis: foliis ellipticis, imo acutis, apice in acumen breve latiusculum recurvum constrictis, chartaceis, marginibus interrupte revolutis subundulatis, supra opace viridibus, nervis tenuibus vix prominulis, subtus opace pallidioribus, ochraceis, costa nervisque prominulis; petiolis tenuiter canaliculatis, imo linea curvata transversali conjunctis, limbo 12plo brevioribus: panicula axillaribus, oppositis, folia superiora æquantibus; pedunculo petiolo triplo longiore, bis dichotome diviso, ramis huic æquilongis, 2–3-floris, cum bracteis oblongis margine membranaceis; pedicellis gracilibus, medio bracteolatis; sepalis parvis, acute oblongis, submembranaceis, ciliatis, singula squamula lata pluridentata intus munitis; corollæ tubo anguste cylindrico, infra medium sensim latiore, glabro, segmentis dolabriformibus, brevioribus, sinistrorsum convolutis, intus pubescentibus; staminibus paullo supra basin insertis; disco nullo; cæteris ut in præcedentibus. In Peruvia: *v. s. in hb. meo* Tarapota (Spruce 4245).

In my specimen, only the upper leaves are present, on axils 4–6 lines apart; they are $1\frac{1}{2}$–2 in. long, $\frac{3}{4}$–1 in. broad, on petioles 2 lines long; the peduncle is 4–5 lines long, its branches 4 lines; the pedicels 5 lines long; the sepals 1 line long; tube of corolla 4½ lines long, segments 3 lines long.

28. PESCHIERA CONCINNA, nob.: ramulis validiusculis, pallidis, angulato-sulcatis, inferne defoliatis et annulatis: foliis heterophyllis, ellipticis, imo acutis, apice in acumen latiusculum plicato-recurvum sensim terminatis, tenuiter chartaceis, supra opace viridibus, minute granulatis, costa sulcata, nervis tenuibus semiimmersis, subtus flavide pallidioribus, costa prominente, nervis rufulis prominulis; petiolis canaliculatis, imo fossulatis et linea transversa conjunctis, limbo 12plo brevioribus: paniculis axillaribus et terminalibus, 2-3-4-fasciculatis, e basi ramosa circa 16-floris, ramis sub 3-floris; pedicellis medio bracteolatis; sepalis parvis, acute ovatis, submembranaceis, intus singulatim squamula pluriliaciniata ad basin munitis; corollae tubo cylindrico, imo paullo latiore, glabro, segmentis dolabriformibus, intus pro dimidia parte inferiore dense pubescentibus, sinistrorsum convolutis; staminibus tubi versus basin insertis. In Peruvia: *v. s. in hb. meo* Tarapota (Spruce 4534).

Axils ¾ in. apart; leaves of unequal length in each node, 5 and 2½ in. long, 2 and 1 in. broad, on petioles 5-3 lines long; the upper pairs smaller; panicles 1¼ in. long; branches of peduncles 3 lines long; pedicels 3-5 lines long; sepals ¾ line long; tube of corolla 7 lines long, segments 4 lines; filaments of stamens ⅛ their length, inserted near the base of the tube; anthers 2-aristate at the base; disk none; 2 free ovaries; style short; rest conforming to the general character.

29. PESCHIERA BLANDA, nob.: ramulis subdichotomis, teretibus, striatis, ad nodos compressis et annulatis: foliis heterophyllis, ellipticis, imo sensim acutis, apice in acumen recurvum longiuscule rostratum subito constrictis, marginibus revolutis, chartaceis, supra viridibus, opacis, leviter corrugulatis, nervis adscendentibus semiimmersis, subtus flavide pallidioribus, opacis, nervis paullo prominulis, petiolis tenuibus, canaliculatis, linea transversali conjunctis, limbo 8-10plo brevioribus: cyma in dichotomiis terminali, circa 12-flora, e basi 3-ramosa, ramis petiolo brevioribus, ramulis paucis, bracteolatis, bi- v. trifloris; pedicellis tenuibus, medio bracteolatis; sepalis parvis, obtuse ovatis, membranaceis, imbricatis, singulis squamula interna trilaciniata munitis; corollae tubo anguste cylindrico, superne intus puberulo, imo ampliore et glabro, segmentis inaequaliter oblongis, tubo brevioribus, glabris, sinistrorsum convolutis; staminibus inclusis; filamentis tenuissimis circa basin tubi insertis; antheris gracilibus, tenuissime biaristatis; disco nullo; ovariis 2, liberis; stylo tenui, brevi, clavuncula incrassata 5-sulcata, imo membrana donata; stigmatibus 2 terminalibus. In Peruvia: *v. s. in hb. meo* Tarapota (Spruce 4209).

A species near the two preceding: leaves in pairs 5 and 4 in. long, or 4 and 3 in. long, 1¾-1¼ in. broad, on petioles 5 and 4 lines long, or on petioles 9-7 and 5 lines long; cyme 1¼ in. long; peduncles 2 lines, their branches 2 lines long; pedicels 3-4 lines long; sepals 1 line; tube of corolla 5 lines long, segments 3½ lines long.

30. PESCHIERA UMBROSA, nob.: *Tabernæmontana umbrosa*, H. B. K. iii. 226: A. DC. *l. c.* p. 375. In Venezuela: *non vidi*.

A tree, with smooth branches; leaves elliptic-oblong, acute at both ends, membranaceous, nerves prominent below, nearly 5 in. long, 2-2¼ in. broad, on channelled petioles ½ in. long, whose margins are conjoined across the node by a very short transverse membrane; corymb subdichotomous, much shorter than the leaves, pedunculated and bracteolated; flowers white, like those of jessamine, pedicellated; sepals lanceolate acute, equal, 6 times shorter than the tube of the corolla, having at their base inside 5 denticulated scales; the tube of corolla 4 lines long, swollen at its base, pubescent in the throat, border-segments a little shorter than the tube, expanded, inæquilateral, roundly obovate; stamens inserted in the base of the tube; anthers linear sagittate, cohering in a cone by adhesion to the clavuncle; 2 ovaries conically pointed, plano-convex, apparently without a disk; the 5 toothed scales mentioned by Kunth belong to the sepals. These characters, especially the position of the stamens, are those of *Peschiera*.

31. PESCHIERA LITORALIS, nob.: *Tabernæmontana litoralis*, H. B. K. iii. 228: A. DC. *l. c.* p. 363. In Campêche: *non vidi*.

Branches smooth, dichotomous; leaves elliptic-oblong, acute at the base, subacuminate, membranaceous, with entire margins, midrib and nerves prominent below, green above, paler beneath, nearly 5 in. long, 2 in. broad, on channelled petioles 4 lines long, their margins conjoined by a transverse line; opposite interpetiolar panicles, shorter than the leaves; peduncle subdichotomous, with few bracteolated flowers 2 in. long; sepals linear-subulate, fleshy, with membranaceous margins, very imbricated, the 2 interior narrower; corolla salvershaped, tube cylindrical and twisting, 4–5 times as long as the calyx, border-segments very expanded, half-obovate, equal, shorter than the tube; stamens inserted upon a pilose ring, near the base of the tube; ovaries 2, ovate.

From its salvershaped corolla with a long tube, with stamens fixed near its base, and its ovaries without a disk, this species well accords with *Peschiera*.

32. PESCHIERA MULTIFLORA, Spruce, MS.: *Tabernæmontana Benthamiana*, Müll. *l. c.* p. 80. In Amazonas: *v. s. in hb. meo et alior. prope Obidos* (Spruce 235).

A suffruticose species 6–10 feet high, with cinereous-brown branchlets, with axils $\frac{1}{2}$–$\frac{3}{4}$ in. apart: the leaves are 3–5 in. long, $1\frac{3}{4}$–$2\frac{7}{8}$ in. broad, on very slender petioles 2–3 lines long; they are very acute at the base, shortly acuminated at the apex: the peduncle of the copious dichotomous corymb is 2–5 lines long, 2 primary branches 4 lines, the secondary 3 lines; the pedicels 2 lines long, with lanceolate bracteoles $1\frac{1}{2}$ line long; sepals 1 line long; tube of corolla 5 lines long, swollen below, narrowed above, pilose within; stamens fixed a little above the base, segments of border broadly dolabriform, subfleshy, 5 lines long, with sinistrorse convolution.

33. PESCHIERA BREVIFLORA, nob.: *Tabernæmontana breviflora*, Müll. *l. c.* p. 79. Prov. Espirito Santo, inter Campos et Victoria: *non vidi*.

A species said to be near *P. multiflora*: leaves elliptic lanceolate, shortly acute at both ends, submembranaceous, subopake above, below veinless, with about 10 distant pairs of nerves; corymbs terminal, compactly many-flowered, divided at the base, a little shorter than the leaves; flowers subsparse; peduncle very short, its branches rather long; bracteoles ovately triangular, subobtuse, short, erect; flowers 6 lines long; sepals acutely triangular, $\frac{2}{3}$ line long; tube of corolla slender, $3\frac{3}{4}$ line long, pubescent within, distinctly broader at its base, where it is staminigerous; disk none; 2 obtusely obovoid ovaries; style double their length.

34. PESCHIERA AUSTRALIS, nob.: *Tabernæmontana australis*, Müll. *l. c.* p. 84. In Brasiliæ prov. australioribus: *non vidi*.

A species said to be near *T. bracteolaris* (*P. hystrix*), differing in its leaves scarcely narrowed at the base, with much shorter petioles, in its acuminated bracts, and a shorter tube in the corolla. Leaves narrowly elliptic oblong, subobtuse at the base, gradually acutely acuminated, submembranaceous, 4–4¾ in. long, 11¾–16 lines broad, on petioles 1¾ line long; corymbs in the dichotomies of the branchlets, densely 20-flowered, with linear acute bracteoles; pedicels 1½ line long; sepals acuminated, with membranaceous margins, ¾ line long; tube of corolla in bud cylindrical, 4 lines long, broader near its base; stamens inserted near its base, in a pilose ring; disk none; ovaries 2, acutely oblong, with a short style; follicles 1½ in. long.

35. PESCHIERA SOLANIFOLIA, nob.: *Tabernæmontana solanifolia*, A. DC. *l. c.* p. 365: Müll. *l. c.* p. 86. In Bahia: *v. s. in hb. Mus. Brit.* Bahia (Blanchet 2724).

A very peculiar species, with thick, 4-angular, fuscous, pubescent branches, densely covered with rather large leaves, and annularly ringed at intervals of 4 lines. The leaves are ovate-oblong, shortly and obtusely acuminated, spathulately and gradually contracted downwards from above the middle, becoming very narrow at the base, where they are subcordate and nearly sessile, are membranaceous, opake green above, puberulous upon about 15–30 pairs of short subpatent nerves conjoined near the margins, pale yellowish below, and densely puberulous, 3½–6¾ in. long, 1⅝–3¼ in. broad above the middle, reduced gradually to a breadth of about 4 lines at the base, on petioles 1–1¼ line long; cymes terminal, puberulous, 40–120-flowered, 3–4 in. long and broad, several times trichotomously divided, each ultimate branchlet about 4 lines long, bearing about 7 almost umbellate approximated flowers on bracteolated pedicels 4 lines long; sepals ovate-lanceolate, 1½ line long; tube of corolla 4¾ lines long, broader at the base, and there staminigerous; segments of border obliquely ovate, 2¼ lines long; no disk; other parts as in the preceding species.

36. PESCHIERA SOLANDRI, nob.: *Tabernæmontana cymosa*, Sol. (non Jaeq.) Primit. Fl. Bras. p. 72: ramulis dichotomis, pallidis, interrupte striatis: foliis ovato-oblongis, imo acutis, apice in acumen obtusulum constrictis, submembranaceis, supra viridibus, pruinoso-opacis, ad costam sulcatis, nervis curvatim patentibus immersis, subtus flavide pallidioribus, opacis, granulatis, costa nervisque prominulis; petiolo tenuissimo, limbo 15–18plo breviore: paniculis axillaribus, tenuiter ramosis, ramis medio bracteolatis 2-floris; pedicellis calyce paullo longioribus; sepalis viridibus, anguste lanceolatis, recurvis, intus squamula plurilacinulata munitis; corollæ tubo calyce 2plo longiore, imo latiore, intus pubescente, segmentis dolabriformibus, tubo 3plo brevioribus, glabris, sinistrorsum convolutis; staminibus paullo supra basin insertis, filamentis tenuibus; disco nullo; ovariis 2, ovatis; cæteris generis. In Brasilia: *v. s. in hb. Mus. Brit.* Rio de Janeiro (Solander).

A species near *P. Spixiana*, differing in its smaller, more lanceolate leaves, on shorter petioles, in its inflorescence and more lanceolate reflexed sepals. The leaves are 3–3½ in.

long, 1–1¼ in. broad, on petioles 2–3 lines long; secondary branchlets of panicle 4 lines long, bracteolated in the middle; tertiary branchlets 3 lines long; pedicels 2 lines long; sepals 1½ line long; tube of corolla in bud 4 lines long.

37. PESCHIERA LOBIFERA, nob.: ramulis dichotomis, pallide brunneis, striolatis, axillis remotis et annulatis: foliis heterophyllis, longe ellipticis, imo acutis, apice in acumen longum et angustatum subito attenuatis, membranaceis, marginibus revolutis subundulatis, supra viridibus, pruinoso-opacis, nervis tenuissimis utrinque prominulis, subtus pallidis, flavicantibus; petiolis tenuibus, caualiculatis, limbo 25plo brevioribus: panicula in dichotomiis, brevi, pedunculo ramisque brevissimis, pedicellis longioribus, bracteolatis; sepalis parvis, obtuse oblongis, margine membranaceis, singulis squamula 3-laciuulata intus munitis; corollæ tubo anguste cylindrico, imo latiore, glabro, segmentis latiuscule dolabriformibus, glabris, tubo brevioribus, expansis, sinistrorsum convolutis; staminibus inclusis; filamentis prope basin tubo insertis; disco nullo; ovariis 2, ovatis; cæteris ut in præcedentibus. In Guiana: *v. s. in hb. Mus. Brit.* Guiana Brit. (Schomb. 138), Surinam (Hostmann 1312).

Axils 3–4 in. apart; leaves 5½ and 4½ in. long, 2¼ and 1¾ in. broad, on petioles 3 and 2 lines long; panicle 1½ in. long; peduncle 2 lines, its branches 1½ line long, each 2-flowered; pedicels 5 lines long; sepals 1 line long; tube of corolla 5 lines long, segments 3½ lines long.

38. PESCHIERA? LINKII, nob.: *Tabernæmontana Linkii*, A. DC. 364: *Tabernæmontana multiflora*, R. & Sch. Syst. iv. 431 (non Sm.). In Brasilia: *non vidi*.

A species with characters obscurely defined. It has smooth dichotomous branchlets, with ovate-lanceolate leaves, acuminated, subrepand, smooth, membranaceous, 3–4 in. long, 1½ in. broad, on petioles 3–4 lines long; axillary corymbs in the dichotomies of the branches, many-flowered, dichotomously divided; sepals obtuse, 1½ line long; tube of corolla 4½ lines long, segments 3 lines long.

39. PESCHIERA PRÆCLARA, nob.: ramulis virgatis, pallide griseis, subangulatis, striatis, sparse lenticellatis, ad nodos remotos dilatatis: foliis majusculis, lanceolato-oblongis, imo acute cuneatis, apice sensim acutis et in acumen lineare reflexum attenuatis, glaberrimis, flaccide chartaceis, supra læte viridibus, opacis, nervis tenuibus semiimmersis, divaricatis, arcuatim nexis, costa tenui, flavida, semiimmersa, subtus pallidioribus opacis, costa prominente, nervis flavidis promiuulis, venis transversis reticulatis; petiolis semiteretibus, imo fuscis, limbo 15plo brevioribus: racemo terminali; pedunculo subtenui tereti, petiolo 4plo longiore, alternatim plurifloro; pedicellis brevibus; sepalis oblongis, obtusis; corolla ignota; disco nullo; ovariis 2, striatis. In Caracas: *v. s. in hb. meo* (Cockburn).

A species with the habit and inflorescence of *Peschiera tenuiflora*, Pöppig (tab. 280), from the same region, but with much larger leaves, having the same texture and venation; the upper internode is 1¾ in. long, the lower one more than 4 in. long; the leaves are 7½–10¼ in. long, 2¼–3¾ in. broad, on petioles 6–9 lines long, not united at their base by a transverse line; the solitary peduncle is 1¼ in. long. The pedicels and calyces were lost after the above memorandum was made; little doubt, however, can be entertained that it is a species very near Pöppig's plant from the Amazonas river, in the same longitude as Caracas.

BONAFOUSIA.

This genus was established by Prof. De Candolle in 1844, upon a single species; but its characters were insufficiently defined. Dr. Müller, in 1860, reduced it into a section of *Tabernæmontana*, with a short character quite useless for the purpose of distinction. It possesses, however, several peculiar features that will maintain the validity of the genus; one of these consists in the remarkable manner of æstivation of the linear-oblong segments of the corolla, where for two-thirds of their length they are suddenly bent inwards and downwards, so that their tips enter the mouth of the tube and embrace the summits of the stamens—a peculiarity manifested also in *Anacampta* and *Anartia*. Müller has given, without any explanation, a drawing of the structure of the flower, where he repeats the mistake of De Candolle in assigning to it a dextrorse æstivation; but in the typical and all the other species, I have found, beyond doubt, that the convolution is sinistrorse. The disk is cylindrical, membranaceous, and adnate. All the species have slender ligneous branches.

BONAFOUSIA, A. DC.: *Tabernæmontana* (in parte) auct.: *Sepala* 5, subparva, ovata, sæpe membranacea, et ciliata, erecta, imbricata, ad basin intus *squamulis* singula singulis denticulatis munita. *Corolla* hypocrateriformis; *tubus* longiuscule cylindricus, superne paullo ventricosus, fauce constrictus; *segmenta* 5, elongata, tubo paullo breviora, parallele subarcuata, obtusa, rotatim explanata, in æstivatione pro tertia parte erecta, nervo oblique ad marginem mucronatim excurrente, et hinc pro reliqua parte subito inflexa, intra faucem descendentia, et stamina in parte involventia, cuncta sinistrorsum convoluta. *Stamina* 5, inclusa; *filamenta* brevissima, in annulum pilosum supra medium tubi inserta; *antheræ* oblongæ, apice acuminatæ, basi biaristatæ; *connectivi* rigidi, in conum subcohærentes. *Discus* cylindricus, membranaceus, ovariis brevior, et his adnatus. *Ovaria* 2, oblonga, fere libera; *stylus* tenuis, apice incrassatus; *clavuncula* crassa, conice oblonga, 5-sulcata et 5-glandulosa, imo membrana expansa suffulta; *stigmata* 2, parva, terminalia. *Folliculi* 2, globose oblongi, utrinque recurvati, faciebus versus angulum dorsalem oblique inclinatis, medio linea crescentiformi signati, ventre valde convexi, sutura intus utrinque inflexa et placentifera dehiscentes. *Semina* plurima, subovata, compressa, dorso pluricostata, ventre canaliculata et hinc *funiculo* pulposo semi-immersa. Cætera ut in *Peschieram* descripta.

Frutices *vel* arbusculæ *Americæ calidioris, ramosi*; folia *opposita, oblonga, glaberrima, petiolata*; paniculæ *axillares, ramosæ, pauciflor*æ.

1. BONAFOUSIA UNDULATA, A. DC. Prodr. viii. 359: *Tabernæmontana undulata*, Vahl (non Mey. nec DC. in p. 368), Ecl. ii. 20, icon. tab. 6; Poir. Dict. vii. 529; Benth. Journ. Bot. iii. 243; Müll. Flor. Bras. fasc. xxvi. p. 70 (nomen), tab. 21 (flos et fructus). In Guiana et ins. Trinidad: *v. s. in herb. Mus. Brit.* Guiana Brit. (Schomb. 42, Anderson); *Poiteau (in fructu)* Acarouari (Sagot 1309).

A species well figured by Vahl. It is a tree 30–40 feet high, with terete branchlets subangular below the axils, which are 3–4 in. apart: the leaves are in equal opposite pairs, regular in form, lanceolate oblong, acute at the base, gradually or more suddenly narrowing at the apex into a long linear acumen; they are submembranaceous, with a slender nerve along the margins, which are crispately undulated, and thus somewhat rigid, bright green above, with many much divaricated fine nerves arcuately conjoined close to the margin, opake and of a more or less bright ochre colour beneath, with slender prominulent nerves, 4½–6½ in. long, including the acumen (9 lines long), 1½–2½ in.

broad, on channelled petioles 3–5 lines long; raceme lateral at the axils, or seated in the dichotomy of the branchlets, on a peduncle 7 lines long, bearing several alternate yellow flowers on pedicels 8 lines long, with small bracts. The sepals are roundish oblong, very imbricated, 2 lines long, each with 3–4 minute scales at the base; the corolla has a cylindrical tube 6 lines long, fleshy and contracted at the mouth, shortly ventricose below it, cylindrical along the middle, and enlarging a little towards the base; the segments are fleshy at their base for a length of 3 lines, are erect in the bud; but then the remaining membranaceous portions, linear, obtuse, are suddenly introflexed, descending into the tube, and there enveloping the upper half of the stamens; they subsequently expand in a rotate form, when they curve sinistrorsely, and are 4 lines long; the stamens, cohering, are fixed in the contraction of the tube and nearly reach the summit; the anthers, disk, style, and clavuncle as in the generic character. The 2 follicles, somewhat spreading, are roundish oblong, inclined and wedge-shaped on the shorter edge, with a raised curved ridge on each side, broadly convex on the ventral side, where they open by a broad, gaping, sutural fissure, are 16 lines long, 9 lines broad; the pericarp is thick, coriaceous, smooth, each follicle enclosing many seeds; the seeds are oblong, acute at one extremity, rounded at the other, and are costately striated, with a hollow channel on one face, where they are attached to a pulpy or fleshy red funicle (arillus of Vahl), which half envelops each seed.

Prof. Müller, as above cited, gives good analytical drawings of the flower, and a figure of the follicle and seed.

Var. *ovalifolia*: the leaves here are of an oval form, acute at the base, cuspidately acuminate, the margins obsoletely crispated, very pallid green on both sides, 5¼ in. long including the acumen (¾ in. long), 3¼ in. broad, on channelled petioles 4 lines long; the inflorescence bears rather larger flowers. In Guiana (Schomb. 42 *bis*).

A drawing of this species, and an analysis of its flower, its follicle, and seeds, are given in Plate VI. B.

2. BONAFOUSIA OBLIQUA, nob.: ramulis tenuibus, pallide brunneis, subsulcatis: foliis oppositis, in paribus fere æqualibus, imo acutis, et hinc uno latere conspicuo obliquis, apice in acumen longiusculum sensim attenuatis, submembranaceis vel chartaceis, planis, marginibus revolutis sæpius integris, aut raro obsolete undulatis, supra læte viridibus, costa sulcata, nervis plurimis prominulis patentim divaricatis, rectis, juxta marginem junctis, subtus flavescentibus, opacis, costa prominente, nervis tenuibus prominulis, venis immersis; petiolis brevibus, imo subfossatis: racemo in dichotomiis laterali, folio 6plo breviore, pluridoro, subhirsutulo; pedunculo sub-4-gono; pedicellis crebre alternis, corrugulatis, calyce 3plo longioribus; sepalis obtuse ovatis, imbricatis, subinæqualibus, scabridulis; corollæ tubo crassiusculo, cylindrico, superne et infra paullo ampliore, intus sub faucem constrictam puberulo, extus scabridulo, segmentis obtuse linearibus, pro tertia parte carnosulis, rectis, pro reliquis duabus partibus in æstivatione subito introflexis et intra faucem descendentibus, demum rotatim explicatis, membranaceis, et purpurascentibus, sinistrorsum convolutis; staminibus in constrictione tubi ex annulo piloso ortis, inclusis, antheris cohærentibus, apice, acuminatis, imo biaristatis; disco cylindrico, submembranaceo, ovariis 2 oblongatis breviore; stylo clavuncula et stigmatibus ut in char. gen.: folliculis ignotis. In Venezuela australi: *v. s. in herb. meo et Mus. Brit.* Rio Casiquiare (Spruce 3119, sub *B. undulata*).

A species very distinct from the preceding: it is arborescent, 18 feet high, lactescent, the axils of the branchlets 2–5 in. apart; leaves 3¾–7 in. long, 1½–2 in. broad, on petioles 1–2 lines long; raceme 1¼ in. long; pedicels 3–4 lines long; sepals 1½ line long; corolla in bud, tube 4½ lines long, its terminal knob 2½ lines long, inflected portions of segments 5½ lines long. According to Spruce the tube is white, the segments and mouth purpurascent (not yellow).

3. BONAFOUSIA LATIFLORA, nob.: *Peschiera latiflora*, Benth. MS.: *Tabernæmontana flavicans*, Müll. (non R. & Sch.) *l. c.* p. 77. In Amazonas, *v. s. in hb. meo et Mus. Brit.* Santarem (Spruce 256).

Evidently a very different plant from that described by Römer and Schultes, which has divaricately dichotomous branches, with flowers on a long peduncle. It has slender divaricate branches; leaves opposite, rarely verticillately ternate, oblong, acute at the base, with a rather long obtuse acumen, pallid and yellowish below, with subprominulent midrib and divaricated nerves, which are reddish; the leaves are unequal in each axil, 2½ and 2¼ in. long, 1 in. and ⅞ in. broad, on slender petioles 2–3 lines long; the upper leaves are smaller, the lower ones larger and more oval. The peduncle, seated in the dichotomy of the branches, is about 3 lines long, bearing about 4 flowers on subumbellate pedicels 4 lines long; sepals acute, 1 line long; tube of corolla very narrow and cylindrical, a little inflated below the mouth, 10 lines long, segments linear oblong, 7 lines long, 2 lines broad, expanded in æstivation, inflected near the middle, the deflected summits reaching the mouth, sinistrorsely convoluted; stamens included in the ventricose portion of the tube; anthers 2-aristate at the base, acuminate at the summit; disk membranaceous, adnate, ⅓ the length of 2 pointed ovaries; style filamentous, reaching the stamens; clavuncle incrassated, oblong, 5-grooved, with a basal umbraculiform appendage; stigmata short.

4. BONAFOUSIA OBLONGIFOLIA, nob.: *Tabernæmontana oblongifolia*, A. DC. *l. c.* p. 368; Müll. *l. c.* p. 74. In Brasilia: *v. s. in hb. Mus. Brit.* Jacobina, prov. Bahia (Blanchet 951, et, sec. DC., Blanchet 2358).

Branchlets slender, pale brown, striolated, with axils 1¾–2¼ in. apart; leaves very patent, lanceolate oblong, somewhat heterophyllous, acute and subinæquilateral at the base, acutely acuminated at the summit, chartaceous, pale green above, with semi-immersed nerves, paler and opake beneath, with a stout midrib and yellow prominulent nerves, 3 and 5¼ in. long at each node, 1½–1¼ in. broad, on slender petioles 4–5 lines long; panicle terminal in the dichotomy of the branchlets; peduncle slender, 4 lines long, the 2 branches at its apex 2 lines long; pedicels few, slender, 6 lines long; oblong sepals obtuse, submembranaceous, spotted with yellow dots, 1½ line long; tube of corolla cylindrical, ventricose in the middle, 9 lines long, its roundish oblique segments being 6 lines long, infolded sinistrorsely in the bud, the extremities descending into the mouth of the tube; stamens seated in the lower contraction of the tube, included in the swollen portion, emanating from as many pilose lines; 2 oblong, pointed, adpressed, smooth ovaries, embraced at their base, for ¼ of their length, by a very thin disk.

5. **BONAFOUSIA ATTENUATA**, nob.: ramulis tenuibus, dichotomis: foliis ellipticis, imo canaliculatim acutis, apice in acumen longe lineare obtusulum recurvum subito attenuatis, tenuiter chartaceis, marginibus subundulatis paullo revolutis, supra læte viridibus, subopacis, nervis tenuissimis, subpatentibus, immersis, subtus flavide pallidioribus, opacis, nervis vix prominulis, omnino eveniis; petiolis tenuibus, canaliculatis, imo fossatis, marginibus linea transversali nexis, limbo 10plo brevioribus: racemo axillari, vel in dichotomiis erecto, folio dimidio breviore; pedunculo brevi, paucifloro; pedicellis calyce 4plo longioribus; floribus majusculis, plerumque caducis; sepalis ovatis, membranaceis, imbricatis, intus squamulis pluribus imo munitis; corollæ tubo cylindrico, supra medium inflato, carnoso, fauce constricto, limbi segmentis lineari-oblongis, pro tertia parte erectis, et dehinc introflexis intra faucem descendentibus, staminum apices amplectentibus, in æstivatione sinistrorsum convolutis, demum expansis; staminibus inclusis, supra medium tubi ad constrictionem affixis, antheris in conum cohærentibus; disco cylindrico, membranaceo, ovariis bis triente brevioribus omnino adnato; stylo clavuncula et stigmate generis. In Guiana Batav. et Brit., et in Cayenne: *v. s. in hb. Mus. Brit.* Surinam (Hostmann 1314); Acaravuary, Guiana (Sagot 993, sub *T. oblongifolia*) ; Cayenne (Martin, sub *T. neriifolia*).

The leaves are 2½–3½ in. long, ¾–1¼ in. broad, on petioles 3–4 lines long; the peduncle is 6 lines long, marked by crowded cicatrices of fallen flowers; pedicels 4–6 lines long; sepals 1 line long; tube of corolla 1 in. long; knob of bud oblong-obovate, linear segments expanded, 8 lines long.

6. **BONAFOUSIA PEROTTETII**, nob.: *Tabernæmontana Perottetii*, A. DC. *l. c.* p. 362. In Guiana Gallica: *non vidi.*

A species apparently near *B. undulata*, with a similar dichotomous habit; leaves acute at the base, with an obtusely linear acumen and undulate margins, 4–6 in. long, 1–2 in. broad, on stoutish petioles broadly channelled, 3 lines long: terminal raceme 5–8 lines long, on a short peduncle, bearing 5–7 flowers, on pedicels 3 lines long, thickened at the apex, bracteolated at the base; sepals ovate, imbricated, unequal; corolla in bud 6 lines long, the tube being pubescent in the mouth. Follicles semi-globular, somewhat compressed, with a lateral curving ridge 1¼ in. long, 1 in. broad; disk and form of segments of corolla unknown.

7. **BONAFOUSIA GUYANENSIS**, nob.: *Tabernæmontana Guyanensis*, Müll. Linn. xxx. 404. In Guyana (Poiteau): *v. s. in herb. Mus. Brit.* Surinam (Miguel, sub *Tab. oblongifolia*).

A species closely allied to the preceding, and said to approach *T. disticha* and *oblongifolia.* It has terete angular branches, with internodes 5–6 in. long, and slender, compressed branchlets, with remote axils: the leaves are oblong elliptic, roundish and suddenly acute at the base, shortly cuspidate at the apex, crenulated on the margins, glabrous, subchartaceous, pallidly green above, with 10–12 pairs of divaricated, ascending, prominulent nerves arcuately conjoined, yellow opake beneath, with prominent reddish nerves, 4¾–7 in. long, 2⅜–3 in. broad, on petioles hoodingly fossate, 1–2 lines long; panicles axillary, compact, 3 in. long, 5–8-flowered on a pubescent peduncle bare for 1 in., dichotomously and shortly branched, and bearing 8 or more closely approximated flowers on pedicels 2½ lines long, supported by acutely ovate ciliolated bracteoles; sepals obtusely obovate, ciliated on the margins, 1½ line long, with an inner deeply 3-laciniated scale;

tube of corolla cylindrical, glabrous, 6 lines long, enlarged at the middle, where it is staminigerous; segments oblong, 8 lines long, inflected below the middle in æstivation, the tips descending into the mouth of the tube; disk tubular, membranaceous, adnate to one half of 2 acute ovaries.

8. BONAFOUSIA OLIVACEA, nob.: *Tabernæmontana olivacea*, Müll. *l. c.* p. 75. In Brasilia septentrionali: *v. s. in herb. meo et Mus. Brit.* San Carlos, Rio Negro (Spruce 3114, sub "*Peschieræ* sp.").

I do not perceive the resemblance of this species to the *T. heterophylla* of Vahl, as stated by Müller, except that, like many other species, it has unequal leaves, which in shape and size are very different; the fuscous, dichotomous branchlets are slender, glabrous, with axils 1-1¼ in. apart; the leaves are oval, or oblong ovate, patently opposite, suddenly acute at their base, hastily terminated by a long, narrow, recurved acumen 4-5 lines long, chartaceous, entire, with subrevolute margins, bright green above, opake, with immersed nerves, pale yellow beneath, opake, with reddish costa, and prominulent patent fine nerves, suddenly conjoined near the margin, 2¾-3 in. long (including the acumen), 1¼-1¾ in. broad, on petioles 5 lines long; raceme in the dichotomy of the branchlets, very short and depauperated, on a peduncle 2 lines long, bearing above 3-4 caducous flowers, and 2 others above them, on bracteolated pedicels 5 lines long; sepals obtusely oblong, somewhat unequal, erect, imbricated, membranaceous, veined, 1¼ line long, with several minute inner scales; the cylindrical tube of the corolla in bud is 7½ lines long, somewhat inflated below the constricted mouth, and near the base, the basal fleshy portion of the segments, forming the knob in æstivation, is 2 lines long, the remaining introflected portion 5 lines long, descending into the tube; stamens as in the preceding species; disk cylindrical, submembranaceous, scarcely as long as the 2 acutely oblong ovaries; style, clavuncle, and stigmata as in the gen. char.; follicles unknown.

9. BONAFOUSIA RUFICOLA, nob.: *Tabernæmontana rupicola*, Benth. in Hook. Journ. Bot. iii. 243; A. DC. *l. c.* p. 362; Müll. *l. c.* p. 74. In Amazonas: *v. s. in herb. meo et alior.* prope Rio Negro (Schomb. 898); Panuré, Rio Uahupes (Spruce 2559), Barra do Rio Negro (Spruce 1463).

A species distinguished by its twice trichotomous branches; leaves almost sessile, elliptic oblong, obtuse and inæquilateral at the base, acuminated at the summit, submembranaceous, entire, subfuscous above, sulcated upon the prominent midrib, many divergent prominulent nerves, with others shorter and intermediate, reticulately veined, beneath yellowish opake, the nerves semi-immersed, 2½-5 in. long, 1-1⅔ in. broad, on channelled petioles 1 line long, very shortly fossated at the base; panicle lateral, 1-2 in. long, on a peduncle 3 lines long, bibracteolated at the base, supporting 3-5 approximated alternate flowers on pedicels 4-5 lines long, shortly bracteolated at the base; sepals ovate obtuse, membranaceous, ciliated on the margin, imbricated, 1 line long, with a broad many-laciniated scale; corolla cylindrical, tube much narrowed in the mouth, thence gradually inflated below, 6 lines long; segments oblique oblong, membranaceous, 9 lines long, 4 lines broad, in æstivation sinistrorsely convoluted, suddenly inflected, the tips entering within the mouth of the tube; stamens seated a little above the middle of the tube on a narrow pilose ring; filaments short pilose; anthers acuminate, biaristate at the base, dorsally pilose; disk cylindrical, 5-sulcate, 5-crenulate, shorter than the two glabrous ovate ovaries; style, clavuncle, and stigmata as in the generic character.

10. BONAFOUSIA POLYNEURA, nob.: *Tabernæmontana rupicola*, var. *Sprucei*, Müll. *l. c.* p. 75. In Amazonas: *v. s. in hb. meo et alior*. Barra do Rio Negro (Spruce 1758, sub "*T. rupicolæ* affinis").

A species distinguished by its more densely foliaceous habit and its polyneurous leaves. Its dichotomous branchlets are rugulose, with axils 1¼–2 in. apart; the oblong leaves, oval and suddenly acute at the base, not inæquilateral, constricted into an acute acumen, are dark rubescent green above, with subcrenulated numerous subpatent nerves 1-2 lines apart, opake and yellowish beneath, with fine nerves, scarcely prominulent, 3–5 in. long, 1¼–2 in. broad, on channelled petioles 1½ line long, transversely conjoined across the axils; raceme lateral, 1 in. long, on an angular peduncle 3 lines long, supporting about 3 flowers on pedicels 2 lines long; roundish, membranaceous sepals, acute, ciliated on the margins, ¼ line long, with an inner trifid scale; tube of corolla cylindrical, fleshy, swollen below the narrow mouth, 5 lines long; segments obliquely oblong, about 8 lines long, 2 lines broad, introflected and convoluted sinistrorsely in æstivation, the extremities descending into the tube; stamens included in the middle of the tube, seated on a pilose ring; ovaries ovate, embraced at the base by a short annular adnate disk; style, clavuncle, and stigmata as in the generic character.

11. BONAFOUSIA RARIFLORA, nob.: *Tabernæmontana rupicola*, var. *oblongifolia*, Müll. *l. c.* p. 74. In Amazonas: *v. s. in hb. meo et alior*. Barra do Rio Negro (Spruce 1005?).

A species differing from *T. rupicola* in its petiolated, very lanceolate leaves, almost nerveless, and a different inflorescence, a more slender habit, with virgated branchlets and distant internodes; the dichotomous slender branchlets are yellowish, striolated, with axils 1¼–2⅓ in. apart; the leaves, subcrenulate, cuneately inæquilateral, with a long acumen, yellowish beneath, are 4½–5 in. long, 1–1¼ in. broad, on very thick petioles ¼ line long, conjoined across the axils; the lateral raceme, on a peduncle 3 lines long, has a stipuliform bract at its base, and supports 3 alternate flowers, on pedicels 4–5 lines long; sepals acute, barely 1 line long; tube of corolla 4½ lines long, narrowed in the mouth; segments dolabriform, 6 lines long, 3 lines broad, simply convoluted sinistrorsely in æstivation; stamens seated on a pilose ring in the constriction of the tube; the rest as in the preceding species.

TABERNÆMONTANA.

This genus was first proposed in 1703 by Plumier in his 'Genera,' p. 18, with a short character, illustrated by a drawing of its flower and fruit. He figured the plant in 1757, with a more copious description of his type, under the specific name of *citrifolia undulata* (Am. ii. 246, tab. 248 B), giving as its synonyms *T. citrifolia lanceolata*, Hort. Cliff., and *T. frutescens*, P. Browne. Linnæus, in his Sp. Pl. (1753) describes the genus

Tabernæmontana with 3 species :—1, *T. citrifolia*, with lanceolate leaves, in Hort. Cliff, with a synonym of Plumier's plant; 2, *T. laurifolia* of Sloane; 3, *T. alternifolia*, a doubtful species of Rheede, Hort. Malab. After this *Tabernæmontana* became the receptacle for a host of heterogeneous species; so that in 1844, Prof. De Candolle enumerated more than 90, after separating four under two new genera, *Peschiera* and *Bonafousia*. Subsequently Prof. Müller removed these into *Tabernæmontana*, adding nearly 40 new heterogeneous species. I have separated and classified most of these 130 species, retaining under *Tabernæmontana* only those corresponding to the characters of the Linnean type, which I carefully examined; these are easily recognized by their hypocrateriform corolla, with sinistrorse æstivation, free slender stamens of a bluish tinge, seated above the middle of the tube, their summits being more or less exserted. The following may be considered to be the characters of the genus as here restricted.

TABERNÆMONTANA, Plum., Linn.: *Sepala parva, oblonga, obtusa aut acuta, quincuncialiter imbricata, sæpe membranacea, 2 exteriora interdum latiora, squamula basali lata 2–4-laciniulata intus munita. Corolla hypocrateriformis; tubus cylindricus; segmenta 5, tubo paullo breviora, imo unguiculata, mox inæqualiter dilatata, sæpius dolabriformia, expansa, æstivatione simpliciter sinistrorsum convoluta. Stamina 5, gracilia; filamenta brevia, supra medium tubi inserta; antheræ fere semper cærulescentes, imo longiuscule biaristatæ, apice cuspidatæ et hinc plus minusve exsertæ. Discus valde membranaceus, sub-5-lobus, ovariis multo brevior, et iis subadhærens. Ovaria 2, oblonga, mutuo applicita. Stylus tenuis, sæpe imo breviter fissus; clavuncula incrassata, oblonga, 5-sulcata, imo appendice submembranacea munita; stigmata 2, brevissima. Folliculi 2, valde divaricati, oblongo-ovales, gibbosi, stipitati, apice retrorsum rostrati, rima ventrali dehiscentes; semina plurima, ovata, dorso striata, ventre concava, hilo mediano affixa, singula funiculis singulis pulposis semi-immersa, quomodo ad placentas suturales seorsum affixa.*

Arbores vel suffrutices Americæ intertropicæ vel in Antillis vigentes, ramis sæpe dichotome divisis; folia opposita, oblonga, acuta, petiolata; cymæ axillares aut terminales, sæpe geminæ; flores albi vel lutei.

1. TABERNÆMONTANA CITRIFOLIA, Plum. Gen. (1703) p. 18, tab. 30; Pl. Amer. (1737) ii. 246, tab. 248 B (excl. syn.); Icon. archetyp. Plum. ined. in Bibl. Banks. tab. 31; Linn. Sp. Pl. (1753) (excl. syn.); A. DC. Prodr. viii. p. 363; Lunan, Jam. ii. 222; Griseb. Fl. B. W. Ind. p. 409 : *Tabernæmontana frutescens*, Sloane, Jam. p. 182. In Antilles: *v. s. in herb. Mus. Brit. Jamaica* (Van Rohr).

A small tree, 15 feet high, with stout branchlets, having axils 2–3 in. apart, all lactescent; leaves rather large, oblong elliptic, cuneate or subacute at the base, somewhat acute at the apex, sides often folded together, margins undulated, bright green above, with about 12 pairs of immersed reddish nerves, yellowish opake beneath, with prominulent midrib and nerves, 3–6¼ in. long, 2–2¾ in. broad, on broadly channelled petioles with membranaceous margins, 3–6 lines long; panicles lateral, often opposite, with 4 branches, each bearing 2 flowers on short pedicels; sepals small, acute; corolla hypocrateriform, tube 8 lines long; segments a little shorter, linear oblong, oblique, sinistrorsely convoluted; stamens inserted below the mouth of the tube; anthers linear, cærulescent, half-exserted, 1½ line long, biaristate at the base; disk shorter than the 2 acute oblong ovaries; style, clavuncle, and stigmata as in the generic character; 2 follicles on a peduncle 1 in. long, oblong, acute, costate, horizontally spreading, 2¼ in. long,

9 lines broad, enclosing several seeds attached to the sutural margins by reddish pulp-like funicles, in which they are half-imbedded.

A drawing of this species, and an analysis of its flower and fruit, are shown in Plate VII. A.

2. TABERNÆMONTANA LANCEOLATA, Linn. in Hort. Cliff. (1737) p. 76 (excl. syn.) ; Sp. Plant. (1753) p. 210 (excl. syn.) ; Jacq. Amer. (1763) p. 38, tab. 175. fig. 13 (flos), excl. syn. ; Lam. Illust. tab. 170 (folium). In Antilles : *v. s. plantam archetyp. in herb. Cliffort. Mus. Brit.* ex Cuba (C. Wright 2948, *in flore et fructu*).

This species has been confounded with the preceding from the time of Linnæus downwards; but the two plants differ obviously in the shape and size of the leaves, their venation, their inflorescence, and in their fruit. Wright's specimen perfectly accords with Linnæus's plant, so that no doubt can exist on the subject. This shows what little attention was paid by Linnæus, in his earlier days, to the exact definition of any species, as in the present case he mixed in one three very different species—(1) *citrifolia*, (2) *lanceolata*, (3) *alternifolia* (a Malay plant described by Rheede). Lamarck gives the leaf of this species in his tab. 170; but the floral parts and seeds are copied from Plumier's 'Genera.'

This is a small tree 8 feet high, with smooth branchlets, having their axils 1¼ in. apart; the leaves are glabrous, subspathulately lanceolate, with a short obtuse acumen, flat, entire, pale green above, sulcated along the midrib, with about 14 pairs of patent immersed nerves suddenly conjoined within the margin, a little paler beneath, opake yellowish, with prominent midrib and very fine straw-coloured nerves, the transversely reticulated veins being immersed, 3–4¾ in. long, 1–1⅜ in. broad, on semiterete, broadly channelled petioles 2–4 lines long; a lateral panicle, on a peduncle 1 in. long, subdivided above into 2 branchlets 9 lines long, bearing alternate flowers on bracteolated pedicels 3 lines long; sepals small, each with an inner multidentate scale; tube of corolla 10 lines long, slender in the middle, ventricose below the mouth, a little swollen at the base, segments 5 lines long, obliquely oblong, sinistrorsely convoluted; stamens fixed in the constriction of the tube, anthers very slender, bluish, half-exserted; disk adnate, sub-5-lobed in the margin, shorter than the 2 pointed oblong ovaries; follicles 2, often solitary by abortion, oblong ovate, compressed, with a sharp recurved point at the apex, rounded along the sutural margin, 1 in. long, 6 lines broad; seeds not very numerous, oval, striated on the dorsal face, deeply channelled on the ventral face, where they are attached to the fleshy funicle ; they are 3 lines long, 2 lines broad.

A drawing of this species, and an analysis of its flower and fruit, are seen in Plate VII. B.

3. TABERNÆMONTANA NERIIFOLIA, Vahl, Ecl. ii. 21; DC. Prodr. viii. 367. In Porto Rico et Venezuela : *v. s. in hb. Mus. Brit.* Cumancoa et Maracaibo (Moritz 357, Sagot 391).

The very lanceolate leaves, slightly heterophyllous, are green above, with an opake granulated surface, with about 20 pairs of short patent nerves, conjoined near the margin, semi-immersed, and without veins, they are ochreously pallid beneath, opake, minutely corrugulated, with slightly prominulent nerves and are veinless; they are

3–3½ in. long, ⅞–1¼ in. broad, on petioles 2–3 lines long; the peduncle, either lateral or in the dichotomy of the branchlets, is 9 lines long, and is divided at its summit into 2 branches, each bearing few flowers; pedicels 2 lines long; sepals ovate oblong, submembranaceous, 1½ line long, with several minute scales inside; tube of corolla narrowly cylindrical, 6 lines long; segments linear-oblong, 5 lines long, simply and sinistrorsely convoluted in the bud; stamens inserted upon a puberulous ring below the mouth of the tube; anthers slender, semi-exserted, cuspidate at the apex, acutely biaristate at the base, of a greenish colour; disk membranaceous, two thirds the length of the 2 acute, oblong, striated ovaries; style slender, incrassated above by a clavuncle, as in the other species.

4. TABERNÆMONTANA AMYGDALIÆFOLIA, Jacq. Amér. 39, tab. 181. fig. 15 (non Seem.); A. DC. *l. c.* viii. 367; Ker, Bot. Reg. tab. 338: *Cestrum nervosum*, Mill. Dict. no. 3. In Nova Granada et Venezuela: *v. s. in hb. Mus. Brit. et Hook.* Carthagena (Miller), S. Martha (Schlim 945), Venezuela (Fendler 1429).

A small lactescent shrub 6 feet high, with dichotomous slender branchlets; leaves lanceolate-oblong, cuneated at the base, acuminate, submembranaceous, pale green above, opake, entire, glabrous, nerves very patent (as in *T. neriifolia*) and immersed, below yellowish, opake, with immersed dark pellucid nerves, with no apparent veins, 2–5 in. long, 9–18 lines broad, on slender petioles 3–6 lines long; racemes in the dichotomies of the branchlets, much shorter than the leaves; peduncle very slender, 1 in. long, bearing 4–5 flowers on alternate pedicels bracteolated at the base, 5 lines long; sepals 1 line long, acute; tube of corolla salver-shaped, 5 lines long, a little broader below the mouth; segments spathulate oblong, expanded, nearly as long as the tube, sinistrorsely convoluted; stamens somewhat exserted in the mouth; 2 free oblong, pointed ovaries, surrounded at their base by a disk ¼ their length; follicles obovate, oblong, green, smooth, about half the size of those of *T. citrifolia*, or less; seeds half-imbedded in pulpy funicles.

5. TABERNÆMONTANA ALBA, Miller, Dict. no. 2, ex Houston, MS.; A. DC. *l. c.* p. 362. In prov. Yucatan: *v. s. in hb. Mus. Brit.* Campeche, Vera Cruz (Houston).

A very distinct species, having spreading, pallid branchlets, with axils ¾–1 in. apart; leaves ovate oblong, somewhat acute at the base, suddenly contracted below the apex into a shortish obtuse acumen, margins subrevolute, chartaceous, green above, and granularly opake, midrib and very spreading nerves of a reddish colour not prominent, beneath opake, of a rusty yellow colour, with a prominent midrib, nerves prominulent, fuscous red, transverse veins immersed; they are 4¾–5¾ in. long, 2–2½ in. broad, on sulcated petioles 5–7 lines long, fossated at the base, and conjoined at the axils by a transverse line; panicle between the terminal leaves, 2 in. long, 1¼ in. broad, with many rather close, somewhat stoutish branches again and again divided; numerous flowers on pedicels 2–4 lines long; sepals small, ovate, imbricated, ¾ line long, each furnished within with 4 linear acute scales; tube of corolla cylindrical, swollen above below the mouth, and there somewhat 5-plicated, is 3 lines long, segments shorter, obliquely oblong, sinistrorsely convoluted; stamens originating in a pilose ring at the contraction of the tube; anthers slender, of a bluish colour, exserted at the apex; a short 5-lobed disk; 2 free, striated, oblong, pointed ovaries; style slender; clavuncle thickish, deeply 5-grooved.

6. TABERNÆMONTANA ACAPULCENSIS, nob.: *Tabernæmontana amygdaleæfolia*, Seem.(non Jacq.) Bot. Her. p. 167: ramulis tenuibus, dichotomis, striolatis: foliis lanceolatis vel oblongo-lanceolatis, imo subcuneatis, apice in acumen longiusculum attenuatis, marginibus crenato-sinuatis, submembranaceis, supra læte viridibus, opacis, minute granulatis, obsolete pilosulis, nervis divergentibus immersis, subtus flavide opacis, granulatis, nervis tenuibus rufescentibus paullo prominulis; petiolo semitereti, limbo 12plo breviore: panicula laterali folio 2–3plo breviore; pedunculo tenui, folio 3plo breviore, sub 4-flora; pedicellis tenuibus, 4plo brevioribus, imo bracteolatis; sepalis parvis, obtuse ovatis, imbricatis, intus squamulis 2 lanceolatis imo munitis; corollæ tubo anguste cylindrico, supra medium paullo ampliore, segmentis oblique oblongis, tubo fere æquilongis, in æstivatione simpliciter sinistrorsum convolutis; staminibus in constrictione tubi insertis, antheris tenuibus semiexsertis; disco tenui, 5-lobo, ovariis 2 oblongis striatis subadnato et triplo breviore; stylo tenui; clavuncula incrassata; stigmatis lobis tenuibus subulatis. In Mexico: *v. s. in hb. Mus. Brit.* Veraguas (Seemann 1221), Acapulco (Pavon), Tehuantepec (Schott 432), Columbia (Cuming 1295).

A shrub 8 feet high, with slender branches, called "jasmin del monte," because of its odoriferous flowers. The leaves are ⅞–3¼ in. long, ½–1½ in. broad, on petioles 2–3 lines long; the panicles are 1½–2 in. long, on slender peduncles 6–9 lines long; pedicels 2–3 lines long; sepals ¾ line long; tube of corolla 7 lines long, segments 5 lines long.

7. TABERNÆMONTANA LAURIFOLIA, Linn. Sp. 308 (non Ker); Miller, Dict. no. 3; Poiret, Dict. vii. 528; Lunan, Jam. ii. 222; A. DC. *l. c.* p. 363; Jacq. Amer. 39; Willd. Sp. i. 1244; Grisebach, Fl. Br. W. Ind. p. 409: *Tabernæmontana frutescens*, Brown, Jam. 181: *Nerium arboreum*, Sloane, Jam. 154; Hist. Jam. ii. 62, tab. 186. fig. 2. In Antilles: *v. s. in hb. Mus. Brit.* Jamaica (Sloane).

A well-known species, but insufficiently described. Sloane's specimen agrees well with his drawing (tab. 186). Lunan describes it as a tree 15 feet high, with a trunk as thick as a man's leg, covered by a smooth whitish bark, and having tortuous branches; its branchlets are curved, with axils 1¼ in. apart; leaves patently opposite along the terminal branchlets, oval-oblong, subacute at the base, suddenly contracted at the apex into a short acumen, lucidly green above, entire on the margins, with several patently divaricating nerves, 4–5 in. long, 2–2¾ in. broad, on straight petioles 1–1½ in. long; panicles lateral, 1–1½ in. long, branching from the base, and bearing several approximated yellow odoriferous flowers, on pedicels 3 lines long; sepals ovate, rounded, membranaceous, veined, imbricated, each having 3 short inner lanceolate scales; tube of corolla narrowly cylindrical, a little wider above, 6–8 lines long; its segments, 5–6 lines long, are obliquely ovate and expanded horizontally on one side, and simply convoluted sinistrorsely in æstivation; the stamens are inserted in the upper portion of the tube; anthers cuspidate at the apex, extending a little beyond the mouth; a semi-5-lobed disk, ⅓ shorter than the 2 free, adpressed, striated ovaries; style slender, surmounted by a thickened, deeply 5-sulcate clavuncle, having a membranaceous expansion at its base, and terminated by 2 subulate stigmata; 2 divaricated ovate follicles, subcompressed, stipitate, horned at the apex.

The *Tabernæmontana laurifolia*, Ker, Bot. Reg. ix. 716, is *Taberna laurina*.

8. TABERNÆMONTANA OCCIDENTALIS, nob.: ramulis pallidis, striatis: foliis oppositis, lanceolato-oblongis, imo acutis, apice in acumen obtusiusculum attenuatis, integris, submembranaceis, supra lætè viridibus, costa tenui nervisque patentibus subimmersis, tenuibus, subtus pallidioribus, costa nervisque paullo prominulis; petiolo supra plano, limbo 50plo breviore: panicula laterali; pedunculo bifido, ramis divaricatis, bracteolatis, 2-floris; pedicellis tenuibus, bracteolatis; sepalis obtuse ovatis, imbricatis, submembranaceis; corollæ tubo cylindrico, subbrevi, segmentis membranaceis oblique oblongis; antheris subcærulescentibus, fere omnino exsertis. In Peruvia: *v. s. in hb. Mus. Brit.?* (Maclean).

A species approaching *T. citrifolia*: its leaves are 4¼ in. long, 1⅜ in. broad, on petioles 1 line long; peduncle 10 lines long; its 2 branches 3 lines; pedicels 4 lines long; sepals 2 lines long; tube of corolla 3 lines long; segments same length and breadth; anthers 1½ line long.

9. TABERNÆMONTANA BERTERII, A. DC. *l. c.* p. 367. In Porto Rico: *non vidi*.

Branchlets pallid; in the lower portions, where the leaves have fallen, they are annulated by a dilated ring; leaves oblong, acute at both ends, 2–3 in. long, 6–12 lines broad, on petioles 4–5 lines long, dilated at the base, and conjoined across the nodes; they are somewhat heterophyllous at the axils, membranaceous, nerves remote and patent; panicles axillary or terminal, shorter than the leaves, on a furcate peduncle, its branches, with few flowers, on pedicels 1 line long, with ovate bracteoles at the base; sepals obtusely ovate, 2 lines long; corolla 1 in. long, the tube constricted in the middle, segments inæquilaterally oblong, shorter than the tube; stamens included, seated in the constriction of the tube. The æstivation of the corolla and other features are unknown; but the species is said to be near *T. amygdalæfolia*.

10. TABERNÆMONTANA UTILIS, Arn. Edinb. Phil. Journ. viii. 318; A. DC. *l. c.* p. 363. In Guiana, Gallica: *non vidi*.

A species said to be near *T. citrifolia*, yielding a lactescent juice, and called "hya-hya" by the natives: leaves oblong, obtuse at the base, suddenly acuminated at the apex, subcoriaceous, glabrous, 4 in. long, 1¾ in. broad, on petioles 6 lines long; cymes axillary, much shorter than the leaves, few-flowered; the lower bracts opposite and foliaceous, upper ones adpressed about the calyx, ciliated; sepals obtuse, ciliated, tube of corolla cylindrical, segments rather short, roundish, simply convoluted; filaments short, seated near the middle of the tube; anthers long and deeply biaristate at the base.

Species of *Tabernæmontana* here excluded and assigned to their proper places:—

Indications: D., De Candolle, Prodr. vol. viii.; B., Müll. Fl. Bras. fasc. xxvi.; L., Müll. Linn. xxx.

T. acuminata, Müll. L. 406 . . . . . = *Peschiera acuminata*.
T. acutissima, Müll. B. 73 . . . . . *Anacampta acutissima*.

T. affinis, Müll. B. 83	= *Peschiera affinis*.
T. amygdalæfolia, Seem. (non Jacq.)	*Tabernæmontana Acapulcensis*.
T. angulata, Müll. B. 72	*Anacampta angulata*.
T. arcuata, R. & P. D. 363	*Merizadenia arcuata*.
T. australis, Müll. B. 84	*Peschiera australis*.
T. Benthamiana, Müll. B. 80	*Peschiera multiflora*.
T. „ Müll. (*bis*) B. 70	*Codonemma calycina*.
T. bracteolaris, Müll. B. 83	*Peschiera hystrix*.
T. breviflora, Müll. B. 79	*Peschiera breviflora*.
T. calycina, Spruce (non Wall.)	*Codonemma calycina*.
T. Catharinensis, D. 365, B. 85	*Peschiera Catharinensis*.
T. cestroides, Nees & Mart.	*Robbia cestroides*.
T. collina, Gardn.	*Peschiera fuchsiæfolia*.
T. congesta, Benth. B. 71	*Anacampta congesta*.
T. cymosa, Jacq. D. 364	*Taberna cymosa*.
T. „ Mart. (non Jacq.)	*Geissospermum Martianum*.
T. „ Soland. (non Jacq.)	*Peschiera Solandri*.
T. discolor, Sw. D. 375	*Taberna discolor*.
T. disticha, A. DC. D. 362	*Taberna disticha*.
T. echinata, Aubl. D. 360	*Peschiera echinata*.
T. „ Vell. D. 360	*Peschiera hystrix*.
T. fallax, Müll. B. 84	*Peschiera fallax*.
T. fasciculata, Poir. D. 375	*Thyrsanthus fasciculatus*.
T. flavescens, R. & Sch. D. 375	*Anartia flavescens*.
T. flavicans, R. & Sch. D. 375, B. 77	*Anartia flavicans*.
T. „ Müll. B. 77	*Anartia flavicans*.
T. frutescens, Sloane, D. 363	*Tabernæmontana citrifolia*.
T. „ P. Br. D. 363	*Tabernæmontana laurifolia*.
T. fuchsiæfolia, A. DC. D. 365, B. 82	*Peschiera fuchsiæfolia*.
T. funiformis, Müll. D. 460, B. 144	*Mitozus funiformis*.
T. „ var. *peduncularis*, Müll.	*Mitozus exilis*.
T. Gaudichaudii, A. DC. D. 365, B. 81	*Peschiera Gaudichaudii*.
T. glabrata, Mart.	*Anartia glabrata*.
T. gracilis, Benth. D. 380	*Malouetia gracilis*.
T. „ Müll. B. 82	*Peschiera gracillima*.
T. grandiflora, Jacq. D. 368	*Stemmadenia grandiflora*.
T. Guyanensis, Müll. L. 404	*Bonafousia Guyanensis*.
T. heterophylla, Vahl, D. 361, B. 76	*Peschiera heterophylla*.
T. „ Benth. D. 361	*Peschiera diversifolia*.
T. Hilariana, Müll. B. 85	*Peschiera Hilariana*.
T. hirtula, Müll. (in parte) B. 78	*Anacampta hirtula*.
T. hystrix, Steud. D. 360	*Peschiera hystrix*.
T. jasminoides, H. B. K. D. 379	*Malouetia jasminoides*.

T. læta, A. DC. (in parte) D. 364 . .	= *Malouetia arborea.*
T. „ Mart. (in parte) D. 364, B. 79	*Peschiera læta.*
T. „ var. *pubescens*, Müll. B. 79 .	*Peschiera florida.*
T. lævigata, Mart. B. 77	*Anartia flavicans.*
T. lævis, Vell. A. DC. D. 375, B. 90 .	*Geissospermum læve.*
T. laurifolia, Ker (non Linn.) D. 363 .	*Taberna laurina.*
T. „ Schott	*Stemmadenia insignis.*
T. Linkii, A. DC. D. 364	*Peschiera Linkii.*
T. litoralis, H. B. K. D. 363	*Peschiera litoralis.*
T. longifolia, Benth. D. 368	*Anacampta longifolia.*
T. lucida, H. B. K. D. 377	*Macoubea,* sp. ?
T. Lundii, A. DC. D. 365, B. 81 . .	*Peschiera Lundii.*
T. (*Odontadenia*) *macrocalyx*, Müll. L. 403	*Codonemma macrocalyx.*
T. macrophylla, Poir. D. 374	*Thyrsanthus macrophyllus.*
T. „ Benth. (non Poir.) B. 75	*Phrissocarpus rigidus.*
T. Meyeri, Don, D. 368	*Anartia Meyeri.*
T. multiflora, R. & Sch. D. 364 . . .	*Peschiera Linkii.*
T. muricata, R. & Sch. D. 361, B. 80 .	*Peschiera muricata.*
T. „ Müll. B. 80	*Peschiera ochracea.*
T. „ Spruce, B. 76	*Phrissocarpus rigidus.*
T. oblongifolia, A. DC. D. 368, B. 74 .	*Bonafousia oblongifolia.*
T. ochracea, Spr. B. 81	*Peschiera ochracea.*
T. odorata, Vahl, D. 379	*Malouetia odorata.*
T. olivacea, Müll. B. 75	*Bonafousia olivacea.*
T. parviflora, Poir. D. 374 . . .	*Thyrsanthus parviflorus.*
T. paucifolia, Müll. B. 87	*Rhigospira paucifolia.*
T. Perottetii, A. DC. D. 362	*Bonafousia Perottetii.*
T. pilifera, Spruce, B. 73	*Anacampta hirtula.*
T. Pöppigii, Müll. L. 405	*Taberna Pöppigii.*
T. populifolia, Poir. D. 374	*Thyrsanthus populifolius.*
T. psychotriæfolia, H. B. K. D. 366 .	*Peschiera psychotriæfolia.*
T. Rauwolfii, A. DC. D. 364, B. 78 .	*Peschiera Salzmanni.*
T. recurva, Sagot	*Anartia recurva.*
T. reticulata, A. DC. D. 366, B. 87 .	*Rhigospira reticulata.*
T. Riedelii, Müll. B. 72 . . .	*Taberna Riedelii.*
T. riparia, H. B. K.	*Malouetia riparia.*
T. rubrostriolata, Müll. B. 71 . . .	*Anacampta congesta.*
T. rupicola, Benth. D. 362, B. 74 . .	*Bonafousia rupicola.*
T. „ var. *oblongifolia*, Müll. B. 75	*Bonafousia rariflora.*
T. „ var. *Sprucei*, Müll. B. 75 .	*Bonafousia polyneura.*
T. Salzmanni, A. DC. D. 362; B. 78 .	*Peschiera Salzmanni.*
T. Sananho, R. & P. D. 363	*Merizadenia Sananho.*
T. sessilis, Vell. B. 96	*Thyrsanthus sessilis.*

T. solanifolia, A. DC. D. 365, B. 86 . =	*Peschiera solanifolia*.
T. Spixiana, Mart. B. 78	*Peschiera Spixiana*.
T. Sprucei, Müll. (in parte) B. 86 . .	*Rhigospira Sprucei*.
T. „ Müll. (in parte) B. 86 . .	*Rhigospira sinuosa*.
T. stenoloba, Müll. L. 407	*Peschiera stenoloba*.
T. subcordata, Linn. Syst. 945 . . .	*Echites umbellata*.
T. submollis, Mart. B. 70	*Anacampta submollis*.
T. tenuiflora, Müll. B. 76	*Peschiera tenuiflora*.
T. ternstræmiacea, Müll. B. 88 . . .	*Rhigospira ternstræmiacea*.
T. tetrastachys, H. B. K. D. 368 . .	*Malouetia tetrastachys*.
T. umbrosa, H. B. K. D. 375 . . .	*Peschiera umbrosa*.
T. undulata, Vahl (non Mey.) . . .	*Bonafousia undulata*.
T. „ Spruce	*Bonafousia obliqua*.
T. „ Meyer, D. 368	*Anartia Meyeri*.
T. versicolor, Müll. B. 146	*Mitozus versicolor*.
T. „ var. *olivacea*, Müll. . .	*Mitozus tenuicaulis*.
T. „ „ *brachystachys*, Müll.	*Mitozus brachystachys*.
T. „ „ *intermedia*, Müll. .	*Mitozus rugosus*.
T. „ *Wulfschlægelii*, Griseb. .	*Anartia Wulfschlægelii*.
T. sp., Benth.	*Malouetia lactiflora*.

TABERNA, DC.

Fifty-nine of the many species of *Tabernæmontana*, enumerated by De Candolle under a section *Taberna*, are mostly of American, with a few of oriental origin, all combined under the single character of a follicular fruit. If we remove from these heterogeneous species all those belonging to *Tabernæmontana* proper, and those belonging to other genera since constituted, we have a remainder, all American, which offer tolerably uniform characters; they are here comprised under a genus *Taberna*.

TABERNA, A. DC. Char. reformat. : *Sepala* 5, parva, ovata, erecta, imbricata, intus squamulis parvis acutis paucis vel pluribus munita. *Corolla* hypocrateriformis ; *tubus* anguste cylindricus; *limbi segmenta* 5, expansa, dolabriformia, sinistrorsum inflexa et convoluta. *Stamina* inclusa, paullo infra medium tubi inserta, subsessilia ; *antheræ* subcohærentes, imo breviter et acute bifurcatæ, apice acuminatæ ; *discus* cylindricus, submembranaceus, margine crenulatus, ovario adnato arcte adglutinatus et eo dimidio brevior ; *stylus* tenuis ; *clavuncula* incrassata, imo membrana indusiata ; *stigmata* 2, parva, terminalia. *Folliculi* 2, sæpius divaricati, oblongi, obtusi, subcompressi, sæpe maculati, plus minusve arcuati, sutura ventrali dehiscentes. *Semina* plurima, in funiculos crassos pulposos semiimmersa. Arbores *vel* suffrutices *Americæ meridionalis*, habitu Tabernæmontanæ.

From the above characters it will be seen that *Taberna* differs from *Tabernæmontana* in the tube of its corolla being swollen in the middle, in the character of its stamens, which are quite included, and in a longer adnate disk. From *Bonafousia* it differs in the shape of its corolla, in the dolabriform segments of its border simply convoluted in æstivation, in the position of its stamens, and in the presence of a disk; from *Peschiera* in the stouter tube of its corolla, in the position of its stamens, in the presence of a disk, and in its smooth (not muricated) fruit.

1. TABERNA CYMOSA, nob.: *Tabernæmontana cymosa*, Jacq. (non Solander) Amer. 39, tab. 181. fig. 14; A. DC. Prodr. viii. 364. Ad Cartagena: *v. s. in herb. Mus. Brit. sine loco (ex hb. Vahl.), et sine flore.*

A species apparently known only to Jacquin, who describes it as a tree 15 feet high, of which the trunk is 6 feet long, its branches furnished with ovate-lanceolate acute, entire or scarcely undulated leaves, 6 in. long, the axillary cymes consisting of a broad, handsome mass of about 40 reddish-white flowers, on slender pedicels 3 lines long; calyx of 5 lanceolate-oblong, flat, erect sepals 2 lines long; tube of corolla narrowly cylindrical, 6 lines long, 1 line broad, a little swollen above the base, the segments being dolabriform, expanded, 5 lines long, 3 lines broad, sinistrorsely convoluted; stamens enclosed in the swollen portion of the tube; follicles 2 (one generally abortive), oblong, recurved, roundly obtuse at the extremity, with a lateral curving ridge on each side, rather large, of a reddish colour, spotted with unequal rusty blotches, 3 in. long, 1¼ in. thick, and containing many seeds, partly enveloped in yellowish succulent funicles.

In the specimen above cited, the leaves quite agree with the description of Jacquin. On it is written (not by Vahl), "*Tab. citrifolia*;" but it is very different from the original drawing of that species furnished by Plumier. In the specimen, the young branch is very slender, the axils ½–1 in. apart; the opposite leaves lanceolate, acute at both ends, 3–4½ in. long, ¾–1 in. broad, on petioles 4–5 lines long.

Figures of this species, in flower and in fruit, are given in Plate VIII. A.

2. TABERNA DISCOLOR, nob.: *Tabernæmontana discolor*, Sw. Prodr. p. 62; Fl. Ind. Occid. p. 535; A. DC. *l. c.* p. 375; Lunan, Jam. ii. 222; Grisebach, Flor. Brit. W. Ind. p. 409. In Antilles: *v. s. in hb. Mus. Brit.* Jamaica (Swartz).

This typical plant agrees with Swartz's description in all respects, except the character of the anthers, "ovatæ," which shape is contrary to that of any of the *Tabernæmontanæ*. I have examined the anthers in the above specimen, and find them to be narrowly oblong, acute and shortly bidentate at the base; stamens inserted above the middle of the tube and quite included, on which account the species is referred to *Taberna*. It is a shrub, 6 feet high, dichotomously branched, with slender 4-angular striated branchlets; leaves elliptic (younger ones lanceolate-ovate), acute at the base, with an obtuse acumen, inequilateral, with undulated margins, green above, very opake, nerves immersed and veinless, sulcated on the midrib, pallid beneath, yellowish, opake, minutely granulated, midrib and nerves prominulent and reddish, 2½–3¼ in. long, 1–1¼ in. broad, on slender channelled petioles 7–9 lines long, fossated at the base and conjoined by a short transverse ridge; peduncle 2 lines long, its branches 5 lines long, each bearing 4–5 flowers, on pedicels 2 lines long, bracteolated at the base; sepals acutely oval, imbricated, with a prominent green nerve and pale membranaceous margins; tube of corolla 6 lines long, segments 3 lines long, inequilateral, ovate at the base, linear and horizontally expanded on the sinister side, simply convoluted sinistrorsely; stamens inserted below the middle of the tube; anthers as before stated; disk very short, membranaceous, investing the base of 2 ovaries; follicles 2, containing many seeds half-immersed in pulpy funicles.

3. TABERNA LAURINA, nob.: *Tabernæmontana laurifolia*, Ker (non Linn.) Bot. Reg. tab. 716; A. DC. *l. c.* p. 363. In Antilles: *v. s. in herb. Mus. Brit.* Jamaica (Shakespear).

De Candolle states that this is very distinct from *T. laurifolia*, Linn., founded on Sloane's plant, differing in its more rounded, cuneated leaves, having the nervation of *T. neriifolia*, and in its much larger flowers, which are white (not yellow), upon a much longer peduncle, bare at its base. It is a lactescent shrub, with stoutish 4-angular branches, apparently much verrucated, with axils $\frac{3}{4}$–1 in. apart; the opposite leaves are roundly obovate, cuneated from the middle to the petiole, with many nearly horizontally patent nerves conjoined along the margin, $2\frac{1}{2}$–$5\frac{1}{2}$ in. long, 1–1$\frac{3}{4}$ in. broad, on slender petioles 6–9 lines long, channelled above, broadly flattened at the base, and there conjoined by a transverse ridge at each node; panicles opposite, on bare peduncles 2 in. long, terminated by 3 alternate, very odoriferous flowers, on thickish pedicels 2 lines long; calyx thickly coriaceous, shortly cupshaped at the base; sepals 5, equal, roundly ovate, convex, imbricated, yellowish green, externally papillose and poriferous, emitting a viscous juice; tube of corolla thickly cylindrical, 9 lines long, 1$\frac{1}{2}$ line broad, segments inequilaterally oblong, very expanded, 9 lines long, 4 lines broad, sinistrorsely convoluted; stamens said to be short and fixed below the middle of the tube,—all being characters conformable with *Taberna*.

4. TABERNA PÖPPIGII, nob.: *Tabernæmontana Pöppigii*, Müller in Linn. xxx. 405. In Peruvia ad Tocache: *non vidi*.

A species with the habit of *T. Sananho*, R. & P., and with internodes as long as the leaves, which are elliptic, obtuse at the base, acuminated at the summit, membranaceous, with 14–16 pairs of arching nerves, concolorous, 8–9 in. long, 3$\frac{5}{8}$–4 in. broad, with petioles 3$\frac{1}{2}$ lines long; peduncle 1$\frac{5}{8}$ in. long, bearing 6–8 slender flowers, which in bud are 6$\frac{3}{4}$–8 lines long, on pedicels 3 lines long; sepals obtusely ovate, ciliolate, with 5–7 internal scales; tube of corolla puberulous within at the insertion of the stamens; ovaries obtusely ovoid, surrounded at the base by an adherent disk.

5. TABERNA DISPARIFOLIA, nob.: ramulis tenuibus, dichotome divisis: foliis plerumque heterophyllis, elliptico-oblongis, imo acutis, apice in acumen longum et angustum subito constrictis, tenuiter chartaceis, supra viridibus, nervis tenuissimis patentim divaricatis vix prominulis, subtus pallidioribus, opacis, costa nervisque rufulis subprominulis; petiolis tenuissimis, canaliculatis, imo vaginatim conjunctis, limbo 12plo brevioribus: racemo laterali aut terminali, brevissimo; pedunculo depauperato, 1–2-floro; pedicellis ei æquilongis; sepalis oblongis, submembranaceis, imbricatis, intus squamulis parvis acutis basalibus munitis: corollæ tubo tenuiter elongato, medio angustiore, segmentis obtuse oblongis, subobliquis, quam tubus dimidio brevioribus, subreflexis, sinistrorsum convolutis; staminibus versus medium tubi insertis; ovariis 2, oblongis, apice liberis, imo pro dimidia parte disco adnatis. In Peruvia: *v. s. in hb. meo et alior.* Tarapoto (Spruce 4611).

A species having the habit and appearance of a *Peschiera*: the axils of its slender dichotomous branchlets are $\frac{1}{2}$–1 in. apart; its opposite leaves 2$\frac{1}{4}$ and 1 or 2$\frac{3}{4}$ and 1$\frac{1}{4}$ in.

long, in each axil, 7-10 lines broad, on petioles 3 and 2 lines long; the peduncle is 5-6 lines long, the pedicels 4-5 lines long; sepals 1 line long; tube of corolla 14 lines long, 1 line broad in the middle; segments 8 lines long, 2½ lines broad, horizontally and simply convoluted sinistrorsely in æstivation; style long and slender, clavuncle incrassated with a basal membranaceous peltate appendage.

6. TABERNA RIEDELII, nob.: *Tabernæmontana Riedelii*, Müll. *l. c.* p. 72. In Amazonas ad Rio Madera (Riedel 1378): *non vidi*.

A shrub 8-10 feet high: subcoriaceous leaves broadly ovate, shortly acute at the base, with a short acute apex, punctulate-scabrous above, pallid below, and of an argillaceous olive colour, with about 15 pairs of nerves, 6¾-10 in. long, 4-5¼ in. broad, on very short petioles; panicle lateral, 8 or 10-flowered, on a scabridly hirsute peduncle, three times as long as the short petioles; pedicels as long as the calyx, with ovate ciliated bracts; sepals broadly ovate and rounded, with ciliated margins, and with many internal basal scales; tube of corolla five times as long as the calyx, 9½ lines long, finely pulverulent and scabrous outside; stamens seated below the middle of tube on a pilose ring; ovaries glabrous, slightly swollen below the middle by an adnate disk.

7. TABERNA DISTICHA, nob.: *Tabernæmontana disticha*, A. DC. viii. 362. In Guiana Gallica: *non vidi*.

Branches terete, yellowish, with internodes shorter than the leaves: leaves distichous, oblong, somewhat acute at the base, acuminate at the apex, membranaceous, 3-5 in. long, 1-2 in. broad, on petioles 2-3 lines long; raceme lateral, on a thick peduncle scarcely longer than the petioles, bearing about 5 approximated flowers, on pedicels scarcely longer than the calyx, with ovate ciliated bracts at their base, ½ line long; sepals obtusely ovate, small; tube of corolla 7 lines long, cylindrical, a little swollen about the middle, segments oblong, shorter than the tube, puberulous on both sides; stamens inserted near the middle of the tube; anthers sagittate, subcoherent at the base; disk agglutinated to the base of 2 ovaries free above. A species said to be near *T. oblongifolia*.

ANACAMPTA [*].

A genus distinguished by its stoutish angular branches, always more or less fistulous; leaves generally large, oblong, rigidly chartaceous, upon stoutish petioles, flat above, deeply and hoodingly fossate at the base, and conjoined across the node by a transverse ridge; short lateral panicles on a stout peduncle bearing above several short branches, each with flowers on short pedicels; calyx generally rather small; tube of corolla cylindrical, stoutish, contracted below the middle at the insertion of the stamens, segments rectangularly prolonged, ¾ the length of the tube, their apices descending into the tube in æstivation, as in *Bonafousia*; disk cylindrical, free, tubular, 5-sulcate, and 5-crenulate; follicles 2, divergent, much compressed, dolabriform, smooth, each containing several ovoid subcompressed seeds attached to the suture by fleshy funicles.

[*] From ἀνακάμπτω (*intreflexo*), from the singular introflexion of the segments of the corolla in æstivation.

ANACAMPTA, nob.: *Tabernæmontana* (in parte) auct.: Sepala parva, rarius majora, oblonga, erecta, imbricata, intus squamula multifida munita. *Corolla* tubulosa; *tubus* cylindricus, supra medium paullulo ampliatus; *segmenta* tubo paullo breviora, plus minusve curvata, ad basin pro tertia parte subrhomboidea, pro reliqua parte lineari-oblonga, hic in æstivatione subito introflexa, apicibus obtusulis intra faucem protensis. *Stamina* inclusa; *filamenta* brevissima, ad constrictionem tubi inserta; *antheræ* lineares, conniventes, cuspidatæ, imo furcis 2 acutis subbrevibus armatæ. *Discus* carnosulus, cylindricus, 5-costatus, margine 5-crenatus, glaber vel hispidulus, ovariis paullo brevior. *Ovaria* 2, oblonga, libera, sæpe pilosa; *stylus* subbrevis; *clavuncula* incrassata, oblonga, imo membrana crispata peltata donata; *stigmata* 2, breviter subulata, terminalia. *Folliculi* 2, dolabriformi-oblongi, subacuti, valde compressi, læves, divaricati, ventre arcuato dehiscentes. *Semina* subpauca, ovata, compressa, dorso crebre striata, asperula, ventre late sulcata et ibi *hilo* centrali notata, funiculo carnoso semivestita aut suspensa.

Arbusculæ *plerumque Brasilianæ, sæpius glaberrimæ;* rami *validiusculi, angulati:* folia *opposita, plerumque majuscula, oblonga, glaberrima, coriacea aut rigide chartacea;* petioli *crassi, supra plani, imo angulosi, striati, superne versus basin cuculla concava muniti, et illic profunde fossati, ad nodos linea transversa nexi;* paniculæ *laterales, subbreviores, pedunculati, apice approximatim ramosæ,* ramis flores 3–4 *breviter pedicellatis gerentibus.*

1. ANACAMPTA CONGESTA, nob.: *Tabernæmontana congesta,* Benth. MS.; *Tabernæmontana rubrostriolata,* Müll. *l. c.* p. 71, tab. 21. fig. 1. In Amazonas: *v. s. in hb. meo et alior.* Santarem (Spruce 232).

Mr. Bentham's specific name is here adopted in preference to the MS. name of Martius, employed by Müller, which does not apply to the present plant, and which probably was given by Martius to some undescribed species. It has stout, dichotomous, subfistulose branchlets, angularly sulcate, and of a yellowish colour: it has large obovate leaves, rounded at the base and suddenly narrowed along the petiole, obtuse towards the summit, and there constricted into a blunt, short acumen, or, by imperfection, round and emarginate there; they are firmly chartaceous, with subrevolute margins, green above, sulcate on the midrib and divergent nerves, yellowish opake below, with prominent costa and reddish nerves, $4\frac{1}{2}$–$7\frac{1}{2}$ in. long, $2\frac{3}{4}$–$4\frac{1}{4}$ in. broad, on stout broad petioles 3 lines long, channelled and deeply fossate at the base, and conjoined across the node by a transverse ridge; panicle lateral and solitary at the axils, 6 lines long, bearing several congested flowers on slender pedicels bracteolated at their base, 2 lines long; sepals ovate, ciliolated, imbricated, 1 line long, having within several lanceolate scales; tube of corolla 7 lines long, staminiferous in the middle, border-segments half as long, dolabriform, sinistrorsely convoluted in æstivation; disk angular, adnate to the ovaries for half their length; fructiferous pedicel much stouter, 5 lines long, supporting 2 gibbous follicles acutely recurved at the summit. These are not yet matured in the specimen; they are smoothly opake, pale brown, $1\frac{3}{4}$–$1\frac{1}{4}$ in. long, $3\frac{1}{4}$ lines broad, and contain about 16 unripe, oval compressed, striated seeds, attached in the middle of the ventral face to a fleshy funicle.

Drawings of this species, in flower and in fruit, are given in Plate IX. B.

2. ANACAMPTA ANGULATA, nob.: *Tabernæmontana angulata,* Mart.; Müll. *l. c.* p. 72, tab. 23. In Amazonas, prov. Pará: *non vidi.*

A well-marked cognate species, with stout dichotomous branchlets, deeply angular-sulcated, compressed, fistulose, dark, puberulous, with axils 3½ in. apart; leaves elliptic-oblong, acute at the base, a long narrow acumen at the apex, glabrous, entire, granularly scabrid on both sides, with about 12 pairs of diverging nerves, 4¾–6 in. long, 3½–3¾ in. broad, on stout channelled petioles, fossated at the base and conjoined by a transverse ridge across the thickened nodes. The panicles are solitary and lateral at the axils, on a stout striated peduncle 9 lines long, bearing 5–7 or more, closely congested flowers, on bracteolated pedicels 2–3 lines long; sepals oblong, 2¾ lines long; tube of corolla 9 lines long; segments gibbously ovoid, 6 lines long; disk cylindrical, surrounding 2 obovoid ovaries.

3. ANACAMPTA ACUTISSIMA, nob.: *Tabernæmontana acutissima*, Müll. Fl. Bras. p. 73. In insulis fluv. Amazones: *non vidi*.

This species is very near the preceding. Its branches are obtusely angular, sub-puberulous; leaves oblong-ovate, obtuse at the base, terminated by a long, narrow, cuspidate acumen, have about 18 pairs of nerves 7 lines apart, are very glabrous, 6¾–8 in. long, 2¾–3¼ in. broad, on petioles 2–2½ lines long (probably deeply fossated and conjoined by a transverse ridge); panicle lateral, on a peduncle 4¾ lines long, bearing from 4 to 7 flowers aggregated on pedicels as long as the calyx, and furnished with triangular, obtuse, puberulous, ciliated bracts; sepals obtusely oblong, glabrous, with ciliated margins, provided with 4 basal scales inside; tube of corolla glabrous outside, pubescent within along 5 longitudinal lines in the middle, where the stamens are inserted; segments oblong, narrowed horizontally, outside furfuraceous at the base, beyond glabrous, convoluted sinistrorsely in æstivation; disk acutely 5-angled, surrounding the ovaries.

4. ANACAMPTA LONGIFOLIA, nob.: *Tabernæmontana longifolia*, Benth. Hook. Journ. Bot. iii. 243; A. DC. *l. c.* p. 368. In Guiana: *v. s. in herb. meo et alior.* Guiana Brit. (Schomb. 292 et 41 bis), Surinam (Miq. sub *T. oblongifolia*), Cayenne (Van Rohr, sub *T. triquetra*).

This must not be confounded with another 41 of Schomburgk's plants, which is *Thyrsanthus laurifolius*. The branchlets are stout, angular, striolated, subfistulose, with axils 1¼–2 in. apart; its subcuneate oblong leaves, acuminate at the summit, are 5–10 in. long, 2–2½ in. broad, on stout deeply fossate petioles 3 lines long, conjoined across the axils by a transverse ridge; inflorescence terminal at the end of a very short 2-leaved branchlet, so that it appears almost axillary; peduncle stout, 1 in. long, divided at its summit into two erect stout portions 1 in. long, each bearing about 20 very closely alternate flowers, most of which are caducous; pedicels 3–4 lines long, issuing from as many imbricating, obsoletely puberulous, oblong, oval bracts 2 lines long, mostly caducous; sepals oblong, obtuse, 2 lines long, each with a 4-dentate scale within; tube of corolla cylindrical, 9 lines long, contracted at the mouth; segments oblong, gibbous, (expanded) 5 lines long, 4 lines broad, sinistrorsely convoluted, their extremities introflexed and descending into the mouth of the tube; stamens inserted above the middle of the tube; ovaries 2, oblong, pointed, free, and half-enclosed within a fleshy, cylindrical, 5-grooved, 5-crenate disk; style, clavuncle, and stigmata as in the generic character.

5. ANACAMPTA SUBMOLLIS, nob.: *Tabernæmontana submollis*, Mart. et Müll. *l. c.* p. 70, tab. 22. In Amazonas: *v. s. in hb. meo et alior*. Rio Negro (Spruce 1666).

A shrub 3–4 feet high, with dichotomous compressed branchlets, the axils 1½–2½ in. apart; leaves lanceolate-oblong, acute at both ends, opake pale green above, yellowish and very opake beneath, with about 16 pairs of paler prominent nerves, 5–7 in. long, 1½–2½ in. broad, on stout petioles 3–5 lines long, deeply channelled, fossate at the base, their margins conjoined across the node by a transverse ridge; panicle lateral, 2 in. long, on a peduncle 1 in. long, with several very short branches bearing flowers on stoutish pedicels 2 lines long, bracteolated at the base; sepals ovate obtuse, 1 line long, with 3 inner small lanceolate scales; corolla tubular; tube cylindrical, very little swollen in the middle, 6 lines long; segments oblong, inequilateral, deeply introflected, the extremities descending into the tube; in æstivation they are sinistrorsely convoluted into a small oval knob 2 lines long; stamens seated in the middle of the tube upon 5 longitudinal pilose lines; anthers acuminate, with 2 slender aristiform basal prongs; disk tubular, fleshy, 5-grooved, 5-crenulate, half the length of the 2 free, oblong, puberulous ovaries; style, clavuncle, and stigmata as in the generic character.

6. ANACAMPTA HIRTULA, nob.: *Tabernæmontana hirtula*, Mart.; Müll. *l. c.* p. 73, tab. 24. Ad Rio Orinoco (Spruce 3660); Santarem, Rio Amazonas (Spruce 2474): *v. s. in hb. meo* Rio Casiquiare (Spruce 3175), Santarem (Spruce 233, sub *T. pilifera*).

A lank species, well represented in the drawing cited. Branches fuscous, fistulose, sharply 4-angular, hirsutulous or subglabrous, lenticellated, with axils 1–2¼ in. apart; leaves oblong-elliptic, acute at both ends, subinequilateral, margins subrevolute, chartaceous, very glabrous, pale green above, yellowish opake beneath, with prominulent patently divaricated nerves terminating in the margin, immersed reticulated veins, 5–10 in. long, 1¾–3¼ in. broad, on channelled petioles 3–5 lines long, fossated at the base, there hooded, leaving a deep oblong hollow, and conjoined across the node by a transverse ridge; panicles lateral and solitary at the nodes, 3 in. long, on a deflected, compressed peduncle 2 in. long, or shorter, bifid at the summit, each branch bearing several approximated flowers on pedicels 2 lines long, shortly bracteolated; sepals ovate, imbricated, 1½ line long, each furnished at its base with very numerous acute scales; tube of corolla cylindrical, spirally twisted, 5 lines long; segments obliquely oblong, 4¼ lines long, deeply introplicated and convoluted sinistrorsely, forming in æstivation a knob 2 lines long; stamens inserted below the middle of the tube; disk cylindrical, sulcate, crenate on the margin, pilose, shorter than the oblong glabrous ovaries.

RHIGOSPIRA *.

A group of plants differing from *Anacampta* in the rigid segments of the corolla—which are erect, and simply convoluted in a pyramidal form in æstivation: their leaves

* From ῥιγόω (*rigesco*), σπεῖρα (*spira*), because of the rigidly pyramidal form of the border of the corolla in æstivation.

are generally very large, rigid, upon short stout petioles, deeply and hoodingly fossate at the base.

RHIGOSPIRA, nob.: *Tabernæmontanæ* sectio *Stenocephalium*, et *Ambellania* (in parte), Müller. *Sepala* ovata, interdum majuscula, valde imbricata, erecta, imo in cupulam brevissimam connata, intus squamulis numerosis 1–2 serialibus munita. *Corolla* tubulosa, mediocris; *tubus* imum versus subdilatatus; *segmenta* tubo paullo breviora, anguste oblonga, erecta, in æstivatione simpliciter et sinistrorsum convoluta. *Stamina* basin versus ad contractionem tubi inserta, inclusa; *filamenta* brevissima; *antheræ* acuminatæ, conniventes, imo breviter et obtusule bifurcatæ. *Discus* cylindricus, carnosus, sæpe hispidulus, 5-sulcatus, ovariis paullo brevior. *Ovaria* 2, oblonga, libera; *stylus* brevissimus; *clavuncula* incrassata, cylindrica, imo peltatim membranacea. *Stigmata* 2, subulata, terminalia.

Suffrutices *Brasilienses*, *plerumque Amazonici*, *rigescentes*; rami *sæpius angulati et fistulosi*; folia *oblonga*, *breviter petiolata*; petioli *crassi imo profunde cucullatim fossati*; paniculæ *laterales*, breves, dense pluriflora; flores *mediocres*.

1. RHIGOSPIRA QUADRANGULARIS, nob.: *Ambellania quadrangularis*, Müll. *l. c.* p. 18: *Hancornia macrophylla*, Spruce MS. In Amazonas, *v. s. in herb. meo* San Carlos, Rio Negro (Spruce 3026).

The branches are acutely 4-angled, 3 lines thick, sparsely verruculose, very fistulose, with remote axils; leaves oblong, rather acute at the base, rounded at the summit, rigidly chartaceous, undulately subplicate, margins subrevolute, dark reddish green above, opake, sulcated along the broad midrib, with about 12 pairs of spreading nerves, arcuately conjoined at the margin, with very numerous transverse veins much reticulated, ferruginously yellow and opake beneath, the midrib very prominent and angular, sulcate along the prominulent nerves, the surface spotted with large fuscous patches, 9 in. long, 3¾–4 in. broad, on stout rigid petioles 1 in. long, striately angular beneath, channelled above, with a short, broad, hooded, basal fosset, their margins conjoined across the node by a prominent ridge; panicle terminal, 5 in. long, spreading above to the same extent, on a bare 4-angular peduncle 3 in. long, trichotomously branched above, branches bare at the base for 1 in., each again trichotomously and shortly divided, the rays severally supporting about 4 subumbellate flowers, on pedicels 2–3 lines long; sepals acute, ¼ line long; tube of corolla 3 lines long, swelling a little above the base, gradually narrowing to the mouth, lined within for ⅔ of its length with 5 densely pilose lines; segments linear oblong, obtuse, 3 lines long, erect, simply convoluted sinistrorsely and somewhat spirally in æstivation, rigid; stamens enclosed, seated in the basal contraction of the tube; anthers acuminate, with 2 obtuse incurving basal prongs; disk cylindrical, striate, crenulate on the margin, enclosing 2 oblong ovaries of its own length; style very short; clavuncle oblong, incrassated with a basal peltate membrane; stigma shortly subulate, terminal.

A drawing of this species, and an analysis of its flower, are shown in Plate X. A.

2. RHIGOSPIRA VENULOSA, nob.: *Hancornia macrophylla*, Spruce MS.: *Ambellania macrophylla*, Müll. *l. c.* p. 18. In Amazonas: *v. s. in herb. Mus. Brit.* Panuré, Rio Uahupes (Spruce 2483).

Müller's specific name is not adopted, in order to avoid confusion with another plant so named by Spruce. It has terete branches, with axils about 2 in. apart; leaves elliptic, subacute at both ends, chartaceous, margins revolute, opake green above, sulcate along the midrib, with more than 50 pairs of prominulent patent parallel nerves arcuately conjoined within the margin, and fine intermediate reticulated veins, ferruginously opake beneath, sulcate along the immersed nerves, 4–6 in. long, 1½–2 in. broad, on channelled petioles 4–5 lines long, deeply fossate at the base, with a hooded margin, angular beneath, and conjoined across the nodes by a transverse ridge; panicle terminal, 3 in. long, on a bare peduncle 9 lines long, with several short branches, each supporting 3 flowers 1¼ in. long, on bracteolated pedicels 3 lines long; sepals acute, 1 line long, each with numerous lanceolate minute inner scales; tube of corolla narrower in the throat, 8 lines long, gradually broader towards the base, 8 lines long, densely pilose for ⅔ its length from the mouth; segments obtusely oblong, 4 lines long, simply sinistrorsely twisted in an obtusely pyramidal form in æstivation; stamens included, inserted at the foot of the pilose ring; anthers acuminate, with 2 obtuse short basal prongs; disk annular, 5-grooved, half the length of the 2 oblong ovaries; rest as in the generic character.

3. RHIGOSPIRA PAUCIFOLIA, nob.: *Tabernæmontana paucifolia*, Spruce; Müll. *l. c.* p. 87. In Amazonas: *v. s. in herb. meo* Panuré, Rio Uahupes (Spruce 2564).

This much resembles the typical species in habit and inflorescence. Its rugous branches are stout and fistulose; its leaves, fuscous and of a reddish hue, are obovate, subacute at the base, obtusely pointed at the apex, flaccidly chartaceous, with parallel divergent nerves terminating in the sinuosities of the margin, ferruginously reddish and opake beneath, with prominent fuscous midrib, nerves, and transverse very reticulate veins, 3½–6½ in. long, 3–4 in. broad, upon stoutish petioles 5–9 lines long, which are angular beneath, deeply fossate at the base, the hollow being margined by an elevated hooded rim, and are connected across the node by a transverse ridge; panicles terminal in the younger branchlets, 2½ in. long, on a bare peduncle 1½ in. long, with an almost capitate head of several flowers, on close spreading branches bare at the base, each bearing 6 or 7 flowers on pedicels 1¼ line long, supported by short acute bracteoles; sepals ovate, 1 line long, ciliolated on the margins, with several inner basal scales; tube of corolla 3 lines long; the segments oblong, 6 lines long, erect, and simply contorted sinistrorsely in æstivation; stamens inserted above the base of the tube upon pilose lines; disk cylindrical, thickish, 5-grooved, hirsutulous, very little shorter than 2 free ovaries.

4. RHIGOSPIRA RETICULATA, nob.: *Tabernæmontana reticulata*, A. DC. *l. c.* p. 366; Müll. *l. c.* p. 87, tab. 27. fig. 2. In Bahia (Blanchet 2336; Riedel 445): *non vidi*.

A species with stout, rigid, subcinereous branches, 4-angular at the apex, branchlets glabrous; leaves patent, obovate, subacute at the base, rounded or obtuse, and mucronulate at the summit, with conspicuous nerves and reticulated veins, 3–5½ in. long, 2–3⅔ in. broad, on petioles 4¾–6 lines long, broad and fossate at the base; panicle terminal, on a peduncle 1¼ in. long, verruculous, with several short subumbellate branches 2½–3¾ lines long, each bearing several close flowers ¾–1 in. long, on pedicels 4 lines long; sepals obtuse, 1½ line long, ciliolated, with very numerous lanceolate

2-serial basal scales; tube of corolla 6 lines long; segments inequilaterally oblong, sinistrorsely convoluted; stamens included; disk cylindrical, crenulate on the margin, half as long as the 2 ovate, pilose ovaries.

5. RHIGOSPIRA SPRUCEI, nob.: *Tabernæmontana Sprucei*, Müll. *l. c.* p. 86, tab. 27. fig. 1. In Amazonas: *v. s. in herb. meo* Panuré, Rio Uahupes (Spruce 2594).

A species well represented in the drawing cited. Its branches, somewhat slender and verruculose, have axils ¾–1½ in. apart; its ovate, subflaccid leaves are 3¼–4½ in. long, 2–2½ in. broad, on rather slender petioles 6–10 lines long, shortly and deeply fossate at the base, the hollow margined by a hooded edge, and connected across the node by a transverse ridge; panicle terminal, 4 in. long, on a bare peduncle 2 in. long, trichotomous at its apex, with branches bare for 1 in. and bearing few flowers at their summits, on pedicels 2¼ lines long, supported by bracteoles 1 line long; sepals ovate, obtuse, imbricate, subscabridulous, with several inner imbricated scales at the base; tube of corolla cylindrical, 5 lines long, pilose in the mouth; segments oblong, subinequilateral, 5 lines long, 2¼ lines broad, subscabridulous within, erect and simply contorted sinistrorsely in æstivation; stamens included, seated on a retrorsely pilose ring a little above the base of the tube; anthers coherent, acuminate, with 2 acute basal prongs; disk cylindrical, thickish, 5-sulcate, densely pilosulous, nearly concealing 2 free ovaries; style short, with an incrassated clavuncle.

6. RHIGOSPIRA SINUOSA, nob.: *Tabernæmontana Sprucei* (in parte), Müll. *l. c.* p. 86. In Amazonas: *v. s. in herb. meo* San Carlos, Rio Negro (Spruce 3693).

A species differing from the preceding in its larger, more rigid leaves, with extremely sinuous margins, always very rounded at the apex, and a more copious inflorescence. The leaves are very acute at the base, sulcate along the midrib, the prominulent fine divergent nerves terminating in the hollow of each sinus, ferruginously and granularly opake beneath, with dark rubiginous prominulent nerves and immersed reticulated veins, 4–6 in. long, 2½–3 in. broad, on stout channelled petioles ¾–1 in. long, shortly and deeply fossate at the base, the fosset surrounded by an elevated hooded edge, partly amplexicaul and connected across the node by a transverse ridge; panicle terminal, 4 in. long, upon an angular fuscous peduncle, spotted with small yellow lenticels, bare at its base for 2½ in., supporting several approximated, lenticellate, spreading branches bracteolated at the base, bare for 3–6 lines, and bearing several congested flowers on pedicels 2–3 lines long, supported by oval bracteoles 1 line long; sepals obtusely ovate, 1½ line long, fusco-pruinose, ciliated on the margins, furnished within at the base with subobsolete scales and ciliated hairs; tube of corolla cylindrical, a little swollen at the base, 3 lines long, with a pilose ring in the mouth; segments fleshy, oblong, subauricular at the base, erect, and simply convoluted sinistrorsely in æstivation, 5 lines long; stamens included, inserted above the base of the tube on 5 pilose lines; anthers acuminate, with 2 slender aristiform basal prongs; disk cylindrical, thickish, 5-grooved, pilose round the margin, and concealing 2 free ovaries; style short, with an incrassated clavuncle.

7. **RHIGOSPIRA TERNSTRŒMIACEA**, nob.: *Tabernæmontana* (?) *ternstræmiacea*, Müll. *l. c.* p. 88. In Amazonas: *v. s. in herb. meo* San Carlos, Rio Negro (Spruce 3035).

A very peculiar plant, which from its compact habit, its large rigid leaves, its dense flowers and larger sepals than usual, might lead to a supposition of its being the type of a distinct genus, as indeed Müller intimated; but these features ought only to be regarded as extreme manifestations of the normal characters of *Rhigospira*. The branch, 4 lines thick, is covered by a fuscous pruinose bark, marked by numerous raised longitudinal ridges connected by transverse muriform lines; and this is lined inside with a stratum of wood ½ line thick, leaving the centre broadly fistulose; the axils are rather close and somewhat dilated; leaves spreading, ovate oblong, suddenly acute upon the petiole, rounded at the summit, thickly coriaceous, very glabrous, with revolute margins, midrib broad and carinate, prominent spreading nerves that terminate in the margin, immersed transverse reticulated veins, yellowish opake beneath, with prominent midrib and nerves, 6–9 in. long, 3–5 in. broad, on stout curving petioles 6–9 lines long, which are deeply fossate within a hooded elevation, and conjoined across the node by a transverse ridge; panicle lateral, 2 in. long, with a congested head of flowers upon a bare deflected peduncle 9 lines long, supporting several short branches, each bearing 3–5 flowers on crowded, bracteolated, short, angular pedicels 1 line long, the bracts 4 lines long, 2 lines broad, adpressed, coriaceous; sepals 5, linear oblong, fuscous red, subcoriaceous, erect, very imbricated, unequal, 4–5 lines long, 2–2½ lines broad, the two exterior shortest, margin pale and undulated, each with very numerous, small, lanceolate scales, in 2 series, within at the base; tube of corolla not quite developed, cylindrical, angular, fleshy, shortly and suddenly broadened at the base, 7 lines long; segments oblong, fleshy, subinequilateral, 7 lines long, 3 lines broad, erect, and sinistrorsely convoluted in æstivation; stamens inserted upon the basal constriction of the tube, 1½ line long, acuminate, obtusely cordate at the base, upon short filaments; disk annular, free, crenate on the margin, half as long as the 2 oblong, pointed, glabrous ovaries.

PHRISSOCARPUS.

A genus proposed for a plant from the Rio Negro, with thick, angular, fistulose branches, and rigid coriaceous leaves on short broad petioles deeply and hoodingly fossate at the base, a short lateral inflorescence, with flowers much resembling those of *Anacampta*, but differing in its follicles, which are muricated, as in *Peschiera*.

PHRISSOCARPUS, nob.; *Tabernæmontanæ* sp., Müll. *Sepala* 5, subparva, obtuse ovata, crassa, margine membranaceo ciliata, imbricata, singulatim squamula trifida intus munita. *Corolla* tubulosa; *tubus* cylindricus, ad medium angustior; *segmenta* triplo breviora, dolabriformia, intus puberula, in æstivatione simpliciter sinistrorsum convoluta. *Stamina* ad annulum retrorse pilosum in constrictionem tubi insita, inclusa; *filamenta* brevissima, retrorse pilosa; *antheræ* lineares, acuminatæ, conniventes, imo acute breviter bifurcatæ. *Discus* tubulosus, margine ciliatus, liber. *Ovaria* 2, conice oblonga, quam discus 2plo longiora. *Stylus* simplex, stamina attingens; *clavuncula* incrassata, cylindrica, imo membrana peltata donata. *Stigmata* 2, subulata, terminalia. *Folliculi* 2, semiovati, crebre echinati;

semina plurima, obovata, apice subacuta, valde compressa, dorso crebre aspere striata, ventre concava, medio hilifera, et hinc funiculo carnoso suspensa.

Frutex Brasiliensis: rami crassi, angulati, fistulosi, cum axillis remotis; folia majuscula, rigida, oblonga, cum petiolis crassis brevibus fossatis; panicula lateralis, brevis, crasse pedunculata, breviter pluriramosa, ramis 2–3-floris.

PHRISSOCARPUS RIGIDUS, nob.: *Tabernæmontana macrophylla*, Müll. (non Poir.) Mart. Fl. Bras. fasc. xxvi. p. 75: *Peschiera muricata*, Benth. (non A. DC.). In Amazonas: *v. s. in hb. meo et alior.* Rio Negro (Spruce 1470).

A well-marked species, with very large leaves, which are unequal at the base, rigidly coriaceous, margins recurved, above fuscous green, opake, minutely corrugulated, with convex interspaces between the sulcate patently divergent nerves arcuately conjoined near the margin, beneath opake ochreous, with very prominent thick reddish midrib and nerves, $8\frac{1}{4}$–$11\frac{3}{4}$ in. long, $3\frac{1}{4}$–$5\frac{1}{4}$ in. broad, on thick petioles only 2 lines long, deeply channelled, with a hooded elevated margin, deeply fossate at the base, and connected across the node by a transverse ridge. Panicle short, erect, lateral at the node, on an obsoletely pubescent stoutish peduncle 9 lines long, very shortly and rather closely branched, each branch bearing 2–3 flowers on stoutish pedicels $1\frac{1}{2}$ line long, supported by a shorter ovate bract ciliolated on the margin; sepals rounded ovate, distinct, 1 line long, with an inner basal 5-fid scale; tube of corolla (in bud) 7 lines long, cylindrical, suddenly narrowed in the middle; segments of the border rhomboidally dolabriform, 3 lines long, sinistrorsely convoluted; stamens inserted in the contraction of the tube, on a retrorsely pilose ring; anthers, disk, style, and clavuncle as in the generic character. Follicles gibbously oval, 1 in. long, 5 lines broad, with a thickly coriaceous pericarp, densely echinated as in *Peschiera*, dehiscing along the convex ventral suture; seeds not numerous, oblong, somewhat pointed at the apex, 5 lines long, $2\frac{1}{2}$ lines broad, longitudinally striated with several asperulous lines, subcompressed, channelled on the ventral face, where they are attached to a pallid fleshy funicle.

A representation of this species, and an analysis of its flower, fruit, and seed are shown in Plate IX. A.

CODONEMMA*.

This genus is proposed for a few plants from the Rio Negro and Guiana, the type of which is the *Tabernæmontana calycina* of Spruce (*T. Benthamiana* bis of Müller). They are distinguished by their large leaves and their inflorescence, the chief peculiarity of which consists in a large campanular calyx, cleft halfway down into 5 oblong imbricated divisions, the fleshy tubular portion being furnished within with numerous lanceolate scales, arranged in several series.

CODONEMMA, nob.: *Calyx majusculus, tubuloso-campanulatus, superne ad medium in lobos 5 subacutos, oblongo-lanceolatos, margine membranaceos, erectos, subinæquales fissus, intus basin versus squamulis*

* From κώδων (*campana*), ἱμμα (*vestis*), on account of its bell-shaped calyx.

numerosis in seriebus 2–4 munitus. *Corollæ tubus* cylindricus, paullo sub medio constrictus, calyce sesqui longior; *segmenta* 5, breviora, rotundato-dolabriformia, æstivatione simpliciter sinistrorsum convoluta. *Stamina* inclusa; *filamenta* brevissima, ad constrictionem tubi inserta; *antheræ* graciles, subliberæ, imo longiusculo biaristatæ, apice cuspidatæ, conniventes. *Stylus* tenuis, stamina attingens; *clavuncula* incrassata, oblonga, profunde 5-sulcata, imo membranaceo-appendiculata; *stigmata* 2, brevissime linearia. *Discus* cylindricus, adnatus, profunde 15-sulcatus, margine obtuse 15-dentatus. *Ovaria* 2, acute oblonga, sulcata, disco 2plo longiora. *Folliculi* 2, oblongo-ovati, divaricati, apice recurvatim rostrati, rugulosi.

Frutices *in America meridionali vigentes*, ramulis *crassis, ad nodos compressis;* folia *majuscula, oblonga, brevissime et crasse petiolata,* petiolis *oppositis, imo fossatis, marginibus linea transversali conjunctis;* paniculæ *ad nodos unilaterales;* pedunculus *apice ramosus, ramis 2-floris;* flores *pedicellati.*

1. CODONEMMA CALYCINUM, nob.: *Tabernæmontana calycina,* Spruce, MS. (non Wall.): *Tabernæmontana Benthamiana* (bis), Müll. *l. c.* p. 70. In Amazonas: *v. s. in hb. meo et Mus. Brit.* San Gabriel, Rio Negro (Spruce 2110).

A plant bearing much the appearance of *Anacampta angulata,* especially in its deeply fossate petioles. The branches are trigonous, dilated at the axils, which are 2½–3¼ in. apart; the leaves are very oblong, subcuneate and inæquilateral at their base, constricted at the apex into a narrow acumen 1 in. in length; they are chartaceous, bright green above, sulcate at the 24 pairs of divergent immersed nerves, which terminate in the reflected margins, paler and yellowish opake below, midrib and nerves prominent, with transversely reticulated veins, 15 in. long, 3–3½ in. broad, on stout channelled petioles 3 lines long, deeply fossate at the base and conjoined across the nodes by a transverse ridge; panicle lateral, fixed 4 lines above each node, on a peduncle barely 1 in. long, bearing 8 or 10 flowers on branchlets 1–2 lines apart, each supporting 2 flowers and 2 bracteoles at its apex, on pedicels 3 lines long; calyx tubular at its base, 9 lines long, divided above into 5 obtuse lobes 3 lines long, the tubular portion being fleshy, and furnished inside with numerous lanceolate scales in several series; the tube of the corolla in bud is as long as the calyx, the segments somewhat shorter, very gibbously ovate, sinistrorsely convolute in æstivation; stamens and disk as in the generic character.

A drawing of this species, and the analysis of its flower, are shown in Plate VIII. B.

2. CODONEMMA MACROCALYX, nob.: *Tabernæmontana (Odontadenia) macrocalyx,* Müll. in Linn. xxx. 403. In Guiana ad Acarouari (Sagot 394): *non vidi.*

A species near the preceding. It is a tall shrub, with subscandent branchlets, very compressed at the nodes; leaves ovate, sometimes acuminate, suddenly constricted at the base upon the petiole, subchartaceous, patent, pale green on both sides, with about 12 pairs of divergent nerves, 6¾–8 in. long, 3¼–4½ in. broad, on thick, short, channelled petioles 1½–2 lines long, fossate at the base, their margins conjoined across the node by a transverse ridge; panicle axillary or terminal, bearing several reddish-yellow odoriferous flowers on a peduncle 9–12 lines long; calyx 7¼ lines long, tubular at its base, and divided halfway down into 5 oblong obtuse lobes, bearing within, at the base, several lanceolate scales; tube of corolla cylindrical, slender, twice the length of the calyx; stamens inserted in the middle of the tube; disk cylindrical, adnate, deeply pluricrenate on the margin; 2 ovate-oblong follicles are described as divaricately reflexed, and acutely recurved at the apex, rugulose.

STEMMADENIA.

This genus was established by Mr. Bentham in 1844, for a few handsome trees with large yellow or white campanular flowers, distinguished by a calyx of 5 large imbricated sepals, furnished inside at their base with numerous (near 100) small lanceolate scales, closely arranged in several series, which gave rise to the generic name. To this genus I have referred the *Tabernæmontana grandiflora* of Jacquin, which fully accords in its characters with the typical species. Miss Drahe's drawing in Mr. Bentham's plate 44 correctly represents the flower with the border-segments convoluted sinistrorsely, as I have found them in all the other species examined by me; and so it is rightly stated in Mr. Bentham's generic character; but in a note he adds, by mistake, that Miss Drahe had erred in this respect in her drawing.

STEMMADENIA, Benth.: *Tabernæmontanæ* sp., Jacq.: *Odontostigma*, Rich. (non Zoll.): Sepala 5, majuscula, obtuse oblonga, inæqualia, quorum 3 exteriora breviora, bracteolis 2 suffulta, submembranacea, intus squamulis lanceolatis numerosissimis pluriseriatis munita. *Corollæ tubus* calyce 2plo longior, latiuscule cylindricus, imo paullulo latior, superne campanulatim ampliatus; *segmenta* 5, ampla, oblique rotundata aut dolabriformia, in æstivatione simpliciter sinistrorsum convoluta. *Stamina* 5, infra medium tubi subsessilia; *antheræ* subcohærentes, cuspidatæ, imo furcis 2 acutis aut obtusiusculis armatæ. *Discus* e lobis 5, marginibus confluentibus, apice crenulatis, suburceolatus, ovaria semitegens. *Ovaria* 2, distincta, oblonga. *Stylus* simpliciter teres; *clavuncula* incrassata, 5-sulcata, imo membrana peltata munita. *Stigmata* 2, terminalia, parva, subglobosa. *Folliculi* 2 (sec. Jacq.), valde divaricati, subcompresse ovati, retrorsum rostrati. Semina *Tabernæmontanæ*.

Arbusculæ *intertropicæ*, *plerumque Mexicanæ*; folia *opposita*, *elliptica*, *petiolata*; racemi *breves*, *pauciflori*, *in dichotomiis foliorum terminales*; flores *majusculi*, *speciosi*, *flavi aut albi*.

1. STEMMADENIA GLABRA, Benth. Bot. Sulph. 425, tab. 44. In America centrali, sinu Fonseca (Hinds): *non vidi.*

A plant with erect stoutish branches and bifurcated branchlets, without stipules; leaves opposite, obovate, obtuse at the base, with a short, suddenly acute constriction at the apex, membranaceous, with subundulate margins, glabrous, green above, more pallid below, costa and 12-16 pairs of nerves prominulent, 5-6 in. long, 2¼-3 in. broad, on petioles 2-4 lines long, sulcate, with the margins conjoined by a transverse ridge across the node; panicle terminal, seated in the dichotomy of the branchlets; peduncle erect, 1 in. long, bearing 3-5 large handsome flowers, on pedicels 4-6 lines long, minutely bracteolated at the base; sepals 5, unequal, 2 inner oblong, nearly an inch long, 3 outer more ovate and shorter, very imbricate, erect, furnished inside with near 100 lanceolate scales closely arranged in 2 series, supported at the base by 2 membranaceous oval bracts 3 lines long. Corolla tubular, nearly 3 in. long; tube 21 lines long, narrower in the lower half, suddenly swelling above into a broader but tubular form, and 7 lines wide in the mouth, below which are 5 longitudinal plicatures alternate with the stamens; segments gibbously oval, crenulate, 14 lines long, 12 lines broad, sinistrorsely convolute in æstivation; stamens seated on the contraction in the middle of the tube, on 5 longitudinal pilose lines; filaments short, glabrous; anthers acute, with 2 somewhat shortish acute basal prongs; disk very short, sub-10-lobed, embracing the base of 2 pointed oblong ovaries for about a quarter of their length; style, clavuncle, and stigmata as in the generic character.

2. STEMMADENIA PUBESCENS, Benth. *l. c.* p. 125; *Bignonia? obovata,* Hook. & Arn. Bot. Beechey's Voy. p. 439. Realejo, Mexico: *non vidi.*

An arborescent species, very near the preceding, with obovate leaves subacute at the base, shortly acuminate, glabrous above, membranaceous, margins entire, below very rigidly pubescent on the obliquely parallel nerves and reticulated veins, 4–6 in. long, on short petioles; racemes terminal, with few flowers 2–3 in. long, on short pedicels; 5 unequal oblong sepals, the 3 outer ones shorter; tube of corolla three times as long as the sepals, swelling above; an expanded border of 5 large, broad, roundish segments.

3. STEMMADENIA MOLLIS, Benth. *l. c.* p. 125. In Guayaquil: *non vidi.*

A species with terete dichotomous branchlets, angular, pubescent; leaves obovate-oblong, narrowed at the base, pubescent above, tomentous below, 4–5 in. long, 1¼–2½ in. broad, on very short petioles; sepals as in the preceding species, the outer ones and the bracteoles pubescent; corolla 3 in. long; tube longer than in the foregoing, more cylindrical, and less inflated.

4. STEMMADENIA GRANDIFLORA, nob.: *Tabernæmontana grandiflora,* Jacq. Am. p. 40, tab. 31, (edit. 8vo) p. 51; Linn. Mant. p. 53; Lam. Dict. vii. 528; Illust. tab. 170. fig. 2 (icon. Jacq. reduct.); A. DC. Prodr. viii. p. 368; Benth. in Journ. Bot. iii. p. 243; in Pl. Hartw. p. 167. no. 1275; Seem. Bot. Her. p. 167; Hook. Bot. Mag. tab. 3226. In Cartagena, Panama et Guiana (sec. Seem. *l. c.*): *in hb. Hook.* Surinam (Hostmann), Venezuela (Linden), Nov. Granada (Linden, Cuming 1124); *v. s. in herb. Mus. Brit.* Panama (Seemann), Guiana (Sagot 389, Schomb. 767).

A tree 8 feet high, with lactescent branches and dichotomous branchlets; leaves elliptic-oblong, cuneate at the base, with a linear recurved acumen, entire, smooth, membranaceous, green above, with very slender nerves arcuately ascending, paler below, the reddish nerves scarcely prominulent, subimmersed, veins reticulated, 2½–4¼ in. long, ¾–1½ in. broad, on slender sulcate petioles 2–3 lines long; a short panicle seated in the dichotomy of the branchlets, on a peduncle 3 lines long, bifurcate, its branchlets being 4 lines long, with several alternate small bracteoles and flowers mostly caducous, the terminal one supporting a single pedicellated flower (rarely 2-flowered); pedicel 2–4 lines long; bracts 1 or 2 beneath the calyx, equally long, foliaceous, truncate at the base; sepals large, membranaceous, very imbricate, 3 interior narrower, oblong, 8 lines long, 2 exterior double their breadth, truncate at their base, pointed, 5 lines long, all furnished at their base inside with numerous approximated pectinate scales united in a ring; corolla hypocrateriform; tube cylindrical, 1¼ in. long, a little swollen and plicate below the mouth; segments of border inequilaterally obovate, or dolabriform, expanded, sinistrorsely convolute in æstivation; stamens rather long, slender, seated above the middle of the tube, their anthers free, biaristate at the base, their acuminate summits nearly reaching the mouth; disk of 5 roundish membranaceous lobes, connate below the margin, ¼ the length of 2 free obovate ovaries; style shortly bifid at the base, simple above; clavuncle thickish, submembranaceously expanded at its base; 2 apical slender stigmata; 2 follicles globosely oblong, divaricately reflexed, with a recurved beak at the apex, 1½ in. long, 10 lines broad, with numerous seeds, as in the other species, half-immersed in fleshy funicles.

This fine species bears all the characters of a *Stemmadenia*, and is extremely different from a true *Tabernæmontana*.

5. STEMMADENIA INSIGNIS, nob.: *Tabernæmontana laurifolia*, Schott, MS. (non Linn. nec Ker). Arborescens, ramulis teretibus, pallidis, glabris, striolatis: foliis oppositis, oblongis, utrinque acutis, chartaceis, supra læte viridibus, opacis, sub lente minute granulosis, nervis plurimis, tenuibus, subpatenter divaricatis, semiimmersis, subtus pallidioribus, costa nervisque flavidis subprominulis; petiolis subtenuibus, limbo 10plo brevioribus: paniculis in ramulis novellis terminalibus, spicatifloris; pedicellis imo et apice bracteolatis, bracteis ovatis, sessilibus; sepalis 5, majusculis, oblongis, subpetaloideis, valde imbricatis, parallele nervosis, intus ad basin squamulis numerosissimis creberrimis munitis; corollæ tubo elongato cylindrico, supra medium subinfundibuliformi; limbi segmentis inæquilateris, oblique rotundatis, valde expansis, in æstivatione sinistrorsum convolutis; staminibus paullo infra medium tubi insertis, acuminatis, basi breviter 2-lobatis, subsessilibus; disco præcedentium, ovariis 2 acute ovatis circumdato; stylo, clavuncula et stigmatibus generis. In Mexico: *v. s. in hb. Mus. Brit.* in Merida cult. (Schott 430).

A handsome species, near the preceding, cultivated in Merida under the name of "laurel." Its branchlets are rather stout, with axils about ½ in. apart; the leaves are 3¾–5½ in. long, 1½–2¼ in. broad, on petioles 4–6 lines long; peduncle less than 1 in. long; pedicels 9 lines long; bracts roundish oblong, 2–3 lines long; unequal sepals 6–8 lines long, 2–3 lines broad; tube of corolla 1⅞ in. long, narrower at the base for the length of 9 lines, somewhat funnel-shaped above, 1 in. broad in the mouth, 3 in. broad at the expanded border; segments 1 in. long, ¾ in. broad. The shape and size of the follicles are not given; but the seeds seem partially invested with a fleshy covering, as the birds are said to devour them greedily.

A figure of this species, and an analysis of its flower, are exhibited in Plate X. B.

6. STEMMADENIA GALEOTTIANA, nob.: *Odontostigma Galeottianum*, Rich. in Sagra, Hist. Cub. xi. 868, tab. 56; Walp. Ann. v. 478. Cuba, circ. Havana in sylvis: *non vidi*.

A tall tree, with slender dichotomous branchlets; opposite leaves oblong, acute at the base, summits acuminate, membranaceous, entire, with divergent nerves, 4¼ in. long, 2 in. broad, on petioles 4 lines long; panicle terminal in the dichotomy of the branchlets, bearing 3–6 large, handsome, yellow, odoriferous flowers; peduncle 6 lines long; pedicels 3 lines long; sepals 5, obtusely oblong, unequal in breadth, membranaceous, laxly imbricate, with a smaller oval bract at the base, and furnished inside with very numerous lanceolate scales in 2 series; corolla broadish-tubular, 2 in. long, narrower within the calyx, the border-segments obliquely inequilateral, roundish, horizontally expanded, 1 in. long and broad, sinistrorsely convolute in æstivation; stamens acute, obtusely bilobed at the base, seated in the contraction of the tube below and alternate with 5 long glands or plicatures of the tube, as in the typical species; disk of 5 connate glands, forming a short tube with a crenate margin, round the base of 2 much longer, free, oblong, pointed ovaries; style slender, terete; clavuncle thick, deeply 5-grooved, with a basal umbraculiform appendage; stigmata short and globose.

7. STEMMADENIA BELLA, nob.: ramulis teretibus, dichotomis: foliis elliptico-ovatis, sæpius conduplicatis, imo acutis, apice recurvatim subito acuminatis, submembranaceis, supra profunde viridibus, opacis, nervis tenuibus vix prominulis; petiolis brevibus, supra planis: racemis opposite axillaribus, vel in dichotomiis ramorum solitariis; pedunculo fere folii longitudine, pæne a basi alternifloro; pedicellis validis, medio et sub calyce bracteolatis; sepalis oblongis, obtusis, membranaceis, medio crassioribus, inæqualibus, valde imbricatis, intus squamulis numerosissimis acute lanceolatis crebre 2–3-seriatis munitis; corolla tubulosa; tubo (parte intra calycem) angustato, superne subcampanulato; segmentis oblique rotundatis, reflexis, in æstivatione sinistrorsum convolutis; staminibus ad contractionem tubi insertis sub lineis 5 pilosis, inclusis; antheris sagittatis; disco annulari, margine vix crenulato, ovariis 2 acutis ¼ breviore; stylo subbrevi; clavuncula dilatatim oblonga, imo membrana donata; stigmatibus brevissimis. In Mexico: *v. s. in hb. Mus. Brit.* Mexico (Brotero 884).

The axils are thickened and 1–1½ in. apart; the leaves are 3–5 in. long, 1¼–3 in. broad, on petioles 3–5 lines long; peduncle ½ in. long, floriferous nearly to the base; flowers 1–2 lines apart; pedicels thick, 3–4 lines long; bract 2 lines long; sepals 5–6 lines long, 2 lines broad; tube of corolla 10 lines long, the contracted basal portion 4 lines long; segments 6 lines long and broad.

8. STEMMADENIA BIGNONIÆFLORA, nob.: *Echites bignoniæflora*, Schl. in Linn. xxvi. p. 372. In Mexico: *non vidi.*

A handsome species, bearing all the characters of this genus. It is a branching shrub, with somewhat slender branchlets, dilated at the axils, with a transverse ridge supporting several prominent stipules, the stems verruculated with broadly oval white lenticels; leaves lanceolately elliptic, acute at both extremities, green, glabrous, with pellucid yellow edges, with 10–12 pairs of arcuately conjoined nerves and reticulated veins, paler beneath, 4 in. long, 1¾ in. broad, on broad petioles with membranaceous edges 3–4 lines long; short racemes at the ends of 2 young axillary branchlets, consisting of 2 pedicellated flowers, upon a short peduncle; pedicels bracteolated at the base; sepals 5, unequal, 6–7 lines long, very imbricated, 2 exterior acutely ovate, 3 interior broader, glabrous, furnished within at the base with a corona of dense small acute scales in 2 series; tube of corolla narrowed at the base, funnel-shaped above, more than 1 in. long, with deltoid segments of nearly the same length; stamens seated in a pilose ring above the bottom of the tube, upon 5 long pilose lines; anthers 2½ lines long, acutely hastate; disk cupular, sub-5-lobed, shorter than the 2 ovaries; style simple; clavuncle subcapitate, terminated by 2 short stigmata.

Species excluded :—
Stemmadenia Guatemalensis, Müller = *Malouetia Panamensis*, Müll.

MERIZADENIA [*].

This genus is proposed for a few South-American plants uniform in their characters, the type of which is the *Tabernæmontana Sananho* of the 'Flora Peruviana.' They are tall trees, with an erect trunk, a branching head with large leaves, all yielding an abundant milky juice.

MERIZADENIA, nob.: *Calyx* parvus. *Sepala* 5, ovata, erecta, imbricata, singulatim squamula 2-dentata intus munita. *Corolla* anguste infundibuliformis; *tubus* cylindricus, supra medium paullo ventricosus, et hinc spiraliter 5-nervosa; *segmenta* spathulato-oblonga, obtusa, obliqua, tubi fere longitudine, latere dextro mucronulata et hinc sub æstivationem subito introplicata, apicibus faucem fere attingentibus, et sinistrorsum convoluta, post expansionem extus omnino deflexa. *Stamina* in parte ventricosa tubi inclusa, subbrevia; *filamenta* brevissima; *antheræ* in conum cohærentes, apice acuminatæ, imo tenuiter 2-furcatæ. *Discus* 5-lobus, lobis erectis, obtusis, discretis. *Ovaria* 2, acute oblonga, libera, disco paullo longiora; *stylus* simplex, tenuis; *clavuncula* incrassata, parvula, ad antheras agglutinata; *stigmata* 2, minima, terminalia. *Folliculi* 2, globosi vel ovati, plus minusve retrorsum rostrati, divaricatissimi, sutura ventrali longitudinali dehiscentes. *Semina* plurima, obovata, dorso plurisulcata, nuda, ventre canaliculata, in sulci medio *hilo* notata, et hinc *funiculo* pulposo affixa et ei semiimmersa, funiculis ad placentas suturales utrinque cohærentibus.

Arbores *Americæ meridionalis*; truncus *crassus, erectus, ramosissimus*; folia *opposita, majuscula, oblonga, acuta, glabra, breviter petiolata*; corymbi *ad nodos solitarii, pedunculati, multiflori*; pedunculus *imo nudus, apice bis trichotome divisus*; flores *mediocres*.

1. MERIZADENIA SANANHO, nob.: *Tabernæmontana Sananho*, R. & P. Flor. Per. ii. 22, tab. 144; A. DC. Prodr. viii. 363. In Peruvia: *non vidi*.

A tree nearly 40 feet high, with a spreading head, an erect trunk, and copious branches, all yielding a copious milky juice. It has stoutish terete dichotomous branchlets, with axils 1½ in. apart; leaves oblong, boatshaped, acute at the base, and with a long, narrow, recurved point, repandly undulated at the margins, with prominent divergent nerves and reticulated veins, 5–6 in. long, 2–2½ in. broad, on stout subtetragonous petioles 3–5 lines long, thickened and fossate at the base, where they are conjoined across the node by a prominent ridge. A single extra-axillary panicle at the nodes, 10-20-flowered, 1¼ in. long, on a stout peduncle 4 lines long, bearing several branchlets 2–3 lines long, each supporting 3 flowers on stoutish pedicels 2 lines long, furnished with small, cordate, rounded bracteoles; calyx 2½ lines long, with 5 rounded sepals; corolla 1¾ in. long, pale yellow, divided halfway into 5 segments; tube cylindrical, angularly striated; segments spathulately oblong, gibbously rounded at the summit, with a strong, nearly median nerve, suddenly and completely deflexed, 10 lines long, 6 lines broad; stamens smallish, biaristate, inserted near the middle of the tube; 2 divaricated follicles subglobose, stipitate at the base, with a short recurved apex, smooth, 2 in. long, 1¼ in. broad, containing many dark obovate compressed seeds costately striated on the dorsal face, 6 lines long, half-imbedded in the fleshy funicles.

[*] From μερίζω (*divido*), et ἀδήν (*glandula*), on account of its divided disk.

2. MERIZADENIA ARCUATA, nob.: *Tabernæmontana arcuata,* ·R. & P. *l. c.* p. 22, tab. 143; A. DC. *l. c.* p. 363. In Peruvia: *non vidi.*

A tree more than 60 feet high, with a spreading head; branchlets stoutish, dichotomous, pallid, subcompressed, with axils 1 in. apart; leaves oblong or lanceolate oblong, pointed at both ends, flat, patent, [with prominulent diverging nerves, 5–6 in. long, 1¾–2 in. broad, on petioles 3–4 lines long, fossulate at the base, and conjoined by a short transverse ridge; panicles 1½ in. long, branching from the base; peduncles slender, 4 lines long, branched, alternately bracteolated, each bearing about 3 alternate flowers; on slender pedicels 3 lines long, furnished with a small acutely ovate bracteole; sepals acutely oblong, 1 line long; corolla pale yellow; tube cylindrical, 6 lines long; segments spathulate-oblong, 5 lines long, 3 lines broad, deflexed; stamens inserted a little below the base of the tube; disk of 5 small free glands; ovaries 2, free to the base, pointed; follicles large, divaricated, oblong, roundish, with an obtuse, reflexed apex, 2¾ in. long, 1¼ in. broad, containing many obovate seeds 4 lines long, dorsally costate, reddish, half-imbedded in scarlet fleshy funicles.

3. MERIZADENIA AMPLIFOLIA, nob.: *Tabernæmontana macrophylla,* Poir. Dict. Suppl. v. p. 276 (non Müll.); A. DC. Prodr. viii. 374. In Guiana: *v. s. in herb. Mus. Brit.* Cayenne (Martin), Guiana (Pollard 10, sub *T. oblongifolia*), Surinam (Hostmann).

A species near *M. arcuata.* Branches compressed, striolated, fistulous, with dilated axils 2 or more inches apart; leaves elongate-oblong, acute at the base, broadish above, suddenly constricted near the summit into a somewhat narrow acumen, undulate and subrevolute at the margins, thinly chartaceous, glabrous, pale green above, granularly rugous, sulcate at the patently divaricate nerves, paler beneath, with prominent midrib and 12 pairs of prominent nerves, 6–9 in. long, 2¼–3¼ in. broad, on rather slender channelled petioles deeply fossulate at the base, and conjoined across the nodes, 3–5 lines long; panicles axillary; peduncles thick, angular, short, alternately 3-branched, each branch bearing several approximated pedicellated flowers, often geminate or subumbellate, its close prominent joints having a short caducous bractlet; pedicels 6 lines long; sepals ovate, obtuse, submembranaceous, 2 lines long; tube of corolla cylindrical, 9 lines long; segments unequally oblong, obtuse, 7 lines long, and quite deflexed, sinistrorsely convolute in æstivation, as in *M. Sananho.*

A drawing of this species, and an analysis of its flower, fruit, and seeds, are shown in Plate XI. A.

ANARTIA [*].

The plants of this small group much resemble in appearance many of the species of *Peschiera* in having unequal pairs of leaves, and a depauperated inflorescence with a salver-shaped corolla; but they differ notably in the longer and more linear form of its segments, inflected downwards, as in *Bonafousia,* and convolute dextrorsely (not sinis-

[*] From ἄναρτιος (*imperfectus*), because of its unequal leaves and impoverished inflorescence.

trorsely) in æstivation; they differ also in the position of the stamens, which are placed in the upper portion of the tube (not in the lower), and in the peculiar form of its disk, which, though distinct, is easily overlooked.

ANARTIA, nob.: *Tabernæmontanæ* sp. auctorum. Sepala 5, parva, sæpius lanceolata, intus ad basin squamulis 2–3 minimis bidentatis munita. Corolla hypocrateriformis; *tubus* tenuiter cylindricus, supra medium paullo inflatus, fauce constrictus; *segmenta* 5, lineari-oblonga, tubo subbreviora, ad medium subito introrsum flexa, et in æstivatione dextrorsum convoluta, demum expansa. *Stamina* subsessilia, supra medium tubi in parte ventricosa inclusa; *filamenta* brevissima; *antheræ* tenuiter lineares, subdiscretæ, imo breviter biaristatæ, apice membrana acuta terminatæ. *Discus* cylindricus, adnatus, truncatus, hyalinus, vix distinguendus. *Ovaria* 2, conice oblonga, disco 2plo longiora. *Stylus* filiformis; *clavuncula* incrassata, breviter oblonga, 5-sulcata, imo appendice membranacea munita; *stigmata* 2, breviter subulata.

Frutices *Americæ callidioris; rami graciles, sæpius dichotomi; folia opposita in quoque nodo valde heterophylla, lanceolata aut oblonga, breviter petiolata; racemi axillares, breves; pedunculus subbrevis, crebriter cicatricosus, et e floribus lapsis sæpe depauperatus; flores persistentes pauci, pedicellati.*

1. ANARTIA MEYERI, nob.: *Tabernæmontana undulata*, Mey. (non Vahl) Esseq. p. 135; A. DC. *l. c.* p. 368: *Tabernæmontana Meyeri*, Don, Dict. iv. 89. In Guiana: *v. s. in hb. Mus. Brit. (sine flore)* Acarouari (Sagot 391, sub *T. oblongifolia*, DC., var. *angustifolia*).

A species certainly different from Vahl's plant, as its leaves are not undulated, its sepals unequal, and the corolla pubescent in the throat, and its leaves are in very unequal pairs. It is a shrub with subflexuous dichotomous branches, the branchlets compressed, with remote axils. The leaves are oblong, acute at the base, constricted at the summit by an obtuse linear acumen, firmly chartaceous, the margins somewhat revolute, of a very pale green above, opake, with immersed patent nerves arcuately conjoined within the margin, yellow and opake below, with immersed nerves, the unequal pairs being 4 and 2 in. long, 7 and 4 lines broad, on channelled petioles 3 and 1½ line long: in the upper axils they are somewhat smaller, and in the same proportions. Meyer says the inflorescence is terminal on a short peduncle, bearing 3 or 4 flowers on short pedicels, each with a basal ovate obtuse concave bracteole; sepals unequal; corolla 1 in. long; tube cylindrical, ventricose below the mouth, which is pubescent; segments oblique, linear oblong, obtuse; anthers included below the mouth of the tube; disk not seen (said to be none); ovaries conical; style simple; clavuncle incrassated, with a basal membranaceous appendage. These characters are quite those of *Anartia*.

2. ANARTIA RECURVA, nob.: *Tabernæmontana recurva*, Sagot, MS. (non Roxb.): ramulis tenuissimis, dichotomis, pallide brunneis, compressis, striolatis, stipula utrinque interpetiolari ad nodos rotundata adpressa membranacea donatis: foliis valde heterophyllis, patentibus vel deflexis, lanceolato-oblongis, utrinque sensim valde acutis, marginibus subrevolutis, subchartaceis, supra pallide viridibus, opacis, ad costam sulcatis, nervis immersis, subtus opace flavicantibus, costa flava prominente, nervis rufulis prominulis; petiolis tenuissimis, canaliculatis, stria transversali basi conjunctis, limbo 12plo brevioribus: paniculis in nodis solitariis lateralibus, circa 12-floris; pedunculo bifurcato; sepalis parvis, acutis, intus squamula parva munitis; corollæ hypocrateriformis tubo cylindrico, infra faucem inflato; segmentis oblongis, medium versus introflexis, in æstivatione dextrorsum convolutis; filamentis brevibus, supra medium tubi insertis; antheris tenuibus, tubi parte ventricosa inclusis,

liberis, imo 2-lobatis, apice acuminatis; disco adnato; ovariis 2 acute oblongis, quam sepala paullo longioribus, striatis; stylo filiformi; clavuncula incrassata, oblonga, 5-sulcata; stigmatibus 2 subulatis. In Guiana: *v. s. in hb. Mus. Brit.* (Sagot 388).

A species very distinct from *A. Meyeri*; it resembles *Peschiera diversifolia* in its lanceolate leaves, but differs in its longer petioles and in its inflorescence. Its axils are 1½ in. apart; the leaves in each pair are respectively 3 and 1 in. long, 8 and 4 lines broad, on petioles 4 and 2 lines long; the peduncle is 4 lines long, its branches somewhat longer, each bearing about 6 bracteolated pedicels 3 lines long; sepals acute, submembranaceous, 1 line long; tube of corolla 8 lines long; its segments oblong, obtusely pointed, 5 lines long, 2 lines broad.

A figure of this species, and an analysis of its flower, are shown in Plate XI. B.

3. ANARTIA GLABRATA, nob.: *Tabernæmontana glabrata*, Mart. MS.: ramulis teretibus, pallidis, striolatis, stipula interpetiolari utrinque ad nodos oblonga obtusa adpressa donatis: foliis elliptico- vel lanceolato-oblongis, imo acutis, apice sensim attenuatis, chartaceis, ad nodos valde heterophyllis, supra viridibus, opacis, costa sulcata, nervis curvatim divergentibus arcuatim nexis, subtus flavescentibus, opacis, crebre granulatis, costa flava prominente, nervis prominulis; petiolis subtenuibus, canaliculatis, imo fossatis, limbo 12plo brevioribus: panicula laterali; pedunculo scabridulo petiolum æquante, depauperato, cicatricibus plurimis e floribus lapsis crebris signato, hinc paucifloro; pedicellis calyci æquilongis, imo bracteolatis; sepalis oblongis, rotundatis, membranaceis, carinatis; corollæ tubo anguste cylindrico, paullo supra medium inflato, ad faucem constricto; segmentis lineari-oblongis, obtusis, tubum fere æquantibus, in æstivatione profundè introflexis et dextrorsum convolutis; staminibus ad constrictionem tubi in annulum retrorse pilosum insitis, inclusis; cæteris ut in char. gen. In Brasilia: *v. s. in hb. meo* Barra do Facaõ (Martius).

An undescribed species, with the nodes of its branchlets 1½–1¾ in. apart; leaves 3–5½ in. long, 1–2 in. broad, on petioles 3–5 lines long; peduncle 6 lines long, cicatrized from the base, bearing towards the summit few alternate pedicels 4 lines long; sepals 1¼ line long; tube of corolla 11 lines long; segments 9 lines long, 2½ lines broad; 2 oblong ovaries embraced for half their length by a tubular hyaline disk, scarcely distinguishable; style very slender, 7 lines long.

4. ANARTIA WULFSCHLÆGELII, nob.: *Tabernæmontana Wulfschlægelii*, Griseb. Fl. Br. W. Ind. p. 409. Jamaica (Wulfschlegel): *non vidi*.

A tortuous shrub, with subquadrangular branchlets marked below with annular nodes where the leaves have fallen off; leaves in unequal pairs, oblong or lanceolate-oblong, acute at the base, with an obtuse acumen, nerves somewhat distant, arcuately conjoined, pairs 2 and 5 in. long, ¾–1¼ in. broad, on petioles 3–8 lines long, conjoined across the node by a transverse ridge; raceme lateral, a little longer than the petiole; sepals ⅔ line long, roundish; tube of corolla 4 lines long; segments obliquely ovate-oblong, obtuse, a little shorter than the tube; stamens inserted in the middle of the tube; anthers 2 lines long; disk scarcely discernible.

A species evidently near the preceding.

5. ANARTIA FLAVICANS, nob.: *Tabernæmontana flavicans*, R. & Sch. Syst. iv. 797; A. DC. *l. c.* p. 375
Müll. *l. c.* p. 77 (excl. synon.), tab. 25. fig. 1: *Tabernæmontana levigata*, Mart. In Brasilia (Hoffm. in herb. Willd.): *non vidi*.

Müller states that the *Peschiera latifolia* (Spruce 236), from Santarem, is identical with Willdenow's plant. Spruce's plant and Müller's drawing are now placed before me side by side; and I can pronounce them to be distinct, not only in a specific point of view, but that they belong to two different genera. Müller's copious description of *Tabernæmontana flavicans* is therefore of no value, as the characters are mainly derived from Spruce's plant. We have no trustworthy evidence in regard to the species in question, except the short character of this plant as quoted by De Candolle; to this we may add Müller's plate 25, above mentioned, which appears to have been made from Willdenow's typical specimen, which coincides sufficiently well with the original description. From these two sources the following diagnosis is drawn up. Müller gives no analysis of the flower; it is therefore probable that he never saw the specimen, and that he obtained his drawing from some other source.

It has very slender, dichotomous, erect branchlets, with axils $\frac{1}{2}$–$1\frac{1}{2}$ in. apart; the opposite leaves, of equal length, are very lanceolate, very acute at the base, with a gradually narrowing blunted acumen, 2–2$\frac{1}{4}$ in. long, 4–5 lines broad, on slender petioles 2$\frac{1}{2}$–3 lines long; the lateral raceme has a peduncle bare at the base for 6 lines, bearing 3–4 alternate flowers above, on bracteolated pedicels 3–4 lines long; sepals acute; tube of corolla 1 in. long, narrowly cylindrical, 1$\frac{1}{2}$ line thick, swelling below the mouth to a breadth of 2 lines; segments oblong, when expanded 1 in. long, 5 lines broad; stamens included and inserted in the constriction, at $\frac{2}{3}$ the length of the tube. These characters are obviously those of *Anartia*; and the species closely approaches *A. recurva*.

6. ANARTIA FLAVESCENS, nob.: *Tabernæmontana flavescens*, R. & Sch. Syst. iv. 797; A. DC. *l. c.* p. 375. In Brasilia: *non vidi*.

A species evidently near the preceding, with broader, more shortly acuminate, oblong leaves 2 in. long; an axillary peduncle, bracteolated, 2 lines long, bearing subumbellate flowers on filiform pedicels 1 in. long; the flowers less than 6 lines long.

7. ANARTIA BOGOTENSIS, nob.: *Echites Bogotensis*, H. B. K. iii. 215, tab. 243; A. DC. *l. c.* p. 474: *Amblyanthera Bogotensis*, Müll. Linn. xxx. 452. In Ecuador, Santa Fé de Bogota: *non vidi*.

A species certainly not belonging to *Amblyanthera*. It is a scandent plant, with straightish, terete, striated, canescently subpubescent branches, with axils 1$\frac{1}{2}$–2 in. apart; leaves oblong, rounded or obsoletely cordate at the base, acuminate, submembranaceous, with entire or subrevolute margins, green and glabrous above, with 2 bifid fleshy, glabrous glands superposed at the base of the midrib, reticulately veined, beneath densely glauco-farinaceous and subpubescent, 2$\frac{1}{2}$ in. long, 11–14 lines broad, on channelled puberulent petioles 3 lines long; 2 opposite racemes, 2$\frac{1}{2}$ in. long, including a short peduncle 2–3fid at the base, each branch bearing several alternate flowers the size of those of *Vinca minor*, on pedicels 4–5 lines long, supported by an acute bract $\frac{1}{2}$ line long; sepals acute, oblong, imbricated, glabrous, with as many alternate inner trifid basal scales; corolla salver-shaped, white, its tube cylindrical, 4 lines long, pilose within; segments obliquely oblong, roundish on one side, with crispate margins, dextrorsely convoluted, rotate, a little longer than the tube; stamens inserted in a pilose ring above the base of the tube; filaments short, pubescent; anthers slender, with a membranaceous apex, acuminate, obtusely and shortly 2-lobed at the base; disk of 5 oblong lobes, hardly discernible; ovaries 2; clavuncle incrassated, 5-grooved, with a peltate membrane at the base.

The species is very near *A. flavicans*.

GEISSOSPERMUM.

This peculiar genus was established in 1849, by Dr. Fr. Allemão, with an excellent description and drawing. Its chief characters reside in its alternate leaves, its extra-axillary inflorescence, the segments of the salver-shaped corolla having a dextrorse convolution, in its cordate anthers, and especially in the structure of the follicles and seeds. Six species are here enumerated, all Brazilian.

GEISSOSPERMUM, F. Allemão: *Sepala* 5, lanceolata aut ovata, subacuta, imo in cupulam brevissimam connata, intus squamula minuta annulo pilorum intermixta instructa. *Corolla* hypocrateriformis *tubus* cylindricus infra faucem paullo inflatus et ibi obsolete plicatus, intus annulo pilorum signatus; *segmenta* oblonga, obtusa, vix inæquilatera, in æstivatione paullo dextrorsum convoluta, tubo subbreviora. *Stamina* 5, inflatione tubi inclusa; *filamenta* brevia, retrorsum pilosa; *antheræ* subovatæ, apiculatæ, imo emarginato-bilobæ. *Discus* urceolatus, membranaceus, ovaria fere abscondens. *Ovaria* 2, ovata, discreta, pilosa; *stylus* simplex; *clavuncula* incrassata, ad antheras agglutinata; *stigmata* 2, breviter obtusa, terminalia. *Folliculi* 2, valde divaricati, oblongi, imo rotundati, apice sensim acutati, baccati, ventre sutura crassa dehiscentes, marginibus profunde introflexis et placentiferis. *Semina* ex utraque placenta 2–5, subcompresse ovata, uno latere, in centro, hilo signata, hoc ad funiculum subcarnosum peltatim affixa, primum in hunc semiimmersâ, dein sua prolongatione a placenta suspensa; *testa* calva, chartacea; *tegmen* membranaceum; *albumen* tenuiter corncum; *embryo* heterotropus eo subbrevior; *cotyledones* 2, cordato-deltoideæ, foliaceæ; *radicula* teres, ad summum spectans, dimidia longitudine cotyledonum.

Arbores *proceri Brasilienses frondosi, vix lactescentes, cortice externo crasso, interno phœrilamellato*; ramuli *bis trichotome divisi, exstipulati; folia alterna, elliptica, petiolata; paniculæ extra-axillares, folii dimidia longitudine; pedunculus brevis, 2-ramosus, ramulis flores plures pedicellatos parvos subumbellatos gerentibus, cunctis sæpius undique pubescentibus.*

1. GEISSOSPERMUM VELLOSII, Fr. Allem. Trab. Soc. Vellos. tab. 7 (excl. syn. Vell.); Müll. Fl. Bras. fasc. xxvi. p. 90 (in parte): *Vallesiæ* sp., Riedel in Man. Agric. Bras. Prov. Rio de Janeiro, in montibus ad altit. 1000 ped. et ultra: *non vidi*.

A tree of great height, the trunk covered with a very thick bark, and an inner lamellar bark, apparently not lactescent; branches flexuous, twice trichotomous, branchlets straight, cinereo-tomentose, becoming smooth; axils ½ in. apart; leaves alternate, subdistichous, elliptic, acute at the base, acuminate, very undulate on the margins, chartaceous, younger ones cinereo-sericeous, with nerves prominulent on both sides, 2–3 in. long, 1–1½ in. broad, on petioles 2–3 lines long; panicle placed 2 lines above or below the axils; peduncle stout, angular, 4 lines long, its 2 branchlets 2 lines long, bracteolated, bearing on their summits each 3–4 fasciculated flowers, on pedicels 1 line long; sepals lanceolate, 1½ line long, connate at the base, cinereo-pilose; tube of corolla cylindrical, angular, pilose outside, glabrous within, except a narrow pilose ring in the contracted mouth, below which it is somewhat swollen, 4 lines long; segments oblong, obtuse, 3 lines long, slightly dextrorsely convolute in æstivation; anthers free, ovate, cordate, on short pubescent filaments; disk very pilose, concealing the ovaries; follicles spreading, 2 in. long, 1 in. broad, with a pericarp 3 lines thick, 2 sutural placentæ agglutinated together, nearly reaching the opposite side of the cell, each bearing on its outer face 4 or 5 seeds, their summits overlapping each other; seeds ovoid, 7 lines long, 4 lines broad, with a central hilum on one face, where they are attached to a fleshy funicle, in which they are half-imbedded; embryo in thin albumen, with 2 cordate cotyledons, and a radicle half their length, pointing to the apex of the follicle.

Dr. Freire Allemão (*loc. cit.*) correctly repudiates the reference of this plant by Riedel to *Vallesia*, on account of its extra-axillary inflorescence, and especially the character of its fruit and seeds.

The analysis of its fruit and seeds (from Allemão), is given in Plate XII. A.

2. GEISSOSPERMUM LÆVE, nob.: *Tabernæmontana lævis*, Vell. Fl. Flum. p. 105, Icon. iii. tab. 18; A. DC. Prodr. viii. 375: *Geissospermum Vellosii*, Müll. in parte (non Allem.) *l. c.* p. 90, tab. 28, quoad fructum: Prov. Rio de Janeiro (in maritimis, circa Tejuca): *non vidi*.

This is a species very different from the preceding, though united with it by Dr. Allemão. It differs in being a much smaller tree, with glabrous (not tomentous) branchlets, in its much narrower lanceolate (not elliptic) leaves retuse (not undulated) on the margins, quite glabrous (not pubescent), in its simple 2- or 3-flowered short raceme (not a divided panicle of 8 flowers), calyx and corolla glabrous outside (not pubescent), in its follicles very acute and reflexed at the apex, in its thicker, glabrous, yellow pericarp replete with a lactescent juice, containing 4 (not 8 or 10) seeds. Dr. Müller (Fl. Bras. fasc. xxvi. p. 90) could only reconcile these differences by inferring that Velloz's details are not to be depended upon as to accuracy; but no one would agree in this opinion who has seen the delicately executed original drawings of Velloz (some of which I possess), which were so roughly copied by the Paris lithographer. In these plates of the 'Flora Fluminensis,' we may rely on the general accuracy of the rough outlines of the plates, as to form and dimensions. In Velloz's plant the very glabrous lanceolate leaves are 2-3 in. long, ¾-1 in. broad, on petioles 1½-2 lines long; the peduncle of the infra-axillary inflorescence is 3 lines long, and supports generally 3, sometimes 2, subalternate bracteolated pedicels 1½-2 lines long; the acuminate glabrous sepals are 1½ line long; corolla yellowish white, glabrous outside, everywhere puberulous within, has a cylindrical tube 6 lines long, with oblong segments 4½ lines long, a little convoluted in æstivation; 2 oblong follicles, spreading, rounded at the base, terminated by a long reflexed acute point, 2½ in. long, 1¼ in. broad, each containing 4 separate seeds, as distinctly stated by Velloz; these are oval, compressed, 8 lines long, 6 lines broad, half-immersed in a white succulent funicle.

3. GEISSOSPERMUM MARTIANUM, nob.: *Tabernæmontana cymosa*, Mart. MS. (non Jacq.): ramulis crassis, subfistulosis, pallidis, subangulatis, striatis, lenticellis albis sparsim verruculosis; axillis

remotiusculis: foliis alternis, lanceolato-oblongis, imo inæquilateris et cuneatis, subobtuse acuminatis, glaberrimis, marginibus retusis, tenuiter chartaceis, supra viridibus, opacis, nervis tenuissimis immersis, subtus flavide opacis, costa nervisque tenuissimis rubellis vix prominulis; petiolo tenui, canaliculato, quam limbus 16plo breviore; foliolis in ramulis novellis inferioribus alternis, in superioribus 4 approximatim verticillatis: paniculis lateralibus et solitariis aut suboppositis, glaberrimis; pedunculis longiusculis, tenuibus, striatis, apice trichotomis, ramis 3-floris; pedicellis tenuibus; sepalis ovatis, acutis; corollæ glabræ tubo cylindrico, intus supra medium piloso, infra faucem paullo inflato, et inde staminifero; segmentis oblongis, obtusis, paullo convolutis, tubo brevioribus; staminibus brevibus; filamentis brevibus; antheris vix acutis, imo cordatis; disco cylindrico, membranaceo, ovaria 2 abscondente; stylo tenui; clavuncula incrassata, subpentagona, glandulifera, apice 5-dentata imo appendice membranacea aucta; stigmatibus 2, breviter rotundatis, apicalibus. In Parahiba Brasiliæ, prov. Rio de Janeiro: *v. s. in hb. meo ex herb. Mart.* sub *Tabernæmontana cymosa*, Mart., Parahiba.

This species much resembles *G. Vellosii* in general appearance. The axils are 2½–3 in. apart; the leaves are 3⅞ in. long, 1¼ in. broad, on petioles 3 lines long; the peduncle of the inflorescence is 3–9 lines long, its 3 branches 9 lines long, each much divaricated, with 3–4 branchlets, each bearing about 4 flowers on pedicels 2 lines long; sepals ¾ line long; tube of corolla 3 lines long; the segments 2 lines long. The specimen is from one of Martius's Brazilian sets, collected by others, and distributed in 1827.

4. GEISSOSPERMUM RAMIFLORUM, Mart.: *Aspidosperma? ramiflorum*, Müll. *l. c.* p. 55. Rio de Janeiro: *non vidi.*

This species bears all the characters of *Geissospermum*, and appears very near the preceding. Müller was persuaded that it accorded ill with *Aspidosperma*. It has ashy black branches, verruculously lenticellated; leaves alternate, elliptic, obtuse or more acute at both ends, very glabrous, membranaceous, fuscous, opake above, with 8–10 pairs of nerves prominulent, very horizontally patent, with others shorter and intermediate, reticulated, 2¾–3½ in. long, 1½–1¾ in. broad, on petioles 5 lines long; panicles lateral, nearly sessile, many-flowered, without pedicels, with a small pubescent bract; sepals ferruginously hirtellous, oblong-ovate acute, 1½ line long; tube of corolla 4½ lines long, fulvo-hirtellous, somewhat inflated above; segments glabrous, oblong-ovate subacute, as long as the tube; ovaries glabrous, with ovules in pairs in 4 series.

5. GEISSOSPERMUM SOLANDRI, nob.: *Wheeleria alternifolia*, Sol. Prim. Flor. Bras. p. 66: ramulis teretibus, lenticellis parvis verruculosis; foliis 3 ultimis minoribus, approximatis, reliquis remotioribus, alternis, ovatis, imo acutis et inæquilateris, superne subrotundatis et in acumen brevissimum obtusum repente constrictis, marginibus vix revolutis, supra viridibus, opacis, minute granulatis, nervis tenuissimis, semiimmersis, subtus ochraceo-pallidioribus, opacis, costa flava prominente, nervis flavidis vix conspicuis; petiolo tenui, quam limbus 5plo breviore: panicula terminali, 2–3-ramosa, ramis fuscis, alternatim paucifloris; pedicellis subbrevibus; sepalis acute ovatis, extus parce hispidulis; corollæ parvæ tubo quam calyx 3plo longiore, extus scabride piloso, intus piloso; segmentis brevibus, ovatis, medio pilosulis, paullo dextrorsum convolutis; staminibus supra medium tubi insertis; antheris acutis, imo cordatis; disco urceolato, ciliato-denticulato; ovariis 2, globosis, pilosulis, disco absconditis; stylo filiformi; clavuncula incrassata glandulifera. In prov. Rio de Janeiro: *v. s. in herb. Mus. Brit. loc. cit. Solander* (A. D. 1768).

This plant bears much resemblance to a *Vallesia*, to which genus Riedel referred *G. Vellosii*. It is a tree with a smooth bark; the axils of its slender branchlets are about ¼ in. apart, except the three terminal ones, which are barely 1 line distant; the leaflets there are about 9 lines long; the leaves of the main branchlets are 2–2¼ in. long, 1½–1¼ in. broad, upon slender petioles 7 lines long; the peduncle of the corymb is 4 lines long, its 3–4 branches 4 lines long, their 2 secondary branches 1½ line long, each bearing 2 small flowers on pedicels ½ line long; the sepals ⅓ line long; the tube of the corolla 1½ line long; the segments ¾ line long; the stamens, upon very short filaments, are enclosed within the mouth of the tube.

These characters all conform with *Geissospermum*, rather than with *Vallesia*; its only peculiarity is the more diminutive size of its flowers.

A drawing of this species, and an analysis of its flower, are seen in Plate XII. A.

The *Wheeleria oppositifolia*, Sol., is described under *Thyrsanthus velutinus*, nob.

6. GEISSOSPERMUM SERICEUM, Benth. & Hook. Gen. ii. 707: *Thyrsanthus sericeus*, Sagot, MS.: ramis subvalidis, dichotomis, ramulis tenuibus: foliis alternis, ellipticis, imo acutis, apice in acumen longiusculum subito constrictis, chartaceis, margine undulatis, supra læte viridibus, opacis, obsolete pilosis, costa prominente, nervis prominulis, venis reticulatis, subtus fulvide opacis, costa nervisque sublanatis; petiolo tenui, sulcato, obsolete puberulo, limbo 9plo breviore: racemis axillaribus, congestifloris, quam folium triplo brevioribus; floribus parvis, ochraceo-pubescentibus; corolla parva; segmentis angustis dextrorsum convolutis. In Guiana: *v. s. in herb. Mus. Brit. loc. cit.* (Sagot 966).

Its branches are 1–2 lines thick, the branchlets more slender, with axils ¾–1 in. apart, with a transverse line across the nodes; leaves 3 in. long, 1¼ in. broad, on a petiole 4 lines long; panicles axillary, ¾–1 in. long, on a stout peduncle 3 lines long, with numerous approximate flowers, all covered with yellow tomentum; pedicels 1 line long; sepals 2 lines long, linear oblong, obtuse; segments of corolla linear, glabrous, 3 lines long.

MALOUETIA.

This genus was established in 1844 by Prof. De Candolle, who placed it in his tribe TABERNÆMONTANEÆ, from which it was separated by Dr. Müller. It has many species, forming trees or erect shrubs, with opposite entire leaves, the nodes generally much dilated by a thick transverse sheath, on which the petioles are inserted; the leaves generally oblong and acute at both ends, or lanceolate, have ascending nerves, which are often furnished below, at the angle of each nerve, with a poriferous gland.

MALOUETIA, A. DC.: *Sepala* 5, parva, acuta, erecta, singula squamula acuta intus munita. *Corollæ tubus* cylindricus, 5-nervis, sæpe spiraliter tortus, medio paullo ventricosus, fauce constrictus, et ibi sæpius squamulis 5 præditus; *segmenta* 5, oblonga, subacuta, simpliciter dextrorsum convoluta. *Stamina* subinclusa, apice sæpius paullo exserta; *filamenta* ad constrictionem tubi inserta; *antheræ* lineares, acuminatæ, in conum cohærentes, imo furcis 2 brevibus acutis armatæ. *Discus* e lobis 5 discretis erectis subacutis; *ovaria* 2, eo paullo longiora, oblonga; *stylus* tenuis stamina attingens; *clavuncula* incrassata cylindrica, imo membrana peltata donata; *stigmata* 2, brevissime linearia, terminalia. *Folliculi* 2, teretes, sæpius divaricati, glabri, aut rarius pilosi, sulco ventrali dehiscentes, suturæ marginibus introflexis in *placentam* cylindricam coalitis. *Semina* lineari-oblonga, valde compressa, glabra, ex una facie *hilo* centrali peltatim affixa, marginibus membranaceis canaliculatim introflexis; *albumen* oblongum, compressum, parcum; *embryo* hoterotropus; *radicula* parva, supera, teres, *cotyledonibus* 2 oblongis 4plo breviōr.

Frutices *plerumque Brasiliani, dichotome ramosi*; folia *opposita, breviter petiolata*; inflorescentia *breviter pedunculata*; flores *plurimi, longe pedicellati, subfasciculati*.

1. MALOUETIA TAMAQUARINA, A. DC. Prodr. viii. 378; Deless. Icon. v. p. 31, tab. 47; Müll. (in parte), Flor. Bras. fasc. xxvi. p. 92: *Cameraria tamaquarina*, Aubl. Pl. Guian. i. 260, tab. 102. In Guiana: *v. s. in herb. Mus. Brit.* Cayenne (Aublet), Guiana (Sagot 1143).

This typical specimen is very different from the two Brazilian plants referred to the same species by Dr. Müller. The leaves have a rufescent hue, with immersed nerves sulcate above, which are slender and prominulent below, with porous glands in their axils.

2. MALOUETIA GUIANENSIS, nob.: *Malouetia tamarquarina*, var. *minor*, A. DC. *l. c.* p. 379: *Cameraria Guianensis*, Aubl. *l. c.* p. 262: *Cameraria lutea*, Lam. Dict. i. p. 573. In Guiana: *v. s. in herb. Mus. Brit.* Cayenne (Aublet).

A species differing from the preceding in its much smaller leaves more acute at the base, rarely with porous glands in the axils of the nerves, in its much smaller flowers, the corolla having a shorter tube. Its slender branches are shining black, and striated; the leaves are lanceolate-oblong, acute at the base, with a narrow, sublinear apex, very entire, chartaceous, opakely green above, with slender subimmersed nerves, opake and rufously brown below, with reddish nerves and midrib little prominent; they are $3\frac{1}{2}$ in. long, 1 in. broad, on slender, black, channelled petioles 2 lines long.

3. MALOUETIA ODORATA, nob.: *Tabernæmontana odorata*, Vahl, Ecl. ii. p. 22 (excl. synon.); A. DC. *l. c.* p. 379; Benth. Lond. Journ. Bot. iii. 343. In Guiana: *v. s. in herb. Mus. Brit.* (Schomb. 951).

This species has dichotomous fuscous branches, compressed and channelled on each edge; leaves lanceolate, with a narrow obtuse acumen, fuscous green above, with immersed nerves, ferruginously opake below, with a darker prominulent midrib, and fine nerves, each with a small porous gland in its axil, $2\frac{1}{2}$–5 in. long, 7–12 lines broad, on petioles $1\frac{1}{2}$–3 lines long; peduncle solitary in each node, bearing 3–4 flowers; pedicels 1 in. long, dark and slender; sepals lanceolate, 1 line long; tube of corolla $3\frac{1}{2}$ lines long; segments oblong, 3 lines long, densely pubescent inside at their base.

4. MALOUETIA TARUMENSIS, Benth. Lond. Journ. Bot. iii. 344. In Guiana: in Mont. Taruma (Schomburgk): *non vidi*.

A species near *M. odorata*. It is a tree 50–60 feet high, with dark, shining, dichotomous branches compressed at the furcations; leaves 5–7 in. long. It is called "hotitjou," and yields an abundant milky juice.

5. MALOUETIA GRACILIS, A. DC. *l. c.* p. 380: *Tabernæmontana gracilis*, Benth. Journ. Bot. iii. 244. In Guiana: *v. s. in herb. meo et alior.* Upper Essequibo (Schomb. 39).

A species with straight striated branches and subdichotomous branchlets, its fuscous branches much thickened at the nodes, forming rough annular rings $\frac{3}{4}$–1$\frac{3}{4}$ in. apart, where the leaves have fallen off. The leaves are lanceolate, rarely oblong, acute and subinequilateral at the base, gradually acuminate at the summit, with subrevolute margins, thinly chartaceous, fuscous above, pale and yellowish below, eglandular, with slender patent nerves suddenly arcuately conjoined within the margins, 2 to 4 in. long, $\frac{1}{2}$–1$\frac{1}{2}$ in. broad, on slender petioles 1$\frac{1}{4}$–3 lines long: 6 or more flowers are crowded on a short axillary peduncle 2 lines long, upon pedicels 3 lines long; 5 acute sepals 1 line long, each with an internal lanceolate scale; tube of corolla narrowly cylindrical, 6–8 lines long, subventricose in the middle; the segments oblique oblong, 6 lines long, 2 lines broad; stamens included in the swollen portion of the tube; fuscous anthers shortly biaristate at the base, with an acute membrane at the summit; a disk of 5 ovate membranaceous lobes longer than the ovaries; 2 follicles, subterete, 1–2 in. long; seeds small, oblong, smooth.

6. MALOUETIA LACTIFLUA, nob.: *Tabernæmontana*, sp., Benth. *l. c.* p. 245; Schomb. Ann. Nat. Hist. i. p. 64: *v. s. in herb. Mus. Brit.* R. Berbice (Schomb. 168) : foliis oblongis, fusco rubro-viridibus, imo subacutis, apice in acumen lineare obtusulum constrictis, chartaceis, marginibus crebre undulatis, supra fusco-viridibus, rubentibus, nervis semiimmersis, opacis, nigro punctulatis, subtus pallidioribus, subferrugineo-opacis, subrugulosis, costa nervisque patentibus, prominulis, rubellis; petiolo tenui, canaliculato, quam limbus 12plo breviore: floribus ignotis.

There can be no doubt that this is a species of *Malouetia*. It is a very lactescent tree, yielding a vegetable milk, used by the natives, and also forms a useful varnish, according to Schomburgk. The leaves are 3 in. long, 1 in. broad, on a petiole 3 lines long.

7. MALOUETIA SCHOMBURGKII, Müll. Linn. xxx. p. 409. In Guiana Brit. Pomaroon (Schomb. 830, 1386): *non vidi*.

A species resembling *M. nitida* in habit. It has dark, slender branches, with axils 1$\frac{3}{4}$–2$\frac{3}{4}$ in. apart, its branchlets being paler; leaves oblong-ovate, acute at both ends, chartaceous, 4–4$\frac{3}{4}$ in. long, 14–20 lines broad, on petioles 9$\frac{1}{2}$–16 lines long; flowers 1 in. long; sepals linear-lanceolate, erect, 1$\frac{3}{4}$ line long; tube of corolla slender above, broader at its base, 6 lines long; segments linear acute, hispidulous within at the base; stamens partly exserted; disk of 5 erect, fleshy, truncated lobes, enclosing 2 ovoid ovaries, hispidulous at their apex; style slender below, 4$\frac{1}{4}$ lines long.

8. MALOUETIA OBTUSIFOLIA, A. DC. Prodr. viii. 379. In Guiana: *v. s. in herb. Mus. Brit.* Cayenne (Martin).

The leaves are stifly chartaceous, with entire, subrevolute margins, of a reddish hue above, opake, with immersed nerves, beneath ferruginous-opake, with slender prominulent nerves having porous glands in their axils, 3$\frac{1}{4}$ in. long, 1$\frac{1}{4}$ in. broad, on petioles 3 lines long; pedicels 5 lines long; sepals 1$\frac{1}{4}$ line long; tube of corolla 5 lines long; segments lanceolate-oblong, 9 lines long, with dextrorse contortion; stamens included, half-exserted at their apex.

9. MALOUETIA LANCEOLATA, Müll. *l. c.* p. 93, tab. 29. fig. 3: *Malouetia tamaquarina*, var. *Brasiliensis*,

A. DC. Prodr. viii. 379. In Brasilia: *v. v.* in montibus Organensibus, *et s. in herb. Mus. Brit. loc. cit.* (Gardner 5547).

I found this species in 1838, in the Organ Mountains, where it forms a shrub 10 feet high, with dichotomous branchlets which are shining, darkly rufescent, striated, fistulose, and compressed at the axils; leaves lanceolate or oblong-lanceolate, gradually acute at both ends, with subrevolute margins, chartaceous, deep green above, subnitid, somewhat granular, with semi-immersed curving nerves, below pallidly flavescent, very opake, with prominent midrib and reddish yellow prominent nerves, having a porous gland in their axils; they are $2\frac{1}{2}$–$3\frac{3}{4}$ in. long, $\frac{3}{4}$–$1\frac{1}{8}$ in. broad, on dark channelled petioles 2–3 lines long. Cyme $\frac{3}{4}$ in. long, solitary at each node, or in the dichotomy of the branches, glabrous; a very short peduncle, thickened at the apex, with scale-like bracteoles, bearing about 12 flowers; pedicels crowded, slender, declinate; sepals small, ovate, submucronate, with membranaceous margins, furnished within with alternate entire or 2-dentate scales; tube of corolla slender, narrowed above, with 5 small fleshy glands in its thickened mouth, 3 lines long; segments oblong obtuse, pubescent at their base, dextrorsely convoluted, 4 lines long; stamens included and inserted a little above the middle of the tube; anthers curvingly sagittate at their base, acute and pilose at the apex; disk of 5 ovate erect lobes, pilose at the apex, and somewhat shorter than the ovaries.

10. MALOUETIA ARBOREA, nob.: *Echites arborea*, Vell. Flor. Flum. p. 114, Icon. iii. tab. 47: *Secondatia arborea*, Müll. *l. c.* p. 110: *Tabernæmontana læta*, A. DC. in parte (non Mart.), Prodr. viii. 364. In Brasilia, prov. Rio de Janeiro, Fazenda de Mendanha (Velloz): *non vidi*.

A species unquestionably belonging to this genus, and differing little from *M. glandulifera*, chiefly in its larger leaves and longer peduncles. Like most other species, it is lactescent, with an erect trunk 8 in. in diameter, with its primary branches dichotomous, spreading, 2 lines thick; branchlets 1 line thick, with axils $1\frac{1}{2}$–$2\frac{1}{2}$ in. apart; leaves opposite, elliptic, acute at both ends, very slender nerves above, the midrib and nerves below being stouter, prominent, with a porous gland in their axils; they are 4–$4\frac{1}{2}$ in. long, $1\frac{1}{4}$–$1\frac{3}{4}$ in. broad, on petioles 2–3 lines long; inflorescence solitary at each node, densely 8-flowered; peduncle $1\frac{1}{2}$ line long; pedicels very slender, 5 lines long; sepals acute, $1\frac{1}{2}$ line long; tube of corolla cylindrical, narrowed above, 5 lines long, with 5 glands in the mouth; segments subequilateral, of a whitish yellow colour, 4 lines long, $1\frac{1}{4}$ line broad; stamens inserted below the mouth and partly exserted; 2 follicles stoutly terete, recurvingly divaricate, lactescent when cut across, 4 in. long, 4 lines thick; seeds many, subimbricated, glabrous, linear-oblong, very compressed, with incurving margins, peltately attached to the inflexed placentæ: this is clearly shown by the inclined section in Velloz's drawing. The loose seed depicted in a separate figure, with a long apical coma, has been placed there in mistake by the Paris lithographer; and this perhaps led Dr. Müller to refer the plant to *Secondatia*; but it belongs most certainly to *Malouetia*. Bentham and Hooker (Gen. ii. 723) agree that it should be excluded from *Secondatia*.

11. **MALOUETIA VIRESCENS**, Spruce; Müller, *l. c.* p. 92. In Amazonas: *v. s. in herb. variis* Panuré, Rio Uahupes (Spruce 2472).

A species near *M. Guianensis*. Branches dark, angular, subcompressed, subverruculose, with axils 1–1½ in. apart; leaves suberect, oblong, acutely obtuse at the base, shortly and obtusely acuminate at the apex, fuscous green above, with immersed fine nerves, ferruginously opake below, with dark midrib and prominulent nerves, in the axils of which a porous gland is most frequently seen, 2–3 in. long, ¾–1¼ in. broad, on petioles 2–3 lines long; axillary peduncle bracteolated, 3 lines long; pedicels slender, 4 lines long; sepals 1 line long; tube of corolla cylindrical, contracted in the middle, border hypocrateriform, segments linear oblong, 4 lines long.

12. **MALOUETIA GLANDULIFERA**, nob.: *Malouetia tamaquarina*, var. *Brasiliensis*, Müll. (non A. DC.) Fl. Bras. xxvi. p. 92. In Venezuelæ confinibus: *v. s. in herb. variis* Rio Casiquiare (Spruce 3305).

A very distinct species. Its erect fuscous branches, dichotomously divided, are subfistulose and interruptedly striated; leaves oblong, acute at the base, obtuse at the apex, margins subrevolute, rigidly chartaceous, green above, opake, impressed-rugulose, nerves immersed, luridly opake below, somewhat paler, midrib and nerves yellowish and prominulent, with a hollow pilose gland in each axil, 2–2¾ in. long, ¾–1 in. broad, on channelled petioles 1½–2 lines long; inflorescence solitary at each node, or in the dichotomy of the branchlets; peduncle 2 lines long, bearing 3 flowers, sometimes reduced to 1; pedicels very slender, 12 lines long; sepals obtusely oblong, imbricately erect, carinate, obsoletely puberulous outside, margins membranaceous, ¾ line long, with oblong fleshy scales within alternate with them; tube of corolla 5 lines long, 1 line broad at its base, ½ line broad at its summit, bearing in its expanding throat 5 obtusely lanceolate fleshy glands; segments of border obtuse-oblong, somewhat inequilateral, opposite the glands, glabrous on both sides, rugulous outside at their base, 5 lines long, 2 lines broad; stamens inserted below and alternate with the glands, partly exserted, quite glabrous; filaments seated on prominent ridges; disk of 5 erect oval fleshy lobes, shorter than the 2 ovaries, which are pilose on their summits; style slender below, with an incrassated clavuncle above; stigmata 2 short lobes; follicles terete, black, 4½ in. long, 2 lines thick; seeds very compressed, oblong, smooth, narrower below, peltately affixed to the placenta by a small ovate hilum.

13. **MALOUETIA MARTII**, Müll. *l. c.* p. 94, tab. 29. In Amazonas: *v. s. in hb. variis* Panuré, Rio Uahupes (Spruce 2435).

A species well distinguished from *M. lanceolata* by its much smaller, very dusky leaves, sharply acuminate, luridly ferruginous beneath, without the usual porous glands, in its darker corolla furfuraceous (not pubescent) within. It bears much the aspect of *M. virescens*. Spruce's plant agrees with Müller's diagnosis; but it is wrongly quoted as from the province of S. Paulo. Its leaves are 2–2¾ in. long, ¾ in. broad, on a petiole 2½–3 lines long; the peduncle is 1 line long, the pedicels 6 lines long; the sepals 1 line long; the tube of the corolla 6 lines long; its segments furfuraceous, 4 lines long, with dextrorse convolution; anthers exserted, furfuraceous.

14. MALOUETIA NITIDA, Spruce; Müller, *l. c.* p. 94. In Amazonas: *v. s. in herb. variis* Barra do Rio Negro (Spruce 1672).

A species differing in appearance from all others. Its branchlets are brown, $2\frac{1}{2}$ lines thick, with many prominent yellow lenticels, and with axils $3\frac{1}{4}$ in. apart; leaves oblong, subacute, and channelled at the base, narrowing gradually upwards and suddenly terminating in a linear acumen $\frac{1}{2}$ in. long, stiffly chartaceous, margins subrevolute, pale green, opake, and rugulous above, yellowish immersed midrib and nerves (about 8 pairs), somewhat paler beneath, opake, rugulous, with prominent midrib and subprominulent fine nerves, veins scarcely visible, $4\frac{1}{2}$–6 in. long, $1\frac{3}{4}$–$2\frac{1}{4}$ in. broad, on channelled petioles $2\frac{1}{4}$ lines long; inflorescence solitary in each axil; peduncle bracteolated, 1 line long, supporting 10–12 subfasciculate flowers; pedicels glabrous, 6 lines long; sepals 1 line long, lanceolate; tube of corolla narrow, contracted in the middle; segments lanceolate, 5 lines long, subpuberulous within at their base, with dextrorse convolution.

15. MALOUETIA FURFURACEA, Spruce; Müll. *l. c.* p. 93. In Brasilia: *v. s. in herb. variis* Barra do Rio Negro (Spruce 1566), San Gabriel, Rio Negro (Spruce 2305).

Its branchlets are somewhat slender, black, striate, dichotomous, with axils 2 in. apart; leaves 4–6 in. long, $1\frac{1}{4}$–2 in. broad, on petioles 2–4 lines long; inflorescence in the dichotomies of the branchlets; peduncle bracteolated, bearing about 6 or 8 fasciculate flowers; pedicels 8 lines long; sepals lanceolate, 1 line long; tube of corolla 4 lines long; linear segments 6 lines long, dextrorsely convolute; 2 terete, smooth, black follicles 12 in. long, $1\frac{1}{4}$ line thick.

16. MALOUETIA AMPLEXICAULIS, Müll. *l. c.* p. 91. In Amazonas: *v. s. in hb. meo* Panuré, Rio Uahupes (Spruce 2595).

A species distinguished by its very large leaves, which give it much the appearance of a *Rhigospira*: these are somewhat unequal in the same node, on one side $3\frac{1}{4}$–5 in. long, $1\frac{1}{2}$–2 in. broad, on the other $5\frac{1}{2}$–8 in. long, $2\frac{1}{2}$–$3\frac{1}{4}$ in. broad, subcordate and subsessile at their base, where they are conjoined by a transverse line, with about 12 pairs of white pubescent nerves, each with a poriferous gland in its axil. A corymb of 6 or 8 flowers fasciculate on short, bracteolated, opposite, extra-axillary nodules, with slender pedicels 5 lines long; the sepals are 1 line long; the very slender tube of the corolla 3 lines long, a little broader below the mouth, with oblong acute segments dextrorsely convolute in æstivation; stamens partly exserted; the disk is fleshy, tubular, crenately lobed on the margin, enclosing 2 pilose ovaries.

17. MALOUETIA RIPARIA, A. DC. *l. c.* p. 380: *Tabernæmontana riparia*, H. B. K. iii. 228. In Nova Granada: *non vidi*.

A lactescent tree, 20 feet high, with smooth dichotomous branches; leaves oblong, narrowly acute at the base, acuminate, with undulate entire margins, membranaceous, with prominent nerves beneath, 4–$4\frac{1}{4}$ in. long, 16–19 lines broad, on channelled petioles scarcely 3 lines long, their margins united by a transverse ridge across the nodes; cymes interpetiolar, opposite at the nodes, on a dichotomous peduncle, and shorter than the leaves, bearing 2 to 4 flowers 1½ in. long, on bracteolated pedicels; sepals smooth, elliptic oblong, obtuse, with undulate membranaceous margins, deeply imbricated, the two interior much narrower; corolla salver-shaped, yellow; tube cylindrical, twisting, 1 in. long, with expanded segments inequilaterally obovate and obtuse, shorter than the tube; anthers sagittate, seated in the middle of the tube; disk fleshy, investing 2 ovaries. Prof. De Candolle rightly placed this species in *Malouetia*, as the kind of inflorescence here indicated is unknown in any plant of the *Tabernæmontaneæ*, but is not uncommon in *Malouetia*: the structure of the flower is that of this genus.

18. MALOUETIA TETRASTACHYA, nob. : *Tabernæmontana tetrastachya*, H. B. K. iii. 227 ; A. DC. *l. c.* p. 368. In Nova Granada : *non vidi*.

A lactescent tree, with smooth, terete branches; leaves oblong, narrowly acute at the base, acuminate, with obsoletely undulate or repand margins, membranaceous, nerves remote, prominent beneath, 6–7 in. long, 2–2½ in. broad, on channelled petioles 6 lines long, their margins conjoined across the node by a transverse ridge; cymes opposite and interpetiolar, much shorter than the leaves; peduncle dichotomously divided into 4 approximated, divaricated, many-flowered spikes; flowers the size of those of jessamine, on close pedicels 3 lines long, bracteolated at the base. This species quite conforms with *M. riparia* in the character of its inflorescence and structure of its flowers.

19. MALOUETIA JASMINOIDES, nob.: *Tabernæmontana jasminoides*, H. B. K. iii. 225 ; A. DC. *l. c.* p. 379. In Venezuela, prope Cumana : *non vidi*.

This species, with flowers like those of jessamine, evidently belongs to this genus, as Kunth suspected; its opposite, oblong leaves, acute at the base, subacuminate, submembranaceous, are 3–4 in. long, 14–18 lines broad, on petioles 3 lines long; in a specimen from Turbaco (perhaps another species) they are 5–6 in. long, 20–21 lines broad, on petioles 6 lines long; peduncle 6–15 lines long, bearing several flowers on slender pedicels 6–7 lines long; sepals ovate, 1 line long; tube of corolla 4 lines long, swollen at the base, the segments being expanded, obovate-oblong, 5 lines long; stamens placed in the mouth of the tube, linear, biaristate at the base; the 2 ovaries surrounded by the disk; style slender; clavuncle adhering to the anthers.

20. MALOUETIA CUBANA, A. DC. Prodr. viii. 379: *Malouetia retroflexa*, Müll. Linn. xxx. 408; Griseb. Fl. Br. W. Ind. p. 412. In Antillis: Cuba, et ins. San Vincente (Guilding).

The descriptions of De Candolle and Müller accord so well together that they denote identically the same species. The leaves are elliptic-oblong, acute at the base, obtusely acuminate, 3–4 in. long, 10–15 lines broad, on petioles 2–3 lines long; the peduncle is 3 lines long, bears 4 to 7 flowers, on slender pedicels 8–10 lines long; sepals subulately lanceolate, reflexed at their apex, 2 lines long; tube of corolla 4 lines long, constricted in the middle; the segments, as large as the tube, are linear, acute, glabrous outside, puberulous within; stamens partly exserted; anthers dorsally hispidulous; disk of 5 erect lobes; ovaries 2, hispidulous at the apex; follicles 12 in. long, 4 lines broad, obtusely attenuated.

21. MALOUETIA PANAMENSIS, Müll. in Van Huerck. Pl. Nov. 185; Benth. & Hook. Gen. ii. 707 : *Stemmadenia Guatemalensis*, Müll. in Linn. xxx. 410. In Panama et Guatemala : *non vidi*.

This species has none of the characters of *Stemmadenia*, but in all respects agrees with *Malouetia*, as Müller himself indicated. Its branches are terete, blackish red, its branchlets compressed; the leaves are oblong, very acute at both ends, submembranaceous, with undulate-repand margins, with 10–12 pairs of divaricate nerves, are near 8 in. long, 2–2¾ in. broad, on petioles 4½ lines long; inflorescence terminal, in two opposite cymes; peduncle extremely short, almost pulviniform, supporting numerous aggregated flowers on stout pedicels 5 lines long, which are as long as the flowers; sepals ovate, obtuse, ciliolated on the margins; tube of corolla cylindrical, constricted in the middle, longitudinally subangular and striate; segments longer than the tube, lanceolate-ovate, furfuraceous above and at their base; stamens inserted in the contraction of the tube; disk cylindrical, of 5 lobes connate at their base, free above, surrounding 2 ovaries, which are somewhat shorter, subpuberulous at their apex, and obtusely ovate.

THYRSANTHUS.

The three genera *Thyrsanthus*, *Parsonsia* and *Forsteronia* are so much alike in habit, kind of inflorescence, and floral structure, that their difference would hardly be recognized, were it not for the divergence observed in the structure of the fruit and seeds. The *Parsonsia* of R. Brown (excluding the American species) was shown to be a distinct genus by De Candolle; but *Thyrsanthus* and *Forsteronia* have been entirely or in part confounded together by most botanists, and even the author of the former genus has renounced it in favour of *Forsteronia* (Gen. ii. p. 710). Notwithstanding this, *Thyrsanthus* appears to me a distinct and tenable genus. It was established by Mr. Bentham in 1841, upon one of Schomburgk's Guiana plants, acknowledged in 1844 by De Candolle, who described six species, one of which was figured in Delessert's Icones. Müller, however, in 1860, cancelled it, absorbing all its species in *Forsteronia*; and Bentham, in 1876, forgetful of his former accurate observations, revoked his genus *Thyrsanthus* in favour of *Forsteronia*. The latter, proposed by Meyer in 1818, was established upon a short diagnosis applicable alike to both these genera; but as two of his species belong to *Thyrsanthus*, a genus then unknown, it follows that his third species (*Echites floribunda*, Sw., *Parsonsia floribunda*, R. Br.) remains the type of *Forsteronia*.

Thyrsanthus comes near *Malouetia*, differing in little else than the character of its inflorescence; and there is no great dissimilarity in the structure of its flower; but in that of its fruit and seeds there is a wide divergence, which enables us at once to distinguish the one from the other. In the absence of this test, there remains the æstivation of the corolla, which shows a dextrorse convolution in one, and a sinistrorse direction in the other. I have observed also a peculiar character in the leaves of all the species of *Thyrsanthus*—the presence of a peculiar granular yellow gland at the junction of the midrib with the petiole, either single or divided, which does not appear in *Forsteronia*.

THYRSANTHUS, Benth. (non Elliot nec Schrank); *Thenardia*, Benth. (non Kunth); *Forsteronia*, Meyer (in parte), Müller, Benth. & Hook. *Sepala* 5, parvula, ovata, subacuta, intus squamulis 2–3 minimis prædita. *Corolla* parva; *tubus* cylindricus; *segmenta* oblonga, subæquilatera, tubo longiora, sæpius intus glabra, raro lanata aut villosa, paullo dextrorsum convoluta, dein subrotata. *Stamina* 5, tubo corollæ inclusa, aut apice semiexserta; *filamenta* brevia; *antheræ* lineari-oblongæ, acuminatæ, imo furcis 2 parallele elongatis armatæ, in conum cohærentes. *Discus* e lobis 5 oblongis, sæpius discretis, ovaria cingens; *ovaria* 2 distincta, eo non rarius longiora; *stylus* brevis, glaber; *clavuncula* cylindrice 5-sulcata, imo membrana peltata indusiata; *stigmata* 2, parva, terminalia. *Folliculi* 2, tenuiter teretes, horizontaliter divergentes, sulco ventrali dehiscentes, suturæ marginibus in *placentam* cylindricam introflexæ. *Semina* plurima, imbricatim suspensa, lineari-oblonga, compressissima, lateribus membranaceis paullo incurvatis, lævia et ecomosa, *hilo* centrali signata; *embryo* incognita.

Frutices *scandentes* Americæ meridionalis, *sæpius glabri*; folia *opposita, rarius ternatim verticillata, oblonga, petiolata*, sæpius glabra; paniculæ *axillares aut terminales, laxe thyrsoideæ aut capitatæ*; flores *numerosi, parvuli, inconspicui.*

1. THYRSANTHUS SCHOMBURGKII, Benth. Hook. Journ. Bot. iii. 245; A. DC. *l. c.* p. 387 : *Forsteronia Schomburgkii*, A. DC. *l. c.* p. 438 (excl. syn.); Müll. Flor. Bras. *l. c.* p. 107 in nota. In Guiana Brit. (Schomb. 37, 57, 556, 557) : *v. s. in herb. meo ex loc. cit.* (Schomb. 537).

This typical species has scandent, rugous, verruculous branches 2 lines thick, with patently divergent branchlets; its opposite leaves have a reddish hue, are obtuse at the base, with a narrow recurved acumen $\frac{1}{2}$ in. long, quite glabrous, palish green above, sulcate along the midrib, which has 2 very minute glands at its base, several oblique subimmersed nerves, beneath rubescently ferruginous, opake, with prominulent nerves and reticulated veins, 3–5 in. long, $1\frac{1}{2}$–$1\frac{3}{4}$ in. broad, on slender channelled petioles 1 line long; panicle terminal, 3 in. long, with opposite ramifications 6 lines long, 4–7 lines apart, dichotomous, each ray bearing an almost capitate cluster of flowers; pedicels 1 line long, with 2 lanceolate bractlets at the base; sepals acute, $\frac{1}{2}$ line long, with 2 minute scales at the base of each within; tube of corolla $\frac{3}{4}$ line long, glabrous, with a narrow pilose ring above its base; the 5 segments linear-oblong, 1 line long, glabrous within, expanded, with dextrorse convolution; stamens inserted in the pilose ring, almost wholly included in it; filaments short; anthers cohering together and to the clavuncle, acute at their summit, 2 obtuse prongs at their base.

2. THYRSANTHUS LAURIFOLIUS, nob.: *Thenardia ? laurifolia*, Benth. *l. c.* p. 246 : *Forsteronia laurifolia*, A. DC. *l. c.* p. 438; Müll. *l. c.* p. 106. In Amazonas : *v. s. in herb. meo* Rio Negro ad Barcellos (Schomb. 953), Rio Negro ad Barra (Spruce 999).

A species very near the preceding, and by mistake referred to *Thenardia*. Its branches are stout, rugous, griseous, glabrous, with divaricating branchlets striate and lenticellate, with axils 1–$1\frac{1}{2}$ in. apart; leaves elliptic oblong, acute, and inequilateral at the base, gradually acuminate, margins somewhat crenulate, chartaceous, very glabrous, glaucous green above, with a slender midrib and subimmersed fine nerves, furnished at the base of the midrib with 2–3 yellow granular glands, ferruginous, opake beneath, with prominent midrib and nerves 4–$4\frac{3}{4}$ in. long, $1\frac{1}{4}$–$1\frac{3}{4}$ in. broad, on subreflexed petioles 3–5 lines long; panicles opposite or terminal, on short peduncles

3–5 lines long, shortly branched, and bearing a capitate cluster of very small, rufously pruinose flowers, 2 lines long, on pedicels ¼ line long, with small bracteoles; sepals subacute, membranaceous, 1 line long; corolla subpuberulous outside; tube 1 line long; segments lanceolate, subreflexed, glabrous inside, dextrorsely convolute in æstivation, 1 line long; disk of 5 smooth, fleshy lobes; follicles 2 (one sometimes abortive), linear, stoutish, 2–3 in. long, containing many oblong flat seeds with narrow winged margins, without any coma.

3. THYRSANTHUS BENTHAMIANA, nob.: *Forsteronia Benthamiana*, Müll. *l. c.* p. 106. In Brasilia: *v. s. in herb. meo et alior.* San Carlos, Rio Negro (Spruce 3481).

A species much resembling the two preceding. Its branches are glabrous, striolate, verrucously lenticellate, with axils 1¼–1¾ in. apart; leaves lanceolate oblong, roundish or subacute at the base, with a very narrow acute acumen, margins revolute, very glabrous, with arcuate, fine, semi-immersed nerves, the midrib at its junction with the petiole showing a yellow granular gland, sometimes split into 2 or more distinct glandules, as in the typical species, ferruginously opake beneath, with a prominent fuscous midrib, prominulent fine nerves and reticulated veins, 4–6¼ in. long, 1⅜–1½ in. broad, on channelled petioles 2–3 lines long; panicles subterminal and axillary, rufescently puberulous, 2½–3 in. long, on a rather slender peduncle bare for 1½ in., bearing above several branchlets ½ in. long, bare at the base for half their length, and bifidly divided, with 3–4 flowers on pedicels 1 line long, and minutely bracteolated; sepals acute, ¾ line long; corolla also pruinosely tomentellous, 2–2¼ lines long, with a very short tube; segments lanceolate, with dextrorse convolution.

4. THYRSANTHUS SPICATUS, nob.: *Forsteronia spicata*, Meyer, Esseq. p. 135; A. DC. *l. c.* p. 437: *Echites spicata*, Jacq. Am. p. 34, tab. 29: *Parsonsia spicata*, R. Br. Mem. Wern. Soc. i. p. 65. In Cartagena (Jacq.): *v. s. in herb. Mus. Brit.* Campeche (Houston).

The plant of Houston agrees well with the drawing of Jacquin, who describes it as a lofty climber, the main stem being 1 in. thick, with alternate remote branches whose axils are nearly 2 in. apart. It exudes a copious milky juice. The leaves are opposite, very spreading, elliptic oblong, roundish at the base, and recurved upon the petiole, with a short suddenly acute reflexed acumen, rigidly chartaceous, with revolute margins, green above, corrugulate, with a flattened midrib and about 10 pairs of divaricate arching nerves, sulcate along them and the immersed reticulated veins, with a large granulated gland at the base of the midrib, pale, ferruginous, and opake beneath, midrib and nerves flattened, reddish, 4½–5¾ in. long, 2½–2¼ in. broad, on channelled petioles 3 lines long; panicles opposite, densely thyrsoid, 1–1½ in. long, ½ in. broad, on short peduncles, bearing very numerous, crowded, subsessile flowers, 2 lines long; sepals ovate, rigid, subimbricated; corolla white, with a very short tube, villous inside; segments acutely oblong, equilateral, with reflexed margins, twice the length of the tube; anthers exserted, conniving in a cone; disk of 5 lobes, as long as the 2 villous ovaries.

5. **THYRSANTHUS GARDNERI**, A. DC. *l. c.* p. 387: *Forsteronia Gardneri*, Müll. *l. c.* p. 100. In Brasilia: *v. s. in herb. meo* prov. Goyaz (Gardn. 3891).

Apparently an erect shrub, having straight terete subpuberulous branches marked with small white lenticels, axils 1¼ in. apart; leaves spreading, oblong, rounded and subcordate at the base, gradually acute and often mucronulate at the apex, very flat, rigidly chartaceous, opake green above, with about 8 pairs of semi-immersed nerves, sulcate on the fine reticulated veins, with 2 small glands at the base of the midrib, glaucous pale beneath, opake, nerves yellow, prominulent, 3–4 in. long, 1–1½ in. broad, on pubescent channelled petioles 1 line long; panicle terminal, laxly thyrsoid, 3¼ in. long, rufously pubescent, branching from the base, branchlets 2¼ in. long, diminishing upwards, again branched, ultimate branchlets 4–6 lines long, bearing several closely approximated flowers on puberulous bracteolated pedicels ½ line long; sepals acute, puberulous, with membranaceous margins, ¼ line long, with 3 minute inner basal scales; corolla reddish, glabrous outside; tube ¼ line long; segments acute, densely lanate within, dextrorsely convolute; anthers subincluded, glabrous, smallish, with 2 parallel obtuse basal prongs; disk of 5 ovate fleshy lobes, shorter than the 2 pilose ovaries.

6. **THYRSANTHUS ADENOBASIS**, nob.: *Forsteronia adenobasis*, Müll. Linn. xxx. p. 412. In Guiana: fl. Pomeroon (Rob. Schomb. 707): *non vidi*.

A species near the preceding, with opposite, sometimes ternate leaves, oval or elliptic, slightly cordate at the base, submembranaceous, glabrous above, with 6–7 pairs of oblique nerves and reticulated veins, showing at the base of the midrib 2 large reddish granular glands, as in the typical species, densely and shortly tomentous beneath, 4–4¾ in. long, 2½–3 in. broad; panicle rigidly pyramidal, deep red, densely puberulous, oppositely branched and again divided, bearing numerous small flowers.

7. **THYRSANTHUS MACROPHYLLUS**, nob.: *Forsteronia macrophylla*, Müll. Linn. xxx. 411: *Tabernæmontana macrophylla*, Poir. Dict. Suppl. v. 276; A. DC. *l. c.* p. 374. In Cayenne: *non vidi*.

A species little known, which must not be confounded with the *Tabernæmontana macrophylla* of Müll., described by me under *Phrissocarpus rigidus*. It has cinereo-pruinose branches; leaves broadly ovate, obtuse, with a short acute acumen, submembranaceous, fuscous green above, glabrous, cinereo-fulvous and pruinose beneath, 5½–6¾ in. long, 3⅜–4 in. broad, on petioles ¼–1 line long; panicle terminal, pyramidally corymbiform, 4 in. long, yellowish puberulous, lower branches elongated, all again branched, and bearing several very small flowers on pedicels 1½–2 lines long; calyx 1 line long; corolla 2¼ lines long, like those in *T. populifolia* and *T. parviflora*.

8. **THYRSANTHUS DIOSPYRIFOLIUS**, nob.: *Forsteronia diospyrifolia*, Müll. Linn. xxx. 415. In Guiana Brit. (Rob. Schomburgk 834): *non vidi*.

A species near the first described, with glabrous branches thickened at the axils, verrucously lenticellate; leaves oblong-elliptic, subobtuse at the base, shortly and obtusely acuminated, coriaceous, with 7–10 pairs of arcuately conjoined nerves, with others shorter and intermediate, smooth above, 3–4 in. long, $1\frac{3}{4}$–2 in. broad, on petioles 2–3 lines long; panicles terminal or axillary, 3–4 in. long, on an elongated angular tomentous peduncle, with many lateral branchlets bare at their base and bearing several small pubescent flowers in heads $4\frac{1}{2}$–6 lines in diameter, on short pedicels, with ovate bracts $1\frac{1}{4}$ line long; flowers $1\frac{1}{2}$–2 lines long.

9. **Thyrsanthus Guyanensis**, nob.: *Forsteronia Guyanensis*, Müll. Linn. xxx. 414. In Guiana Brit. (Schomb. 821–1466) : *v. s. in herb. Mus. Brit.* (Sagot 1067).

A species differing from all the preceding in its slighter habit. It has slender branchlets, verrucously lenticellate, with axils about 1 in. apart; leaves elliptic, acute at the base, suddenly constricted at the summit into a shortish obtuse acumen, subcoriaceous, margins revolute, pale green above, with divaricate slender nerves, the midrib near the petiole charged with a yellow granular gland as in the typical species, pale reddish yellow beneath, opake, slender nerves prominulent, mostly with a pore in their axils as in *T. Schomburgkii*, 2–$2\frac{1}{2}$ in. long, $\frac{7}{8}$–1 in. broad, on channelled petioles $1\frac{1}{4}$ line long; panicle pyramidal, 2 in. long, its branches on a quadrangular rachis bearing several (4–6) subumbellate, very small flowers, on pedicels 1 line long, all ferruginously puberulous; sepals acute, with ciliate margins, 1 line long; corolla 2 lines long; tube $\frac{1}{2}$ line long, puberulous; segments lanceolate, hirsutulous outside, with dextrorse æstivation, glabrous inside, with median nerve obsoletely puberulous.

10. **Thyrsanthus corymbosus**, nob.: *Forsteronia corymbosa*, A. DC. (non Mey.) *l. c.* p. 437 : Griseb. Fl. Br. W. Ind. p. 412 : *Echites corymbosa*, Jacq. Amer. p. 34, tab. 30; Sw. Obs. 105. In Antillis : *v. s. in hb. Mus. Brit.* Jamaica (Dr. Wright).

A twining species, growing to the height of 20 feet; very lactescent, with divided glabrous branches, the axils being 1 in. apart; leaves elliptic, somewhat rounded and obsoletely cordate at the base, subacute at the summit, entire, glabrous, green above, with prominulent red, arching nerves, and transverse, much reticulated veins, with 2–3 distant small glands at the base of the midrib, pallid beneath, 2–$2\frac{1}{2}$ in. long, $\frac{3}{4}$–$1\frac{1}{4}$ in. broad, on slender petioles 3–4 lines long; panicle terminal, divided into two principal branches $1\frac{3}{4}$ in. long, which are much divided into many approximated branchlets 9 lines long, each on a bare pedunculate support $2\frac{1}{4}$ lines long, and bearing above 8 crowded bracteolated divisions, forming a corymbulose head, each division again divided into about 7 pedicellated flowers; bracts linear-lanceolate, membranaceous, red, obsoletely pubescent, $1\frac{1}{2}$ line long; pedicels pubescent, $\frac{1}{2}$ line long; sepals linear-acuminate, very membranaceous, red, pubescent at the base, obsoletely pilosulous outside above, 1 line long; corolla $1\frac{3}{4}$ line long; tube $\frac{1}{2}$ line long; segments obtusely oblong, membranaceous, red, subreflexed, $1\frac{1}{4}$ line long, with dextrorse convolution; stamens inserted in a pilose ring within the tube, exserted; anthers scarcely cohering, connivent, with a broad membrane at the apex, and 2 parallel short obtuse lobes at the base; disk of 3 free oblong erect lobes, as long as the 2 ovaries, pubescent at the apex; 2 elongated obtusely terete follicles, horizontally divaricate, 8 in. long; seeds numerous, oblong, subscriceous under a lens, otherwise, according to Jacquin and De Candolle, without a coma Swartz says they have a setose pappus, meaning their setosely hairy covering. Grisebach states they have a rusty coma; but that applies to his *Forsteronia Alexandri*. The flower, beyond all doubt, belongs to *Thyrsanthus*, and not to *Forsteronia*.

11. THYRSANTHUS CORYMBIFERUS, nob.: *Thenardia ? corymbosa*, Benth. Hook. Journ. Bot. iii. 246: *Forsteronia corymbosa*, Mey. Esseq. p. 134, excl. synon. (non A. DC. nec Griseb.): *Forsteronia Schomburgkii*, A. DC. *l. c.* p. 438 (non Benth.): *Forsteronia lancifolia*, Müll. (in parte), *l. c.* p. 106. In Guiana (Schomb. 247): *non vidi*.

This certainly is not a *Thenardia*; but it accords with the genus *Thyrsanthus* of Bentham, and is near the preceding species. It is subscandent, with smooth branchlets somewhat pilose at the summits; leaves oval-oblong, obtuse and subcordate at the base, narrowly obtuse and mucronate at the apex, membranaceous, glabrous above, with glands at the base of the midrib, as in *T. Schomburgkii*, subglabrous beneath, reticulated, 2-3 in. long, 1-1½ in. broad, on puberulous petioles; panicle terminal, short, densely flowered; flowers on pedicels shorter than the calyx; sepals lanceolate, without an internal scale; tube of corolla short, with a pilose staminiferous ring in the mouth; segments acute; anthers long, exserted, with 2 basal obtuse forks.

12. THYRSANTHUS AUBLETIANUS, nob.: *Apocynum umbellatum*, Aubl. Pl. Guian. i. p. 275, tab. 108: *Forsteronia Schomburgkii*, var. *umbellata*, A. DC. *l. c.* p. 438: *Thenardia umbellata*, Spreng. Syst. i. 636; G. Don, Dict. iv. 80. In Cayenne: *non vidi*.

A sarmentose species, very distinct from *T. Schomburgkii*. The leaves, according to Aublet, are rounded at the base, terminated by a long acumen, 2½-3¼ in. long, 1-1½ in. broad, smooth above, cinereo-tomentous below, on petioles 3-4 lines long; corymb terminal, 1 in. long and broad, on a naked peduncle 9 lines long, with many flowers subumbellate on the ends of its branchlets, which are 2-bracteolate at their base, the pedicels being also bracteolated; flowers 2 lines long, of a reddish colour; tube of corolla short; the segments rounded-oblong; stamens inserted in the mouth of the tube; anthers adhering to the clavuncle.

Aublet's specific name has not been adopted, to prevent confusion with the *Echites umbellata* of Jacquin, or that of Kunth.

13. THYRSANTHUS ACOUCI, nob.: *Apocynum Acouci*, Aubl. *l. c.* p. 274, tab. 107: *Apocynum apiculatum*, Lam. Dict. i. p. 214: *Forsteronia Acouci*, A. DC. Prodr. viii. p. 437. In Guiana: *v. s. in herb. Mus. Brit.* Cayenne (Aublet).

This is a scandent species, with slender glabrous branchlets. Its lanceolate oblong leaves, horizontally spreading, are somewhat acute at their base, constricted above into an obtuse acumen, thinly chartaceous, with subrevolute margins, palish green and opake above, glauco-pulverulent, closely granulated with dark polished dots, semi-immersed fine nerves, and sulcate upon the finely reticulated veins, with 2 small yellow glands at the base of the midrib, lateritious and opake beneath, with prominulent nerves, 3½-4 in. long, 1-1½ in. broad, on deeply channelled petioles 1 line long; panicles terminal and geminate, or axillary, 3 in. long, pubescent, bare at the base for ¾ in., oppositely branched at intervals of 9 lines, branchlets 9 lines long, again divided above the middle, bearing above several lax flowers on bracteolated pedicels ¼ line long; sepals acute, pilose, margins membranaceous, ¾ line long; corolla 1½ line long; segments ovate, as long as the tube, sublanate within, with dextrorse æstivation; stamens subincluded.

14. **THYRSANTHUS GRACILIS**, Benth. Hook. Journ. Bot. iii. p. 246; A. DC. *l. c.* p. 387. In Guiana Brit. ad Curassawaka: *v. s. in herb. meo* (Schomburgk 608).

A species near the preceding, with verrucously lenticellate branches 2½ lines thick, and very slender horizontal branchlets with axils 2-3 in. apart; leaves oblong-ovate, rounded and subcordate at the base, suddenly narrowed towards the summit into a narrow obtuse acumen, submembranaceous, glabrous, opake green above, sulcate along the midrib and fine diverging nerves, reticulately veined, with 2 minute glands at the base of the midrib, ferruginously opake beneath, with scarcely prominulent nerves, 3-3½ in. long, 1⅜-1¾ in. broad, on slender spreading petioles 2 lines long; panicle terminal, 4-5½ in. long, subthyrsoid, very laxly and remotely branching from the base, branches diverging, 2½ in. long, diminishing upwards, very glabrous, again alternately divided, the branchlets bearing many lax or subfasciculated flowers, on bracteolated pedicels 1 line long; flowers very small, like those of the preceding species.

15. **THYRSANTHUS POPULIFOLIUS**, nob.: *Tabernæmontana populifolia*, Poir. Dict. Suppl. i. p. 276; A. DC. *l. c.* p. 374. In Carolina et Georgia: *v. s. in herb. Mus. Brit.* Georgia (Marshal).

A species with slender dichotomous branches. Its leaves are broadly ovate, subacute at the base, shortly acuminate, subchartaceous, almost glabrous above, pale and opake beneath, shortly and rigidly pilose, 1¾ in. long, 1¼ in. broad, on petioles scarcely 1 line long; panicles axillary, 2¼ in. long, on a peduncle bare for 1¼ in., branching above, branches 6-9 lines long, again shortly branched, and bearing numerous small flowers on pedicels 2 lines long; sepals lanceolate, subrecurved, 1 line long, with several very minute inner scales; corolla glabrous; tube contracted in the middle, 1½ line long; segments oblong ovate, 1¼ line long, with dextrorse convolution; stamens almost wholly included within the tube; anthers cuspidate, with 2 long acute basal prongs; style, stigma, and disk as in the generic character.

16. **THYRSANTHUS DIFFORMIS**, nob.: *Echites difformis*, Walth. Fl. Carol.; Pursh, Fl. Un. St. i. 178; Ellis, Sk. i. 312: *Echites puberula*, Mich. Fl. Bor. Amer. i. 120; Poir. Dict. Suppl. ii. 537: *Forsteronia difformis*, A. DC. *l. c.* p. 437: *Secondatia difformis*, Benth. & Hook. Gen. ii. 710. In Carolina et Florida: *v. s. in herb. Mus. Brit.* Florida (Chapman).

A slender climbing species, with pubescent branches; leaves lanceolate elliptic, acute at the base; acuminate, membranaceous, pale green above, opake, obsoletely puberulous, with slender immersed pellucid nerves and reticulated veins, with a granular yellow gland at the base of the midrib, very pellucid, opake beneath, puberulous on the midrib and nerves, 1½-3 in. long, 6-12 lines broad, on channelled petioles 2 lines long; panicles axillary, glabrous, 2½ in. long; peduncle slender, bare at the base for 1 in., above very laxly branched, lower branches 1¼ in. long, again branching and bearing about 5 lax flowers on slender bracteolated pedicels 2 lines long; sepals acuminately lanceolate, margins pellucid, 1¼ line long, each with 2 lanceolate inner scales; corolla 3¾ lines long; tube 2½ lines long; segments 1¼ line long, acutely oblong, membranaceous, with dextrorse convolution, all glabrous; stamens almost wholly included, inserted in a pilose ring; anthers acuminate, with 2 long slender basal prongs; disk of 5 oblong lobes, as long as the 2 glabrous ovaries; 2 follicles, slender, acute, glabrous, 6-8 in. long.

This species, in its inflorescence and floral structure, closely resembles the preceding from the same region, both being quite in accordance with *Thyrsanthus*; it is therefore neither a *Forsteronia* nor a *Secondatia*, more especially differing from the latter in its slender follicles, the seeds of which are not said to be comose.

17. THYRSANTHUS PYRIFORMIS, nob. In Antillis: *v. s. in herb. Mus. Brit.* Cuba (Sagra 141).

A species near the two following. It has slender, pallid, striolate, dichotomous branches, with axils 1-1½ in. apart; leaves obovate, subcuneate below the middle, rounded and mucronulate at the summit, very glabrous, thinly chartaceous, flat, palish green above, opake, finely corrugulate, fine ascending nerves scarcely prominulent, with 2 minute glands at the base of the subimmersed midrib, pale yellow and opake beneath, the slender nerves scarcely visible, 2-2½ in. long, 1⅜-1⅝ in. broad, on slender channelled petioles 4-5 lines long; panicle terminal, 2½ in. long, on a peduncle bare at the base for 6 lines, bifid, and again dichotomously branched, each branch bifid and bearing 2 fascicles of small, approximate flowers on pedicels 1½ line long, supported by acute membranaceous bracteoles ⅓ line long, all slightly puberulous; sepals obtusely oblong, with membranaceous margins, puberulous within along the nerve, ⅔ line long; corolla reddish, glabrous, 2½ lines long; tube 1½ line long; segments 1 line long, oblong, with dextrorse convolution; stamens mostly included; anthers apiculate, with 2 long parallel basal prongs; disk of 5 free oblong lobes, as long as the 2 puberulous ovaries.

18. THYRSANTHUS PARVIFLORUS, nob.: *Tabernæmontana parviflora*, Poir. Dict. Suppl. v. 276; A. DC. *l. c.* p. 374. In Amer. meridionali: *non vidi*.

A species near *T. populifolius*, with slender branchlets; leaves oval-lanceolate, obtuse at the base, acuminate, glabrous, dark green above, yellowish beneath, 2 in. long, 1 in. broad, petiolated; panicles terminal, geminate, subcymose, bearing many subumbellate small flowers, on short bracteolated pedicels.

19. THYRSANTHUS FASCICULATUS, nob.: *Tabernæmontana fasciculata*, Poir. Dict. vii. 531; A. DC. *l. c.* p. 375. In Cayenne: *non vidi*.

A species near the preceding. Its leaves are ovate-lanceolate, obtusely acuminate, 2-3 in. long, 1½ in. broad, petiolated; panicles cymose, axillary, divided, with many small flowers fasciculate at the ends of each ramification; tube of corolla 2-3 lines long, with linear segments.

20. **Thyrsanthus pubescens**, nob.: *Forsteronia pubescens*, A. DC. *l. c.* p. 436; Müll. *l. c.* p. 104. In Brasilia: *v. s. in herb. meo*, Ceará (Gardner 1761).

Its branches are oppositely ramose, studded with small white verrucous lenticels, subpubescent, the axils being 1–2 in. apart; leaves obovate, subacute or obtuse at the base, rounded or emarginate at the mucronulate apex, flaccidly chartaceous, green above, subpubescent, with yellowish slender midrib and oblique nerves, with 2 collateral fulvous glands among the hairs at the base of the midrib, pale beneath and covered with fine short tomentum, especially on the nerves and transverse veins, between which are very numerous fascicles of short hairs, $3-4\frac{3}{4}$ in. long, $1\frac{3}{4}-2\frac{1}{4}$ in. broad, on pubescent petioles 3–7 lines long; panicle terminal, spiciform, 4 in. long, covered with reddish pubescence, alternately branched at intervals of 2–4 lines, with short branches, the lower ones 1 in. long, diminishing upwards, each on a bare support, carrying an almost capitate head of small dense flowers on bracteolated pedicels $\frac{1}{2}$ line long; sepals acute, $\frac{3}{4}$ line long; corolla $2\frac{1}{4}$ lines long; the acute segments $1\frac{1}{4}$ line long, with dextrorse convolution; stamens glabrous, half-exserted; anthers acuminate, furnished at the base with 2 parallel prongs.

21. **Thyrsanthus affinis**, nob.: *Forsteronia affinis*, Müll. *l. c.* p. 100, tab. 30. In prov. Alt. Amazonas et confinibus: *v. s. in herb meo* Tarapota (Spruce 4493).

Spruce's plant agrees sufficiently with Müller's drawing. The branchlets are slender, subquadrangular at the summit, striolate, with small lenticels, the axils $\frac{1}{2}$–1 in. apart; leaves oblong elliptic, subacute at the base, as in the drawing (not cordate as in the text), with a short, abrupt, subacute acumen, very glabrous, rigidly membranaceous, darkish green above, subopake, sulcate along the midrib and oblique slender nerves, with 2 whitish glands at the base of the midrib, pale ferruginous and opake beneath, with prominulent red midrib and nerves, finely reticulated veins, $3\frac{1}{2}-4\frac{1}{4}$ in. long, $1\frac{1}{4}$–2 in. broad, on sulcate petioles $3-3\frac{1}{4}$ lines long; panicle terminal, 4 in. long, remotely and very laxly branching from the base; lower branches slender, 2 in. long, bare at the base for half their length, again branched, branchlets 3–4 lines long, bearing at their summits few very small flowers on bracteolated pedicels 1 line long, all glabrous; sepals ovate acuminate, pruinose, $\frac{1}{2}-\frac{3}{4}$ line long; corolla pruinose, $1\frac{1}{2}$ line long; segments acute, twice as long as the tube, woolly within, dextrorsely convolute; anthers dorsally pilose, half-exserted; disk of 5 oblong lobes, as long as the 2 glabrous ovaries.

22. **Thyrsanthus placidus**, nob. In Alta Amazonas: *v. s. in herb. Mus. Brit.* Tarapota (Spruce 4295).

A species very near the preceding, differing in its pubescent leaves and spicate inflorescence; branches very slender, puberulous, with axils $\frac{3}{4}$–1 in. apart; leaves elliptic, acute at the base, constricted at the summit into a short acumen, flaccid, green and subglabrous above, with immersed slender nerves, with 2 small glands at the base of the midrib, paler beneath, yellow, covered with short soft pubescence, especially on the prominulent nerves, 3 in. long, $1\frac{3}{4}$ in. broad, on pubescent channelled petioles 2 lines long; panicle terminal, $3\frac{1}{2}$ in. long, thyrsoid, pubescent, on a short peduncle, with branches $\frac{1}{2}$ in. long, 2–4 lines apart, spreading, again divided, each bracteolated branchlet bearing 3–5 approximated flowers on bracteolated pedicels 1 line long; sepals acutely ovate, puberulous, 1 line long; corolla subglabrous, 2 lines long; segments ovate, a little shorter than the tube, submembranaceous, smooth, with dextrorse convolution; stamens more than half-included, anthers with 2 long basal prongs.

23. THYRSANTHUS GLABRESCENS, nob.: *Forsteronia glabrescens*, Müll. *l. c.* p. 102. In Brasilia australiore, *v. v. et sicc. in herb. meo* (n. 3942) Rio de Janeiro, Botafogo; *v. s. in herb. Mus. Brit.* prov. S. Paulo (Bowie and Cunningham).

Its branches are interruptedly striate, sublenticellate, oppositely branched, branchlets slender, striolate, with axils 1–1½ in. apart; leaves often scarcely opposite, elliptic oblong, obtuse at the base, ending in a sudden sharp acumen, submembranaceous, fuscous rufescent green above, often marked by many small white leprous dots, with about 7 pairs of semi-immersed oblique nerves, and with 2 small yellowish glands at the base of the midrib, opake and subferruginous beneath, with prominulent reddish midrib, nerves, and reticulated veins, 2½–3¼ in. long, 1¼–1¾ in. broad, on petioles 3 lines long; panicle terminal, pyramidally thyrsoid, laxly branched, 3½ in. long; peduncle slender, bare at the base for 4–6 lines, branches somewhat spreading, ¾–1 in. long, diminishing upwards, again laxly divided, bearing many lax flowers on bracteolated pedicels 1–1½ line long, all subglabrous or shortly puberulous; sepals ovate, subobtuse, 1 line long, each with 3 minute inner basal scales; corolla glabrous outside, 1½ line long; segments lanceolate, as long as the tube, woolly within; anthers semi-exserted, bifurcate at the base; disk of 5 free lobes, nearly as long as the 2 glabrous ovaries.

24. THYRSANTHUS BRACTEATUS, nob.: *Echites bracteata*, Vell. Fl. Flum. p. 112, Icon. iii. tab. 41 (non Kunth): *Echites Velloziana*, A. DC. *l. c.* p. 474: *Forsteronia bracteata*, Müll. *l. c.* pp. 106–453. In prov. Rio de Janeiro: *v. v. et sicc. in herb. meo* (n. 4025) montibus Organensibus (*in flore et fructu*).

A scandent species, with rigid subflexuous rufescent branches, oppositely divided, branchlets more slender, verrucously lenticellate, with axils 1–1½ in. apart, all covered with dense, short, ferruginous pubescence; leaves spreading, oblong ovate, shortly cordate at the base, with a very short obtuse or acute acumen, rigidly chartaceous, with revolute margins, dark green above, opake, sulcate on the pilosulous midrib and oblique nerves, with 2 or more small glands among the rigid hairs at the base of the midrib, ferruginously opake beneath, hispidly pilose upon the prominent midrib and nerves, the hairs rufous and spreading, 1¾–2¾ in. long, ⅞–1¼ in. broad, on stout villous petioles 1½–2 lines long; raceme terminal, 1 in. long, densely hirsute, on a stoutish peduncle 9 lines long, bearing an oblong capitate head of small flowers, all rufously hirsutulous, on horizontal stout pedicels ½ line long, at first approximately spicate, afterwards more remote, the lower ones supported by lanceolate bracts 2 lines long, the upper ones by acutely deltoid bracteoles ½ line long; sepals acute, subpilose, 1 line long; corolla subpilose outside, glabrous within, 2 lines long; tube 1½ line long; segments membranaceous, ½ line long; stamens small, apices subexserted; disk of 5 oblong free lobes, a little shorter than the 2 subpilose ovaries; follicles 2, horizontally divaricate, black, sparsely pilose, terete, straight, 2 in. long, 1 line thick, subacute at the apex, each enclosing many imbricate seeds on a narrow cylindrical placenta emanating from the ventral suture; seeds acutely oblong, 3 lines long, $\frac{1}{4}$ line broad (immature), with pellucidly membranaceous margins, reddish, marked on the ventral face by the hilum, and without the indication of a coma; embryo unknown.

A drawing of this species, with its floral and carpological analyses, is given in Plate XIII. B. The latter analysis agrees precisely with Mr. Bentham's description of his typical species in Hook. Journ. Bot. iii. 246.

25. THYRSANTHUS MULTINERVIUS, nob.: *Forsteronia multinervia*, A. DC. *l. c.* p. 437; Müll. *l. c.* p. 104; *Wheeleria oppositifolia*, Solander, Prim. Fl. Bras. p. 66. In Brasilia, prov. Rio de Janeiro: *v. s. in herb. Mus. Brit.* Rio de Janeiro (Solander, A.D. 1786), Rio Parahybuna (Gardner 5543).

A species described by De Candolle from a plant collected by Gomez in the neighbourhood of Rio de Janeiro, with which the above specimens well agree. It is a climbing plant, with subflexuous, ferruginously pilose, lenticellate branches, the axils 1 in. apart; leaves ovate oblong, subobtuse at the base, acutely acuminate and mucronulate, submembranaceous, green with a reddish hue above, with about 12 pairs of parallel subascending nerves and transverse reticulated veins, sparsely pilose, especially on the nerves, with 2 distinct glands at the base of the midrib almost concealed by the hairs, more densely pilose beneath, 3–5 in. long, 1–1$\frac{3}{4}$ in. broad, on pubescent petioles 2–3 lines long; inflorescence axillary on a subdeflexed peduncle 4 lines long, subcapitate, 1 in. in diameter, consisting of very numerous small flowers on very approximate branchlets bare at the base for 3 lines, each bearing about 8 crowded subspicate flowers on pubescent pedicels 1 line long, each furnished with a small lanceolate bract; sepals acutely oblong, puberulous, $\frac{3}{4}$ line long; corolla glabrous, 2 lines long; tube only $\frac{1}{2}$ line long, bearing within a dense ring of white hairs; segments oblong, submembranaceous, of a red colour, smooth on both sides, a small tuft at the base of the median nerve, with dextrorse convolution, the right inside margin involute; stamens inserted on the pilose ring; filaments very short; anthers oblong, small, shortly bicleft at the base, terminated by an inflexed membranaceous point; disk 5-lobed, as long as the 2 pilose oval ovaries.

A species near *T. bracteatus*.

26. THYRSANTHUS BRASILIENSIS, nob.: *Forsteronia Brasiliensis*, A. DC. *l. c.* p. 436; Müll. *l. c.* p. 102: *Echites torquata*, Cas. (?) Pl. Bras. n. 1601. In Brasilia: *v. s. in hb. meo* (n. 5057), Pernambuco (Gardner 1059).

An erect shrub, 5 feet high, with slender, rufescent, glabrous, lenticellate branchlets, having axils 1 in. apart; leaves opposite, oblong, narrower below the middle, rounded at the base, suddenly contracted at the summit into an obtuse acumen, submembranaceous, glabrous, darkish green above, sulcate on the midrib, with 2 small glands at its base, nerves semi-immersed, somewhat paler beneath, with prominulent reddish nerves and reticulated veins, 1$\frac{3}{4}$–2$\frac{3}{4}$ in. long, 9–18 lines broad, on puberulous channelled petioles 2 lines long; a subglobose panicle 6 lines in diameter, on a peduncle 3 lines long, bearing many small agglommerated flowers on pedicels $\frac{1}{2}$ line long, and an acute bract of the same length; sepals lanceolate, 1 line long; corolla 2 lines long, with a very short tube, having a pilose ring in its mouth; segments lanceolate, with dextrorse convolution, reddish, almost glabrous, obsoletely pubescent on the median nerve; stamens exserted. Gardner's specimen agrees with the characters given by De Candolle and Müller. Casasetto's plant probably belongs elsewhere, as it appears to be a twining species.

27. THYRSANTHUS RUFUS, nob.: *Forsteronia rufa*, Müll. *l. c.* p. 100, tab. 31. In Brasilia: *v. v. et sicc. in herb. meo* (n. 4039) ex montibus Organensibus; *v. s. in herb. Mus. Brit. ex eodem loco* (Gardner 530), *in herb. meo* (n. 2411) *sine loco* (Ackermann).

I collected this species in company with Gardner in January 1838. It is tolerably well figured by Müller (*l. c.*). The branches and branchlets are ferruginously tomentous, with axils 1–1½ in. apart; the leaves are oblong-ovate, obtuse and rounded at the base, constricted near the summit into a short subacute acumen, chartaceous, entire, green and opake above, with many divaricately ascending nerves arcuately conjoined, puberulous on the midrib, paler beneath, pubescent, with yellow prominulent nerves, 3½–3¾ in. long, 1½–1¾ in. broad, on pubescent petioles 3–4 lines long; the panicles, nearly erect, are opposite in the axils, or geminate at the ends of the branches, subpyramidal, 5¼ in. long, branching from near the base at intervals of about ½ in., closer gradually upwards, lower branches 1 in. long, bare and bracteolated at the base, again and again divided, all furnished with narrow acute bracteoles 4 lines long; flowers in each branch numerous, subcongested, on pedicels 2 lines long; sepals acute, externally pubescent, 1½ line long, with few inner bifid scales; corolla 4½ lines long, its tube cylindrical, 1½ line long; segments acutely oblong, reddish, membranaceous, slightly puberulous inside, with dextrorse convolution, 3 lines long; stamens exserted; filaments short, membranaceous; anthers 2 lines long, linear, membranaceous at the apex, with 2 obtuse basal prongs; disk 5-lobed, as long as the 2 pilose ovaries; style very short, with a thickened clavuncle as usual. The fruit is unknown.

Müller ascribes to this species 2 follicles more than a foot long, strangulated at remote intervals into 5 or 6 seminiferous lobes containing several seeds with a long apical coma; but these belong to his *Forsteronia montana*, a plant also from the Organ Mountains, which he confounded with it, and which has a very similar habit and inflorescence. This latter plant is fully described in a subsequent page, under that name.

28. THYRSANTHUS SESSILIS, nob.: *Echites sessilis*, Vell. Fl. Flum. p. 111; Icon. iii. tab. 35; A. DC. *l. c.* p. 476: *Tabernæmontana sessilis*, Vell. *l. c.* p. 106: *Malouetia sessilis*, Müll. *l. c.* p. 96. In Brasilia: *v. s. in herb. Mus. Brit. sine loco* (Claussen).

The two plants recorded by Velloz under the same specific name are evidently identical; and Claussen's specimens agree well with them. The floral characters are not those of *Malouetia*, but they accord in all respects with *Thyrsanthus*. Velloz found one of the plants at Cairurú, near Paraty, in the province of Rio de Janeiro, the other near Itagoahy, in the same province. It is a scandent species, with dichotomous, flexuous, verruculously lenticellate, lactescent branches, the axils being 1–4 in. apart; the leaves are elliptic oblong, roundish at the base, and suddenly constricted upon the petiole, shortly acuminate, patently recurved, thinly chartaceous, very glabrous, obscure green and opake above, with scarcely prominulent midrib and oblique nerves, with 2 small long glands at the base of the midrib, ferruginously opake beneath, with prominulent and reticulate veins, 3–4 in. long, 1½–2 in. broad, on deeply channelled reflexed petioles 3–4 lines long; the inflorescence is axillary, or in the dichotomy of the branches, 1 in. long, consisting of 8 or 10 approximate flowers on a slender peduncle 3 lines long, all glabrous, upon pedicels 2–3 lines long, supported by an acutely ovate membranaceous bracteole 1 line long; sepals acutely ovate, submembranaceous, 1 line long, each with three minute inner basal scales; corolla red, glabrous outside, 4 lines long; tube 3 lines long, pilose in the throat; segments subovoid, membranaceous, 1 line long, with dextrorse convolution; stamens partly exserted; anthers acuminate, with 2 long, slender, parallel basal prongs; disk of 5 oblong free lobes, nearly as long as the 2 ovaries.

29. THYRSANTHUS CREBRIFLORUS, nob.: ramulis teneris, teretibus, fuscis, lenticellis parvis flavidis creberrime maculatis: foliis ovatis, imo subacutis, apice sensim vel abruptius acute acuminatis, glaberrimis, submembranaceis, supra fusce viridibus, costa plana, imo glandulis 2 parvis munita, nervis tenuissimis, violaceis, adscendenti-divaricatis, venisque reticulatis utrinque fere immersis, subtus opace brunnescentibus; petiolis fuscis, glabris limbo 12plo brevioribus: panicula terminali, subthyrsoidea, quam folium paullulo breviore, e basi alternatim ramosa; pedunculo flavide pubescente, ramis divisis, creberrime plurifloris, pedicellis brevissimis, bracteolatis; sepalis parvis, ovatis, flavide membranaceis, obsolete puberulis; corollæ tubo brevissimo, segmentis oblongis 2plo longioribus, glabris, rufescentibus, dextrorsum paullulo convolutis; staminibus subexsertis; cæteris ut in *T. myriantho*. In Brasilia, prov. Rio de Janeiro ad Rio Parahybuna, montibus Organensibus: *v. s. in herb. Mus. Brit. ex l. c.* (Gardner 5013).

A species near the preceding. Its branchlets are very slender, with axils near 1 in. apart; leaves 2–2¼ in. long, 10–12 lines broad, on petioles 2 lines long; panicle 1¾ in. long; its branches ½ in. long, diminishing upwards; pedicels ⅛ line long, supported by a bracteole of the same length; sepals ½ line long; tube of corolla 1 line long; segments 1½ line long. The rest as in *T. myrianthus*.

30. THYRSANTHUS MYRIANTHUS, nob.: *Forsteronia floribunda*, Müll. (non Meyer) *l. c.* p. 96. In Brasilia, prov. Minas Geraës: *v. s. in herb. meo et alior*. Arraial das Mercês (Gardner 5012).

The specimen above quoted is Gardner's 5012 (not Gaudichaud's, as Müller by mistake states). Its branches are fistulous, compressed, lenticellate, fuscous-reddish, with axils 2–2½ in. apart, each node furnished with 3 distinct interpetiolar stipules; leaves ternate, spreading, oblong-elliptic, subacute at the base, narrower and mucronately obtuse at the summit, submembranaceous, glabrous, darkish green above, with a flattened fuscous midrib, and about 9 pairs of arcuated nerves, each with a small concave gland within its axil, and a more or less concrete granular gland at the base of the midrib, concolorous beneath, with reddish prominulent nerves and reticulated veins, 4¼–4½ in. long, 1⅜–2 in. broad, on channelled lenticellate petioles 1 line long; panicle terminal, somewhat spreading, 8 in. long, bearing innumerable very small flowers on a peduncle bare for 7 lines, then oppositely branched at intervals of 1½ in., gradually diminishing upwards, branches very slender, arcuately ascending, bare at the base for some distance, bracteolated, each alternately divided, the branchlets bearing several laxly

P

alternate flowers, on pedicels 1–1½ line long, minutely bracteolated; sepals subacute, membranaceous, glabrous, ¼ line long, each with 3 minute inner scales; corolla 2 lines long, dark red, glabrous; tube ⅔ line long; segments 1¼ line long, equilateral, glabrous outside, pubescent inside on the median nerve, with a slight dextrorse convolution; stamens exserted; disk of 5 free, broadly ovate lobes, as long as the 2 conical ovaries, hairy at the summit.

31. THYRSANTHUS LUSCHNATII, nob.: *Forsteronia Luschnatii*, Müll. *l. c.* p. 98. In Brasilia, prov. Rio de Janeiro: *non vidi*.

A species near the preceding, with cinereous glabrous branches; leaves ternate, ovate, subacute at the base, shortly acuminate, rigidly membranaceous, cinereo-fuscous, with slender, scarcely prominulent nerves, 2⅜–2¾ in. long, 1¼–1⅜ in. broad, on petioles 3–4 lines long; inflorescence as in the preceding species, obsoletely pubescent.

32. THYRSANTHUS MERIDIONALIS, nob.: *Forsteronia meridionalis*, Müll. *l. c.* p. 98. In Brasilia, prov. Rio Grande do Sûl ad S. João Baptista (Sellow): *non vidi*.

A species approaching the two preceding, with obsoletely tomentellous branches; leaves ternate, ovate-lanceolate, cordate at the base, with a long acute acumen, submembranaceous, blackish green above, dark olive green beneath, minutely pubescent and scabridulous, 2⅛–2½ in. long, 6–8¼ lines broad, on petioles 2¼ lines long; inflorescence as in the preceding species, with innumerable, minute flowers.

33. THYRSANTHUS EMBELIOIDES, A. DC. *l. c.* p. 387; Deless. Icon. v. 21, tab. 48: *Forsteronia embelioides*, Müll. *l. c.* p. 97, tab. 50, fig. 2. In Brasilia, prov. Minas Geraës: *v. s. in herb. meo et alior*. Catas Altas (Gardner 5014).

A species differing from *T. Luschnatii* in its smaller and paler leaves, which exactly resemble those of *T. difformis*. Its branches are very slender, glabrous, and rufescent, with axils 1–1½ in. apart; leaves ternate, ovate-oblong, acute at the base, obtuse or suddenly constricted at the apex into a short acumen, membranaceous, glabrous, of a palish green above, sulcate along the midrib, immersed pellucid nerves, with a longitudinal granular gland hidden in hairs within the basal plicature, paler, yellowish and opake beneath, with subprominent midrib, and reddish fine pellucid nerves and reticulated veins, 1–2¼ in. long, 7–9 lines broad, on slender petioles 3–5 lines long; panicle terminal, laxly branched, as in *T. myrianthus*, 3 in. long, 2 in. broad, bearing innumerable very small flowers, on pedicels 1–1½ line long; sepals membranaceous, ¼ line long; corolla of a reddish hue, pruinose, membranaceous; tube ½ line long; segments roundish, 1½ line long; rest as in the generic character.

34. THYRSANTHUS PILOSUS, A. DC. *l. c.* p. 387: *Echites pilosa*, Vell. Fl. Flum. p. 112; Icon. iii. tab. 38: *Forsteronia pilosa*, Müll. *l. c.* p. 99. In Brasilia, prov. Rio de Janeiro: *non vidi*.

A species near *T. myrianthus*, with stoutish branches, shortly dichotomous at the apex, with axils 1–1½ in. apart; leaves ternate, lanceolate-oblong, narrower and obtuse at the base, with a long, gradually acute summit, 3½–5 in. long, ¾–1¼ in. broad, on spreading petioles 2 lines long; panicles terminal, thyrsoid, 4 in. long, 1 in. broad, with several opposite divergent branchlets 2–3 lines apart, 1 in. long, shortening upwards, again branching, each branchlet bearing about 6 alternate flowers, on pedicels ½ line long; flowers 2 lines long; segments of border puberulous inside.

The *Thyrsanthus sericeus* of Sagot is referred by Bentham and Hooker (Gen. ii. 707) to *Geissospermum*.

ROBBIA.

This genus was first established by Prof. De Candolle in 1844, upon a Brazilian plant which had been previously noticed by Martius as a species of *Tabernæmontana*. The genus was clearly defined by De Candolle, and well figured by Delessert, who added to it analytical details of the structure of the flower and the seed; but notwithstanding this, Dr. Müller ignored the genus, wrongly regarding the typical plant as a species of *Malouetia*.

I have here added another species; but I will first correct a few errors in the recorded details. De Candolle attributes to the segments of the corolla a sinistrorse convolution; but I have found this to be dextrorse, as is correctly shown in the analysis of Delessert. In this analysis there is an omission of the 5 scales which close the mouth of the corolla, which De Candolle rightly mentions. These scales are placed opposite to the segments, are rounded, fleshy, ciliated on their margins, and united in an annular ring. The anthers are enclosed for three fourths of their length within the tube, where they appear almost sessile; but their long filaments are agglutinated to the tube, where they form 5 ridges covered by retrorse white hairs; upon the back of the anthers may be seen a line of rigid hairs. I found also the tube of the corolla puberulous within, towards its base. I remarked also that the inner integument of the seed is distinct, though adhering to the testa, and that the embryo is enveloped in thin albumen.

1. ROBBIA CESTROIDES, A. DC. *l. c.* p. 445; Deless. Icon. v. 23, tab. 52: *Malouetia cestroides*, Müll. *l. c.* p. 94, tab. 29. fig. 2: *Tabernæmontana cestroides*, Nees et Mart. Nov. Act. xi. p. 83. In prov. Bahia et Ilheos (Blanchet 1578 et 1738): *v. s. in hb. Mus. Brit.*

This species certainly does not belong to *Malouetia*. It is a glabrous shrub, 6 feet high, with slender dichotomous branches, its axils being 1½–2 in. apart; leaves elliptic or lanceolate oblong, acute at both ends, terminated by a short obtuse acumen, submembranaceous, very glabrous, pale green above, with very fine, semi-immersed, eglandulous nerves and reticulated veins, ochraceous opake beneath, with reddish prominulent midrib and nerves, 1½–2¾ in. long, 7–9 lines broad, on slender petioles 3 lines long; panicles in the opposite axils, with fasciculate flowers borne on a peduncle scarcely 1 line long; pedicels slender, 4–5 lines long, with a small basal bracteole; sepals subacute, ¼ line long; tube of corolla gradually swelling downwards, narrower upwards, with 5 small glands in the throat, it is 3 lines long, including the short campanular expansion of the throat; segments linear oblong, acute, 6 lines long, simply and dextrorsely convolute, rotately expanded, recurved at the apex; stamens included within the throat, seated on 5 pilose lines; disk of 5 oblong free lobes, half as long as the 2 pilose obtusely oblong ovaries; style slender, bearing a clavuncle membranaceous at its base, adhering to the anthers; 2 short, erect, terminal stigmata; 2 divaricate follicles, terete or subfusiform, 3 in. long, 2½ lines thick, arcuate; seeds without an apical coma, oblong, subcompressed, with a central hilum on one face, densely covered all over with erect cottony hairs, which extend far beyond the apex; embryo in thin albumen, with 2 linear-oblong flat cotyledons 8 times as long as the narrow terete superior radicle.

A drawing of this species, with its floral analysis, is shown in Plate XII. B.

2. ROBBIA GOSSIPINA, nob.: ramulis quadrangulatis, dichotomis, ad nodos compressos dilatatis: foliis oppositis, ellipticis, imo acutis, apice in acumen lineare obtusum attenuatis, marginibus subundulatis, tenuiter chartaceis, supra viridibus, sublucentibus, ad nervos sulcatulis, subtus fulvide pallidioribus, opacis, costa rubella prominula, nervis adscendenti-divaricatis, cum glandula cava in quaque axilla, venis reticulatis immersis; petiolis tenuibus, canaliculatis, margine nodi insertis, limbo 12plo brevioribus; pedunculo fructifero axillari et subterminali, quam petiolus 3plo longiore: folliculis 2, paullo divaricatis, subulato-teretibus, apice obtuso incurvatis, sutura ventrali dehiscentibus, marginibus introflexis placentiferis; seminibus plurimis, ventre subconcavis et curte pilosis, medio hilo oblongo peltatim affixis, dorso pilis lanatis longissimis erectis densis ultra apicem extensis; embryone heterotropo, in albumine incluso, cotyledonibus oblongis, foliaceis, quam radicula supera teres 6plo longioribus. In prov. Rio de Janeiro: *v. s. in herb. Mus. Brit.* Itagoahy (Bowie et Cunningham).

The opposite leaves are fixed on the edges of the prominent transverse compressed nodes, which are ¾ in. apart; the leaves are 3–4 in. long, 1½-1½ in. broad, on petioles 3–4 lines long, and are conspicuous for the concave glands seen beneath in the axil of each nerve. The fructiferous peduncle is 9 lines long, terminated by 2 suberect, terete, tapering follicles 2¾ in. long, 2¼ lines broad, containing numerous cottony seeds densely covered by long, soft, ascending hairs, which extend 6 lines beyond the summit, being very short towards the base; the testa is 9 lines long, 1½ line broad, very compressed; the raphe and hilum are seen on the middle of one face.

A drawing of this species, with its follicles, and analysis of its seeds, are seen in Plate XII. C.

3. ROBBIA MACROCARPA, nob.: *Echites ? macrocarpa*, Rich. (uon Wallich) Fl. Cub. p. 94; Walpers Ann. v. 495. In ins. Cuba: *non vidi*.

This species cannot belong to any other genus than *Robbia*, with which it agrees well in all its essential characters. It is glabrous, with an erect, branching, woody stem, the branches being virgate; the leaves are ternately verticillate, elliptic-oblong, very obtuse, coriaceous, below finely reticulated, marked by many close impressed dots, on longish petioles; flowers aggregated in a cyme. As in the preceding species, one of its follicles is abortive, the other being very elongated and narrow, more than 18 in. long, 2 lines broad, containing many oblong-linear compressed seeds covered all over with very long white hairs.

SKYTANTHUS.

A genus first proposed by Meyen in 1834, upon a Chile plant. A second species was described by Prof. De Candolle in 1844, as the type of his genus *Neriandra*—an excellent analysis, under the latter name, being shown in Delessert's Icones. Its fruit and seeds, however, were then unknown. Müller, in 1860, described a third species, and at the same time figured the fruit and seeds of De Candolle's species. The genus is distinguished by the long setaceous termination of its anthers—a feature also occurring in *Nerium* and *Strophanthus*, in the tribe *Stipecomeæ*: it is also notable for the total absence of a disk. The fruit consists of 2 long slender follicles, containing many imbricate, oblong, glabrous, compressed seeds winged at both extremities, without an apical coma, and peltately attached by a central hilum to the inflected placenta. This structure places the genus in the tribe *Robbieæ*.

1. SKYTANTHUS ACUTUS, Meyen, Reise i. 376; Endl. Gen. Suppl. p. 1396; A. DC. *l. c.* p. 488 : *Skytalanthus acutus*, Schauer, Nov. Act. xix. Suppl. i. 361; Gay, Chile, iv. 385 ; Walp. Rep. vi. 478 : *Neriandra angustifolia*, A. DC. *l. c.* p. 422. In Chile ad Copiapo : *non vidi*.

A low shrub, with a subprostrate or procumbent stem, and terete pubescent branches ; leaves approximated, opposite or alternate, lanceolate, subcuneate at the base, obtuse, with a recurved mucronate apex, entire, coriaceous, with revolute margins, midrib immersed above, prominent beneath, opakely glaucous above, farinaceously puberulous below, 1½–2 in. long, 2–3 lines broad, on petioles 2–4 lines long ; cymes axillary or terminal, shorter than the leaves, on a trichotomous peduncle, few-flowered, with minute bracts ; pedicels 3 lines long ; sepals acute, as in the pedicels hirtellous, 1½ line long ; tube of yellow corolla 7 lines long, villous within ; segments oval, of the same length, puberulous outside; anthers exserted, with long apical appendages ; 2 long, terete, compressed subulate, falcate, velvety follicles, horn-shaped, giving to the plant the name of "cuernecilla."

2. SKYTANTHUS HANCORNIÆFOLIUS, nob. : *Neriandra hancorniæfolia*, A. DC. *l. c.* p. 422 ; Deless. Icon. v 22, tab. 50; Müll. *l. c.* p. 63, tab. 50. fig. 1. In prov. Bahia, Jacobina, in montibus : *non vidi*.

A shrubby species, with terete glabrous branches ; leaves opposite or subalternate, oblong, cuneate at the base, subacute towards the apex, nerves approximate, patently parallel, slender, 1½–2 in. long, 7–9 lines broad, on very slender petioles 4–7 lines long ; panicles dichotomous in opposite axils, slender, 2–2¼ in. long ; pedicels 4 lines long, slender, with a very minute basal bracteole ; sepals acutely linear, imbricated, 1¼ line long, without inner scales ; tube of corolla 3 lines long, narrowly cylindrical ; segments 6 lines long, oblong, subreflexed, dextrorsely convolute ; stamens seated in the middle of the tube, with long, exserted apical appendages, spirally twisted together ; disk none ; 2 free ovaries ; follicles 2, terete, puberulous, horizontally expanding, extrorsely arching, 8 in. long, 2 lines broad; seeds oblong, winged all round, 8 lines long, 2 lines broad, with a central hilum, peltately attached on each side of a solid torose placenta.

3. Skytanthus Martianus, nob.: *Neriandra Martiana*, Müll. *l. c.* p. 62, tab. 18: *Habsburghia comans*, Mart. Pl. Bras. Medic. In Brasilia, ad Rio San Francisco: *non vidi*.

This is said to resemble much the preceding species; and it comes from near the same locality. It differs only in the form and pubescence of its leaves; the axils are ¾–1 in. apart; the leaves are oblong-elliptic, subacute at both ends, pubescent at first, afterwards glabrous above, with close patent nerves, 1¾–2⅜ in. long, 6–7 lines broad, on petioles 5 lines long; peduncle ¾ in. long, twice trichotomously divided.

4. Skytanthus Havanensis, nob.: *Neriandra Havanensis*, Müll. Linn. xxx. 401. In Havana (Sagra 274): *non vidi*.

A species with very slender branches, trichotomously divided, with axils 4 in. apart; leaves broadly ovate, inequilateral, and suddenly acute at the base, terminated by a short, oblique, acute, often recurved acumen, glabrous, with many close, parallel, straight nerves conjoined near the margin and ¾–1 line apart; they are 2–2⅞ in. long, 1½–1¾ in. broad, on petioles 6 lines long; panicles trichotomously branched, shorter than the leaves, bearing 12 to 18 flowers, on slender pedicels 2 to 4 times as long as the calyx; sepals broadly ovate, rounded and mucronulate at the apex, 1¼ line long; tube of corolla 3¼ lines long, campanulate in the mouth; segments 5¾ lines long, triangularly inequilateral; anthers small, ovoid, terminated by filiform appendages of nearly equal length, twisted together; ovaries short, glabrous.

The *Neriandra suberecta*, A. DC., founded on the *Echites suberecta*, Sw. et And. (non *Echites suberecta*, Jacq.), belongs to my genus *Chariomma*. It is referred by Bentham and Hooker (Gen. ii. 705), to *Urechites*, here confounding the two plants figured by Andrews and Jacquin under the same name, which are very distinct.

In p. 28 I have alluded to a mistake imputed by Messrs. Bentham and Hooker to Müller, in regard to the supposed identity of *Cameraria* and *Skytanthus*; but I find this not to be Müller's mistake, but one of the many blunders of Prof. Grisebach, who in his Cat. Pl. Cub. n. 16, p. 170, confounds together *Cameraria latifolia* and *Neriandra Havanensis*.

Chariomma [*].

Most of the plants forming this group were placed, doubtfully, by De Candolle, in *Neriandra*, a genus since abandoned; and they certainly differ widely in several respects. *Neriandra* (now *Skytanthus*, by right of priority) has a rather small hypocrateriform corolla, with narrow segments; the stamens are seated below the mouth, and the twisted appendages are exserted; there is no disk. On the other hand, in *Chariomma* the corolla is larger (often very large), with broad dolabriform segments, the stamens are wholly included, being inserted below the middle of the tube, and there is a conspicuous disk. The type is the *Echites suberecta* of Swartz and Andrews (not of Jacquin).

Chariomma, nob. *Sepala* 5, acute lanceolata, membranacea, erecta, valde imbricata, intus singulatim squamulis 3 parvis acutis ad basin prædita. *Corolla* sæpius majuscula; *tubus* pro tertia parte imo

---

[*] From χάρις (*gaudium*), ὄμμα (*facies*), from its large handsome flowers.

cylindricus, superne campanulatus, fauce nudus ; *segmenta* 5, latissime dolabriformia, angulo sinistro acuto, dextrorsum convoluta, subrotatim expansa. *Stamina* 5, omnino inclusa ; *filamenta* breviter linearia, margine pilosa, ad contractionem tubi inserta ; *antheræ* lineares, subacute bifurcatæ, apice in appendices 4plo longiores, tenuissime lineares, spiraliter tortas prolongatæ. *Discus* e lobis 5 oblongis carnosis constans. *Ovaria* 2, oblonga, disco 2plo longiora. *Stylus* subtenuis ; *clavuncula* incrassata, imo in membranam late peltatam expansa. *Stigmata* 2, obtusa, sæpe pilosa, terminalia. *Folliculi* 2, longi, teretes. *Semina* plurima, imbricata (non alata), compressa, apicem versus lanuginosa, ecomosa.

Suffrutices *Antillani et Columbienses, subscandentes ; folia opposita, interdum ternata aut verticillata, ovata vel oblonga, breviter petiolata ; paniculæ terminales aut axillares ; flores speciosissimi, lutei vel albi.*

1. CHARIOMMA SURRECTA, nob.: *Echites suberecta*, Sw. (non Jacq.) Observ. p. 104; Andrews in Bot. Repos. tab. 187; Sims, Bot. Reg. xxvii. tab. 1064, var. β; Lunan, Hort. Jam. ii. 144: *Nerium sarmentosum* (2), P. Browne, Jam. p. 180: *Neriandra suberecta*, A. DC. Prodr. viii. 422: *Hæmadictyon suberectum*, Don, Dict. iv. 23: *Urechites neriandra*, Griseb. Fl. B. W. Ind. p. 415. In Antillis: *non vidi*.

This species has been confounded with the *Echites suberecta* of Jacquin by every botanist, from Swartz downwards (except De Candolle), both plants being natives of Jamaica; but this differs in many essential particulars, especially in its inflorescence, with large yellow flowers, in the position of its stamens, terminated by long twisting filiform appendages, and the presence of a disk. It grows in savannas, flowering all the year round, is a shrubby plant, charged with milky juice, and, when supported by other shrubs, grows to a height of 10 feet, but in the open savannas to only 3 or 4 feet, sometimes even to only 1 foot. Its branching stem is glabrous, the branches straight, weak, terete, pubescent, the dilated axils 2–3 in. apart; opposite leaves ovate, rounded at the base, subobtuse and mucronate at the apex, subcoriaceous, entire, with very revolute margins, above nitid, reticulated, somewhat pallid beneath, subhirsutulous, 2¼ in. long, 1½–1⅜ in. broad, on channelled puberulous petioles 3 lines long; racemes lateral at the nodes, 2–2½ in. long; peduncle bare for the length of 1–1½ in., trifid above, and bearing 5–7 opposite flowers on pedicels 2–4 lines apart and 3–5 lines long, each with a basal bracteole 3–4 lines long; sepals linear acuminate, hirsute, 3–4 lines long; corolla very large; tube cylindrical, 15 lines long, contracted near its base for a quarter of its length, swelling above, 5 lines broad in the mouth, hispidly pubescent externally, with red striate lines within; segments roundly dolabriform, acute at the sinister angle, dextrorsely convolute, rotately expanded, smooth inside, membranaceous, yellow, 12 lines long, 9 lines broad; stamens seated in the contraction of the tube, included; filaments short, pilose; anthers linear, corneous below and bifurcate, prolonged at the summit into very long filiform appendages, spirally twisted together, and nearly reaching the mouth; disk of 5 oblong, free, crenate lobes, surrounding the 2 small ovaries; style short and slender, clavuncle incrassate; stigmata 2, obtuse, terminal. The 2 follicles, according to Swartz, are very long, terete and pubescent. Sloane says they are set together like bull's horns. They contain several imbricate seeds, lanuginous towards the apex, as in *Elytropus* and *Skytanthus*.

The whole plant is extremely poisonous.

The specific name is changed to *surrecta*, that it may no longer be confounded with the *Echites suberecta* of Jacquin (non Sw.).

A drawing of it, with its floral analysis, is given in Plate XV. B.

2. CHARIOMMA DOMINGENSIS, nob.: *Echites Domingensis*, Sw. Prodr. p. 52; Fl. Occid. i. 529; Jacq. Coll. i. p. 73; Icon. Rar. tab. 53; A. DC. *l. c.* p. 452: *Echites heterophylla*, Gmelin, Syst. i. 437: *Urechites Jamaicensis*, Griseb. Fl. Br. W. Ind. p. 416. In Antillis: *non vidi*.

A very slender, branching, climbing plant, growing to a height of 10 feet, with filiform, terete, pubescent, lactescent branchlets; leaves ovate-oblong, rounded or subcordate at the base, acute at the summit, entire, rigidly chartaceous, glabrous above, nerved and reticulately veined, pale ferruginous beneath, and scabridly pubescent, those of early growth narrowly linear and 3 in. long, those of permanent production 1–1½ in. long, 6 lines broad, on short pubescent petioles; panicles axillary, subracemose, shorter or longer than the leaves, on bifid peduncles, each branch bearing few large odoriferous yellow flowers; sepals subulately linear, erect, subhirtous, 4 lines long; tube of corolla 1 in. long, cylindrical below for a length shorter than the sepals, swelling above, and spreading to a breadth of 5 lines in the mouth, which is villous inside and subpentagonous; segments large, obliquely inequilateral, undulated on the margin, 12 lines long, 10 lines broad; stamens seated at the contraction of the tube, enclosed; anthers linear, with long slender apical appendages, spirally twisted together; disk of 5 roundish yellow lobes, embracing the 2 ovaries; style short; clavuncle incrassate, 5-lobed; stigmata 2, globose.

This species evidently belongs to *Chariomma* (not to *Skytanthus*), on account of its inflorescence with large yellow flowers, the position of its stamens, and the presence of a conspicuous disk.

3. CHARIOMMA MUCRONULATA, nob. In ins. San Thomas, *v. s. in herb. Mus. Brit. ex loc. cit.* (Rhyons, sub *Echites erecta*).

A species near *C. Domingensis*, differing in the size and shape of its leaves and in its smaller flowers. It has rather slender terete branches, with axils 1¼ in. apart; leaves opposite, oblong, narrower towards the roundish base, broader and rounded at the mucronulate summit, chartaceous, with subcrenulate revolute margins, pale green above, very opake, with about 8 pairs of scarcely prominulent fine ascending nerves, opake and subochraceous beneath, with a flattened midrib, prominulent nerves, and finely reticulated veins, 2–2¼ in. long, ¾–1 in. broad, on channelled petioles 2 lines long; inflorescence axillary, as long as the leaves, on a bifid peduncle, each branch bearing 3 or 4 flowers on finely hirsutulous pedicels 3 lines long; sepals linear, acuminate, membranaceous, hirsutely pilose outside, 3 lines long, ¼ line broad, pilose along the nerve within, with 2 or 3 very minute internal scales; tube of corolla 7 lines long, stoutish, narrower at its base for 2½ lines, spreading above to a breadth of 6 lines; segments dolabriform, 6 lines long, and as broad, acute at the sinister angle, and dextrorsely convolute, subvillous outside, as well as the tube; stamens inserted in the constriction of the tube, and altogether included; filaments pilose; anthers ovate, shortly bifurcate at the base, expanded at the summit into long slender appendages, spirally twisted together, and scarcely reaching the mouth; disk of 5 ovate fleshy lobes, half the length of 2 acutely oblong ovaries; style shortish, clavuncle incrassate, with a basal peltate membrane; stigmata 2, pilose; 2 erect follicles, slender, terete, arching, conjoined at the apex, near 3 in. long, 1 line thick.

4. CHARIOMMA FLAVA, nob.: *Dipladenia flava*, Hook. Bot. Mag. tab. 4702; Müll. in Linn. xxx. 445; Walp. Ann. v. 496. In Nova Granada (Purdie), in Kew cult.: *non vidi*.

A scandent plant, closely resembling the typical species in its habit and inflorescence, more especially in its stamens terminated by long setiform appendages; there can be no hesitation, therefore, in placing it here, especially as Sir William Hooker did not observe its disk. Its terete branches are firm, pilose when young; its axils $\frac{3}{4}$ in. apart; its opposite leaves ovate, subacute at the base, shortly and acutely constricted at the apex, submembranaceous, younger ones pilose, 2-2$\frac{3}{4}$ in. long, 1-1$\frac{1}{2}$ in. broad, on petioles 4-6 lines long; raceme axillary or terminal, with 2 or 3 showy yellow flowers, or only a single one by abortion, all sericeo-pilose; peduncle 6 lines long; bracts foliaceous, 4 lines long; pedicels 4 lines long; sepals subulate, 4 lines long; tube of corolla 1 in. long, narrowly constricted below the middle; segments broadly dolabriform, 1 in. long and broad; stamens included, their long twisting appendages reaching the mouth.

5. CHARIOMMA NOBILIS, nob.: *Dipladenia nobilis*, Lemaire, Ann. Soc. Gand. iii. 331, tab. 152; Van Houtte, Fl. des Serres, v. 437; Paxton, Mag. Bot. xvi. 66, cum icone; Walp. Ann. iii. 44; Müll. Fl. Bras. *t. c.* p. 130. In Brasilia, prov. S. Catharina: *non vidi*.

A handsome species, only known as a cultivated plant. It approaches *C. flava* in its elongated twisting anthers. It has several erect stems growing out of a tuberous root, which are green, glabrous, and lactescent; leaves small, ovate, subcordate, with a short obtuse acumen, shining above, with numerous parallel nerves; racemes opposite, with large, tricoloured flowers; sepals small, gibbous at the base, recurved at the apex; tube of corolla 3 in. long, narrowly cylindrical at its base for the length of 1 in., funnel-shaped above, and costate, yellow below, dark purple within the mouth; segments unguiculate, broadly dolabriform, uncinately acute, of a pale rose-colour; stamens inserted in the constriction of the tube; anthers very elongated at the apex, and there spirally twisted together.

The plant is certainly not a *Dipladenia*.

6. CHARIOMMA VERTICILLATA, nob.: *Apocynum scandens, amplissimo flore luteo*; *Plumieria fol. ovato-oblongis*, Plum. Amer. i. p. 21, tab. 29: *Nerium oleander*, Lunan (in parte), Hort. Jam. ii. 181. In Jamaica: *non vidi*.

A handsome species, differing from all the preceding in its larger, verticillate leaves, and broad terminal corymb of several large handsome flowers. From Plumier's drawing, the stem has ternate branches, subscandent, with axils 4 in. apart; the lower leaves are opposite, the intermediate and terminal quaternately verticillate; they are ovato-elliptic, oblong, subobtuse at the base, terminated by a short acumen, rigid, with entire margins, and arcuately conjoined nerves patently divaricate, 3-4 in. long, 1$\frac{3}{8}$-1$\frac{3}{4}$ in. broad, on stout petioles 3 lines long; terminal panicle sessile, trifidly branching from its base, each branch on a peduncle ¾–1 in. long, bearing 3 yellow flowers, on pedicels 3 lines long, supported by linear bracts; sepals acutely oblong, 6 lines long; tube of corolla 2¾ in. long, narrowed below the middle, campanularly expanding above; segments rhomboidally dolabriform, 1¼ in. long and broad. There are indications in the rough drawing of the long setiform expansions of the anthers. According to Lunan, the leaves are poisonous and acrid, and the disk of 5 lobes tridentate at the apex.

7. CHARIOMMA SCANDENS, nob.: *Apocynum scandens flore nerii albo*, Plum. Descr. Plants Amer. p. 82, tab. 96. In insul. S. Domingo et Martinico: *non vidi*.

A lactescent, sarmentaceous shrub, with opposite cinereous branches 2 lines thick, with axils 4¼–5¼ in. apart; leaves opposite, oblong, gradually narrower towards the base and decurrent on the petiole, roundish above and suddenly terminating in a short mucronate point, entire, rigidly chartaceous, bright green above, with about 15 pairs of parallel patent arching nerves, darker beneath, 2¼–3½ in. long, 1¼–1¼ in. broad, on petioles 5–6 lines long; raceme lateral, on a peduncle ¾–1¼ in. long, bearing on its summit 3–4 verticillate flowers, or more often a solitary flower by abortion; bracts short, linear; pedicels 6 lines long; sepals oblong, subacute, 3 lines long; tube of corolla 2 in. long, contracted below the middle, funnel-shaped above, of a reddish colour; segments white, dolabriform, uncinate at one angle, 12 lines long, 9 lines broad; follicles terete, parallel, erect, acute, 8 in. long, 1½ line thick, subconjoined at the apex; seeds many, clothed on their surface with dark reddish soft hairs.

Although so little of the floral structure is known, it is manifest from its habit, its large handsome corolla like that of an oleander, with broad dolabriform segments uncinate on one angle, that it belongs to this genus, with which it agrees in the character of its follicles, as indicated by Swartz. The exserted appendages of the anthers are seen in Plumier's rough figure, by error 8 in number. It is a species evidently congeneric with his *Apocynum scandens*, last described.

ELYTROPUS.

A genus established in 1860, by Dr. Müller, upon the *Echites pubescens*, Hook. and Arn., a plant from Chile, and which comprises few species. These are mostly shrubs, with opposite, ovate or elliptic leaves, upon short petioles, and very short, few-flowered axillary panicles; they bear 2 compressed linear follicles, with several imbricated seeds, without any apical coma, which are much flattened, clothed above the middle with many ascending soft hairs, which extend far beyond the apex, and are peltately attached in the middle to intruding placentæ. Each seed contains an embryo in thin albumen, with foliaceous cotyledons, and a terete radicle of the same length.

1. ELYTROPUS PUBESCENS, nob.: *Echites pubescens*, Hook. & Arn. (non R. & Sch.) Bot. Beechy Voy. p. 34; Journ. Bot. i. 286: *Elytropus Chilensis*, Müll. (in parte), in Linn. xxx. 440. In Chile: *v. s. in herb. meo* (n. 20758), Valdivia (Bridges 661).

A species much stouter than the others following, which have been confounded with it. Its branches are brown, compressed, striate, glabrous, the younger branchlets puberulous; the axils are 1¼ in. apart; leaves ovate or ovate-oblong, roundish at the base, and subcordate, subacuminate, coriaceous, dark green above, corrugulate, glabrous, with slender immersed nerves, yellowish opake beneath, granulated midrib and nerves prominulent and pubescent, without apparent veins, 2–2¼ in. long, 1–1¼ in. broad, on stoutish pubescent petioles 2–3 lines long; racemes short, axillary, ¾ in. long, on a very short peduncle, bearing 2–3 alternate approximate flowers; pedicels very short, bracteolated; sepals obtusely oblong, pilose outside; corolla with a short tube; segments spathulately oblong, longer than the tube, with simple dextrorse convolution; stamens inserted near the base of the tube; anthers acuminate, with 2 basal aristate prongs; disk of 5 free, erect lobes, nearly as long as the 2 ovaries; 2 erect, terete follicles, pilose, 3½ in. long, the sutural margins introflexed and seminiferous; seeds oblong, compressed, with a small central hilum, furnished dorsally above the middle with dense erect hairs extending far beyond the summit.

A drawing of this species, with an analysis of its flower, fruit, and seeds, is shown in Plate XIV. A.

2. ELYTROPUS CHILENSIS, Müll. Bot. Zeit. 1860, p. 21, cum icone; Linn. xxx. 440: *Echites Chilensis*, A. DC. Prodr. viii. 468; Gay, Chile, iv. 387. In Chile: *v. s. in herb. meo* (n. 20337); ad Chillan (Germain, *in flore et fructu*).

A climbing species, near the preceding, but easily distinguished by the very dilated nodes of its branches, which are ¾ in. (sometimes 2 in.) apart; the branches are reddish brown and softly pubescent; leaves oblong-ovate, rounded at the base, gradually acute above the middle, rigidly chartaceous, with revolute margins, pale green above, sulcate along the nerves, the younger ones sparsely hirsute with hairs globose at the base, pallidly flavid beneath, very opake, subrugulous, midrib and nerves very prominent, and patently hirsute, 1¼–2¼ in. long, ⅝–1¼ in. broad, on stoutish, recurved, rigidly hirsute petioles 2–4 lines long; flowers geminate or solitary in the axils on patently pilose pedicels 3 lines long, each bearing 3 alternate acute bracteoles; sepals acute, pale green, pubescent, 3 lines long, 1⅓ line broad; corolla glabrous, with a cylindrical tube 2½ lines long; segments ovate, 4 lines long, 2½ lines broad, with simple dextrorse convolution; rest as in the preceding species; 2 follicles, parallelly erect, linear, compressed, subtorulose, flavidly pubescent, when not quite ripe 3 in. long, 1½ line broad, often conjoined at the apex.

3. ELYTROPUS PTARMICUS, nob.: *Echites Chilensis*, Müll. (in parte) *l. c.* p. 440: *Echites ptarmica*, Pöpp. Gen. iii. 69, tab. 278: *Vinca sternutatoria*, Pöpp. MS. *in herb.* Chile australis, ad Antuco (Pöppig): *non vidi.*

A low shrub, with several procumbent or scandent ramose hirsute branches, about 1 foot long; the oval leaves, obtuse or slightly cordate at the base, obtusely acute at the summit, pubescent beneath and hirsute along the midrib, are 2–3½ in. long, 1–1⅝ in. broad, on petioles 2–3 lines long; 1 or 2 flowers on a short axillary peduncle, with decussate oblong bractlets 1 line long; pedicels 1½ line long; sepals acutely oblong, subinequilateral, pubescent, ciliato-denticulate on the margins, 4 lines long; corolla 4 lines long, tubular, with a border of 5 ovate-oblong, nearly equilateral segments dextrorsely convolute in æstivation; stamens seated a little above the base of the tube on short pubescent filaments; anthers hairy behind, included, and nearly as long as the tube; disk of 5 obtusely ovate truncated lobes, as long as the ovaries; style short, incrassated at its summit by a cylindrical clavuncle, having a 5-cleft indusium at its base; stigmata 2, shortly rounded; 2 follicles, spreading, terete, pointed, glabrous outside. A species well known to the natives under the name of "quilmay," being used to produce sneezing.

4. ELYTROPUS HETEROPHYLLUS, nob.: *Elytropus Chilensis*, Müll. (in parte) *l. c.* p. 440: *Echites heterophyllus*, Miquel in Linn. xxv. 653. In Chile, prov. Valdivia (Lechler): *v. s. in herb. meo* (n. 7914), Chiloë (Capt. King).

Captain King's plant does not appear to differ from that of Lochler, as described by Miquel. The branches are dark red, terete, scabridly granulous, not dilated at the axils, which are 1-1½ in. apart; leaves opposite, in equal pairs, but the pairs vary in size, the lower ones largest, they are elliptic, narrower and obtuse at the base, acuminate and mucronate at the summit, rigidly chartaceous, with very revolute margins, green above, glabrous, subrugulous, flavidly opake beneath, punctate-rugulous, hairy on the midrib and 8 pairs of ascending prominulent nerves, scabridulous to the touch; the pairs of leaves are respectively 2⅞, 1¾ in. long, 6, 11 lines broad, on slender, patent, puberulous petioles 4-6 lines long; flowers solitary in the opposite axils, on slender pedicels 4-6 lines long, each bearing about 3 pairs of opposite bracteoles; sepals linear, acute, very membranaceous, subglabrous, or ciliolate, 2½ lines long, ¾ line broad, with alternate acute inner scales; tube of corolla 3½ lines long; segments oblong, 3½ lines long, 2 lines broad, with simple dextrorse convolution; rest as in the other species. Miquel attributes to it 2 follicles, erect, subtorulose, acute at each end, 3 in. long.

5. ELYTROPUS SPECTABILIS, nob.: *Echites spectabilis*, Stadelm. Bot. Zeit. 1841, Beibl. 44; A. DC. *l. c.* p. 462; Müll. *l. c.* p. 153. In Amazonas, Rio Negro et Rio Solimoës; in regione Japurensi: *non vidi.*

A plant evidently congeneric with the *Echites ptarmica* of Pöppig. It has a stoutish, terete, subtomentous trunk, with climbing thickish branchlets covered with fuscous pilose hairs, and with distant internodes; the opposite large leaves are oblong, slightly cordate at the base, with a short narrow acumen, membranaceous, of a dark olive hue, with subrevolute margins, opake on both sides, glabrous, with 10 pairs of divaricate nerves arcuately conjoined near the margins, without any apparent veins, 10-12 in. long, 4-5½ in. broad, on petioles 1⅔-2 in. long; inflorescence in opposite axils, as long as the petioles; peduncle 3 lines long, supporting 8 slender pedicels 5¾-7½ lines long, covered with from 16 to 20 linear-subulate bracts 3 lines long, the last 5 alternate with the sepals, all clothed with velvety tomentum, and terminated by a single flower, 2-2½ in. long; sepals linear-subulate, pubescent, 4-5 lines long, each with an internal basal tridentate scale; corolla white, with a cylindrical tube constricted below the middle, with a border of 5 expanded obliquely ovate segments, somewhat shorter than the tube, glabrous; disk of 5 erect lobes as long as the 2 ovaries; 2 straight erect follicles, 10 in. long, 3¾ lines broad; seeds scarcely observed. These characters are quite analogous to those of *Elytropus ptarmica*, differing in an inflorescence of 8 instead of 2 pedicellate flowers.

ERIADENIA*.

A peculiar genus, founded upon an erect shrub with opposite leaves, marked by immersed closely parallel nerves, as in *Nerium* and *Hancornia*. In habit and inflorescence it resembles *Rhodocalyx*, having rufescent sepals with parallel nerves, a long tubular corolla, its segments similarly contorse, sagittate anthers, a disk of 5 free fleshy lobes, a style with a similar clavuncle, follicles of the same shape and size; but it differs in many essential particulars, especially in the want of an apical coma in the seeds.

ERIADENIA, nob. *Sepala* 5, ovata, parallele nervosa, extus pilosa, singula squama lata ciliata 2–3-lacinulata intus munita. *Corolla* hypocrateriformis, tubo anguste cylindrico, longo, recto, utrinque glabro, intus paullo infra faucem glandulis 5 breviter oblongis donato, limbi segmentis 5, glandulis alternis, inæquilateris, trapezoideo-linearibus, tubo æquilongis, intus horizontaliter plicatis et dextrorsum convolutis. *Stamina* 5, paullissime supra basin tubi inserta, subsessilia; *antheræ* lineares, sagittatæ, apice longe cuspidatæ, imo tenuiter parallele 2-furcatæ, medio extus puberulæ, intus anguste 2-loculares. *Discus* 5-lobus, lobis liberis, erectis, ovatis, extus brevissime pilosis, margine crebre ciliatis. *Ovaria* 2, ovata, disco æquilonga, puberula. *Stylus* brevissimus, subvalidus, striatus, 2-sulcatus, apice clavuncula conica 10-sulcata imo 5-dentatim expansa incrassato; *stigmata* 2, acute linearia, foliacea, erecta. *Folliculi* 2, tereti-cylindrici, subcurvati, subtorulosi; *semina* pauca, compressissima, lineari-oblonga, apice rostrata, subimbricata, *hilo* parvo centrali peltatim affixa, pilis rufulis rigidis densissime patentim villosa.

Frutex Peruvianus; folia opposita, ovata, patentissime et parallele nervosa, petiolata; inflorescentia *extraaxillaris, racemosa;* pedicelli *alterni, bracteolati;* flores *majusculi, rubri.*

ERIADENIA OBOVATA, nob.: ramulis subfistulosis, erectis, angulato-sulcatis, epidermide tenui laxa striata: foliis oppositis, cuneato-obovatis, apice rotundatis, et in acumen mucroniforme obtusum repente constrictis, coriaceis, marginibus integris revolutis, supra profunde viridibus, subnitentibus, nervis patentissimis crebre parallelis utrinque omnino immersis, costa sulcata, subtus flavide opacis, costa prominente; petiolo canaliculato, quam limbus 8plo breviore: racemo laterali; pedunculo foliis dimidio breviore; pedicellis circa 8, alternis, imo bracteolatis, calyce 2plo longioribus; sepalis brevibus, obtuse oblongis, extus puberulis, marginibus glabris et membranaceis; corolla hypocrateriformi; tubo longe cylindrico; segmentis 5, imo trapezoideis, medio mucronatis, dein lineariexpansis, tubo subæquilongis, rubris: cæt. ut in char. generico. In Peruvia alta: *v. s. in herb. meo et alior.* Tarapota (Spruce 4303).

Its straight branchlets have axils 1 in. apart; the leaves are 2½–3 in. long, 1¼–1¾ in. broad, on rather slender petioles 4 lines long, united transversely by a line on each side; the peduncle is about 1¼ in. long, bearing about 8 or 10 alternate flowers on pedicels 5 lines long, each with an acute ovate bract two thirds of its length; the sepals are 2 lines long; the tube of the corolla 12 lines long, 1½ line broad; segments 11 lines

* Ab ἔριον (*lana*), ἀδήν (*glandula*), from its hairy disk.

long, 3 lines broad at the base, 1 line broad beyond the middle; the glands in the throat are ½ line long; the stamens, 4 lines long, are seated 1 line above the base of the tube; the lobes of the disk and ovaries are 1¼ line long, the style and stigmata 2 lines long; the follicles are 4 in. long, the pericarp subcoriaceous, pale within, with many parallel nerves, impressed where the seeds make it somewhat torulose; the seeds are linear-oblong, rostrate, 7 lines long, densely covered on both sides by reddish long hairs spreading in all directions, but without any apical coma.

A drawing of this species (with an analysis of its flower, fruit and seeds) is given in Plate XIV. B.

RHABDADENIA.

A very peculiar genus, established by Dr. Müller in 1860, upon two Brazilian plants, one collected by Pohl on the coasts of S. Brazil, the other the *Echites biflora* of Jacquin, which he confounded with *Echites paludosa*, a distinct species, well described and figured by Vahl. Dr. Grisebach regarded *Rhabdadenia* as identical with *Laubertia* A. DC., a very distinct genus. The generic character is detailed in Prof. Müller's monograph, and the typical species well analyzed in his plate 52. Its most peculiar character lies in the structure of the seed, which has no coma properly speaking, as in the *Echiteæ*; but the apex of the testa is prolonged into a slender tubular rostrum two-thirds of its length, and is further lengthened by long setaceous erecto-divergent fine hairs, which spring from this rostrum everywhere, from the base to the apex, as in a feather. This brings the genus near *Robbia*, which, though furnished with a brush of long silky hairs issuing from below the apex, has no such rostrum.

Other very distinctive characters reside in the habit of the plants, and in the very peculiar kind of inflorescence. The branches are erect, and subscandent, sometimes spirally twining; the opposite leaves somewhat distant, not very large, often cordate at the base, upon shortish petioles; the lateral axillary inflorescence has a long slender peduncle, bearing on its apex 2 shortish pedicels, each supporting a single handsome flower; sometimes this peduncle is 2-fid, each branch bearing 2 similar pedicellate flowers; and rarely one of the pedicels falls off, leaving a 3-flowered panicle; rarely the common peduncle has 2 or more short branches, each bearing geminate pedicellate flowers: in all cases these branches or pedicels have no bracts, or, seldom, a few rudiments of them*. The sepals are small, lanceolate or oblong, bearing within, at the base of each, 2 or 3 acute scales. The corolla is contracted at the base to a narrow cylindrical tube, above which it is much more broadly cylindrical or funnel-shaped, with a border of ovate dolabriform segments, simply convolute dextrorsely in æstivation; stamens seated in the contraction of the tube, upon short filaments pilose behind; the corneous connectives of the anthers are shortly 2-lobed at the base, with a long pointed apex, and pilose behind; disk of 5 erect, oblong, fleshy, free lobes, rounded or emarginate at the apex, very shortly connate at the base; 2 free ovaries about their length;

---

* Dr. Müller, in obscure terms, describes this peculiar kind of inflorescence, "sub-umbellato-contracta, oligantha, vel laxius bostrycina."

style shortly bifid at the base, very slender above; clavuncle oblong, cylindrical, incrassated, 5-grooved and nectariferous, somewhat fimbriated at its apex, having at its base a broad umbraculiform appendage; stigma of 2 short oval lobes at the apex; 2 follicles, straight, terete, suberect or horizontally divaricate, dehiscing along each ventral suture, which is inwardly inflected along the margins, forming 2 linear coriaceous placentæ; seeds numerous, fusiformly linear, compressed, with a small central hilum upon one face, and having at the apex the long, peculiar, brush-shaped rostrum, as before described; the embryo imbedded in waxy albumen, is teretely cylindrical, with 2 cotyledons many times shorter than the superior radicle, and nearly of the same thickness.

The following appears to me a correct list of the genuine species, after the rejection of some others enumerated by authors.

1. RHABDADENIA POHLII, Müll. Fl. Bras. *t. c.* p. 174, tab. 52. In Brasilia, prov. Rio de Janeiro: *v. v. et sicc. in herb. meo* (n. 3437 et 4024). Magé: *v. s. in hb. Mus. Brit.* Magé (Gardner 536). I have not seen its fruit, which is well depicted by Müller.

A low shrub, with slender twining branches, with opposite, spreading, acutely lanceolate leaves, narrowly cordate at the base, 2¾ in. long, 7 lines broad, on a slender petiole 3 lines long; inflorescence lateral at each axil, on a very slender peduncle 3 in. long, bearing 2 slender pedicels 3 lines long, 2-bracteolate at their base, each supporting a single purple flower; sepals acutely linear, 3½ lines long, each with 3 acute distinct scales subconnate at the base (not deficient according to Müller); the contracted portion of the tube of the corolla is 5 lines long, 1 line broad, suddenly swelling into an almost cylindrical form, 1¼ in. long, 6 lines in diameter; segments dolabriform, 9 lines long and broad, mucronate at the apex, simply convolute dextrorsely in æstivation; stamens inserted in the contracted portion of the tube; anthers broadly bifid and acute at the base; disk of 5 erect, free, obtuse, oblong lobes, somewhat shorter than the 2 free ovaries; style slender, expanded at the apex into a thick, 5-grooved, 5-glandular clavuncle, furnished at its base with a broad membranaceous umbraculiform appendage: the 2 terete divergent follicles, as figured by Müller, are 3¾ in. long, 2 lines thick; seeds 9 lines long, with the addition of a brush-like rostrum of twice that length.

2. RHABDADENIA PALUDOSA, nob.: *Echites paludosa*, Vahl (non H. B. K., nec Don, nec Griseb.), Eclog. ii. p. 19, Icon. tab. 5; A. DC. *l. c.* p. 467. In Brasilia septentrionali (Van Rohr): *v. s. in herb. meo, et Mus. Brit.* Maranhão (Gardner 6060).

Van Rohr collected plants in all the provinces of Guiana, including that of Brazil; and Maranhão may be said to be within the same floral region. Gardner's specimen well accords, in every respect, with the good description and drawing of Vahl, taken from Van Rohr's plant, and is unquestionably a *Rhabdadenia*. I have alluded to Grisebach's plant under the name of *Echites paludosa* Vahl, when describing *Rhabdadenia nervosa*. Müller wrongly refers Gardner's plant to *Rhabdadenia biflora*, certainly a very different species.

This is a small shrub, with erect, slender, virgate, striate branches, whose dilated axils are 1¼–2 in. apart; the opposite leaves are erect, lanceolate-oblong, acute at the base, sharply mucronulate, opake, rubescent or cinnamon-coloured above, paler beneath, with subimmersed midrib and nerves, 2–3 in. long, 4–9 lines broad, on slender petioles 3 lines long; the peduncle of the axillary inflorescence is simple, erect, 2 in. long, or longer, bearing 2 suberect pedicels 5–8 lines long; sepals acute, 1 line long; corolla altogether 1¾ in. long, the contracted portion of the tube 6 lines long, at which height the stamens are inserted, the upper portion of the tube is of the same length, funnel-shaped, and 5 lines broad in the mouth; the segments dolabriform, mucronate at the apex, 9 lines long, 4 lines broad, with dextrorse convolution; stamens inserted in the constriction of the tube on a pilose ring; anthers cohering, 2 lines long, obtusely bifid at the base; disk of 5 fleshy, obtuse, erect lobes scarcely conjoined at the base, as long as the 2 free ovaries; follicles 2, suberect, supported by the persistent calyx, terete, 2½ in. long, 1½ line thick; seeds slender, fusiform, striolate, ½ line broad in the middle, 13–15 lines long, independently of their apical rostrum, which is 12 lines long, and is furnished from the bottom to the top with long, penniform, crowded, silky hairs, without any apical coma.

A drawing of this species, exhibiting the peculiar structure of the seed, is given in Plate XV. A.

3. RHABDADENIA LAXIFLORA, nob.: *Echites suberecta*, Grisebach (non Jacq. nec Sw.) in parte, Pl. Cub. Wr. p. 520; Cat. Pl. Cub. p. 171, n. 43; Revis. Cat. Pl. Cub. n. 1890. In Antillis: *v. s. in herb. Mus. Brit.* Cuba (C. Wright 400, sub *Echites suberecta*, Jacq.).

A plant unquestionably belonging to *Rhabdadenia*, and generically distinct from either of the species described by Jacquin and Swartz. Its branches are somewhat slender, branching, terete, pubescent, with axils ¾–1 in. apart; opposite leaves oblong-ovate, obtusely roundish at the base, rounded and frequently mucronulate by the shortly excurrent nerve, entire, chartaceous, darkish green of a rufescent hue above, opake, obsoletely puberulous, sulcate along the midrib, with 5 pairs of divergent, arching, semi-immersed nerves, with others shorter and intermediate, and finely reticulated veins, whitish yellow beneath, opake, subvelutinous, with reddish costa, nerves, and fine reticulations, 1¾–2 in. long, ⅞–1 in. broad, on channelled pubescent petioles 1½ line long; racemes axillary, solitary at the nodes, about 5 in. long, on an erect peduncle, bare at its base for 2½ in., bearing upwards about 5 alternate flowers, on pubescent stoutish pedicels 6 lines long, at intervals of 6 lines, supported by lanceolate bracteoles 1¼ line long; sepals lanceolate-acuminate, erect, membranaceous, puberulous, reddish, 4 lines long, ¾ line broad at the base, with 3 short acute inner scales; corolla handsome, of a reddish hue; tube 1¼ in. long, narrowed at the base for 5 lines, broadly cylindrical above and 4 lines broad, slightly pubescent outside, glabrous within; segments dolabriform, 9 lines long, 6 lines broad, dextrorsely convolute; stamens seated in the contraction of the tube; filaments membranaceous, glabrous, 1 line long; anthers ⅘ lines long, acuminate, with 2 acute, incurved, subparallel basal prongs; disk of 5 fleshy, oblong, truncated lobes, concealing the 2 ovaries; style slender, 4 lines long; clavuncle incrassate, with a basal peltate membrane; stigmata very short; 2 follicles, suberect, subincurved, terete, smooth, 5–6 in. long; seeds linear, 4 lines long, continued by a very slender rostrum 3½ lines long, which is plumosely covered by fine silky hairs 3–6 lines long.

4. **RHABDADENIA BIFLORA**, Müll. Fl. Bras. *t. c.* p. 175: *Echites biflora*, Jacq. Amer. p. 30, tab. 21; A. DC. Prodr. viii. p. 450; Griseb. Fl. Br. W. Ind. p. 415: *Echites Ehrenbergii*, Schlect. Linn. xxvi. 666: *Rhabdadenia Ehrenbergii*, Müll. Linn. xxx. 454. In America tropicali: *v. s. in hb. Mus. Brit.* ins. Carib. (Jacquin, typ.); Cayenne (Sagot 387); Manglares de Sisal (Schott 812); Jamaica (Dr. Wright).

A shrub, yielding a lactescent juice, with scandent, slender, fistulous branches, often climbing to a height of 20 feet; branches with axils 2–3 in. apart; leaves very patent, obovate, acute at the base, rounded and mucronate at the apex, 2–3 in. long, 1–1½ in. broad, on petioles 4–6 lines long; the peduncle of the axillary inflorescence is 6 lines long, bearing 2 apical pedicels 6 lines long, supported by acute bracteoles; sepals subequal, oval, 3 lines long, 2 lines broad, marked by parallel nerves and reticulated veins; the contracted portion of the tube of the corolla is 8 lines long, above it is funnel-shaped and 8 lines long, 6 lines broad in the mouth; segments dolabriform, 9 lines long, 7 lines broad, with simple dextrorse convolution; stamens seated on a pilose ring in the mouth of the contracted portion of the tube; filaments short, partially adnate; anthers obtusely bifid at the base, acute and pilose at the apex; disk of 5 erect ovate lobes, scarcely connate at the base, as long as the 2 free ovaries; style slender; clavuncle ovate, 5-angular, 5-glandular, expanded at its base into a membranaceous umbraculiform appendage; 2 stigmata, small, terminal; 2 follicles, terete, suberect, 3½ in. long, 2 lines thick, subcohering at the summit; seeds linear, terminated at the apex by a long brush-shaped caudal rostrum, as in *Rh. Pohlii*.

5. **RHABDADENIA CAMPESTRIS**, nob.: *Echites campestris*, Vell. Flor. Flum. p. 113, Icon. iii. tab. 43; A. DC. Prodr. viii. 475: *Amblyanthera campestris*, Müll. *l. c.* p. 149. Brasilia, prov. Rio de Janeiro (Velloz, in apricis): *non vidi*.

This is a subscandent species, with stoutish branches, and axils 2 in. apart; leaves elliptic, gradually acute towards the summit, narrower below the middle, rounded or obsoletely cordate at the base, hirsute above, pubescent beneath, 4–5 in. long, 2–2¾ in. broad, on petioles 3 lines long; the inflorescence is terminal at the end of very young branchlets, consisting of a stoutish pubescent peduncle 4 lines long, bearing a single sessile orange-coloured flower; the sepals are lanceolate, pubescent, 6 lines long; the funnel-shaped tube of the corolla is contracted cylindrically at the base to a diameter of 3 lines, swelling upwards to the mouth, which is 6 lines broad, and is 1½ in. long, pubescent outside; segments obliquely rounded, 11 lines long and broad, dextrorsely convolute; the 5 lobes of the disk are free, nearly as long as the ovaries.

6. **RHABDADENIA MADIDA**, nob.: *Echites madida*, Vell. Fl. Flum. 112, Icon. iii. tab. 42; A. DC. *l. c.* p. 474: *Amblyanthera madida*, Müll. *l. c.* p. 150. In Brasilia, prov. Rio de Janeiro australiore in via Paciencia ad San Paulo tendens (Velloz, in sylvis madidis): *non vidi*.

A species, without doubt, belonging to this genus, and near *R. Pohlii*, differing in its broader leaves and solitary flower. In the latter species the basal lobes of the leaves overlap one another, hiding the sinus; in this species these lobes are rounder and broadly gaping. It is a climbing glabrous plant, with slender twining branches, having its axils about 3 in. apart; the leaves are oblong, broadly cordate at the base, and terminate in a shortish obtuse acumen; they have about 12 pairs of divergent nerves, are 3–3¾ in. long, 1–1¼ in. broad, on spreading slender petioles 3–4 lines long; the inflorescence consists of a single flower, solitary in each axil, on a slender erect peduncle 2 in. long, with a terminal pedicel 3 lines long, supported by a linear bracteole 2½ lines long; sepals acute, 3 lines long; corolla of a purplish red colour, glabrous; tube 1¼ in. long, cylindrically narrowed at its base for 8 lines, funnel-shaped above, 7 lines broad in the mouth; segments obtusely dolabriform, 6 lines long and broad, dextrorsely convolute; stamens included and inserted in the constriction of the tube; anthers cohering in a cone: the rest as in *R. Pohlii.*

7. RHABDADENIA NERVOSA, nob.: *Apocynum nervosum,* Miller, Dict. (1768) n. 9: *Echites (Laubertia) paludosa,* Griseb. (non Vahl) in Flor. Brit. W. Ind. p. 415. In Antillis et America tropicali, sec. Griseb. in Cat. Pl. Cub. C. Wright, 33 (Wright 2954); in Revis. ejusd. Cat. 1885 (C. Wright 2954): *v. s. in herb. Mus. Brit.* Carthagena (specim. typ. *ex herb. Miller*).

This is evidently the same species, with oval mucronulate leaves, described by Grisebach as the "*Echites paludosa,* Vahl," a blunder scarcely exceeded by any of the several errors of the former author in his enumeration of the apocyneous plants of the Antilles. It is difficult to understand how so glaring a mistake could have been made; for Vahl's excellent description and drawing are so precise, that no botanist ought to have erred on the subject.

Apparently an erect shrub, with subscandent branches, the axils being 1½–2 in. apart; the opposite leaves are ovate-oblong, obtuse (often oblique) at the base, broadly rounded at the summit, frequently emarginated, always suddenly mucronulate, thinly chartaceous, with scarcely revolute margins, very opake above, subferruginous, sulcated along the midrib, with very slender immersed nerves, opake and darkly ochraceous beneath, with blackish nerves scarcely prominulent, 1¾–3½ in. long, ¾–1¾ in. broad, on slender, straight, channelled petioles 4–9 lines long; raceme terminal, on a peduncle 3–4 in. long, bearing about 5 alternate flowers on slender pedicels 4–6 lines long, each with a slender linear basal bracteole; sepals linear-oblong, with parallel nerves, 2–2½ lines long, ¼ line broad; a handsome yellow corolla; tube 1¾ in. long, narrowed cylindrically at its base for 9 lines, funnel-shaped above; segments dolabriform, 9 lines long: the rest as in *R. Pohlii.*

8. RHABDADENIA CORDATA, nob.: *Apocynum cordatum,* Miller, Dict. (1768) n. 10; Houston, Icon. n. 8, pl. 44. fig. 5, 10 et 11; A. DC. *l. c.* p. 440: *Periploca scandens,* Miller, Dict. n. 10. Vera Cruz: *v. s. in herb. Mus. Brit.* (specim. in hort. Milleri cult. ex pl. ab Houstonio introducta) in fructu.

The above specimen undoubtedly belongs to *Rhabdadenia.* The slender subscandent pale brown branch has its axils 2½ in. apart; the leaves are oblong, roundish and obsoletely cordate at the base, rounded and mucronulate at the apex, entire, with subrevolute margins, dark green above, with immersed nerves, yellowish opake beneath, with scarcely prominulent nerves, 2½ in. long, 1 in. broad, on slender petioles 4 lines long; inflorescence axillary, with a terete peduncle half as long as the leaves, bearing

2 flowers on pedicels one third of its length; flowers large, yellow; sepals small, acute; tube of corolla narrowly cylindrical below for one third of its length, suddenly campanulate above; segments half as long as the tube, expanded, inequilaterally oblong; fructiferous peduncle 6 lines long, the pedicels 3 lines long; the persistent sepals 1¼ line long; 2 terete follicles acute at both ends, very divaricate, subreflected, 4½ in. long, 3 lines broad in the middle; seeds like those of *R. Pohlii.*

9. **Rhabdadenia macrostoma,** Müll. Linn. xxx. 435: *Echites macrostoma,* Benth. in Hook. Journ. Bot. iii. p. 248; A. DC. Prodr. viii. 453. In Guiana Brit. et Surinam (Schomb. 329 and 556): *non vidi.*

A scandent plant with oval mucronulate leaves, obsoletely pubescent above, rufescently tomentellous beneath, 1½–3½ in. long, 10–18 lines broad, on petioles 2–3 lines long; peduncle of the axillary inflorescence longer than the leaves, often bearing 2 flowers on pedicels 2–3 lines long; sepals linear-subulate, 1½ line long, reflexed; corolla rose-coloured; contracted portion of tube 6 lines long, inflated portion 20 lines long, 8 lines broad, subcylindrical; segments broad; stamens inserted in a pilose ring at the sudden contraction of the tube; disk of 5 free, erect lobes, as long as the 2 ovaries; follicles terete, 4 in. long.

Müller states that the sepals have no inner basal scales.

10. **Rhabdadenia barbata,** nob.: *Echites barbata,* Desv. Prodr. Pl. Ind. Occid. p. 416 ; A. DC. *l. c.* p. 453: *Urechites barbata,* Müll. Linn. xxx. 447: *Echites (Urechites) barbata,* Griseb. Fl. Br. W. Ind. p. 416. In Antillis: *non vidi.*

A species seen alone by Desvaux, and known to us only by his imperfect description. De Candolle did not see it; and the determinations of Müller and Grisebach are mere guesses, founded on a chance observation in the 'Prodromus.' From Desvaux's account the characters of the inflorescence and the form of the corolla are certainly more in accord with those of *Rhabdadenia* than of *Urechites.* It is an erect shrub, with pubescent branches; the leaves are obovate, submucronate, glabrous, with distant oblique nerves; panicle on a long peduncle supporting few flowers; sepals subulate, pilose; tube of corolla barbately pilose, narrow below for the length of the calyx, thence swelling upwards.

11. **Rhabdadenia ? lucida,** nob.: *Echites lucida,* R. & Sch. Syst. iv. 796; A. DC. *l. c.* p. 475: *Odontadenia lucida,* Müll. *l. c.* p. 120 in adnot, et in Linn. xxx. p. 453. In Orinoco: *non vidi.*

Apparently a scandent plant from Willdenow's herbarium; leaves elliptic-oblong, subcordate at the base, obtuse at the summit, lucid above; inflorescence a solitary flower, on an elongated pedicel, as in the *Echites madida,* Vell. Icon. iii. tab. 42, and as sometimes occurs in *R. Pohlii.*

Species excluded:—

R. *Sagræi,* Müll. Linn. xxx. 435, 447; *Echites Sagræi,* A. DC. *l. c.* p. 456 . . . . = *Angadenia Sagræi.*

R. Cubensis, Müll. *l. c.* p. 435 (Linden 1716) . . = *Angadenia Havanensis.*
R. Lindeniana, Müll. *l. c.* p. 437 (Linden 1700-
    1823) . . . . *Angadenia Lindeniana.*
R. Wrightiana, Müll. *l. c.* p. 438 (C. Wright 399)   *Angadenia Valenzuelana.*
R. Berterii, Müll. *l. c.* p. 446; Linn. xxvi. 665;
    A. DC. *l. c.* p. 447 . . . . *Angadenia Berterii.*

LAUBERTIA.

A genus established by Prof. De Candolle in 1844, upon a single Peruvian species. This is a climbing plant, with terete branches, opposite or ternately verticillate leaves, ovate-elliptic, acuminate, obtuse at the base, obliquely penninerved, 4 in. long, 1½ in. broad, on petioles 5 lines long. It has a terminal inflorescence upon a long peduncle, bearing many alternate flowers on pedicels ½ in. long; 5 sepals, without inner scales; tube of corolla 9 lines long, cylindrical for the length of 6 lines, swelling above; segments dolabriform, 3 lines long, with sinistrorse convolution; stamens seated on the contraction of the tube, the anthers acuminate, extending beyond the mouth, bidentate at the base; disk urceolate, as long as the 2 free ovaries, subcrenulate on the margin, unequally and shortly cleft in one or two places; style simple; clavuncle subcapitate, with a basal undulated membranaceous expansion; 2 slender follicles, 18 in. long, 1-2 lines thick, containing many seeds 12 lines long, rostrate at their apex for ¼ of their length, and there densely and plumosely furnished with long hairs, as in *Rhabdadenia*, the hairs extending 1 in. above the apex, which has no real coma. The species which bears the specific name *Boissieri*, was found in the herbarium of Pavon, without mention of its locality.

The species of *Laubertia* enumerated by Grisebach all belong to *Rhabdadenia* or *Angadenia.*

URECHITES.

A genus established by Müller in 1860 [*]; but no figured analysis has been given of it. The origin of the generic name is not stated; and there is nothing in its structure that can explain this ambiguity. He describes three Mexican species, and a fourth from the West Indies, the *Echites suberecta* of Jacquin (not of Swartz and Andrews). The fruit consists of 2 curving follicles, as figured by Jacquin, who simply describes the seeds as oblong, and acute at both ends; by Müller these are said to be linear, ovoid, imbricate, acuminate, costate, pilose all over, the superior hairs far extended beyond a slender rostrum, from which they chiefly originate pinnately, as in a feather, after the manner seen in *Rhabdadenia*; the seeds were too immature to show the embryo. The numerous seeds, in the language of Müller, are "in placenta demum membranacea plurilamellosa numerosa, quibus junctæ sunt squamulæ tot quot semina peculiares cymbi-

[*] Bot. Zeit. 1860, p. 23.

formes, utrinque longe subulato-acuminatæ, glabræ, in quibus semina ipsa nidulantur anguste lineari-ovoidea, apice acuminata, basi rotundiora, tota superficie dense sericeo-pilosa, et longitrorsum pluricostulata, ad apicem radicularem sericeo-comosa; coma longius breviusve stipitata, cum spermadermio haud articulata."

There is one important omission in these circumstantial details, no mention being made of the manner of attachment of the seeds, whether suspended by a funicle, as in *Stipecoma*, or peltately affixed by a central hilum, as in *Rhabdadenia*. We may fairly incline to the latter view, because Müller thus describes the ovules in each ovary, " amphitropa, in placenta ventrali lamelloso-bifida, pluriserialia." The above mode of placentation is quite unexampled; and we have no reason to doubt the correctness of such minute details. Perhaps some degree of analogy may exist in the processes I have described in the placenta of *Stipecoma*.

Messrs. Bentham and Hooker, after an interval of sixteen years, are the only botanists who have acknowledged this genus (Gen. ii. 727); but in their diagnosis they singularly omit all mention of the extraordinary placentation of the fruit; they merely describe the seeds as having a plumose rostrum.

1. URECHITES KARWINSKII, Müll. Linn. xxx. 440. In Mexico: *non vidi*.

2. URECHITES ANDRIEUXII, Müll. *l. c.* p. 442. In Mexico: *non vidi*.

3. URECHITES SUBERECTA, Müll. *l. c.* p. 444: *Echites suberecta*, Linn., Jacq. Am. p. 82, tab. 26 (non Sw. nec Andr.); A. DC. *l. c.* p. 453; Schlect. Linn. xxvi. 666: *Laubertia urechites* (*Echites suberecta*), Griseb. Fl. Brit. W. Ind. p. 415. In Jamaica et San Domingo: *non vidi*.

A plant full of milky juice, 10 feet high when supported by other bushes, but in the open fields scarcely more than 1 to 3 feet in height. It has slender branches, with axils ¾–1 in. apart; opposite leaves ovate-elliptic, subacute at the base, summits rounded and mucronate, glabrous, sometimes scabrous beneath, 1¾–2¼ in. long, ⅞–1 in. broad, on petioles 1 line long; panicle subterminal, 1½ in. long; peduncle 8 lines long, branched, few-flowered; pedicels 6 lines long, pilose, with small lanceolate bracts; sepals subulately lanceolate, pilose outside, deciduous, 4 lines long, 2 lines broad, sparsely pilose outside, with a few pointed basal scales; corolla 1½ in. long; tube below narrowly cylindrical, 1 line broad for the length of 4 lines, thence suddenly enlarging in a cylindrical form and 4 lines broad; segments glabrous, dolabriform, 8 lines long, 7 lines broad; stamens seated in the contraction of the tube in a pilose ring, the filaments being short and glabrous; anthers acute at the summit, shortly 2-lobed (not aristate) at the base, lobes obtuse, incurved, and they are slightly scabrous on the back; disk of 5 ovate fleshy emarginated lobes, as long as the 2 free ovaries; style slender, shortly bifid at the base, clavuncle thickened, 5-grooved, glandular, with a basal membranaceous peltiform appendage; 2 stigmata, short and terminal; 2 follicles, erect, slender, subincurved, fuscous, 4 in. long, 2 lines thick. The peculiar placentation and structure of the seeds are fully described above, as quoted from Müller.

This species has been confounded by most botanists with the *Echites suberecta*, Swartz and Andr. (non Jacq.); Swartz (Observ. p. 104) makes the same mistake; Hook. and

Benth. (Gen. ii. 728) do the same. Swartz and Andrews's plant, the *Neriandra suberecta* of A. DC. is here referred to my genus *Chariomma* (see p. 111).

Species excluded:—

Urechites Jægeri, Müll. Linn. xxx. 442.	= *Laseguea Jægeri*.
U. Domingensis, Müll. *l. c.* 447	*Chariomma Domingensis*.
U. barbata, Müll. *l. c.* 447	*Rhabdadenia barbata*.
U. Neriandra, Griseb. Fl. Br. W. Ind. p. 415 . .	*Chariomma surrecta*.

ODONTADENIA.

A genus established by Mr. Bentham in 1841*, who placed it in the tribe *Plumerieæ*; he did not find ripe seeds in the fruit examined by him. Prof. De Candolle arranged the genus in the *Tabernæmontaneæ*, between *Bonafousia* and *Peschiera*†. Dr. Müller located it in the *Echiteæ*, next to *Anisolobus*‡, but afterwards he made it a section of *Tabernæmontana* §. It must, however, be placed in a very different position, on account of its long anatropus seeds, which have neither a pulpy funicle nor a coma. A distinguishing feature among its many peculiar floral characters is the disk, which is conically cylindrical, fleshy, divided halfway into 5 erect lobes, which are again cleft into 2 to 5. obtuse teeth. The fruit consists of 2 (or more often, by abortion, 1 only) oblong, stoutish follicles, containing each about 100 long, terete seeds, without any apical coma, imbricatively erect, attached by a small basal hilum to 2 septiform membranaceous placentas extending halfway across the cell. The embryo is encased in a thin corneous albumen, has 2 linear narrow cotyledons with a terete radicle one tenth of their length, which points to the basal hilum.

As several heterogeneous species have been recorded which ought to be excluded, I will here enumerate only those which legitimately belong to the genus.

1. ODONTADENIA SPECIOSA, Benth. Hook. Journ. Bot. iii. 240; Müll. (in parte) Fl. Bras. *t. c.* p. 117; A. DC. Prodr. viii. 360. In Guiana: *v. s. in hb. Mus. Brit.* Berbice (Schomb. 309).

A handsome species, with stoutish terete branches with axils 2-2½ in. apart; leaves oblong-lanceolate, subacute towards the base, gradually narrowing above acuminately, margins undulated, subrevolute, chartaceous, dark green above, quite glabrous, patently spreading, with about 16 pairs of fine yellow nerves running straight to the margin, hepatic brownish beneath, opake, with an elevated striolate midrib and prominent nerves with obsolete veins, 6 in. (or more) long, 2-2½ in. broad, on rather slender channelled petioles 5-6 lines long; panicles axillary or terminal; pedicels 6-8 lines long; sepals 4 lines long, spreading, obtusely broad, with waving membranaceous margins; corolla 2 in. long; tube 1¼ in. long, ventricose at the base for 4 lines below the constriction, broadly campanulate above, glabrous; segments oblong, spread-

* Hook. Journ. Bot. iii. 242. † Prodr. viii. 359.
‡ Mart. Flor. Bras. fasc. xxvi. 116. § Linn. xxx. 402.

ing to a diameter of more than 2 in.; stamens inserted in a pilose ring in the constriction of the tube; anthers 4 lines long, connivent, pilose with long white hairs behind and on the margins; disk of 5 subconnate lobes denticulate at the apex, longer than the 2 enclosed ovaries; styles free near their base, connate above; follicles 5 in. long, 1½ in. broad, tapering towards the summit; seeds, upwards of 100, linear oblong, 1¼ in. long in an unripe state.

2. ODONTADENIA GRANDIFLORA, nob.: *Odontadenia speciosa*, Müll. (in parte) *l. c.* p. 117: *Hæmadictyon grandiflorum*, A. DC. (non Griseb.) *l. c.* p. 426: *Echites grandiflora*, Mey. Esseq. p. 131: *Echites insignis*, Spr. Syst. i. 632: *Echites Meyeriana*, R. & Sch.: *Echites macrantha*, R. & Sch. Syst. iv. 793. In Guiana, Para et Panama: *v. pl. s. et fruct. in herb. Mus. Brit.* Panama (Hayes, *in flore*), ins. Mechiana, Pará (J. G. Smith, *fruct. solus*).

A climbing species, with terete, smooth branches, having axils 1½–2 in. apart; opposite leaves, broadly obovate, shortly narrowing at the base, obtuse at the apex, very glabrous, entire, with prominent nerves, and handsomely reticulated veins, 6 in. long, 4–5 in. broad, on petioles 11 lines long; panicle axillary, branched, shorter than the leaves, many-flowered, pedicels spreading, 3-bracteolate at the base, each supporting a single large flower; sepals roundly ovate, imbricated, 2 exterior somewhat larger; corolla 3 in. long, yellowish red; tube cylindrical, shortly swollen at the base below the constriction, and there obsoletely pentagonous, campanular above; segments obtusely oblong, spreading; stamens seated at the contraction of the tube, filaments very short, channelled; anthers linear lanceolate, connivent, sagittately 2-lobed at the base, glabrous behind, with a small tuft of hairs in the front, at the insertion of the filament; disk of 5 compressed dentate lobes, confluent at the base, enclosing 2 ovate ovaries; style shortish, bipartite at the base; clavuncle oblong, pentagonous, with a peltate membrane at the base; stigmata 2, short and distinct; follicle (I saw only a loose one) 6 in. long, 1¼ in. broad, opening by a ventral suture; pericarp thickish, coriaceous; placentas 2, distinct, submembranaceous, 6 lines broad, studded closely with cicatrices, denoting the points of attachment of the seeds; seeds very numerous, linearly terete, subincurved, erect, with a basal hilum, 2½–3 in. long, 2½ lines thick, obtusely pointed at the apex; testa rugulous, subcoriaceous, formed of fine transverse crystalline cells, showing on one side along its entire length, a narrow raphe containing many white spiral threads; inner integument thin and membranaceous, covering a thin pergameneous albumen 2¼ in. long; the embryo 1¾ in. long, has 2 flat linear cotyledons 18 lines long, 1 line broad, with a basal slender terete radicle 3 lines long.

This species, confounded with the preceding, is readily distinguished from it by having leaves twice as broad, obtuse (not acuminate) at the summit, by its petioles of twice the length, by its much larger corolla, and other particulars.

A drawing of it, and an analysis of its flower, fruit, and seeds, are given in Plate XVI., where the seeds in figs. 10 and 11 are thicker than they ought to be; in fig. 9 this is better shown.

3. ODONTADENIA FORMOSA, nob.: *Odontadenia grandiflora*, Miq. (non Mey.) Stirp. Surin. Sel. p. 166; Walp. Ann. iii. 35: ramulis pallidis, opacis, striolatis; foliis elliptico-oblongis, imo a medio cunea-

tim angustatis, apice in acumen longiuscule angustum obtusulum subito constrictis, chartaceis, marginibus subrevolutis, glaberrimis, supra pallidissimis, opacis, nervis tenuibus subprominulis, venis crebre transversis, subtus concoloribus, nervis venisque prominulis; petiolo subtenui, quam limbus 12plo breviore: racemis axillaribus, glabris, folio dimidio brevioribus; pedunculo alternatim plurifloro; floribus speciosis; pedicellis tenuibus, calyce 3plo longioribus; sepalis obtuse ovatis, marginibus membranaceis; corolla præcedentis; staminibus in constrictionem infra medium insertis; antheris anguste linearibus, subconniventibus, apice cuspidatis, imo longiuscule divergenti-biaristatis, per medium dorsi crebre patentim villosis; disco quam calyx dimidio breviore, fere ad basin 5-lobo, lobis 6-denticulatis, ovariis æquilongo. In Guiana et Surinam: *v. s. in herb. Mus. Brit.* Acaouari (Sagot 283).

A species differing from *O. speciosa* in its extremely pallid, oblong subcuneate leaves, with a long, narrow, obtusely linear acumen, and in its axils only 1 in. apart; the leaves are 6½–7 in. long (including the acumen 9 lines long), 2⅜–2¾ in. broad, on petioles 6–8 lines long; peduncle 1 in. long; slender pedicels 6–7 lines long; ovate sepals 2¼ lines long, 1¼ line broad; corolla 2½ in. long.

4. ODONTADENIA HARRISII, nob.: *Dipladenia Harrisii*, Purdie, in Hook. Bot. Mag. tab. 4825; Walp. Ann. v. 496: *Dipladenia Harrisonii*, Müll. Linn. xxx. 446: *Cycladenia Harrisonii*, Lemaire, in Van Houtte, Illust. Hort. (1855) Miscel. p. 7: *Odontadenia speciosa*, Griseb. (non Benth.), Fl. Brit. W. I. p. 416.

A magnificent cultivated species, much resembling *O. speciosa*. Its oblong leaves have a narrow obtuse acumen, become gradually narrower from the middle towards the base, where they are slightly cordate, have many diverging nerves, are 14 in. long, 5½ in. broad, on petioles 7 lines long; its panicle is copiously flowered; pedicels 6–8 lines long; sepals oval, subacute, 4 lines long; tube of corolla funnel-shaped, 2 in. long, widening in the mouth to a breadth of near 1 inch, the border expanding to a diameter of 3¼ in., the segments being dolabriform, dextrorsely convolute, 1⅛ in. long and broad; lobes of disk denticulate, enveloping the ovaries.

The following species should be excluded from the genus, and thus transferred:—

Odontadenia hypoglauca, Müll. Fl. Br. *l. c.* p. 118 = *Angadenia hypoglauca*.
O. hypoglauca, Müll. tab. 35 A, p. 118 . . . . *A. majuscula*.
O. nitida, Müll. p. 118 . . . . *A. nitida*.
O. cordata, A. DC. p. 360, Müll. *l. c.* p. 119 . . *A. nitida*.
O. Pöppigii, Müll. p. 119 . . . . *A. Pöppigii*.
O. geminata, Müll. (in parte) p. 119 . . . . . *A. geminata*.
O. geminata, var. *elegans*, Müll. p. 120 . . . . *A. elegans*.
O. coriacea, Müll. Linn. xxx. p. 450 . . . . . *A. coriacea*.
O. macrocalyx, Müll. Linn. xxx. p. 403 . . . *Codonemma macrocalyx*.
O. angustifolia, A. DC. p. 360 . . . . *Mitozus linearis*.
O. lucida, Müll. *l. c.* p. 120 . . . . *Rhabdadenia lucida*.
O. speciosa, Griseb. (non Benth.) *l. c.* p. 416 . . *Odontadenia Harrisii*.

MACROSIPHONIA.

Of this genus, one of the handsomest and most peculiar of the family, several species have been enumerated by different botanists, who have not been quite in accord respecting them. I will here, therefore, endeavour to point out those which may be received as valid species. On account of its very large flowers it is here placed at the head of the *Echiteæ*. From their hollow or herbaceous stems they are all (perhaps) annual plants, springing from a perennial tuberous rootstock.

1. MACROSIPHONIA VELAME, Müll. *l. c.* p. 138, tab. 42 : *Echites Velame*, St.-Hil. Mém. Mus. xii. 324 ; Stadelm. Bot. Zeit. 1341, Beibl. 61 ; A. DC. *l. c.* p. 471. In Brasilia, prov. Minas Geraës : *v. s. in herb. meo ex loc. cit.* (Claussen).

A species so-called from its vernacular name, derived from its velvety clothing. It has a tuberous perennial root, producing several (perhaps annual) erect, fistulous, woolly, simple stems, 1–2 feet high, with axils $\frac{3}{4}$–1 in. apart ; leaves elliptic-oblong, subcordate at the base, acute towards the apex, and mucronate, densely clothed above with white arachnoid hairs, and covered beneath with dense woolly, yellowish, long tomentum, undulate on the margins, 1$\frac{3}{8}$–2$\frac{1}{2}$ in. long, $\frac{5}{8}$–1$\frac{1}{2}$ in. broad, on woolly petioles 1 line long ; peduncle solitary in one of the upper axils, erect, stoutish, densely lanate, 1–2 in. long, supporting 2 flowers on pedicels 3 lines long, furnished at the base with a slender subulate bract 7 lines long ; sepals subulately linear, gradually broader at the base, with involute margins, tomentous outside, glabrous within, 9 lines long, each with 6–8 minute internal scales ; tube of corolla 3–4 in. long, narrowly cylindrical, densely tomentous, swollen above for $\frac{1}{4}$ of its length into a tubular expansion 5 lines broad, smooth inside, with 5 woolly lines below the contraction, upon which the stamens are inserted ; segments glabrous inside, woolly at the base outside, roundish, subspathulate, 1 in. long and broad, crenulately crispate on the margin ; disk of 5 oblong lobes, shorter than the 2 glabrous oblong ovaries ; 2 follicles, erect, terete, subtorulose, pilose, 8 in. long, 2 lines thick.

2. MACROSIPHONIA GUARANITICA, Müll. *l. c.* p. 139 : *Echites Guaranitica*, St.-Hil. Bull. Soc. Philom. 1824, p. 77 ; Mém. Mus. xii. 324 ; A. DC. *l. c.* p. 472 (in parte). In Brasilia, prov. Rio Grande, ad Missiones S. Francisco de Borja : *non vidi.*

A species much like the preceding. Its simple erect stems are covered with long, slender, entangled, white hairs ; leaves broadly ovate or oblong, subcordate at the base, shortly cuspidate and mucronate at the apex, margins scarcely revolute, subpilose above, incano-tomentous beneath, 1$\frac{1}{4}$–1$\frac{5}{8}$ in. long, 1–1$\frac{5}{8}$ in. broad, obsoletely petiolate ; raceme 1–5-flowered, on a peduncle often very long, all covered with arachnoid tomentum, bracts narrowly linear, 2–3 times shorter than the sepals ; sepals very narrow, linear, arachnoid, 6 or 7 times shorter than the tube of the corolla, villous within, with 2–6 basal scales ; tube of corolla slender for $\frac{5}{6}$ or $\frac{6}{7}$ of its length, the rest campanularly dilated ; segments obovate, as long as the swollen portion of the tube, crispate ; ovaries glabrous ; coma 3 times as long as the seeds.

3. MACROSIPHONIA LONGIFLORA, Müll. *l. c.* p. 140, tab. 48: *Echites longiflora*, Desf. Mém. Mus. v. 275, tab. 20; St.-Hil. Mém. Mus. xii. 324; Stadelm. Bot. Zeit. 1841, Beibl. 64; A. DC. *l. c.* p. 471; *Echites grandiflora*, Hook. Arn. (in parte), Jo. Bot. i. 286: *Echites augusta*, Vell. Flo. Flum. 114, Icon. iii. tab. 48. In Brasilia, confinibus prov. Rio de Janeiro, S. Paulo, et Minas: *v. s. in herb. meo*, Minas Geraës (Claussen).

This species has a thick rootstock, bearing several erect, simple, woolly, fistulous stems, 12–15 in. high, sometimes with 2 opposite lateral branches 6 in. long, with smaller leaves; axils $\frac{1}{2}$–1 in. apart; opposite leaves subimbricate, lanceolate-oblong, subcordate at the base, gradually acuminate, chartaceous, with undulated reflexed margins, opake and almost glabrous above, sulcate along the midrib, nerves, and veins, densely covered beneath with yellowish soft tomentum, 1–1¾ in. long, 5–9 lines broad; on woolly petioles $\frac{1}{2}$ line long; peduncle simple, nearly terminal, 6–12 in. long, pubescent, or reddish and subglabrous, bearing 2 flowers at the apex 2 in. apart (or sometimes only a single flower), on pedicels 3 lines long, furnished below with 3 linear bracts 3–6 lines long; sepals very narrow, very acuminate, or setaceous at the reflected apex; tube of corolla slender, cano-tomentous, 5–6 in. long, swelling in a campanular form for $\frac{1}{4}$ of its length; segments obliquely roundish, 1¼ in. long and broad, with crispate margins, border when expanded 2¾ in. in diameter; the 2 erect, subtorulose, lanate follicles are 7½ in. long; seeds compressed, linear oblong, 5 lines long, apical coma 9 lines long.

4. MACROSIPHONIA MARTII, Müll. *l. c.* p. 138: *Echites virescens*, Stadelm. (non St.-Hil.), Bot. Zeit. 1841, Beibl. 63. In Brasilia: *v. s. in herb. meo*, prov. Goyaz (Gardner 3312).

The stem is erect, 2 feet high, including the flowers, all covered with white soft hairs, the axils being 6–9 lines apart; the leaves are opposite, nearly erect, and subimbricate, oblong, obtusely acute, subcordate at the base, chartaceous, the margins crenately revolute, above darkish green, opake, convex between the sulcate immersed nerves and transverse veins, shortly and sparsely pilose, densely covered beneath with white woolly tomentum, midrib reddish, nerves immersed, 1½–2½ in. long, 8–10½ lines broad, on petioles $\frac{1}{2}$–1 line long; peduncle terminal, erect, sparsely clothed with reddish tomentum, 7 in. long, bearing above from 3 to 5 suberect flowers, on pedicels 3 lines long, 1 in. apart, with 3 subsetaceous bracts 6 lines long; sepals very narrow, subulate, subreflexed at the apex, 7 lines long; tube of corolla slender, 3 in. long, swelling for $\frac{1}{4}$ its length in the mouth in a cylindrical form, covered with whitish pubescence; segments obovate, for the most part glabrous, but tomentous at their base, the margins crispately crenate; follicles 6 in. long; seeds 5½ lines long, with an apical coma of the same length.

The species differs from *M. longiflora* only in a terminal, stouter, longer, 5-flowered peduncle, the mouth of the shorter tube of the corolla being swollen in a narrower and more tubular form.

5. MACROSIPHONIA VIRESCENS, Müll. *l. c.* p. 139: *Echites virescens*, St.-Hil. Bull. Soc. Philom. 1824, p. 77; Mém. Mus. xii. 324; A. DC. *l. c.* p. 472 (in parte). In Brasilia ad Campos Geraës, prov. S. Paulo: *non vidi*.

Stem erect, subsimple, densely covered with ferruginous curling tomentum, bare of leaves upwards; leaves opposite, lanceolate, shortly acuminate, subcordate at the base, margins subrevolute, opake above, covered with whitish small pimples, below clothed with whitish tomentum, hirsute on the midrib, 2–2¾ in. long, 7½–9½ lines broad, on petioles 2–4 lines long; peduncle 4–4¾ in. long; sepals 9½–11½ lines long, with numerous inner scales; corolla 4¼ in. long, softly puberulous; tube slender, swollen in the mouth for ⅓ of its length in a subcampanular form; segments as long as the swollen portion of the tube; ovaries clothed with woolly hairs; follicles 10 in. long, torulose, nearly smooth.

A species near *M. longiflora*, principally differing in its clothing.

6. MACROSIPHONIA VERTICILLATA, Müll. *l. c.* p. 140: *Echites petræa*, St.-Hil. Mém. Mus. xii. 321; A. DC. *l. c.* p. 472. In Brasilia: *non vidi*.

A species growing in the extreme south-western portion of the province of Rio Grande, as far as Montevideo, and in Uruguay. It is a suffruticose, erect plant, its stem dichotomous at the apex, from 6 to 18 in. high, covered with dull red softly hirsute hairs, its lower leaves ternate or quaternate, upper ones opposite, closely imbricated, linear lanceolate, acute at the apex, obtusely cordate at the base, margins very revolute, subrugous above, sparsely hirsute with reddish hairs, beneath cano-tomentous, with a prominent midrib which is reddishly hirsute, 8–16 lines long, 1–5 lines broad, on petioles ¼–½ line long; peduncle in the axils or dichotomy of the stem, solitary, 1-flowered, 2½–6 in. long; pedicel short, with 3 or 4 bracts 3 lines long, cano-tomentose; sepals acutely lanceolate, tomentously pilose; corolla 3½–4½ in. long, with an elongated slender tomentous tube, gradually dilated and reddish at its summit, villous within at the contraction of the tube, where the stamens are inserted; segments roundish, inequilateral, with crispate margins; 2 slender follicles (6 in. long in the immature state), subarcuate, torulous, acute, pubescent.

7. MACROSIPHONIA PINIFOLIA, nob.: *Macrosiphonia verticillata*, var. *pinifolia*, Müll. *l. c.* p. 141: *Echites pinifolia*, St.-Hil. Mém. Mus. xii. 325; A. DC. *l. c.* p. 471. In prov. Goyaz, et in confinibus prov. Minas et St. Paulo: *non vidi*.

A valid species, though regarded as a mere variety of the preceding by Müller. It is remarkable for its very small hispid leaves; its stem is erect, hispid, scarcely 8 in. high; its leaves are very crowded, verticillately quaternate, narrowly linear, with revolute margins, hispid above, cano-tomentous beneath, 6–9½ lines long, ¼–1 line broad; the peduncle varies from 4 to 6¾ in. in length; tube of corolla extremely long, according to its age; segments crispate. The flower is odorous.

8. MACROSIPHONIA PROSTRATA, nob.: *Echites multifolia*, nob. olim in Trav. ii. p. 531: *Echites grandiflora*, Hook. var. *minor*, Journ. Bot. i. 286. In regione Argentina, (Pampas) prov. Cordova: *v. v. et sicco in herb. meo* (Punta de Agua).

A very pretty species, collected by me in 1825, when I made coloured drawings of it, with copious descriptions. It has a napiform root, throwing out several slender, simple, prostrate pilose stems, less than a foot long, sometimes shortly branched near the base, the axils 6–8 lines apart, bearing in each 3 verticillate linear-oblong membranaceous leaves, acute at the summit, bisinuately truncate at the base, with subrevolute margins, bright green and sparsely pilose above, sulcate on the midrib, of a yellowish tinge beneath, with many snow-white hairs, midrib and nerves reddish, 8–12 lines long, 2–3 lines broad, on slender pilose petioles $\frac{1}{2}$ line long; flowers solitary in many of the axils, on a peduncle 6 lines long, bearing in its middle 5 erect verticillate bracts the size and shape of the sepals; sepals linear-lanceolate, acute, of a reddish hue, subpilose, 7 lines long, 1 line broad; corolla large, hypocrateriform; tube 5½ in. long, funnel-shaped in the mouth for ¼ of its length, narrowly cylindrical below, 1¼ line broad, and of a greenish hue; 5 segments, rotately expanded, obliquely trapezoid, 15 lines long, 10 lines broad, the sinister margin thickened and of a bright red colour, archingly and dextrorsely curved, the rest pure white, and crispate on the margin; they close into a pentagonal twisting cone in the evening and again expand on the next morning; the stamens are inserted on a pilose ring at the constriction of the tube; the filaments are very short, the anthers oblong, yellow, 4 lines long, obtuse at the base, curving outwards, cohering by agglutination with the clavuncle, terminated by triangular membranes, all connivent in the axis; disk of 5 erect, acute lobes, half the length of the 2 acute oblong, subpilose ovaries; style slender, 4½ in. long, bearing a green pentagonal oblong clavuncle, having a lacerated peltate membrane at its base, and terminated by 2 minute stigmata; follicles 2, erect, subterete, striate, subtorulose, afterwards glabrous, 8 in. long, 2 lines broad; pericarp subcoriaceous, red outside, yellow inside, these nitid and finely striate; seeds many, reddish, compressed, dorsally striate, subpilose, channelled on the ventral face, with a longitudinal raphe, 4 lines long, 2 lines broad, dorsally striate, sub-pilose, crowned with an apical coma 15 lines long, consisting of many dense erect reddish hairs; embryo in corneous albumen, with a superior terete radicle ½ line long and oblong subobtuse cotyledons 2 lines long, 1¼ lines broad.

Drawings of this species, in flower and in fruit, with the analysis of the flower, fruit, and seeds, are given in Plate XVII.

Species excluded :—

  Macrosiphonia hypoleuca, Müll. . . . = *Rhodocalyx hypoleucus*, nob.
  M. suaveolens, Mart. & Gall. . . . . *Rhodocalyx suaveolens*, nob.

STIPECOMA.

This genus was elaborated by me in 1837, under another name, for some new species which I had collected, and illustrated by drawings and analyses taken from the living plants. Dr. Müller published the genus in 1860, upon *Echites peltigera*, A. DC., which he described and figured in the 'Flora Brasiliensis,' not recognizing two other species described by him under *Echites*. His generic name is not quite consistent, because the coma of the seed is not stipitated, properly speaking, but springs from the long rostrate summit of the testa. Messrs. Bentham and Hooker (Gen. ii. 724) quite misunderstood the carpological characters of the genus, which they had derived from Müller, who was unacquainted with the real structure. The following is a more correct diagnosis.

Stipecoma, Müll. (char. emendat.). *Sepala* lineari-oblonga, longiuscula, obtusa, tenuiter membranacea, reticulata, erecta, intus ad basin squamulis singulis alternatim munita. *Corolla* tubulosa; *tubus* calyce longior, cylindricus, crasse carnosus, imo latior, ad medium subito constrictus, superne inflatus, 5-sulcato-plicatus, fauce coarctatus, aut lævior et subcampanulatus; *segmenta* 5, oblonga, rotundatim inæquilatera, versus angulum sinistrum acuta, rotatim expansa, dextrorsum convoluta, tubo subæquilonga. *Stamina* 5, inclusa; *filamenta* subbrevia, crassa, flexuosa, ad constrictionem tubi inserta; *antheræ* majusculæ, rigidæ, imo divaricatim biaristatæ, apice acutissimæ, in conum conniventes, et ad clavunculam cohærentes. *Discus* 5-lobus, lobis obtuse oblongis, carnosis, quam ovarias paullo brevioribus. *Ovaria* 2, oblonga, subacuta; *stylus* tenuis, *clavuncula* crasse cylindrica 5-sulcata, imo membrana peltata suffulta, stamina attingens; *stigmata* terminalia, parvula, tenuia. *Folliculi* 2, majusculi, teretes, longi, subarcuati, apice cohærentes, sutura ventrali dehiscentes; pericarpium crassum, rigidum; *placenta* maxima, tenuiter chartacea, medio longitrorsum carinata (*carina* intra suturam affixa, demum soluta), utrinque latissime extensa, et in tubi formam voluta, marginibus vix approximatis, hinc undique libera, extus lævis, intus costellis prominulis 10 (utrinque 5 carinæ parallelis) remote articulatis munita; *articulis* tot quot *semina* (circiter 60); singulatim *funiculo* brevi semen pendendo et *appendice* mitræformi velata donatis; *vasæ spirales* medulla costellarum permeantes, per funiculos raphesque continuatæ, demum in chalazis basalibus evanidæ; *testa* elliptico-oblonga, chartacea, glabra, dorso convexa, ventre canaliculata, et hinc *raphe* longitudinali a funiculo ad *chalazam* basalem continua signata, apice in rostrum breve constricta, superne in annulum *micropylen* ambientem et comiferum incrassata; *coma* testæ longitudinis, e pilis elasticis sericeis, erecta; *albumen* testæ conforme, durum; *embryo* anatropus, inclusus; *cotyledones* 2, oblongæ, foliaceæ, canaliculatim incurvæ; *radicula* supera, teres, his triplo longior.

Frutices *scandentes Brasilienses*: folia *opposita, crassa, late ovato-oblonga, profunde peltata, petiolata*; racemi *axillares, longiusculi, pendentes, tomentosi, ramosi*; pedunculi *bractea magna foliosa donati, plurifiori*; pedicelli *bibracteolati*; flores *speciosi, lutei*.

1. **Stipecoma peltigera**, Müll. Fl. Bras. xxvi. p. 176, tab. 53: *Echites peltigera*, Stadelm. Bot. Zeit. 1841, Beibl. 21; A. DC. *l. c.* p. 447: *Echites tropæolifolia*, A. DC. *l. c.* p. 447. In Brasilia, prov. Cuyaba, Minas Geraës et Bahia: *non vidi*.

The type, and only species described by Müller as belonging to the genus; several others, however, are described by him under *Echites* which he did not recognize. This is a delicate climbing species, very different in appearance from the others, which generally have very large leaves and bunches of handsome flowers. Its slender flexuose branches have axils 2–3 in. apart; its leaves opposite, oblong-ovate, peltate, rounded at the base, suddenly acuminate and mucronate at the apex, rigidly membranaceous, with revolute margins, rorid and cinereously reddish above, glaucously opake below, and covered with very minute whitish dots, $2\frac{1}{2}$–3 in. long, $1\frac{1}{4}$–$1\frac{1}{2}$ in. broad, on angular slender petioles $1\frac{1}{8}$ in. long, fixed peltately $\frac{1}{2}$–$\frac{5}{8}$ in. above their base; the panicles are terminal in the dichotomy of the ultimate pair of leaves in the young branchlets, $1\frac{1}{2}$–$2\frac{3}{8}$ in. long; peduncle 8 lines long, divided into 2 branches of the same length, each bearing about 6 flowers, on pedicels 8 lines long; flowers reddish, $9\frac{1}{2}$ lines long; sepals roundly ovate, obtuse, glabrous, with ciliolate margins, 1 line long, with a small basal bifid scale alternate with each; corolla glabrous; tube cylindrical, contracted in the middle, where it is staminigerous, 6 lines long; segments dolabriform, 4 lines long and broad; anthers acuminate, 2-aristate at the base, hispid dorsally; lobes of disk subconnate at the base, nearly as long as the 2 pilose ovaries; 2 follicles, straight, terete, acuminate, 4 in. long, ¼ in. thick; seeds with a slender rostrum half their length, terminated by a coma as long as the seed.

2. STIPECOMA PELTATA, nob.: *Echites peltata*, Vell. Fl. Flum. p. 110, Icon. iii. tab. 32; A. DC. (in parte) *l. c.* p. 465; Müll. (in parte) *l. c.* p. 159 (excl. tab. 53. fig. 2). In Brasilia, prov. Rio de Janeiro, in montibus: *non vidi*.

Velloz found this species on the confines of that province, on the road leading from Cunha to Santa Cruz. The plants cited by Müller as constituting it belong to another species (*mucronata*), which I found in the Organ Mountains; and it is manifest that neither he nor De Candolle had seen Velloz's plant, which has much larger leaves and a different inflorescence. This species has much larger leaves than any of the others (if we except *S. macrocalyx*). Its branches are more than 3 lines thick; the oblong-ovate leaves are orbicular at the base, shortly acute at the summit, quite glabrous, 9½ in. long, 6½ in. broad, the insertion of the stout petiole (3 in. long) being 2 in. from the base; opposite axillary racemes, shorter than the young leaves from which they spring; the peduncle 1 in. long, bears about 3 alternate flowers, supported by as many oblong bracts 5 lines long; the pedicels, 6 lines long, bear in the middle 2 acute bracteoles 2¼ lines long; sepals acutely oblong, 9 lines long, 2⅓ lines broad; corolla large, sulphur-coloured; tube cylindrical, stoutish, constricted in the middle, 1⅓ in. long; segments spathulate-oblong, inequilateral, obliquely truncate, 1 in. long, 5 lines broad; stamens seated in the contraction of the tube; anthers acute, 4 lines long; disk sub-5-lobed, as long as the ovaries, which they embrace; 2 follicles teretely cylindrical, a little arcuate, conjoined firmly at the summit, smooth, 8 in. long, 9 lines thick; seeds acutely oblong, 1 in. long, including a rostrum of half their length; apical coma 1 in. long.

3. STIPECOMA PLICATA, nob.: *Echites plicata*, A. DC. *l. c.* p. 454: *Echites peltata*, Müll. (non Velloz) *l. c.* p. 159. In prov. Rio de Janeiro, ad ped. Mont. Organ.: *v. s. in herb. meo* (22. 206) *ex loc. cit. sine flore* (Mrs. Fry).

The above specimen agrees in all respects with the diagnosis of De Candolle; the inflorescence I have not seen. It is a climbing plant, with flexuose, fistular, angular, striate branches, sparsely covered with fulvous tomentum, its axils being 1½–2 in. apart; leaves ovate-oblong, rounded and plicately undulate at the base, suddenly narrowed at the summit by an acute reflexed acumen, chartaceous, margins cartilaginous and sub-revolute, above olive-green, opake, finely corrugulate, with 7 basal radiating nerves, and 7 pairs of lateral divergent immersed nerves, below fulvo-ochraceous, opake, obsoletely tomentous, with prominent reddish costa and straight nerves, all arcuately conjoined within the margin, and immersed transverse veins; they are 3½–5 in. long, 1¾–2¼ in. broad, on stout petioles 1–1¼ in. long, inserted ½–⅝ in. within the margin, patent or subdeflexed at the base. The inflorescence, according to De Candolle, is axillary, short, 1- or 2-flowered, subtomentous, on a very short peduncle, with 2 or 4 bracts 3 lines long; pedicels 6 lines long; sepals obtusely oblong, glabrous, shorter than the pedicels; corolla yellow, glabrous; tube 9 lines long, thicker above the calyx, and there pilose and staminigerous within;

segments elliptic, somewhat shorter than the tube; lobes of disk obtusely oblong, as long as the 2 ovaries.

4. **Stipecoma pulchra**, nob.: scandens, ramis crassis, demum glabris, ramulisque fistulosis, teretibus, validis, in axillis compressis et dilatatis, dense ochraceo- et floccoso-tomentosis: foliis profunde peltatis, late ovatis, imo rolundatis et undulatis, apice in acumen brevissimum acutum subito constrictis, marginibus integris, subretusis, revolutis, chartaceis, supra profunde viridibus, glabris, opacis et rugulose granulatis, nervis basalibus 7 radiantibus, lateralibus utrinque 6, patentim divaricatis, cunctis intra marginem arcuatim nexis, subimmersis, eveniis, subtus ochraceo-tomentellis, costa valida, nervis prominentibus transversim venosis; petiolis crassis, teretibus, longiusculis, ochraceo-tomentosis, imo sæpe gyratim tortis: inflorescentia insigni, laterali, valde elongata, undique fulvo-tomentosa; pedunculo crasse tereti, fasciculis 2-4 remotis ramulosis instructo; ramulis plurimis, congestim multifloris, dense imbricatim bracteatis; bracteis magnis, elliptico-oblongis, acutis, inferioribus majoribus sæpe foliola simulantibus; pedicellis ex axillis bractearum enatis, validis, et eis æquilongis, imo 2-bracteolatis, bracteolis lanceolatis paullo brevioribus; sepalis lineari-oblongis, acutis, membranaceis, margine undulatis, obsolete pilosis, intus squamulis paucis minutissimis donatis; corolla glabra; tubo cylindrico sepalis sesquilongiore, medio valde constricto; segmentis inæquilateri-oblongis, acutis, expansis, æstivatione dextrorsum convolutis; staminibus ad constrictionem tubi insertis, inclusis; filamentis subbrevibus, carnosulis; antheris corneis, apice cuspidatis, imo divergenter biaristatis; disco 5-lobo, lobis carnosis viridescentibus, rotundatis, imo connatis, ovaria 2 rotundata circumcingentibus; stylo brevi, tenui; clavuncula crassa, cylindrica, 5-sulcata, glutinosa, et imo membrana lata horizontali munita, stigmatibus 2 minimis. Rio de Janeiro, v. v. ad Morro Flamengo, et sicc. in herb. meo (3877).

I found this fine species in flower in 1837. The branches are $\frac{1}{4}$ in. thick, have axils 9 in. apart; leaves 5$\frac{1}{4}$–7 in. long, 3$\frac{1}{4}$–5$\frac{1}{4}$ in. broad, the insertion of the petiole $\frac{3}{4}$–1 in. above the base, the acute acumen $\frac{1}{4}$ in. long and broad, the petioles 4–5 in. long; the ripe axillary panicles are 5$\frac{1}{2}$ in. long, with about 6 branches, peduncle bare at the base for 1 in., branches 1 in. long, bearing upwards many crowded flowers; bracts many, 6 lines long, 2 lines broad; pedicels 4 lines long; sepals 6 lines long; tube of corolla 9 lines long; segments 6 lines long, 3 lines broad; anthers 3 lines long; disk and ovaries 1 line long; style 3 lines long, clavuncle $\frac{1}{2}$ line long.

A drawing of this species, with its floral analysis, is shown in Plate XVIII.

5. **Stipecoma mucronata**, nob.: *Echites peltata*, Müll. in parte (non Velloz), *l. c.* p. 159, tab. 53. fig. 2 (semen): scandens, ramulis teretibus, crassiusculis, fistulosis, adultis subglabris, junioribus fulvo-tomentosis, axillis dilatatis paullo compressis: foliis profunde peltatis, ovatis, imo orbiculatis, undulato-subplicatis, apicem versus rotundatis et in acumen lineare brevissimum obtuse mucronatis, marginibus vix revolutis, chartaceis, supra olivaceo-viridibus, sparse pubescentibus, nervis basalibus 7 radiantibus, lateralibus utrinque 5 paullo divergentibus marginem versus arcuatim nexis, paullo prominulis, reticulato-venosis, subtus ochraceis, densius tomentosis, costa nervisque rubescentibus prominentibus; petiolis crassis, tomentosis, sensim deflexis, peltatim affixis: racemis axillaribus, quam folium dimidio brevioribus, fulvo-tomentosis; pedunculo alternatim 6-floro, bracteato; pedicellis remotiusculis, sub medium 2-bracteolatis; floribus majusculis; sepalis linearibus, obtusulis, nervoso-membranaceis, glabris, pedicellum fere æquantibus, intus squamulis 3 acutis singulatim munitis; corolla glabra; tubo crassiusculo, cylindrico, medio constricto, ad faucem subito ampliato; segmentis magnis, oblongis, subtruncatis, inæquilateris

membranaceis, nervoso-reticulatis, tubi longitudine, æstivatione dextrorsum convolutis: folliculis 2, teretibus, arcuatis, apice nexis, seminibus ut in *S. ovata*. In Brasilia, prov.Rio de Janeiro, ad Cantagallo: *v. v. et sicco in herb. meo* (4055), *in flore et fructu*, montibus Organensibus.

The fistular branches 2½ lines thick, narrow, curvingly upwards, with axils 6 in. apart; leaves 3½–5 in. long, 2⅝–4 in. broad, on reflexed petioles 12–15 lines long, inserted 1 in. above the basal margin; raceme 1–2 in. long; peduncle flexuose, 1 in. long, bearing 6 alternate flowers on pedicels 4–6 lines long, bibracteolate in the middle; bracteoles linear, 2–3 lines long; sepals spathulately linear, subobtuse, 5 lines long, 1 line broad; tube of corolla greenish red, 16 lines long; segments pale rose-colour, 8 lines long, 5 lines broad; fructiferous peduncle, thickened, 1 in. long, supporting 2 arching follicles (not arrived at half their maturity) 4 in. long, 2 lines broad.

Specimens of this plant were sent to Müller from Cantagalla, by Peckholt, the seeds of which were figured by the former under *Echites peltata*. The soft flexible coma of these seeds are gathered by the natives and called *painha de penna*, being used as a substitute for feather-down, samples of which were shown in the London International Exhibition in 1862.

6. STIFFCOMA MACROCALYX, nob.: *Echites macrocalyx*, Müll. *l. c.* p. 160. In prov. Bahia (Blanchet, Sello 1665): *non vidi.*

A species near that figured by Velloz, growing in damp shady places. Its branches are ferruginously tomentous; its large leaves are broadly ovate, with a short cuspidate acumen, peltately fixed on long petioles, subcoriaceous, above fuscous green, and slightly pubescent, below ochraceously fuscous, opake, densely tomentous on the nerves, which are arcuately conjoined within the margin; they are said to be larger than those of *S. speciosa*, nob. The opposite racemes, scarcely longer than the petioles, bear 2 or 3 greenish-yellow flowers, each pedicel supported by 2 bracts, all as long as the calyx; sepals oblong-ovate, acute, erect, membranaceous, ferruginously pubescent, 1–1¼ in. long, each with an inner deeply multilaciniate basal scale; corolla glabrous, 2¾ in. long; tube stout, cylindrical, campanulate in the mouth; segments half its length, broadly ovate or subrotund; anthers hairy behind; lobes of disk free, as long as the 2 tomentous ovaries.

7. STIFECOMA SPECIOSA, nob.: scandens, ramulis crassiusculis, fistulosis, striatis, ferrugineo-tomentosis, axillis dilatato-compressis: foliis profunde peltatis, oblongo-obovatis, imo orbiculatis et undulatoplicatis, apice subito acuminatis, concavis, molliter crassiusculis, marginibus subrevolutis, supra fusco-viridibus, opacis, obsolete puberulis, nervis 7 basalibus radiantibus, lateralibus utrinque 8 recte divergentibus, cunctis intra marginem arcuatim nexis, prominulis, subtus ochraceo-pallidioribus, opacis, subtomentosis, costa nervisque rufulis, venis tenuissimis transversis immersis; petiolis crassiusculis, tomentosis, teretibus, longiusculis, flexuosis, deflexis: paniculis axillaribus, petiolo 2plo longioribus; pedunculo petiolum æquante, apice 3-ramoso, ramis fastigiato-plurifloris, multibracteatis; bracteis linearibus; pedicellis ad medium lineari-bibracteolatis; sepalis linearilanceolatis, quam pedicelli vix brevioribus, erectis, membranaceis, sparse puberulis; corolla speciosa, flava, glabra; tubo cylindrico, crassiusculo, quam sepali 2plo longiore, hinc valde constricto, superne subcampanulato; segmentis tubum æquantibus dolabriformibus, venosis, expansis, æstivatione dex-

trorsum tortis et convolutis; staminibus ad contractionem tubi insertis. In Rio de Janeiro, *v. v.* in montibus Organensibus, *in herb. meo* (4056).

I found this species in flower in January 1838. The fistulose scandent branches are ¼ in. thick, with axils 7 in. apart; the opposite leaves are 3½–6 in. long, 2¼–3¾ in. broad, on petioles 1¾–2 in. long, which are inserted ¾–1 in. above the base of the blade; panicle spreading, 3–4 in. long, subtomentous; peduncle bare at the base, 2 in. long; its 3 branches ¾ in. long, each bearing 5–6 approximate flowers, on pedicels bracteate at their base, bibracteate in the middle, 8 lines long; bracts 6 lines long, 1 line broad; sepals the size of the bracts, reticulately veined, each having within at the base a small alternate scale; tube of corolla 1 in. long; segments 9 lines long, 4 lines broad; anthers slender, 4½ lines long, acutely acuminate, and sharply biaristate at the base, subpuberulous behind; disk 5 free fleshy roundish lobes nearly as long as the 2 roundish glabrous ovaries; style slender; clavuncle incrassate, glandular, supported upon a peltate membranaceous appendage.

8. STIPECOMA OVATA, nob.: scandens, ramis strictis, crassis, teretibus, striatis, fistulosis, pallidis, cinereopruinosis, sparse lenticellatis; axillis remotis, linea transversali notatis: foliis ovatis, imo orbicularibus et undulato-plicatis, apice sensim late acutis et mucronatis, marginibus revolutis, crassiuscule chartaceis, supra fusco-viridibus, opacis, corrugulatis, costa nervisque immersis, subtus flavide ferrugineis, opacis, corrugulatis et granulosis, obsolete tomentosis, nervis basalibus 7 radiantibus, lateralibusque utrinque 7 prominulis, versus marginem arcuatim nexis; petiolo vix crasso, angulato, corrugulato, imo cirrose reflexo: pedunculo fructifero crasso, petiolum æquante; folliculis 2 subpedalibus, paullo arcuatis, teretibus, striatellis, cinereo-nigrescentibus, apicibus subangustatis arcte jugatis: cæteris ut in char. generico. In Brasilia: *v. v. in fructu*, montibus Organensibus, *in herb. meo* (4058); *v. s. in herb. Mus. Brit.* Itagoahy (Bowie and Cunningham).

The branches are 3 lines in thickness, very fistulose, rigid, with axils 8 in. apart; the leaves are 4¼–5¼ in. long, 3–4 in. broad, on petioles 1¼–1½ in. long, inserted ¾ in. within the border. The fructiferous peduncle, with the cicatrices of 2 abortive flowers, is 1½ in. long; the follicles are 10½ in. long; the seeds (including the long glabrous rostrum 6 lines) are 14 lines long, 1 line broad, with an apical spreading coma 13 lines long; funicle beneath the ring of the coma very short, but distinct.

The follicles in Bowie and Cunningham's specimen, not yet ripe, are 7½ in. long, 4 lines broad.

A drawing of this species in fruit, showing the carpical structure, and the analysis of its seeds are given in Plate XIX.

9. STIPECOMA PARABOLICA, nob.: scandens, foliis subpeltatis, oblongis, imo rotundatis, supra medium sensim angustioribus, apice in acumen sublineare acutum recurvulum attenuatis, marginibus integris subrevolutis, crassiuscule chartaceis, supra profunde viridibus, glabriusculis, nervis immersis, ad insertionem petioli glandula rotundata signatis, subtus opacis, ferrugineo-pruinosis; petiolo tenui, recurvato, 6plo breviore quam limbo, paullo intra marginem subtus peltatim affixo: cæteris ignotis. In Brasilia: *v. s. in herb. Mus. Brit.* prope San Paulo (Bowie and Cunningham), *sine flore et fructu.*

The leaves are 4½ in. long, 2 in. broad, on a somewhat slender petiole ¾ in. long, inserted 1 line within the margin.

RHODOCALYX.

This genus comprises several low-growing plants, for the most part springing out of ligneous tuberose rhizomes, producing several short stems, knotty and bracteolate at the base, bare and erect above, where they are furnished with few opposite broadish leaves, either subsessile or petiolate. The inflorescence consists of one or few flowers, axillary or terminal in the sinus of the two ultimate leaves; these are supported by slender pedicels, bracteolate at the base; the sepals are rather large, often of a reddish hue, submembranaceous, reticulately veined, acute, sometimes subcordate at the base, with an inner, broad, deeply laciniulate scale; the corolla is salver-shaped; tube narrowed at the base for the length of the calyx, funnel-shaped above; segments oblong, one-third of its length, with dextrorse convolution; stamens seated in the constriction of the tube; anthers linear, acute, subcohering, with 2 short basal prongs; style filiform; clavuncle thickened, cylindrical, with a basal peltiform appendage. But the chief peculiarity is the manner in which its seeds are suspended from the lamellar placentæ of 2 terete follicles; these are imbricate, oblong, subcompressed, dorsally convex and cancellately reticulated, concave on the ventral face, where they are marked with a raphe running from top to bottom, which at its summit is extended into a filiform funicle 6 times the length of the seed, and by which the latter is suspended from the placenta; the seed is crowned by an erect coma 5 times its length; the anatropous embryo is imbedded in albumen, its 2 oblong foliaceous cotyledons, laterally incurved, are 3 times as long as the more slender terete superior radicle.

The presence of a distinct funicle, by which the seed is suspended, brings this genus into proximity with *Stipecoma*; but it wants the long peculiar rostrum, seen in the seed of the latter genus; in other respects it is extremely different.

1. RHODOCALYX ROTUNDIFOLIUS, Müll. Fl. Bras. xxvi. p. 173, tab. 51. In Brasiliæ prov. central.: *v. s. in herb. meo*, Minas Geraës (Claussen).

This plant, in the herbarium, may at first sight be mistaken for the *Dipladenia illustris*, var. *rotundifolia*, of Müller; but it may be recognized by the presence of its lower bracteiform leaves, by its smaller flowers, larger (not lanceolate) sepals, a shorter tube of the corolla, which is a little longer than the sepals. It has been wrongly regarded as identical with the *Echites erecta* of Velloz (which is *Laseguea erecta*, Müll.). Its ligneous rhizome is horizontal, sending from one extremity several short erect stems, scarcely a foot long, bearing towards the base a few opposite acute bracteiform scales (abortive leaves), and, above the middle, 2 or 3 pairs of leaves about 2 in. apart; the leaves are suborbicular, with a very short acumen, pale green above, thickly clothed with a whitish tomentum, with about 4 pairs of distant immersed nerves, $1\frac{3}{4}$–$2\frac{3}{4}$ in. long, $1\frac{1}{4}$–$2\frac{3}{4}$ in. broad, with a pubescent petiole 1 line long. The inflorescence is tomentous, 2–$4\frac{1}{2}$ in. long, on a straight peduncle bearing about 4 pairs of opposite flowers (sometimes reduced to a single one) on pedicels 10 lines long, each furnished at the base with a bract nearly of its length, acutely oblong, glabrous, with ciliated margins; sepals oblong, acute, reticulated, 8 lines long, 4½ lines broad; tube of corolla constricted in the middle, cylindrical, 10 lines long; segments acutely and obliquely ovate, 4 lines long, 3½ lines broad; stamens arising from a pilose ring at the constriction of the tube; anthers acute, shortly bilobed at the base, connivent in a cone; disk of 5 oblong fleshy lobes nearly the length of the 2 oblong ovaries; style slender, bearing a thick oblong clavuncle with a lacerated membrane at its base, terminated by 2 short obtuse stigmata; follicles, according to Müller, terete, 4 in. long, 3½ lines thick; seeds oblong, truncated (not rostrate), 2 lines long, 1 line broad, compressed, surmounted by a copious coma 18 lines long, and suspended by a rigid funicle 21 lines long.

A drawing of the follicle and of its seed is shown in Plate XX. A.

2. RHODOCALYX CRASSIFOLIUS, nob.: *Amblyanthera crassifolia*, Müll. *l. c.* p. 143: *Echites crassifolia*, Spruce MS. In Brasilia; Rio Negro: *v. s. in hb. meo*, prope San Carlos (Spruce 3136).

This, certainly, is not an *Amblyanthera*. Apparently it is a dwarfish erect shrub, with a stem only a few inches high, seemingly springing from a tuberous root, as in the preceding species. This stem is divided at its summit into 2 or 3 suberect, stoutish, reddish, angularly compressed, sparsely hirsutulous branches, 3–3½ in. long, each terminated by only 2 opposite patent leaves, which are oblong, cordate, rounded at the summit, rigidly coriaceous, with subrevolute margins, glabrous, reddish green above, with immersed nerves, below opake, reddish ochreous, nerveless, with sparing dark dots, midrib prominent; on different branches they are respectively 2¼ and 3⅜ in. long, 1½ and 1⅞ in. broad, on stout petioles 1 line long; peduncle terminal, 2 lines long, bearing about 2 flowers on slender pedicels 8 lines long; sepals acute, 8 lines long, 2 lines broad, of a reddish colour, thickly membranaceous, sparsely pilose; tube of corolla fleshy, cylindrical, constricted in the middle, sparsely pilose, 20 lines long; segments spathulate-oblong, oblique, dextrorsely convolute, 8 lines long, 4 lines broad; stamens inserted in the constriction of the tube; filaments pilose; disk 5-lobed, half as long as the 2 ovaries.

A drawing and analysis of the flower of this species are given in Plate XX. A.

3. RHODOCALYX LANUGINOSUS, nob.: *Echites lanuginosa*, Mart. et Gall. Bull. Acad. Brux. xi. 357; Walp. Rep. vi. 477. In Mexico: *non vidi*.

A species with an erect, branching, tomentose stem; leaves roundish, entire, subcordate, pale green above, densely covered beneath with soft woolly tomentum, as in *R. rotundifolius*, less than 1 in. long, on very short petioles; flowers solitary in the axils, on a short pedicel; tube of corolla 2½ in. long.

4. RHODOCALYX SUAVEOLENS, nob.: *Echites (Macrosiphonia) suaveolens*, Mart. et Gall. Bull. Acad. Brux. xi. 356; Walp. Rep. vi. 477. In Mexico: *non vidi*.

This plant cannot belong to *Macrosiphonia*, on account of its habit, locality, and inflorescence. It is congeneric with the preceding, and accords well with *Rhodocalyx*. It has an erect, branching, pubescent stem; the leaves are oblong, entire, with revolute margins, pubescent above, snowy tomentose beneath, 2 in. long, 5–6 lines broad, almost sessile; flowers axillary, solitary, on pedicels shorter than the leaves; corolla white, salver-shaped, with a subtomentous tube 1½ in. long; segments 6 lines long.

5. RHODOCALYX HYPOLEUCUS, nob.: *Echites hypoleuca*, Benth. Pl. Hartw. pp. 23 et 33; A. DC. Prodr. viii. 472: *Macrosiphonia hypoleuca*, Müll. Linn. xxx. 452. In Mexico (Hartweg 193): *non vidi*.

Dr. Müller regarded this species as belonging to *Macrosiphonia*—which opinion cannot be maintained, for the reasons given in the description of the two preceding species. It approaches *R. suaveolens*. It has 2 or 3 erect puberulous stems, 6 in. high, rising from a thickish root; leaves ovate-oblong, sublanceolate, subcordate, sparsely puberulous above, covered with white tomentum below, 10–18 lines long, 4–7 lines broad, on petioles 1 line long; peduncle terminal in the sinus of the ultimate pair of leaves, and shorter than they, with 1 or 2 bracts at the base of 1 or 2 flowers; bracts 3–4 lines long, tomentous; pedicels as long as the peduncle, pubescent; sepals linear-lanceolate, velutinous, 4–5 lines long, 1 line broad; corolla white; tube cylindrical, velutinous, 1½–1¾ in. long, subventricose above the middle, and contracted in the mouth, which is yellowish; segments obovate, half as long as the tube, with reddish margins; disk of 5 oblong lobes, of which 2 are subconnate at the base, half as long as the 2 ovaries.

6. RHODOCALYX CRASSIPES, nob.: *Echites crassipes*, Rich. Fl. Cub. xi. p. 91: Walp. Ann. v. p. 494. In Cuba, circa Janasi (Sagra): *non vidi*.

A climbing species, with very slender, glabrous branches; leaves oblong-lanceolate, narrow, obtuse at both ends, mucronate, coriaceous, with immersed nerves, petiolate; inflorescence axillary, 1-flowered, on a short thick pedicel; sepals oblong-lanceolate, acute, glabrous; corolla 2 in. long; tube swelling above the middle; segments obovate-oblong, obtuse; stamens inserted in the constriction of the tube.

7. RHODOCALYX CALYCOSUS, nob.: *Echites calycosa*, Rich. Pl. Cub. p. 94; Griseb. Pl. Wright. Cub. p. 520, in Cat. Pl. Cub. p. 194 (sub *Laseguea*); Walp. Ann. v. 495. In Cuba, Santiago (Linden 1783): *v. s. in herb. Mus. Brit.* Cuba (Wright 1877).

The specimen above-mentioned agrees with Richard's diagnosis in all essential respects. That description however, by a typical error, states that the segments of the corolla are 1¼ to 4 times *longer* than the tube, instead of 3 times *shorter*. Grisebach copies this error.

It is a subscandent shrub, with slender, twining, ferruginously hirsute branchlets, having axils about 6 in. apart; leaves broadly elliptic, subacute at the base, shortly acuminate, pale green and sparsely pilose above, ferruginous and hirsutulous beneath, with reddish prominulent nerves and reticulated veins, 4–5 in. long, 2–2¼ in. broad, on pubescent petioles 5–6 lines long; racemes lateral, puberulous, 5 in. long, on a peduncle bare at the base for 1¼ in., bearing upwards 4 or more lax flowers on slender pubescent pedicels 9 lines long, each supported by a linear adpressed pilose bract 6 lines long, 2 lines broad; sepals linear, acuminate, pale and submembranaceous, puberulous, ciliated, 7 lines long, 2 lines broad (one of them sometimes a little broader), each with an inner basal broad pectinate scale; tube of corolla narrow at the base for about half its length, broadly campanulate above, membranaceous, white, 1¼ in. long; segments roundish, dolabriform, with a sharp tooth on one side, retusely sinuate on the upper margin, 7 lines long, 6 lines broad; stamens seated on a broad rigidly pilose ring in the contraction of the tube; disk cleft into 5 subacute lobes, nearly as long as the 2 glabrous oblong ovaries.

Grisebach regarded this species as a *Laseguea*; but the size and shape of the corolla, and other characters, forbid such a reference.

8. RHODOCALYX CINEREUS, nob.: *Echites cinerea*, Rich. Fl. Cub. xi. p. 93; Walp. Ann. v. p. 494. In Cuba (Sagra): *nón vidi*.

A shrub with an erect stem, bearing several virgate branches, densely cinereo-hirsute; leaves small, ovate, obtuse and subcordate at the base, acuminate, cinereo-hirtulous on both sides, on almost obsolete petioles; flowers axillary, solitary, pedicellate; sepals subulately linear, hirsute; corolla hypocrateriform, with a slender hirsute tube, slightly swollen near the middle; segments broadly ovate, very obtuse, rotate, puberulous, somewhat longer than the tube; follicles 2, straight, parallel, acute, cinereo-hirtous, 3 in. long; seeds narrow oblong, compressed, terminated by a longer coma, and suspended by a long funicle.

9. RHODOCALYX COCCINEUS, nob.: *Echites coccinea*, Hook. Arn. Journ. Bot. i. 286: *Echites Hookeri*, A. DC. *l.c.* p. 476; Müll. Fl. Bras. xxvi. p. 161: *Dipladenia coccinea*, Müll. *l.c.* p. 132. In Brasilia austr. prov. Rio Grande, fluv. Jacuhy, in saxosis (Tweedie 791): *non vidi*.

A species much resembling *R. rotundifolius*. Very few characters are given of it; but it is said to be an erect shrub, rising from a root having 5 or 6 black tubers like potatoes; leaves elliptic, obtuse at the base, acute, very glabrous; peduncle terminal, bearing a corymb of rich scarlet flowers, the size of those of the oleander, on bracteate pedicels; sepals large, subulate, half the length of the tube of the corolla; follicles linear, glabrous.

From my analysis of a kindred species received from Tweedie, from the same locality, little doubt can exist that this plant belongs to *Rhodocalyx*.

10. RHODOCALYX OVATUS, nob.: *Echites coccinea*, var. β. *ovata*, Hook. Arn. *l. c.* In Brasilia austr. prov. Rio Grande: *v. fol. sicc. in herb. meo*, fluv. Jacuhy (Tweedie).

The single loose leaf accompanying the specimens sent to me by Tweedie, quite agrees with the description above cited. It merely states that the leaves are broader, subrotund-elliptic, and that the flowers are paler; the leaf received is orbicularly ovate, rounded at the base, emarginate and broadly mucronate at the apex, entire margins subrevolute, chartaceous, very glabrous, reddish green above, sulcate along the midrib, with fine immersed diverging nerves and reticulated veins, ferruginously opake beneath, with subprominent midrib and prominulent nerves, 3¼ in. long, 1⅝ in. broad, on a slender rigid petiole 8 lines long.

11. RHODOCALYX TWEEDIANUS, nob. In Brasilia austr.: *v. s. in herb. meo*, prov. Rio Grande ad fluv. Jacuhy (Tweedie).

Two specimens of this species were sent to me in 1835 by Tweedie; both evidently indicate that the stems are simple, probably not more than 8 to 12 in. high; the stem is slender, pale brown, fistulose, very glabrous, $\frac{1}{4}$ line thick, the nodes scarcely dilated, bearing 6 or 8 setiform stipules on each face; in the specimen with a perfect flower the terminal internode in its whole extent is 6 in. long; in the younger specimen, with the flower in bud, the terminal internode is $1\frac{1}{2}$ in., the intermediate internode $2\frac{3}{4}$ in., the lower one only $\frac{3}{4}$ in. long; the opposite leaves are oblong-ovate, obtuse or emarginately cordate at the base, rounded and emarginate, or abruptly acuminate at the summit, submembranaceous, opake green above, with immersed very fine divergent nerves, yellowish opake beneath, the midrib, nerves, and fine transversely reticulated veins reddish and little prominulent, 2–$2\frac{3}{4}$ in. long, 1–$1\frac{3}{4}$ in. broad, on slender petioles 5–8 lines long; the terminal solitary flower, seated in the sinus of the ultimate leaves, has no peduncle, the pedicel is 10 lines long, supported by 2 basal lanceolate membranaceous bracts 3 lines long; sepals acutely lanceolate, submembranaceous, with undulate margins, erect, pale reddish, 4 lines long (one a little broader), each with a lanceolate ciliated inner basal scale; corolla apparently red, with a tube 10 lines long, narrowed at its base for 2 lines, thence rather narrowly funnel-shaped above, with obovate inequilateral rhomboid obtuse segments, finely reticulately nerved, 9 lines long, 4 lines broad; stamens seated on a dense pilose ring in the contraction of the tube; filaments short, retrorsely pilose; anthers subcohering, linear, with a membranaceous apex, obtusely and shortly bilobed at the base; disk of 5 free oblong lobes, shorter than the 2 acutely oblong glabrous ovaries; style reaching the anthers, with a thickened clavuncle membranaceously peltate at the base, terminated by 2 short stigmata.

These characters all correspond with *Rhodocalyx*, and in no way accord with *Dipladenia*. The shorter inferior internode in Tweedie's specimen indicates that the plant, as in the several preceding species, is very short in stature, and its stems simple.

12. RHODOCALYX CUNEIFOLIUS, nob.: caulibus e basi binis, humilibus, striatis, pallidis, puberulis; foliis basalibus oppositis, acute ovatis, bracteiformibus, sequentibus gradatim majoribus, reliquis obovatis, infra medium cuneatim angustatis, apice rotundiusculis et subito mucroniformi-apiculatis, rigide chartaceis, utrinque sparsim subpuberulis, costa hirsutula, marginibus ciliatis, concoloribus, nervis immersis divergentibus et crebre parallelis, fere sessilibus: racemo terminali, pedunculo quam folium sesqui longiore; floribus 4, alternatim oppositis; pedicellis imo bracteolatis, calyce paullo longioribus, breviter puberulis; sepalis lineari-acuminatis, membranaceis, valde imbricatis, sparsim pilosulis, margine ciliatis, intus squamula bidentata munitis; corolla hypocrateriformi; tubo supra basin pro quarta parte anguste cylindrico, superne ventricoso, quinqueplicato, fauce subconstricto, extus puberulo; segmentis late dolabriformibus, rotatis, tubo tertia parte brevioribus; staminibus ad contractionem tubi in annulo piloso insertis; filamentis antice affixis, gossypinis; antheris apice membranaceis, imo aristis 2 obtusis parallelis quam filamenta paullo brevioribus munitis; disco fere ad basin in lobos 5 carnosos apice emarginatos fisso; ovariis 2 acuminatis discum paullo excedentibus; stylo tenui, imo breviter bifisso, cruribus cum ovariis articulatis; clavuncula crassa, 5-sulcata, imo peltato-membranacea; stigmatibus brevibus terminalibus. In Brasilia: *v. s. in herb. meo* (n. 16894), Minas Geraës (Claussen).

The above specimen, with the aspect of a *Dipladenia*, is only 7 in. long, with a straight, erect stem, with the fragment of another conjoined at the base. The basal opposite leaves are diminished to the size of small ovate bracts; in the superior axils they are only 3 lines long; the superior three pairs, 1 in. apart, are erect, 1¼–1½ in. long, 6–9 lines broad above the middle, on petioles scarcely 1 line long. The terminal panicle has an erect peduncle bare at its base for 2½ in., and bears, above, 4 flowers ¾ in. apart, on bracteolate pedicels 7 lines long; sepals 5 lines long; basal contraction of tube of corolla 5 lines long, its entire length being 21 lines; segments 7 lines long, 5 lines broad; the colour of the flower is apparently purplish red; the stamens are inserted 6 lines above the base of the tube, on a densely pilose ring; the anthers acuminate, rigid, with 2 basal obtuse parallel prongs; the compressed filaments are fixed in front above the sinus of the forks, as in *R. crassifolius*, with which its floral characters correspond in all respects.

PRESTONIA.

This genus was established by Robert Brown in 1811, upon one of the rare plants collected by Banks and Solander at Rio de Janeiro in 1768. This, however, was only imperfectly described by that celebrated botanist, as he failed to observe the peculiar structure of the fruit, which was also unknown to Kunth, De Candolle, Endlicher, Müller, and the authors of the 'Genera Plantarum.' The latter botanists (*op. cit.* ii. p. 709) amalgamated with it the genus *Hæmadictyon*, because in both cases the tube of the corolla is furnished in the mouth with a callous ring and 5 free narrow linear appendages. Under the head of *Hæmadictyon* the reasons will be given more fully for refusing to adopt this conclusion. One good discriminating character has been overlooked, viz. the presence of several small stipules upon the transverse ridge at each node, and the involucel of several stipuliform scales where the peduncle of the inflorescence rises laterally out of the ring, which are always wanting in *Hæmadictyon*. In the latter genus the peduncle of the raceme is always simple; in *Prestonia* it is very shortly branched, each branch densely furnished with almost sessile flowers, forming a capitate head, and the fruit is an elongated coriaceous 2-celled capsule. The inflorescence and floral structure are well illustrated in Delessert's 'Icones' (v. tab. 51), with one oversight, the 2-celled ovary being shown as 2 distinct ovaries. The following is offered as a more correct diagnosis of the genus.

PRESTONIA, R. Br.: *Hæmadictyon* (in parte) auct. *Sepala* 5, acute oblonga, imbricata, æqualia, aut minora et coriacea vel majora et submembranacea, singula intus squamulis singulis latis apice denticulatis munita. *Corolla* hypocrateriformis; *tubus* late cylindricus, calyce paullo longior, fauce subconstrictus et illic *annulo* calloso integro vel *callis* plurimis minutis in seriem simplicem dispositis signatus, et sub faucem appendicibus 5 squamaceis cum segmentis alternis præditus; *segmenta* 5, acute inæquilatera aut dolabriformia, tubo subbreviora, dextrorsum convoluta. *Stamina* 5, e pilis medio tubi orta; *filamenta* brevissima; *antheræ* lineares, in conum subcohærentes, apice acuminatæ, imo incurvatim biaristatæ, apicibus interdum subexsertis. *Discus* cylindricus, margine crenulatim paullo quinqui fido, ovarium obtegens. *Ovarium* ovatum, 2-loculare, loculis utrinque pluriovulatis; *stylus* filiformis; *clavuncula* breviter oblonga, 5-glandulosa, imo indusio peltiformi munita; *stigmata* 2, parva, obtusa, terminalia. *Fructus* capsularis, fusiformi-cylindricus, superne angustior, apice breviter nodosus, utrinque sulcatus; *pericarpium* crasso-coriaceum, 2-loculare, per *dissepimentum* bilamellare ad sulcos septicide dehiscens, marginibus ad axem sutura longitudinali introflexis et placentiferis. *Semina* plurima, oblonga, compressa, superne suspensa, coma æquilonga coronata; *testa* dorso corrugata, ventre planata et *raphe* longitudinali vasis spiralibus repleta munita; *embryo* anatropus, in *albumen* tenue viride immersus; *cotyledones* 2, oblongæ, membranaceæ; *radicula* his triplo brevior, tenuiter teres, supera.

Frutices *Americæ meridionalis scandentes, plerumque dense villosi, rarius glabri; ramorum axillæ dilatatæ, remotiusculæ, linea transversa notatæ, et utroque latere pluristipellatæ; folia oblonga vel elliptica, opposita, integra, nervosa, tomentosa vel glabra, cum petiolis linea transversa nexis: cyma unilateralis; pedunculus ex involucello stipellarum ortus, apice brevissime ramosus, ramis densifloris, corymbam capitatam simulantibus; flores subparvi, subpedicellati, bracteolati: fructus villosus,* pericarpio *crasse coriaceo*.

1. PRESTONIA TOMENTOSA, R. Br. Mem. Wern. Soc. i. 69; A. DC. *l. c.* p. 429; Müll. Fl. Bras. xxvi. p. 163 (in parte). In Brasilia: *v. s. in herb. Mus. Brit.* Rio de Janeiro (Solander).

This typical specimen, collected by Solander in 1768, has scandent branches, covered with yellow tomentum, with axils 6 in. apart; the opposite oblong leaves, oval at the base and there scarcely cordate, diminish gradually towards the summit, and are terminated by a narrow very acute acumen, are fuscous green above, sparsely pilose, with short rigid hairs seated upon minute scabrid glandules, are sulcate along the immersed nerves and transverse veins, clothed beneath with extremely dense, soft, woolly, yellow tomentum which conceals the under surface, $4\frac{1}{2}$–$5\frac{1}{2}$ in. long, $1\frac{3}{4}$–$2\frac{1}{2}$ in. broad, on thick, woolly petioles 2 lines long; inflorescence lateral, very tomentous, on a peduncle 3 lines long, shortly divided, the branchlets bearing many flowers aggregated into a globular head 1 in. in diameter; pedicels 2 lines long, villous, bracteoles linear, acute, villous, 2 lines long, 1 line broad; sepals acutely oblong, densely villous on both sides, 6 lines long, $2\frac{1}{4}$ lines broad, each with an opposite, inner, externally villous, somewhat acute scale $1\frac{1}{4}$ line long, 3-denticulate at the apex; tube of corolla pilose outside, 8 lines long, appendages as in the generic character; the segments, glabrous within, are 5 lines long; stamens included, shortly excurrent; filaments retrorsely hispid behind; anthers subcoherent; disk urceolate, with a margin of 5 broad emarginated teeth, enclosing a pilose 2-celled ovary; capsule as in the generic character, of a greyish colour, retrorsely pilose, $2\frac{3}{4}$ in. long, 9 lines broad, reduced above to $1\frac{1}{2}$ line, and terminated by a globular knob 2 lines broad; seeds oblong, fusiform, compressed, rugous on the dorsal face, with a white longitudinal raphe on the ventral side, 5 lines long, 1 line broad, with an apical coma of erect reddish hairs, in 2 series, 6 lines long.

It may be greatly doubted whether the specimens of Pohl from the province of Goyaz, and of Claussen from Minas Geraës, as quoted by Müller, are identical with Solander's plant. De Candolle, who refers to Claussen's specimen, was dubious on the subject, though he had not seen the typical plant. Müller's description, without a knowledge of the type, is sufficiently at variance with it, as its leaves are of a yellowish golden green, fulvo-tomentous above on the nerves and margins, of a different size, and on longer petioles; the pedicels are longer, as are also the sepals, and as long as the tube of the corolla; the calycine scales are bidentate: these are conditions sufficiently different from the typical specimen.

A drawing of this plant, and an analysis of its flower, fruit, and seeds, are shown in Plate XX. B.

2. PRESTONIA LATIFOLIA, Benth. in Hook. Journ. Bot. iii. 250; A. DC. *l. c.* p. 429; Deless. Icon. v. 22, tab. 51; Müll. *l. c.* p. 167. In Guiana: *v. s. in herb. meo et alior.* Pirara (Schomb. 755).

A climbing shrub, with branches 2 lines thick, covered with dense yellow woolly tomentum, the axils 6 in. apart, being traversed between the petioles by an arching rib, furnished with several small toothlike hairy stipules; leaves ovate, navicularly plicate, recurved, and subcordate at the base, roundish at the summit, with a short, abrupt, often recurved acumen, opake-green above, scabridulous, shortly and softly pubescent, hirsutulous on the yellow slender nerves, beneath covered with dense yellowish tomentum, the midrib, stoutish nerves, and transverse veins of a reddish hue, $3\frac{1}{2}$–5 in. long, 2–3 in. broad, on thick pubescent petioles 2–$2\frac{1}{2}$ lines long. The peduncle of the tomentous corymb is stout, reflected, 1 in. long, issuing from one side of the node between the stipules upon the transverse ridge, and bearing a capitate head of many flowers, $1\frac{1}{2}$ in. in diameter; sometimes it happens that many of the flowers disappear, giving it the appearance of a few-flowered raceme; the thick pedicels are 1 line long, supported by tomentous acutely linear bracts 3 lines long; the sepals acutely oblong, are hairy on both sides, 5 lines long, 2 lines broad, each with an inner broad pluridentate scale; the tube of the corolla is cylindrical, stout, pilose, 7 lines long, with 5 semiexserted linear appendages; segments inequilateral, oblong, acute on one angle, 4 lines long, $2\frac{1}{2}$ lines broad, hairy outside; stamens inserted in the middle of the tube, with subcohering anthers shortly exserted at the apex; disk urceolate, its margin split into 5 short crenate lobes, somewhat longer than the ovary.

3. PRESTONIA IPOMÆIFOLIA, A. DC. *l. c.* p. 429. In Cayenne: *non vidi.*

A species scarcely differing from the preceding; leaves ovate, rounded at the base, abruptly cuspidate, pilose above, hispidly rufo-tomentous beneath, with more patent nerves, 4–6 in. long, 2–3 in. broad, on petioles 2–3 lines long; inflorescence capitate, rufo-tomentous; sepals pilose on both sides, 5 lines long; tube of corolla 6 lines long; disk urceolate, twice as long as the ovary, with crenulate lobes.

4. PRESTONIA GLABRATA, H. B. K. iii. 222: *Hæmadictyon glabratum*, A. DC. Prodr. viii. 427. In America centrali, ad Guayaquil (Bonpland): *v. s. in herb. Mus. Brit.* Panama (Seemann 1062).

The above specimen, referred by Seemann in his Botany of the Herald p. 168, to the Brazilian type *P. tomentosa*, R. Br., is certainly very different. He there seems to have overlooked the plant in his collection which is here described as *P. Seemanni*. *P. glabrata* is a climbing species, with pale brown glabrous branches, with axils about 5 in. apart; leaves obovate-oblong, broader below the middle, narrower towards the base, which is rounded and shortly cordate, the summit suddenly constricted into a short acute acumen, margins subrevolute, chartaceous, reddish green above, opake, sulcate on the midrib and on 10 pairs of ascending nerves, and on the transversely reticulated veins, ferruginously opake beneath, with prominent red midrib nerves and veins, scabridulous to the touch, $3\frac{1}{4}$–$4\frac{1}{4}$ in. long, $1\frac{3}{4}$–$2\frac{1}{4}$ in. broad, on patent slender petioles 8–12 lines long; raceme solitary and lateral, as long as the leaves, on a peduncle bare at its base, bearing above several flowers on slender hirtellous pedicels 3 lines long; sepals lanceolate, acuminate, erect, very membranaceous, glabrous, hirtellous at the base, 4 lines long, $\frac{3}{4}$ line broad, each with a broad acute inner scale; tube of corolla cylindrical, broadening a little upwards, 8 lines long, with a crenate annular ring in the mouth, and below it 5 linear membranaceous appendages partly exserted; stamens seated a little above the middle of the tube on hirtellous filaments; anthers acuminate, reaching the mouth, with 2 long slender divaricating prongs at their base; disk 5-lobed, about as long as the ovary.

5. PRESTONIA SEEMANNI, nob.: *Prestonia tomentosa*, Seem. (non R. Br.) in Bot. Her. p. 168. Panama, in uliginosis: *v. s. in herb. Mus. Brit. ex loc. citat.* (Seemann).

A species distinct from *P. tomentosa*. Its leaves are oblong-ovate, rounded and subcordate at the base, above the middle narrowing gradually and attenuated into a sharp point, chartaceous, bright green above, pilose, with curving ascending prominulent nerves, paler beneath, densely covered with yellow tomentum, 5–$3\frac{3}{8}$ in. long, $1\frac{3}{4}$–$2\frac{1}{2}$ in. broad, on tomentous petioles 2 lines long; inflorescence lateral, covered with long sericeous hairs, with many flowers congested into a globular head, upon a shortish peduncle; pedicels hairy, 4 lines long; sepals 6 lines long, lanceolate-ovate, covered on both sides with long soft hairs, each with a long 3-denticulate scale, pilose outside; tube of corolla cylindrical, membranaceous, with parallel nerves, pilose outside, 6 lines long; segments oblong, rigidly hirsute, especially at the apex, with very long, yellow, rigid hairs; stamens exserted beyond the linear appendages of the throat; disk urceolate, submembranaceous, $1\frac{1}{2}$ line high, its short marginal lobes tridenticulate, twice as long as the ovary.

6. PRESTONIA CALYCINA, Müll. *l. c.* p. 162. In Brasilia, prov. Minas Geraës (St.-Hilaire): *non vidi*.

This handsome species must not be confounded with *Hæmadictyon calycinum*, Benth. Its branches are densely clothed with rigid retrorse ferruginous hairs, the older ones subglabrous; leaves broadly ovate-elliptic, rounded and plicate at the base, shortly acuminate, rigidly membranaceous, darkish brown above, sparsely puberulous, with villous margins, below rigidly tomentous, 4–$4\frac{3}{4}$ in. long, $2\frac{1}{4}$–$3\frac{1}{2}$ in. broad, on petioles $1\frac{1}{2}$ line long; axillary inflorescence capitate, on a peduncle 7 lines long, and covered with ferruginous hairs; bracts acuminate, sparsely pilose, $9\frac{1}{2}$–$10\frac{1}{4}$ lines long; sepals acuminate, pilose, as long as the bracts, each with an internal oblong 2–3-denticulate scale; corolla $1\frac{1}{2}$ in. long; tube a little swollen at the base; segments ovate, somewhat shorter than the tube, the linear appendages in the throat bilobed and papillous; stamens a little exserted; disk urceolate, cleft halfway down into 5 entire lobes.

A species said to be near *Prestonia Surinamensis*.

7. PRESTONIA HIRSUTA, Müll. *l. c.* p. 162, tab. 48. In Brasilia, prov. San Paulo: *non vidi*.

The branches are covered with reddish rigidly hirsute hairs glandular at their base; leaves broadly ovate, rounded and slightly cordate at the base, acuminate, chartaceous, fuscous-green above, sparsely pilose, covered beneath with erect sericeous hairs, $3\frac{1}{2}$–7 in. long, 2–$5\frac{1}{2}$ in. broad, on petioles 3 lines long; the axillary inflorescence hirsute, with flowers congested into a head $2\frac{1}{2}$ in. in diameter, on a peduncle 6 lines long; pedicels 4 lines long; sepals acutely oblong, puberulous, $8\frac{1}{2}$ lines long; corolla $1\frac{1}{4}$ in. long; tube with an annular ring and subexserted appendages in the mouth; segments half the length of the tube, obliquely oblong; anthers biaristate at the base, acuminate, upon short filaments; disk urceolate, 5-grooved, with 5 short apical lobes; ovary half the length of the disk.

8. PRESTONIA LUTESCENS, Müll. *l. c.* p. 164. In Brasilia, prov. Minas Geraës (Claussen 1957): *non vidi*.

A species with the tomentous covering and general appearance of *P. tomentosa*. Leaves oblong, or lanceolate-ovate, pilose above, covered beneath with a dense yellow tomentum, $2\frac{3}{8}$–4 in. long, $1\frac{1}{4}$–2 in. broad, on petioles 2–3 lines long; peduncle $2\frac{1}{2}$–$7\frac{1}{4}$ lines long; sepals $5\frac{3}{4}$ lines long, pilose; corolla yellow, pilose, 1 in. long, its tube 6 lines long; anthers and appendages somewhat exserted; disk urceolate, 3 times as long as the ovary, with 5 short terminal crenulate lobes; ovary pilose at the apex.

9. PRESTONIA BAHIENSIS, Müll. *l. c.* p. 164. In Brasilia, prov. Bahia (Blanchet 24 *bis et* 3776): *non vidi*.

A species resembling the preceding. Its branches are covered with ferruginous or yellow retrorse hairs; leaves broadly elliptic, obtuse and subcordate at the base, shortly acuminate or emarginate at the summit, above softly fulvo-hirsute, $2\frac{3}{4}$–$4\frac{1}{2}$ in. long, 2–$3\frac{1}{4}$ in. broad, almost sessile; inflorescence axillary, with capitate flowers as in the typical species; disk urceolate, with 5 short crenulate lobes, as long as the ovary.

10. PRESTONIA LANATA, Müll. *l. c.* p. 164. In Brasilia, prov. Minas Geraës (St.-Hilaire) : *non vidi*.

A species resembling *P. tomentosa*, but with larger, narrower leaves. Its branches are covered with more patent yellowish tomentum; leaves oblong, or lanceolate-ovate, narrowing towards the obtuse base, gradually acuminate to the apex, membranaceous, fuscous above, covered with yellow hairs, beneath densely woolly with whitish silky tomentum; inflorescence capitate, on a short peduncle, all densely fulvo-piloso; sepals elongated, acuminate; tube of corolla densely sericeous; appendages exserted; disk urceolate, 5-lobed, a little longer than the ovary.

11. PRESTONIA SURINAMENSIS, Müll. in Linn. xxx. 433. In Surinam : *non vidi*.

A species near *P. ipomœifolia*, with softer tomentum. Branches covered with short reddish hairs; leaves broadly ovate, narrower and obtuse at the base, with a short acumen, membranaceous, fuscous above, sparsely pilose, villous on the immersed nerves, ferruginous hirsute on the margins, beneath covered with short fulvous tomentum, 6–10 in. long, $3\frac{1}{2}$–$6\frac{1}{4}$ in. broad, on petioles 5 lines long; axillary inflorescence capitate,

u 2

on a peduncle 10 lines long, all ferruginously pilose; bracts acutely and broadly ovate, 5 lines long; pedicels 6 lines long; sepals broadly ovate, 5½ lines long, hirsutulous on both sides; corolla 10–12 lines long, sericeously villous outside; tube ¾ of that length; appendages linear, lanceolate, obtuse, densely papillous, and with the stamens partly exserted; disk urceolate, crenately 5-lobed on the margin, as long as the ovary.

12. PRESTONIA CEARENSIS, nob.: volubilis, ramis subtenuibus, luteo-pubescentibus: foliis oblongis, imo rotundatis et subcordatis, superne sensim acute acuminatis, tenuiter chartaceis, marginibus revolutis et subcrenulatis, supra pallide viridibus, subglabris, ad nervos immersos sulcatis et flavide puberulis, subtus ferrugineo-puberulis, nervis venisque reticulatis densius flavide hirsutulis: inflorescentia laterali, capitata, pubescente; pedunculo reflexo; floribus congestis, pedicellatis; sepalis acute oblongis, tubo corollæ brevioribus, extus hirsutis, intus squama lata lineari extus hirsuta munitis. In Brasilia, prov. Ceará: *v. s. in herb. Mus. Brit.* Crato (Gardner *sine numero*).

Axils 5 in. apart; leaves 3–5¾ in. long, 1–2¼ in. broad, on pubescent petioles 2 lines long; reflexed peduncle 6 lines long, bearing a capitate head of flowers 1¾ in. in diameter; pedicels 4 lines long; sepals 5 lines long; tube of corolla 7 lines long; segments 4 lines long; stamens inserted in the middle of the tube on a pilose ring; cohering, acuminate; anthers and appendages semiexserted.

13. PRESTONIA MOLLIS, H. B. K. iii. 221, tab. 242: *Hæmadictyon molle*, A. DC. *l. c.* p. 427. In Peruvia, prov. S. Juan de Bracamoras: *v. s. in herb. meo* Chachapoyas (Mathews).

Mathews's specimen agrees with Kunth's drawing. It is a climbing plant, with very slender tortuous subangular branches, with axils 3½–4 in. apart, and having a transverse ridge, with about 4 pectinated small stipules on each face; leaves oblong-elliptic, obtuse or subtruncated at the base, and with a short suddenly acute acumen, pale green above, subscabridulous, somewhat trinerved at the base, with other 5 pairs of fine divaricated nerves, which are scabridly pilose, paler, yellowish, opake beneath, scabridly puberulous, especially on the midrib and nerves, 2–3 in. long, ¾–1¼ in. broad, on scabridulous petioles 3–6 lines long; corymb solitary and lateral at the nodes, 2½ in. long, on a bare slender peduncle rising out of the pectinated ring, 1 in. long, 2–3fid above, and bearing a congested head of flowers on slender pedicels 4–6 lines long, each with an acute linear membranaceous bract 4 lines long; sepals acutely oblong, very membranaceous, reticulated, subimbricate, 6 lines long, 1¾ line broad, each with a small inner triangular scale; tube of corolla a little swollen at the base, much contracted in the middle, of thin texture, glabrous, 10 lines long, with an almost obsolete disjointed ring in the mouth, and below it 5 spathulate-linear appendages semiexserted; segments falcately oblong, subacute, 8 lines long; stamens inserted in a pilose ring in the middle of the tube, on slender filaments; anthers acuminate, with 2 long, sharp, subdivaricated prongs, the summits partly exserted; disk of 5 small, rounded, fleshy lobes, half-connate at the base, as long as the ovary.

Kunth was wrong in describing the lobes of the disk as distinct from the base, and the ovary as divided: he was in error in figuring a thick ring in the mouth of the corolla.

14. PRESTONIA LÆTA, nob.: scandens, ramulis teretibus, fistulosis, pallidis, striolatis, hirsutulis cum pilis imo tuberculatis; axillis remotis, ad lineam transversam stipulis plurimis subsetaceis munitis: foliis ovalibus, imo rotundatis, vix cordatis, apice in acumen acutum subito constrictis, submembranaceis, marginibus ciliatis vix revolutis, supra viridibus, subnitentibus, in costa sulcatis, nervis prominulis venisque transversum reticulatis fusco-rufescentibus, et parcissime pilosis, subtus læte flavis, opacis, glabris, sed costa nervis venisque rufo-tomentellis; petiolis brevibus, rufo-puberulis: corymbo laterali, quam folium 3plo breviore; pedunculo valido, dense pubescente, imo stipellis involucellato, apice 2-ramoso, ramulis congestim plurifloris; pedicellis calyce paullo longioribus, bracteola ¼ breviore suffultis; sepalis majusculis, oblongis, subito cuspidatis, membranaccis, viridulis, extus parce pilosis, undulatis, intus squama lata tridenticulata munitis; corollæ glabræ tubo validiuscule cylindrico, fauce annulo integro, et subtus appendicibus 5 lanceolatis apice exsertis instructo; segmentis rhomboidco-ovatis, angulo sinistro acutis, tubo brevioribus; staminibus ex lineis 5 pilosis medio tubi insertis; antheris acuminatis, imo biaristatis; disco urceolato, carnoso, apice breviter 5-lobo, ovario longiore; stylo tenui; clavuncula incrassata, oblonga, 5-glandulosa, imo membrana peltata instructa; stigmate terminali, brevi, oblonge bilobo. In Brasilia: *v. v. et s. in herb. meo* Rio de Janeiro, Monte Corcovado.

A species with its fistulous branches 2 lines thick, having stipuliferous axils 8 in. apart; leaves 4–5 in. long, 2½–3¼ in. broad, on petioles 2 lines long; peduncle of corymb 9 lines long, its branches 3 lines long; pedicels rather stout, 4–6 lines long; sepals 6 lines long, 3 lines broad; tube of corolla 7 lines long, 2 lines broad; segments 4 lines long, 3 lines broad; filaments 1 line long; anthers 2¼ lines long.

15. PRESTONIA MEGALAGRION, nob.: *Hæmadictyon megalagrion*, Müll. *l. c.* p. 170: *Echites megagros*, Vell. Fl. Flum. p. 110, Icon. iii. tab. 33. In Brasilia, prov. Rio de Janeiro, Campo Grande (Velloz): *v. s. in herb. Mus. Brit.* Itagoahy (Bowie and Cunningham).

A handsome species, agreeing in habit and inflorescence with *Prestonia*. Its scandent branches are subtomentous, lactescent, with axils 5–6 in. apart, furnished with stipules; leaves opposite, patent or reflected, broadly ovate-oblong, roundish at the base, shortly acuminate and mucronate at the apex, subplicate, crenulate, and ciliate on the margins, fuscous green above, obsoletely pilose, sulcate along the arching divaricated nerves, yellow hispidulous along the slender immersed midrib, beneath ferruginously opake, patently hispid on the midrib and prominent nerves, 6½–7½ in. long, 2½–4½ in. broad, on stout hispid petioles 3–4 lines long; corymb solitary and lateral at each node, hispidly pilose, on a stout reflected peduncle 9 lines long, rising out of a stipuloid involucel, shortly 3–4-branched at the apex, and bearing numerous flowers aggregated in a head 2 in. in diameter; pedicels densely tomentous, recurved, 4 lines long, supported by linear hispid bracteoles 1¼ line long; sepals oblong, acuminate, pilose on both sides, 7 lines long, 2 lines broad, each with an inner broadly ovate truncated scale denticulate at the apex; tube of corolla yellowish, pruinosely pubescent, 8 lines long, its mouth with an annular ring, and beneath it 5 subulate subexserted appendages; segments inequilaterally oblong, acute, 6 lines long; stamens as in the preceding species; disk urceolate, submembranaceous, with an emarginately 5-lobed margin, longer than the included 2-lobed ovary.

APTOTHECA.

This genus is proposed for a plant from Cuba, described by Grisebach under the name of *Thyrsanthus corylifolia*:—but which has an elongated 2-locular capsule, of the shape and structure of that of *Rhaptocarpus odoriferus*, an axillary, sessile, short, spicately capitate head of very small subsessile flowers; 5 small sepals, each with a simple acute internal scale; a corolla with a tube about the length of the calyx, with oblong segments somewhat longer, having a sinistrorse convolution, little imbricated in æstivation; 5 stamens upon slender filaments, seated at the base of the tube, and exserted anthers slightly coherent; no disk; and a roundish 2-celled ovary.

APTOTHECA, nob.: *Thyrsanthus*, Griseb. in parte: *Sepala* 5, parva, obtuse oblonga, intus squamula acuta singulatim donata. *Corollæ tubus* cylindricus, calycem subæquans, fauce retrorsum pilosus, membranaceus; *segmenta* 5, obtuse oblonga, rotata, æstivatione paullo imbricata et sinistrorsum convoluta. *Stamina* 5; *filamenta* filiformia, tubum æquantia, ad ejus basin inserta; *antheræ* lineares, vix cohærentes, apice membrana lata acuta munitæ, imo in furcas 2 parallelas obtusas breves fissæ. *Discus* nullus. *Ovarium* rotundatum, 2-loculare; *stylus* tenuis; *clavuncula* conice oblonga, imo 5-lobulata; *stigma* breviter acute 2-lobum. *Capsula* elongata, utrinque sulcata, 2-locularis, dissepimento bilamellari septicide dehiscens, septis per medium longitudinaliter hiantibus, marginibus introflexis et placentiferis; *semina* plurima, linearia, compressa, raphe longitudinali prominente signata, glabra, apice coma longiore coronata.

APTOTHECA CORYLIFOLIA, nob.: *Forsteronia corylifolia*, Griseb. in Cat. Pl. Cub. p. 171 (1856): *Thyrsanthus corylifolius*, Griseb. in Pl. Wr. Cub. part. ii. 519 (1862). In Cuba: *v. s. in herb. Mus. Brit.* Guantanamo (Wright 1664, *in flore et fructu*).

A scandent plant, with slender, straight, glabrous branches, its axils being $1\frac{1}{2}$–2 in. apart; leaves oval, rounded or subacute at the base, suddenly constricted at the apex into a short acumen, thinly chartaceous, bright green above, opake, obsoletely puberulous, sulcate and pilosulous along the midrib, with fine yellow nerves, paler beneath, opake, costa, nerves, and veins prominent, pubescent, the axils of the nerves bearded with a tuft of white hairs, $2\frac{3}{4}$–$4\frac{1}{4}$ in. long, $1\frac{3}{4}$–2 in. broad, on slender pubescent petioles 2–3 lines long. The inflorescence, $1\frac{1}{2}$ in. long, consists of numerous approximate small flowers, agglomerated towards the summit, on pedicels $\frac{1}{4}$ line long; sepals acutely ovate, pale, sparsely puberulous on both sides, each with an acute inner scale $\frac{1}{2}$ line long; tube of reddish corolla 1 line long, with a densely pilose ring in the throat; segments obliquely oblong, pilose in the middle on both sides, rotate, $1\frac{1}{4}$ line long; stamens with slender filaments as long as the tube, and fixed at its base, 1 line long; anthers the same length, their summits subexserted; ovary globose, pilose at the apex, $\frac{1}{3}$ line long. Capsule 8 in. long, $3\frac{1}{2}$ lines broad, deeply 2-sulcate; seeds many, 5 lines long, linear, flat, with a linear prominent raphe; apical coma yellow, 7 lines long.

Grisebach considered this plant to be near *Thyrsanthus spicatus*.

A drawing of the plant, and an analysis of its fruit and seeds, are given in Plate XXI. B.

RHAPTOCARPUS*.

This genus is proposed for some anomalous species of *Echites*, distinguished by their bilocular elongated capsular fruit, like two follicles agglutinated together, as in *Prestonia*, the seeds being crowned by a long coma. The floral characters are derived from the examination of a plant of Weir's collection, specifically identical with one figured by Velloz in the 'Flora Fluminensis;' but I have not seen the fruit.

RHAPTOCARPUS, nob.: *Sepala* 5, acuta, submembranacea, imo in cupulam brevem crasse gibbosam connata, singula squama lata, ad medium in lacinias 4 obtusas fissa intus donata. *Corolla* tubulosa; *tubus* sepalis 2plo longior, ventricosus, fauce constrictus, undique nudus; *segmenta* 5, oblique dolabriformia, pro tertia parte tubo longiora, æstivatione simpliciter dextrorsum convoluta. *Stamina* 5, fauce inclusa; *filamenta* brevissima, glabra; *antheræ* in conum conniventes, vix exsertæ, imo breviter bilobæ, apice acuminatæ. *Discus* 5-lobus, lobis carnosis obtusis, ovario subbrevior. *Ovarium* oblongum, 2-loculare. *Stylus* tenuis, tubo corollæ paullo brevior; *clavuncula* crassa oblonga, imo annulata, 5-sulcata; *stigma* breviter bilobum. *Capsula* elongata, tereti-cylindrica, utrinque sulcata, 2-locularis, dissepimento bilamellari per sulcos septicide dehiscens, septis medio longitudinaliter hiantibus, marginibus introflexis et placentaribus. *Semina* plurima, fusiformia, compressa, dorso costata; *coma* ampla, erecta, 2plo longior.

Frutices *Brasilienses scandentes*: folia *opposita*, *ovata*, *breviter petiolata*; inflorescentia *in quoque nodo solitaria*, *lateralis*; pedunculus *bifissus*, ramulis *longiusculis*, *spicatim plurifloris*.

1. RHAPTOCARPUS ODORIFEROUS, nob.: *Echites odorifera*, Vell. Fl. Flum. i. 109; Icon. iii. tab. 28; A. DC. Prodr. viii. 468; Müll. *l. c.* p. 156. In Brasilia: *v. s. in herb. Soc. Reg. Hort. et meo in flore*, prov. S. Paulo (Weir 474).

The specimen above quoted agrees perfectly with the drawing of Velloz. It is a scandent plant, with flexuose, fistulose, fuscous branches, sparsely covered with short reddish hairs, with axils 3 in. apart; leaves ovate-oblong, rounded and subcordate at the base, gradually narrower upwards, and mucronately acuminate, with retuse subrevolute margins, subchartaceous, above fuscous, opake, granular and sparsely pilose, especially on the immersed nerves, beneath ferruginous, opake, finely granulate, obsoletely pubescent, with darker prominent subpilose nerves, 3¼–4 in. long, 1¾–2¼ in. broad, on stout petioles 1½ line long; inflorescence lateral at the nodes, elongated, ferruginously velutinous, on a peduncle 1½ in. long; its 2 floriferous branches 2¼ in. long, each bearing about 12 alternate pedicellate flowers; pedicels 6–7 lines long, with a slender linear bract 1½ line long; sepals narrow, acuminate, 2 lines long; tube of corolla glabrous, red, 8 lines long, membranaceous, ventricose, contracted for 2 lines below the mouth; segments red, whitish at the top, dolabriform, 4 lines long and broad; anthers 3 lines long, included; disk 2 lines long; capsule, according to Velloz, 11 in. long, ½ in. broad, pendulous.

A drawing of this plant, and an analysis of its flower, fruit, and seeds, are shown in Plate XXI. A.

* From ῥάπτω (*consuo*), καρπός (*fructus*), because the elongated capsule resembles two confluent follicles.

2. **Rhaptocarpus didymus**, nob.: *Echites didyma*, Vell. *l. c.* p. 109, Icon. iii. tab. 27; A. DC. *l. c.* p. 468; Müll. *l. c.* p. 155. In Brasilia, prov. Rio de Janeiro (Velloz): *non vidi*.

This species, from Velloz's drawing, agrees with the preceding in its bifurcate inflorescence, and in its capsular fruit. Its flexuose branches have axils 5 in. apart; leaves elliptic-oblong, acute at both ends, 7–7½ in. long, 3–3¼ in. broad, on petioles 5 lines long; peduncle 2 in. long, its 2 branches 2 in. long, each bearing many approximate flowers towards the extremity; the pedicels, bracteolate at the base, are 4–5 lines long; the acute sepals of the same length; tube of corolla pale yellow, ventricose in the middle, 5 lines long; segments 5 lines long; anthers exserted; disk of 5 oblong lobes; the compressed straight capsule is 10 in. long, bisulcate, and nearly ½ in. broad.

Rhaptocarpus coalitus, nob.: *Echites coalita*, Vell. *l. c.* p. 112, Icon. iii. tab. 40; A. DC. *l. c.* p. 458; Müll. (in parte) *l.c.* p. 155 (excl. tab. 50. fig. 4). In Brasilia, prov. Rio de Janeiro (Velloz): *non vidi*.

A species closely allied to the two preceding. Its scandent branches have axils 3 in. apart; leaves ovate-oblong, rounded or obtuse at the base, subacute above, 3½–4 in. long, 1½–2 in. broad, on petioles 3 lines long; raceme solitary and lateral in each node, 2 in. long, bearing many approximate flowers from near its base, on pedicels 4–5 lines long; sepals acutely oblong, 4 lines long; tube of yellow corolla 4 lines long, ventricose above, and again constricted in the mouth; segments subregular, 3 lines long; anthers included; capsule siliquiform, subtorulose, pendulous, 7 in. long, 3 lines broad, bisulcate; seeds acutely oblong, compressed, 5 lines long, with an apical coma 9 lines long.

Müller, without any knowledge beyond the description of Velloz, regarded this species as identical with the *Echites Vautherii* A. DC.; but the latter differs essentially in its much smaller, more lanceolate leaves, glanduliferous at the base of the midrib and at the axils of the nerves, its more elongated racemes, and especially in its fruit.

4. **Rhaptocarpus Martii**, nob.: *Echites Martii*, *l. c.* p. 153. In Brasilia, prov. Bahia, ad Joazeivo: *non vidi*.

A species with slender glabrous branches; leaves lanceolate, acute at both ends, submembranaceous, fuscous, with 5–6 pairs of immersed nerves, veinless, 2–3 in. long, 5–8 lines broad, on petioles 1–1½ line long; axillary or terminal raceme ⅞–1⅝ in. long, on a short peduncle subglobose at the base, bearing 12–18 closely approximate flowers, on pubescent pedicels 4¼ lines long, supported by lanceolate bracts 2 lines long; sepals narrow-oblong, subobtuse, erect, half the length of the tube of the corolla, each with an internal, broad, 3–5-denticulate scale; corolla 9 lines long, with a fuscous, cylindrical, hirsutulous tube, pubescent within, the segments shorter than it; anthers glabrous; disk 5-lobed.

Müller says this species is distinguished from his *Echites coalita* (non Vell.) by its longer calyx, half the length of the tube of the corolla, its erect (not recurved) sepals. By *E. coalita* he refers to Gardner's plant from Crato (my *R. apiculata*). From the latter it appears also to differ in its submembranaceous, shorter, narrower, lanceolate leaves, acute at both ends, and by its shorter inflorescence.

5. RHAPTOCARPUS APICULATUS, nob.: *Echites coalita*, Müll. in parte (non Vell. nec DC.), *l. c.* p. 155. In Brasilia, prov. Ceará: *v. s. in herb. Mus. Brit.* Crato (Gardner 1754).

A species very distinct from Velloz's *E. coalita*, and from *E. Vautherii*, A. DC., which Müller mingled together: he quotes Gardner's number 1755 instead of 1754, the former being *E. versicolor*, Stadelm. It is a scandent plant, with pallid, rather slender, fistulous, glabrous, striolate, tortuous branches, with axils 6 in. apart; leaves ovate, rounded at both ends, but suddenly constricted at the apex into a short, acute, almost mucronate point, subcoriaceous, with entire revolute margins, subfuscous above, finely corrugulated, with immersed indistinct nerves, ferruginously opake below, glabrous, the nerves scarcely prominulent, 3½–4 in. long, 1½–1¾ in. broad, on rather slender channelled petioles 5–6 lines long; raceme axillary, reflected, nearly 2 in. long, bearing from the base many approximate flowers, which are almost umbellately close towards the extremity; the very slender pedicels are 4–5 lines long; calyx truncate and shortly cupular at the base, cleft into 5 sepals; sepals submembranaceous, linear-oblong, obtuse and recurved at the apex, 2 lines long; tube of corolla narrow, a little swollen near the base, 5 lines long, its segments 3 lines long; disk of 5 fleshy oblong lobes, nearly as long as the ovary; the capsule, in a very young half-matured state, is terete, flattened, bisulcate, 1¼ in. long, supported by the calyx.

DIPLADENIA.

A genus established in 1844 by Prof. A. De Candolle. It consists of several species, mostly low suffruticose plants, with simple erect stems, which are fistulous, and grow out of tuberiform roots; they have few, but large, handsome campanular flowers. I have separated from it many of the species, here described under *Homaladenia* and *Micradenia*, which differ in many essential characters, and which also possess a 2-lobed disk; but in *Dipladenia* these lobes are larger and broader, and the anthers are cordate at the base, not expanded into two long basal prongs.

Besides the above exceptions, *Carruthersia* and *Kopsia* have a 2-lobed disk.

1. DIPLADENIA ILLUSTRIS, A. DC. Prod. viii. 483; Müll. (in parte) Flor. Bras. fasc. xxvi. p. 125 (excl. icon. in tab. 38): *Echites illustris*, Vell. Flor. Flum. p. 114, Icon. iii. tab. 49. In Brasilia, prov. São Paulo: *v. s. in herb. meo* Itú (Weir 118); in prov. São Paulo (Ackermann).

Velloz found this fine species in the mountains bordering on the provinces of Rio de Janeiro and São Paulo. Velloz's figure well represents the plant. The stem, rising out of a large gongyloid root, is 8 in. high, pubescent, 2½ lines thick, simple, erect, fistulous, with glandless axils 1½ in. apart, bearing 3 opposite pairs of leaves in the upper portion, which are slightly divergent, ovate-oblong, subcordate at the base, shortly and suddenly acuminate at the apex, submembranaceous, puberulous on both sides, more densely beneath, with about 10 pairs of somewhat patent nerves conjoined near the margins, with others shorter and intermediate, 2¾–3 in. long, 2–2¼ in. broad, on broad pubescent petioles 1 line long; on the basal portion are 2 pairs of opposite folioles (well shown by Velloz) which are 6–10 lines long, 2½–3 lines broad. The raceme is terminal, 4–5 in. long, erect, bearing 1 terminal and 4 opposite flowers about 1 in. apart, on pedicels 6 lines long, all pubescent; sepals lanceolate, acuminate, 4 lines long, 1¼ line broad, puberulous, each with 3 acuminate inner scales; corolla puberulous, pale red; tube 1½ in. long, narrowly contracted at the base for 5 lines, funnel-shaped above; segments roundly dolabriform, acute at one angle, 1¼ in. long, 1 in. broad; stamens seated on a pilose ring at the constriction of the tube; filaments ½ line long; anthers 3½ lines long, obtusely emarginate at the base; disk of 2 rounded lobes, as broad and long as the ovaries; 2 follicles, erect, terete, 5–6 in. long; seeds linear, 5 lines long, surmounted by a coma 7 lines long.

A drawing of this plant in flower and in fruit, with an analysis of its flower, and a figure of the seed, are shown in Plate XXII.

2. DIPLADENIA VELUTINA, A. DC. *l. c.* p. 483 : *Dipladenia gentianoides*, var. *velutina*, Müll. *l. c.* p. 124 : *Echites velutina*, Stadelm. Bot. Zeit. 1841, p. 72. In Brasilia, prov. São Paulo : *v. s. in herb. meo,* prov. S. Paulo (Ackermann).

A species with much the habit of the preceding. It has an erect cano-hirsute, fistulous stem, near a foot high, 1½ line thick, bearing about 3 pairs of opposite leaves at the simple axils which are 3–4 in. apart; leaves ovate, rounded at the base, mucronate at the apex, chartaceous, with many parallel nerves, as in *D. illustris*, niveo-pubescent above, cano-hirsute beneath, especially on the midrib and nerves, 2–2½ in. long, 1½–2 in. broad, on a broad pilose petiole 1½–2 lines long; raceme terminal, erect, lanately pubescent, on a peduncle 1 in. long, bearing on its summit 3 flowers on pedicels 6 lines long; sepals acuminate, pubescent, 4 lines long; tube of corolla 1 in. long, narrowly cylindrical below for half of its length, funnel-shaped above; segments dolabriform, 6 lines long.

3. DIPLADENIA SANCTA, A. DC. *l. c.* p. 484; Müll. *l. c.* p. 126: *Echites sancta*, Stadelm. *l. c.* p. 59. In Brasilia, prov. Bahia, ad Monte Sancta: *v. s. in herb. meo,* prov. Bahia ad Serra de Piedade (Ackermann).

Müller, who did not see the plant, states that its stem ·is 3–4 *feet* high, evidently a mistake for as many *inches*; for in two of my specimens it is only 3 in., and in the other 7 in. high, being erect, compressed, fistulous, 2 lines broad, retrorsely pilose above, more glabrous below, with axils 2 in. apart; leaves opposite, suberect, broadly ovate, subcordate at the base, roundish at the apex, and suddenly subacute, mucronulate, fuscous greenish above, opake, with subrevolute margins, 10 pairs of divergent nerves arcuately conjoined, with as many shorter and intermediate, a little paler and brownish beneath, corrugulate, somewhat glabrous, with long patent white hairs along the midrib, 2¾–4¾ in. long, 1¾–2¼ in. broad, on stout hairy petioles 1 line long; raceme terminal, 2–3 in. long, the peduncle, patently pubescent, bearing laxly about 6 alternate flowers on stoutish pedicels 5 lines long; 2–3-bracteolate at the base; sepals linear, very acuminate, 4–5 lines long, reddish, membranaceous, each with 3 small acute basal scales;

corolla whitish red below, red above, glabrous; tube 11 lines long, narrowly cylindrical for half its length, funnel-shaped in the upper portion, pubescent within the mouth; segments dolabriform, 10 lines long; stamens seated on a pilose ring at the constriction of the tube; filaments capillary, barbate at the summit, 3 lines long; anthers linear acute, obtusely 2-lobed at the base; disk of 2 lobes, as broad and long as the 2 ovaries; style slender, retrorsely barbate; 2 follicles erect, terete, scarcely torulose, glabrous, 4–4¼ in. long, 1¾ line broad; seeds sigmoid, scabrid, 2½ lines long, surmounted by a yellow coma of equal length.

4. DIPLADENIA SCABRA, Müll. *l. c.* p. 128 : *Dipladenia illustris,* var. *glabra,* Müll. *l. c.* p. 125, tab. 38. In Brasilia austr.: *v. s. in herb. meo,* Tucundiva, prov. São Paulo (Weir 369).

An erect species, with a straight, subglabrous, fistulous stem, scarcely more than 1 line thick, with axils about ½ in. apart; leaves subimbricate, suberect, obovate-oblong, slightly cordate at the base, roundish at the apex, with a mucronate acumen, subchartaceous, with a slightly revolute margin, opake green above, minutely scabrid, midrib prominent, with 10-12 pairs of divergent arcuately conjoined nerves, and others shorter intermediate, concolorous beneath, and nearly glabrous, 2–2¼ in. long, ⅞–1⅜ in. broad, on petioles 1 line long; raceme terminal, 5 in. long, on a subglabrous peduncle, bare at the base for 2 in., bearing upwards of 6–8 alternate flowers on stoutish pedicels 6 lines long, supported by 1 or 2 linear-lanceolate bracts 4–5 lines long; sepals linear-lanceolate, membranaceous, 6 lines long, each with 3–4 minute acute inner scales; tube of corolla 9 lines long, narrowly cylindrical at the base for half its length, funnel-shaped above, glabrous outside, pubescent within; segments oblong, acute, inequilateral, 9 lines long and broad; stamens seated on a niveous pilose ring in the contraction of the tube, 3 lines long; filaments short, pilose; anthers linear acute, obtusely bilobed at the base; the two lobes of the disk large, as long and as broad as the two ovaries.

My specimen agrees exactly with the description and drawing of Müller, except in its leaves being a trifle broader; it certainly offers no resemblance to *D. illustris*; it is represented by Müller as growing out of a napiform tuber 5 in. long and 1¾ in. thick.

5. DIPLADENIA GARDNERIANA, A. DC. *l. c.* p. 483 : *Dipladenia illustris,* var. *pubescens,* Müll. *l. c.* p. 125. In Brasilia: *v. s. in herb. meo,* prov. Goyaz (Gardn. 3311).

This species offers little resemblance to *D. illustris*. It has an erect, subangular, fistulose, glabrous stem, apparently 8 in. high, with axils 2 in. apart; leaves few, opposite, oblong, roundish and subcordate at the base, gradually acute towards the apex, thinly chartaceous, shortly hirtulous on both sides, concolorous, with a prominent sulcate midrib and many divergent immersed nerves, 4–5 in. long, 1¾–2¼ in. broad, on petioles 1 line long; raceme terminal, 7 in. long; peduncle bare at the base for 3½ in., bearing upwards about 4 alternate flowers, on bracteated pedicels 6 lines long; sepals subulate, acuminate, 5 lines long; tube of corolla 1 in. long, narrowly cylindrical for half its length, glabrous, funnel-shaped above; segments broadly dolabriform, acutely uncinate, 1½ in. long, 1 inch broad; stamens inserted on a pilose ring at the constriction of the tube; disk of two rounded subtruncate lobes, half as long as the two ovaries.

6. DIPLADENIA ALEXICACA, A. DC. *l. c.* p. 484: *Dipladenia illustris*, var. *glabra*, Müll. *l. c.* p. 126: *Echites alexicaca*, Stadelm. *l. c.* p. 68. In Brasilia, prov. Bahia (Blanch. 3382) : *non vidi*.

A species with a napiform, tuberous root, throwing out several erect, simple stems; leaves obovate-orbiculate, rounded at the base, very shortly acute, 2–2½ in. long, nearly of the same breadth, on petioles 1½ line long; raceme terminal, few-flowered, on bracteated pedicels 6–10 lines long; corolla 1½ in. long, rose-coloured.

7. DIPLADENIA ANDROSÆMIFOLIA, A. DC. *l. c.* p. 484: *Dipladenia illustris*, var. *glabra*, Müll. *l. c.* p. 126. In Brasilia, prov. Bahia ad Igreja Velha (Blanch. 3582 in parte) : *non vidi*.

An erect, compressed stem, 12 in. high; leaves broadly elliptic, obtuse and cordate at the base, cuspidate at the apex, pale green above, glabrous, with many approximate parallel nerves, 1¼ in. long, 1–1¼ in. broad, on petioles 1 line long; raceme terminal, on a peduncle bearing 5–6 rose-coloured flowers, on pedicels 6 lines long, supported by lanceolate bracts 2 lines long; sepals lanceolate acuminate, 4 lines long, each with 2 inner bidentate scales; tube of corolla 1 in. long, contracted for half its length in a cylindrical form; disk of 2 broadly rounded lobes, half as long as the 2 ovaries.

8. DIPLADENIA VENULOSA, Müll. *l. c.* p. 126. In Brasilia, prov. Minas Geraës: *non vidi*.

A species near *D. sancta*: stem 2¼ lines thick, somewhat thickened at the approximate axils; opposite leaves ovate, cordate, subobtuse at the apex, chartaceous, very glabrous, with 12–15 pairs of parallel nerves, veins reticulated, 2¾–4¼ in. long, 1¼–2¼ in. broad, on petioles 1 line long; raceme lateral, as long as the leaves, with 3–5 large flowers, on pedicels nearly 1 in. long, with bracts 3 lines long; sepals linear-lanceolate, 4–5⅔ lines long, with several simple inner scales more or less combined at the base; tube of corolla 1¾ in. long, contracted in a narrow cylinder for 10 lines; segments broadly dolabriform, 12 lines long, 9 lines broad.

9. DIPLADENIA ROSA CAMPESTRIS, Lemaire in Van Houtte, Flor. des Serr. iii. 256; Walp. Ann. i. 504. *Dipladenia illustris*, var. *pubescens*, Müll. *l. c.* p. 125: *Echites rosa campestris*, Hügel, Parad. Vindob. fasc. 5, cum icon. In Amer. trop.: patria ignota (forsan Brasilia).

Root tuberous, woody, with erect, simple stems, which (with the leaves) are velvety pubescent, and 18 in. high; leaves oval, with a short, recurved, mucronate point at the apex, midrib thickish, with numerous approximately parallel nerves; large, handsome flowers, of a pale rose colour; tube campanulate above, yellow within and in the mouth stellately striped, 1¾ in. long, narrowly cylindrical at its base for one third of its length, subcampanular above, glabrous; segments oblique, dolabriform, shortly uncinate, patent, undulate.

ANGUSTIFOLIA: a group with narrow elliptic leaves, none of which are known to me.

10. DIPLADENIA SPIGELIÆFLORA, Müll. *l. c.* p. 122, tab. 37: *Echites spigeliæflora*, Stadelm. *l. c.* p. 58: *Dipladenia pulchella*, A. DC. *l. c.* p. 485: *Echites pulchella*, Gardner in Hook. Icon. tab. 470. In prov. Goyaz: *non vidi*.

11. DIPLADENIA LINEARIS, Müll. *l. c.* p. 123. In Brasilia, prov. Minas Geraës: *non vidi*.

12. DIPLADENIA GENTIANOIDES, A. DC. *l. c.* p. 484; Müll. *l. c.* p. 124, tab. 37. In Brasilia, prov. São Paulo: *non vidi*.

13. DIPLADENIA LONGILOBA, A. DC. *l. c.* p. 485: *Dipladenia spigeliæflora*, var. *longiloba*, Müll. *l. c.* p. 122. In Brasilia, prov. Minas Geraës: *non vidi*.

14. DIPLADENIA SAPONARIA, A. DC. *l. c.* p. 485: *Dipladenia xanthostoma*, Müll. *l. c.* p. 123. In Brasilia, prov. São Paulo: *non vidi*.

Species exclusæ.

D. xanthostoma, Müll. Flor. Bras. xxvi. p. 123	= *Temnadinia xanthostoma.*
D. flava, Hook.; Müll. Linn. xxx. p. 445	*Chariomma flava.*
D. nobilis, Lem.; Müll. Fl. Bras. xxvi. p. 130	*Chariomma nobilis.*
D. coccinea, Müll. *l. c.* p. 132	*Rhodocalyx coccineus.*
D. Harrisoni, Hook.; Müll. Linn. xxx. p. 446	*Odontadenia Harrisii.*
D. crassinoda, Müll. Fl. Br. xxvi. p. 132	*Micradenia crassinoda.*
D. crassinoda, Lindley; A. DC. *l. c.* p. 486	*Micradenia nodulosa.*
D. atroviolacea, A. DC. *l. c.* p. 484	*Micradenia atroviolacea.*
D. Sellowii, Müll. *l. c.* p. 128	*Micradenia Sellowii.*
D. Martiana, Müll. *l. c.* p. 127	*Micradenia Martiana.*
D. acuminata, Hook.; Müll. *l. c.* p. 129	*Micradenia acuminata.*
D. splendens, A. DC. *l. c.* p. 676; Müll. *l. c.* p. 130	*Micradenia splendens.*
D. urophylla, Hook., Müll. *l. c.* p. 131	*Micradenia urophylla.*
D. Riedelii, Müll. *l. c.* p. 131	*Micradenia Riedelii.*
D. Moricandiana, Müll. *l. c.* p. 129	*Micradenia Moricandiana.*
D. fragrans, A. DC. *l. c.* p. 483; Müll. *l. c.* p. 130	*Micradenia fragrans.*
D. tenuifolia, A. DC. *l. c.* p. 482	*Homaladenia tenuifolia.*
D. tenuifolia, var. *puberula*, A. DC. *l. c.* p. 482	*Homaladenia puberula.*
D. linariæfolia, A. DC. *l. c.* p. 482	*Homaladenia tenuifolia.*
D. pastorum, A. DC. *l. c.* p. 482	*Homaladenia pastorum.*
D. peduncularis, A. DC. *l. c.* p. 482	*Homaladenia peduncularis.*
D. polymorpha, var. *brevifolia*, Müll. *l. c.* p. 122	*Homaladenia brevifolia.*
D. polymorpha, var. *peduncularis*, Müll. *l. c.* p. 122	*Homaladenia vincæflora.*
D. Fendleri, Müll. Linn. xxx. p. 417	*Prestoniopsis Fendleri.*

MICRADENIA.

A series of plants, first placed in a group distinct from *Dipladenia* by Prof. DeCandolle in 1844. These are distinguished from the former by their habit, especially in the incrassated axils of the branches, furnished with a whorl of warty glands between the petioles, in the pedicels of the flowers spirally twisted, in the anthers with long, obtuse, parallel, basal prongs, in the much shorter disk, seldom attaining more than a quarter of the length of the ovaries, in the incrassated placenta of the follicles, from which are suspended many flat imbricate seeds having a nearly obsolete coma of short scale-like hairs. It forms a very good genus, well-marked by constant and uniformly peculiar characters.

MICRADENIA, A. DC.: *Sepala* 5, subparva, valde acuminata, quincuncialiter imbricata, intus ad basin squamulis 2 bidentatis munita, persistentia. *Corolla* majuscula; *tubus* glaber, pro ¼ parte crassior angustissime cylindricus, dein ampliatus, cylindrice campanulatus, sæpius submembranaceus; *segmenta* 5, rhomboideo-dolabriformia, latere mucronata, tubo sæpius 3plo breviora. *Stamina* ad contractionem tubi in annulo piloso inserta; *filamenta* subbrevia, niveo-pilosa; *antheræ* lineari-oblongæ, acutæ, basi in furcas 2 obtusulas parallele lineares fissæ. *Discus* e lobis 2 oppositis, brevissime latis, rotundatis, quam ovaria sæpius 4plo brevioribus. *Ovaria* 2, acute oblonga, lobis disci alterna; *stylus* tenuis, imo fissus, cruribus cum ovario articulatis; *clavuncula* incrassata, 5-sulcata, imo membrana peltata indusiata, ad antheras cohærens; *stigmata* 2, minima, acuta, terminalia. *Folliculi* 2, erecti, curvati, teretes, sutura ventrali dehiscentes, marginibus introflexis in placentam cylindricam coalitis; *semina* plurima, parva, compressissima, obspathulata, *raphe* tenui æquilonga summo suspensa; *coma* brevissima, e pilis paucis brevissimis, subpaleaccis.

Suffrutices *Brasilienses, ramosissimi;* rami *subsarmentosi, sæpe flexuosi;* axillæ *sæpe approximatæ, valde incrassatæ,* glandulis *plurimis carnosis verticillatim munitæ;* folia *opposita, elliptico-oblonga, sæpius longiuscule petiolata;* racemi *axillares vel terminales, pauciflori;* flores *speciosi, albi, rosei vel atro-purpurei;* pedicelli *spiraliter torti.*

1. MICRADENIA CRASSINODA, A. DC. *l. c.* p. 486: *Echites crassinoda*, Gardn. Lond. Journ. Bot. i. 544: *Dipladenia crassinoda*, Müll. (non Lindl.) *l. c.* p. 132. In Brasilia, prov. Rio de Janeiro: *v. v.* in summo Monte Corcovado: *v. v. et sicc. in herb. meo* (3137); *in hb. Mus. Brit.*; *v. s.* ex eodem loco (Gardner, 250).

I collected this plant in 1836, in company with Gardner. It is of low growth, with many straggling, sarmentose, stout branches, subfistulose, covered irregularly with a lax epidermis, somewhat corrugately striate, very incrassate in the approximate axils, which are only 3–6 lines apart, 3–4 lines broad, bearing on each side, between the petioles, 4–6 subulate warty excrescences, often pectinately combined together; leaves lanceolate-oblong, acute at both ends, glabrous, subcoriaceous, green above, with semi-immersed divergent nerves, beneath ferruginously opake, with immersed nerves, $2\frac{1}{4}$–$3\frac{1}{4}$ in. long, 5–12 lines broad, on slender channelled petioles 2 lines long; axillary racemes $1\frac{1}{2}$–3 in. long, with a bracteolated peduncle 9 lines long, bearing about 5 alternate white flowers, on spirally twisted pedicels 6–9 lines long, obsoletely bracteolated at the base; sepals lanceolate, sharply acute, with pellucid margins, having within 2 bifurcate basal scales; tube of corolla 2 in. long, narrowly cylindrical at the base for a length of 4 lines, funnel-shaped above, with subtruncate, dolabriform segments 10 lines long, 9 lines broad; stamens 4 lines long, inserted at the contracted portion of the tube, on a densely pilose ring; anthers purplish, coherent, with 2 parallel, obtuse, basal spurs; follicles 2, erect, incurved, slender, terete, 2½–3 in. long, 1½ line thick; immature seeds 1¼ line long, very compressed, obspathulate, fixed round a thickish placenta, with a deciduous coma of few silky hairs the length of the testa.

A drawing of this species, in flower and fruit, with the analysis of its flower and a figure of its seed, are given in Plate XXIII.

2. MICRADENIA ATROVIOLACEA, nob.: *Echites atroviolacea*, Stadelm. Bot. Zeit. 1841, p. 76; Gardn. Lond. Journ. Bot. i. 544: *Dipladenia atroviolacea*, A. DC. *l. c.* viii. 484; Müll. Flor. Bras. xxvi. p. 127. In Brasilia prov. Rio de Janeiro, in montibus circa Tejuca, ad Pedra Bonita: *v. v. et sicc. in herb. meo* (3186); *v. s. in herb. Mus. Brit.* (Gardner 249, ex eodem loco).

I found this plant on one of the spurs of the Tejuca range, in company with Gardner, in 1836. It is a low, bushy plant, growing on rocky ground, with many, rather slender subsarmentous branches, having approximate axils 4–6 lines apart, charged between the petioles with several small warty excrescences, as in the former species; the leaves are lanceolate-oblong, subacute at the base, gradually or suddenly constricted near the apex into a narrow acumen, subcoriaceous, pale green above, with a prominent fine midrib and scarcely visible nerves, paler opake beneath, with a reddish prominulent midrib and immersed nerves, 1½–2 in. long, 6 lines broad, on slender channelled petioles 3–5 lines long, the leaves being erect and much imbricated near the ends of the branchlets; racemes axillary, pedunculate, bearing about 4 alternate flowers, on slender, spirally twisted pedicels 6–8 lines long; sepals acuminately subulate, with membranaceous margins, 2½ lines long; tube of corolla 18 lines long, narrowed and scarlet at the base for a length of 8 lines, above that suddenly bell-shaped cylindrically, where it is white, with reddish irregular stripes; segments rhomboid-oblong, of a dark, dull red-brown colour, 8 lines long, 6 lines broad, expanding above the mouth; stamens nearly sessile at the contraction of the tube; anthers purple, cohering, each with 2 obtuse, parallel, basal spurs.

Var. *ovata*, nob.: *Echites atropurpurea*, Lindley, in Paxton Mag. Bot. (1842); Bot. Reg. vol. xxix. (1843), tab. 27; A. DC. *l. c.* p. 486. It differs in its more ovate leaves, 1¼–1½ in. long, 9–11 lines broad, on slender petioles 5–6 lines long; its flowers are exactly as those above described; so that the different colouring given by Lindley must be due to hot-house cultivation.

I found this on the same spot and also at Pavuna, near Iguassu, in the same province.

3. MICRADENIA NODULOSA, nob.: *Dipladenia crassinoda*, Lindley (non Gardner), Bot. Reg. xxx. tab. 64: *Dipladenia Martiana*, var. *glabra*, Müll. *l. c.* p. 128. In Brasilia: *v. s. in herb. Mus. Brit.* prov. Minas Geraës, ad Pico de Itabira (Sellow): *non vidi*.

A climbing plant, with very flexuose, hairy, dichotomous branches, having axils 2–4 in. apart, which are much incrassate and charged on each face between the petioles with about 6 subulate, reflexed, warty glands; leaves ovate-elliptic, rounded at the base, with a short acute acumen, thinly chartaceous, slightly revolute on the margin, olive-green above, opake, obsoletely puberulous, shortly hispid on the deeply sulcate midrib, with about 14 pairs of patent arcuately conjoined nerves, with others shorter and intermediate, ferruginously opake beneath, obsoletely puberulous, midrib and nerves prominulent, 2¼–3 in. long, 1⅜–1¾ in. broad, on slender channelled petioles 4–5 lines long; raceme axillary, glabrous, on a peduncle 3 in. long, bearing many alternate flowers 2–3 lines apart on spirally twisted pedicels 8 lines long; sepals acute, 2 lines long; dark-red tube of corolla 12 lines long, narrowly cylindrical at the base for 4 lines, funnel-shaped above, yellowish in the throat; segments rose-coloured, rhomboid, and broadly dolabriform, 9 lines long and broad; stamens seated on a pilose ring in the contraction of the tube, on short barbate filaments; anthers acute, with 2 parallel, aristiform, basal prongs; disk of two flat, rounded lobes ¼ the length of the 2 subulate ovaries. No details are given by Lindley.

4. MICRADENIA RIEDELII, nob.: *Dipladenia Riedelii*, Müll. *l. c.* p. 131. In prov. Rio de Janeiro, Cabo Frio (Riedel): *v. v. et sicc. in herb. meo* (4021) prope Magé et Macahé; *v. s. in herb. Mus. Brit.* Magé (Gardn. 537).

The above plant, collected by me in 1836, corresponds with the description given by Müller of the Cape-Frio plant, from nearly the same locality. It is a rather low shrub, with glabrous, pallid, striate, often flexuous branches, with more or less approximate axils ½–2 in. apart, much incrassate and charged with several acute warty glands between the petioles; leaves broadly ovate or oblong, subacute and plicate at the base, roundish and suddenly contracted at the summit into an acute acumen 2 lines long, chartaceous, with thin, subrevolute margins, fuscous green and very opake above, with semi-immersed fine nerves, opake and reddish ferruginous beneath, the nerves being scarcely prominulent, 1¾–3 in. long, 1–1¾ in. broad, on slender petioles 6–9 lines long; racemes 2, terminal, on bare peduncles ½–1 in. long, bearing upwards about 7 alternate flowers, on spirally twisted pedicels, 3 lines apart and 2¼–4 lines long, with a small, acute, deciduous bract; sepals acuminate, 2 lines long, with pellucid margins; tube of corolla 1¼ in. long, narrowly contracted and scarlet at the base for a length of 5 lines, broadly funnel-shaped and paler above, with membranaceous segments, rhomboidally dolabriform, mucronate, 6–7 lines long, and of a rose colour; stamens inserted in the constriction of the tube; filaments niveo-tomentose; anthers cohering, of a reddish colour, with 2 basal, obtuse, parallel prongs; disk of 2 very short rounded lobes, one sixth the length of the 2 conical, oblong ovaries.

5. MICRADENIA HIRSUTULA, nob. In Brasilia: *v. s. in herb. meo* (Claussen, sine loco).

An erect species, apparently of low stature, the specimen being 8 in. high, the basal portion being divided into 2 branches, one of which is broken off; it is clothed with whitish retrose or patent hairs; the upper axils 1½ in. apart, with warty excrescences ¼ line long; the leaves are subovate, gradually rounded or subcordate at the base, roundish below the summit and constricted into a broadish acute point, rigidly chartaceous, sparsely and rigidly pilose above, with approximate, parallel, fine, immersed nerves, subferruginously opake below, sparsely pubescent, hirsutulous on the prominent midrib, 1⅜–1¾ in. long, 7–10 lines broad, on pubescent broad petioles 1½–2 lines long; the terminal raceme has a straight, stoutish, pubescent peduncle 2¼ in. long, bearing 3–4 distant, alternate flowers, on pilose pedicels 6 lines long, supported by an acute bract 2 lines long; sepals acutely lanceolate, submembranaceous, reddish, glabrous, 5 lines long, curving at the apex; tube of corolla 1¼ in. long, very narrow, and scarlet for the length of 8 lines, then swelling into a cylindrical bell-shape, whitish, with red stripes, subplicate; segments of a deep-red chocolate-colour, oblong, with nearly parallel sides, obliquely truncate at the summit, 7 lines long, 3½ lines broad; stamens seated in the constriction of the tube, springing out of a dense cottony ring; anthers yellow, with 2 basal, obtuse, parallel prongs. It is a species widely differing from all others.

6. MICRADENIA SELLOWII, nob.: *Dipladenia Sellowii*, Müll. *l. c.* p. 128. In Brasilia: prov. Minas Geraës (Riedel 1448), Itacolumi (Riedel 2768): *non vidi*.

A slender species, with small narrow leaves like those of *M. atroviolacea*: the branches are long, slender, and flexuous, with glands in the axils between the petioles; the leaves are oblong-elliptic, obtusely acute at both ends, subcoriaceous, with revolute margins, of a dark reddish green, 1⅜–2¼ in. long, 7–9½ lines broad; raceme subterminal, longer than the leaves, bearing 3–6 large flowers like those of *M. Martiana*; tube of corolla purple, with rosy-red segments.

7. MICRADENIA UROPHYLLA, nob.: *Dipladenia urophylla*, Hook. Bot. Mag. tab. 4414; Müll. *l. c.* p. 131. In Brasilia: *v. v.* in montib. Organ.; *v. s. in herb. Mus. Brit.* ex eodem loco (Gardner 5817).

A climbing species, collected by me in 1828 at an elevation of 3500 feet; Gardner found it in the same locality in 1841. The cultivated plant was received in 1848 from Mr. Veitch's collector, probably from the same locality. Its flexuous branches are pale brown, subangular, striate, fistulous, glabrous, 1½ line thick; the axils subdilated, 1½–2¾ in. apart, are charged at the nodes on each face with about 6 subulate fleshy glands 1–2 lines long; the opposite leaves are oblong (in Gardner's specimen more ovate), rounded and plicate at the base, suddenly constricted at the apex into an obtuse narrow, caudate acumen, submembranaceous, fuscous green above, opake, sulcate along the midrib and about 10 pairs of diverging nerves and transverse veins, pallid brown beneath, with prominulent nerves, 3½–4½ in. long, 1½–2 in. broad, on slender striolate petioles 6–9 lines long; racemes solitary and lateral at the nodes, 4 in. long; on a slender, patent or recurving peduncle 1¼ in. long, bearing above about 4 alternate flowers on slender spirally twisted pedicels 9 lines long, each with a linear bracteole 2 lines long; sepals lanceolate, 1¼ line long; tube of corolla 1⅜ in. long, contracted below into a narrow cylindrical form 4 lines long, upwards funnel-shaped, and 6 lines broad in the mouth, of a salmon-red colour; segments oblong-acute, somewhat equilateral, reflexed at the apex, 6 lines long, 3 lines broad; disk of 2 lobes one third the length of the 2 ovaries.

8. MICRADENIA MARTIANA, A. DC. *l. c.* p. 485: *Echites Martiana*, Stadelm. Bot. Zeit. 1841, p. 31: *Dipladenia Martiana*, Müll. *l. c.* p. 127 (excl. syn.). In prov. Bahia: *non vidi*.

A scandent plant, with flexuous glabrous branches (younger ones hirsutulous), much incrassate at the approximate thickened axils, which present between the petioles 4 oblong, subcordate, cuspidate, red, reflexed, warty glands, 1–2¼ lines long; leaves obovate-oblong, subcordate, cuspidate, coriaceous, with revolute margins, rough above, velvety beneath, with oblique nerves and transverse veins, 1½–3¼ in. long, 10–18 lines broad, on petioles 1–2 lines long; racemes terminal or axillary, glabrous, as long as the leaves, bearing 3–5 purplish red flowers 2 in. long, on pedicels 12 lines long; sepals subulate, glabrous, 6 lines long, having 2 internal, basal, bifid scales; tube of corolla 1⅛ in. long, much narrowed at the base as far as the middle, thence funnel-shaped; segments rhomboidally orbicular, crispate along the edge; 2 follicles 3¼ in. long.

9. MICRADENIA MORICANDIANA, A. DC. *l. c.* p. 486: *Dipladenia Moricandiana*, Müll. *l. c.* p. 129. In Brasilia, prov. Bahia: *non vidi*.

A species distinguished by its smaller leaves on short petioles, and smaller flowers; subscandent, slender branches, puberulous above with short retrorse hairs; approximate axils much incrassate, and charged on each face between the petioles with 4 warty ovate glands 1⅛ line long; leaves obovate, obtuse at the base, mucronate, coriaceous, fuscous, glabrous, nerved but veinless, 1–1¼ in. long, 6–9 lines broad, on puberulous petioles 2 lines long; racemes axillary, glabrous, longer than the leaves, bearing 2 or 3 yellow flowers on thick, rigid, spirally twisted pedicels 6 lines long; sepals subulately ovate, 1⅛ line long, each with 2 inner basal bifid scales; tube of corolla 1 in. long, contracted at the base below the middle, swelling in a funnel-shape above; segments obscurely ovate, dolabriform, with undulated margins; stamens inserted in the contraction of the tube; disk of 2 rounded lobes much shorter than the 2 ovaries.

10. MICRADENIA FRAGRANS, nob.: *Echites fragrans*, Stadelm. Bot. Zeit. 1841, p. 71: *Dipladenia fragrans*, A. DC. *l. c.* p. 483: Müll. *l. c.* p. 130, tab. 39. In Brasilia, prov. Bahia: *non vidi*.

A species near the preceding, but with more rigid and straighter branches, and larger flowers. Its branches are glabrous, terete, much incrassate at the axils, which are 2–2½ in. apart, and charged on each side, between the petioles, with about 8 large, subulate, warty glands soon caducous; leaves elliptic or obovate, rounded or obtuse at the base, suddenly acuminate at the summit, chartaceous, smooth, reddish green, 2¾–3¼ in. long, 1½–2 in. broad, on slender petioles 9–10 lines long; racemes terminal or axillary, on a peduncle 1 in. long, bearing upwards about 7 white flowers on alternate pedicels 12–15 lines long; sepals ovate-acuminate, 2 lines long, with 2 inner basal bifid scales; tube of corolla 18 lines long, narrowed at the base for one third of its length, thence swelling in a campanular form to a breadth of 8 lines in the mouth; segments rhomboidally ovate, dolabriform, mucronate, 18 lines long, 12 lines broad; stamens seated in the contraction of the tube, with purplish anthers, having at their base 2 parallel obtuse prongs as long as the filaments; disk of 2 rounded lobes ⅓ the length of the 2 ovate ovaries; follicles 9¼ in. long, 1¾ line thick. Müller mentions a variety from the province of Minas, with ternate leaves, which may be regarded as a distinct, undescribed species.

11. MICRADENIA ACUMINATA, nob: *Dipladenia acuminata*, Hook. Bot. Mag. tab. 4828: Müll. *l. c.* p. 129 In Brasilia, montib. Organ.; in caldario culta: *non vidi*.

This splendid species is only known from a plant received from the Organ Mountains, and raised by Veitch. From its large flowers and long sepals, it approaches *Dipladenia*; but its climbing habit, the presence of subulate warty glands at the axillary nodes, the twisted pedicels, the small size of the lobes of the disk, all prove that it really belongs to *Micradenia*. It is described as a climbing shrub, everywhere glabrous, with axils 1½ in. apart, charged at the incrassate nodes on each face with 2 laciniate, subulate, diverging glands 2-3 lines long; leaves opposite, elliptic-ovate, cordate at the base, shortly acuminate, submembranaceous, with divergent nerves and reticulated veins, 3½–4 in. long, 1½–1¾ in. broad, on stoutish petioles 6 lines long; raceme terminal, pendent, 6 in. long, bearing 8 alternate flowers, on bracteolate, spirally twisted pedicels 1 in. long; sepals lanceolate, subulate, erecto-patent, 9 lines long, each with an inner lanceolate scale; corolla large, its border spreading to a diameter of 4 in.; tube 2½ in. long, whitish, narrowed cylindrically at the base for half its length, funnel-shaped above, streaked deep red in the mouth; segments rhomboidally dolabriform, with a long uncinate acumen, of a deep rose-colour, dextrorsely convolute, expanded, 2 in. long, 1¼ in. broad; stamens seated at the constriction of the tube, cohering, glabrous; disk of two fleshy, flat, rounded lobes, less than half the length of the 2 oblong ovaries; style slender, clavuncle incrassate, 5-grooved, agglutinated to the anthers.

12. MICRADENIA SPLENDENS, A. DC. *l. c.* p. 676; Müll. *l. c.* p. 130: *Echites splendens*, Hook. Bot. Mag. tab. 3976. In Brasilia, montib. Organ. et in caldario cult.: *non vidi*.

A climbing species near *M. acuminata*, but with larger leaves; probably it is only a variety of it. It has terete, glabrous branches, with incrassate axils 3½ in. apart; leaves elliptic, cordate at the base, acuminate, subcoriaceous, undulating on the margins, glabrous above, with very numerous, divergent, parallel, immersed nerves, very pubescent beneath, nerves prominent, 4-8 in long, 1½-3 in. broad, on extremely short petioles; racemes axillary, on a peduncle shorter than the leaves, bearing 4-6 large showy flowers on pedicels bracteate at the base, 6-12 lines long; sepals subulate, acuminate, reflexed at the summit, 6 lines long; tube of corolla white, glabrous, hairy within, narrowly cylindrical for 6 lines, funnel-shaped above, 1½ in. long; segments of a deep rose-colour, broadly dolabriform, uncinately toothed, 1½ in. long and broad, all expanding to a diameter of 4 in.; stamens inserted at the constriction of the tube; anthers shortly and obtusely 2-lobed at the base; disk of 2 rounded emarginate lobes one third the length of the 2 ovaries.

HOMALADENIA.

A very distinct group of plants, placed by Prof. DeCandolle in *Dipladenia*; but they differ in their habit, in their short erect stems densely covered above with pine-like leaves, terminal flowers with a smallish hypocrateriform corolla, with a narrow cylindrical tube and a rotate border; stamens included within the mouth of the tube; anthers shortly cordate at the base; disk of 2 ovate glands as long as the ovaries; seeds with a double coma, the inner hairs twice the length of the seeds,—characters quite at variance with those of *Dipladenia*.

HOMALADENIA*, nob.: *Dipladenia* (in parte) auctorum. Sepala acuta vel longe acuminata, imbricata, intus squamulis 2 minimis ad basin munita. Corolla hypocrateriformis; *tubus* tenuiter cylindricus, ad faucem vix latior; *segmenta* rhomboideo-dolabriformia, triplo breviora, rotata, dextrorsum convoluta. *Stamina* intra faucem inclusa, sæpe ex annulo niveo-piloso orta; *filamenta* pilosa; *antheræ* his duplo longiores, apice acutæ, imo breviter cordatæ, in conum conniventes. *Discus* opposite bilobus, lobis anguste oblongis. *Ovaria* 2, acuta, his alterna et paullo longiora; *stylus* tenuis; *clavuncula* incrassata, 5-sulcata, imo membrana peltata indusiata; *stigmata* 2, parva, terminalia. *Folliculi* 2, tenuiter teretes, subtorulosi, erecto-patentes. *Semina* plurima, oblonga, sæpe pilosa; *coma* dupla, erecta, pilis inferioribus duplo longioribus, exterioribus multo brevioribus; *embryonis radicula* supera.

Suffrutices *valde humiles, Brasilienses vel Guianenses*: radix *crassa, dauciformi-tuberosa, apice caulos plurimos emittens*; caulis *simplex, sæpius tenuissimus, erectus, imo nudiusculus, apicem versus crebre foliosus*; folia *opposita, anguste linearia aut lanceolato-oblonga, erecta, imbricata, rarius remotiora, brevissime petiolata*; racemus *terminalis, pauciflorus*; flores *parvi, rarius mediocres*.

1. HOMALADENIA TENUIFOLIA, nob.: *Dipladenia tenuifolia*, A. DC. Prodr. viii. 482: *Dipladenia polymorpha*, var. *tenuifolia*, Müll. Fl. Bras. xxvi. 121: *Echites tenuifolia*, Mikan, Flor. Bras. fasc. 3; Stadelm. Bot. Zeit. 1841, p. 53. In Brasilia, prov. Rio de Janeiro, Minas Geraës et Goyaz: *v. s. in herb. meo* prov. Goyaz (Gardner 3888).

A species with an erect filiform stem, 6–9 in. high, bare at its base, sending out a short lateral branchlet; axils ¾–1 in. apart; leaves opposite, narrowly linear, subincurved, acuminate, fleshy, margins revolute, glabrous above, puberulous beneath, 1½–2¾ in. long, barely ¼ line broad, on petioles 1 line long; raceme terminal; peduncle bearing 4 alternate flowers 6–9 lines apart, on pedicels 3–4 lines long, with basal bracteoles 1 line long; sepals acute, 1 line long; tube of corolla very slender, 6 lines long, a little swollen at the mouth, within which the stamens are enclosed; segments obliquely oblong, rotate, 3 lines long, 2 lines broad; the glabrous follicles (which I have not seen) are 4 in. long, 1 line broad, scarcely torulose; seeds 4 lines long; coma, outer row 6 lines long, inner series 12 lines long.

A drawing of this plant, in flower and in fruit, is shown in Plate XXIV A.

2. HOMALADENIA LINARIÆFOLIA, nob.: *Dipladenia linariæfolia*, A. DC. *l. c.* p. 482. In Brasilia, prov. Bahia: *non vidi*.

A slender stem 4–5 in. high, hirsutely puberulous, throwing out other branchlets from its base; leaves narrowly linear, obtuse at the base, acuminate, rigid, with revolute margins, subglabrous, 1–1½ in. long, ¾ line broad, erect; terminal peduncle 1–1½ in. long, bearing about 3 flowers, on pedicels scarcely ¼ line long; sepals subulately lanceolate, 3 lines long; tube of corolla 7–8 lines long, very slender, thicker in the mouth, within which the stamens are enclosed, seated on a pilose ring; segments obliquely oblong, 4 lines long, 2–2¼ lines broad.

3. HOMALADENIA PASTORUM, nob.: *Dipladenia pastorum*, A. DC. *l. c.* p. 482: *Dipladenia palymorpha*, var. *tenuifolia*, Müll. *l. c.* p. 121: *Echites pastorum*, Stadelm. *l. c.* p. 52: *v. s. in herb. meo* Minas Geraës (Claussen 256).

A tuberous root, throwing out several slender, puberulous, simple stems, 6 in. high,

* From ὁμαλὸς (*planus*), ἀδὴν (*glans*), from the flat shape of the lobes of the disk.

nearly bare of leaves above the base, densely foliiferous above the middle ; leaves approximate, erect, imbricate, acute at the base, acuminate, glabrous, with revolute margins, 1½ in. long, 1¼ line broad, nearly sessile; raceme terminal, rather short, bearing about 3 flowers on a bare peduncle 1 in. long; pedicels with a lanceolate bract 2 lines long, glabrous, 3–4 lines long; sepals acutely lanceolate, 2 lines long ; tube of corolla slender, 7 lines long, slightly swollen at the mouth; segments falcate, rotate, scarlet, 4 lines long, 1¼ line broad ; stamens placed within the mouth and inserted in the contraction of the tube; disk of 2 flat, semiorbicular lobes, as long as the 2 ovaries; 2 terete, subtorulose follicles ; seeds 3 lines long, with a yellowish coma twice that length.

4. HOMALADENIA PEDUNCULARIS, nob. : *Dipladenia peduncularis*, A. DC. *l. c.* p. 482 : *Dipladenia polymorpha*, var. *peduncularis*, Müll. *l. c.* p. 122 : *Echites peduncularis*, Stadelm. *l. c.* p. 54. In Brasilia, prov. Minas Geraës : *v. s. in flore in herb. meo* (Claussen 252).

Stems simple, scarcely 6 in. high, sparsely puberulous, slender, bare for a short distance below, above crowded with leaves, which are erect, narrowly linear, acute at both ends, margins revolute, hirto-pilose above, opake beneath, 1½–1¾ in. long, ½ line broad, on slender petioles ¼ line long ; peduncle axillary, slender, 1¼–2¼ in. long, bearing 3–4 flowers on pedicels 6 lines long, each with a lanceolate bract 1 line long; sepals lanceolate, erect, imbricate, 2–2¼ lines long; slender tube of corolla 6 lines long ; narrow segments 2 lines long; disk of 2 broadish lobes, as long as the 2 ovaries; follicles torulose, 3 in. long.

5. HOMALADENIA PUBERULA, nob. : *Dipladenia tenuifolia*, var. *puberula*, A. DC. *l. c.* p. 482 : *Dipladenia polymorpha*, var. *puberula*, Müll. *l. c.* p. 121. In Brasilia, prov. Goyaz et Piauhy : *v. s. in herb. meo*, Piauhy (Gardner, 2229).

A very dwarfish species, the rather stout, erect stems being only 3–6 in. high, glabrous, very rugous, with 2 or 3 patent lateral branches 1–2 in. long, densely beset with imbricate, narrow, acuminate, linear leaves with revolute margins, darkish above, yellowish and pubescent beneath, 4–8 lines long, ⅛–⅙ line broad, on short, slender petioles ; peduncle terminal, slender, puberulous, 1¼ in. long, bearing 3 alternate flowers on pedicels 2 lines long, with an acute basal bract ¾ line long ; sepals lanceolate, 1 line long ; tube of corolla slender, 5 lines long ; segments 4 lines long.

This appears to me a peculiar and very distinct species.

6. HOMALADENIA BREVIFOLIA, nob. : *Dipladenia polymorpha*, var. *brevifolia*, Müll. *l. c.* p. 122. In Brasilia, prov. Minas Geraës : *non vidi*.

Stems erect, simple, very short, densely foliiferous ; leaves broadly elliptic or oblong-ovate, 5–12 lines long, 3–7 lines broad ; inflorescence on a very long peduncle. A species widely differing from all others, and approaching the preceding.

7. HOMALADENIA VINCÆFLORA, nob. : *Dipladenia vincæflora*, Van Houtte, Fl. Serres, ii. p. 8, tab. 6 ; Walp. Rep. vi. 742 : *Dipladenia polymorpha*, var. *peduncularis*, Müll. *l. c.* p. 122. In prov. Minas Geraës : *non vidi*.

A species with a tuberous root, throwing out several erect, subbranching, low, slender stems, having 2–4 minute subulate stipules at the axils ; leaves extremely small, linear lanceolate, fleshy, glabrous, with revolute margins, ½–2 in. long, 2½–5 lines broad; racemes axillary, on a very long naked peduncle, bearing 1 or more flowers; sepals short; corolla hypocrateriform, with a long, narrow, cylindrical tube, swollen a little below the mouth; segments rotate, roseate red; disk of 2 orbicular lobes.

PRESTONIOPSIS.

This is a very good genus, established by Müller, in 1860, upon the *Echites pubescens* of Willdenow (*non* Hook.), one of Humboldt's plants, the exact locality of which was not known; but this I find is Bogotá. The plant was first noticed by Willdenow, under a short account stating that it had an axillary subumbellate inflorescence. Müller has given a copious floral character of it from a specimen stated to be incomplete; my examination of Mutis's plant confirms the correctness of Müller's details in every particular. He observes that, although it offers a slight resemblance to *Prestonia* in habit and aggregated flowers, it is very dissimilar in its floral structure; and he points to *Laseguea* as its nearest ally. According to my view, the genus must be placed in the *Dipladenieæ*, on account of its bilobed disk. In habit it approaches *Micradenia*; and in the small size of its flowers it offers some similarity to *Homaladenia*. The calyx consists of 5 narrow, very acuminate sepals of unequal length, quincuncially imbricate, and furnished within with a basal, bidentate scale; the tube of the corolla is cylindrical, as long as the sepals, and narrowed at its base for a quarter of its length; segments as long as the tube, narrowly oblong, and erect, dextrorsely convolute in æstivation; stamens seated at the constriction of the tube; filaments short, glabrous, affixed to a tuft of white hairs in the sinus of the anthers; anthers sublinear, with an apical membrane, and shortly cordate at the base, cohering in a cone by their agglutination to the clavuncle; disk of 2 broadish, flat, opposite lobes, shorter than the 2 free ovaries; a short style surmounted by a very thick 5-grooved clavuncle, indusiate at its base by a narrow membrane; stigmata 2, short and terminal; 2 follicles, subulately terete, rather stout, subdivaricate; seeds many, subulately terete, with a very erect apical coma nearly twice its length.

1. PRESTONIOPSIS PUBESCENS, Müller, Bot. Zeit. 1860, p. 22, tab. 1 (in parte infer.) figs. 1–6; id. Linn. xxx. p. 439: *Echites pubescens* (non Hook. & Arn.), Willd. in R. & Sch. iv. p. 796; Kunth. Nov. Gen. iii. 453; A. DC. Prodr. viii. 476. In Nova Granada: *v. s. in herb. Mus. Brit.* Bogotá (Mutis).

This is said to be a scandent shrub; its branches are somewhat stout, lenticellately verrucose, pubescent, compressed, and dilated at the nodes by a transverse ridge; axils 2–3 in. apart; leaves opposite, subpatent, oblong-ovate, cordate at the base, acutely acuminate, darkish green above, with immersed nerves, pubescent, yellowish opake beneath, nerves prominent, 3¼ in. long, 1¾ in. broad, on pubescent petioles 5 lines long; inflorescence axillary, on a peduncle 9½ lines long; flowers very numerous, in a subcapitate head, on pedicels obsoletely pilose, 3 lines long, each with 2 acute bracts 1½ line long; sepals linear-lanceolate, very acuminate, unequal in length, 4–5 lines long, quincuncially imbricate, pilose outside, with an internal, bidentate, linear scale; tube of corolla cylindrical, 6 lines long; segments erect, oblong, 6 lines long, dextrorsely convolute in æstivation; stamens inserted in the short basal constriction of the tube, on 5 tufts of white hairs; anthers linear, shortly cordate at the base; disk of two opposite, rounded, fleshy lobes, alternate with and half the length of the 2 free ovaries; style very short, clavuncle adhering to the anthers, conical, 5-grooved, with a basal expanded membrane; stigmata 2, subulate.

A drawing of this species, with its floral analysis, is given in Plate XXIV B.

2. PRESTONIOPSIS HIRSUTA, nob.: ramulis subtenuibus, strictis; axillis remotis; foliis oppositis, ovatis, imo profundiuscule cordatis, apice angustioribus et in acumen breve subito constrictis, chartaceis, marginibus vix revolutis, supra fusco olivaceis, glabris, in nervis venisque transversim et crebre reticulatis sulcatis, et ibi albide hirsutulis, subtus sordide ferrugineis, undique puberulis, nervis venisque prominulis breviter hirsutis, petiolo tenui, quam limbus 5plo breviore: panicula capitata, puberula, in nodis solitaria; pedunculo elongato, tenuiter tereti, apice confertifloro; pedicellis bracteis calyceque æquilongis et hirsutulis; bracteis linearibus acutis; sepalis eis similibus, marginibus rubris reflexis; corollæ tubo cylindrico, subtenui, calyci æquilongo, intus lineis 5 albide pilosis munito; segmentis æquilongis, lineari-oblongis, cum tubo extus sparsim pilosis, in æstivatione dextrorsum convolutis; staminibus ad contractionem basalem tubi enatis; antheris imo cordatis, apice acuminatis, in conum subcohærentibus; disci lobis 2, oppositis, rotundatis, ovariis alternantibus et dimidio brevioribus; stylo brevissimo; clavuncula conica 5-sulcata, imo membrana donata; stigmatibus 2, subulatis, terminalibus. In Venezuela: *v. s. in herb. Mus. Brit.* Tovar (Moritz).

A species near the preceding. Its axils are 5½ in. apart; leaves 3¾ in. long, 2¾ in. broad, on petioles 8 lines long; peduncle 3 in. long; pedicels 4 lines long; bracts 3 lines long, unequal; sepals 2¼–3 lines long; tube of corolla 4 lines long; segments of the same length.

3. PRESTONIOPSIS VENOSA, nob.: ramulis tenuibus, teretibus; foliis ovatis, imo obtuse rotundatis, caniculatim plicatis et recurvis, apice in acumen breve obtusum repente constrictis, rigide chartaceis, marginibus subrevolutis, supra fusco-viridibus, glabris, in nervis adscendentibus et venis transversis valde reticulatis profunde sulcatis, et hinc subbullatis, subtus concoloribus, rigide pubescentibus, costa nervis venisque prominentibus, petiolo piloso, canaliculato, quam limbus 8plo breviore: inflorescentia terminali; pedunculo tereti, quam folium breviore, crebre multifloro; pedicellis tenuissimis, apice subito crassioribus, puberulis; sepalis lanceolatis, 2 exterioribus longioribus, membranaceis, extus puberulis, intus squamula munitis; corolla glabra; tubo cylindrico, quam calyx duplo longiore, imo brevissime angustiore, intus infra faucem lineis 5 albido-pilosis signato; segmentis carnosulis, linearioblongis, extus sparse pilosulis; staminibus ad contractionem basalem tubi insertis; antheris longe apiculatis, imo breviter bilobis; disco bilobo, lobis rotundatis, ovariis 2 alternis et dimidio brevioribus. In Venezuela: *v. s. in herb. Mus. Brit.* Tovar (Moritz).

This species differs from the preceding in its leaves subacute at the base and there conduplicate; axils 1½ in. apart; leaves 2–2¼ in. long, 1¼–1½ in. broad, on petioles 3 lines long; peduncle 1 in. long; head of flowers 1 in. in diameter; pedicels 3 lines long; sepals narrowly lanceolate, 2 lines long; tube of corolla 3 lines long, with 5 pubescent lines below the mouth; segments 2½ lines long, puberulous inside at the base, with a dextrorse convolution.

4. **Prestoniopsis Fendleri**, nob.: *Dipladenia Fendleri*, Müll. Linn. xxx. 417. In Venezuela, Tovar (Fendler 1030) : *non vidi*.

A species near the two preceding. It is a subscandent shrub, with glabrous verrucose branches, the younger ones puberulous; leaves broadly ovate or elliptic, cordate at the base, shortly cuspidate at the apex, glabrous above, with 6–8 pairs of divergent nerves and reticulated veins, incano-tomentose beneath, 2¾–4¼ in. long, 1½–3 in. broad, on petioles ⅔–1⅜ in. long; raceme lateral or subterminal, on a peduncle 2 in. long, bearing a head of densely aggregated, small, pubescent flowers, on pedicels 5–7 lines long, supported by narrow linear-lanceolate bracts of the same length; sepals linear-lanceolate, imbricate, pubescent, 3¼ lines long, each with a basal 2-3fid scale; corolla not yet expanded, nearly 1 in. long; tube pubescent, contracted near the base, where it is staminigerous, pubescent in the mouth; segments rather narrow, elongate, with ciliated margins, 1¾ line broad; disk 2 ovate lobes, half as long as the 2 ovaries.

Anisolobus.

A genus established by DeCandolle in 1844. Its chief distinctive character (whence its name) is a large calyx of 5 unequal, oblong, obtuse, erect, membranaceous sepals, quincuncially imbricate, the 2 outer ones being smaller. Müller, regardless of this prominent feature, described and figured some of its species as belonging to *Odontadenia*, a genus with which he was evidently unacquainted. This mistake was afterwards copied by the authors of the 'Genera Plantarum' (ii. 723), who, without sufficient reflection, absorbed *Anisolobus* into *Odontadenia*; the latter is a genus widely remote, with which *Anisolobus* can claim no affinity whatever. It was founded by Mr. Bentham, in 1841, upon very sound data.

The generic character of *Anisolobus* is here remodelled from the careful analysis of those species which I have been able to examine.

Anisolobus, A. DC.: Müll. (in parte). *Calyx* majusculus. *Sepala* 5, valde inæqualia, quorum 2 exteriora minora, quincuncialiter et insigniter imbricata, oblonga, obtusa, membranacea, imo crassiora, intus *squamulis* 2 bidentatis singulatim munita. *Corolla* tubulosa; *tubus* longiusculus, infra medium angustatus, superne infundibuliformis; *segmenta* falcatim dolabriformia, in æstivatione pro tertia parte erecta, angulo sinistro acutata, dehinc subito introflexa, intra tubum descendentia, apicibus antheras attingentes, demum expansa et dextrorsum convoluta. *Stamina* 5, ad constrictionem tubi inserta, inclusa; *filamenta* subbrevia, linearia, membranacea; *antheræ* anguste lineares, cuspidatæ, imo in furcas 2 longiusculas fissæ. *Discus* urceolatus, margine denticulatus, ovaria sæpius occultans. *Ovaria* 2, oblonga; *stylus* tenuis; *clavuncula* incrassata, pentagone cylindrica, glandulosa, ad antheras conglutinata, imo indusiata; *stigmata* 2, parva, oblonga, terminalia. *Folliculi* 2, oblongi, crassiusculi, fusiformes, horizontaliter divergentes, glabri vel pubescentes, sutura ventrali dehiscentes; *semina* plurima, linearia, *coma* sericea 3–4plo longiore coronata.

Suffrutices *Americæ meridionalis, sæpius scandentes*; rami *ad nodos stipulacei*; folia *opposita, oblonga, breviter petiolata*; racemi *vel paniculæ laterales aut terminales, sæpe geminati*; flores *pedicellati et bracteolati*.

1. ANISOLOBUS PEROTTETII, A. DC. Prodr. viii. p. 395; Müll. Fl. Bras. xxvi. p. 115. In Guiana (Perottet): *non vidi*.

A species, with straight, verrucate branches, furnished on each side of the nodes with 2 small stipules; leaves distichous, oblong, acute at the base, acuminate, furnished with many close nerves and reticulated veins, 3 in. long, 1-1¼ in. broad, on petioles 3 lines long; calyx 3¾ lines long; corolla 2 in. long.

The description of the plant from Maranhão under this name, by Müller, differs from that of DeCandolle in several respects, indicating a specific difference, its leaves being 5¼-9½ in. long, 1⅛-1½ in. broad, on petioles 4¼-5¼ lines long; while his variety *obtusa*, from Matto Grosso, appears still more distinct.

2. ANISOLOBUS SALZMANNI, A. DC. *l. c.* p. 395; Müll. *l. c.* p. 113. In Brasilia, prov. Bahia: *non vidi*.

A scandent plant, with glabrous branches, the branches pubescent at the summits; leaves opposite (but not distichous), ovate or oblong-ovate, very obtuse at the base, somewhat blunt at the acuminate apex, coriaceous, glabrous, shining, fuscous-green above, pallid beneath, with darker nerves, 4¾-7 in. long, 2-3 in. broad, on petioles 3¾-4 lines long; racemes terminal, densely flowered, on a short peduncle furnished with numerous roundly ovate bracts; pedicels twice the length of the petioles; sepals broadly oblong, 3¾-5½ lines long, unequal, much imbricated, subciliate, with a few internal basal scales; tube of corolla 1 in. long, enlarging at the base and upwards; segments about the same length; disk entire (but doubtfully according to DeCandolle), 2-3 lines long, concealing the ovaries; Müller states that it is partially cleft into 5 crenulate lobes.

3. ANISOLOBUS DISTINCTUS, nob.: ramulis crassiusculis striolatis, axillis remotiusculis stipulaceis: foliis late ovatis aut oblongis, imo rotundatis, interdum circa petiolum brevissime acutatis, apice in acumen late lineare obtusum repente constrictis, integris, rigidule chartaceis, supra rufule viridibus, nervis nigris arcuatim nexis subimmersis, subtus flavide opacis, nervis fulvidis venisque transversis valde reticulatis vix promiuulis; petiolo fusco, semitereti, quam limbus 8plo breviore: racemis terminalibus geminatis, pedunculatis; pedunculis nudis apice laxe 8-10-floris; pedicellis oppositis, imo breviter bracteolatis, ultimis congestis; sepalis oblongo-ovatis, valde imbricatis, extus puberulis, intus pruinosis, squamulis paucis basalibus munitis; corollae tubo cylindrico, paullo sub medium constricto, superne sublatiore, extus pruinoso; segmentis oblique oblongis, dextrorsum convolutis; disco urceolato ad medium 5-sulcato, margine denticulato, ovaria 2 pilosula paullo superante; staminibus ad contractionem tubi insertis, inclusis. In Guiana: *v. s. in herb. Mus. Brit.* (Schomburgk 212).

Axils 3¼ in. apart; leaves 5-6 in. long, 3-3½ in. broad, on rather stout petioles 8 lines long; panicles 3 in. long; bare peduncles 9 lines long; pedicels 4 lines long; sepals, very young, 2½ lines long, roundish; corolla, in bud, 1 in. long.

4. ANISOLOBUS OBLONGUS, nob.: ramulis teretibus, subtenuibus, glabris, ad nodos stipularibus: foliis elongato-oblongis, imo obtusis, superne sensim acutis, marginibus subundulatis, chartaceis, supra fusco-viridibus, pruinoso-opacis, in costa sulcatis, ad nervos immersos subpuberulis, subtus hepatice flavescentibus, opacis, costa nervis venisque transversis reticulatis rubidulis valde prominentibus; petiolis semiteretibus, sulcatis, limbo 15plo brevioribus: racemo terminali, alternatim 5-6-floro; floribus pro genere speciosis, flavis. In Brasilia: *v. s. in herb. Mus. Brit.* Itagoahy (Bowie & Cunningham).

The slender branch has axils about 1 in. apart; leaves 5½ in. long, 1½ in. broad, on petioles 6 lines long; raceme about 3 in. long, on a bare peduncle 1¼ in. long; bearing several large yellow subapproximate flowers on slender twisted pedicels 8 lines long; sepals unequal, obtuse, 3½–5 lines long, 2 lines broad; the lower narrowed portion of the tube of the corolla 7 lines long, 1¼ line broad, upper moiety 7 lines long; segments 7–9 lines long; anthers 4 lines long; disk urceolate, 5-grooved, margin denticulated, a trifle longer than the 2 ovaries.

A drawing of this species, and an analysis of its flower, fruit, and seed, are shown in Plate XXVI.

5. ANISOLOBUS STADELMEYERI, Müll. *l. c.* p. 113 (in parte) : *Echites densevenulosa*, Stadelm. Bot. Zeit. 1841, p. 47; A. DC. *l. c.* p. 464. In Brasilia, prov. Rio de Janeiro: *v. s. in herb. Mus. Brit.* mont. Organ. (Gardner 5820).

Probably a shrub, with scandent, slender, dark, pubescent branches, with axils 3⅛ in. apart, having caducous stipules; leaves elliptic-oblong, obtusely acute and emarginate at the base, furnished at the apex with a short subacute acumen, rigidly chartaceous, fuscous-green above, obsoletely puberulous, with slender immersed nerves, paler beneath, glaucous-pruinose, subhirsute on the prominent midrib and nerves, veins closely reticulated, 3¾ in. long, 1⅝ in. broad, on petioles 3 lines long; panicles in opposite axils, on a slender naked pubescent peduncle 1½ in. long, twice trichotomously branched, each branch bearing about 3 flowers, on pedicels with small bractlets and 4–6 lines long; sepals obtusely oblong, membranaceous, with ciliate margins, sparsely pilose, 3½–4 lines long, 1–1½ line broad, unequal, imbricate; corolla 2½ in. long; tube cylindrical, suddenly constricted below the middle; segments dolabriform, rounded on the dexter side, simply convolute in the bud; stamens seated at the constriction of the tube; anthers linear, narrow, somewhat shortly bifurcate at the base; disk urceolate, 5-sulcate, and denticulated on the margin, concealing the 2 ovaries.

6. ANISOLOBUS HEBECARPUS, Müll. *l. c.* p. 112, tab. 33. figs. 1 & 3 : *Echites hebecarpa*, Benth. MSS. In Amazonas: *v. s. in herb. meo* Santarem (Spruce 681).

An erect shrub, different from the preceding species, with very straight, subfistular, glabrous, opake branches, striate, rendered somewhat scabrous by many short, prominent, obtuse lenticels, with 2 stipules on each side between the petioles; leaves oblong-ovate, subcordate at the base, roundish towards the summit, and there constricted suddenly into a short acumen, chartaceous, opake above, with immersed nerves and transversely reticulated fine veins, paler beneath, pruinously opake (not pubescent), midrib and nerves prominent, 3–5¾ in. long, 1½–2½ in. broad, on stout, recurving, glabrous petioles 3–5 lines long; panicle lateral, 3–5 in. long, on a deflected peduncle 6–18 lines long, divided at its apex into 2 parallel floriferous branches, each bearing about 6 alternate flowers; bracts linear-oblong, reddish, submembranaceous, margins glabrous, 3 lines long; pedicels 3–6 lines long; sepals oblong, obtuse, glabrous, membranaceous, imbricate, 4–6 lines long, with an internal, subulate, bidentate scale; corolla handsome, deep rose-colour; tube 20 lines long, narrowly cylindrical for half its length, fleshy, pubescent inside, campanular and glabrous above; segments obliquely very inequilateral, with an acute tooth near the sinister angle, dextrorsely convolute, 9 lines long and broad; stamens seated on a densely lanate ring in the contraction of the tube; anthers cohering, 3 lines long, acuminate, acutely biaristate at the base; disk urceolate, denticulate on the margin, shorter than the 2 pointed ovaries; style slender, 10 lines long; clavuncle incrassate, membranaceous at its base; follicles horizontally divergent, fusiformly terete, glabrous, 5¼ in. long, 3½ lines thick; seeds numerous, 4½ lines long, with an erect apical coma 15 lines long.

7. ANISOLOBUS ZUCCARINIANUS, nob.: *Echites Zuccariniana*, Stadelm. Bot. Zeit. 1841, p. 76; A. DC. *l. c.* p. 471: *Anisolobus hebecarpus*, var. *erectus*, Müll. *l. c.* p. 112. In Brasilia, prov. Goyaz et Cuyaba: *non vidi*.

A shrub much less in height than Spruce's plant, with narrower pubescent leaves on shorter petioles, and tomentous inflorescence. It has stoutish, softly pubescent branches, with axils 1 in. apart, having 2 acute stipules on each face; opposite leaves erect, oblong-elliptic, cordate at the base, shortly cuspidate and mucronate at the apex, chartaceous, puberulous above, velutinous beneath, with prominent costa, nerves, and transversely reticulated veins, 2¾–5 in. long, 1¾–2½ in. broad, on petioles 1–4 lines long; panicle lateral, covered with yellowish or whitish tomentum, densely many-flowered; pedicels niveous, 6–8 lines long; bracts ovate, acute, 1–1½ line long; sepals oblong, very unequal, obtuse, membranaceous, pubescent, ciliate, 4–6 lines long, with an inner, bidentate, subulate scale; tube of corolla 15 lines long, narrowly cylindrical for half its length, funnel-shaped above, tomentous within; segments subunguiculate, deltoid, very inequilateral, with an uncinate tooth on the sinister angle, 9 lines long, 9 lines broad, with a falciform expansion, dextrorsely convolute; stamens inserted in the contraction of the tube; anthers cohering, cuspidate, biaristate at the base; disk urceolate, crenately denticulate on the margin, concealing the 2 subglobose ovaries; follicles teretely fusiform, densely pubescent.

8. ANISOLOBUS PULCHERRIMUS, nob.: *Echites pulcherrima*, Pohl, in Icon. Sel.: *Anisolobus hebecarpus*, var. *scandens*, Müll. *l. c.* p. 112, tab. 33. fig. 2. In Brasilia, prov. Goyaz ad Coralinha (Pohl 1383): *non vidi*.

A shrub with an erect short pubescent stem, with glabrous, flexuous, slender, subprostrate branches; leaves elliptic, cordate at the base, shortly cuspidate, softly puberulous above, velutinous beneath, 4½–5 in. long, 2½ in. broad, on petioles 4 lines long; raceme lateral or terminal, bearing many alternately approximate flowers, on pedicels 6–8 lines long; bracts ovate, 1–1½ line long; sepals oblong, very obtuse, membranaceous, unequal, 3½–4½ lines long, very imbricate, each with an inner basal 2-dentate scale; tube of corolla 15 lines long, narrowly cylindrical at the base for half its length, swelling above; segments rhomboid-obovate, acutely dolabriform, subcrispate; stamens seated in the contraction of the tube; anthers cohering, acuminate, biaristate at the base; disk 5 fleshy, sulcate lobes, crenulate on the margin.

9. ANISOLOBUS POHLIANUS, nob.: *Echites Pohliana*, Stadelm. Bot. Zeit. 1841, p. 73; A. DC. *l. c.* p. 470. In Brasilia, prov. Minas Geraës: *non vidi*.

A species near the preceding; being a low shrub with a glabrous stem 18 in. high, having scandent, hirsutulous branches; leaves ovate-oblong or linear-oblong, rounded or subcordate at the base, acute or shortly cuspidate at the apex, glaucous green above, ciliate on the margins, 3–3¼ in. long, 10–18 lines broad, on ciliate petioles 2 lines long; raceme terminal, elongate, few-flowered; pedicels 6–8 lines long; bracts cuspidately lanceolate, 3 lines long; sepals 3½–4¼ lines long, with 2 approximate bidentate inner scales; tube of the corolla narrowed below for half its length, funnel-shaped above, 2 in. long; segments oblong, inequilateral; stamens inserted at the constriction of the tube; disk urceolate, denticulate on the margin, nearly concealing 2 ovate-oblong ovaries.

10. ANISOLOBUS PSIDIIFOLIUS, nob.: *Echites psidiifolia*, Mart., Stadelm. in Rat. Fl. (1841), Beibl. 46; A. DC. *l. c.* p. 453; Müll. *l. c.* p. 160. In Brasilia, prov. Bahia: *non vidi*.

This species is placed here because of its large unequal sepals and other conformable characters. It has pubescent branches with remote stipular axils; narrow oblong leaves shortly acuminate, subcordate at the base, pubescent, 2–2½ in. long, 10–15 lines broad, the petioles being 2 lines long; several flowers aggregated upon a peduncle 1⅓ in. long; pedicels ebracteolate, 3–4 lines long; sepals oblong, truncate, membranaceous, pubescent, ciliate, 4–6 lines long, 3–4 lines broad, with as many internal, broad, denticulate scales; cylindrical tube of corolla 8–10 lines long; segments dolabriform, roundish; stamens inserted in the middle of the tube; anthers rigid, acute, shortly bilobed at the base; disk urceolate, 5-grooved, as long as the ovaries.

11. ANISOLOBUS PUNCTICULOSUS, Miq. Stirp. Surin. p. 158; Walp. Ann. iii. 37: *Echites puncticulosa*, Rich. in Act. Soc. Hist. Nat. Paris, 1792, p. 107; A. DC. *l. c.* p. 473. In Surinam et Cayenne: *non vidi*.

A shrub with obtusely 4-angled verruculose branches, having short, ovate, deciduous stipules at the nodes; leaves ovate or elliptic-ovate, with a short, broad, emarginate acumen, coriaceous, with about 5 pairs of nerves, reticulate, petiolate; panicle terminal, shortly puberulous, on a peduncle bearing several approximate flowers; sepals broadly ovate, obtuse, outer ones puberulent, inner ones somewhat longer, more scarious, and subglabrous; disk urceolate, contracted at the obsoletely repand-denticulate margin.

12. ANISOLOBUS HOSTMANNI, Miq. Stirp. Surin. p. 159; Walp. Ann. iii. p. 38. In Surinam: *non vidi*.

A shrub, with subcylindrical branches, roughly verruculose, with deciduous stipules; leaves elliptic, subobtuse at both ends, coriaceous, with nerves and reticulate veins, petiolate; panicle axillary or terminal, shorter than the leaves, puberulous, on a short peduncle; sepals ovate, obtuse, puberulous, outer ones somewhat shorter, inner ones more glabrous, each with an inner bifid scale; corolla 2¼ in. long, its tube slender, subcampanulate above the middle; segments roundish-ovate.

13. ANISOLOBUS FOCKEI, Miq. Stirp. Surin. p. 159; Walp. Ann. iii. 38. In Surinam: *non vidi*.

A shrub with obtusely tetragonous, verruculose branches, with several ciliate, setiform deciduous stipules; leaves ovate-elliptic or oblong, acute at the base, obtusely acuminate, the larger ones subinequilateral, subcoriaceous, obliquely nerved and reticulate, petiolate; panicles axillary, mostly opposite, the lower ones with a long, the upper ones with a shorter peduncle, trichotomously divided, puberulous; flowers pedicellate, supported by ovate, ciliolate, puberulous bracteoles; sepals obtuse, ciliolate; tube of corolla thickened at the base, constricted in the middle, funnel-shaped above.

14. ANISOLOBUS RUBIDULUS, nob.: glaberrimus, ramulis tenuibus, rubescentibus, striolatis; axillis stipulis parvis utrinque munitis: foliis oppositis, ellipticis, imo obtusis, apice sensim acuminatis, chartaceis, supra pallide viridulis, rufescentibus, nervis subpatentibus, arcuatim nexis, subimmersis, subtus paullo pallidioribus, nervis tenuibus prominulis, venis transversis valde reticulatis; petiolo tenui, sulcato, quam limbus 15plo breviore: panicula terminali, trichotome divisa, multiflora; pedicellis tenuibus, petiolo duplo longioribus; sepalis 5, oblongis, obtusis, rubidulis, marginibus membranaceis, valde imbricatis, adpressis, subinæqualibus, singulatim squamulis 2 intus munitis; corollæ tubo imo anguste cylindrico, superne infundibuliformi; segmentis oblongo-dolabriformibus, expansis; staminibus in contractionem tubi insertis; disco cylindrico, 5-sulcato, obtuse denticulata, ovariis 2 oblongis pilosulis paullo breviore. In Guiana: *v. s. in herb. Mus. Brit.* Cayenne (Martin).

A slender plant, with axils 1 in. apart; leaves 2½–3¾ in. long, 1¼–1½ in. broad, on petioles 2–3 lines long; panicle 2 in. long, spreading; pedicels 6 lines long; sepals 2¼ lines long, 1 line broad; tube 11 lines long, contracted from the middle downwards; segments 5 lines long and broad.

ANGADENIA.

This genus is proposed for a small group of fruticose plants, erect or scandent, chiefly referred by Müller to *Odontadenia* and *Anisolobus*, differing from the former in their floral and carpical characters, and from the latter in their small, equal, coriaceous sepals, and in the shape and mode of æstivation of the segments of the corolla, and other features.

ANGADENIA*, nob.: *Sepala* 5, parva, æqualia, subacuta, coriacea, marginibus sæpe angustissime pellucidis, quincuncialiter subimbricatis, intus *squamulis* totidem bidentatis munita. *Corolla* tubulosa; *tubus* pro dimidia parte infera anguste cylindricus, superne infundibuliformi-campanulatus; *segmenta* dolabriformia, angulo sinistro acuta, latere altero rotundatim expansa, æstivatione simpliciter dextrorsum convoluta. *Stamina* 5, inclusa, ad constrictionem tubi inserta; *filamenta* brevia, complanata; *antheræ* cuspidato-lineares, imo in furcas 2 breves acutas fissæ; clavunculæ agglutinatione in conum cohærentes. *Discus* majusculus, vasiformis, crassus, ore denticulatus. *Ovaria* 2, acute oblonga, discum paullo superantia. *Stylus* tenuis; *clavuncula* incrassata, cylindrica, imo membrana peltata apophysata; *stigmata* 2, minima, acuta, terminalia. *Folliculi* 2, robuste fusiformes, horizontaliter divaricati, sutura ventrali dehiscentes. *Semina* plurima, linearia, *coma* densa, longa, erecta, penicilliformi coronata.

Frutices *Americæ meridionalis ramosi; rami sæpe scandentes ad nodos breviter stipulacei: folia opposita, ovata vel elliptico-oblonga, sæpe cordata, coriacea, petiolata; paniculæ axillares aut terminales, pluriflora; flores subspeciosi, pedicellati.*

1. ANGADENIA HYPOGLAUCA, nob.: *Echites hypoglauca*, Stadelm. Bot. Zeit. 1841, p. 123; A. DC. *l. c.* p. 448: *Odontadenia hypoglauca*, Müll. (in parte) Fl. Bras. xxvi. p. 118, tab. 35 B. In Brasilia, prov. Bahia et Pernambuco: *non vidi*.

A climbing plant, with slender, flexuous, glabrous branches, having axils 5 in. apart, bearing on their transverse ridge 2 thick ovate or linear-oblong glands; leaves ovate-oblong, cordate at the base, rounded and emarginate at the summit, very glabrous above,

* From ἄγγεα (*vasa*), ἀδήν (*glandula*), from its urceolated disk.

glauco-velutinous beneath, 3½–5¼ in. long, 2¼–3¼ in. broad, on petioles 2–3 lines long; racemes axillary and terminal, opposite, about as long as the leaves, on a very slender flexuous peduncle bare at the base for the length of 1 in., bearing above 5 to 8 alternate, rather distant flowers on slender pedicels 6–8 lines long, twisted, and bracteolate at the base; sepals oblong, imbricate, 2 lines long; corolla hypocrateriform; tube cylindrical, slightly contracted in the middle, 1½ in. long; segments rotate, dolabriform, 9 lines long, 4 lines broad; stamens seated a little above the middle of the tube, and reaching the mouth, with 2 short divergent prongs at the base; disk urceolate, fleshy, with very numerous fine denticulations on the margin, some few of them deeper than the others, shorter than the 2 conical, oblong, glabrous ovaries.

2. ANGADENIA MAJUSCULA, nob.: *Odontadenia hypoglauca*, Müll. (in parte) *l. c.* p. 118, tab. 35 A. fig. 1. In Amazonas: *v. s. in herb. Mus. Brit.* Santarem (Spruce 696).

A species distinct from the preceding. It has stouter, flexuous branches, with axils 4 in. apart; leaves ovate-oblong, deeply cordate at the base, rather obtuse and suddenly mucronate at the summit, margins subrevolute, of a palish green above, but pubescent on the midrib and nerves, of which there are 10 pairs divergent and prominulous, furnished with transversely reticulate immersed veins, beneath very opake and yellowish glaucous on the midrib and nerves, 3–6 in. long, 1⅜–3¼ in. broad, with a basal sinus 2–5 lines deep, on glaucous channelled petioles 3–6 lines long; racemes axillary, opposite, on stoutish peduncles naked at the base for 1⅓ in., bearing above about 8 opposite flowers on very slender pedicels 7 lines long; sepals ovate, subacute, 2½–3 lines long, each furnished with 2 bifid internal scales; tube of corolla 11 lines long, narrowly cylindrical, contracted in the middle; segments dolabriform, 8 lines long; stamens seated in the contraction of the tube; anthers acuminate, with 2, somewhat divergent, basal prongs; disk shortly cleft into 5 or 10 striate, denticulate lobes, as long as the 2 glabrous ovaries.

3. ANGADENIA SYLVESTRIS, nob.: *Echites sylvestris*, A. DC. *l. c.* p. 464: *Echites grandiflora*, Stadelm. (non Meyer) Bot. Zeit. 1841, p. 49: *Odontadenia sylvestris*, Müll. (in parte) *l. c.* p. 117 (excl. tab. 35 A. fig. 2). In Brasilia, Rio Japuré in sylvis (Martius): *non vidi*.

This species is evidently not a true *Odontadenia*, but, like the *O. hypoglauca* of Müller, belongs to this group. DeCandolle described it from the *Echites grandiflora* of Stadelmeyer, who wrongly confounded it with Meyer's plant of the same name from Guiana. The plant seems to have been collected by Martius, near the river Japuré, a region south of the Rio Negro. Müller united it with another plant collected by Sagot in Guiana, which is the *Echites coriacea* of Bentham, here described under the following species; we must therefore reject the specific character and the floral analysis of Müller, and trust wholly to that given by DeCandolle. Its branches are obtusely 4-angled, and their axils remote; the leaves are cuneately obovate, with a short, mucronate acumen, membranaceous, marked beneath with prominent midrib and nerves and obliquely transverse veins, 5–8 in. long, 2–4 in. broad, on petioles less than 1 inch long; panicles axillary, shorter than the leaves, on peduncles often 3 in. long, bearing many flowers on pedicels 3 lines long, minutely bracteolate; sepals obtusely ovate, 3 lines long, with inner trifid scales; corolla 2¼ in. long, yellowish red, its tube somewhat ventricose within the calyx, narrowly cylindrical and constricted below the middle, funnel-shaped above; segments trapezoid; stamens inserted in the constriction of the tube, with connivent anthers; disk vasiform, finely denticulate on the margin, striolate, fleshy, and concealing the 2 subulate ovaries.

4. ANGADENIA CURURU, nob.: *Echites Cururu*, Mart. Pl. Med. tab. 64; Stadelm. Bot. Zeit. 1841, p. 78; A. DC. *l. c.* p. 470: *Anisolobus Cururu*, Müll. *l. c.* p. 112, tab. 34 (excl. var.): *Anisolobus Kappleri*, Miq. Stirp. Surin. p. 159. In Amazonas, Rio Coari, Ega et Rio Negro: *non vidi*.

A species from the same region as the preceding, to which it is nearly allied. Müller's drawing is copied from that of Martius above cited; and it is stated to be near *A. Amazonica* in its leaves and inflorescence. Its stoutish branches are trichotomously or oppositely divided, fuscous, verruculous, with axils 2–2¾ in. apart; leaves elliptic, subacute at both ends, or with a suddenly contracted, short, obtuse acumen, subcoriaceous, fuscous above, glabrous, subnitid, with about 10 pairs of diverging nerves and finely reticulated veins, paler beneath, 3¾–4¾ in. long, 1½–2 in. broad, on petioles 3–7 lines long; panicles opposite, axillary, longer than the leaves, on a bare peduncle 2 in. long, erect, above trichotomously branched, each branch bearing about 6 flowers on bracteolate pedicels 5–6 lines long; sepals small, ovate, acute, pubescent, thickish, imbricate, 2 lines long, each with a small inner, bidentate scale; tube of corolla subglabrous, 14 lines long, narrowly cylindrical at its base for one third of its length, widening a little above; segments trapezoidally dolabriform, with crispate margins, 9 lines long, 6 lines broad; stamens seated in the contraction of the tube; anthers acuminate, with 2 shortish, acute, subdivergent, basal prongs, hirtulous dorsally; disk urceolate, enclosing the 2 somewhat shorter, acutely ovate, glabrous ovaries.

5. ANGADENIA GRANDIFOLIA, nob.: *Echites Cururu*, var. *grandifolia*, Stadelm. *l. c.* p. 78; A. DC. *l. c.* p. 470: *Anisolobus Cururu*, var. *grandifolius*, Müll. *l. c.* p. 113. In Amazonas, Rio Solimoës: *non vidi*.

A species differing from the preceding in the unusual size of its leaves, which are more oblong, 7¼–10 in. long, 3¼–4 in. broad; the inflorescence is 5 in. long; other particulars are not given. It seems to differ little from the *Anisolobus Perottetii*, Müll. (non A. DC.).

6. ANGADENIA AMAZONICA, nob.: *Echites Amazonica*, Stadelm. Bot. Zeit. 1841, p. 50; A. DC. *l. c.* p. 464: *Echites bicornis*, Spruce, MSS.: *Echites verrucosa*, R. & S. Syst. iv. 795: *Anisolobus Amazonicus*, Müll. *l. c.* p. 114. In Amazonas, ad Panuré Rio Uahupes (Spruce 2503): *v. s. in herb. Mus. Brit.* Rio Guaïnia (Spruce 3550).

A species scarcely differing from *A. Cururu*. Its branches are more slender, brownish, striolate, glabrous, subverrucose, with axils 1¾ in. apart, having a short stipule on each side of the petioles; leaves elliptic, narrower towards the base, roundish at the summit, and suddenly constricted into an acute acumen, opakely fuscous above, with 10 or 12 pairs of divergent nerves, and transverse veins finely reticulate, yellowish opake beneath, with reddish prominent midrib and nerves, 4½–5½ in. long, 1¼–2¼ in. broad, on petioles 4–5 lines long; panicles opposite or subterminal, pubescent, on a naked peduncle 1¼ in. long, bearing several branches 4–6 lines long, supporting several subapproximate flowers on pubescent pedicels 6 lines long, with minute ovate bracteoles; sepals obtusely oblong, with submembranaceous margins, 1¼ line long, ¾ line broad; tube of corolla 15 lines long, narrow below for one third of its length; segments dolabriform, $4\frac{1}{2}$ lines long; stamens seated on a pilose ring at the constriction of the tube; anthers slender, linear, acute, with 2 short, subdivergent, basal prongs; disk urceolate, fleshy, denticulate on the margin, and nearly concealing the 2 free ovaries.

7. ANGADENIA LATIFOLIA, nob.: *Anisolobus Amazonicus*, var. *latifolius*, Müll. *l. c.* p. 114: *Odontadenia*, sp., Benth. MSS. In Brasilia, *v. s. in herb. meo*, Panuré, Rio Uahupes (Spruce 2503).

A species very distinct from the preceding. Its branches are compressed, opake, substriate, dilated at the axils, which are $1\frac{1}{2}$ in. apart, and thickened by a transverse ridge, bearing 2 or more acute stipules, often caducous; leaves very broadly ovate, rounded, but shortly and very suddenly acute upon the petiole, roundish towards the summit and suddenly constricted into an obtusely cuspidate acumen, rigidly chartaceous, with subundulated margins, opakely fuscous above, with curving immersed nerves, and transverse veins very finely reticulated between them, paler and ferruginously opake beneath, with prominent reddish nerves and veins, $4-4\frac{1}{2}$ in. long, $2\frac{1}{2}-3$ in. broad, on curving, stoutish, channelled petioles 5–6 lines long; terminal or subaxillary panicles on peduncles 5–8 lines long, each bearing about 10 flowers on slender pedicels 9 lines long; sepals ovate, subacute, unequal, very imbricate, 2 lines long; tube of corolla subpuberulous, narrowed below for half its length, slightly swelling above, 7 lines long; segments obliquely ovate, $2\frac{1}{2}$ lines long; disk cupular, cleft halfway into 5 subacute lobes shorter than the 2 ovaries.

The species differs from *A. Amazonica* in its much broader, less acuminate, more rigid leaves, and in its geminate terminal panicles bearing fewer flowers.

8. ANGADENIA SPRUCEI, nob.: *Anisolobus Sprucei*, Müll. *l. c.* p. 114: *Odontadenia*, sp., Benth. MSS. In Amazonas: *v. s. in herb. meo* prope Panuré, Rio Uahupes (Spruce 2553).

A species near the two preceding, with stout straight branches, having their axils $2\frac{3}{4}-3\frac{1}{2}$ in. apart, bearing on each face 2–4 lanceolate membranaceous stipules 1 line long, very caducous; leaves oblong-elliptic, gradually narrowing towards the base from the middle, suddenly contracted at the more rounded summit into a sublinear obtuse acumen, chartaceous, with subrevolute margins, reddish fuscous and opake above, with black midrib and immersed nerves, ochreous-brown below, midrib and nerves reddish, subprominulent, with closely transverse reticulate veins, 4–5 in. long, $1\frac{1}{2}-2$ in. broad, on petioles 3–4 lines long; panicles axillary, single or geminate and terminal, on peduncles 9–15 lines long, trichotomously branched, each branch bearing 2–3 alternate flowers, on pedicels 4–6 lines long, furnished with 2 small bracts; sepals broadly ovate, very imbricate, ciliate on the margins, 2 lines long; tube of corolla 10 lines long, the contracted basal portion of the tube being 3 lines long; segments broadly oblong, 4 lines long; stamens inserted at the contraction of the tube; disk urceolar, with many denticulate teeth on the margin, half the length of 2 conical oblong ovaries.

A drawing of this species, and an analysis of its flower, are given in Plate XXVII. A.

9. ANGADENIA COGNATA, nob.: *Anisolobus cognatus*, Müll. *l. c.* p. 113: *Echites cognata*, Stadelm. Bot. Zeit. 1841, p. 79; A. DC. *l. c.* p. 470. In Brasilia, Rio Japuré: *non vidi*.

A species with glabrous branchlets; leaves ovate or oblong-ovate, subacute at the base, shortly and obtusely acuminate, submembranaceous, nitid and fuscous above, with prominulent nerves and transversely reticulated veins, $4\frac{3}{4}$–7 in. long, 2–$3\frac{1}{4}$ in. broad, on petioles 6–8 lines long; panicle terminal, glabrous, many-flowered, on pedicels longer than the calyx; sepals broadly ovate, ciliate, 3–$3\frac{3}{4}$ lines long; tube of corolla $2\frac{3}{8}$–$2\frac{3}{4}$ in. long, glabrous, cylindrical for one fourth of its length, subcampanulate above, with broad segments one half of its length; stamens seated on the contraction of the tube, included; anthers somewhat hairy, sagittate; disk urceolate, partly cleft into 5 denticulate lobes, scarcely as long as the 2 cano-tomentous ovaries.

10. ANGADENIA PRUINOSA, nob. In prov. Piauhy: *v. s. in herb. Mus. Brit.* Oeiras (Gardner 2232).

An undescribed species near the preceding, with scandent, slender, flexuose, dichotomous branches, the axils 1–2 in. apart; leaves ovate-elliptic, rounded at the base, with a shortish acute or obtusulous acumen, thinly chartaceous, with margins scarcely revolute, dark rubiginous green above, opake, with slender immersed nerves and delicate reticulated veins, puberulent beneath, griseous, finely granulate, the nerves fuscous, scarcely prominulent, 2–$2\frac{1}{4}$ in. long, 1–$1\frac{1}{2}$ in. broad, on slender, griseous, margined petioles 3 lines long; fructiferous raceme short, 9 lines long, bearing 2 follicles, horizontally divaricated, thickly cylindrical, 5 in. long, 6 lines thick; seeds many, black, compressed, rostrate, 9 lines long, 1 line broad, crowned by a white, erect, thick, pencil-like coma 21 lines long.

The follicle and seeds exactly correspond with those of *A. hebecarpus*, showing that it belongs to this genus.

A drawing of this species, with its fruit and seeds, is shown in Plate XXVII. B.

11. ANGADENIA CORIACEA, nob.: *Echites coriacea*, Benth. (non Blume) in Hook. Journ. Bot. iii. 249; A. DC. *l. c.* p. 467: *Odontadenia coriacea*, Müll. Linn. xxx. 450: *O. sylvestris*, Müll. (in parte) *l. c.* p. 117 (inclus. tab. 35 A. fig. 2 bis). In Guiana Brit., Pirara (Schomb. 738), Acouari (Sagot 383): *non vidi.*

A species, as before stated, confounded by Müller with *A. sylvestris*. It is a slender, glabrous climbing plant, resembling *A. elegans* in many respects. Leaves ovate-oblong, obtuse at the base, shortly acuminate, glabrous, coriaceous, elegantly veined, with nerves little prominent; panicle ramose, on a stoutish peduncle, bearing few flowers laxly disposed, on stoutish pedicels; sepals obtuse; tube of corolla nearly an inch long, funnel-shaped above the middle.

No dimensions are given, either of the leaves or parts of the inflorescence.

12. ANGADENIA NITIDA, nob.: *Echites nitida*, Vahl, Ecl. ii. 19, Icon. tab. 13; A. DC. *l. c.* p. 453: *Odontadenia nitida*, Müll. *l. c.* p. 118; Griseb. Fl. Brit. W. Ind. p. 416: *Odontadenia cordata*, A. DC. *l. c.* p. 360. In Guiana. *v. s. spec. typ. in herb. Mus. Brit.* Cayenne (Van Rohr).

A climbing, glabrous species, with slender substriate branches, having their axils 3 in. apart; leaves oblong, with parallel sides, rounded and cordate at the base, obtuse at the summit, with a short mucronate point, entire, submembranaceous, glabrous, nitid above, glauco-ferruginous beneath, with divaricate nerves and very reticulate veins, 3–4 in. long, 1–$1\frac{3}{4}$ in. broad, on slender petioles 4–6 lines long; raceme axillary, on a glabrous, slender, recurved peduncle 2 in. long, bearing at the summit a thyrse 2 in. long, consisting of from 8 to 15 opposite flowers on slender pedicels 6–9 lines long, bracteolate at the base; sepals ovate, acute, 2¼ lines long, furnished with several minute internal scales; tube of corolla 1½ in. long, narrowly cylindrical and contracted in the middle, widening above; segments roundish, 4 lines long; stamens seated in the contraction of the tube; anthers narrow, with 2 divergent prongs at the base as long as the filaments, acuminate at the summit, pubescent behind, half exserted; disk 10-striate, unequally divided and subdenticulate on the margin, three fourths the length of the 2 oblong glabrous ovaries.

13. ANGADENIA ELEGANS, nob.: *Echites elegans*, Benth. in Hook. Journ. Bot. iii. 249; A. DC. *l. c.* p. 466; *Odontadenia geminata*, Müll. (in parte) *l. c.* p. 119. In Amazons: *v. s. in herb. Mus. Brit.* Rio Negro (Schomb. 965).

A climbing plant, with dichotomous slender branches, having dilated axils 1–2¼ in. apart; leaves glabrous, oblong, rounded at the base, sharply acuminate at the summit, chartaceous, margin subrevolute, dark green above, midrib sulcate, with divaricate nerves and closely transverse prominulent veins, fulvous opake beneath, nerves and veins prominent, 2½–3 in. long, 1 in. broad, on slender channelled petioles incrassate at the base, 4 lines long; racemes axillary, on slender divaricately dichotomous peduncles 9 lines long, each bearing 3–6 flowers, sometimes reduced to 2, on slender pedicels 7 lines long; sepals acutely ovate, glabrous, 1¼ line long, with submembranaceous margins; tube of corolla cylindrical, 12 lines long, 1 line broad; segments broadly dolabriform, shorter than the tube, yellow, red in the mouth; disk urceolate, fleshy, denticulate and shortly 10-cleft on the margin, a little shorter than the ovaries.

14. ANGADENIA GEMINATA, nob.: *Echites geminata*, R. & Sch. Syst. iv. 795; A. DC. *l. c.* p. 475: *Odontadenia geminata*, Müll. (in parte) *l. c.* p. 119. In Brasilia: *v. s. in herb. meo et alior*. San Carlos, Rio Negro (Spruce 3152).

A species distinctly described by Römer and Schultz, and different from the preceding, varying from it in its broader ovate leaves shortly acuminate but not mucronate at the apex, undulated on the margin, with more nerves. It has very slender flexuose branches, with axils, not dilated, about 2½ in. apart; leaves divaricate or reflexed, oblong-ovate, rounded at the base, suddenly and shortly acuminate, margin cartilaginous, crenately undulate, green above, with a slender midrib and numerous close, subpatent, thin prominulent nerves, with transversely reticulated veins, yellowish opake beneath, with prominent nerves and veins, 2¼–3¼ in. long, 1¼–1¾ in. broad, on slender petioles little incrassate at the base, 5 lines long; racemes opposite, on compressed peduncles bare at the base for 1 in., each bearing above 6 flowers in 3 geminate pairs 4–6 lines apart, on slender pedicels 10 lines, the upper ones 6 lines long; sepals as in the preceding; tube of the corolla slender, a little swollen in the mouth, 13 lines long; segments broadly dolabriform, 9 lines long and broad; stamens seated in the middle of the tube; anthers with 2 basal prongs, somewhat divergent; disk as in the preceding species.

15. ANGADENIA PÖPPIGII, nob.; *Odontadenia Pöppigii*, Müll. *l. c.* p. 119: *Echites bifurcata*, Pöpp. MSS. In Amazonas, Rio Teffé, prope Ega (Pöpp. 2866) : *non vidi*.

A plant with slender glabrous branches, much resembling *A. geminata*: leaves elliptic, obtuse at the base, roundish at the summit, with a short cuspidate acumen, subcoriaceous, glabrous, shining and fuscous green above, rufescently opake beneath, nerves and veins prominulent on both sides, $3\frac{1}{2}$–$4\frac{3}{4}$ in. long, $1\frac{3}{8}$–$2\frac{3}{4}$ in. broad, petiolate; panicle axillary, spreading, much longer than the leaves, bearing numerous flowers on slender pedicels 3 or 4 times as long as the calyx; sepals obtusely ovate; tube of corolla cylindrical, narrowed below, contracted in the middle, a little wider above; segments nearly half the length of the tube; anthers dorsally glabrous; disk as in the preceding species.

16. ANGADENIA RETICULATA, nob.; scandens; ramulis tenuibus, flexuosis, pubescentibus; axillis remotis: foliis ellipticis, imum versus sensim angustioribus, cordatis, apice acumine repente mucroniformi apiculatis, marginibus revolutis, supra opacis, fusce viridibus, scabridule punctulatis, nervis immersis, subtus opacis, fusce ochraceis, costa nervisque tenuibus fuscis prominentibus, venis transversis insigniter reticulatis; petiolis brevibus, canaliculatis, hirsutis: racemo laterali, spicatifloro; pedicellis brevibus; sepalis ovatis, acutissimis; corollæ tubo ad medium cylindrico, sursum subcampanulato; staminibus in contractione tubi in annulum lanatum inserta. In Brasilia : *v. s. in herb. Mus. Brit.* N. S. d'Abadia, prov. Goyaz (Gardn. 4271) ; Maranhão (Gardn. 6058).

Axils $2\frac{1}{2}$–$3\frac{1}{4}$ in. apart; leaves $2\frac{1}{4}$–3 in. long, 1–$1\frac{1}{2}$ in. broad, on petioles 2–$2\frac{1}{2}$ lines long, the basal lobes being 1 line deep; raceme $2\frac{1}{2}$ in. long, on a peduncle 9 lines long; flowers 1 line apart; pedicels $\frac{1}{2}$ line long; sepals 1 line long; tube of corolla $1\frac{3}{4}$ in. long; segments 6 lines long, 5 lines broad; disk striate, crenate on the margin.

17. ANGADENIA ALMADENSIS, nob.: *Echites Almadensis*, Stadelm. *l. c.* p. 28; A. DC. *l. c.* p. 464: *Amblyanthera palustris*, var. *Almadensis*, Müll. *l. c.* p. 146. In Brasilia, prov. Bahia et Pernambuco; *v. s. in herb. Mus. Brit.* prov. Pernambuco (Gardn. 1060).

A species with subhirsute branches, having remote axils; leaves obovately oblong, narrowing towards the base and there auriculately cordate, cuspidate-acuminate, submembranaceous, with revolute margins, light green and opake above, scabridulous or adpressed pilosulous, with immersed nerves, beneath flavescent and opake, hirtulous, with prominulent slender nerves, 2–5 in. long, $1\frac{1}{2}$–3 in. broad, on petioles 8–15 lines long; raceme lateral, 4 in. long, sparsely hirsute, bearing many flowers, on pedicels 3 lines long; sepals lanceolate, membranaceous, $2\frac{1}{4}$ lines long, with an inner deltoid bidenticulate scale; corolla $2\frac{3}{4}$ in. long, glabrous, reddish-coloured; tube cylindrical as far as the middle, then funnel-shaped; segments inequilaterally oblong, subacute, dextrorsely convolute, marked near the base and within the tube with many interrupted yellow lines; stamens inserted at the contraction of the tube in a narrow pilose ring; anthers coherent, acuminate, and nearly reaching the mouth, acutely biaristate at the base; disk fleshy, striate, denticulate on the margin, half the length of the 2 oblong ovaries; style filiform; clavuncle oblong, with a peltate membrane at its base.

18. ANGADENIA ELLIPTICA, nob. In Brasilia : *v. s. in herb. Mus. Brit.* Paranaguá (Gardner 2663).

A climbing species, with slender, striate, glabrous branchlets, with axils 1-2 in. apart; leaves ovate-oblong, rounded at the base, suddenly and shortly acute at the summit, submembranaceous, rufescent and shining above, with a pale slender midrib and nerves, palish green and opake beneath, obsoletely puberulous, with prominulent midrib and nerves, 2¾ in. long, 1¼ in. broad, on very slender petioles 4 lines long; raceme lateral, not more than 1 in. long, bearing about 5 flowers; sepals oblong, subobtuse, with pellucid margins; tube of corolla 5 lines long; segments oblong, 3 lines long; anthers acuminate, bifurcate at the base; disk urceolate, striate, denticulate on the margin.

19. ANGADENIA BERTERII, nob.: *Echites Berterii*, A. DC. *l. c.* p. 447; Schlecht. in Linn. xxvi. p. 665: *Rhabdadenia Berterii*, Müll. in Linn. xxx. p. 435. In insula San Domingo: *non vidi*.

A climbing plant, with retrorsely hispidulous branches; leaves approximate, ellipticobovate, subacute at both ends, mucronulate, coriaceous, glabrous, 1¼–2 in. long, 10–12 lines broad, on petioles scarcely 2 lines long; raceme terminal, many-flowered, glabrous; pedicels 5–6 lines long, with bracts 1 line long; sepals narrow, acutely lanceolate, 2½ lines long, each with 2 small inner scales; corolla yellowish, 1¼ in. long; tube narrow below for the length of 4 lines, dilated above, pilose within the mouth; stamens inserted in the contraction of the tube, on a pilose ring; anthers biaristate; disk tubular, narrowed and crenate in the mouth, near 1 line long; style simple; clavuncle incrassate, 5-grooved, dilated at the base; stigmata small, slender.

This plant appears to conform to *Angadenia*, on account of the shape of the disk and other characters; it appears to have little affinity with *Rhabdadenia*.

20. ANGADENIA LINDENIANA, nob.: *Rhabdadenia Lindeniana*, inclus. var. *angustifolia*, Müll. *l. c.* p. 438. In Cuba: *v. s. in herb. meo* (Linden 1699. No. 1700 et 1823 mihi invisa).

A very slender climbing species, with axils 1-3 in. apart, and bearing two minute stipules on each face; the leaves are elliptic-oblong, roundish at the base, constricted at the summit into an acute subrecurving acumen, darkish opake green above, with revolute margins, sulcate along the midrib, nerves immersed, ferruginously opake beneath, with prominent midrib and prominulent fine nerves, 1–1¼ in. long, 4–7 lines broad, on scabridulous petioles 1–1½ line long; panicle lateral, glabrous, on a bare, slender deflected peduncle 12–15 lines long, divided at its apex into 2 floriferous branches of nearly the same length, bearing each about 7 alternate flowers, on pedicels 3–5 lines long, with a small setaceous bract; sepals acutely lanceolate, with membranaceous margins; tube of corolla narrow at the base for one third of its length, swelling above, glabrous; segments dolabriform, simply folded dextrorsely in æstivation, expanding horizontally; stamens seated at the contraction of the tube; anthers cohering, dorsally hispidulous, acuminate, biaristate at the base; disk cylindrical, margin 5-crenate, concealing the 2 ovaries; style slender; clavuncle incrassate, 5-grooved, with a dilated basal membrane; stigmata short, terminal.

In Linden's No. 1700 and 1823 (which I have not seen) the leaves are somewhat larger, but all the characters are essentially the same.

21. ANGADENIA SAGRÆI, nob.: *Echites Sagræi*, A. DC. *l. c.* p. 450; Griseb. Fl. Br. W. Ind. pp. 415, 416: *Rhabdadenia Sagræi*, Müll. Linn. xxx. p. 435. In Cuba: *non vidi*.

A species bearing much the appearance of *Mesechites myrtifolia*; it has extremely slender scabridulous branches, pilose towards the ends; opposite ovate-oblong leaves, narrowly cordate at the base, acute and mucronate at the apex, margins revolute, coriaceous, glabrous, with immersed nerves, 6–9 lines long, 4–5 lines broad, on very short petioles; raceme terminal, shortly pedunculate, bearing at its apex 3–4 alternate flowers on pedicels 4–6 lines long, with subrevolute bracts 1 line long; flowers 9–10 lines long; sepals acutely ovate, glabrous, 1¼ line long; tube of corolla 3 lines long, narrower below the middle, swelling above; stamens inserted in the contraction of the tube; anthers pilose behind; disk urceolate, with undulate margins, as long as the 2 ovaries; follicles very slender, terete, 3–4 in. long.

22. ANGADENIA VALENZUELANA, nob.: *Echites Valenzuelana*, Rich. Pl. Cub.; Griseb. in Pl. Wright. Cub. p. 520: *Rhabdadenia Wrightiana*, Müll. *l. c.* p. 438. In Cuba, *v. s. in herb. Mus. Brit.* Monte Verde (Wright 399).

A species, according to Grisebach, near *A. Lindeniana*; it also approaches *A. Sagræi* in habit. A small tree, with very slender, dichotomous, compressed, dark-red cinereo-glabrous branches, with axils 3 lines apart; opposite lanceolate leaves, cuneately narrowed upon the petiole, roundly obtuse and emarginate at the apex, chartaceous, with revolute margins, glabrous, nitid, dark green above, corrugulate, sulcate along the midrib, opake and dealbate beneath, with immersed darkish nerves and reticulated veins 1–1¾ in. long, 5–6 lines broad, on slender channelled petioles 1½ line long; raceme lateral, nearly as long as the leaves, depauperated, with 2 flowers on slender pedicels 4¾ lines long; flowers rose-coloured; sepals ovate, obtuse, 2 lines long; corolla 9½ lines long; tube contracted below the middle; segments paler, rhombic ovoid, 3½ lines long; stamens seated in the contraction of the tube; anthers hispidulous behind; follicles 2, erect, terete, slightly arcuate, 4¾ in. long, 1¼ line thick; seeds many, pale brown, linear oblong, compressed, with white verrucular stripes on the back, pale (with a raphe) on the ventral side, 3 lines long, with a simple coma of the same length.

This species is referred by Benth. & Hook. (Gen. ii. 725) to *Mandevilla*; but this reference cannot be maintained.

23. ANGADENIA HAVANENSIS, nob.: *Rhabdadenia Cubensis*, Müll. *l. c.* p. 435. In Cuba, Saltadero (Linden 1716): *non vidi*.

A species near *A. Cubensis*, with extremely slender, fuscous, patently pubescent branches; leaves linear-lanceolate, suddenly contracted and obtuse at the base, acute at the apex, membranaceous, dark olive-green above, subglabrous, rufescent beneath, and pubescent on the midrib, 1–1¼ in. long, 2–3 lines broad, on petioles 1 line long; raceme lateral, subglabrous, longer than the leaves, pedunculate, bearing above 6–8 flowers on alternate slender pedicels 4¾ lines long, with a minute acute basal bract; sepals ovate, acute, 6 lines long, imbricate, with 1 or 2 subulate inner scales; corolla 1–1¼ in. long; tube narrow below the middle, campanulate above; segments inequilaterally oblique, near half the length of the tube; stamens inserted in the contraction of the tube;

anthers dorsally hispid; disk urceolate, submembranaceous on the margin, which is crenulate, exceeding the 2 acutely ovoid ovaries.

24. ANGADENIA CUBENSIS, nob.: *Echites Cubensis*, Griseb. in Revis. Pl. Cub. Cat. No. 1887. In Cuba: *v. s. in herb. Mus. Brit.* Cuba (Wright 2955).

A species very near *A. Lindeniana*; a subscandent plant, with more remote axils; leaves roundish, scarcely cordate, acute, dark green above, with paler margins, pallid brown beneath, with immersed nerves $1\frac{1}{2}$–$1\frac{3}{4}$ in. long, 7–8 lines broad, on petioles 1 line long; inflorescence not stated; sepals acute, with 2 small acute inner scales; tube of corolla 7 lines long, narrow below the middle, widening upwards; segments dolabriform, dextrorsely convolute, 6 lines long, 5 lines broad, unequally expanded; stamens inserted in the contraction of the tube; anthers glabrous, acute, shortly 2-lobed at the base, on shortish pilose filaments; disk tubular, subconical, submembranaceous, 5-sulcate.

25. ANGADENIA PRIEURII, nob.: *Echites Prieurii*, A. DC. *l. c.* p. 458: *Amblyanthera Prieurii*, Müll. in Linn. xxx. p. 448. In Guiana Gallica (Le Prieur 241): *non vidi*.

A species with tortuous, scabridly pubescent branches; leaves elliptic, subcordate, acuminate, coriaceous, very glabrous, shining above, velutinous beneath, 3 in. long, 14–16 lines broad, on petioles 2 lines long; peduncle shorter than the leaves, bearing many densely congested flowers, on pedicels a little shorter than the calyx; sepals acutely ovate, puberulous outside, each with an inner obtuse scale; corolla hypocrateriform, glabrous; tube narrowly cylindrical, contracted in the mouth, 10–11 lines long, with a ring of retrorse hairs above the middle; segments half as long as the tube; stamens inserted in the pilose ring; anthers acute; disk urceolate, nearly entire or undulate on the margin; follicles 2, erect, torulose, glabrous, 3–4 in. long; seeds with a rufescent coma.

26. ANGADENIA PANDURATA, nob.: *Echites pandurata*, A. DC. *l. c.* p. 458: *Amblyanthera pandurata*, Müll. in Linn. xxx. p. 448. Ad Oaxaca (Andrieux 245): *non vidi*.

A species with pubescent branches; leaves fiddle-shaped, lower portion broader and cordate, shortly acuminate, pubescent, membranaceous, undulate, hoary beneath, 2–4 in. long, $1\frac{1}{4}$–2 in. broad, on petioles 6–9 lines long; racemes shorter than the leaves, simple, pubescent, bearing many flowers on pedicels 3 lines long; sepals obtusely ovate; corolla $1\frac{1}{4}$ in. long, glabrous; tube narrowly cylindrical, a little swollen above; segments half its length; stamens inserted on a pilose ring at the contraction of the tube; anthers obtusely bilobed at the base; disk cylindrical, 5-striate, shorter than the ovaries.

PERICTENIA*.

This genus is proposed for a handsome Peruvian plant of Spruce's collection, distributed under the name of *Echites stipellaris*. This approaches *Dipladenia* in habit; its axils are furnished with a pectiniform ring of long stipules, as in *Mandevilla*; the segments of the corolla are elongated horizontally, and introplicate in æstivation, so that their tips descend into and far below the mouth of the tube, as in *Bonafousia*.

* From περί (*circum*), κτείς (*pecten*), from the pectiniform ring of stipules at the nodes.

PERICTENIA, nob. *Sepala* 5, subparva, oblonga, obtusa, valde imbricata, marginibus submembranaceis, singula intus squamulis 2 acute 2-dentatis munita. *Corolla* hypocrateriformis; *tubus* longe et anguste cylindricus, supra breviter ampliatus; *segmenta* 5, pro tertia parte trapeziformia, subito angustata et longe horizontaliter protensa, rotata, in æstivatione inflexa et intra tubum descendentia, dextrorsum convoluta. *Stamina* 5, paullo supra basin tubi inserta; *filamenta* brevia, retrorsum niveo-pilosa; *antheræ* lineares, acutissimæ, dorso pilosulæ, imo in furcas 2 longe aristatas tenuissimas fissæ. *Discus* urceolatus, sub medium in lobos 5 oblongos obtusos pilosulos divisus. *Ovaria* 2, parva, globosa, dense niveo-hispidula, disco inclusa; *stylus* brevis, validiusculus; *clavuncula* incrassata, 5-sulcata, imo indusiata; *stigmata* 2, parva, terminalia.

Frutex *Peruvianus subhumilis, erectus*; stipulæ *plurimæ, aristato-lanceolatæ, ad nodos pectinatim sitæ*; folia *pauca, opposita, ovata, utrinque acuta, breviter petiolata*; racemi *folio multibreviores, pauciflori, simpliciter vel opposite axillares et terminales, pedunculati*; flores *speciosi, breviter pedicellati, bracteolati*.

PERICTENIA STIPELLARIS, nob.: *Echites stipellaris*, Spruce, MSS. Caule erecto, rigido, fistuloso, valde compresso, profunde 4-sulcato, fusco, brevissime rufo-hirtello, lenticellis longis flavidis notato; axillis 3, floriferis, ad nodos dilatatos stipulis plurimis setaceo-linearibus pectinatim erectis munitis: foliis late ovatis, imo subacutis, apice in acumen brevissimum obtusulum repente constrictis, marginibus subundulatis, supra viridibus, ad costam et nervos pilosulis, nervis recte divaricatis et arcuatim nexis, subtus flavide opacis, pubescentibus, costa nervisque prominulis; petiolis profunde canaliculatis, quam stipulæ haud longioribus: paniculis axillaribus, oppositis aut solitariis, vel terminalibus; pedunculo longiusculo, flavide tomentoso, tereti, apice incrassato et hic brevissime dichotomo; ramis bibracteolatis, crebriter pauciflorís; floribus ut in char. generico. In Peruvia alta: *v. s. in herb. meo ex* Tarapota (Spruce 4900).

A very peculiar plant, with much the habit of *Dipladenia Gardneriana*. Its erect fistular stem, nearly 10 in. long, is bare at its base for the length of 6 in., the upper portion being interrupted by 3 foliiferous nodes 1¼, 1, and ¾ in. apart respectively, each node being furnished with a ring of 12 aristiform stipules 5–6 lines long (3 placed close together on each side of the petiole); opposite leaves 5–5½ in. long, 3–3¾ in. broad, on petioles 5 lines long; opposite peduncles 1½–2 in. long, 8-flowered; 2 divaricating branches 4–4¼ lines long; bracts half that length; pedicels 3 or 4 close together, 3 lines long, pilose, bibracteolate; sepals 2¼ lines long, obtuse, pilosulous on both sides, with membranaceous margins; corolla glabrous; tube 16 lines long, 2 lines broad, swelling towards the mouth to a breadth of 4 lines; segments 10 lines long; stamens inserted 1 line above the base of the tube; slender anthers 4½ lines long; filaments as long as the aciculate basal prongs.

A representation of this species, and an analysis of its flower, are given in Plate XXVIII.

MANDEVILLA.

This genus was established in 1840 by Dr. Lindley, upon a single species, the only one hitherto known; it was figured and described by him and Sir Wm. Hooker, by both from living plants. It was not adopted by De Candolle; but Endlicher accepted it. It has more lately been acknowledged by the authors of the 'Genera Plantarum,' but upon terms which cannot be admitted; for they absorb into it the *Amblyanthera* of Müller, a valid genus, utterly discordant with it. *Mandevilla* is distinguished from the latter by its much more slender habit, its branches very weak, twining, or simply subdichotomous, furnished at its rather remote nodes with a pectinate ring of fleshy slender stipules; the inflorescence is lateral and pendulous, upon an elongated bare peduncle, bearing above a few large campanulate laxly secund flowers, upon pedicels without bracts, thus differing from the peculiar characteristics of *Amblyanthera*.

MANDEVILLA, Lindl. *Sepala* 5, lanceolato- vel lincari-oblonga (quorum 1 sæpe latius), erecta, intus ad basin squamula lata pectinatim denticulata vel ciliata munita. *Corolla* tubulosa; *tubus* imo anguste cylindricus, superne campanulatim inflatus; *segmenta* late dolabriformia, dextrorsum convoluta. *Stamina* 5, in contractionem tubi inserta; *filamenta* retrorsum hispida; *antheræ* lineares, apice membrana apiculatæ, imo breviter 2-lobæ, in conum conniventes. *Discus* urceolatus, membranaceus aut carnosus, margine ad tertiam vel dimidiam partem 5fidus, ovariis subbrevior. *Ovaria* 2, libera. *Stylus* filiformis; *clavuncula* oblonga, 5-sulcata, imo membrana peltata expansa; *stigmata* 2, parva, terminalia. *Folliculi* 2, longi, teretes; *semina* plurima, oblonga, compressa, *raphe* longitudinali signata; *coma* apicalis, molliter sericea, expansa, testa triplo longior.

Frutex *Americæ meridionalis, volubilis vel scandens*; ramuli *rubtenues*, axillis *dilatatis*, stipulis *plurimis acutissimis pectinatim erectis munit*; folia *petiolata, ovato-oblonga, imo sæpe cordata, subtus plerumque pubescentes*; racemi *axillares aut terminales, longe pedunculati, interdum abortione ad florem unicum reducti*; flores *pedicellati, speciosi, albi vel coccinei*.

MANDEVILLA SUAVEOLENS, Lindl. Bot. Reg. xxvi. p. 36, tab. 7; Hook. Bot. Mag. 67, tab. 3797; Paxton Mag. 16, tab. 290; Endl. Gen. Suppl. i. p. 1396: *Echites suaveolens*, A. DC. (non Mart. & Gall.), Prodr. viii. p. 452. In Buenos Ayres cult.: *non vidi*.

A twining plant, with large odoriferous flowers, sent home by Tweedie in 1840, from Buenos Ayres, where he found it cultivated under the name of *Jasmin de Chile*. It has subglabrous branches about the thickness of a crow's quill, with axils 3¼ in. apart, furnished on each side with 6 acute fleshy stipules 2 lines long, united in a pectinate ring; leaves oblong, cordate at the base, acute, submembranaceous, glabrous above, paler beneath and glaucous, with hairy tufts in the axils of the brown nerves, the veins very reticulate, 2½ in. long, 1¾ in. broad, the basal sinus 2-3 lines deep, on petioles 1-2 lines long; raceme lateral, pendent, on a glabrous peduncle bare at its base for 2 in., bearing above several alternate flowers on ebracteate secund pedicels about ¼–½ in. apart, 9 lines long; flowers cream-coloured, odoriferous, 2¼ in. long; sepals lanceolate, erect, subimbricate, 4 lines long, each with a broad pectinate scale within, as long as the disk; tube of corolla 1¼ in. long, narrowed cylindrically at the base for half its length; segments dextrorsely convolute, broadly dolabriform, the sinister angle acute, sinuate above, rounded, 1 in. long, 9 lines broad; stamens seated in the contraction of the tube, on a densely pilose ring; filaments retrorsely hispid; anthers oblong, cohering, with a membranaceous apex, obtusely bilobed at the base; style slender; clavuncle incrassate, oblong, 5-grooved, with a basal peltate membrane; stigmata 2, small, erect; disk of 5 fleshy, oblong, truncate lobes, shorter than the 2 pointed oblong ovaries; follicles 2, terete, parallel, pendent, 1-1½ foot long; seeds with an apical coma.

AMBLYANTHERA.

This genus, proposed by Müller in 1860, has not been acknowledged by other botanists. The name was given on account of the short, obtuse, basal lobes of its anthers—a character of no distinctive value, as this is also seen in many other genera. As mentioned in a preceding page (p. 183), *Amblyanthera* was suppressed by the authors of the 'Genera Plantarum' (ii. p. 726), and absorbed into *Mandevilla*, which is an essentially different genus : in the former the plants are very bushy, the branches, wanting the peculiar stipules of the latter; the only plant known of *Mandevilla* is, on the contrary, a very slender climber, with a different inflorescence. *Amblyanthera* has a condensed panicle of many flowers, on short pedicels hidden by large, broad, foliaceous bracts, much imbricated—a feature only approached by *Laseguea*, where the bracts are linear and very narrow. *Amblyanthera*, however, when properly restricted, constitutes a very good genus. Müller evidently was not aware that, besides the basal lobes, the rest of each anther is formed upon a peculiar plan; the want of this knowledge led him to unite with it a host of heterogeneous species, a list of which is here appended. Müller, in his illustrations of *Amblyanthera*, gives a correct representation of one of the species in his plate 45; but his plate 44 represents a very different plant, which I have referred to my genus *Mitozus*.

The following is an amended diagnosis of the genus, according to my own observations.

AMBLYANTHERA, Müll. (in parte), char. emendato. *Sepala* 5, acutissime lineari-lanceolata, erecta, submembranacea, paulo quincuncialiter imbricata, intus squamula deltoidea vel ovata inæqualiter laciniulata singulatim munita. *Corolla* majuscula; *tubus* cylindricus, sub medium angustatus, intus ad constrictionem lineis 5, vel annulo retrorsum piloso donatus, superne campanulatus; *segmenta* 5, dolabriformia, angulo sinistro acuta, latere altero horizontaliter rotundata, æstivatione dextrorsum convoluta, demum expansa, tubo breviora. *Stamina* 5, inclusa, annulo piloso insita; *filamenta* subbrevia, linearia; *antheræ* longiusculæ; *connectivum* membranaceum, late lineare, coloratum, apice acutum, medio loculis 2 parvis ovatis collateralibus polliniferis signatum, margine sub medium callo magno incrassatum; *callus* superne hippocrepiformis, inferne truncatus et in lobulos 2 breves obtusos fissus. *Discus* urceolatus, carnosus, usque ad medium in lobos 5 obtusos fissus; *ovaria* 2, acute oblonga, disco paullo longiora; *stylus* filiformis; *clavuncula* incrassata, oblonga, longitudine 5-glandulosa, imo *appendice* membranacea signata, mox ad antheras adglutinata, his hinc in conum cohærentibus; *stigmata* 2, parva, acuta, terminalia. *Folliculi* 2, teretes, torulosi, subarcuati, apice interdum nexi, valde pilosi; *placenta* e marginibus suturæ ventralis introflexis, anguste lineares; *semina* plurima oblonga, ad ventrem concavum *raphe* longitudinali signata; *coma* pilis rufulis sericeis 2-3plo longioribus coronata.

Frutices *plerumque Brasilienses, valde ramosi; ramuli sæpe fistulosi, flexuose subscandentes, hirsuti, cum axillis remotis; folia opposita, oblonga, imo sæpius cordata, acuminata, eglandulosa, pubescentes vel subhirsuta, petiolata; racemi singulatim laterales; pedunculus elongatus, supra medium crebre pluriflorus; pedicelli breves, imo bracteati; bractea magna, foliosa, ovata, longe cuspidata, stipitata, pedicello 3–4plo longior; flores majusculi, coccinei vel lutescentes, sæpius extus niveo-tomentosi.*

1. AMBLYANTHERA HIRSUTA, nob. : *Echites hirsuta*, Velloz, Fl. Flum. p. 113, Icon. iii. tab. 44 (non R. & Sch., nec Stadelm. nec Hook.): *Echites Fluminensis*, A. DC. Prodr. viii. p. 452 : *Amblyanthera Fluminensis* (in parte), Müll. Fl. Bras. xxvi. p. 149. In prov. Rio de Janeiro, Boa Vista, circa Itagoahy (Velloz) : *v. s. in herb. Mus. Brit.* Itagoahy (Bowie & Cunningham, *in flore et fructu*).

The above specimen, from the same locality, is quite in accordance with Velloz's drawing in regard to the length of the internodes, the size and shape of the leaves, and the character of the inflorescence, differing only in the fruit, which corresponds with that of the genus as given by Müller. Velloz's drawing of the follicle is that of an Asclepiad, as he himself indicated, and is probably that of an undescribed *Schubertia*, the plants of which much resemble those of *Amblyanthera*. This species is confounded by Müller with his *A. Fluminensis*; but the two species are very distinct. This has scandent, flexuous, hirsutulous branches, the axils being $3\frac{1}{4}$–$4\frac{1}{2}$ in. apart; leaves opposite, oblong, a little narrower towards the base, where they are auriculately cordate and eglandulose, rather suddenly acuminate at the summit, fuscous green above, opake, hirsutely pubescent, with about 11 pairs of patently divaricate fine immersed nerves, yellowish brown and opake, beneath more densely hirto-pubescent (with simple hairs), more especially on the scarcely prominulent midrib and nerves, 3–4 in. long (including the basal lobes 2 lines deep), $1\frac{3}{4}$–$1\frac{5}{8}$ in. broad, on rather slender patent pubescent petioles 6 lines long; raceme lateral at the nodes, 3 in. long, hirsutulous, on a somewhat patent peduncle bare at the base for 1 inch, bearing above about 6 alternate flowers on stoutish tomentous pedicels 3 lines long, each supported by an oblong elliptic stipate bract acuminate at the summit, hirsutulous, 9 lines long, 4 lines broad; sepals narrowly subulate, lanceolate, membranaceous, smooth inside, tomentous, with white hairs outside, 3 lines long, 1 line broad at the base, ciliate on the margins, with an inner multilacinulate scale; corolla scarlet, niveo-lanate in the bud; tube afterwards sparsely pubescent, yellowish within, cylindrical, campanulate above the middle, 9–10 lines long; segments dolabriform, acute at one angle, plicately crenate along the margin, reddish yellow, subglabrous, 5 lines long and broad; stamens seated in the contraction of the tube, upon 5 densely lanate niveous lines; anthers 1 line long, with a scarlet connective pointed at the summit, obtusely emarginate or shortly bilobed at the base, cohering in a cone round the clavuncle; disk half cleft into 5 emarginate lobes, shorter than the 2 pointed pubescent ovaries; follicles torulously terete, very arcuate and conjoined at the apex, hirsute, $4\frac{1}{2}$ in. long, 2 lines broad; seeds many, pilose, oblong, compressed, 3 lines long, crowned by an erect reddish coma 9 lines long.

2. AMBLYANTHERA FLUMINENSIS, Müll. *l. c.* p. 148, tab. 45 (excl. syn.). In prov. Rio de Janeiro ad Oliveira, in Serra de Macacú et in mont. Organensibus : *non vidi*.

A more lax species than the preceding, and confounded with it. It has fuscous flexuous branches clothed with yellowish hispid hairs, the axils being 6–$6\frac{1}{2}$ in. apart; leaves elliptic-oblong, gradually narrower below the middle, auriculately cordate at the base, truncate and mucronate at the apex, or with a short, rather blunt acumen, submembranaceous, above green, opake, subpilose on both sides, ciliate on the margins, with 15 pairs of subascending nerves, beneath reddish, opake, patently hispidulous along the prominulent midrib and nerves, $3\frac{1}{4}$–6 in. long, $1\frac{3}{4}$–$2\frac{3}{4}$ in. broad, on hirsute petioles 3–$4\frac{1}{4}$ lines long; a lateral raceme at the nodes, densely pubescent, 4 in. long, on a thickish peduncle bare below for 2 in., bearing upwards 6 or 7 alternate flowers about 3 lines apart, on pedicels 3 lines long, supported by as many foliaceous bracts, rhomboidally ovate, subacute at the base, narrowly acuminate, pubescent, 9 lines long, 4 lines broad; sepals subulately lanceolate, externally pilose, ciliate on the margins, 5 lines long, 1 line broad at the base, each with an internal semicircular denticulate scale; a handsome corolla, niveo-pilose outside; tube cylindrical below the middle, campanular above, 13 lines long;

segments dolabriform, with a prominent tooth at the sinister angle, membranaceous, 8 lines long, 7 lines broad, sigmoidly shaped above; stamens seated on a woolly ring in the middle of the tube; stamens as in the preceding; disk and other parts as in the generic character; follicles unknown.

3. AMBLYANTHERA CLAUSSENII, nob.: *Echites Fluminensis*, var. *Claussenii*, A. DC. *l. c.* p. 452: *Amblyanthera Fluminensis*, var. *Claussenii*, Müll. *l. c.* p. 149. In Brasilia, prov. Minas Geraës ad Cachoeira do Campo (Claussen): *v. s. in herb. meo* (Claussen 250).

A climbing plant, with flexuous, slender, patently pubescent, fistulous branches, 1 line thick, with axils $4\frac{1}{2}$–7 in. apart, rarely with a very slender, unilateral, very pubescent branchlet; leaves ovate, rounded and deeply cordate at the base, with rounded lobes, contracted below the apex into a subulately linear recurving acumen, fuscous green and opake above, remotely hispid with rigid hairs bulbose at the base, patently cano-hirsutulous along the midrib, with about 16 pairs of divergent nerves and others shorter and intermediate, with transversely reticulated veins, ciliate on the margins, paler beneath, and more densely hispidulous, especially on the nerves, $2\frac{1}{2}$–$4\frac{1}{2}$ in. long (including the basal lobes 3 lines long), $1\frac{1}{4}$–2 in. broad, on retrorsely hispid petioles 2 lines long; raceme solitary, lateral at the nodes, 3–4 in. long, patently hirsute, on a stoutish divergent peduncle bare at the base for 1–$1\frac{1}{4}$ in., bearing upwards about 12 alternate flowers on hirsute pedicels 2 lines long, each supported by a large foliaceous ovate bract, substipate at the base, with an elongated, very narrow, incurved linear point, with coloured nerves, densely pubescent beneath, 10 lines long, 4 lines broad; sepals subulately linear, very acute, with a reddish membranaceous margin, smooth inside, puberulous outside, 6 lines long, 1 line broad at the base; corolla of a deep scarlet colour when in bud, densely clothed with white woolly hairs, afterwards subglabrous; tube cylindrical as far as the middle, funnel-shaped above, 10 lines long; segments rhomboidal, much veined, uncinately acute at the sinister angle, horizontally spreading on the dexter side, 6 lines long, 4 lines broad; stamens seated in the contraction of the tube, on a densely woolly niveous ring.

A representation of this species, with an analysis of its flower, is shown in Plate XXV.

4. AMBLYANTHERA HISPIDA, Müll. *l. c.* p. 147, tab. 44. fig. 2. In Brasilia australiore: *v. s. in herb. Mus. Brit.* sine loco (Sellow, *in fructu*).

A climbing species, with simple, terete, flexuous, hirsute branches; leaves oblong-ovate, narrower below the middle, deeply cordate at the base, with rounded lobes, gradually or more suddenly acuminate, chartaceous, fuscously olive-coloured above, opake, subsparsely hispid, with adpressed soft hairs seated upon prominent rugous points, with about 12 pairs of divergent semi-immersed nerves, ferruginously pallid and opake beneath, densely hirsutulous, especially on the midrib and nerves, and on the transverse veins with patent more rigid hairs, $4\frac{3}{4}$–$5\frac{3}{4}$ in. long, $2\frac{1}{4}$–$2\frac{5}{8}$ in. broad, on patently hispid petioles 5 lines long; raceme (according to Müller) axillary, as long as the leaves, pubescent, on a peduncle bare at the base for $1\frac{1}{4}$ in., bearing several flowers on stout subreflected pedicels, supported by as many linear-lanceolate pubescent bracts as long as the pedicel and calyx; sepals linear-lanceolate, subpubescent, $3\frac{1}{2}$–$4\frac{1}{2}$ lines long, 1 line broad at the base, each with an inner, ovate, subcrenate scale; tube of corolla cylindrical, more slender in the middle, campanular above, white externally, yellow inside with reddish stripes, pubescent outside, 17 lines long; segments dolabriform, puberulous outside, acute at the sinister angle, horizontally expanded on the other, 7 lines long and broad, deeply sigmoid on the upper margin; follicles arcuate, torulosely terete, conjoined at the apex, sparsely clothed with long yellow hairs, 5½ in. long; seeds numerous, oblong, dorsally convex and puberulous, deeply channelled on the ventral face, and there marked by a white longitudinal raphe nearly reaching the base, 4 lines long, 1 line broad, with a reddish sericeous apical coma 9 lines long.

A drawing of the follicles, and the analysis of the seed, are given in Plate XXV. figs. 13 to 18.

5. AMBLYANTHERA OVATA, nob.: ramis simplicibus, scandentibus, flexuosis, fistulosis, pallide brunneis, pubescentibus; axillis remotis: foliis late ovatis, imo rotundatis, integris et subplicatis, aut vix cordatis, apice emarginatis aut subito in acumen acutum constrictis, supra fusco-viridibus, opacis, breviter adpresse hirtulis, pilis imo scabridule bulbosis, nervis tenuissimis utrinque circa 15 subpatule divaricatis, subtus flavide opacis, dense et breviter tomentosis, costa nervisque prominulis molliter hirsutis, venis conspicue transversis et reticulatis; petiolis tenuibus, puberulis, quam limbus 3–4plo brevioribus: racemo solitario, ad nodos laterali, quam folium 2plo longiore; pedunculo valido, pro tertia parte basali nudo, superne valde incrassato et alternatim plurifloro; pedicellis brevibus, subreflexis, puberulis, bracteis ovalibus tomentosis suffultis; sepalis subparvis, lanceolatis, puberulis; corolla nondum explicata flavida, undique molliter niveo-lanata; tubo cylindrico medio angustiore, superne vix inflato. In Bolivia? *v. s. in herb. meo*, sine loco.

A distinct species, with branches 1 line thick, the axils 4–6 in. apart; leaves 2¼–2¾ in. long, 1½–2 in. broad, on slender petioles 8–9 lines long; raceme 4 in. long, on a stout peduncle 1¼ line thick below, 2 lines thick above, bare at the base for 1 in.; flowers alternate, 3 lines apart, on pedicels 2 lines long, supported by oval bracts 4 lines long; sepals 2½ lines long; corolla in bud 1¾ in. long; tube 11 lines long; follicles (in a very immature state) densely niveo-tomentous.

6. AMBLYANTHERA CILIATA, Müll. Fl. Bras. xxvi. p. 146; Linn. xxxi. p. 449: *Echites ciliata*, Stad. Bot. Zeit. 1861, p. 32; A. DC. Prodr. viii. p. 459. In prov. Bahia, ad Caiteté: *non vidi*.

A climbing species with glabrous branches, and patent branchlets hispidulous towards their base, with remote axils; leaves oblong-ovate, narrowed and cordate at the base, acuminate, rigidly membranaceous, glabrous above, with about 11 pairs of slightly arching and very slender reticulated veins, ciliate on the margins, paler beneath, hispid along the midrib and nerves, 3½–5 in. long, 1½–2¼ in. broad, on petioles 6–10 lines long, the upper pairs shortest; raceme axillary, erect, on a short peduncle, with many flowers on rigid puberulous pedicels 2 lines long, supported by narrow, linear-lanceolate, long-acuminate bracts with ciliate margins 11 lines long; sepals ovate-lanceolate, long-acuminate, margins ciliate, 3¾ lines long, each with a small ovate inner scale; tube of corolla 12 lines long, cylindrical below, subcampanulate above the middle; segments subtrapezoid ovate, 1¾ line long; disk of 5 truncate-ovate concave lobes, shorter than the ovaries; follicles torulose, glabrous, 4 in. long, 2¼ lines broad; seeds as long as the coma.

A species probably belonging to *Laseguea*.

7. AMBLYANTHERA BRIDGESII, Müll. in Linn. xxx. p. 420. In Bolivia (Bridges, Cuming 120): *non vidi*.

A glabrous plant, with spreading verruculose branchlets; leaves oblong-ovate, or ovate-lanceolate, or ovate, cordate at the base, with a long acumen, membranaceous, glabrous above, with 6-8 pairs of divergent prominulent nerves nearly conjoined close to the margins, with reticulated, pellucid, fuscous veins, $2\frac{3}{4}$–4 in. long, 1–1$\frac{3}{4}$ in. broad, on petioles 7$\frac{1}{2}$ lines long; racemes axillary, longer than the leaves, glabrous, on a peduncle $3\frac{1}{2}$–4$\frac{3}{4}$ in. long, bearing laxly many flowers, on glabrous pedicels 7–9 lines long, supported by sublinear subglabrous bracteoles $3\frac{1}{2}$–4$\frac{1}{2}$ lines long; sepals narrow, linear-lanceolate, subglabrous, of the same length, each with an inner, deeply bifid, subulate scale; corolla in bud 1$\frac{3}{8}$ in. long; tube narrowed below, contracted in the middle; segments dimidiato-obovate, length unknown; stamens inserted in the contraction of the tube on a retrorsely pilose ring; disk of 5 truncately ovate lobes, three times shorter than the oblong-ovoid acuminate ovaries.

A species also probably belonging to *Laseguea*.

8. AMBLYANTHERA MORITZIANA, Müll. in Linn. xxx. p. 421. In Columbia (Moritz 31): *non vidi*.

A scandent species, with hirto-pubescent branches and branchlets; leaves broadly ovate, or obovate, cordate at the base, with a short acumen, rigidly membranaceous, with 5–6 pairs of divergent prominulent nerves and transverse veins, $2\frac{3}{8}$–4$\frac{3}{4}$ in. long, 1$\frac{3}{4}$–2$\frac{1}{4}$ in. broad, on petioles 7 lines long; racemes axillary, a little longer than the leaves, glabrous, on a peduncle 1$\frac{1}{4}$ in. long, bearing many flowers 1$\frac{3}{8}$ in. long on pedicels 4–6 lines long, supported by linear spathulate bracts 1 in. long; sepals acuminately oblong, rugous outside at the base, each with an inner crenately dentate truncate scale; tube of corolla narrow as far as the middle, dilated upwards; segments obovoid, less than half the length of the tube; stamens seated in the contraction of the tube; anthers short, glabrous; disk of 5 oblong lobes, connate at the base, nearly as long as the glabrous cylindrically ovoid ovaries.

9. AMBLYANTHERA SCHLIMII, Müll. *l. c.* p. 419. In Nova Granada, prov. Ocanna (Linden, Schlim 575): *non vidi*.

A species differing from the preceding in its smaller, narrow, lanceolate leaves and shorter racemes; its slender fuscous branches are pubescently hirtous, 1–1$\frac{1}{2}$ line thick; leaves linear-lanceolate, obtuse or subcordate at the base, narrowing above into an obtuse acumen, subcoriaceous, glabrous above, blackish, shining, reticulately rugous, covered beneath with velutinous, woolly, white or yellowish hairs, with 15–18 pairs of horizontally-spreading nerves, 1$\frac{5}{8}$–2$\frac{3}{4}$ in. long, 2$\frac{3}{4}$–4$\frac{1}{4}$ lines broad, on petioles 1–1$\frac{1}{2}$ line long; racemes lateral, shorter than the leaves, on a short peduncle bearing many dense flowers on pedicels supported by triangularly ovate acuminate bracts; sepals triangularly ovate, acuminate, subcarinate, 1 line long, each with an inner, deltoid, denticulate scale; corolla in the whole 1 in. long, yellow; tube narrowly cylindrical for half its length, dilating above, pubescent or glabrous; segments obliquely ovate, acute on one edge, much shorter than the tube; stamens seated in the contraction of the tube, upon a retrorsely pilose ring; disk cup-shaped, half-cleft into 5 lobes, nearly as long as the glabrous oblong-ovoid ovaries.

10. AMBLYANTHERA FENDLERI, Müll. *l. c.* p. 417. In Venezuela, prope Tovar (Fendler 1032): *non vidi*.

A species, from its densely bracteate brush-like raceme, evidently belonging to this genus, with which it agrees in its other characters. It has griseo-pubescent branches, darkish branchlets 1–1½ line thick; leaves narrow-lanceolate, cordate at the base, gradually acuminate, rigidly membranaceous, palish green above, glabrous, shining, with 9–12 pairs of diverging straight nerves arcuately conjoined, veinless, cano-pubescent beneath, 2⅔–3¼ in. long, 7–9½ lines broad, on petioles 1½–3 lines long; racemes axillary, a little longer than the leaves, on a short peduncle bearing many dense flowers on alternate pedicels, thicker above, 3 lines long, the lower ones caducous, supported by linear-lanceolate acuminate bracts 5 lines long; sepals ovate-acuminate, puberulous, each with an inner oblong laciniulate scale; corolla in the whole 1¾ in. long; tube narrowly cylindrical for two thirds its length, campanulate above, pilose; segments shorter, broadly ovate; stamens seated in the contraction of the tube; disk 5-cleft, as long as the smooth ovoid ovaries.

11. AMBLYANTHERA SPRUCEANA, Müll. Fl. Br. xxvi. p. 143: *Echites Javitensis*, Benth. (non Kunth) MSS. Prope Panuré, Rio. Uahupes (Spruce 2863): *non vidi*.

It is an erect plant, with glabrous, rigid, angular branches, and subtomentellous branchlets; leaves oblong-elliptic, obtuse at the base, shortly acuminate, subcoriaceous, fuscous green above, glabrous or scabridly hirtellous, with about 12 pairs of divergent dark-red nerves and reticulated veins, sparsely subhirtellous beneath, 2⅔–3¼ in. long, 1–1¾ in. broad, on slender petioles 5–7 lines long; raceme subterminal, in young state 2¼ in. long, puberulous, with a simple, straight, stout peduncle 1¼–1¾ line thick, bearing many densely spicate flowers, which are almost sessile, and supported by as many elongated, carinately navicular bracts 9½ lines long, with a long, incurved acumen; sepals 1¾ line long, broadly ovate, obtuse, each with an inner, broad, unequally denticulate scale; corolla (yet in bud) 10½ lines long, tomentellous; tube cylindrically contracted below the middle, a little broader above; segments inæquilateral; disk 5-cleft, nearly as long as the ovaries.

Species assigned to Amblyanthera *by Müller, here excluded and referred to their proper places.*

(Indications: B.=Flor. Bras. fasc. xxvi.; L.=Linnæa, vol. xxx.)

A. acutiloba, L. 447	= *Echites acutiloba.*
A. andina, L. 425	*Echites andina.*
A. Andrieuxii, L. 422	*Echites Andrieuxii.*
A. angustifolia, L. 447	*Mesechites linearifolia.*
A. antennacea, L. 448	*Laseguea antennacea.*
A. Benthami, L. 451	*Homaladenia angustifolia.*
A. Bogotensis, L. 452	*Anartia Bogotensis.*

A. brachyloba, L. 423	= *Echites brachyloba*.
A. campestris, B. 149; L. 453	*Rhabdadenia campestris*.
A. chlorantha, L. 454	*Echites chlorantha*.
A. citrifolia, L. 450	*Echites citrifolia*.
A. congesta, L. 450	*Echites congesta*.
A. convolvulacea, L. 447	*Echites convolvulacea*.
A. convolvulacea, L. 430	*Echites mexicana*.
A. crassifolia, B. 143	*Rhodocalyx crassifolia*.
A. Cuyabensis, B. 145; L. 450	*Mitozus Cuyabensis*.
A. Fluminensis, var. *Stadelmeyeri*, B. 149	*Temnadenia Stadelmeyeri*.
A. foliosa, L. 427	*Laseguea foliosa*.
A. funiformis, B. 146; L. 449	*Mitozus funiformis*.
A. Guianensis, L. 448	*Echites Guianensis*.
A. Karwinskii, L. 426	*Echites Karwinskii*.
A. leptophylla, B. 142; L. 448	*Mitozus leptophyllus*.
A. macrophylla, L. 449	*Exothostemon macrophyllum*.
A. madida, B. 150; L. 453	*Rhabdadenia Pohlii*.
A. membranacea, L. 423, 448	*Echites membranacea*.
A. Mexicana, L. 424	*Echites Mexicana*.
A. microcalyx, L. 428, 448–453	*Echites microcalyx*.
A. microcalyx, L. 454	*Mesechites jasminiflora*.
A. Oaxacana, L. 447	*Mesechites Oaxacana*.
A. palustris, B. 145	*Temnadenia palustris*.
„ „ var. *Almadensis*, B. 146	*Temnadenia Almadensis*.
A. pandurata, L. 448	*Angadenia pandurata*.
A. Pavonii, L. 450	*Echites hirsuta*.
A. Prieurii, L. 448	*Angadenia Prieurii*.
A. suaveolens, L. 447	*Mandevilla suaveolens*.
A. subsagittata, L. 453	*Echites subsagittata*.
A. subsessilis, L. 447	*Echites subsessilis*.
A. tomentosa, L. 450	*Temnadenia tomentosa*.
A. torosa, L. 446	*Mesechites torosa*.
A. tubiflora, L. 454	*Echites tubiflora*.
A. versicolor, B. 146; L. 449	*Mitozus versicolor*.
„ „ var. *glabrata*, B. 147; L. 449	*Mitozus tenuicaulis*.

ECHITES.

This genus was first proposed by P. Browne in 1756 for a Jamaica plant, and was so named because its follicular fruit assumed the form of a viper (ἔχις). At that early period no precise genus was known, and species were defined in two or three words. Though Browne gave ample details of his species, Jacquin was the first to give a regular diagnosis of the genus *Echites*. Linnæus in 1764 acknowledged *Echites* under very similar circumstances; so that his definition of the genus is of little value. This example was followed by other botanists, who continued to heap up in this genus a great number of plants bearing little relation to the true type, thus creating great confusion up to the present time.

The order *Apocyneæ* was not proposed until 1789, and then vaguely, as Jussieu included in it all the *Asclepiadeæ*, *Loganiaceæ*, and other groups of plants. It was not till 1811 that the celebrated Rob. Brown remedied this confusion by separating and defining the *Apocyneæ* and the *Asclepiadeæ* as distinct families, in the former of which the genus *Echites* is enumerated in terms differing little from those of Jacquin. The genus, still ill-defined, continued to increase in the number of species, when, in 1844, Prof. De Candolle enumerated 177 species, a number soon after considerably increased by Müller, all proposed without any relation to the structural peculiarities of the original type.

In this memoir I have endeavoured to separate the legitimate species, amounting to about 40, from the mass of above 200 of those recorded by authors. The plants of true *Echites* may be distinguished not only by the floral characters, but by having several pointed glands, arranged transversely across the nodes in the usual place of stipules, and in having similar glands at the base of the midrib of the leaves at their junction with the petioles. The following is an amended diagnosis of the genus.

ECHITES, P. Browne, Jam. p. 18; Jacq. Amer. p. 29; Linn. Sp. Pl. (1764) in parte; R. Brown, Mem. Wern. Soc. i. p. 396. *Sepala* 5, parva, acuta, intus singulatim squama profunde plurilacinulata munita; *corolla* tubularis; *tubus* longiusculus, imo breviter et anguste cylindricus, supra latior, subquinquangularis, hinc sæpe spiraliter tortus, fauce subconstrictus; *segmenta* 5, truncatim dolabriformia, oblonga vel tubo breviora, dextrorsum convoluta. *Stamina* ad constrictionem tubi inserta; *filamenta* tenuia, subbrevia; *antheræ* rigide lineares, acuminatæ, imo in furcas 2 breves acutas fissæ. *Discus* e lobis 5 obtuse linearibus, carnosulus; *ovaria* 2 illum subæquantia; *stylus* tenuis; *clavuncula* incrassata, oblonga; *stigmata* 2, parva, terminalia. *Folliculi* 2, aut erecti vel horizontaliter divaricati, anguste teretes, sutura ventrali debiscentes. *Semina* plurima, lineari-oblonga, compressa, rugulosa, funiculo brevissimo *raphe* continuo suspensa, *coma* sericeo-pilosa paullo longiore coronata.

Frutices *scandentes Americæ intertropicæ;* ramuli *ad nodos glandulis acutis plurimis præditi;* folia *opposita, petiolata, ovata aut oblonga, ad costam petiolum versus glandulis carnosulis munita;* inflorescentia *axillaris, sæpe bifida;* flores *plurimi, pulchri, pedicellati, umbellatim aut congestim aggregati;* pedicelli *brevissime bracteolati.*

1. ECHITES OVATA (scandens foliis ovatis), P. Browne, Hist. Jam. p. 182: *Apocynum folio rotundo,* Sloane, Jam. 1207, tab. 131. fig. 2, Cat. Jam. p. 89: *Apocynum scandens,* Catesb. Carol. i. p. 58, tab. 58. In Antillis: *v. s. in herb. Mus. Brit.* Jamaica (Shakespear, Houston).

The original type of the genus, which is fully described by Dr. Browne, and well figured by Sloane and Catesby. It grows on the dry (not moist) parts of the savannas of Jamaica; its scandent flexuose branches have axils $1\frac{1}{4}$ in. apart; leaves ovate, rounded at the base, subacute at the apex, rigidly membranaceous, dark green above, paler and opake beneath, with about 11 pairs of subdivergent, parallel, prominent nerves arcuately conjoined, $2-2\frac{1}{2}$ in. long, $1\frac{1}{2}-2\frac{1}{4}$ in. broad, on channelled petioles 3–6 lines long; raceme lateral, short, on a deflexed peduncle 4–6 lines long, bearing 2–5 aggregated pale yellow flowers, on pedicels 6 lines long; sepals acute, 1–1½ line long; tube of corolla narrowly cylindrical towards the base and near the summit, where it is spirally twisted, ventricose in the middle, 15 lines long, subpilose within; segments obovately dolabriform, crispate on the margins, 7 lines long and broad, with dextrorse convolution; stamens inserted on a pilose ring on the lower constriction of the tube; disk of 5 oblong fleshy lobes, half the length of the 2 ovate glabrous ovaries; follicles 2, terete, horizontally divaricate, outwardly subarcuate, 8 in. long, 3 lines thick towards the base, obtuse, and 2 lines thick towards the apex; seeds many, oblong, dorsally costate, thinly rostrate at the summit, with a longitudinal raphe, from the apex of which they are suspended, 4 lines long, with an apical, spreading, softly sericeous yellowish coma 10 lines long.

2. ECHITES UMBELLATA, Jacquin (non H. B. K.), Amer. p. 30, tab. 22; Linn. Sp. Pl. (in parte) 307, Syst. iii. p. 331; A. DC. Prodr. viii. p. 447; Griseb. Fl. Br. W. Ind. p. 414; Lunan, Jam. ii. p. 145: *Tabernaemontana subcordata*, Linn. Syst. p. 945: *Periploca (Nerium) oblongo-cordata*, Plum. Amer. ii. p. 210, tab. 216. fig. 2. In Antillis: *non vidi*.

This marked species is well depicted by Jacquin and Plumier, and is very different from the plant described by Kunth. In Jamaica it grows in the moist parts of the savanna. It is a twining plant, climbing to a height of 15 feet, exuding a clear, glutinous and poisonous juice; its branchlets are slender, glabrous, with axils 4 in. apart; leaves oblong, deeply cordate at the base, subacute at the summit, dark green above, with about 14 pairs of patently divaricate nerves arcuately conjoined near the undulate margin, pale ferruginous beneath, with prominulent nerves and reticulated veins, 3¼–4 in. long, 1½–2 in. broad, on petioles 5 lines long; inflorescence lateral, on a peduncle 1¾ in. long, supporting 4–7 flowers on umbellate pedicels 6 lines long, pluribracteolate at their base; sepals acute or acuminate, 1¼ line long, each with 2 acute inner scales; tube of corolla 12–15 lines long, narrowly cylindrical at the base and summit for a length of 5 lines, there spirally twisted, longitudinally 5-nerved, of a greenish colour; segments white, deltoidly dolabriform, with crenulate margins, 7 lines long and broad, dextrorsely convolute; stamens on very short filaments, seated on the lower constriction of the tube; disk of 5 fleshy oblong lobes, shorter than the 2 conical ovaries; follicles 2, terete, oblong, horizontally divaricate, obtuse, 8 in. long, 4 lines thick, containing many oblong seeds thinly rostrate at the apex, 6 lines long, surmounted by an erect apical coma 9 lines long.

3. ECHITES OBLIQUA, nob.: *Echites umbellata*, H. B. K. (non Jacq.) Gen. iii. p. 212 (excl. syn.): *Apocynum obliquum*, Miller, Dict. No. 8. In Antillis, Cuba (Bonpland): *v. s. in herb. Mus. Brit.* Jamaica (Houston).

A climbing species with terete branches, having its axils 1½ in. apart; opposite leaves suborbicular, roundish at the base, retuse, with a very short acute acumen at the summit, rigidly membranaceous, darkish green above, with many parallel, oblique, divergent nerves and reticulated veins, beneath opake, paler, pruinose, with prominent nerves, 2–2¼ in. long, 1½–2 in. broad, on petioles 4–6 lines long; raceme lateral at the nodes, on an erect peduncle ½–1 in. long, supporting 4–5 flowers on subumbellate pedicels 6 lines

2 c

long, with as many basal bracteoles; sepals lanceolate, acuminate, spreading, 1½ line long; tube of corolla narrowly cylindrical at the base and at the summit, where it is spirally twisted, subventricose in the middle, subsericeo-puberulous within, 18 lines long; segments obovate-oblong, inequilateral, crispate on the margin, 6 lines long, 4 lines broad, expanded, with dextrorse convolution; stamens seated on a pilose ring at the lower constriction of the tube 6 lines above the base; filaments very short; anthers linear, sagittate, acuminate, with two obtuse parallel basal prongs; disk of 5 linear emarginate lobes, half as long as the 2 glabrous ovate ovaries; follicles 2, patently divaricate, in the immature state 3 in. long, and then obsoletely torulose, afterwards perhaps longer and straighter; seeds many, comose.

4. ECHITES LONGIFLORA, nob.: *Echites umbellata*, var. *longiflora*, Griseb. in Pl. Cub. Wr. p. 520; Cat. Pl. Cub. No. 34. In Cuba: *v. s. in herb. Mus. Brit.* Cuba (C. Wright 1661).

A distinct climbing species, distinguished by its solitary axillary flower; its twining branchlets are slender, with axils 3 in. apart; leaves opposite, ovate-oblong, narrowed towards the base, and there obtuse, with a recurving channelled acute acumen, green above, with about 16 pairs of subimmersed divergent nerves arcuately conjoined, yellowish opake beneath, with prominulent slender nerves and reticulated veins, 3¾ in. long, 1⅞ in. broad, on recurving petioles 6 lines long; inflorescence axillary, 1-flowered, on a very slender erect peduncle 1¼ in. long, pluribracteolate at the base, continuous with the pedicel, which is ¼ in. long; sepals acutely lanceolate, erect, 1⅓ line long; corolla of a greenish-yellow colour; tube 20 lines long, narrowly cylindrical above and at the base, ventricose in the middle; segments obovate-oblong, inequilateral, 5-8 lines long, 4 lines broad; follicles 2, terete, horizontally divaricate, 3 in. long, nearly 2 lines thick.

5. ECHITES LUTEA, Vell. Fl. Flum. p. 109, Icon. iii. tab. 25; A. DC. *l. c.* p. 467; Müll. *l. c.* p. 159. In Brasilia prov. Rio de Janeiro, versus Itagoaby: *v. s. in herb. meo* (Claussen, *sine loco*).

This specimen agrees with the drawing of Velloz. It is a scandent species, very near *E. umbellata*, has slender, flexuose, subhispidulous branches, with thickened axils 5 in. apart, having 3 obtuse glands on each face across the nodes, half-concealed by the hairs; the opposite leaves are deflected, oblong-lanceolate, narrowed at the base and there subobtuse, sharply acute at the summit, chartaceous, with very revolute margins, scabridly hirsute above, with divergent arching nerves, beneath ferruginously opake, pubescent and patently hirsute along the midrib and nerves, 6-7 in. long, 1½-2 in. broad, on reflexed petioles 5-6 lines long; raceme lateral, on a suddenly deflected puberulous peduncle 1 in. long, divided above into 2 branches bearing many approximate or subumbellate flowers, on bracteolate pubescent pedicels 9 lines long; sepals acuminate, subpilose outside, margins membranaceous, 2 lines long; tube of corolla 16 lines long, narrowly cylindrical at its base for half its length, widening above, and there spirally twisting as in *E. umbellata*, sparsely pilose; segments rhomboidally dolabriform, 8 lines long, with subcrenulate margins; stamens seated on the constriction of the tube; anthers acuminate, shortly bifurcate at the base; disk of 5 fleshy lobes, 2 lines long, equal to 2 ovate ovaries.

6. ECHITES CONVOLVULACEA, A. DC. *l. c.* p. 451 : *Amblyanthera convolvulacea*, Müll. in Linn. xxx. p. 447 (non 430). In Peruvia et Bolivia: *v. s. in herb. Mus. Brit.* Lacarejo, Sorate (Mandon 1472).

A climbing species, with slender glabrescent branchlets, with axils 3–4 in. apart, charged on each side with 3–4 rounded glands; leaves ovate, cordate at the base, with rounded lobes somewhat folded, terminated by a long, suddenly cuspidate acumen, membranaceous, subglabrous above, with subscandent semi-immersed nerves, bearing at the base of the midrib 3–5 subulate glands, cinereo-puberulous beneath, $3\frac{1}{2}$–$5\frac{1}{2}$ in. long, 2–$2\frac{3}{4}$ in. broad, on pubescent petioles 5–9 lines long; panicle simply racemose, lateral at the axils, 8 in. long, on a glabrous peduncle bare at the base for $3\frac{1}{2}$ in., bearing several alternate or secund flowers on pedicels 9 lines long, supported by lanceolate bracteoles: sepals lanceolate, gibbous at the base, submembranaceous, pilose outside, 6–7 lines long, 1 line broad, each with a broad deeply and acutely laciniated scale; corolla glabrous, tube 1 in. long, narrower below for one fourth of its length, subventricose in the middle; segments oblong, obliquely inequilateral, 5 lines long, glabrous, with dextrorse convolution; stamens seated in a pilose ring in the contraction of the tube; filaments short, retrorsely pilose; anthers subcoherent, 5 lines long, membranaceous above, with 2 short obtuse basal lobes; disk of 5 oblong lobes, emarginated at the summit, shorter than the 2 oblong pointed ovaries; follicles 2, terete, straight, subparallel, 7 in. long, $1\frac{1}{4}$ line thick; placenta $\frac{1}{2}$ line broad; seeds many, oblong, compressed, pruinose, with a longitudinal raphe, 4 lines long, $\frac{3}{4}$ line broad, surmounted by a softly sericeous spreading coma 9 lines long.

A drawing of this species, showing an analysis of its floral and carpological structure, in given in Plate XXIX.

The *Amblyanthera convolvulacea* of Müller belongs to his variety *pubescens* from Mexico.

7. ECHITES PALLIDA, nob.; *Echites* sp., Benth. in Plant. Hartweg. p. 120. In Ecuador: *v. s. in herb. Mus. Brit.* Guayaquil (Hartweg 670).

A species with terete branches, the axils 3 in. apart, furnished on each face with 2 acute stipules; leaves ovate, roundishly truncate and broadly subcordate at the base, gradually acute above the middle, glabrous, very membranaceous, above pale green, opake, 5 converging nerves near the base, with others lateral and ascendingly divergent and prominulent, beneath equally pallid, midrib prominent, nerves and transverse veins little prominent, $3\frac{1}{2}$ in. long, $2\frac{3}{4}$ in. broad, on rather slender, yellowish, channelled petioles 10 lines long; racemes terminal, binate, shorter than the leaves, on suddenly reflected peduncles bare at the base for 9 lines, thence bearing several crowded spicate flowers, with imbricate, membranaceous, lanceolate bracts, each 6 lines long; pedicels 4 lines long; sepals lanceolate, very membranaceous, pale, 6 lines long, 1 line broad, each with a roundish ciliate inner scale, all quite glabrous. The corolla had fallen off, leaving in its place 2 very immature follicles supported by the sepals and disk cleft nearly to the base into 5 oblong submembranaceous lobes ; these immature follicles are flattened, linear, straight, pale yellow, pruinosely pilose, $1\frac{1}{2}$ in. long, 1 line broad.

8. ECHITES MEMBRANACEA, A. DC. *l. c.* p. 457. In Peruvia (Pavon): *non vidi*.

A plant with straight, elongated, tomentous branches; leaves oval, cordate, acutely mucronate, very membranaceous, puberulous above, with several prominent glands along the midrib, hirsutulous beneath, especially on the nerves and veins, 3 in. long, 1½ in. broad, on petioles 5 lines long; raceme lateral, tomentous, 5 in. long, bearing many alternate flowers on pedicels 3 lines long; sepals ovate, subulate, 4 lines long, gibbous at the base, with an inner acute scale; tube of corolla 9 lines long, hirsute; segments glabrous, obovate-oblong; disk quinquefid, with obtuse lobes, somewhat shorter than the ovaries.

A species near *E. hirtiflora*.

9. ECHITES CHLORANTHA, Schl. in Linn. xxvi. p. 663. In Venezuela, prope Maiquetia: *v. s. pl. fructif. in herb. meo*, sine loco, forsan Caraccas (Cockburn).

Schlectendahl describes this species as a shrub, 10 feet high, with verrucose terete branches and glabrous branchlets, subhirsute when young; leaves broadly ovate, obtuse at the base, shortly acuminate at the apex, glabrous, with subrevolute margins, nearly concolorous, sulcate on the midrib, the base of which is furnished with 2 erect, subulate, fleshy glands, midrib and nerves prominent beneath, 3–4 in. long, 1½–2½ in. broad, on sulcate petioles 6–9 lines long; panicle lateral, on a thick peduncle 1–3 lines long, divided into 2 short branches bearing several flowers on glabrous, spirally twisted pedicels 4 lines long; sepals oblong, obtuse, ciliate, imbricate, 3 lines long, with an inner basal emarginated or laciniulate scale; tube of corolla rufescent, cylindrical, 8 lines long, slightly swollen below the middle more constricted portion, narrowly campanulate above, with a border of shortish segments of a greenish hue, acutely and horizontally extended or subreflected; stamens inserted in the pilose contraction of the tube; disk of 5 obtuse, fleshy lobes, as long as the ovaries; follicles 2, terete, 8 in. long, 2 lines thick, glabrous; seeds 6 lines long, acute at both ends, puberulous, with a coma of reddish soft hairs 10 lines long.

In the fructiferous plant the branches are stout, with opposite, spreading, flexuose branchlets 1 line thick, tapering upwards, rugously striolate and lenticellate, with axils 3 in. apart, charged with several glandular stipules; the leaves are of the same size and shape as those of Schlectendahl's plant, agreeing in all respects, except that the petioles do not exceed a length of 6 lines; the peduncle is 3 lines long, bifurcate, each division bearing 2 horizontally divergent terete follicles, striolate, densely lenticellate, 7½ in. long, 3 lines thick, tapering to an obtuse apex 2 lines broad, slightly arcuate; seeds dorsally striolate, flat on the ventral face, with a longitudinal raphe 6 lines long, and an apical rufescent coma 10 lines long.

It is a species near *Echites acuminata*, R. & P.

10. ECHITES GLANDULOSA, R. & P. Fl. Per. ii. p. 19, tab. 135: *Hæmadictyon glandulosum*, A. DC. *l. c.* p. 427: *Prestonia Peruviana*, Spr. Syst. i. p. 637. In Peruvia ad Muñas: *non vidi*.

A climbing plant, with tomentous branchlets; axils 3–5 in. apart, having at the nodes several subulate fleshy glands in the place of interpetiolar stipules; leaves ovate, rounded and deeply cordate at the base, acute at the summit, with a bullate surface above, and much reticulated divergent nerves, canescently tomentous below, with reddish prominent nerves, furnished at the base of the midrib adjoining the petiole with several subulate glands; they are 3–4¾ in. long (including the sinus 6–9 lines deep), 2–3¾ in. broad, on stoutish petioles 4–6 lines long; panicle lateral, longer than the leaves, 6–7-flowered; flowers albescent, on alternate pedicels 6 lines apart, with a small basal bract; sepals acute, 4–5 lines long, submembranaceous, each with a row of lanceolate inner basal scales; tube of corolla 2½ in. long, cylindrical, somewhat contracted in the middle, funnel-shaped above, with a border of 5 obliquely oblong segments, 13 lines long, 6 lines broad, having a large internal spot at their base; stamens inserted in a pilose ring in the contraction of the tube; disk of 5 free lobes, half the length of the 2 pointed oblong ovaries.

This species is placed in *Prestonia* by Bentham and Hooker (Gen. ii. p. 709) on account of the supposed 5 large scales in the mouth of the corolla, as figured by Ruiz and Pavon; but these are mere discoloured spots, or they would have been otherwise described.

11. ECHITES ACUMINATA, R. & P. *l. c.* p. 19, tab. 134 a; A. DC. *l. c.* p. 449. In Peruvia ad Cuchero: *non vidi.*

A slender climbing plant, with axils about 1½ in. apart, having 4 intrapetiolar stipules truncate and acutely emarginate; its opposite oblong leaves are suddenly acute at their summit, slightly cordate at their base, where they have 5 fleshy acutely subulate glands at the base of the midrib (3 central, 2 lateral); they are glabrous, with about 10 pairs of divaricate nerves, 2¾–3 in. long (including the sinus, scarcely more than 1 line deep), 1⅜–1¼ in. broad, on petioles 4 lines long; racemes solitary in the axils or geminate, 9–10-flowered; peduncle 3 lines long; pedicels often geminate, of a purple colour, twisted, 6 lines long, with 3 bractlets at the base; sepals oblong, pointed, 3–4 lines long, with many internal lanceolate basal scales; corolla white inside, purplish outside, its tube cylindrical, contracted in the middle, and again narrowed in the mouth, 1 in. long; segments subreflected, ovate, inequilateral, with a long, narrow, horizontal expansion; stamens cohering, inserted in the contraction of the tube; disk of 5 free fleshy lobes, half the length of the subulately oblong ovaries; follicles 2, slender, terete, subadherent at the apex, nearly straight, near 7 in. long, 2 lines thick; seeds slender, 6 lines long, crowned by a fulvous coma 4 lines long.

12. ECHITES LAXA, R. & P. *l. c.* p. 19, tab. 134 b; A. DC. *l. c.* p. 451. In Peruvia ad Pillao: *non vidi.*

A climbing species having angular subvillous branchlets, with internodes 3¼–4½ in. apart, and there furnished with many glandular stipules; leaves ovate, subcordate at the base, acute at the summit, glabrous above, villous about the sinus, midrib and nerves prominent and villous below, and there furnished at the base of the midrib (at its junction with the petiole) with many subulate fleshy glands, 3½–4 in long, 2–2½ in. broad, on villous petioles 9–11 lines long; racemes lateral, long, pendent on a slender peduncle bare at its base for the length of 4 in., bearing 3 alternate, somewhat remote flowers on bracteolate pedicels 7-10 lines long; sepals linear-oblong, acute, imbricate, furnished within at their base with a dense row of small lanceolate scales; large handsome yellow corolla; tube 2 in. long, cylindrical for half its length, funnel-shaped above, and 6 lines wide in the mouth; segments oblong, horizontally expanded and curvingly pointed, dextrorsely convolute; stamens fixed in the middle of the tube; disk of 5 free lobes, much shorter than the 2 acutely oblong ovaries; style filiform; clavuncle incrassate, with 2 short subulate stigmata.

13. ECHITES SUBSAGITTATA, R. & P. (non Griseb.) *l. c.* p. 19; A. D.C. *l. c.* p. 475. In Peruvia ad Cuchero : *non vidi*.

A climbing, glabrous species, with very long, granulose, reddish, branching stem; branches filiform, with many close stipuloid glands about the axils; opposite leaves oblong, subsagittate at the base, acuminate, with ciliated margins, glanduliferous near the sinus below, and on short pubescent petioles; raceme short, lateral, few-flowered; pedicels with a small deciduous bracteole at the base; sepals acute.

A species near the preceding. The plant under this name, from Trinidad, with torulose follicles, vaguely considered by Grisebach (Fl. Br. W. Ind. p. 413) to be the same as *E. hirsuta*, H. B. K., is the *Echites microcalyx*, A. DC.

14. ECHITES HIRSUTA, R. & P. *l. c.* p. 19, tab. 136: *Echites Pavonii*, A. D.C. *l. c.* p. 463: *Prestonia hirsuta*, Spr. Syst. iv. 637. In Peruvia ad S. Antonio de playa grande, Chicoplaya : *non vidi*.

A climbing species with extremely slender, twisting, hirsute branches, with several slender interpetiolar glands; leaves oblong-ovate, acuminate, shortly cordate at their base, and furnished with 1 or 2 oblong acute glands at the sinus, densely villous below, 4–4½ in. long, 2–2¼ in. broad, on villous petioles 5 lines long; raceme lateral, 5–6 in. long, with many alternate yellow flowers, on pedicels 5 lines long, with lanceolate bracts 4 lines long; sepals acute, 3 lines long; tube of corolla 1½ in. long, contracted in the middle; segments obliquely oblong, 1 in. long, expanded; stamens shortish, seated in the middle of the tube; anthers cohering; disk of 5 lobes, half as long as the 2 ovaries; follicles 2, subacutely terete, subadhering at the apex, 4–5 in. long, 1½ line thick; seeds with an apical coma.

This must not be confounded with the *Echites hirsuta* of Richard, or that of Velloz.

15. ECHITES ACUTILOBA, A. DC. *l. c.* p. 451. In Peruvia : *non vidi*.

A climbing plant, with slender glabrous branchlets; leaves oblong, cordate, acuminate, membranaceous, subglabrous, with 2–3 glands at their base, 2–2½ in. long, 11–15 lines broad, on puberulous petioles 5–7 lines long; a simple lateral raceme, as long as the leaves, glabrous, with alternate pedicels, supported by much shorter linear bractlets; sepals linear-lanceolate, ciliate at their base, 3½ lines long; tube of corolla 7 lines long, cylindrical, somewhat contracted in the middle; segments narrowly oblong, one third the length of the tube; stamens seated on a pilose ring in the contraction of the tube; disk of 5 linear lobes, longer than the ovaries.

16. ECHITES SUBSESSILIS, A. DC. *l. c.* p. 451. In Peruvia: *non vidi*.

A species near *C. glandulosa*, with glabrous branches; leaves broadly elliptic, cordate, acuminate, membranaceous, glabrous above, with 4–5 acutely subulate glands near the sinus, puberulous below, with prominent nerves, 5 in. long, 3 in. broad, on thick petioles, shorter than the basal lobes, which are thus somewhat amplexicaul; raceme lateral, as long as the leaves, glabrous, with alternate pedicels 6 lines long, each with a basal bracteole half its length; sepals obtusely ovate; tube of corolla 8 lines long, 3 times as long as the sepals, cylindrical, somewhat contracted below the middle; segments ovate-oblong, half the length of the tube; stamens seated in the contraction of the tube on a pilose ring; anthers obtusely bilobed at the base; disk of 5 roundish, free lobes, half as long as the 2 ovaries.

17. ECHITES MONTANA, H. B. K. iii. 213; A. DC. *l. c.* p. 465. In Peruvia, circa Pasto: *non vidi*.

A climbing species, with hirsutulous branches; axils with several not very prominent interpetiolar glands; leaves elliptic-oblong, cordate, shortly acuminate, submembranaceous, green above, scabridly hirsutulous, with 3 or more subulate glands near the base of the midrib, beneath softly cano-hirtulous, 2¼–2½ in. long, 15–16 lines broad, on channelled pubescent petioles 6 lines long; raceme lateral, near 1 in. long, on a hirsute peduncle 5 lines long, bearing upwards 4–8 flowers on pubescent pedicels 4–5 lines long; bracteole small; sepals ovate-lanceolate, hirsute at the base, 1½ line long; corolla salver-shaped, glabrous; tube 7 lines long, constricted in the middle; segments obliquely ovate, roundish, crispate, rotate, yellow above, whitish below; stamens seated on a pilose ring in the contraction of the tube; anthers cohering, acuminate, obtusely bilobed at the base; disk of 5 short truncated lobes, shorter than the 2 oblong ovaries; follicles slender, terete, glabrous, fuscous, 7½ in. long, enclosing many comose seeds.

18. ECHITES LITOREA, H. B. K. *l. c.* p. 212; A. DC. *l. c.* p. 448. In ins. Cuba: *non vidi*.

A climbing plant with umbellate flowers, as in the typical species; it has slender, terete, glabrous branchlets, its axils furnished with many glabrous subulate glands in the place of stipules; opposite leaves oblong, rounded at both ends, with a short acute mucronate point, submembranaceous, glabrous, green above, with parallel nerves and much reticulated veins, paler beneath, 15–16 lines long, 7–8 lines broad, on channelled petioles 1½ line long; raceme lateral, on a glabrous peduncle ½–1 in. long, bearing on its summit 2–5 subumbellate flowers on pedicels 4–6 lines long, bracteolate at their base; sepals ovate-lanceolate, 1½ line long; corolla salver-shaped; tube constricted in the middle; segments obliquely ovate, crenulate, one third the length of the tube; stamens inserted in the constriction of the tube; disk of 5 roundish lobes, one third shorter than the 2 oblong ovaries; style slender; clavuncle agglutinated to the connivent anthers.

19. ECHITES RIPARIA, H. B. K. *l. c.* p. 214; A. DC. *l. c.* p. 466. In Nova Granada, fluv. Magdalena: *non vidi*.

A species closely allied to *E. montana*, with slender hirtellous branchlets, its axils charged with many subulate, ciliate glands in lieu of stipules; leaves ovate-oblong, cordate, acute, entire, submembranaceous, green and subglabrous above, bearing near the base of the midrib several successive subulate glabrous glands, beneath softly hirto-pubescent, 20-21 lines long, 12 lines broad, on channelled pubescent petioles 3 lines long; raceme lateral, pubescent, 1½ in. long, bearing about 6 flowers 9-10 lines long, on bracteolate pedicels 3 lines long; bracts pilose, lanceolate, 2 lines long; sepals lanceolate, pubescent, imbricate, spreading, with acute inner scales; corolla cylindrical; tube 6 lines long, swelling upwards; segments roundish, dolabriform, crispate, rotate, shorter than the tube; stamens seated in the constriction near the middle of the tube; anthers coherent, lanceolate; disk of 5 short truncate lobes, shorter than the 2 oblong ovaries.

20. ECHITES CONGESTA, H. B. K. *l. c.* p. 214; A. DC. *l. c.* p. 466: *Amblyanthera congesta*, Müll. Linn. xxx. 450. In Ecuador, prov. Popayan: *non vidi*.

A scandent species, with hirsute terete branches, marked with many white lenticels; axils charged with many depressed, ciliated, dentiform glands in the usual place of stipules; leaves roundly ovate, cordate, shortly acuminate, submembranaceous, above green, sparsely pilose, with parallel nerves and much reticulated veins, bearing about 4 subulate glabrous glands in succession near the base of the midrib, canescently hirto-pubescent beneath, 3-3½ in. long, 2-2½ in. broad, on channelled hirto-canescent petioles 8-9 lines long; raceme lateral, on a hairy peduncle 1½ in. long, bearing a capitate head of closely aggregated, small, odoriferous flowers, on pilose pedicels 3-4 lines long, with lanceolate bracts; sepals linear-lanceolate, hairy outside, half the length of the tube of the corolla; corolla white, size of that of jessamine; tube cylindrical, rugosely contracted above the base, pubescent within; segments unequally oblong, obtuse, crispate on the margins, a little longer than the tube, subreflexed; stamens inserted on a pilose ring above the base of the tube; anthers cohering, lanceolately acuminate, obtusely bilobed at the base; disk of 5 short lobes, as long as the 2 oblong glabrous ovaries.

21. ECHITES CITRIFOLIA, H. B. K. *l. c.* p. 216; A. DC. *l. c.* p. 465: *Amblyanthera citrifolia*, Müll. Linn. xxx. p. 450. In Nova Granada, prov. Mariquita: *non vidi*.

A slender species, with elongated glabrous branchlets, having remote axils, charged with many short, irregular, smooth, tooth-like glands; opposite leaves ovate-oblong, rounded or obsoletely cordate, acuminate, glabrous, rigidly membranaceous, with revolute margins, shining above, with subparallel nerves and reticulated veins, the nerves beneath prominulent, 3 in. long, 15-17 lines broad, on channelled petioles 2-3 lines long, bearing at their junction with the blade 2 subulate glabrous glands; raceme lateral, 1½ in. long, on a peduncle divided at its apex into two branches, each bearing many pedicellate flowers; sepals ovate, acuminate, imbricate, glabrous, six times shorter than the tube of the corolla, which is salver-shaped; tube cylindrical and constricted in the middle; stamens seated on a pilose ring at the constriction of the tube; anthers acuminate, obtusely 2-lobed at the base, and cohering round the clavuncle.

22. ECHITES HIRTIFLORA, A. DC. *l. c.* p. 456. In Peruvia (Pavon): *non vidi*.

A climbing species, with tomentous branches; leaves elliptic, cordate, very acuminate, membranaceous, subpubescent above, with many glands on the midrib, scabridly pubescent beneath, 2 in. long, 10–12 lines broad, on petioles 2 lines long; raceme lateral, tomentous, longer than the leaves, bearing many alternate flowers on pedicels 2 lines long; sepals ovate, subulate, gibbous at the base, glabrous, with an inner basal acutely ovate scale; tube of corolla 9 lines long, subcylindrical, hirsute; segments oblong-ovate, shorter than the tube; anthers obtusely subbilobed at the base; disk of 5 obtuse lobes, a little shorter than the two glabrous ovaries.

23. ECHITES MANSOANA, A. DC. *l. c.* p. 448: *Mesechites sulphurea,* Müll. *l. c.* p. 151, tab. 46 (excl. syn. Velloz). In Cuyaba et Matto Grosso: *non vidi.*

As stated elsewhere, this is a species certainly different from the *Echites sulphurea.* It is a climber, with slender terete branches, their axils being $4\frac{1}{4}$–$5\frac{3}{4}$ in. apart; leaves oblong, obtuse at the base, roundish, with a short obtuse acumen, coriaceous, margins revolute, spreading nerves and veins scarcely visible, having a broad gland divided into 4 or 6 obtuse lobes at the base of the midrib, 3–4 in. long, 10–18 lines broad, on petioles 4–5 lines long; raceme lateral, shorter than the leaves, subcapitate, on a peduncle 5 lines long, divided at the apex into two branches, each bearing many approximate flowers, on twisted pedicels 3–5 lines long, supported by short acutely oval bractlets; sepals obtusely elliptic, ciliolate, $2\frac{1}{2}$ lines long, each with an internal tridentate scale; tube of corolla 8 lines long, contracted in the middle; segments roundish, 3 lines long and broad, dextrorsely convolute; stamens seated in the contraction of the tube; anthers linear, with a short incurved apex, shortly and obtusely 2-lobed at the base; disk of 5 obtusely ovoid lobes as long as the ovaries; style filiform; clavuncle incrassate, oblong, with a basal membranaceous appendage.

24. ECHITES VAUTHIERI, A. DC. *l. c.* p. 457: *Echites coalita,* Müll. (non Vell.) *l. c.* p. 155, tab. 50. fig. 4 (semen): *Echites sulphurea,* Vell. Fl. Flum. p. 109, Icon. iii. tab. 26: *Mesechites sulphurea,* Müll. in parte, *l. c.* p. 151. In prov. Rio de Janeiro, in montib. Organ. (Vauthier 78); Velloz: *v. s. in herb. Mus. Brit.* prov. Rio de Janeiro (Bowie et Cunningham, *in fructu*).

A climbing species with slender, terete, twice trichotomous branches, with axils 2–4 in. apart; leaves lanceolate-oblong, subacute at the base, acutely acuminate, mucronate, subcoriaceous, with revolute margins, pale green above, finely corrugulate, with about 6 pairs of divergent subimmersed nerves, charged beneath with several ovate-oblong and subulate fleshy glands, yellowish opake beneath, nerves scarcely visible, $2\frac{1}{2}$–$3\frac{1}{2}$ in. long, $\frac{3}{4}$–$1\frac{1}{4}$ in. broad, on petioles 2–3 lines long; racemes axillary, 2 in. long, on a bare peduncle 3 lines long, bearing about 7 subapproximate flowers on pedicels 3–6 lines long, supported by short lanceolate bracteoles; sepals oblong-acute, 3 lines long, gibbous at the base, with an inner ovate denticulate scale; corolla yellow; tube cylindrical, 6 lines long; segments obovate, inequilateral, 3 lines long; stamens seated on a pilose ring in the middle of the tube; disk of 5 obtuse lobes, somewhat conjoined at the base, shorter than the ovaries; follicles 2, on a short stout peduncle, horizontally spreading, cylindrical, subobtuse at the base, straight, fuscous, striolate, $5\frac{1}{2}$ in. long, 4 lines broad below the middle, tapering upwards to a breadth of 2 lines at the rounded apex; seeds many, linear-fusiform, compressed, dorsally convex and rugosely striate, flat on the ventral face, 4 lines long, with a longitudinal raphe and a spreading coma of soft whitish hairs 8 lines long.

This species was confounded by Müller with *Echites Mansoana* A. DC., a very different plant with more ovate leaves, from Cuyaba; it is extremely distinct from the *Echites coalita* of Velloz.

25. ECHITES TRIFIDA, Jacq. (non Müll. nec Griseb.) Amer. p. 31, tab. 24; A. DC. *l. c.* p. 454; II. B. K. iii. p. 216; Seem. Bot. Her. p. 168 (excl. syn.). Ad Carthagena (Jacquin); Cumana (Bonpland): *v. s. in herb. Mus. Brit.* Panama (Seemann 161).

A climbing lactescent species, with slender terete glabrous branchlets, with axils 2–2¾ in. apart, charged with a few obtuse glands between the petioles; leaves ovate-oblong, rounded or obtuse at the base, acute or acuminate, submembranaceous, reddish green and opake above, nerves semi-immersed, scabridulous to the touch, with a broadish, dusky, ciliolate gland at the base of the midrib, paler and yellowish opake beneath, with immersed fine reddish nerves and reticulated veins, 2–3 in. long, ¾–1¼ in. broad, on extremely slender channelled petioles 3–6 lines long; raceme lateral, on a peduncle 3 lines long, trifid at its apex, each branch bearing about 5 approximate flowers on pedicels 3–4 lines long, minutely bracteolate; sepals oblong, scarcely acute, imbricate, fleshy, with diaphanous margins, 2 lines long, with an inner broad pluridentate scale; tube of corolla cylindrical, of a dark purple colour, 10 lines long, swelling a little above the middle; segments of a greenish hue, obliquely oblong, 6 lines long, 4 lines broad, rotate; stamens inserted on a pilose ring at the contraction of the tube; anthers linear, with an acute membrane at the apex, and 2 parallel obtuse lobes at the base; disk of 5 obtuse lobes, half the length of the 2 pointed glabrous ovaries; style long and filamentous; clavuncle conically oblong, with a membranaceous indusium at its base, terminated by 2 subulate stigmata.

26. ECHITES TUBULOSA, Benth. Journ. Bot. iii. 249; A. DC. *l. c.* p. 454: *Mesechites trifida*, Müll. (in parte) *l. c.* p. 151: *Echites trifida*, Griseb. *l. c.* p. 413. In Amazonas et Guiana Brit.: *v. s. in herb. meo et alior.* Guiana (Schomb. 311), Rio Solimoës (Spruce 1348).

A climbing species, differing from *E. trifida*, Jacq., in its larger leaves upon longer petioles, and its inflorescence: branches terete, sulcate, obsoletely puberulous, lenticellate, with axils 4–6 in. apart and transversely glanduliferous; leaves oblong-ovate, roundish or subcordate at the base, shortly acuminate, submembranaceous, glabrous, with many patently divaricate immersed nerves, midrib sulcate, bearing at its base 2–3 superposed ovate acute adpressed glands, opake beneath, pallidly ochraceous, fine reddish prominulent nerves reticulately veined, 3–5 in. long, 1¼–2 in. broad, on suddenly deflexed petioles 6–12 lines long; raceme lateral, on a peduncle 6 lines long, divided at the apex into 2 branches 9 lines long, each bearing numerous approximate flowers, on minutely bracteolate pedicels 4–6 lines long; sepals acutely oblong, with membranaceous margins; corolla rose-coloured; tube 12 lines long, swelling above the middle; segments broadly dolabriform, 3 lines long; stamens inserted on a pilose ring at the contraction of the tube; follicles free, 8–10 in. long according to Mr. Bentham.

27. ECHITES VERAGUENSIS, Seem. Bot. Her. p. 168. In Veraguas, Volcan Chiriqui (Seemann): *non vidi.*

A climbing species, resembling *E. laxa*, with pubescent branchlets, afterwards glabrescent; leaves ovate-oblong, cordate, acuminate, glabrous above, with many glands at the base, glabrous beneath, but villous in the axils of the nerves, $3\frac{1}{2}$–4 in. long, 1-$1\frac{1}{2}$ in. broad, on petioles 1 in. long; raceme lateral, bearing 5–8 flowers on pedicels supported by acutely ovate bracteoles; sepals acutely ovate; corolla $2\frac{1}{4}$ in. long; tube yellow, constricted below the middle, somewhat funnel-shaped; segments dark purple, obliquely obovate, obtuse; stamens inserted on a pilose ring at the constriction of the tube; filaments pilose; anthers glabrous.

28. ECHITES SURINAMENSIS, Miq. Stirp. Surin. Select. p. 155; Walp. Ann. iii. p. 42. In Surinam: *non vidi.*

A plant referable to this group on account of its bidentate glandular stipules and the presence of bicuspidate glands at the base of the leaves; its branches are fuscous, glabrous, and smooth; its branchlets subpuberulous, with bidentate stipules around the nodes; the leaves are elliptic-oblong or lanceolate, shortly acute, rounded at the base, glabrous above, with bicuspidate glands at the base of the midrib, paler beneath, with about 8 pairs of subobsolete nerves; raceme lateral; peduncle bifid, with smooth branchlets and smooth, ovate, rounded, subciliolate bracteoles; sepals ovate, subciliate; tube of corolla cylindrical, staminigerous above the middle, a little bell-shaped in the mouth, with a border of 5 shortish segments.

29. ECHITES MICROCALYX, A. DC. *l. c.* p. 456; Schlecht. Linn. xxvi. p. 662: *Echites subsagittata*, Griseb. (non R. & P.) *l. c.* p. 413: *Amblyanthera microcalyx*, var. *trichantha*, Müll. Linn. xxx. 448. In Venezuela prope Caracas: *non vidi.*

A climbing plant, 8 feet high, with very slender puberulous branches; leaves oblong-ovate, cordate, acutely acuminate, membranaceous, subglabrous above, the midrib charged with many dark fleshy glands, pilose beneath, $1\frac{1}{2}$–$2\frac{1}{2}$ in. long, 7-10 lines broad, on slender petioles 2 lines long; peduncle of the raceme pubescent, shorter than the leaves, bearing above 4–6 approximate flowers, on pedicels 3 times as long as the calyx; sepals linear-lanceolate, ciliate on the margins, scarcely 2 lines long, gibbous at the base, with an acutely ovate inner scale; corolla $1\frac{1}{4}$ in. long, pubescent, with white patent hairs; tube cylindrical, 9-10 lines long, broader above the middle; segments half as long as the tube; stamens seated near the contraction of the tube, on a pilose ring of white retrorse hairs; anthers $2\frac{1}{2}$ lines long, shortly 2-lobed or emarginate at the base, acuminate above, cohering.

The *Echites subsagittata*, Griseb. (non R. & P.), from Trinidad, belongs here. The floras of the latter island and the opposite coast of Venezuela are largely identical.

30. ECHITES BRACHYLOBA, nob.: *Amblyanthera brachyloba*, Müll. Linn. *l. c.* p. 423. In Peruvia, Paranahunanco (Mathews 820): *non vidi.*

A plant evidently belonging to this genus, on account of the glands on its leaves. It has very slender puberulous branchlets; leaves ovate, cordate at the base, obtuse at the summit, membranaceous, sparsely and minutely puberulous above, the midrib charged at its base with many subulate glands, puberulous beneath and subsericeous on the midrib and nerves, $2\frac{1}{4}$–$2\frac{3}{4}$ in. long, $1\frac{1}{4}$ in. broad, on petioles $5\frac{3}{4}$ lines long; raceme much longer than the leaves, on an elongated peduncle, densely flowered above, on approximate puberulous pedicels $3\frac{1}{4}$–$4\frac{1}{4}$ lines long, supported by acutely lanceolate bracteoles one half to three fourths shorter than the pedicels, and afterwards reflexed; sepals triangularly ovate, puberulous, $1\frac{1}{2}$–2 lines long, with 5–8 inner acute scales; corolla, in the whole, $8\frac{1}{2}$ lines long; tube glabrous, cylindrical for half its length, a little swollen above; segments short, ovate, obtusely rounded, much shorter than the tube; stamens inserted in the contraction of the tube upon a sericeous woolly ring; anthers short, glabrous; disk of 5 free ovate lobes, nearly as long as the obtusely ovoid ovaries.

31. ECHITES ANDINA, nob.: *Amblyanthera Andina*, Müll. Linn. xxx. p. 425. In Nova Granada, Andibus Quitensium (Jameson 101) : *non vidi*.

A species belonging to this genus because of the glandular midribs of its leaves. It is said by Müller to be near *E. microcalyx* and *E. acutiloba*, before described. It has very slender, puberulous branches, with axils 2 in. apart; leaves ovate or oblong-ovate, narrowed and cordate at the base, shortly acuminate, membranaceous, olive-green above, opake, puberulous, with 7–10 pairs of nerves, reticulately veined, the midrib charged at its base with many subulate glands, paler beneath, and softly cano-pubescent, $1\frac{5}{8}$–$2\frac{1}{4}$ in. long, 7–12 lines broad, on petioles $2\frac{3}{4}$ lines long; racemes axillary, scarcely as long as the leaves, on a peduncle $7\frac{1}{4}$ lines long, bearing 5–7 flowers on pedicels $4\frac{3}{4}$ lines long, supported by linear-lanceolate bracteoles half their length; sepals ovate-lanceolate, subobtuse, puberulous, $1\frac{3}{4}$–$2\frac{1}{4}$ lines long; corolla altogether 1 in. long; tube 7 lines long, cylindrical for half its length, a little swollen above; segments narrowly obovate, acuminate, half as long as the tube; stamens seated in the contraction of the tube; disk of 5 broadly ovate lobes, half as long as the ovaries.

32. ECHITES ALBIFLORA, nob.: *Peschiera? albiflora*, Miq. Stirp. Surin. Sel. p. 165 ; Walp. Ann. iii. p. 63. In Surinam : *non vidi*.

This species has few of the characters of a *Peschiera*; and as it bears most of the essential features existing in *E. umbellata*, I have placed it here.

Its branches are terete; the branchlets subtetragonous, with membranaceous angles, glabrous, having several ovate acute, coriaceous interpetiolar stipules conjoined across the nodes; leaves oblong or elliptic, acute at the base, suddenly contracted at the summit, with a recurved acute acumen, membranaceous, glabrous, with about 20 pairs of patent curving nerves, and very short petioles; racemes axillary, on a bifid peduncle, with short bracteolate pedicels; sepals lanceolate, obsoletely puberulous, with few internal basal scales; tube of corolla long and slender, with ovate-oblong acute segments as long as the tube; stamens inserted in the middle of the tube.

33. ECHITES DISADENA, Miq. Stirp. Surin. Sel. p. 156 ; Walpers, Ann. iii. p. 43. In Surinam : *non vidi*.

A species congeneric with the preceding. It has glabrous branchlets; leaves oblong or elliptic-ovate, obtuse at the base, with a short acute acumen, coriaceous, with about 8 pairs of curving spreading nerves, reticulated, with 2 approximate, ovate, entire erect concave glands at the base of the midrib; raceme lateral, short, or longer, with twisted pedicels 3 times as long as the calyx; sepals ovate, somewhat acute, ciliolate; tube of corolla cylindrical, somewhat funnel-shaped in the mouth, with shortish segments; follicles terete, subcurving, 3 in. long; seeds with a yellowish coma.

34. ECHITES VENENOSA, Stadelm. Bot. Zeit. 1841, p. 66; A. DC. *l. c.* p. 470. In Brasilia, prov. Bahia: *non vidi.*

A pubescent shrub, with broadly ovate leaves, rounded at the base, shortly cuspidate, with membranaceous ciliate margins, glaucous green above, velvety hirsute, with about 20 pairs of nerves, furnished near the base with several stipuliform glands, 2¼ in. long, 15-20 lines broad, on petioles 1½ line long; peduncle terminal, sub-2-flowered, on pedicels 4-5 lines long, with a pubescent bract of the same length, cristate along the middle; sepals lanceolate, membranaceous, 4-5 lines long, ciliate above, with an inner bifid scale; corolla large, rose-coloured; tube contracted in the middle, funnel-shaped above; segments inequilateral, broadly obovate, subacute; stamens inserted in the middle of the tube; disk of 5 trapezoidal lobes, half as long as the 2 ovate-oblong ovaries. The plant is poisonous to cattle.

35. ECHITES JAPURENSIS, Stadelm. *l. c.* p. 19; A. DC. *l. c.* p. 454: *Mesechites Japurensis*, Müll. *l. c.* p. 152. Inter fluv. Japuré et Negro, in sylvis: *non vidi.*

A climbing species, with slender, glabrous, flexuose branches and remote axils; leaves broadly ovate or oblong, narrowed and obtuse at the base, cuspidately acuminate, subcoriaceous, with a single gland at the base of the midrib, 4-4½ in. long, 2-2½ in. broad, on petioles 3-4 lines long; raceme terminal, subsessile, bearing many flowers on minutely bracteolate pedicels, 3-4 lines long; sepals obtusely oblong, as long as the pedicels, with 2 inner trapezoidal crenato-dentate scales 1 line long; tube of corolla 1 in. long; segments obovate; stamens inserted in the middle on the contraction of the tube; disk of 5 lobes, half as long as the 2 oblong puberulous ovaries.

36. ECHITES MEXICANA, nob.: *Amblyanthera Mexicana*, Müll. Linn. xxx. p. 424. In Mexico, prope Victoria (Karwinsky 9): *non vidi.*

This species is placed in this genus, as it is said by Müller to be close to *E. microcalyx* and *E. Andina*; but no mention is made of any glands upon the leaves or axils. It is suffruticose, with suberect branches, and very slender, flagelliform branchlets; leaves ovate-lanceolate, narrowed and subcordate at the base, subacuminate, membranaceous, puberulous or glabrous, with 4-5 pairs of nerves, and others shorter and intermediate, reticulately veined, midrib flattened, 1⅜-2 in. long, 9¾-10¾ lines broad, on petioles 2¼ lines long; raceme lateral, 2 in. long, on a slender peduncle 5-7¼ lines long, bearing many flowers on slender pedicels 4½-5 lines long, supported by linear-lanceolate bracteoles 1½-1¾ line long; sepals ovate-lanceolate, acuminate, subrecurvingly spreading at the apex, as long as the pedicels, with 4-6 inner subulate scales; tube of corolla narrowly cylindrical for one third of its length, swelling above; segments narrow, obliquely obovate; stamens seated on the contraction of the tube; anthers glabrous; disk of 5 lobes, as long as the 2 obtusely ovoid glabrous ovaries.

37. ECHITES TUBIFLORA, Mart. & Gall. Bull. Acad. Brux. xi. 358; Walp. Rep. vi. 476 : *Amblyanthera tubiflora*, Müll. *l. c.* pp. 423, 454. Circa Mexico : *non vidi.*

A scandent species with very slender branches ; leaves lanceolate, cordate, acuminate, glabrous above, cinereo-tomentous beneath, on short petioles ; racemes bearing many large reflected flowers ; calyx of 5 glabrous sepals, one quarter the length of the corolla ; corolla subtubular, with short, very obtuse rotate segments ; follicles 2, long, slender, appressed.

Müller states that this species is near *E. brachyloba* and *E. convolvulacea.*

38. ECHITES KARWINSKII, nob.: *Amblyanthera Karwinskii*, Müll. *l. c.* p. 426. In Mexico meridionali (Karwinsky 473 & 1347) : *non vidi.*

A peculiar species, evidently belonging to this genus on account of the glands on the midribs of the leaves and the characters of its flowers. It is a prostrate plant, having the habit of *Echites torosa*, Jacq., with ascending, slender, subscandent, erect branches 1 foot long, which are reddish-fuscous and obsoletely griseo-puberulous ; leaves oblong-ovate or lanceolate-spathulate, narrowed and obtuse at the base, shortly acute at the summit, membranaceous, fuscous, glabrous, shining above, with 4–6 pairs of nerves and others intermediate, reticulately veined, the midrib charged with 2–3 glands, 1–1¼ in. long, 2¾–7 lines broad, on petioles 1 line long ; racemes axillary, as long as or longer than the leaves, glabrous, on a peduncle 5–6 lines long, bearing many flowers on rigid pedicels 3 lines long, supported by linear-lanceolate bracteoles 1½ line long ; sepals ovate-lanceolate, acuminate, orange-coloured, with dark spots and hyaline margins, 2¾ lines long, with 4–7 inner subulate scales ; corolla in the whole 9½ lines long ; tube cylindrical for half its length ; segments rhomboidally obovate, acute at one angle ; anthers short ; disk of 5 obtuse lobes, as long as the 2 obtusely ovoid ovaries.

39. ECHITES ANDRIEUXII, nob.: *Amblyanthera Andrieuxii*, Müll. *l. c.* p. 422. Circa Oaxaca (Andrieux 249) : *non vidi.*

A subscandent species, near *S. Karwinskii*, with terete, glabrous, reddish, subverrucose branchlets 1 line thick ; branches at the base (and probably the axils) surrounded by a ring of scaly glands, densely foliaceous above ; leaves narrowly obovate, or obovate-lanceolate, acute at both ends, rigidly membranaceous, fuscous, hirto-puberulous above, with about 6 pairs of nearly obsolete nerves, yellowish beneath and softly pubescent, 9½–15 lines long, 3¼–7 lines broad, on petioles 1½–2¼ lines long ; racemes axillary, a little longer than the leaves, subglabrous, a little deflexed, simple, bearing few pedicellate flowers, the 2 lower ones opposite, the rest alternate, on rigid pedicels 1–1½ line long, supported by lanceolate puberulous bracteoles of the same length ; sepals ovate-lanceolate, puberulous outside, with membranaceous margins, 1¾ line long, having as many subulate inner scales ; corolla altogether 5¾–7 lines long ; tube rather broadly cylindrical, somewhat thicker at the base, swelling campanularly above to a breadth of 2 lines ; segments rhomboidally obovate, half as long as the tube ; disk of 5 free obtusely oblong lobes, as long as the 2 ovoid ovaries.

40. ECHITES LANATA, Mart. & Gall. Bull. Acad. Brux. xi. p. 359; Walp. Rep. vi. p. 476. In prov. Oaxaca: *non vidi*.

A species said to resemble *Echites montana* of Kunth, with pubescent branches; leaves obovate, cordate, acuminate, coriaceous, densely pubescent above, woolly beneath, sessile; racemes axillary, longer than the leaves, bearing several lax pedicellate flowers, rather less than 1 inch long; sepals obtusely ovate, glabrous; corolla hypocrateriform; stamens included.

41. ECHITES LINEARIS, Velloz, Fl. Flum. p. 111, Icon. iii. tab. 36: *Forsteronia? linearis*, Müll. *l. c.* p. 107. In Brasilia, prov. Rio de Janeiro, ad Santa Cruz (Velloz): *non vidi*.

A plant known only to Velloz. It is a stoutish climber, with slender flexuose branchlets, having axils 2–4 in. apart; leaves oblong-elliptic, acute at the base, acuminate, 4–4½ in. long, 1½–2¾ in. broad, on stoutish reflexed spreading petioles ¾–1 in. long; raceme terminal, simple, spicately flowered, 4 in. long, on a peduncle bare at the base for 1½ in., bearing upwards about 15 simple, alternate, rather small flowers on pedicels 2 lines long, supported by 2 opposite, small, acute bracts; sepals acute, 1 line long; corolla (apparently in bud) 5 lines long, yellow; tube very short; segments linear-subulate, erect, 3 lines long; stamens partly exserted; disk of 5 free lobes surrounding the 2 oblong ovaries; style short; clavuncle incrassate.

Müller, who did not see this plant, refers it doubtfully to *Forsteronia*; but it differs from that genus in its simple, spicate inflorescence with alternate larger flowers. For the same reasons it cannot belong to *Thyrsanthus* nor to *Exothostemon*. From *Echites* proper it differs in its undeveloped flowers, by its very short tube and subexserted stamens; but it accords in its spicate inflorescence. Till more is known of it, the species will remain in *Echites*, with an exceptional development in the shape of its corolla. The opposite bracteoles at the base of the pedicels are omitted by the Paris draughtsman; but they are shown in the analytical figure.

TEMNADENIA.

A group of species, uniform in their characters, mostly climbing plants with opposite elliptic leaves generally cordate at the base and pubescent; inflorescence more frequently lateral, on a deflexed peduncle supporting 2 floriferous branches bearing several pretty flowers; fruit of 2 terete very woolly follicles, conjoined at the apex.

TEMNADENIA *, nob. *Sepala* 5, lanceolata, tenuiter acuminata, margine membranacea, quincuncialiter imbricata, intus *squamula* sublaciniata singulatim munita. *Corolla* subhypocrateriformis; *tubus* cylindricus, parallele striatus, sæpe sub medium subito constrictus, superne infundibuliformis, fauce nudus aut in gula carnosula crebre costulatus, vel raro in lineola transversa contractus. *Segmenta* 5, oblonga, oblique et rotundate dolabriformia, horizontaliter expansa et dextrorsum convoluta. *Stamina* 5, inclusa, ad constrictionem tubi inserta; *filamenta* brevia, pilosa, ex annulo piloso orta; *antheræ* lineares, acuminatæ, in conum subcohærentes, imo acute bifurcatæ. *Discus* cylindricus, fere ad basin quinquefissus, lobis oblongis obtusis emarginatis; *ovaria* 2, subæquilonga aut paullo longiora. *Stylus* tenuis; *clavuncula* incrassata, cylindrica, imo membranula peltata

* From τέμνω (*scindo*), ἀδήν (*glanda*), from its disk cleft into 5 segments nearly to the base.

indusiata; *stigmata* 2, minima, terminalia. *Folliculi* 2, teretes, apice conjuncti, densissime albotomentosi; *semina* plurima, comosa.

Suffrutices *Americæ meridionalis, plerumque Brasilienses*; rami *sæpe alte scandentes*; folia *opposita, elliptica, acuta, imo sæpius cordata, brevipetiolata*; inflorescentia *racemosa*; pedunculus *lateralis, deflexus, apice parallele 2-ramosus, ramis undique plurifloris*; flores *plerumque rosei aut violacei pedicellati et breviter bracteolati.*

1. TEMNADENIA VIOLACEA, nob.: *Echites violacea*, Vell. (non Müll.), Flora Flum. p. 110, Icon. iii. tab. 31; A. DC. *l. c.* p. 459; Stadelm. *l. c.* p. 34. In Brasilia, prov. Rio de Janeiro, circa Itagoahy (Velloz): *v. s. in herb. Mus. Brit.* Rio de Janeiro (Solander); *in herb. Reg. Hort.* ex prov. Saõ Paulo (Weir 122).

A scandent species, with dark costately striate scabridulous branches; axils 3–4 in. apart, dilated, with a short stipule on each side of the petioles; leaves oblong, rounded and deeply cordate at the base, gradually acuminate or more suddenly acute at the summit, submembranaceous, above fuscous green, opake, scabridly pruinose, with immersed nerves, beneath opake, yellowish hepatic, scabrid, and rigidly hirsutulous, 2½–4 in. long, 1¼–2 in. broad, on reflexed pubescent petioles 2 lines long; raceme lateral at the axils, 4 in. long; peduncle deflexed, 1¼ in. long, bifid at the summit, each branch bearing about 10 alternate flowers, on patent subpilose pedicels 6 lines long, having an acute bract ¾ line long at their base; sepals ovate, acuminate, subpilose, reddish, 3 lines long, 1¼ line broad, each with 3 small lanceolate inner scales; corolla 2¼ in. long, violet below, upper portion of a deep rose-colour; tube 15 lines long, cylindrical and ventricose at the base for a length of 6 lines, there suddenly constricted, rather broadly cylindrical or infundibuliform above, sparsely pilose outside; segments dolabriform, 10 lines long, 9 lines broad, subcrispate on the margins, with dextrorse convolution; stamens inserted in the constriction of the tube, on a retrorsely pilose niveous ring; anthers 2½ lines long, cohering in a cone, very acuminate, subhirsute behind, with 2 acute stoutish basal lobes; disk fleshy, cleft for more than half its length into 5 emarginated lobes as long as the 2 globular ovaries; style slender; clavuncle incrassate, with a basal membranaceous expansion. Follicles terete, striate, said by Weir to be 6 in. long; seeds oblong, with a long rostrum as in *Stipecoma*, dorsally convex, and interruptedly costulate, concave on the ventral face, 5½ lines long, 1¼ line broad, with a linear raphe, crowned by a spreading silky coma 11 lines long.

2. TEMNADENIA BICRURA, nob.: *Echites varia*, Müll. (non Stadelm.) *l. c.* p. 157 (excl. var. *purpurea* et *sulphurea*), tab. 47. In Brasilia, prov. Rio de Janeiro: *v. v. et sicc. in herb. meo* (no. 1587 et 4020).

The drawing above figured in the 'Flora Brasiliensis' was taken from a plant introduced into the Paris Garden from Rio de Janeiro. I found it in a living state at distant places in that province in 1830 and 1838, and then made drawings of it, its chief peculiarity consisting in its long pendent bifid raceme; its tortuous branches are fuscous, striate, and shortly hirsute, with dilated axils 4–5 in. apart, furnished on each side of the petioles with 2 small acute stipules; opposite leaves ovate or oblong-ovate, rounded or somewhat acute at the base, suddenly constricted into a short mucronulate acumen, membranaceous, subundulate on the margins, above fuscous green, opake, obsoletely velutinous, with very fine prominulent nerves, beneath yellowish ferruginous, very opake, puberulous, with rubescent prominulent nerves, 3–4 in. long, 1½–2¼ in. broad, on tortuous pubescent petioles 2–3 lines long; inflorescence lateral at the axils, about 6 in. long, on a stoutish velutinous reflexed peduncle 1¾ in. long, bearing at its apex 2 equal racemose subflexuose branches 2½–3½ in. long, spicate, with numerous alternate flowers 1–2 lines apart, on pedicels 6–9 lines long, with a setaceous bractlet at their base 1–2 lines long; sepals acuminate, recurved at the apex, 5 lines long, each with an acute bidentate basal scale; tube of corolla darkish red, 10 lines long, somewhat broadly cylindrical, much contracted in the middle; segments broadish, inequilaterally rounded, dolabriform, with a dextrorse convolution, 4 lines long, 4 lines broad, of a palish yellow colour; stamens inserted at the contraction of the tube, on a narrow ring of retrorse white hairs; anthers cohering in a cone, very acuminate, with 2 long, divergent, incurving, aristiform basal forks; disk fleshy, split nearly to the base into 5 emarginate, striate lobes as long as the 2 globose ovaries; style slender; clavuncle incrassate, 5-sulcate, with a basal peltate membrane, and terminated by 2 small obtuse stigmata; follicles unknown.

3. TEMNADENIA LOBBIANA, nob.: *Echites hirsuta*, Hook. (non Rich., nec R. & P., nec Stadelm.), Bot. Mag. tab. 3997 : *Echites lasiocarpa* (in parte), inclus. var. *Lobbiana*, A. DC. *l. c.* p. 464. In Brasilia, prov. Rio de Janeiro: *v. v.* circa Magé, *et sicc. in herb. meo* (4022).

This species was figured by me from a living plant in 1836; and with this the plant introduced from Rio de Janeiro at a later date, and figured by Sir Wm. Hooker, well accords. It is a scandent species, with terete flexuose hirsute branches, its woolly subdilated axils 4 in. apart, with 2 linear pubescent stipules on each face 1 line long; the opposite leaves are elliptic-oblong, cordate at the base, somewhat suddenly constricted into a short cuspidate acumen, entire margins subundulate and subrevolute, deepish green above, opake, shortly and sparsely puberulous above, with prominulent nerves, beneath pale yellowish, opake, pubescent, the slender prominulent nerves being patently pilose, 4–4½ in. long (including the rounded basal lobes 3 lines deep, and the acumen 5 lines long), 2–2¼ in. broad, on patently pubescent petioles 6–9 lines long; a single lateral raceme at the nodes, on a stoutish woolly deflexed peduncle 6 lines long, bearing upwards about 6–8 approximate flowers on yellowish woolly pedicels 3 lines long, each supported by a short ovate bract; sepals lanceolate, hispidly pubescent, erect, 4 lines long, each with an internal broad denticulate scale; corolla rather large, with a border of a pale yellow colour, with red striate lines in the throat; tube reddish, 16 lines long, narrowed at the base for 7 lines, sparsely pubescent, above funnel-shaped; segments dolabriform, deeply uncinate at the left angle, dextrorsely convolute, 6 lines long and broad; stamens seated on a densely pilose ring at the contraction of the tube; anthers cohering in a cone, biaristate at the base; disk rather deeply cleft into 5 fleshy oblong emarginate lobes, a little shorter than the 2 acute pubescent ovaries; style slender; clavuncle large, 5-grooved, with a basal peltate membrane; follicles 2, linear, compressed, conjoined at the apex; in my specimen these are immature, densely covered with white woolly hairs, 1½ in. long (when matured, 6 in. long); seeds with a yellowish coma.

A drawing of this plant in flower and fruit, together with figures of the seed of *T. violacea*, are shown in Plate XXX.

4. TEMNADENIA LASIOCARPA, nob.: *Echites lasiocarpa*, A. DC. *l. c.* p. 463 (excl. 2 var.). In Brasilia, prov. Cuyaba: *non vidi*.

A climbing species, growing in hedges. Leaves ovate or ovate-oblong, narrower at the base, and there auriculately cordate, cuspidate at the apex, undulate on the margin, obsoletely pilose above, adpressed hirsute beneath, 3–5 in. long, 1¾–2¼ in. broad, on petioles 6 lines long; racemes axillary, half as long as the leaves, bearing many flowers on pedicels 3 lines long; sepals subulately linear, with pellucid margins, each with a truncate scarcely dentate scale; corolla incano-villous outside, with a yellow tube 1 in. long, narrowed in the lower half, funnel-shaped above, with obovate segments; disk of 5 oblong obtuse lobes; follicles 2, terete, erect, torulose, subconjoined at the apex, ferruginously hirsute; seeds with an ochraceous coma.

A very well-marked species.

5. TEMNADENIA STELLARIS, nob.: *Echites stellaris*, Lindl. Bot. Reg. tab. 1664; A. DC. *l. c.* p. 457 (excl. pl. Gardn. 1060): *Echites varia*, Müll., var. *rosea*, *l. c.* p. 158. In Brasilia, prov. Rio de Janeiro: *v. s. in herb. Mus. Brit.* in mont. Organ. fluv. Parahyba (Gardn. 5544).

A scandent species, well represented in the drawing above cited, taken from a cultivated plant obtained from Rio de Janeiro, which corresponds with Gardner's cited specimen: it is near *T. biorura*. Its slender branches cinereo-pubescent, have dilated substipular axils 4–5 in. apart; opposite leaves elliptic, gradually very narrow towards the recurved subplicate base, which is there cordate, or rather bilobed, gradually acuminate at the apex, membranaceous, ciliate on the margin, light green above, opake, softly and shortly puberulous, with subimmersed slender nerves, paler beneath, of a reddish fulvous colour, opake, pubescent, patently pilose on the scarcely prominulent midrib and nerves, 2¾–3½ in. long, 1¼–1½ in. broad, on pubescent petioles 4 lines long; raceme lateral at the nodes, 3 in. long, including the suddenly deflexed peduncle of half that length, bearing beyond numerous approximate flowers on slender pubescent pedicels 4 lines long, supported by minute bracts; sepals linear, acuminate, pubescent, 4 lines long, each with 3 unequal acute basal scales; corolla tubular; tube 9 lines long, dark-red, swelling upwards and downwards from the middle, where it is considerably contracted, marked by parallel nerves; segments subfleshy, dolabriform, acute at the sinister angle, dextrorsely convolute, 6 lines long, 4 lines broad, of a yellowish pink colour, marked in the mouth with several radiating, confluent, stellated dark-red patches; stamens seated in the contracted portion of the tube, on a narrow retrorsely pilose ring; anthers cohering in a cone, very acuminate, with 2 divergent, incurved, long, aristiform basal prongs, hirsutulous behind; disk fleshy, slit nearly to the base into 5 obtuse lobes, as long as the 2 rounded ovaries; style slender; clavuncle oblong, incrassate, with a basal peltate membrane; follicles not known.

6. TEMNADENIA SECUNDIFLORA, nob.: *Echites secundiflora*, A. DC. *l. c.* p. 457. In Mexico: *non vidi*.

A subscandent plant, with slender, pallid, glabrous branches; leaves oblong-ovate, cordate, acuminate, membranaceous, 2 in. long, 9–10 lines broad, on petioles 3 lines long; racemes simple, axillary, pendulous, 6 in. long, fructiferous at the base, bearing above several alternate secund flowers, on pedicels 2 lines long, supported by lanceolate bracts 1 line long; sepals broadly lanceolate, acuminate, 2–3 lines long; tube of corolla 1 in. long, greenish yellow, narrow at the base; segments obovate-oblong, crispate, subreflexed, 6 lines broad, yellowish, with crimson spots at their base; follicles linear, torulose, subcoherent at the apex, 4–5 in. long.

A species in habit, inflorescence, and spotted corolla approaching *T. stellaris*.

7. TEMNADENIA PALLIDIFLORA, nob.: *Echites Franciscea*, Hook. (non Lindl.), var. *pallidiflora*, Bot. Mag. 76, tab. 4547: *Echites varia*, Müll. (non Stadelm.), var. *sulphurea*, *l. c.* p. 158. In Brasilia, prov. Rio de Janeiro, inter Magé et Freichal: *v. v. et sicco in herb. meo* (No. 4031).

My specimen agrees well with Sir Wm. Hooker's drawing of a plant received from Rio de Janeiro, and cultivated in the Botanic Garden of Paris. It is a climbing species, near *T. bicrura*, with slender, terete, softly puberulous branches, with axils 3–3½ in. apart; leaves opposite, oblong, narrowing below the middle, cordate and obtusely bilobed at the base, suddenly constricted at the summit into a short acute acumen, submembranaceous, pale green above, rigidly and sparsely pilose above, the hairs growing out of scabridly globular prominences, ciliate on the margin, opake, and pale yellowish beneath, the reddish midrib, nerves, and transversely reticulate veins prominulent and furnished with long white very patent hairs, 2–3 in. long, $\frac{7}{8}$–1¼ in. broad, on suddenly reflexed cano-tomentose petioles 3–5 lines long; raceme lateral, as long as the smaller leaves, on a hirsutely pubescent peduncle 9 lines long, bearing upwards about 10 alternate subapproximate flowers, on hairy deflexed pedicels 2 lines long, with a short acute basal bract; sepals linear-lanceolate, very attenuated at the summit, thickly pilose outside, with membranaceous margins, each with an inner denticulate scale; corolla of a pale yellow colour, marked by roseate spots in the mouth, densely niveo-tomentose outside; tube cylindrical, 12 lines long, contracted 5 lines above the base, subcampanulate above; segments deltoid, dolabriform, with an acute tooth at the sinister angle, roundly expanded at the other side, and dextrorsely convolute, 4 lines long and broad.

8. TEMNADENIA LEPTOLOBA, nob.: *Echites leptoloba*, Stadelm. Bot. Zeit. 1841, Beibl. i. p. 157; A. DC. *l. c.* p. 456. In sylvis Rio Japuré et Rio Negro: *non vidi*.

A shrub with a striate stem and subfiliform, terete, glabrous branches, having remote axils; leaves ovate, membranaceous, upper ones narrower, cuneate at the base, cuspidate at the apex, lower ones subobtuse at the base and acute above, 3–4½ in. long, 2–2½ in. broad, on petioles 6–9 lines long; racemes axillary, longer than the leaves; peduncle bifid; pedicels 6 lines long, supported by ovate-lanceolate bracts, scarcely 1 line long; sepals ovate-lanceolate, patent, 2 lines long, each with an inner, trapezoidal, obsoletely bidentate scale ¼ line long; corolla yellow, glabrous; tube striate, 6 lines long, constricted at the mouth; segments oval, undulate, 3 lines long; disk of 5 oblong lobes, longer than the 2 ovaries; follicles 2, more than a foot long, subtorulose, sometimes conjoined at the apex.

This plant, from its habit, bifid raceme, from the tube of its corolla constricted below the mouth, its disk, and its follicles conjoined at the apex, agrees with *Temnadenia*, and seems near *T. secundiflora*.

9. TEMNADENIA CORDATA, nob.: *Echites cordata*, A. DC. *l. c.* p. 451. In Mexico (Mocin et Sessé, cum icon. ined.) : *non vidi*.

A climbing species with flexible, terete, pilose branches; leaves ovate, acuminate, cordate at the base, ciliate, pilose, 3 in. long, 18–20 lines broad, on petioles 3 lines long; racemes axillary, shorter than the leaves, on a simple pilose peduncle bearing several alternate flowers spicately disposed on pedicels 3 lines long, supported by lanceolate bracteoles 1 line long; sepals lanceolate, acuminate, 3 lines long; corolla yellow; tube cylindrical, 8 lines long, narrowed a little below the middle, smooth in the mouth; segments ovate, acute, 3 lines long and broad; anthers conniving in a cone in the middle of the tube; style pilose; stigma bilobed; disk of 5 free linear lobes.

This plant bears all the characters of *Temnadenia*, and appears to be near *T. secundiflora* and *T. glaucescens* from the same country.

10. TEMNADENIA FRANCISCEA, nob.: *Echites Franciscea*, Lindl. (non Hook.) Bot. Reg. xxxiii. tab. 34; A. DC. *l. c.* p. 452: *Echites violacea*, Müll. (non Vell.) *l. c.* p. 158, tab. 50. fig. 3 (flos) : *Echites varia*, Müll. (non Stadelm.), var. *purpurea*, *l. c.* p. 158 : *Echites Maximiliana*, Stadelm. Bot. Zeit. 1841, p. 43; A. DC. *l. c.* p. 462. In Brasilia, prov. Bahia: *v. s. in herb. Mus. Brit.* ad Penedo, Rio San Francisco (Gardner 1354); Rio San Francisco (Blanchet 2865).

Gardner's specimen from Penedo agrees well with Lindley's drawing. It is a handsome scandent plant, with flexuose puberulous branches, and axils 3 in. apart; leaves ovate, plicate and obsoletely cordate at the base, mucronately acute, velutinous on both sides, 3–3¼ in. long, 1¾–2 in. broad, on pubescent petioles 3 lines long; raceme lateral, pubescent, on a suddenly deflexed peduncle bare for the length of 1 in., thence densely many-flowered on pedicels 4–6 lines long; sepals acuminate, 2–3 lines long, with 5 inner lanceolate scales at the base of each; corolla 20 lines long, rose-coloured, with 5 stellular, yellow, oblong patches in the mouth; tube glabrous, constricted a little below the middle for 6 lines, 14 lines long; segments rhomboidally dolabriform, 6 lines long, 9 lines broad, rotate; stamens inserted at the contraction of the tube; anthers coherent, acuminate, pilose dorsally, biaristate at the base; disk partly cleft into 5 oblong emarginate lobes, nearly as long as the 2 ovate ovaries.

11. TEMNADENIA XANTHOSTOMA, nob.: *Echites xanthostoma*, Stadelm. Bot. Zeit. 1841, p. 55; A. DC. *l. c.* p. 468 : *Dipladenia xanthostoma*, Müll. *l. c.* p. 123 (excl. syn.). In Brasilia, prov. Saõ Paulo : *non vidi*.

Müller wrongly regarded this plant as identical with *Dipladenia saponariæ*, A. DC.; but it cannot belong that genus, as its disk shows. It has a short erect stem, with approximate leaves, which are oblong-lanceolate, contracted towards the base, acuminate, mucronate, glabrous, the superior ones spathulate, 1½ in. long, 6-8 lines broad, on petioles 1 line long; peduncle terminal, 2 in. long, bearing a few purplish scarlet flowers yellow in the mouth, on bracteolate pedicels 4-6 lines long; sepals acuminate, 6 lines long; tube of corolla 1 in. long; segments 6-8 lines long, 2 lines broad; stamens inserted in the middle of the tube, with membranaceous tips; disk of 5 erect lobes, subciliate.

12. TEMNADENIA PALUSTRIS, nob.: *Echites palustris*, Salzmann: *Echites tomentosa*, var. *laticordata*, A. DC. *l. c.* p. 463: *Amblyanthera palustris*, Müll. *l. c.* p. 145. In Brasilia, prope Bahia (Salzmann) : *non vidi*.

A climbing plant, with branches covered with yellow shaggy hairs, its axils remote; leaves oblong-elliptic, openly cordate at the base, with a long acute acumen, membranaceous, darkish above, sparsely hirsute, more densely hirsute beneath, 4-5 in. long, 2 in. broad, on petioles 1 in. long; raceme lateral, on a long rigid peduncle, fulvo-hirsute, bearing about 12 large flowers on pedicels 3 lines long, with lanceolate-ovate bracts 3 lines long; sepals acuminately ovate, hirsute, 6 lines long, with an inner multidentate scale; corolla yellow, 2 in. long; tube narrowly cylindrical for two thirds of its length, broadly campanulate above, sericeo-pilose within; segments half its length; disk sub-5-lobed, shorter than the 2 ovaries; follicles 2, terete, obtuse at the base, torulose, hirsute, 4 in. long, conjoined at the apex; seeds 2-3 lines long, comose.

This species is near *T. lasiocarpa*, and must not be confounded with the *Rhabdadenia paludosa* (*Echites paludosa*, Vahl), nor with the *Echites paludosa*, H. B. K.

13. TEMNADENIA SEMIDIGYNA, nob.: *Echites semidigyna*, Berg, in Abh. Ulyssingen (Flushing), iii. p. 588, cum icone; Gmelin, Syst. Veg. iv. p. 436; A. DC. *l. c.* p. 474. In Guiana Batava: *v. s. in herb. Mus. Brit.* Surinam (Anderson, ex hb. Rudge).

Anderson's specimen agrees with the description and drawing of Berg. It is a climbing plant, having terete branches, roughly striate, with axils 1½-2 in. apart; leaves elliptic-oblong, acute at both ends, acuminate, chartaceous, green and concolorous on both sides, 4-6 in. long, 1-2 in. broad, on slender petioles 4-6 lines long; racemes axillary and opposite, 4 in. long, on a very slender peduncle thickened at the summit, minutely bracteolate at the base, 3 lines long; sepals obtusely oblong, imbricate, 2 lines long, with several inner basal scales; tube of corolla cylindrical, narrower below the middle, somewhat swollen in the mouth, 10 lines long; segments obliquely oblong, 5 lines long, 2 lines broad; stamens inserted on the contraction of the tube; filaments very short, pubescent; anthers acuminate, sagittate at the base, pilose behind; disk urceolate, cleft into 5 oblong, obtuse, emarginate lobes, longer than the 2 subglobose ovaries; style slender, shortly bifid at the base; clavuncle oblong, 5-sulcate, expanded at the base, and adhering to the anthers.

14. TEMNADENIA TOMENTOSA, nob: *Echites tomentosa*, Vahl, Symb. fasc. iii. p. 44, Icon. tab. 5; A. DC. *l. c.* p. 463; Benth. Journ. Bot. iii. p. 247: *Amblyanthera tomentosa*, Müll. in Linn. xxx. p. 450. Prope Cayenne: *non vidi*.

A plant with tortuous, slender, hirsute branches, with axils 1½-2 in. apart; opposite leaves obovate-elliptic, diminishing below the middle into 2 narrow, cordate, incumbent lobes, gradually acuminate, flatly hirsute above, scabridulous beneath, adpressed pilose on the prominulent nerves and veins, $2\frac{1}{2}$–3 in. long, 1–1$\frac{1}{2}$ in. broad, on petioles 4–5 lines long; raceme lateral, pilose; peduncle hirsute, 9 lines long, bearing upwards many approximate flowers on pubescent pedicels 4 lines long; sepals narrowly lanceolate, glabrous, 5 lines long; tube of corolla 21 lines long, contracted at the base for 7 lines, funnel-shaped above, cinereo-pubescent; segments dolabriform, 9 lines long, 6 lines broad; stamens inserted on a pilose ring in the contraction of the tube; follicles brown, terete, torulous, acute at both ends, subglabrous, 7–9 in. long; seeds 6 lines long, with a rufescent coma 11 lines long.

15. TEMNADENIA GLAUCESCENS, nob.: *Echites glaucescens*, Mart. & Gal. Acad. Brux. xi. p. 358; Walp. Rep. vi. p. 476. Circa Oaxaca, in montibus : *non vidi*.

A species with scandent glabrous branches; leaves ovate, cordate, acute, petiolate, glaucous beneath; racemes axillary, longer than the leaves, with an elongated peduncle bearing 3–4 secund pedicellate flowers; sepals small, lanceolate; corolla funnel-shaped, 1$\frac{1}{2}$ in. long; tube narrowed at the base for half an inch, broadening above; segments roundish; anthers included; disk of 5 free lobes.

16. TEMNADENIA SOLANIFOLIA, nob.: *Hæmadictyon? solanifolium*, Müll. *l. c.* p. 171, tab. 49. In Brasilia, prov. Rio de Janeiro (Schüch, Akermann): *v. s. in herb. Mus. Brit.* circa Itagoahy, *in flore*; prov. S. Paulo, *in fructu* (Bowie and Cunningham).

The plant above cited agrees with the description and drawing of Müller; and though its flowers are somewhat smaller, they bear all the characters of *Temnadenia* and none of the essential features of *Hæmadictyon*, wanting the peculiar corona and the buccal appendages of the latter genus, in which it is doubtfully placed by Müller. It is a subscandent plant, with subflexuose ferruginously puberulous branches incrassate at the axils, which are 3–4 in. apart; leaves elliptic, obtuse or subacute at the base, constricted into an acute or obtuse mucronulate acumen at the summit, chartaceous, with revolute margins, finely corrugulate and fuscous green above, subasperously granulate, with about 8 pairs of slender divergent immersed nerves, yellowish opake beneath, granularly scabridulous, with obsolete hairs on granules upon the midrib and nerves, which are fuscous and prominulent, $2\frac{1}{2}$–$4\frac{1}{2}$ in. long, 1$\frac{1}{2}$–1$\frac{5}{8}$ in. broad, on slender pilose channelled petioles 3–4 lines long; panicle lateral, ferruginously puberulous, on a terete peduncle 6 lines long, bifid at the apex, each branch bearing about 6 opposite flowers on slender spirally twisted pedicels 3–6 lines long, with a small linear basal bracteole; sepals narrowly lanceolate, subpuberulous, with ciliolate margins, 3 lines long, each with an inner broadish subdentate scale; tube of corolla 6 lines long, a little ventricose above the middle, cylindrical above, where it is fuscous, thickish, and marked within the throat by 10 subpuberulous lines, but without corona or buccal appendages; segments rounder on one side, simply convolute dextrorsely, 3 lines long; stamens inserted on a pilose ring at the lower constriction of the tube; anthers slender, coherent, rigid, acuminate, with 2 acute basal prongs; disk of 5 erect emarginate lobes, as long as the 2 ovate ovaries; follicles 2, nearly straight, terete, subparallel, suddenly inflected near the apex, seemingly as if they had been there conjoined, black, opake, lenticellate, 2¾ in. long, 1 line thick; seeds many, linearly fusiform, ¾ line long, compressed and subchannelled on the ventral face, which bears a longitudinal raphe terminating in a point by which they are attached to the placenta, striate on the dorsal face; a widely spreading sericeous coma of fine soft hairs, 12 lines long, with an outer series of hairs of half that length.

17. TEMNADENIA CORRUGULATA, nob.: volubilis, ramulis tenuissimis: foliis elliptico-oblongis, imo subacutis, acuminatis, marginibus subrevolutis, undulatis, flaccide chartaceis, utrinque minutissime corrugulatis, supra læte viridibus, ad costam nervisque sulcatis, ad basin costæ glandula munitis, subtus flavide opacis, subscabridulis, costa nervisque fuscis et prominulis, eveniis, petiolo tenui: racemis lateralibus, simplicibus, quam folium quadruplo brevioribus; floribus subapproximatis; pedicellis tenuibus, calyce paullulo longioribus; sepalis lanceolato-linearibus, puberulis, intus squamula obtusa donatis; corollæ tubo cylindrico, parallele nervoso, quam calyx duplo longiore; segmentis inæquilatere deltoideis, quam tubus dimidio brevioribus, dextrorsum convolutis; staminibus medio tubi insertis; antheris longe cuspidatis, basi tenuiter biaristatis; disci lobis emarginatis, ovaria æquantibus: cæteris ut in præcedentibus. In Brasilia: *v. s. in herb. Mus. Brit.* Rio de Janeiro, in montibus (Bowie et Cunningham).

A species closely approaching the preceding. The axils of its slender branches are 3 in. apart; leaves 2–3¼ in. long, ¾–1¼ in. broad, on petioles 5 lines long; raceme 1 in. long' with about 10 congested flowers on pedicels 2½ lines long; sepals 1½ line long; tube of corolla 6 lines long, its throat exactly as in the last species; the segments 2½ lines long and broad. It differs from the preceding in its more corrugulate leaves, not folded at the base, in its shorter raceme on a shorter peduncle, smaller flowers, in its erect sepals, with a rounded internal scale, and in its longer disk.

18. TEMNADENIA PARVIFLORA, nob.: *Hæmadictyon parviflorum*, Benth. Pl. Hartw. p. 355. In Nova Granada, circa Pandi (Hartweg 1053): *non vidi*.

A plant bearing all the appearance of a *Prestonia*, as Mr. Bentham observed. Its scandent branches are softly and rufously tomentose, its axils furnished with many setiform stipules; leaves ovate-oblong, narrowed below the middle, acute at the base, acuminate, softly chartaceous, villous above, sericeo-tomentous beneath, 4–7 in. long, 2–4 in. broad, on petioles 6–12 lines long; corymb terminal, on a divided peduncle bearing numerous flowers in a densely capitate head 1–3 in. in diameter, on thickish subfasciculated tomentose pedicels 3 lines long; sepals membranaceous, very acuminate, velutino-tomentose, 2¼ lines long, each with an inner bifid or 2 simple scales; corolla villous outside; tube nearly 3 lines long, its mouth fleshy, without appendages; segments nearly as long as the tube, oblong-lanceolate, glabrous; stamens seated on a pilose ring in the middle of the tube; filaments short; anthers included, the tips scarcely exserted; disk of 5 connate bifid lobes as long as the villous ovaries; follicles less than a foot long, clothed with rufo-velutinous hairs; seeds with a long apical coma.

19. **TEMNADENIA RIEDELII**, nob.: *Hæmadictyon Riedelii*, Müll. *l. c.* p. 170. In Brasilia, prov. S. Paulo, ad Sorocaba (Riedel 1973): *v. s. in herb. meo* Campinas (Weir 75).

Weir's plant is from the same province as that of Riedel's. It is a climbing species, with stoutish, flexuose, pale, subfistulose branches, covered with a short yellow tomentum, with dilated axils 5 in. apart, furnished along the transverse ridge with several pectinoid stipules; leaves ovate, at the base suddenly and acutely constricted upon the petiole, with an abrupt acute acumen, submembranaceous, pallid green above, with short dense yellow pubescence on the flattened midrib and on 5-6 pairs of arching prominulent nerves and transversely reticulated veins, beneath of a yellowish hue, shortly tomentellous, especially on the little prominulent nerves and veins, 4¾ in. long, 2½-3 in. broad, on stout floccose petioles 9 lines long; corymb solitary and lateral at the nodes, with a peduncle rising out of an involucel of scales, 1 in. long, somewhat 2-branched, each branch laxly flowered, puberulous; flowers mostly geminate upon slender pedicels 6 lines long, with corresponding opposite linear-oblong bracts of the same length; sepals oblong, acuminate, pilose on both sides, 5-7 lines long, 2 lines broad, each with an inner broadly ovate truncate scale denticulate at the apex; tube of corolla broadish, cylindrical, reddish, glabrous, 6 lines long, thickish in the mouth, without appendages; segments oblong-ovate, inequilateral, 4 lines long, 2½ lines broad, glabrous; stamens inserted upon 5 pilose lines in the middle of the tube; anthers acuminate, 3¼ lines long, with 2 basal divaricate prongs 1 line long.

20. **TEMNADENIA TENUICULA**, nob.: ramis tenuiculis, teretibus, subglabris; axillis remotis, dilatatis, cum stipulis parvis acutis 2 vel plurimis pectinatim dispositis: foliis lanceolato-oblongis, imo obtusis et obsolete cordatis, apice gradatim augustatis et breviter acuminatis, supra fusco-viridibus, nitidulis, parenchymate ruguloso, nervis tenuissimis, arcuatis, subimmersis, subtus fere concoloribus, opacis, nervis vix prominulis; petiolis tenuibus, patentibus: corymbo laterali, solitario, quam folium breviore; pedunculo crassiusculo, imo squamulis involucellato, apice 2-3-furcato, ramis congestim pluriflorus et capitatis; pedicellis tenuibus, quam calyx duplo longioribus, bracteola parva acuta suffultis; sepalis lineari-oblongis, submembranaceis, acutis, intus squama late triangulari munitis; corolla subparva; tubo cylindrico, quam calyx duplo longiore, fauce interrupte callosa, appendicibus nullis; segmentis inæquilatere ovatis, acutis, tubo ¼ brevioribus; staminibus annulo piloso in medio tubi insertis; antheris linearibus, acutis, faucem vix attingentibus, imo furcis 2 incurvis brevibus armatis, dorso pruinosis; disco urceolato, in lobos 5 apice denticulatos inciso, quam ovarium longiore. In Brasilia: *v. v. et sicc. in herb. meo* (no. 4050), Rio Paquequer, in montibus Organensibus.

I found this plant in flower in Jan. 1838. It approaches *T. solanifolia* in habit, differing in its smaller leaves, and flowers aggregated in a more capitate head; its branches are only ½ line thick, its axils 3½-4½ in. apart, with many stipules ¼ line long; leaves 1½-3 in. long, ½-¾ in. broad, on petioles 2-2½ lines long; corymb 1¼ in. long; peduncle bare for ⅔ in., its branches many-flowered from the base on pedicels 4-5 lines long; sepals 2½-3 lines long, 1 line broad; tube of corolla narrower in the middle, 5 lines long; segments 3 lines long, 2 lines broad; anthers 2½ lines long.

21. **TEMNADENIA ANNULARIS**, nob.: *Prestonia annularis*, G. Don, Dict. iv. p. 84; *Echites annularis*, Linn. fil. Suppl. 166: *Hæmadictyon? annulare*, A. DC. *l. c.* p. 428. In Surinam: *non vidi*.

A climbing species, with opposite petiolate leaves 1 foot long; corymb axillary, on a bifid peduncle; sepals oblong, erect, concave; tube of corolla cylindrical, longer than the calyx, with a prominent ring in the mouth, concave beneath, apparently without appendages; segments obliquely roundish, emarginate, rotate; disk of 5 small ovate lobes.

From its bifid peduncle and flowers without faucial appendages, it probably belongs to this group.

22. TEMNADENIA QUINQUANGULARIS, nob.: *Echites quinquangularis*, Jacq. Amer. p. 32, tab. 25; A. DC. *l. c.* p. 468: *Prestonia quinquangularis*, Spr. Syst. i. p. 637. Ad Carthagena: *non vidi*.

A climbing species, with scabridulous branches, the axils $5\frac{1}{4}$ in. apart; leaves opposite, elliptic-obovate, obtuse at the base, subacute at the reflexed summit, nerves divergent, $2\frac{1}{4}$–3 in. long, $1\frac{3}{4}$–$1\frac{7}{8}$ in. broad, on patent slender petioles 3 lines long; raceme lateral, not quite as long as the leaves; peduncle bare for 1 in., bearing above 12–16 subalternate flowers on reflexed pedicels 3 lines long; sepals acuminate, reflexed at the apex, 2 lines long; corolla greenish-yellow, with a white cylindrical tube, broader at its base, 9 lines long, pentagonal above, and somewhat thickened in the mouth, without any apparent appendages; segments obovate, obliquely truncate, 4 lines long; stamens inserted above the inflated portion of the tube on a pilose ring; anthers lanceolately acuminate, hastate at the base, cohering in a cone, which fills the upper portion of the tube; disk 5-lobed, as long as the ovaries.

De Candolle considered this species quite foreign to *Prestonia*, and not conformable with *Hæmadictyon*; the flowers were regarded by him as agreeing with those of his *Echites cordata* (*Angadenia nitida*, antè, p. 177).

MITOZUS*.

An extensive natural group of plants, one of the most uniform in its characters among the *Echiteæ*, easily recognizable by their extremely slender branchlets. They disagree utterly with *Anisolobus* and *Amblyanthera*, to which some of the species have been referred by Müller. The *Echites funiformis* of Velloz may be regarded as the type. The almost filiform branchlets are dilated at the somewhat remote nodes, and there furnished with 2 small caducous stipules; the leaves are opposite, generally rather small, glabrous, oblong, often cordate at the base, pointed at the summit, upon short, slender petioles; the inflorescence is lateral, upon a long or shorter peduncle, bearing several alternate flowers on minutely bracteolate pedicels; calyx small; corolla salver-shaped, rather small or of moderate size, with dextrorse convolution. Its chief peculiarity is its disk, which is tubular, submembranaceous, 5-grooved, entire on the margin or arched between the grooves, quite or nearly concealing 2 free ovaries. The fruit consists of 2 long, very slender follicles, smooth, often torulose, either free or conjoined at the apex; seeds with a simple sericeous coma.

MITOZUS, nob. *Calyx* parvus; *sepala* 5, acuta aut obtusa. *Corolla* mediocris; *tubus* infra medium cylindricus, superne amplior; *segmenta* oblique ovata, tubo dimidio breviora, in æstivatione dextrorsum

* From μίτος (*filum*), ὅζος (*ramus*), from its funiform branches.

convoluta. *Stamina* ad constrictionem tubi inserta; *filamenta* complanata, dense puberula; *antheræ* lineares, cuspidatæ, imo in furcas 2 parallelas obtusas fissæ, dorso hispidulæ. *Discus* e lobis 5 carnosis, truncatis, subconnatis. *Ovaria* 2, disco paullo longiora. *Stylus* tenuis; *clavuncula* oblonga, imo membrana peltata suffulta; *stigmata* 2, terminalia, minima. *Folliculi* 2, tenuiter teretes, liberi et erectiusculi, aut arcuati et apice nexi. *Semina* plurima, oblonga, *raphe* longitudinali notata; *coma* ampla, elastice expansa, duplo longior.

Suffrutices *Americæ meridionalis, debiles, sæpius volubiles;* folia *opposita, mediocria, oblonga, sæpe cordata, acuta, subbreviter petiolata;* racemi *laterales, alternatim plurifori;* flores *mediocres, pedicellati;* fructus *follicularis.*

1. MITOZUS EXILIS, nob.: *Amblyanthera funiformis*, var. *pedunculata*, Müll. Fl. Bras. xxvi. p. p. 144. In prov. Rio de Janeiro, ad Magé: *v. v. et sicc. in herb. meo* (no. 3436).

This plant, which I found in 1837, is evidently identical with Müller's variety above cited; but it is a species extremely different from that of Velloz. Its very twining branches are extremely slender, scarcely ¼ line thick, dilated at the axils, the lower ones being 3 in., the upper ones 1½–2 in. apart, and furnished with 2 almost obsolete stipules; its oblong-ovate leaves are cordate at the base, contracted near the summit into a long, narrow, acute acumen, submembranaceous, pale green above, with slender immersed nerves, yellowish-opake beneath, with immersed reddish nerves, 1–1¾ in. long, 6–9 lines broad, on petioles 3–4 lines long; raceme lateral, on a peduncle 1 in. long, slender, bearing at its apex 6–8 flowers alternately approximate, on pedicels 5 lines long, with a small bracteole at their base; sepals ovate, acute, 1 line long; tube of corolla (still in bud) cylindrical below, swelling above, 12 lines long; segments 6 lines long, with dextrorse convolution; stamens inserted in the constriction of the tube, on a pilose ring; anthers acuminate, dorsally subhispid, with 2 narrow, parallel, obtuse basal prongs; disk of 5 fleshy truncated connate lobes, as long as the 2 conical ovaries; fructiferous peduncle 1 in. long; pedicel 9 lines long; follicles 2, arcuate and conjoined at the summit, 3 in. long, ¾ line thick; seeds 2 lines long, with a spreading, reddish-yellow coma 3½ lines long.

A drawing of this plant, in flower and in fruit, is given in Plate XXXI.

2. MITOZUS GUANABARICUS, nob.: *Echites Guanabarica*, Casar. Nov. Stirp. Pl. Rio Jan. No. 1483: *Echites microphylla*, A. DC. (non Stadelm.) in parte, Prodr. viii. p. 459 : *Amblyanthera funiformis*, Müll. *l. c.* p. 144 (excl. syn. Velloz), var. *microphylla* (in parte), tab. 44. fig. 1. In prov. Rio de Janeiro, Cabo frio (Pohl) ; circa Rio de Janeiro (Riedel) : *v. v.* ad pedem montium Organ. *et sicco in herb. meo* (no. 4029, *in fructu*).

My specimen quite agrees with Müller's drawing, which was probably made from Riedel's specimen. It is a climbing species, very near the preceding, with very slender, funiform, dichotomous branches, the axils being 1½–2 in. apart, and bearing 2 minute stipules; the leaves are oblong, rounded at the base, suddenly narrowed at the summit into a much longer acute acumen, chartaceous, with subrevolute margins, pale-green above, with reddish immersed fine nerves, paler and yellowish-opake beneath, with a prominent yellow midrib, the nerves scarcely visible, 1½–2 in. long, 8–10 lines broad, on petioles 5–6 lines long; fructiferous peduncle 2¼ in. long, with the cicatrices of few flowers above; elongated pedicel 1 in. long; follicles arcuate, divaricate, striate, subtorulose, 5 in. long, 1 line thick; seeds and coma as in the preceding species; the inflorescence similar, bearing yellow flowers.

3. MITOZUS FUNIFORMIS, nob.: *Echites funiformis*, Vell. Fl. Flum. p. 109, Icon. iii. tab. 29; A. DC. *l. c.* p. 460: *Amblyanthera funiformis*, Müll. Fl. Bras. xxvi. p. 144. In Brasilia, insulis Ilha grande et S. Catherina: *non vidi*.

This species certainly does not belong to *Amblyanthera*; it has been confounded by Müller with others collected by me, here described. In the drawing of the 'Flora Fluminensis' the Paris artist, who roughly copied the fine drawings of Velloz, has made the branches in the plate cited far too stout, as the name *funiformis* clearly indicates, and as the branchlet on the right-hand side of the plate shows. The branches are slender, dilated at the axils, which are $1\frac{1}{4}$–2 in. apart, and bear 2 minute stipules; the leaves are ovate, cordate at the base, narrowing above the middle into an acute acumen, are 2–$3\frac{1}{4}$ in. long, 1–$1\frac{3}{4}$ in. broad, on petioles 4–5 lines long; the panicle is lateral, on a bare slender peduncle 2–4 in. long, bearing above about 10 alternate flowers on slender pedicels 6–9 lines long; sepals acutely ovate, $1\frac{1}{4}$ line long; tube of corolla $1\frac{1}{2}$ in. long, campanularly widening above the middle; segments 8 lines long, 7 lines broad; stamens inserted in the contraction of the tube; disk urceolate, 5-grooved, with a shortly crenate 5-lobed margin, a little shorter than the 2 oblong ovaries; style slender, 9 lines long; clavuncle incrassate, on a peltate membrane; follicles 2, straight, terete, parallel, nearly erect (not conjoined at the apex), $4\frac{3}{4}$–5 in. long, 2 lines broad; seeds oblong, 4 lines long, coma 8 lines long.

4. MITOZUS MICROPHYLLA, nob.: *Echites microphylla*, Stadelm. *l. c.* p. 35; A. DC. *l. c.* p. 459. In Brasilia, prov. Bahia et S. Paulo: *non vidi*.

A species notable for its small leaves, and distinct from the preceding. It is a scandent plant, with very slender glabrous branches, having its axils furnished with 2 dentiform stipules; the opposite leaves are ovate-oblong, rounded and cordate at the base, gradually acute or acuminate, green above, ferruginous beneath, with prominent midrib and nerves, which are parallelly divergent and barbate in their axils, the veins reticulated, 10–20 lines long, 8–10 lines broad, on pilose petioles $2\frac{1}{2}$–3 lines long; raceme lateral, 2 in. long, on a slender peduncle 1 in. long, bearing about 7 subapproximate alternate flowers, on pedicels 3–4 lines long, supported by a small acute bract; sepals acute, $1\frac{3}{4}$ line long, with an inner denticulate scale; tube of corolla 18 lines long, narrowed at its base for 7 lines, thence campanulate; segments yellow, rhomboidally ovate, inequilaterally dolabriform, 9 lines long and broad, dextrorsely convolute; stamens seated at the contraction of the tube; anthers cohering, membranaceous at the summit, shortly bilobed at the base; disk urceolate, its margin scarcely 5-cleft, crenulate, as long as the ovaries; follicles slender, cylindrical, smooth, pendulous, 7 in. long.

5. MITOZUS BLANCHETII, nob.: *Echites Blanchetii*, A. DC. *l. c.* p. 448; Müll. *l. c.* p. 157. In Brasilia (Blanchet 3223A), Bahia: *non vidi*.

A climbing species with stout branches; branchlets slender, subtetragonous, flexuose, cinereo-fuscous; axils ciliolate; leaves elliptic, obtuse at both ends, chartaceous, with revolute margins, having above immersed, almost evanescent nerves, beneath punctulate-scabrid, with short sparse soft hairs, 3–4 in. long, 1½–2 in. broad, on thick petioles 4 lines long; raceme lateral, shorter than the leaves; peduncle thick, stiff, glabrous, bearing many densely crowded smallish flowers, on pedicels viscidly puberulous, nearly 9 lines long, thickened above; sepals obtusely ovate, scarcely 1 line long, altogether with about 8 minute internal scales; tube of corolla narrowly cylindrical for half its length, 8 lines long, a little swollen above; segments obliquely ovate, 4 lines long; ovaries enclosed within an urceolate disk of 5 truncated subconnate lobes.

6. MITOZUS GRACILIPES, nob.: *Anisolobus? gracilipes*, Müll. *l. c.* p. 115: *Echites gracilipes*, Stadelm. Bot. Zeit. 1841, p. 22; A. DC. *l. c.* p. 455. In Brasilia, prov. Minas Geraës: *v. s. in herb. Mus. Brit.* Serra de Araripe (Gardner 1756).

A twining shrub, with slender flexuose branchlets, lenticellate and ferruginously subhirsute; leaves elliptic or lanceolately oblong, obtuse at the base, shortly acuminate, rigidly membranaceous, dark green, opake, and glabrous above, paler and hirsute beneath, with darker nerves, 2–3½ in. long, 10–20 lines broad, on petioles 3 lines long; raceme lateral, on a slender peduncle 6–8 lines long, with many minute caducous bractlets; flowers on twisted, slender, puberulous pedicels; sepals lanceolate, acuminate, 2¾ lines long, unequal, puberulous, with membranaceous ciliate margins; corolla 10¼ lines long; tube longer than the sepals, pubescent, funnel-shaped above, contracted near the middle, and there staminigerous; segments sparsely pubescent on both sides, with white margins, half as long as the tube; disk urceolate, margin shortly cleft into 5 fleshy lobes, half as long as the 2 ovaries.

7. MITOZUS TENELLUS, nob.: *Odontadenia angustifolia*, A. DC. *l. c.* p. 360. In Guiana Gallica: *non vidi.*

A climbing glabrous plant, not to be confounded with the *Echites angustifolia* of Bentham or with that of Poiret. Leaves oblong-lanceolate, obtuse and subcordate at the base, very acute, 4 in. long, ½–¾ in. broad, on petioles 6 lines long; panicle lateral, nearly 4 in. long, on a dichotomously divided peduncle, bearing many flowers on reflexed pedicels 6 lines long; sepals obovate-oblong, 2 lines long; tube of corolla 9 lines long, lower part pilose within and staminigerous in the middle; disk urceolate, of 5 fleshy truncate lobes, unequally connate, a little shorter than the 2 ovaries.

It certainly does not belong to *Odontadenia*; it is a species apparently very close to the preceding.

8. MITOZUS LEPTOPHYLLUS, nob.: *Echites leptophylla*, A. DC. *l. c.* p. 455: *Echites linearifolia*, Stadelm. (non Hamilt.), *l. c.* p. 18. In Brasilia, prov. Bahia et Goyaz: *v. s. in herb. Mus. Brit.* Mission Douro (Gardner 3517).

A subscandent plant, with very slender striate branches, the axils 2½–3 in. apart; opposite leaves linear-oblong, shortly cordate at the base, subacute and mucronate at the summit, with revolute margins, rigidly coriaceous, sulcate above along the middle, convex on each side of the midrib, pale green above, sparsely and softly pubescent, with about 12 pairs of patent arcuate immersed nerves, pale yellow and pruinosely velutinous beneath, with immersed nerves, 2–4 in. long, 3–4 lines broad, on stoutish pilosulous petioles 1–2 lines long; raceme lateral, 1–1½ in. long, pubescent, bearing 4–5 alternate flowers on pedicels 6 lines long, supported by linear setiform bracteoles; sepals lanceolately subulate, 1¼ line long, with an inner 3-dentate scale; corolla handsome, dark-red; tube 2 in. long, narrowed at the base for half its length, thence enlarged into a broad funnel-shape, glabrous, its mouth yellow; segments violaceous, rhomboidally oval, inequilaterally oblique, subdolabriform, crispate, 4 lines long and broad; stamens seated on a niveously pilose ring in the contraction of the tube; anthers membranaceous at the apex, obtusely bifurcate at the base; disk urceolate, 5-sulcate, margin 5-notched, surrounding the 2 ovaries.

A species closely allied to the two preceding.

9. MITOZUS TENUICAULIS, nob.: *Echites tenuicaulis*, Stadelm. *l. c.* p. 40; A. DC. *l. c.* p. 462: *Amblyanthera versicolor*, var. *olivacea*, Müll. *l. c.* p. 147. In Brasilia, prov. Bahia et Amazonas: *v. s. in herb. meo et Mus. Brit.* S. Gabriel, Rio Negro (Spruce 2206).

A distinct species, with twining, very slender, striate, subpuberulous branches, with prominent transverse axils 4 in. apart; leaves lanceolately oblong, very much narrower towards the base, which is shortly and narrowly cordate, with a long, very acuminate, subciliate summit, rigidly chartaceous or subcoriaceous, with revolute margins, glabrous and polished above, of a deep olive-green colour, corrugulate and sulcate along the hispidulous, very slender, immersed midrib, nerves, and veins, fulvously opake and pruinosely velutinous beneath, with prominent slender midrib, nerves, and reticulated veins, 2¾–3½ in. long, ⅞–1 in. broad, on villous petioles 4 lines long; raceme lateral, 1½ in. long, on a peduncle as thick as the branch, 6 lines long, bearing above about 12 alternate flowers of a pale-rose or yellowish colour, pubescent outside, about the size of those of *M. versicolor*.

10. MITOZUS VERSICOLOR, nob.: *Echites versicolor*, Stadelm. Bot. Zeit. 1841, p. 38; A. DC. *l. c.* p. 461: *Amblyanthera versicolor*, Müll. (in parte), *l. c.* p. 146. In Brasilia, prov. Bahia et Ceará: *v. s. in herb. meo*, prov. Ceará, ad Crato (Gardner 1755).

This species certainly does not belong to *Amblyanthera*, but is congeneric with all the preceding. It is a climbing plant, with extremely slender, twining, reddish, hirsutulous branches; its axils, 3–4 in. apart, are furnished with 2 small acute stipules on each face; expanded opposite leaves, oblong-ovate, cordate at the base, suddenly or more gradually acute and cuspidate at the apex, submembranaceous, pale or darker green above, opake, scabridulous and hirsutulous on the midrib and nerves, beneath incano-pallid or ochraceously opake, shortly or obsoletely velutinous, with a reddish prominent midrib, prominulent fine nerves and reticulated veins, 2–3¼ in. long, 1–1⅓ in. broad, on pubescent petioles 3–4 lines long; raceme lateral, nearly as long as the leaves, on a peduncle as slender as the branch, 6 lines long, charged above with about 14 alternate flowers on pedicels from 1½ to 6 lines long, supported by slender lanceolate bracts 1½ line long; sepals acute, 1⅓ line long, with an inner rhombic, 3-denticulate scale; corolla white, of a yellowish, roseate or purplish hue, all cano-pubescent outside; tube 16 lines long, narrowed at the base for the length of 9 lines, campanular above; segments rhomboidally ovate, dolabriform, acute within the sinister angle, dextrorsely convolute, 9 lines long and broad; stamens seated on a retrorsely pilose ring in the contraction of the tube; anthers cohering, membranaceous at the apex, obtusely bifurcate at the base, nearly as long as the 2 ovaries.

The leaves on their lower side bear much the peculiar appearance of those of *M. brachystachyus.*

11. MITOZUS RUGOSUS, nob.: *Echites rugosa*, Benth. Journ. Bot. iii. p. 248; A. DC. *l. c.* p. 460: *Amblyanthera versicolor*, var. *intermedia*, Müll. *l. c.* p. 146. In Guiana (Schomb. 350): *non vidi.*

A scandent species, its older branches glabrous, the younger scabridly puberulous; leaves oblong, roundly emarginate or subcuneate at the base, shortly acuminate, subcoriaceous, rugous and scabridly pubescent above, or subsequently smooth, cano-tomentose beneath, or afterwards nearly smooth, 2 in. long, petiolate; peduncle of raceme stout, spicately many-flowered; bracts lanceolately subulate, not exceeding the calyx; pedicels very short; sepals short, very acute, each with a broadly ovate inner scale; corolla yellow, with a cylindrical tube 1 in. long, spreading above; segments broad; stamens seated on a pilose ring in the contraction of the tube; disk urceolate, of 5 oblong fleshy obtuse lobes, partly subconnate.

Müller regarded this plant as a variety of *E. versicolor.*

12. MITOZUS BRACHYSTACHYUS, nob.: *Echites brachystachya*, Benth. Journ. Bot. iii. p. 248; *Amblyanthera versicolor*, var. *β, intermedia*, Müll. *l. c.* p. 146. In Guiana Brit.: *v. s. in herb. meo* (Schomb. 350, in errore) *et in herb., Mus. Brit.* (Schomb. 565).

A climbing species, with very slender flexuous pubescent branches, with ciliate axils 3–4 in. apart; leaves elliptic-oblong, auriculately cordate at the base, acute and mucronate at the summit, membranaceous, dark green above, opake, finely puberulous, nerves immersed, palish green beneath, opake, cano-tomentellous, with fine reddish prominulent nerves, transverse veins very reticulated, 2–3 in. long, $\frac{3}{4}$–$1\frac{1}{4}$ in. broad, on pubescent petioles 2–3 lines long; raceme lateral, 2 in. long, on a stout scabrid peduncle 1 in. long, bearing above many spicate flowers on alternate pedicels, pubescent, 2 lines long, with acute bracts; sepals triangularly acute, recurved at the apex, gibbous at the base, 2 lines long, each with 2 inner acute scales; tube of corolla 20 lines long, narrowly contracted at the base for 4 lines, broadly funnel-shaped above, membranaceous, often plicated into a narrower space; segments inequilateral, broadly dolabriform, 9 lines long and broad; stamens seated in the contraction of the tube, on a dense white pilose ring; disk urceolate, fleshy, with a 5-cleft margin surrounding the ovaries.

A species very near *M. versicolor* in the peculiar appearance of its leaves.

13. MITOZUS SYMPHITOCARPUS, nob.: *Echites symphitocarpa*, Mey. Ess. p. 132; A. DC. *l. c.* p. 467; Griseb. Flor. Brit. W. Ind. p. 414 (sub *Synechites*). In Guiana, Essequibo: *non vidi.*

A climbing species near *M. brachystachyus*, with simple cirrus-like shining branches, subscabridly rufescent, with white lenticels; leaves opposite, patent, elliptic-ovate, obtuse, sagittately cordate, with an acute sinus at the base (younger ones there almost entire), acute or acuminate, subscabrid above, tomentose beneath, reticulately veined, on curving petioles ⅛ in. long; racemes lateral, simple, pubescent, 2 in. long; sepals puberulous, subulate, acuminate; corolla 2 in. long, glabrous, yellow, variegated with white and red; tube cylindrical, swollen above the base, campanulate near the mouth, marked inside with several white, retrorsely sericeous lines; segments acuminately uncinate at the angle; stamens inserted above the base of the tube; filaments compressed, thickened and subpilose; anthers subsagittate at the base, erect, and cohering; disk urceolate, of 5 fleshy subconnate lobes, enclosing 2 oval ovaries; style as long as the filaments; clavuncle subglobose, terminated by 2 stigmata; follicles 2, terete, torulose, 5 in. long, 3 lines broad, conjoined at the curving summits.

The plant described by Grisebach under the same name, probably belongs to some other species.

14. MITOZUS CUYABENSIS, nob.: *Echites Cuyabensis*, A. DC. *l. c.* p. 462: *Amblyanthera Cuiabensis*, Müll. *l. c.* p. 145. In Cuyaba: *non vidi*.

A species with slender, virgate, hirtellous branches, with remote axils; leaves elliptic, obtuse and subcordate at the base, very acuminate, rigidly membranaceous, subglabrous, with parallel divergent nerves, 5 in. long, 1½–2 in. broad, on petioles 4–5 lines long; raceme as long as the leaves, scabro-hirtellous, on a thick angular peduncle, bearing many flowers on pedicels 1½–2 lines long, supported by ovate-subulate bracteoles 1–2 lines long; sepals ovate-acuminate, subglabrous, 2 lines long, each with an inner simple or bifid scale; corolla glabrous; tube cylindrical below the middle, funnel-shaped above, 1½ in. long; segments 1 in. long; disk urceolate, of 5 fleshy subconnate lobes, half as long as the 2 puberulous ovaries; follicles 2, subtorulose, glabrous, 7–9 in. long, 1½ line thick; seeds with a deep-yellow coma.

This is said by Müller to be near his *E. versicolor*, var. *glabrata*.

15. MITOZUS CONCINNUS, nob.: ramulis tenuissimis, pallidis, striolatis; foliis patentibus, ovato-oblongis, imo rotundato-obtusis, apice acutis, tenuiter chartaceis, marginibus revolutis, supra viridibus, impresse corrugulosis, nervis arcuatis immersis, subtus flavescenti-opacis, costa, nervis venisque transversim reticulatis vix prominulis; petiolis tenuibus, quam limbus 20plo brevioribus: racemis axillaribus, simplicibus, quam folium triplo brevioribus, glabris, plurifloris; pedicellis tenuissimis; sepalis linearibus, submembranaceis, singulis squamula lata intus munitis; corollæ tubo cylindrico; segmentis deltoideis, quam tubus triplo brevioribus; staminibus medio tubi insertis; antheris acuminatis, basi parallele furcatis; stylo tenui; clavuncula crasse cylindrica; stigmatibus 2, obtusis, terminalibus. In Brasilia, prov. Alagoas: *v. s. in herb. Mus. Brit.* Penédo, Rio S. Francisco (Gardner 1353).

A very slender climbing plant, with axils 3 in. apart; leaves 2½–2¾ in. long, ⅞–1 in. broad, on petioles 1¼ line long; pedicels 3 lines long; sepals 1 line long; tube of corolla 6 lines long; segments 3 lines long and broad; disk urceolate, of 5 fleshy subconnate lobes.

16. MITOZUS BREVIPES, nob.: *Echites brevipes*, Benth. in Pl. Hartw. p. 216: *Mesechites brevipes*, Müll. in Linn. xxx. p. 454. In Nova Granada: *v. s. in herb. Mus. Brit.* Rio Mesa, prov. Bogota (Hartwegg 1195).

A climbing species with very slender terete branches; leaves subpatent, ovate-oblong, rounded at the base, and there obsoletely cordate, acutely acuminate, rigidly chartaceous, margins subrevolute, fuscous green above, sulcate along the yellowish midrib and nerves, which are arcuately conjoined near the margin, palish beneath, with reddish prominent midrib and nerves barbate in their axils, transversely veined, 2½–2¾ in. long, 1¼–1⅜ in. broad, on petioles 2 lines long; axillary racemes 1½ in. long, bearing several flowers, on bibracteolate pedicels 2 lines long; sepals acutely lanceolate, 1 line long, each with a bidentate internal scale; tube of corolla narrow, contracted in the middle, 4–5 lines long; segments 1½–2 lines long, dextrorsely convolute; stamens inserted in the middle of the tube on a pilose ring; anthers with 2 very narrow parallel obtuse forks at the base; disk urceolate, of 5 obtuse lobes, subconnate, as long as the sepals, and half the length of the ovaries; style filiform; clavuncle incrassate, supporting 2 short stigmata; follicles 2, on a peduncle 1½ in. long, slender, subparallel, terete, somewhat torulose, 7 in. long; seeds linear, compressed, 3 lines long, with a reddish coma 6 lines long.

A species very near the preceding.

17. MITOZUS SCABRIDULUS, nob. In Brasilia, *v. s. in herb. Mus. Brit.* ad Rio de Janeiro, Santa Thereza (Bowie & Cunningham).

A scandent species: its branches are slender, with axils 2–2½ in. apart; leaves patently opposite, ovate, truncately obtuse at the base, where they are shortly constricted upon the petiole, suddenly narrowed at the summit into a short acumen, rigidly chartaceous, with very revolute margins, fuscous-green above, finely corrugulate, sulcate along the semi-immersed oblique nerves and very reticulate veins, with granular glands at the base of the yellow carinate midrib, flavidly opake beneath, with prominent fuscous slender midrib and nerves, shortly scabrid over their surface, 1¾–2¼ in. long, 1–1¼ in. broad, on slender fuscous scabridulous petioles, 3–4 lines long; racemes axillary, 1½–2¼ in. long, with a flexuose rachis, shortly pedunculate at the base, and bearing many close flowers spicately disposed on slender subrecurved twisted scabridulous pedicels 3 lines long, supported by acute minute bracteoles; sepals linear, acuminate, gibbous at the base, subreflexed at the apex, subscabrid, 2 lines long; corolla yellow, scabridulous outside, glabrous within, 3 lines long; tube 2 lines long; segments dolabriform, membranaceous, 1 line long, dextrorsely convolute; stamens almost included; anthers very slender, glabrous, acuminate, with 2 long slender basal prongs; disk of 5 subconnate lobes, a little shorter than the 2 glabrous ovaries.

18. MITOZUS DISCOLOR, nob.: *Echites discolor*, Moritz, MSS. In Venezuela, sine loco (Moritz 1299): *in herb. meo.*

A species nearly approaching the preceding; its branches are somewhat slender, fistulous, scabridly pubescent, with axils 2½ in. apart; leaves opposite, suberect, lanceolate-oblong, narrowed towards each extremity, very shortly and narrowly subcordate at the base, with an apical narrow linear acumen, subchartaceous, margins scarcely revolute, fuscous green and opake above, with an impressed punctulate surface, scabridulous, with immersed nerves, beneath covered with a pubescent tomentum not very dense, with a pale prominulent midrib, 2¼ in. long, 3 lines broad, on hirto-pubescent petioles 2 lines long; panicle axillary, 1¼ in. long, all hirto-puberulous, on a peduncle 3 lines long, furnished above with 6–8 subsecund alternate flowers, on pedicels 2 lines long, each supported by a setiform puberulous bract 3 lines long; sepals acute, puberulous, 1 line long, terminated by a setiform appendage of the same length. The corolla had fallen away; but another was seen in an extremely young state covered with dense ferruginous tomentum.

19. MITOZUS MEXICANUS, nob.: *Prestonia Mexicana*, A. DC. l. c. p. 429. In Mexico ad Oaxaca (Andrieux 251) : *non vidi.*

A climbing species, with broadly ovate leaves, rounded and subcordate at the base, suddenly acuminate at the apex, pubescent above, rufo-tomentose beneath, 4–6 in. long, 3–4 in. broad, on petioles 2–4 lines long; inflorescence rufo-tomentose; sepals pubescent on both sides, 7 lines long, with an inner short ovate-truncate denticulate scale, glabrous inside; tube of corolla a little longer than the calyx, its mouth 5-sulcate, furnished with 5 small glands, without appendages; stamens inserted on a retrorsely pilose ring in the middle of the tube; disk urceolate, 5-sulcate, with 5 crenate teeth on the margin, or, in other words, of 5 subconnate lobes.

20. MITOZUS JAMAICENSIS, nob.: *v. s. in herb. Mus. Brit.* Jamaica (Dr. Wright).

A species having very slender twining branches, with axils ½–1 in. apart; leaves oblong, cordate at the base, acute and shortly acuminate, with revolute margins, chartaceous, green above, corrugulate, opake, with immersed nerves, ferruginously opake beneath, with a reddish prominulent hirsute midrib and rubescent smooth nerves and much-reticulated veins, 1–1½ in. long, 7–10 lines broad, on petioles 1–2 lines long; raceme axillary, 4 lines long, on a very slender peduncle 1½ in. long, bearing upwards several alternate flowers on filiform pedicels 9 lines long; sepals ovate-lanceolate, 1 line long; corolla dark-red; tube cylindrical, contracted below the middle, 10 lines long; segments obliquely obtuse, undulate on the margins, dextrorsely convolute, 4 lines long; stamens inserted above the base of the tube; anthers linear, acuminate, with 2 subacute basal prongs; disk urceolate, of 5 oblong roundish lobes connate at the base.

SECONDATIA.

This genus was established by Prof. A. De Candolle in 1844, and afterwards illustrated by Prof. Müller in the 'Flora Brasiliensis.' It consists of a few slender scandent species, the branches minutely crenulate across the nodes, with extremely small intrapetiolar stipules, opposite petiolate leaves, and a terminal, very short raceme, furnished with few very inconspicuous flowers on a short divided peduncle. The fruit is peculiar in shape, consisting of 2 suberect follicles, broad and fusiform, woody, containing many seeds, with a long elastic coma of numerous spreading hairs, recurving outwards in a trumpet-form.

The *Secondatia arborea*, Müll. (*Echites arborea*, Velloz) is referred to *Malouetia*, antè, p. 89.

SECONDATIA, A. DC. *Sepala* 5, parva, acuto-ovata, subæqualia, imbricata, intus squamulis totidem minutis alternis aut oppositis irregulariter sitis munita. *Corolla* subparva; *tubus* subbrevis, imo constrictus, superne paulissime ampliatus, intus pilosulus; *segmenta* trapezoideo-dolabriformia, apice sinuato-truncata, tubum æquantia aut superantia, expansa, in æstivatione dextrorsum convoluta. *Stamina* imo tubi inserta et eidem subæquilonga; *filamenta* subbrevia, glabra; *antheræ* lineares, in conum cohærentes, apice acuminatæ, imo in aristis 2 tenues paullo divergentes fissæ, dorso hirsutæ. *Discus* urceolatus, fere ad basin in lobos 5 obtusos fissus; *ovaria* 2, subglobosa, disco paullulo breviora. *Folliculi* 2, fusiformi-oblongi, aut ovatiores, validi, sublignosi, divaricatim erecti, sutura ventrali dehiscentes, et ibi placentiferi; *placenta* coriacea, striata; *semina* numerosa, lineari-oblonga; *coma* magna, e pilis longis elasticis subrevolutim curvatis; *embryo* in *albumine, cotyledonibus* semiteretibus, quam *radicula* supera triplo longioribus.

Suffrutices *intertropici, plerumque Brasiliani, subscandentes, glabri*; folia *opposita, oblonga, plerumque parvula, petiolata*; inflorescentia *terminalis, breviter racemosa, pluri- vel pauciflora*; flores *inconspicui.*

1. SECONDATIA DENSIFLORA, A. DC. Prodr. viii. p. 445; Müll. Fl. Bras. xxvi. p. 108, tab. 32 (anal. floris et fructus). In Brasilia, prov. Cuyaba et Goyas: *v. s. in herb. Mus. Brit.* Cuyaba (Manso, *ex herb. Martius*); *in herb. meo* prov. Goyas (Gardner 3325).

Prof. De Candolle unites with this a specimen from Guiana, a species alluded to by Bentham (Lond. Journ. Bot. iii. p. 250, sub Schomb. 599). Müller joins with it other plants from Minas and Guiana; but from the differences in the diagnoses of De Candolle and of Müller, and from the discordance in the floral analysis of the latter from that I observed in Manso's specimen, we may conclude that two, if not three, species have been confounded together by Müller. The following description of the species is given from a careful examination of the specimens of Manso and Gardner. Müller's floral analysis therefore relates not to this species, but to another, either from Minas or Guiana.

It is apparently a scandent plant, having somewhat slender, curving, subfistulose, sublenticellate, striate, glabrous branches, with axils 1¼ in. apart, and a small acute stipule on each side of the opposite petioles; leaves ovate-oblong, roundish or subacute at the base, suddenly constricted at the summit into a narrowish subacute acumen, the margins sinuously undulating, thinly chartaceous, glabrous, green above, midrib prominulent, with 12 pairs of fine distinct divergent nerves, free and somewhat arching but not conjoined within the margin, a little darker beneath, opake, with prominulent nerves and scarcely visible transverse veins, 3–4 in. long, 1¼–2 in. broad, on subpatent channelled petioles 4–5 lines long; panicle terminal, in the sinus between the ultimate pair of leaves, nearly 1 in. long, biramose at the base, the branches divided and bearing from 20 to 40 small flowers on approximate alternate pedicels 2–3 lines long, supported each by a bracteole the size of the sepals; sepals ovate, obtuse, with ciliate membranaceous margins, ¾ line long; corolla hypocrateriform; tube cylindrical, inside glabrous in the middle towards the base, but thickly pilose in the mouth, 4 lines long; segments ovate, slightly dolabriform, dextrorsely convolute, 2 lines long, 1½ line broad; stamens seated near the base of the tube; filaments short, puberulous; anthers linear, 2¼ lines long, very acuminate, with 2 parallel basal prongs; disk urceolate, cleft halfway into 5 obtuse lobes nearly as long as the ovaries; follicles 2, subdivergent, often solitary by abortion, with a thickish ligneous pericarp, fusiformly oblong, broadish, 5 in. long, 1¼ in. broad in the middle; seeds many (as in the gen. char.), 8½ lines long, surmounted by a white, widely spreading, recurving coma 18 lines long.

A drawing of this species, in flower and in fruit, is shown in Plate XXXII.

2. SECONDATIA FLORIBUNDA, A. DC. p. 446; Müll. *l. c.* p. 109. In Brasilia, prov. Bahia, ad Jacobina (Blanchet 3370): *non vidi*.

A scandent glabrous species, with slender terete branches; leaves elliptic, very obtuse at the base, with a lanceolately cuspidate apex; nerves pellucid, with finely reticulated veins, 2½ in. long, 15–17 lines broad, on petioles 4–5 lines long; panicles spreading, trichotomously divided, a little longer than the leaves, with branches 8–9 lines long, bearing many flowers on very slender pedicels 4–5 lines long, supported by lanceolate bracts ½ line long; sepals a little larger than the bracts, lanceolate; tube of corolla glabrous, 3 lines long; segments oblong, a little longer than it; disk of 5 dentate lobes, a little shorter than the ovaries.

3. SECONDATIA POLIOSA, A. DC. *l. c.* p. 446; Müll. *l. c.* p. 109, tab. 32. fig. 1. In Brasilia, prov. Bahia, ad Jacobina (Blanchet 3685) et prov. Ceará: *v. s. in herb. Mus. Brit.* Oeiras (Gardner 1762).

A glabrous species, differing from the two preceding in its smaller, more approximate leaves acute at both extremities, with many transversely reticulated veins, 1½–1¾ in. long, 7–8 lines broad, on petioles 2–3 lines long; terminal panicles more compact, much shorter than the leaves, with branches 3–4 lines long, bearing many flowers on slender pedicels 2–3 lines long; sepals acute, ½ line long; tube of corolla 2¼ lines long; segments oblique-oblong, rotate, 2½ lines long.

4. SECONDATIA FERRUGINEA, nob.: *Echites ferruginea*, Rich. Fl. Cub. xi. p. 92; Walp. Ann. v. p. 494. In Cuba, Guanabacos (Sagra): *non vidi*.

A species with a weak branching stem, and slender, red, hirtous branchlets; leaves small, obtusely elliptic or obovate, obtuse at the base, glabrous above, subferruginously opake beneath, on short petioles; inflorescence terminal, bearing 3 or many flowers upon rather long pedicels, glabrous; sepals ovate-acuminate; corolla small, yellow, funnel-shaped, with a narrow tube nearly three times as long as the sepals; follicles 2, erect, parallel, acute, 3–4 in. long, 1 in. broad.

5. SECONDATIA SCHLIMIANA, Müll. in Linn. xxx. p. 416. In Nova Granada ad Ocanna (Schlim 510): *non vidi*.

A species with glabrous, terete, obscurely reddish, lenticellate branchlets, with axils 4–5 in. apart; leaves elliptic, acute at the base, cuspidately acuminate, nerves with transverse veins much reticulated, 2–2¾ in. long, 9½–16½ lines broad, on petioles 5–6 lines long; a spreading terminal panicle 1½ in. long, much divided, puberulous, many-flowered; flowers on rigid pedicels 3 lines long; sepals 1¼ line long; tube of corolla glabrous, hispid within, 2¾ lines long; segments obliquely ovoid, glabrous; anthers dorsally pubescent; disk 5-lobed, as long as the ovaries.

6. SECONDATIA PERUVIANA, Pöpp. Nov. Gen. iii. p. 71, tab. 281. In Peruvia, ad Cuchero: *non vidi*.

This is described as a climbing plant, hanging from the summit of trees 30–40 feet high, having many branches 3–4 in. thick, intertwining, covered with a dark rough bark. Its branchlets are slender, straight, smooth, their axils scarcely dilated, 1½–2 in. apart, bearing 2 extremely small stipules; the leaves are elliptic, broadish at the base, and suddenly narrowed upon the petiole, acutely acuminate, subundulate on the margins, membranaceous, smooth above, glaucous beneath, with fine divergent nerves and transverse veins, 4 in. long, 2 in. broad, on slender petioles 5 lines long; panicles opposite, axillary, shorter than the leaves; peduncle slender, 1 in. long, its summit divided into 2 slender branches, with a solitary pedicellate flower in the dichotomy, each branch 1½ in. long, bearing 6–8 alternate flowers on bracteolate pedicels 1¼ line long, laxly disposed; sepals acutely ovate, 1 line long; tube of corolla stoutishly cylindrical, 9 lines long, 5-sulcate, narrowed in the middle and contracted in the mouth, which is there furnished with a pilose ring; segments obtusely oblong, inequilateral, dextrorsely convolute, 2½ lines long; stamens seated a little above the base of the tube; anthers acuminate, divided at the base into 2 acute subdiverging prongs; style extremely short, stoutish; clavuncle incrassate, claviform, with a membranous basal appendage; disk urceolate, 5-lobed on margin, shorter than the 2 unilocular ovaries; follicles 2, oblong, very divaricate, in an immature state plano-convex, containing numerous imbricate seeds, too much injured by insects for their structure to be ascertained.

All these characters seem to favour the conclusion of Pöppig, that the plant belongs to *Secondatia*.

HAPLOPHYTON.

A genus established by Prof. De Candolle in 1844 (Prodr. viii. p. 412), upon a Mexican plant in Pavon's herbarium and a drawing of the same by Mocinno et Sesse, named *Echites cimicifuga*. It is a shrubby plant, subherbaceous, with very slender terete, erect, dichotomous, puberulous branches; leaves subopposite, subdistichous, narrowly ovate-acuminate, thinly membranaceous, puberulous, with hairs arising from vesicles, glandular in the axils of the oblique nerves, veinless, 2–2¾ in. long, 8–10 lines broad, on petioles 1–1½ line long; flowers geminate in the dichotomies of the branchlets, on puberulous pedicels three times as long as the petioles; sepals linear-acuminate, 2 lines long, erect, without inner scales, subpilose outside; corolla hypocrateriform, 9 lines long, pale yellowish; tube 4 lines long, cylindrical, broader in the middle, glabrous in the mouth and at the base, otherwise internally pilose; segments oblong-obovate, more than twice the length of the tube, simply sinistrorsely convolute; stamens inserted in the middle of the tube on slender filaments; anthers linear, obtuse, shortly and roundly bilobed at the base; disk none; style filiform; stigma capitate, 2-lobed; follicles 2, narrowly terete, erect, straight, striate, at first subpuberulous, 2 in. long; seeds many, linear-oblong, crowned with a coma of equal length.

The specimen is from Tehuantepec (Andrieux 250).

MESECHITES.

This is a valid genus, when restricted within the uniform limits indicated by the several species here described. It was established in 1860 by Müller, who unfortunately figured as its type the *Echites Mansoana* of De Candolle, from Matto Grosso, a plant before enumerated (*suprà*, p. 201); with this he confounded, as a mere variety, the *Echites sulphurea* from Rio de Janeiro, well figured by Velloz, a very different plant (*Echites Vauthieri*, DC.). *Mesechites*, however, is well figured by Jacquin in the plates 27 and 28 of his 'Stirpium Americanarum.'

The following is a reformed diagnosis of the genus.

MESECHITES, Müll. (in parte): char. emend. *Sepala* parva, æqualia, acuta aut obtusa, intus squamula acuta singulatim munita. *Corolla* hypocrateriformis; *tubus* cylindricus, infra medium tenuiter angustatus, superne paullo latior; *segmenta* 5, dolabriformia, tubi dimidia longitudine, rotatim expansa, dextrorsum convoluta. *Stamina* ad medium tubi inserta, inclusa; *filamenta* brevia; *antheræ* subcohærentes, oblongæ, membrana acuta apiculatæ, imo in furcas 2 obtusas divisæ. *Discus* e lobis 5 liberis, aut basi brevissime nexis; *ovaria* 2, disco longiora; *stylus* gracilis, stamina attingens; *clavuncula* incrassata, conice oblonga, subpentagona, imo membrana lacerata munita; *stigmata* 2, linearia, terminalia. *Folliculi* 2, lineares, sæpius torosi, erecti. *Semina* acuta vel obtuse linearia, *coma* sericea coronata.

Herbæ *repentes, vel* suffrutices *humiles Americæ calidioris*; folia *opposita, sæpe cordata*; racemi *sæpius axillares, pauciflori*; flores *subparvi, sæpius rubescentes.*

1. MESECHITES REPENS, nob.: *Echites repens*, Jacq. Amer. p. 33, tab. 28; Lam. Dict. ii. p. 340; A. DC. Prodr. viii. p. 449 (excl. syn.); Schlecht. Linn. xxvi. p. 666; Griseb. Fl. Br. W. Ind. p. 414. In Antillis: *non vidi*.

A species notable for its narrow-lanceolate leaves and bifid peduncle, with small red flowers. It is a procumbent plant, with slender glabrous branches, incrassate at the axils, which are 1–2 in. apart, and which often throw out suckers that take root; leaves lanceolate, subcordate at the base, acute, 1¼ in. long, 3 lines broad, on petioles 1½ line long; raceme axillary, as long as the leaves; peduncle 1 in. long, divided at its summit into 2 branches, each bearing 2–3 flowers on pedicels 1 line long, all bracteolate; sepals slender, 1 line long; corolla red, its narrow cylindrical tube swelling above, 7 lines long; segments dolabriform, 4 lines long and broad; disk of 5 rounded lobes, distinct, half as long as the ovaries; follicles linear, torulose, 6 in. long.

2. MESECHITES TORULOSA, nob.: *Echites torulosa*, Linn. Sp. Pl. (in parte), p. 307; Lam. Dict. ii. p. 339 (excl. syn. et tab. 174); Sw. Obs. p. 105; Griseb. Fl. Brit. W. Ind. p. 414: *Echites torosa*, Jacq. Amer. p. 33, tab. 27; A. DC. *l. c.* p. 449; Griseb. *l. c.* p. 414: *Amblyanthera torosa*, Müll. in Linn. xxx. p. 446. In Antillis: *v. s. in herb. meo, in flore*, Jamaica (Heward) : *in herb. Mus. Brit.* Campêche (Schott 673 in flore).

The above plants agree well with the drawing of Jacquin above cited. Linnæus suppressed the name *torosa*, substituting for it that of *torulosa*, although he quoted the more copious description and drawing of Jacquin to explain his own laconic character.

Both were equally wrong in adopting as its synonym the *Nerium sarmentosum* of P. Browne, which is *Mesechites myrtifolium*. Swartz, who well described Jacquin's plant, avoided this mistake, considering that the drawing of the latter better represented the species than that of Browne.

It is a subscandent plant, with an abundant lactescent juice; its branches are very slender, smooth, bifid towards the summit, with axils $1\frac{1}{2}$–$2\frac{1}{2}$ in. apart; the opposite leaves are patent, oblong, narrowing towards the base, acute and mucronulate at the apex, opake-green above, with about 8 pairs of diverging nerves, sulcate on the reticulated veins, pale glaucous beneath, opake, midrib pale and prominulent, with immersed nerves, 1-2 in. long, 4–7 lines broad, on scabridulous petioles $1\frac{1}{3}$ line long; raceme axillary, very short, on a peduncle 2 lines long, bearing 3 to 6 alternate smallish flowers on capillary pedicels $2\frac{1}{4}$ lines long; sepals sharply acuminate, subreflexed at the apex, glabrous, 2 lines long, $\frac{1}{4}$ line broad; tube of corolla slender, a little swollen in the middle, 6 lines long; segments broadly dolabriform, rotate, with dextrorse convolution, 4 lines long, 3 lines broad, of a pale rubescent colour; follicles 2, erect, terete, acuminate, torulose, with small oblong comose seeds.

3. MESECHITES LANCEOLATA, nob.: *Nerium foliis lanceolatis*, Plum. Amer. i. p. 20, tab. 27. fig. 1: *Echites repens*, A. DC. in parte (non Jacq.), *l. c.* p. 449. In America tropica: *non vidi*.

A twining species, extremely different from *M. repens*: it has terete, very flexuose slender branches, with axils $1\frac{1}{4}$–$1\frac{1}{2}$ in. apart; leaves very patently opposite, lanceolately oblong, roundish at the base, subobtusely narrowed at the summit, with about 8 pairs of divergently ascending nerves curvingly connected near the margin, 2–$2\frac{1}{4}$ in. long, 6–$6\frac{1}{4}$ lines broad, on petioles 2 lines long; raceme lateral, on a peduncle $1\frac{1}{2}$ in. long, bearing on its summit 3–4 subapproximate flowers on pedicels 2 lines long; sepals small, subacute; tube of corolla slender, 8 lines long; segments dolabriform, 4 lines long and broad, rotately expanded, with dextrorse convolution; follicles 2, pendulous, slender, subarcuate, very torose, 7 in. long; seeds smallish, with an apical coma 6 lines long.

This species differs from *M. torulosa* in its long, simple, flexuose branches, larger and less acute leaves, and a raceme upon a lengthened peduncle, and longer flowers.

4. MESECHITES ANGUSTIFOLIA, nob.: *Echites angustifolia*, Poir. (non Benth.) Dict. Suppl. ii. p. 537; A. DC. *l. c.* p. 449; Schl. Linn. xxvi. p. 665. In Antillis ad San Domingo: *non vidi*.

The very slender twining branches are glabrous and lactescent; the opposite leaves are long and extremely narrow, glabrous, entire, almost sessile, linear, rounded at the base, acute at the summit, marked by a midrib and 2 simple parallel nerves, more than 3 in. long, 2 lines broad; inflorescence axillary, very short, on a slender, bifid, 2-flowered puberulous peduncle; flowers small, white; follicles 2, very slender, torulose, compressed, glabrous, 6-8 in. long.

5. MESECHITES LINEARIFOLIA, nob.: *Echites linearifolia*, Ham. Prodr. Pl. Ind. Occid. p. 31; A. DC. *l. c.* p. 449. In Hispaniola, Cap. Henrici: *non vidi*.

A lactescent species near the preceding, differing principally in its white flowers. Its slender funiform branches are glabrous; leaves linear, very narrow, mucronate, on very short petioles; peduncles axillary, filiform, shorter than the leaves, with 2 floriferous branches, each bearing several small white flowers.

6. MESECHITES ANGUSTATA, nob.: *Echites angustifolia*, Benth. (non Poir.), Hook. Journ. Bot. iii. p. 247. In Guiana Brit.: *v. s. in herb. Mus. Brit.* prope cataractam Kaietur (Appun).

This species was found by Schomburgk in the sandstone region near Mount Roraima, and afterwards by Appun at the great fall of Kaietur on a tributary river of the lower Essequibo. It is a shrubby plant, with thickish branches and slender subflexuose branchlets, with axils ¾–1 in. apart; leaves opposite or ternate, patent, lanceolate-oblong, obtusely narrowed toward the base, obtuse and mucronulate at the apex, subcoriaceous, with very revolute margins, subnitid above, deeply sulcate along the midrib, with many very patent immersed nerves, opake and yellowish beneath, with a very prominent reddish midrib, and semi-immersed nerves, 1–1½ in. long, 1½–2¼ lines broad, on channelled petioles 1 line long; raceme with a flexuose rachis, bearing smallish flowers, on short thick pedicels; sepals acutely oblong, ¾ line long; corolla scarlet, salver-shaped; tube 1 in. long, narrower below the middle, somewhat broader above; segments more orange-coloured, obliquely ovate, 3 lines long, 2 lines broad; stamens inserted in the contraction of the tube upon a pilose ring; filaments slender; anthers obtusely bilobed at the base; disk of 5 free oblong lobes as long as the ovaries; follicles 2, slender, terete, arcuate, conjoined at the apex.

7. MESECHITES SUBCARNOSA, nob.: *Echites subcarnosa*, Benth. Hook. Journ. Bot. iii. p. 247: *Mandevilla subcarnosa*, Benth. & Hook. Gen. ii. p. 727. In Guiana Brit. circa Roraima (Schomburgk): *v. s. in herb. Mus. Brit.* prope cataractam Kaietur (Appun).

A glabrous shrubby species, near the preceding, with a stoutish subfleshy stem and slender scandent fuscous branchlets; these are thickened across the approximate axils, which are 1½ line apart; leaves opposite, lanceolate-elliptic, somewhat attenuated towards each extremity, with a short subobtuse acumen, margins subrevolute, chartaceous, dark green above, with 6 pairs of distant horizontally patent nerves conjoined near the margins, as in *Plumeria*, with immersed transversely reticulate veins, ochreously paler beneath, opake, with a fuscous prominulent midrib and nerves, nearly 2 in. long or longer, 5 lines broad, on slender channelled petioles 2 lines long; raceme with several subspicate flowers on short pedicels; sepals acute, 1½ line long; corolla salver-shaped, tube a little wider above; fructiferous peduncle 6 lines long, closely cicatrized; follicles 2, slender, terete, subtorulose, 4–4½ in. long, 1 line thick; seeds 4 lines long, linear, with a reddish spreading coma 6 lines long, the outer hairs somewhat shorter.

The above details accord well with Mr. Bentham's description. The authors of the 'Genera Plantarum' (ii. p. 727), however, regard this plant as belonging to *Mandevilla*; but if we compare one with the other it will be seen that they are utterly at variance in almost every character, so that this view must be discarded.

8. MESECHITES MYRTIFOLIA, Müll. (in parte) Linn. xxx. p. 445: *Echites myrtifolia*, R. & Sch. (non Poir.) Syst. iv. p. 795; A. DC. *l. c.* p. 473: *Echites torulosa*, Lam. (in parte) Dict. ii. p. 332; Illust. tab. 174. fig. 1: *Nerium sarmentosum* (4), P. Browne, Jam. p. 181, tab. 16. fig. 2. In Antillis: *v. s. in herb. Mus. Brit.* Jamaica (Houston, in fructu).

A slender, low, weakly species with twining glabrous or scabridulous branches, the axils being ¾ in. apart; leaves subpatently opposite, elliptic-ovate, obsoletely subcordate at the base, subacute and mucronate at the apex, chartaceous, with subrevolute margins, green above, opake, with immersed divergent nerves, yellowish opake beneath, with prominent red midrib and nerves, veins transversely reticulated, 14 lines long, 7 lines broad, on slender petioles 1½ line long; inflorescence terminal or axillary, on a peduncle 9 lines long, bearing beyond several alternate flowers on pedicels 2½–3 lines long; sepals linear acuminate, 1½ line long; corolla salver-shaped, rose-coloured; tube slender, a little swollen in the middle, 6 lines long; segments dolabriform, 5 lines long, 3 lines broad, rotate; stamens enclosed in the middle of the tube; follicles 2, on a peduncle 4 lines long, extremely slender, terete, substriate, torulose, 6 in. long, 1½ line broad, enclosing several comose seeds.

Müller united into one species this and the following; but this differs in its larger and more ovate leaves, and its corolla with a tube more than double the length of the other.

A drawing of this species, in flower and fruit, showing its floral analysis, is given in Plate XXXIII. A.

9. MESECHITES ROSEA, nob.: *Echites rosea*, A. DC. *l. c.* p. 450; Griseb. in Pl. Cub. p. 520. In Cuba: *v. s. in herb. Mus. Brit.* Cuba (La Sagra 142 in flore, Wright 1662 in fructu).

A climbing species with scabrid slender branches, filiform above, with axils ¾–1¼ in. apart; leaves patently opposite, rarely ternate, ovate-oblong, rounded and obsoletely cordate at the base, rounded and mucronulate at the summit, subcoriaceous, with revolute margins, green above, with obscure immersed nerves, beneath yellowish-opake, with very prominent midrib and diverging nerves (about 8 pairs), 9 lines long, 3–5 lines broad, on slender petioles ½ line long; raceme axillary, short, on a peduncle bearing 2–3 rose-coloured flowers on very slender pedicels 2 lines long; sepals acute, 1 line long; corolla hypocrateriform; tube narrowly cylindrical, 12 lines long, slightly ventricose above the middle; segments inequilaterally ovate, very rotate, 6 lines long, 4 lines broad, with dextrorse convolution; stamens inserted in the middle of the tube; disk of 5 oblong obtuse lobes, shorter than the ovaries; follicles 2, subcompressed, torulose, 9 in. long, 2 lines broad, on a peduncle 6 lines long.

10. MESECHITES BROWNEI, nob.: *Echites torosa*, var. *Brownei*, A. DC. *l. c.* p. 449; Müll. Linn. xxx. p. 446: *Echites Brownei*, Griseb. *l. c.* p. 414. In America tropica: *v. s. in herb. Mus. Brit.* Campêche (Houston), Cuba (Schott 38).

A species differing in all respects from *M. torulosa*, especially in the size and shape of its leaves and in its inflorescence. The branches and branchlets are very slender, scandent; the leaves subapproximate, appearing remote from the falling-off of the intervening leaves; they are subpatently opposite, broadly ovate-elliptic, obtuse and cordate at the base, suddenly briefly acute and mucronate at the summit, very membranaceous, smooth on the margins, opake-green above, with very slender subimmersed nerves, pallidly yellowish and opake beneath, with nerves scarcely prominulent, $2\frac{1}{4}$–$2\frac{3}{4}$ in. long, $1\frac{1}{2}$–$1\frac{3}{8}$ in. broad, on slender petioles $2\frac{1}{2}$–3 lines long; racemes axillary, on a very slender peduncle $2\frac{1}{4}$ in. long, bearing several alternate yellow flowers $1\frac{1}{2}$ line apart, on pedicels bibracteolate in the middle, 4 lines long; sepals acute, 1 line long; 2 slender pendent follicles, 9 in. long, subtorose, with many lengthened interruptions.

11. MESECHITES HASTATA, nob.: volubilis, ramulis tenuissimis, flexuosis, puberulis, cum axillis remotis; foliis oblongis, imo angustioribus, cum sinu angusto cordatis, apice acuminatis, submembranaceis, marginibus planis, supra laete viridibus, costa nervisque puberulis, subtus fere concoloribus, sparsim pilosulis, costa flavida, pubescente, prominula, petiolis brevibus hirsutulis; racemis lateralibus, folio longioribus, pedunculo pro tertia parte nudo, supra crebre alternatim multifloro; pedicellis imo breviter acute bracteolatis; sepalis brevibus, acutis; corolla hypocrateriformi; tubo cylindrico, medio constricto; segmentis rotatis, oblongis, quam tubus triplo brevioribus. In Cuba: *v. s. in herb. Mus. Brit.* Hacienda Saragosa (Schott 674).

The axils of the very slender branchlets are $2\frac{1}{2}$–5 in. apart; leaves $1\frac{1}{4}$–$1\frac{3}{4}$ in. long, 8–10 lines broad, on petioles $2\frac{1}{4}$ lines long, the narrow basal sinus being 1 line deep.
It is a species approaching *M. Brownei*.

12. MESECHITES DICHOTOMA, nob.: *Echites dichotoma*, H. B. K. iii. p. 217; A. DC. *l. c.* p. 465. In regno Quitensi, prov. Bracamoros: *non vidi*.

A climbing species, with glabrous terete branchlets; leaves ovate-oblong, cordate, acuminate, submembranaceous, entire, glabrous, very reticulately veined, nearly 5 in. long, $2\frac{1}{4}$ in. broad, on channelled petioles 3 lines long; raceme lateral, near 6 in. long, on an elongated peduncle, bearing 2 branches, each furnished with many flowers on glabrous pedicels 6 lines long, but twice that length in the fruit; sepals ovate-lanceolate, shorter than the tube of the corolla; corolla salver-shaped, of a bluish or violet colour; tube constricted near the middle; stamens inserted in the constriction of the tube; anthers cohering, acute, subsagittate; disk 5-cleft, shorter than the 2 ovaries; follicles pendulous, terete, torulose, glabrous, 6 in. long, containing many comose seeds.

13. MESECHITES GUAYAQUILENSIS, nob.: *Echites Guayaquilensis*, Benth. Pl. Hartw. p. 119. In Ecuador: *v. s. in herb. Mus. Brit.* Guayaquil (Hartweg, no. 669).

A slender twining plant, with pubescent branches; leaves ovate, narrowly cordate at the base, subacute, membranaceous, opake, margins ciliate, puberulous above, with fine immersed nerves, paler and opake beneath, subpuberulous, with fuscous midrib and nerves scarcely prominulent and pilose, $1\frac{3}{4}$ in. long, 8 lines broad, on very tomentose petioles $1\frac{1}{2}$ line long; raceme lateral, longer than the leaves; peduncle $1\frac{1}{4}$ in. long, bare at the base for 3 lines, bearing above 6–8 alternate spicate flowers on pedicels 1 line long; sepals acute, $\frac{3}{4}$ line long, each with an internal bidentate scale; tube of corolla slender, tomentous, subinfundibuliform above the middle, 8 lines long; segments ovate, inequilateral, subacute, 3 lines long, 2 lines broad; stamens seated on a pilose ring in the middle of the tube; anthers membranaceously apiculate, shortly bilobed at the base; disk of 5 obtusely oblong fleshy lobes.

14. MESECHITES HIRTELLA, nob.: *Echites hirtella*, H. B. K. iii. p. 213 (non Benth.); A. DC. *l. c.* p. 465. In Nova Granada, prope Mariquita: *non vidi*.

A climbing species, with extremely slender striate shaggy branchlets; leaves oblong, narrowed and cordate at the base, mucronate and acute at the apex, entire, submembranaceous, hirsute on both sides, reticulately veined, with a minute gland at the bottom of the midrib, 2–2⅜ in. long, ¾–1 in. broad, on reddish pilose channelled petioles 2 lines long; raceme lateral, hirtellous, near 2 in. long, on a peduncle 6 lines long, bearing upwards many flowers on pedicels with much shorter lanceolate bracteoles, pilose; sepals ovate, acuminate, imbricate, hirtellous; corolla salver-shaped, yellow, pilose outside; its tube 9–10 lines long, somewhat contracted in the middle, swelling above, with five small red spots in the mouth; segments obliquely inequilateral, obovate, crispate, rotate, half as long as the tube; stamens seated in the constriction of the tube; anthers acuminate, cohering; follicles very slender, subtorulose, rostrate at the apex, glabrous, 5–6 in. long; seeds fusiform, with an apical coma.

15. MESECHITES OAXACANA, nob.: *Echites Oaxacana*, A. DC. *l. c.* p. 451; Benth. Pl. Hartw. p. 350, sub n° 492: *Amblyanthera Oaxacana*, Müll. in Linn. xxx. p. 417. In Mexico, prov. Oaxaca: *non vidi*.

A climbing plant, with slender branchlets; leaves ovate, subcordate, acuminate, membranaceous, with many approximate nerves, reticulated, with 2 small glands at their base, 2–2½ in. long, 9–12 lines broad, on slender petioles 4 lines long; racemes axillary and terminal, as long as the leaves, on a slender peduncle bearing few flowers on pedicels a little longer than the calyx; sepals lanceolate; tube of corolla 5 times as long as the sepals, cylindrical, a little swollen above; segments shorter than the tube; stamens seated above the middle of the tube; disk of 5 acute lobes, longer than the ovaries; follicles 2, 5 in. long, erect, linear, somewhat torulose.

This plant certainly does not belong to *Amblyanthera*, and does not harmonize with the *Echites hirtella*, Benth.

16. MESECHITES BIRTELLULA, nob.: *Echites hirtella*, Benth. (non H. B. K.) Pl. Hartw. p. 67. In Mexico: *v. s. in herb. Mus. Brit.* Puente de Gia (Hartweg 492).

A species near *M. torulosa*, and very different from *Echites hirtella*, H. B. K., which is said by Bentham to be identical with *Echites Oaxacana*, A. DC. It is a twining plant, with filiform glabrous branches, having axils 1–1¾ in. apart; leaves lanceolate-oblong, obtuse and emarginately cordate at the base, gradually narrowing from the middle into a very long acute acumen, membranaceous, pale green above, opake, shortly puberulous, and scabridulous to the touch, with slender midrib and inumersed nerves, paler, with a yellowish hue, and opake beneath, obsoletely puberulous, with slightly prominent reddish midrib and nerves and very reticulate veins, 2¼ in. long, 9 lines broad, on petioles 3 lines long; raceme lateral, 1 in. long, on a slender peduncle bare for half its length, 3 lines long; branchlets alternate, bearing 2 flowers each on pedicels 4 lines long; sepals acuminate, 1½ line long; tube of corolla 10 lines long, slender below, widening a little above the middle; segments dolabriform, acute on one side, rounded on the other, 4 lines long, dextrorsely convolute; stamens inserted on a pilose ring in the middle of the tube; filaments retrorsely pilose; anthers emarginate at the base, acuminate, cohering; disk of 5 obtuse linear fleshy lobes.

17. MESECHITES JASMINIFLORA, nob.: *Echites jasminiflora*, Mart. & Galeotti, Bull. Acad. Brux. xi. p. 357; Walp. Rep. vi. p. 476. In Mexico: *non vidi*.

A twining species, with slender puberulous branches; leaves lanceolate, cordate, acuminate, subglabrous above, softly pubescent beneath, on short villous petioles; racemes axillary, pedunculate, longer than the leaves, bearing yellow flowers; sepals small; corolla salver-shaped, 1 in. long; stamens included; follicles very long, torulose. A species near *M. torosa*, with somewhat broader leaves and larger flowers.

18. MESECHITES GUIANENSIS, nob.: *Echites Guianensis*, A. DC. *l. c.* p. 458: *Amblyanthera Guianensis*, Müll. in Linn. xxx. p. 448. In Cayenne: *non vidi*.

A climbing plant with elongated terete scabrid branchlets; leaves ovate or lanceolate, cordate, acuminate, membranaceous, glabrous, having several glands above and near the petiole, reddish nerves and veins, 3–4 in. long, 10–18 lines broad, on petioles 2–3 lines long; raceme lateral, glabrous, nearly as long as the leaves, bearing many spicate flowers on pedicels 1½ line long, supported by lanceolate bracts 3 lines long; sepals ovate, subulate, 2 lines long, with an inner 4-dentate scale; tube of corolla 14 lines long, a little broader below the middle, swelling above; segments half as long as the tube; stamens inserted on a hirsute band at the constriction of the tube; disk of 5 obtuse lobes; follicles torulose, glabrous, patently recurved, 5 in. long, 3 lines broad.

19. MESECHITES ANDRIEUXII, nob.: *Amblyanthera Andrieuxii*, Müll. *l. c.* p. 422. In Mexico, prope Oaxaca (Andrieux 249): *non vidi*.

A somewhat scandent species, with terete, glabrous, reddish, subverrucose branches 1 line thick, with branchlets very scaly at the base, copiously leafy above; leaves narrowly obovate or obovate-lanceolate, acute at both ends, rigidly membranaceous, fuscous, hirto-puberulous above, with about 6 pairs of divergent nerves, obsoletely veined, yellowish beneath, softly pubescent, 9½–13 lines long, 3¼–7 lines broad, on petioles 1½–2¼ lines long; racemes axillary, a little longer than the leaves, subdeflexed, subglabrous, bearing many small flowers, the 2 lower ones opposite, the others alternate, on rigid pedicels 1–1½ line long, supported by puberulous lanceolate bracteoles of the same length; sepals ovate-lanceolate, puberulous outside, with membranaceous margins, 3 lines long, with 4–8 inner subulate scales; corolla in the whole 5¾–7 lines long; its cylindrical tube broader at the base, swelling above to a breadth of 2 lines; segments rhomboidally obovate; disk of 5 free ovate obtuse lobes, as long as the glabrous ovoid ovaries.

ANECHITES, Griseb.

This was proposed as a subtribe of the genus *Echites* by Grisebach in 1864, for a group of plants, chiefly natives of the Antilles, much resembling *Mesechites* in habit, differing chiefly in having narrow linear acuminate anthers, with two long parallel needle-like forks at their base, and in the lobes of the disk united at their base into a cup. Grisebach describes the segments of the corolla as sinistrorse; but I have found them to be dextrorsely convolute.

ANECHITES, Griseb. (char. reformato). *Sepala* 5, lanceolata, intus squamulis totidem obtusis sæpius denticulatis munita. *Corolla* hypocrateriformis; *tubus* anguste cylindricus; *segmenta* 5, oblonga, inæquilatera, rotata, dextrorsum convoluta. *Stamina* medio tubi inserta, inclusa; *filamenta* tenuia. *Antheræ* anguste lineares, apice cuspidatæ, imo furcis 2 brevibus armatæ. *Discus* suburceolatus, usque ad medium vel ultra in lobos 5 fissus; *ovaria* 2, libera, longiora. *Stylus* filiformis; *clavuncula* incrassata. *Folliculi* 2, lineari-teretes, paralleli; *semina* comosa.

Plantæ *Antillanæ vel Brasilienses, humiles, volubiles aut scandentes;* folia *opposita ovata aut oblonga, interdum cordata, petiolata;* racemi *axillares, simplices, pedunculati;* flores *pauci, alterni, pedicellati.*

1. ANECHITES ADGLUTINATA, nob.: *Echites adglutinata*, Jacq. (non Burm.) Amer. p. 31, tab. 23; A. DC. *l. c.* p. 448: *Echites circinalis*, Griseb. (non Sw.) Fl. Brit. W. Ind. p. 414. In Antillis: *v. s. in herb. Mus. Brit.* S. Domingo (Swartz); S. Lucia (sine nom.).

A climbing plant, with slender glabrous branches; leaves broadly ovate, rounded at the base, round and emarginate at the summit with a short mucronate point, rarely subobtuse, pallidly membranaceous, glabrous, pale green above, yellowish opake beneath, with reddish midrib and nerves scarcely prominulent, $2\frac{1}{4}$–$3\frac{1}{4}$ (sometimes 4) in. long, $1\frac{1}{2}$–$2\frac{1}{4}$ in. broad, on petioles 3–4 lines long; racemes axillary, $1\frac{1}{2}$ in. long including the bare peduncle (9 lines long), which supports about 5 alternate flowers on pedicels 1 line long; sepals acute, $\frac{1}{2}$ line long; tube of corolla cylindrical, a little swollen in the middle, 4 lines long; segments oblong-lanceolate, 3 lines long; stamens inserted above the middle of the tube; anthers cuspidate, included, bidentate at the base; disk shorter than the 2 free ovaries; follicles 2, terete, agglutinated at the apex.

2. ANECHITES CIRCINALIS, nob.: *Echites circinalis*, Sw. Flor. Ind. Occid. i. p. 533; ejusd. Prodr. p. 52: A. DC. *l. c.* p. 466; Griseb. *l. c.* p. 414: *Echites adglutinata*, Griseb. (non Sw.), *l. c.* p. 414: *Hæmadictyon circinalis*, Don, Dict. iv. p. 83. In Hispaniola et Jamaica: *v. s. in herb. Mus. Brit.* Jamaica (Shakespear).

A slender scandent plant, with glabrous branches and distant axils; leaves ovate-oblong, obtusely rounded at the base, gradually acute, yellowish green above, sulcate along the reddish midrib, nerves reddish, immersed, margins very revolute, scabridulous above, pale yellow beneath, opake and glabrous, with prominent reddish midrib, nerves, and veins, $1\frac{3}{4}$–2 in. long, 10 lines broad, on petioles 3 lines long; raceme lateral, glabrous, on a bare peduncle 2–3 in. long, erect, bearing many white flowers on alternate or, often, geminate pedicels 1 line long, with small acute bracteoles; sepals lanceolaté, erect,

½ line long; tube of corolla cylindrical, 3 lines long, narrower at the base for one third of its length, with a row of villous scales in the throat; segments linear-oblong, crispate along the margins, 2½ lines long, somewhat twisted dextrorsely, rotate; stamens seated at the constriction of the tube; filaments slender; anthers included, acuminate, shortly bidentate at the base; disk of 5 lobes; style, clavuncle, and stigmata as in the generic character; follicles 2.

The *Echites circinalis*, Griseb. (non Sw.) is said by the authors of the 'Genera Plantarum,' ii. p. 725, to be a cultivated specimen of *Holarrhena antidysenterica*.

The *Echites circinalis*, Müll., does not belong to this species: it is the *Echites leptoloba*, Stadelm. (*Mitozus*, nob.), and the *Echites revoluta*, A. DC. *l. c.* p. 457 (*Anechites revoluta*, nob.).

A drawing of this species, showing its floral analysis, is given in Plate XXXIII.B.

3. ANECHITES THOMASIANA, nob.: *Echites circinalis*, var. *Thomasiana*, A. DC. *l. c.* p. 466; Schlecht. (non Sw.), Linn. vi. 731. In umbrosis ins. S. Thomæ: *non vidi*.

A species differing from *A. circinalis* in its leaves acute at both extremities, in its longer racemes, with pubescent peduncle, calyx, and corolla, in its more revolute sepals, and its corolla twice the size, with the tube scarcely ventricose.

4. ANECHITES ASPERUGINIS, nob.: *Echites asperuginis*, Sw. Prodr. p. 52; Flor. Ind. Occid. i. p. 531; Griseb. Pl. Wr. Cub. p. 519; Cat. Pl. Wr. p. 170, n. 10: *Echites circinalis*, Griseb. (non Sw.), var. *adglutinata*, Fl. B. W. Ind. p. 414: *Echites lappulacea*, var. *asperuginis*, A. DC. *l. c.* p. 448. In Antillis: *v. s. in herb. Mus. Brit.* S. Domingo (Swartz, specim. typicum); Cuba (Wright 1663).

A scandent plant, with slender hispid branches; the axils are 2¼–3 in. apart; leaves elliptic-oblong, acute at both ends, or obtusely acute and gradually more acuminate, very membranaceous, green above, sparsely subhispid, with hairs globular at their base, with fine nerves, paler and glabrous beneath, with black dots corresponding to the hairs of the upper surface, prominent yellow midrib, patently hirsute, nerves little prominulent, 2–3 in. long, 9–15 lines broad, on slender petioles 5–7 lines long; racemes axillary, longer than the leaves; peduncle slender, 4½ lines long, bearing upwards 4–6 flowers on slender hirsutulous pedicels 6 lines long; sepals acutely lanceolate, 1½ line long, glabrous; corolla white, its tube slender, subpentagonous, twice the length of the sepals; segments obtusely ovate; stamens inserted in the middle of the tube; lobes of disk oblong, emarginate, half the length of the 2 ovaries; 2 slender terete follicles.

5. ANECHITES LAPPULACEA, nob.: *Echites lappulacea*, Lam. Dict. ii. p. 341; A. DC. *l. c.* p. 448: *Nerium caule volubili*, Plum. Amer. i. p. 19, tab. 26 (excl. syn.). In S. Domingo: *non vidi*.

A sarmentose plant, with a thick repent root and many stoutish climbing branches, which are verrucose; leaves ovate-oblong, subcordate, with an obtuse apical acumen, shining above, densely hispid beneath, 4 in. long, 1¾ in. broad, on glabrous petioles 5–9 lines long; racemes axillary, nearly 10 in. long, upon a hispid peduncle; flowers spicate in opposite pairs on pedicels ¾–1 in. apart (fructiferous pedicels 1–1½ in. apart);

corolla white, 7–9 lines long; sepals glabrous, one third the length of the pedicels, acutely ovate; tube of corolla 3–4 times as long as the sepals; segments roundly obovate, as long as the tube; fructiferous pedicels opposite, bearing 2 erect reddish follicles densely hispid at each extremity with hooked rigid hairs, glabrous in the middle, teretely linear, 3 in. long, 2 lines thick; the seeds comose.

De Candolle considers, on the authority of Poiret, that *E. asperuginis*, Sw., is a mere variety of this very distinct species; but this seems inadmissible. Bentham and Hooker (Gen. ii. p. 708) repeat the same inference.

6. ANECHITES REVOLUTA, nob.: *Echites revoluta*, A. DC. *l. c.* p. 457; *Echites circinalis* (in parte), Müll. (non Sw.) in Flor. Bras. xxvi. p. 154. In Brasilia, prov. Cuyaba: *non vidi*.

A plant very distinct from that of Swartz: it has very slender scandent stems; its leaves are oblong, acute, 2–3 in. long, ¾–1 in. broad, plicately folded at the base, on petioles 3 lines long; raceme axillary, on a bare peduncle 1 in. long, bearing above 8–10 flowers; sepals linear-lanceolate, with an inner multidentate scale; tube of corolla cylindrical, 7 lines long; segments longer than the tube; stamens inserted in the middle of the tube, above its broad pilose lining; disk of 5 lobes, connate at the base, longer than the ovaries.

EXOTHOSTEMON.

A genus, proposed by G. Don for a group of Orinoco and Columbian plants, described by Kunth under a distinct section of *Echites*. In habit and in their peculiar inflorescence they approach *Laseguea*, but differ from it in their corolla, with a more slender tube, pilose in the mouth, and in their much broader segments, more especially in their wholly exserted stamens, a peculiarity which gave rise to the generic name. They are slender scandent plants, with a fruit of 2 terete torulose follicles, with comose seeds. Messrs. Bentham and Hooker are undoubtedly wrong in amalgamating *Exothostemon* with *Prestonia* (Gen. ii. p. 709), the two genera being widely distinct: in the one the inflorescence consists of a densely ramified panicle, often capitate, in the other a long narrow raceme with adpressed bracts; in the one the mouth of the corolla-tube is furnished with scales and a fleshy annular ring, which are wanting in the other; one has a fruit of 2 free terete follicles, the other has a long cylindrical 2-celled capsule with septicidal dehiscence; the coma of the seeds is simple in the one, double in the other.

EXOTHOSTEMON, G. Don: *Echites* (an nov. genus?), H. B. K., A. DC.: *Prestonia* (in parte), Benth. & Hook. Char. reformatus. *Sepala* 5, ovata, acuminata, erecta, submembranacea, colorata, reticulato-venosa, imo squamula intus munita. *Corolla* hypocrateriformis; *tubus* anguste cylindricus, ad faucem brevissime dilatatus, ubi annulo piloso donatus; *segmenta* dolabriformia, angulo uno acuminata, altero late rotundata. *Stamina* annulo piloso inserta; *filamenta* brevia; *antheræ* lineares, in conum cohærentes, sæpius omnino exsertæ, acuminatæ, imo breviter emarginato-bilobæ. *Discus* suburceolatus, in lobos 5 carnosos fere ad basin fissus. *Ovaria* 2, disco circumdata. *Stylus* simplex; *clavuncula* incrassata, 5-angulata, imo membrana lacerata munita, ad antheras agglutinata; *stigmata* 2, parva, terminalia. *Folliculi* 2, teretes, sæpe torulosi, sutura ventrali dehiscentes, margine placentiferi; *placenta* linearis, demum soluta; *semina* plurima, oblonga, dorso convexa, margine incurva, ventre sulcata ; *coma sericeo-pilosa, duplo longior, decidua ; albumen tenue, caruosum ; embryo inclusus ; cotyledones 2, foliaceæ, oblongæ, obtusæ ; radicula supera, cylindracea.*

Suffrutices *Americæ intertropicæ* ; ramulis *tenuibus scandentibus, cum* axillis *remotis ;* folia *opposita, oblonga, acuminata, imo sæpe cordata, glabra aut hirsuta, sæpe* glandulis 2–4 *carnosis ad costæ basin munita, petiolata ;* racemi *laterales, rarius terminales, aspergilliformes, multiflori ;* flores *mediocres, crebre alternatim spicati, pedicellati ;* bracteæ *lanceolatæ, sæpe majusculæ, coloratæ, reticulatæ.*

1. EXOTHOSTEMON BRACTEATUM, G. Don, Dict. iv. p. 82 : *Echites bracteata,* H. B. K. iii. p. 217 (non Vell.) ; A. DC. *l. c.* p. 458.   In Nova Granada, Mariquita : *non vidi.*

A climbing species, with subfiliform villous branches, having remote axils ; leaves elliptic, cordate at the base, rounded and mucronately cuspidate at the apex, flat, entire, membranaceous, reticulately veined, above green, pubescently hirtellous, with about 4 glabrous subulate glands at the base of the midrib, beneath softly and canescently tomentose, 1¾–2 in. long, 13–14 lines broad, on channelled villous petioles 4–5 lines long ; raceme lateral, aspergilliform, under 3 in. long, on a villous peduncle bearing few rather large flowers on alternate hairy pedicels 1½ line long, each with a coloured, reticulate, hirtellous, acuminate bract narrowed at the base, near an inch long ; sepals acuminately lanceolate, subequal, flat, erect, 4 or 5 times shorter than the tube of the corolla, each with an inner deltoid scale ; corolla orange-coloured, hairy outside, its cylindrical tube pubescent inside, shortly cup-shaped in the mouth, and there furnished with a pilose staminigerous ring ; segments oblong, inequilateral or dolabriform, with an acute tooth at one angle, rounded at the other ; stamens seated on a pilose ring in the mouth of the tube ; anthers cohering, quite exserted.

The only flower examined by Kunth was in bud.

2. EXOTHOSTEMON JAVITENSE, G. Don, *l. c.* p. 82 : *Echites Javitensis,* H. B. K. *l. c.* p. 220 ; A. DC. *l. c.* p. 461.   In Venezuela, Missiones del Orinoco (Bonpland) : *non vidi.*

A lactescent shrub, with terete glabrous branches ; leaves elliptic-oblong, rounded at the base, shortly acuminate, membranaceous, with entire subrevolute margins, green above, smooth, reticulately veined, paler beneath, minutely scabridulous, 4–4½ in. long, 1¾–2 in. broad, on glabrous channelled petioles 5–6 lines long ; raceme spicatiform, lateral, erect, glabrous, 6 lines long ; peduncle covered from near the base with numerous approximate, nearly sessile, spreading flowers, the size of those of *Vinca rosea,* each supported by an acutely oblong, glabrous, coloured, deciduous bract 1 in. long ; sepals short, roundly ovate, obtuse, glabrous, subimbricate, coloured, ciliate, each with an inner basal scale ; corolla glabrous, its tube cylindrical, green, 1 in. long, lined below the mouth with a sericeo-pilose ring ; limb funnel-shaped, cleft into 5 inequilateral reflexed segments cuspidate at one angle, rounded at the other, sericeo-pilose about the mouth ; stamens inserted in the top of the tube ; anthers quite exserted, acuminate, shortly 2-lobed at the base, cohering in an erect cone ; disk of 5 fleshy lobes, subconnate at the base, nearly as long as the ovaries ; follicles, in the immature state, slender, cylindrical.

This and the preceding species differ from all the following in their very long bracts, thus showing an approach of the genus towards *Laseguea.*

3. EXOTHOSTEMON MOLLISSIMUM, Don, *l. c.* p. 82: *Echites mollissima*, H. B. K. *l. c.* p. 218; A. DC. *l. c.* p. 461. In Nova Granada ad Honda: *non vidi*.

A climbing plant, with filiform hairy branches, having remote axils; leaves oblong, rounded and cordate at the base, cuspidately acuminate, flat, membranaceous, above green and hispidly pubescent, reticulately veined, canescent beneath, with soft shaggy hairs, 2-2¼ in. long, 10-12 lines broad, on channelled tomentose petioles 4-5 lines long; raceme lateral, shorter than the leaves, pedunculate, hirtellous; bracts lanceolate, as long as the pedicel and calyx; pedicels hairy, 1½ line long; sepals acutely ovate, erect, 1 line long, each with an inner lanceolately ovate scale: corolla yellow, hirtellous; tube 8-9 lines long, cylindrical, a little wider in the mouth, where it is sericeously pilose; segments inequilateral, shortly acute at one angle, rounded at the other; stamens inserted in the mouth of the tube, exserted; filaments short, broader above, pilose inside; anthers linear, glabrous, emarginately bilobed at the base; disk urceolate, glabrous, partially cleft into 5 obtuse lobes, enclosing 2 ovaries; style, clavuncle, and stigmata as in the generic character; follicles 2, slender, terete, torulose, hairy, 3 in. long; seeds comose.

4. EXOTHOSTEMON MACROPHYLLUM, G. Don, *l. c.* p. 82: *Echites macrophylla*, H. B. K. (non Roxb.), *l. c.* p. 218; A. DC. *l. c.* p. 461. Rio Orinoco: *non vidi*.

A slender species, with terete hairy branches; leaves subovate, elliptic, cuspidate, cordate at the base, entire, membranaceous, above adpressed pilose, reticulately veined, beneath canescent, hirto-pubescent, 5 in. long, 2¼ in. broad, on tomentose channelled petioles 6 lines long; raceme lateral, much shorter than the leaves, pedunculate, few-flowered; bracts ovate-oblong, hairy, as long as the pedicel and calyx, canescently tomentose; sepals hairy, shorter than the tube of the corolla, acuminately ovate, with an internal scale; corolla not larger than that of *Vinca rosea*, pubescently hairy outside; tube cylindrical, a little swollen at the staminiferous sericeo-pilose ring in its mouth; segments inequilateral; stamens inserted in the pilose ring, exserted; filaments, anthers, and other parts as in the preceding.

5. EXOTHOSTEMON GRACILE, G. Don, *l. c.* p. 82: *Echites gracilis*, H. B. K. *l. c.* p. 219; A. DC. *l. c.* p. 460. Rio Orinoco: *non vidi*.

A climbing species, with filiform hairy branches, having very remote axils; leaves oblong-lanceolate, upper ones lanceolate, acuminate, rounded and cordate at the base, flat, above glabrous, shining, green, reticulately veined, beneath paler, hirtellous, with prominent nerves, 2-2¼ in. long, 3-7 lines broad, on shaggy channelled petioles 2 lines long; raceme lateral, including the peduncle 3 in. long, bracteate, all hirtellous; pedicels 1½ line long, subulate; bracts of the same length; sepals hairy, ovato-lanceolate, with a deltoid inner scale; corolla yellow, glabrous, its tube cylindrical, 8 times as long as the sepals, a little swollen in the mouth, which is lined with a sericeo-pilose ring; segments inequilateral, cuspidately acuminate at one angle, rounded at the other; stamens inserted in the pilose ring, exserted: the rest as in the preceding species.

6. EXOTHOSTEMON SPECIOSUM, G. Don, *l. c.* p. 82: *Echites speciosa*, H. B. K. iii. p. 219; A. DC. *l. c.* p. 460. Rio Orinoco: *non vidi*.

A slender climber, with filiform branches, the younger ones hirtellous, all with remote axils; leaves oblong, acuminate, rounded and cordate at the base, membranaceous, green and glabrous above, reticulately veined, beneath paler and hirtellous, with prominent nerves, $2\frac{1}{2}$–$2\frac{3}{4}$ in. long, 9–11 lines broad, on hairy channelled petioles 3 lines long; raceme lateral, pedunculate, 2 in. long, all hirtellous, its rachis flexuose; bracts 2 lines long; pedicels 4 lines long; flowers yellow, 2 in. long; sepals acutely oval; tube of corolla 9–10 lines long, sericeo-pilose in the mouth; stamens and other parts as in the preceding species; follicles 2, terete, fuscous, smooth, pointed, 7 in. long, the sutural placenta afterwards free; seeds oblong, 5 lines long, dorsally convex and pilosulous, channelled on the opposite face; coma sericeous, ferruginous, deciduous.

7. EXOTHOSTEMON PALUDOSUM, G. Don (in parte), *l. c.* p. 83: *Echites paludosa*, H. B. K. (non Vahl), iii. p. 221. In Cuba: *non vidi*.

A climbing species, with striate terete glabrous branches; leaves oblong or oblong-linear, acute at the base, acute or shortly acuminate at the apex, membranaceous, entire, glabrous, reticulately veined, with a prominent midrib beneath, 2–$2\frac{1}{4}$ in. long, 4–11 lines broad, on glabrous channelled petioles 4–5 lines long; raceme terminal, 2 in. long, pedunculate, bearing 2 to 4 geminate flowers on pedicels 4 lines long; sepals acutely oblong, glabrous, reticulately veined, 3 lines long; corolla glabrous, its tube cylindrical, much longer than the sepals, its segments as in the last species; the stamens inserted on a pilose ring in the throat; the anthers exserted, bearded: the rest as in all the preceding species.

A species confounded with the *Echites* (*Rhabdadenia*) *palustris*, Vahl, which it much resembles in habit, but differs in the narrow cylindrical tube of the corolla with a pilose ring in the throat, on which the exserted stamens are seated.

8. EXOTHOSTEMON SERICEUM, nob.: *Prestonia sericea*, Mart. & Galeot. Bull. Acad. Brux. xi. p. 360; Walp. Rep. vi. p. 473. In Mexico, prope Oaxaca: *non vidi*.

A climbing plant, with villous branches: leaves ovate-lanceolate, subcordate, acuminate, villous and scabridulous above, flavescent and sericeo-tomentose beneath, subsessile; panicle axillary, with a bifid peduncle longer than the leaves, fulvo-tomentose, each branch corymbiferous; bracts linear-acuminate; sepals rather large, cordately ovate, acuminate, villous; corolla salver-shaped; tube sericeously villose; segments obovate; stamens half-included, semi-exserted; no appendages in the mouth of the tube.

9. EXOTHOSTEMON CONTORTUM, nob.: *Hæmadictyon contortum*, Mart. & Gal. Bull. Acad. Brux. xi. p. 360; Walp. Rep. vi. p. 473. In Mexico, prope Oaxaca: *non vidi*.

A subscandent species; leaves oval, subcordate, acuminate, pubescent above, puberulo-velutinous beneath; panicles axillary, on a bifid peduncle longer than the leaf, each branch bearing many congested flowers; corolla salver-shaped, red, 1 in. long; tube elongated, somewhat twisted; segments roundly ovate, reflexed; stamens exserted.

THENARDIA.

This genus was established by Kunth in 1818, with a good figure and an ample description. It has numerous large flowers on a slender axillary peduncle, and many long slender pedicels aggregated into an umbellate corymb: the flower has 5 lanceolate sepals, and a corolla with an extremely short narrow tube and a border of 5 gibbously ovoid segments, patently expanded, with a simple dextrorse convolution; the stamens are long and wholly exserted. The chief peculiarity of the genus consists in a syngenesious union of its broad membranaceous filaments into a tube in the middle, while their extremities are quite free; they are seated in the mouth of the short tube of the corolla, and are attached above to the anthers; these have a long indurated connective with 2 long basal prongs, and terminated above by a soft triangular expansion, all valvately conniving at the apex to form the stegium which covers the stigma. The style is slender and terminated by the incrassate clavuncle, which is pentagonal and nectariferous, peltate below, with a membranaceous laciniulate margin, and is surmounted by a globose stigma, in accordance with the usual structure of the family; this was not understood by Kunth, who figured the adherent ruptured portions of the base of the clavuncle as expanded extensions of the filaments—a mistake arising from its appearance in the dried flower. Kunth did not see its bifollicular fruit; this was described by De Candolle from a Mexican drawing, where they are fusiform, 6 in. long, 4–5 lines broad, containing many obovoid seeds with an apical coma.

1. THENARDIA FLORIBUNDA, H. B. K. Nov. Gèn. iii. p. 210, tab. 240; A. DC. Prodr. viii. p. 425. In Mexico indigena et in hort. cult.: *non vidi*.
2. THENARDIA? SUAVEOLENS, Mart. & Galeotti, Bull. Acad. Brux. xi. p. 359; Walp. Rep. vi. p. 473. In Mexico, prov. Mechoacan: *non vidi*.

A doubtful species.

The two plants from Guiana, placed in *Thenardia* by Mr. Bentham, belong to his genus *Thyrsanthus*.

FORSTERONIA.

Under *Thyrsanthus* it is related how that genus has been confounded with *Forsteronia* by Müller, and their numerous respective species promiscuously intermingled by him. Meyer, in founding the genus *Forsteronia* in 1818, before the establishment of *Thyrsanthus*, equally confounded together the few species enumerated by him, so that his generic character is not exact. De Candolle in 1844 offered a much better diagnosis than that of Müller (1864); but the following appears to me a still more correct resumen of its characters. There is a remarkable degree of similarity in the external habit of the plants and in the character of the inflorescence in the two genera, the flowers in both cases being too minute to render their difference easily perceptible; but there can be no mistake in the respective characters of the follicles and seeds.

FORSTERONIA (char. reformat.), Meyer, A. DC., et Müll. (in parte). *Sepala* 5, parva, obtusa vel acuta, erecta. *Corolla* parva; *tubus* brevissime cylindricus, sæpe intus pilosus; *segmenta* 5, oblonga, erecta, submembranacea, vix imbricata, marginibus demum subrevolutis, æstivatione minime sinistrorsum convoluta, sæpe intus dense villosa. *Stamina* 5, tubo inserta; *filamenta* brevia, complanata, pilosula; *antheræ* omnino exsertæ, in conum conniventes, apicibus membranaceis inflexis; *connectivum* corneum, imo in furcas 2 paullo divergentes fissum. *Discus* in lobos 5 liberos divisus. *Ovaria* 2 distincta, paullo breviora. *Stylus* tenuis, brevis; *clavuncula* incrassata; *stigmata* 2, brevia, terminalia. *Folliculi* 2, teretes, torulosi, nunc interrupte et longe strangulati, sutura ventrali dehiscentes. *Semina* oblonga, ventre concava, et raphe longitudinali notata; *coma* paullo longior, sericea, decidua.

Suffrutices *Antillani, plerumque Brasilienses*; ramuli *tenues, sæpius scandentes*; paniculæ *axillares aut terminales, sæpius multum divisæ spiciformes aut laxiuscule ramosæ, multiflores*; flores *minimi, sæpius dense aggregati*.

1. FORSTERONIA FLORIBUNDA, Meyer, Esseq. p. 135 (non Müll.); A. DC. Prodr. viii. p. 437; Griseb. Fl. W. Ind. p. 412: *Echites floribunda*, Sw. Prodr. p. 52; Fl. Ind. Occid. p. 534: *Parsonsia floribunda*, R. Br. Mem. Wern. Soc. i. p. 65; G. Don, Dict. iv. p. 79. In Antillis: *v. s. in herb. Mus. Brit.* Jamaica (Swartz, Wright, Masson).

The typical specimen shows this to be a true *Forsteronia*. It is a shrub with flexuose, slender, scandent, glabrous branches; its opposite leaves are oval or oblong-ovoid, obtuse at the base, gradually acute and obtusely mucronate at the apex, the margins subrevolute, subcoriaceous, glabrous, deep green above, subnitid, sulcate along the midrib, with about 12 pairs of patently diverging nerves, with others shorter and intermediate, all semiimmersed, yellowish and opake beneath, with a prominent reddish midrib and scarcely prominulent fine nerves, $2\frac{1}{2}$–3 in. long, 1–1½ in. broad, on petioles 2–3 lines long; panicles axillary and terminal, shorter than the leaves, much divided, their branchlets 3 lines long, bearing numerous very small white flowers on slender pedicels 2 lines long; sepals ovate-acute, ¼ line long; corolla 3 lines long, externally pruinose; tube ¼ line long, villous inside; segments lanceolate, equilateral, membranaceous, very villous inside towards the base, sinistrorsely subconvolute; anthers exserted, connivent, villous; disk of 5 oblong glabrous lobes, as long as the pubescent ovaries.

2. FORSTERONIA PAVONII, A. DC. *l. c.* p. 438. In Peruvia (Pavon): *v. s. in herb. Mus. Brit.* Tarapota (Spruce 4908).

Spruce's plant agrees well with the short description of De Candolle. The branches are dichotomous, the branchlets spreading, glabrous, shining black, slender, striolate, with axils 1 in. apart; leaves oblong, subacutely obtuse at the base, gradually acuminate, thinly chartaceous, glabrous, pale green above, with fine immersed nerves, paler beneath, opake, midrib flat, reddish, with scarcely prominulent nerves, 2 in. long, 9–12 lines broad, on slender spreading channelled petioles 2 lines long; panicles terminal in the young branches, spicately racemose, 2 in. long, on a peduncle bare at its base for 9 lines, its approximately divided branches bearing very numerous condensated minute flowers on pedicels ½ line long; sepals ovate, subacute, pale and membranaceous, with small inner scales; corolla less than 2 lines long, glabrous outside; tube extremely short, sericeous within; segments oblong, glabrous, the inner median nerve puberulous; stamens exserted, fixed in the middle of the tube; disk of 5 distinct free lobes, concealing 2 pilose ovaries.

3. FORSTERONIA REFRACTA, Müll. Fl. Bras. xxvi. p. 97. In Brasilia, prov. centralibus: *v. v. et sicc. in herb. meo* (n. 4026, in flore et fructu) montibus Organensibus.

A scandent shrubby species, with glabrous, fuscous, trichotomous patent branches and slender branchlets, all verruculous with crowded raised yellow lenticels, the axils $\frac{3}{4}$ in. apart; leaves elliptic, obtuse or subacute at the base, contracted at the summit into a subobtuse acumen, flaccidly chartaceous, glabrous, opake green above, with 6 pairs of fine diverging nerves and reticulated veins, paler beneath, with prominulent yellow nerves, $1\frac{1}{2}$–$2\frac{1}{4}$ in. long, $\frac{3}{4}$–1 in. broad, on slender glabrous petioles 2 lines long; racemose panicles at the end of the young branchlets, about as long as the leaves, covered with yellow tomentum; peduncle terete, lenticellate, bearing several opposite patent or refracted branchlets at intervals of $\frac{1}{2}$ in., and about 6 lines long, each with very short secondary branchlets bearing several approximate almost sessile flowers; petals obtusely ovate, $\frac{1}{4}$ line long; corolla 2 lines long, its tube $\frac{1}{2}$ line long; segments linear-oblong, puberulous outside, with rigid villous hairs inside, expanded and reflexed at the apex; stamens upon short filaments inserted within the tube; anthers as long as the tube, wholly exserted, their membranaceous summits connivent at the truncate apex, coriaceous and shortly bilobed at the base, all glabrous; style slender, short; clavuncle thick, club-shaped; stigmata short, terete, terminal; follicles 2, pendent, free, torose, striolate-sulcate, acute, 10–13 in. long, the seminiferous lobes fusiform, 5 lines long, 2 lines thick, alternating with as many strangulations $\frac{1}{2}$–$\frac{3}{4}$ line thick, 8 to 12 lines long, glabrous, fuscous; seeds linear-oblong, 5 lines long, crowned by a persistent rufescent, sericeous, very spreading coma 9 lines long.

A drawing of this species, in flower and in fruit, is shown in Plate XXXV. B.

4. FORSTERONIA MINUTIFLORA, Müll. *l. c.* p. 99. In Brasilia, loco ignoto (Claussen 1955): *v. s. in herb. meo* (n. 8064), filio lecto ad Iguassu, prov. Rio de Janeiro.

This plant agrees with Claussen's, as described by Müller, in the shape of its leaves and its inflorescence; only the leaves are somewhat smaller; the branches are glabrous, fuscous, the younger ones paler and puberulous; leaves ovate-lanceolate, obtuse or subcordate at the base, gradually and acutely acuminate, submembranaceous, dark green above, opake, of a rufescent hue, younger ones subpubescent, $1\frac{1}{2}$–$2\frac{1}{4}$ in. long, 4–7 lines broad, on slender petioles $2\frac{1}{4}$–3 lines long (in Claussen's plant the leaves are $2\frac{1}{4}$–$3\frac{3}{4}$ in. long, 11–12 lines broad, on petioles 2 lines long); raceme terminal, $2\frac{1}{2}$–3 in. long, narrowly subpyramidal, with many patent or subrefracted branchlets again closely divided, bearing very numerous minute flowers on very short slender pedicels; sepals extremely minute, puberulous; corolla pubescent, $\frac{3}{4}$ line long, tube extremely short.

The plant bears no resemblance to the *F. meridionalis* of Müller, as stated by him; it comes nearer to his *F. Riedelii*.

5. **Forsteronia montana**, Müll. *l. c.* p. 101. In Brasilia, prope Rio de Janeiro, in montib. ad Estrella: *v. s. in herb. Mus. Brit. in fructu*, prov. Rio Janeiro (Bowie & Cunningham 72) : *flores non vidi.*

This species, described by Müller, is scandent, with slender, glabrous, fuscous branches, densely verruculose; leaves broadly ovate, roundish and subcordate at the base, suddenly and shortly acuminate at the apex, membranaceous, glabrous, fuscous-green above, with about 5 pairs of ascending semiimmersed nerves and reticulated veins, pale ferruginous and opake beneath, with subprominulent nerves, and sulcate over the immersed reticulated veins, 4–5¼ in. long, 2¼–2¾ in. broad, on rather slender channelled petioles not 6 lines long; inflorescence terminal (or lateral at the ends of the younger branches), pyramidal, with few ramifications, each branchlet rather laxly flowered, the flowers nearly 2 lines long, on short bracteolate pubescent pedicels; sepals acutely ovate, half the length of the corolla, pubescent, ciliolate on the margins, without inner scales; corolla ferruginously tomentellous; tube very short; segments oblong-ovate, erecto-patent, hispidulous within, twice the length of the tube; stamens exserted; anthers rigidly hairy behind; disk 5-lobed; follicles 2, 14 in. long, torose, glabrous, fuscous, having about 8 very narrow long strangulations between as many subacutely ovate seminiferous swellings, which are subnitid and costately striate outside.

6. **Forsteronia Sellowii**, Müll. *l. c.* p. 101. In Brasilia meridionali (Sellow 396), prov. Rio Janeiro (Riedel 1101) : *v. s. in herb. Mus. Brit.* Brazil (Sellow).

A scandent plant, whose branches are cinereous, trichotomous; branchlets slender, fuscous, glabrous; leaves oblong-ovate or ovate-lanceolate, subacute at the base, shortly acuminate, submembranaceous, subglabrous, or obsoletely puberulous, opakely pallid-green above, glaucous, with 5–6 pairs of fine prominulent nerves, with others intermediate, all arcuately conjoined, pale-green beneath, with reddish prominulent nerves and reticulate veins, 2⅜–3¼ in. long, 10–12 lines broad, on slender glabrous petioles 3–4 lines long; panicle subterminal, 3 in. long, branching from near the base, the lower branches short, increasing upwards, where the branchlets are again divided and thickly flowered; flowers approximate, on slender pubescent pedicels 1 line long; sepals acutely ovate, puberulous, ¾ line long; corolla fulvo-puberulous outside, 2 lines long; tube very short, it and the acutely ovate segments hispid inside.

7. **Forsteronia Riedelii**, Müll. *l. c.* p. 103. In Brasilia, prov. Rio de Janeiro, ad Estrella (Riedel) : *v. s. in herb. Mus. Brit.* Iguassu, prope Estrella (Bowie & Cunningham).

A slender climbing plant, with glabrous, striate, brown branchlets, their axils 1 in. apart; leaves oblong-lanceolate (upper, young ones narrowly lanceolate), acute at the base, with a short broadish subobtuse acumen, membranaceous, scabridulous, fuscous-green above, with 4–6 pairs of remote ascending nerves, subferruginous beneath, opake, with prominulent reddish nerves and densely reticulate veins, 2–2⅝ in. long, 6–10 lines broad, on slender petioles 2–3 lines long; panicle racemose, terminal on the young branches, 2¼ in. long, oppositely branched at distances of 6 lines; branches ½–1 in. long, bare at the base, patent, again shortly divided and bearing several approximate flowers on pedicels 1 line long; sepals acutely ovate, subpilose, ¼ line long; corolla subpilose, 2 lines long; tube very short.

8. **FORSTERONIA AUSTRALIS**, Müll. *l. c.* p. 103. In Brasilia australiore, prov. São Paulo (Sellow): *v. s. in herb. Mus. Brit.* Brasilia merid. (Sellow, Bowie and Cunningham).

Branches slender, fuscous, sparsely verruculose, glabrous, with axils 1½–3 in. apart; leaves elliptic or obovate, obtuse or subacute at the base, with a suddenly constricted acute acumen, flaccidly chartaceous, very glabrous, above fuscous-green, with about 9 pairs of prominulent diverging nerves and immersed reticulated veins, brownish opake beneath, with prominulent nerves and veins, 2½–3½ in. long, 1½–2¼ in. broad, on slender channelled petioles 3–4 lines long; panicle terminal in the young branchlets, 2¼ in. long, oppositely branching from the base, and again divided; branchlets ¾ in. apart, sublaxly many-flowered on bracteolate tomentellous pedicels 1½–2 lines long; sepals ovate, obtuse, tomentellous, with ciliolate margins; corolla 2–2¼ lines long; tube very short; segments obliquely ovate, densely pilose inside.

9. **FORSTERONIA OBTUSILOBA**, Müll. Linn. xxx. p. 413. In Caracas: *non vidi.*

A species said to be near *F. australis*, with reddish fuscous branchlets; leaves ovate, somewhat acute at the base, shortly acuminate, very glabrous, membranaceous, 2 in. long, 1⅔ in. broad, on petioles 1½–2 lines long; panicle terminal, 2¾ in. long, pyramidal, patently and shortly branched, the branchlets again divided and densely flowered; corolla 2 lines long, glabrous, with a very short tube hispid in the mouth; segments acutely oblong, shortly tomentellous; disk of 5 nearly free obtuse lobes; ovaries ovoid, subtomentellous at the apex.

10. **FORSTERONIA ACUTIFOLIA**, Müll. Fl. Bras. xxvi. p. 99. In Brasilia ad Rio de Janeiro: *v. s. in herb. Mus. Brit. l. c.* (Sellow, Bowie and Cunningham).

It has a twining branch, with a resilient bark; branches very slender, pale brown, lenticellate, more or less puberulous; leaves ovate-oblong, subacute at the base, suddenly acutely acuminate at the summit, chartaceous, glabrous above, fuscous green, with 7 pairs of slender, scarcely prominulent, divergent nerves and transverse reticulate veins, darkly ferruginous beneath, subpuberulous, with reddish prominulent nerves, 3 in. long, 1⅔ in. broad, on very slender petioles 5 lines long; panicles axillary and terminal, 3 in. long, bare at the base for ¼ in., rather narrow, densely ferrugineo-puberulous, with short branches 4–6 lines apart, divided and bearing many very small approximate flowers on slender pedicels ¾ line long; sepals acutely ovate, ¾ line long; corolla 2 lines long, tube very short.

11. **FORSTERONIA PROTENSA**, nob.: *Forsteronia acutifolia*, var. *pubescens*, Müll. (non A. DC.) *l. c.* p. 99. In Brasilia circa Rio de Janeiro (Sellow): *v. s. in herb. Mus. Brit. ex l. c.* (Sellow, Bowie and Cunningham).

A scandent species, with slender flexuose branchlets, pale brown, striolate, and lenticellate, with axils 1½ in. apart; leaves elliptic-oblong, acute at the base, suddenly constricted towards the apex into a long, straight, linear, obtusulous acumen, chartaceous, glaucous opake and fuscous-green above, with about 7 pairs of slender, diverging, semi-immersed nerves, arcuately conjoined, paler, opake, and ferruginous beneath, puberulous, 3 in. long including the linear acumen (4 lines long, 1 line broad), 1¼ in. broad, on channelled petioles 3 lines long; panicles axillary and terminal, 3 in. long, laxly branched, branches subdivergent, 4–6 lines apart, 12 lines long, bare at the base, again divided and bearing numerous very small flowers on bracteolate pedicels ½ line long, all shortly puberulous; sepals acute, ¾ line long; corolla 2 lines long; tube extremely short; segments oblong, three times as long as the tube; stamens exserted.

12. FORSTERONIA THYRSOIDEA, Müll. *l. c.* p. 105 : *Echites thyrsoidea*, Vell. Fl. Flum. p. 111, Icon. iii. tab. 37. In Brasilia, prov. Rio Janeiro, ad Santa Cruz: *non vidi.*

A scandent species, with stoutish hirsute branches 4 lines thick, with axils 4½ in. apart, whence issue more slender branchlets divaricating nearly at a right angle, 9 in. long, hirtous, lenticellate, the axils 2 in. apart; the leaves on the branchlets (sometimes not quite opposite) are elliptic, rounded or roundish at the base, constricted near the apex into a subobtuse acumen, with about 12 pairs of very fine diverging nerves and many transverse reticulated veins, hirsutulous beneath, 3–3¼ in. long, 1¼–1¾ in. broad, on slender pubescent petioles 1½–2 lines long; inflorescence terminal, on a peduncle ½ in. long, supporting a pyramidal floral mass 2 in. long, 10 lines broad at the lower part, gradually pointed upwards, consisting of a number of densely approximate branchlets crowded with many very small yellowish flowers, each mostly concealed by its own small lanceolate bract; flowers scarcely more than 2 lines long; pedicels very short; sepals acutely lanceolate; tube of corolla extremely short; its segments 2 lines long, subacute; stamens quite exserted: subsequently the floral peduncle becomes elongated and thickened, producing 3 long pedicels 6 lines apart, each supporting 2 elongated pendent follicles 9½ in. long, having about 6 narrow strangulations, the intervals being fusiformly oblong, seminigerous, 2 lines broad, dehiscing in the usual manner; seeds conically oblong, subpilose, 5 lines long, 1⅓ line broad, with a spreading coma 8 lines long.

A species near *F. montana.*

13. FORSTERONIA DIVARICATA, nob. : ramis validiusculis, pallide brunneis, verruculoso-lenticellatis, remote divaricatim opposite ramosis, ramis tenuioribus incurvatis, iterum breviter ramulosis, ramulis tertiariis brevibus, foliatis et floriferis : foliis ellipticis, in paribus tribus, imo subrotundatis, apice breviter acutis, chartaceis, supra fusco-viridibus, opacis, scabridulis, ad nervos sulcatis, nervis utrinque 6, divergenti-adscendentibus, immersis, subtus pallidioribus, opacis, costa nervisque fulvis prominentibus, patentim hirtulis, breviter petiolatis : paniculis in ramis tertiariis terminalibus, a basi trichotomis, ramis adscendenti-divaricatis, curvatis, imo nudis, superne ramulosis et crebriter plurifloris; floribus congestis, hirsutulis, pedicellatis; sepalis parvis, acutis; corolla hispidula, tubo brevissimo. In Brasilia, prov. Rio de Janeiro : *v. s. in herb. Mus. Brit. ex l. c.* (Bowie and Cunningham, n. 72).

This plant has many of the characters of the *Echites thyrsoidea* of Velloz, the preceding species, but is more glabrous and its inflorescence more diffuse, and has smaller leaves. The main branch is 1 line thick, with axils 2½ in. apart; the primary branchlets issue from these axils nearly at a right angle, curving upwards, being 3 in. long, all glabrous, have their axils 1½ in. apart, and bear at their summits a terminal raceme; leaves 1⅞ in. long, 9 lines broad, on hirsute petioles 1 line long, opposite upon the short secondary branchlets, which are 6 lines apart; raceme spreading, consisting of 3 branches, nearly 3 in. long, all issuing from the base, where they are bare for 1 in., bearing upwards at intervals of 6 lines lateral branchlets 8 lines long, bare for half that length, which bear upwards a mass of approximate flowers more or less spreading, and all hirsutulous; pedicels 1 line long; sepals ¾ line long; corolla 2 lines long, with an extremely short tube; follicles said to be more than 1 foot long.

14. FORSTERONIA OVALIFOLIA, nob.: *Echites ovalifolia*, Poir. Dict. Suppl. ii. p. 535; A. DC. *l. c.* p. 473. In Antillis: *v. s. in herb. Mus. Brit.* Hispaniola (Swartz).

This specimen agrees with Poiret's description: its leaves are opposite, obovate, subcuneately narrowed towards the base, rounded, mucronate at the shortly narrowed summit, of a laurel-like texture, very dark green above, glabrous, rigidly coriaceous, sulcate along the midrib and 5 pairs of divergent slender yellow nerves, nitid, with a thick corrugulate parenchyma, pale yellow and opake beneath, granular and sparsely puberulous, with prominent midrib and nerves, the veins wholly immersed, 1½–1⅜ in. long, 9–10 lines broad, on slender channelled petioles 3 lines long; panicles axillary, longer than the leaves, puberulous, much branched, branches 6 lines long, again subdivided, with very numerous small flowers on bracteolate pedicels ½ line long; sepals subobtusely ovate, puberulous, ⅓ line long; corolla in bud 2 lines long, shortly puberulous; tube very short; rest as in the preceding species.

15. FORSTERONIA ROTUNDIUSCULA, nob. In Brasilia: *v. s. in herb. Mus. Brit. in fructu* (Sellow).

A species very near the preceding: branches slender, terete, glabrous, dichotomous, axils about 1 in. apart; leaves orbicular, sometimes plicate, slightly cordate at the base, suddenly constricted at the apex into a short acute acumen, fuscous green above, finely rugulose, with immersed very fine nerves, paler and brownish beneath, opake, obsoletely puberulous, with prominulent fine nerves, 1¼ in. long, 1¼ in. broad, on slender petioles 1 line long; inflorescence axillary; fructiferous peduncle 9 lines long; glabrous follicles 2, terete, 5 in. long, 1 line broad, much arched and conjoined at the apex; seeds many, linear-oblong, 4 lines long, compressed, striated dorsally, with a white longitudinal raphe along the ventral face; coma reddish, sericeous, 6 lines long, suberect, and caducous.

LASEGUEA.

A very good genus, established in 1844 by Prof. De Candolle, well illustrated by Delessert in his 'Icones,' and by Dr. Müller in the 'Flora Brasiliensis,' as well as by Velloz in the 'Flora Fluminensis.' Its several species have frequently (perhaps always?) knotty tuberose roots, from which spring one or more simple, stoutish, erect, subherbaceous stems, with axils not very remote; the leaves are opposite, ovate or oblong, often cordate, on stoutish petioles; raceme lateral or subterminal, forming an elongated brush-like spike, signalized by several imbricate bracts partly concealing as many inconspicuous flowers, which have a tubular corolla with small rounded segments 3–4 times shorter than the tube. De Candolle, in his description of the genus, assigns a sinistrorse convolution to the segments of the corolla, which is not correct; but Müller rightly gives them a dextrorse direction.

LASEGUEA, A. DC. (char. emend.) *Sepala* 5, ovato-acuminata, submembranacea, intus squamula integra vel irregulariter dentata singulatim munita; *corolla* tubulosa; *tubus* cylindricus, calyci æqualis vel longior, medio paullo constrictus, et ibi annulo piloso intus donatus; *segmenta* 5, inæquilatera, oblique ovata, angulo sinistro acutiora, tubo 3–4plo breviora, dextrorsum convoluta. *Stamina* inclusa, ad medium tubi annulo piloso inserta; *filamenta* brevissima, margine villosa; *antheræ* lineari-oblongæ, in conum cohærentes, apice membrana apiculatæ, imo cordatæ vel obtusæ et brevissime bilobæ. *Discus* e lobis 5 obtusis, ovariis dimidio brevior; *stylus* filiformis; *clavuncula* incrassata, imo membrana peltata munita; *stigmata* 2, parva, terminalia. *Folliculi* 2, tenuiter teretes, erecti, vix curvati, sæpe longissimi. *Semina* numerosa, subimbricata, lineari-oblonga, apice truncata, striolata; *coma* erecta, seminis sesquilongitudine, e pilis mollibus confecta.

Plantæ Americæ intertropicæ, raro extratropicæ plerumque Brasilianæ, a radice sæpe tuberoso ortæ; ramuli *subherbacei, vel sublignosi, scandentes*; folia *opposita, ovato-oblonga, sæpe cordata, subbreviter petiolata*; racemi *axillares vel subterminales, pedunculati, crebre multiflori, aspergilliformes, imbricatim bracteati*; flores *mediocres, inconspicui, pedicellati.*

1. LASEGUEA GUILLEMINIANA, A. DC. Prodr. viii. p. 481; Deless. Icon. v. p. 23, tab. 53: *Laseguea erecta*, var. *Guilleminiana*, Müll. Fl. Bras. fasc. xxvi. p. 135, tab. 41. In Brasilia, prov. centralib: *v. s. in herb. Mus. Brit.* Minas Geraës (Claussen).

This plant has a stout erect pubescent stem, with axils ½ in. apart; its decussately opposite leaves are oval, mucronate at the apex, cordate at the base, pubescent beneath, with prominent nerves and reticulate veins, 3–4¼ in. long, 2–3 in. broad, on petioles 1 line long; raceme elongated, 4–8 in. long, pyramidal, bare at the base, densely flowered, clothed with imbricating lanceolate bracts, each 5 lines long, supporting a single pedicellate flower; pedicels twisted, pubescent, 6 lines long; sepals glabrous, lanceolate, 9 lines long, 1 line broad at the base; tube of corolla cylindrical, 8 lines long; segments 1½ line long, acute, dextrorsely convolute; stamens inserted on a pilose ring above the middle of the tube, included; filaments short; anthers coherent in a cone; disk of 5 truncated lobes, half as long as the 2 ovaries.

2. LASEGUEA ERECTA, Müll. (in parte) *l. c.* p. 135: *Laseguea acutifolia*, A. DC. Ann. Sc. Nat. 1844, p. 261; Walp. Rep. vi. p. 477: *Echites erecta*, Vell. Fl. Flum. p. 113, Icon. iii. tab. 45. In Brasilia, ad Encrucilhada, prope conterminam prov. Rio de Janeiro et S. Paulo: *non vidi*.

An erect shrub, about 18 in. high, with a stout semiherbaceous pubescent stem, bearing a single branchlet, the axils being 2 in. apart; leaves decussately opposite, erect, subovate, cordate at the base, narrowing upwards into a subacute point, margins undulate, beneath pilose, with prominent subascending nerves, 3–4 in. long, 1¾–2¼ in. broad, on petioles 2 lines long; racemes axillary and terminal, narrowly spicate, on a peduncle 4 in. long in flower (longer in fruit), with very approximate flowers, signalized by many imbricate adpressed acute bracts 4 lines long; pedicels 4 lines long; sepals lanceolate, 6 lines long; tube of corolla 8 lines long; segments acute, 2 lines long; stamens included, cohering in a cone; follicles 2, erect, parallel or slightly curved, 5 in. long, 1½ line thick.

3. LASEGUEA EMARGINATA, A. DC. *l. c.* p. 481; Müll. *l. c.* p. 136: *Echites emarginata*, Velloz, *l. c.* p. 113, Icon. iii. tab. 46. In Brasilia: *v. s. in herb. Mus. Brit.* prov. central, (Claussen).

A species near the preceding, having a tuberous root, an erect stem with few short branches and with axils 2-3 in. apart, everywhere pubescent; leaves ovate, subcordate at the base, emarginate at the summit, scabrid above, sulcate along the nerves, paler and pubescent beneath, with prominent midrib and very ascending reddish nerves, 2-2¾ in. long, 1⅓-1¼ in. broad, on petioles 2 lines long; racemes axillary and terminal, narrowly cylindrical, 6 in. long, pubescent; peduncle quadrangular, clothed with many imbricating acutely lanceolate coloured bracts 6 lines long; pedicels 6-8 lines long; sepals linear, 8' lines long; tube of corolla greenish white, cylindrical, gradually narrower upwards, 6 lines long; segments oval, 2 lines long, with dextrorse convolution; stamens included in the upper portion of the tube.

4. LASEGUEA GLABRA, A. DC. in Ann. Sc. Nat. 3ᵉ sér. i. p. 262; Walp. Rep. vi. p. 477. In Brasilia, prov. Rio Grande do Sul: *non vidi*.

A species evidently distinct from any of the preceding: it is an erect shrub, everywhere glabrous; leaves approximate, acutely ovate, the nerves patently prominent beneath, with reticulate veins, 3 in. long, 1¼ in. broad; raceme terminal, cylindrical, erect, glabrous, 1 in. long, bearing many approximate flowers furnished with acutely oblong bracts 6 lines long, 1¼ line broad, covering pedicels 4 lines long; sepals obtusely oblong, 6 lines long.

5. LASEGUEA OBLIQUINERVIA, A. DC. Ann. Sc. Nat. 3ᵉ sér. i. p. 261; Walp. Rep. vi. p. 477: *Laseguea Guilleminiana*, var. *obliquinervia*, Müll. *l. c.* p. 135. In Brasilia, prov. S. Paulo: *non vidi*.

An erect plant, with branches densely and fasciculately pilose; leaves obovate, obtuse, mucronulate at the apex, subglabrous above, with oblique nerves and reticulated veins, incano-pubescent beneath, 2⅓-3 in. long, 2-2¼ in. broad, subsessile; raceme 5 in. long; peduncle bare at the base, bearing above many flowers on straight pedicels 6 lines long, covered by linear-lanceolate subglabrous bracts of the same length; sepals linear-lanceolate, subglabrous, narrower at the base, 10 lines long, 1 line broad.

6. LASEGUEA VILLOSA, nob.: ramulis substrictis, dense pilosis; axillis subremotis: foliis oblongis, imum versus angustioribus, et hic profundiusculè cordatis, apice repente et longè cuspidatis, supra fusco-viridibus, sparsè et longè pilosis, subtus ferrugineo-opacis, pilosulis, ad nervos prominentes sparsè hirsutis; petiolis tenuibus, longè pilosis: racemo laterali, subrecurvo, imo pedunculato, mox aspergilliformi, cum bracteis numerosis longiusculis imbricatis, multifloro; floribus subparvis; bracteis oblongis, longè cuspidatis, membranaceis, nervo mediano puberulis; pedicellis brevissimis, hispidulis; sepalis angustè lanceolatis, cuspidatis, medio pilosulis; corolla tubulosa, lutea, fauce sanguinea; tubo subbrevi, bractea paullò longiore, imo ampliore, pilosulo; segmentis brevibus, dextrorsum convolutis. In America centrali: *v. s. in herb. Mus. Brit.* Nicaragua (Seemann 95).

The axils are 3⅓ in. apart; the leaves 6¼ in. long including the basal sinus (6 lines deep), 2¾ in. broad, on petioles 1 in. long; raceme 3½ in. long; peduncle bare at the base for 1¼ in.; bracts 6 lines long, 1 line broad; pedicels 1½ line long; sepals 4 lines long; corolla in bud 6 lines long.

7. LASEGUEA ANTENNACEA, nob.: *Echites antennacea*, A. DC. *l. c.* p. 456. In Peruvia (Pavon): *non vidi*.

A species with scabridly pubescent terete branches; leaves oblong, subcordate, acuminate, scabrid above, with several glands at the base of the limb, velutinous beneath, 4 in. long, 1¼ in. broad, on petioles 3 lines long; raceme lateral, arcuate, 2-3 times as long as the leaves, scabridly puberulous, bearing many almost sessile flowers, partly concealed by as many bracts, which are oblong, mucronate, membranaceous, reddish, 6-8 lines long, 2-3 lines broad; sepals acuminately ovate, 2 lines long, with an inner dentate scale; corolla scabridulous, red; tube 1 in. long, a little narrowed in the middle; segments shorter than the tube; stamens inserted in the constriction of the tube; disk urceolate, thick, a little shorter than the ovaries; follicles arcuate, torulose, converging at the apex, 6 in. long; seeds 4 lines long, with a rather long reddish coma.

This species is placed in *Laseguea* on account of its general character, its inflorescence, and more especially the form of its disk; it is evidently near the preceding species.

8. LASEGUEA BICOLOR, nob.: *Echites bicolor*, Miq. Stirp. Surin. Sel. p. 154; Walp. Ann. iii. p. 42. In Surinam: *non vidi*.

A plant possessing all the characters of *Laseguea*: its branches are scabrescent; the leaves ovate or elliptic-ovate, roundish and shortly cordate at the base, shortly acuminate, subscabrid above, pilose on the midrib above with hairs globular at their base, beneath subsericeously pubescent, on very short petioles; racemes axillary, cylindrical, densely spicate, as long as the leaves, puberulous, furnished with many imbricating lanceolate bracts as long as the pedicel and calyx; pedicels short; sepals linear, subequal, puberulous, each with an inner obtuse or denticulate scale; tube of corolla slender, puberulous, somewhat dilated at the base; segments acutely ovate, shorter than the tube.

9. LASEGUEA LATIUSCULA, nob.: suberecta, ramis rigide teretibus, cum axillis remotis: foliis oppositis, oblongis vel ovatis, imo oblique rotundatis, apice late ellipticis, et in acumen subbreve cuspidatum subito constrictis, submembranaceis, margine ciliatis, supra profunde viridibus, ad costam nervosque puberulis, subtus rufescentibus, præsertim ad costam et nervos subhispidulis; petiolis brevibus, canaliculatis, puberulis: racemo laterali, quam folium subbreviore, erecto, imo pedunculato, mox aspergilliformi, bracteis crebre imbricatis, adpresse erecti, lineari-lanceolatis, cuspidatis, quam pedicellus calyxque triplo longioribus, glabris, rubris, marginibus submembranaceis; pedicellis brevissimis; sepalis cuspidato-lanceolatis, subinæqualibus, glabris, intus squamula lata apice 3-5-denticulata munitis; corolla tubulosa, carnosula, rubidula; tubo cylindrico, medio vix coarctato; segmentis membranaceis, ovalibus, subacutis, inæquilateris, quam tubus triplo brevioribus, dextrorsum convolutis: staminibus ad medium tubi annulo retrorsum piloso insertis; antheris cohærentibus, apice membranaceis, imo in furcas 2 parallele obtusas subbreves divisis; disco cylindrico, lobis 5, apice truncatis; ovariis 2, acute oblongis, discum excedentibus; stylo filiformi; clavuncula incrassata:

folliculis 2, erectis, parallelis, teretibus; seminibus comosis. In Cayenne: *v. s. in herb. Mus. Brit.* (Van Rohr).

The rigid upright branches are 1 line thick, with axils 4 in. apart; leaves 3¾–4¼ in. long, 2½–2¾ in. broad, on petioles 2½–3 lines long; raceme 3 in. long, on an erect peduncle bare at its base for one third of its length, thence furnished with numerous imbricate bracts 6 lines long, 1 line broad; pedicels 1 line long; sepals 1½ line long; tube of corolla 9 lines long; segments 4 lines long, 3 lines broad; the 2 follicles are 6¼ in. long, 1¾ line broad; the seeds are linear-oblong, 6 lines long, 1 line broad, terminated by an erect coma 9 lines long.

A drawing of this species, with its floral and carpological analysis, is shown in Plate XXXV. A.

10. LASEGUEA VENUSTULA, nob.: ramulis substrictis, brunneis, scabridule pruinosis; axillis remotiusculis: foliis oppositis, obovato-oblongis, infra medium angustioribus, imo in lobos 2 obtuse angustos auriculato-cordatis, apice recurvule attenuato-acuminatis, marginibus tenuiter cartilagineis, supra fusco-viridibus, scabridule pruinosis, ad costam sulcatis, nervis immersis, subtus fusce hepaticis, opacis, obsolete scabridulis, costa nervis venisque transversim reticulatis rubidulis prominulis; petiolo canaliculato, scabrido, quam limbus 12plo breviore: racemo laterali, quam folium subbreviore, ad medium pedunculato, sursum aspergilliformi, multifloro; bracteis lanceolatis, crebre imbricatis, scabridulis, marginibus membranaceis, quam calyx triplo longioribus; pedicellis brevibus; sepalis lanceolatis, acuminatissimis, scabridulis, intus squamula lata apice 3-denticulata munitis; corollæ tubo cylindrico, carnosulo, superne pro tertia parte subampliato, quam calyx multo longiore; segmentis oblongis, dolabriformibus, dextrorsum convolutis, quam tubus triente brevioribus; staminibus annulo niveo-piloso ad contractionem tubi insertis; antheris cohærentibus, apice membranaceis, imo in furcas 2 obtusas breves divisis; disco urceolato, in lobos 5 emarginatos breviter fisso; ovariis 2, oblongis, paullo brevioribus; stylo filiformi; clavuncula incrassata, imo membranacea. In Cayenne: *v. s. in herb. Mus. Brit.* ex loc. cit. (Van Rohr).

A species near the preceding, but with larger, narrower leaves; axils 2–3 in. apart; leaves 3–4½ in. long, 1–1¾ in. broad, on petioles 3–4 lines long; raceme 2½ in. long, on a peduncle half that length; bracts 4 lines long, 2 lines broad, very approximate, erect; pedicels ½ line long; sepals 1¼ line long; tube of corolla 9 lines long; segments 3 lines long and broad.

11. LASEGUEA SUBSPICATA, nob.: *Echites subspicata*, Vahl, Ecl. ii. p. 18; A. DC. *l. c.* p. 467. In America centrali (Van Rohr): *non vidi*.

A species near the preceding. A climbing plant, with smooth terete branchlets; leaves patently opposite, oblong, subcordate at the base, attenuated at the apex, very glabrous, shining, very entire, reticulately veined, beneath with a prominent reddish midrib, 4–5 in. long, on obsoletely villous petioles 6 lines long; raceme lateral, glabrous, on a peduncle thickened above, and then extending in a brush-like form, nearly as long as the leaf, with very approximate flowers, and having many dark imbricating linear-lanceolate bracts with membranaceous margins longer than the pedicel and calyx; pedicels very short; sepals lanceolate, glabrous; corolla glabrous, with a cylindrical tube 1 in. long, shortly swollen near the throat.

12. **Lasegura foliosa**, nob.: *Amblyanthera foliosa*, Müll. in Linn. xxx. p. 427. Prope Mexico (Giesbrecht) : *non vidi*.

A species, according to Müller, resembling the preceding : its branches are 18 in. long, with terete glabrous remote branchlets densely foliaceous ; leaves subsessile, erect, obovate, cordate at the base, gradually acuminate, membranaceous, dusky, subglabrous above, with 6–8 pairs of divergent prominulent nerves subarcuately conjoined, reticulately veined, hirtellous along the nerves, puberulous on the margins, $3\frac{1}{4}$–$4\frac{3}{4}$ in. long, $1\frac{1}{4}$–$1\frac{3}{4}$ in. broad, on petioles $1\frac{3}{4}$ line long; racemes axillary, shorter than the leaves and concealed by them, glabrous, with many small flowers upon a short peduncle, on pedicels 4 lines long, supported by acuminate linear-lanceolate bracts $3\frac{1}{4}$ lines long ; sepals linear or triangular-lanceolate, acuminate, ciliate on the margins, $3\frac{1}{4}$–$3\frac{3}{4}$ lines long, with 4–8 inner subulate scales; corolla in the whole $9\frac{1}{2}$ lines long, its tube narrowed at the base for two thirds of its length, widening above ; its segments rhomboidally obovate, short; anthers short; disk half-cleft into 5 obtuse lobes, as long as the ovoid glabrous ovaries.

13. **Lasegura pubiflora**, nob.: erecta, ramulis compressis, puberulis: foliis elliptico-oblongis, imo subacutis, apice in acumen breve constrictis, chartaceis, marginibus revolutis, utrinque sparse puberulis, supra viridibus, ad costam sulcatis, nervis impressis, subtus flavescentibus, opacis, nervis vix prominulis, venis valde reticulatis ; petiolis limbo 5plo brevioribus : racemis axillaribus, crebre spicatifloris, undique pilis mollibus longis sparsim puberulis, bracteis spathulato-lanceolatis, imbricatis, erectis, membranaceis ; pedicellis brevioribus ; sepalis acutissime linearibus, membranaceis ; corollæ tubo quam calyx triplo longiore, apice' paullo ampliato, extus dense niveo-piloso, intus glabro ; segmentis membranaceis, oblique rotundatis, dextrorsum convolutis, margine exteriore pilosis ; staminibus supra medium tubi inclusis ; filamentis brevibus, pilosis ; antheris linearibus, apiculatis, imo breviter obtuse bilobis ; disco 5-lobo, lobis obtusis, ovariis 2 pilosis æquilongo. In Antillis :
v. s. in herb. Mus. Brit. Jamaica (Dr. Wright, sub *Echites suberecta*).

Leaves $1\frac{1}{4}$–$1\frac{3}{4}$ in. long, 7–9 lines broad, on petioles 3–4 lines long ; raceme 4 in. long ; bracts 4 lines long, 1 line broad, 5–6 lines distant ; pedicels 4 lines long ; sepals $3\frac{1}{4}$ lines long, $\frac{1}{2}$ line broad ; tube of corolla 9 lines long ; segments 3 lines long and broad.

14. **Lasegura Pentlandiana**, A. DC. Ann. Sc. Nat. 3⁰ sér. i. p. 262 ; Walp. Rep. vi. p. 478. In Bolivia, ad Illimani : *non vidi*.

A scandent species, allied to the two preceding : branches glabrous below, puberulous above ; leaves ovate or acutely ovate, glabrous above, incano-pubescent beneath, 2 in. long, 1–$1\frac{1}{2}$ in. broad, on petioles 6–10 lines long; bracts of raceme 4 lines long ; pedicels 5 lines long ; sepals 6 lines long, less than 1 line broad.

15. **Lasegura Hookeri**, Müll. Fl. Bras. xxvi. p. 136 : *Parsonsia? bracteata*, Hook. Arn. Journ. Bot. i. p. 287 ; A. DC. *l. c.* p. 402. In Brasilia, prov. Rio Grande do Sul (Tweedie 88).

A strong climbing plant, with acutely ovate-cordate leaves, pubescent beneath, 2–3 in. long, on short petioles ; racemes axillary, 8 in. long, spicately flowered ; flowers approximate, numerous, on short pedicels, which are hidden by as many imbricating lanceolate bracts ; sepals lanceolate, as long as the bracts ; tube of corolla of the same length ; segments small, ovate, erect; stamens included, seated on a pilose ring above the base of the tube; disk of 5 lobes, surrounding the ovaries.

This species is placed by Messrs. Bentham and Hooker (Gen. ii. p. 725) in *Odontadenia*, to which genus it is seen to bear no relation whatever.

16. LASEGUEA LEPTOCARPA, nob.: *Parsonsia leptocarpa*, Hook. Arn. Journ. Bot. i. p. 287. In Brasilia, prov. Rio Grande do Sul.

A species near the preceding, climbing to the top of the highest trees. It has pubescent branches, with glabrous, oval, obtuse, membranaceous leaves on short petioles; raceme terminal, subsessile, covered closely with imbricating, small, acutely oval bracts; tube of corolla nearly twice the length of the sepals, pilose within towards the base; its segments lanceolate, rotate; lobes of the disk acute; follicles 1–2 feet long, less than a line thick. These are all the particulars recorded, from which it is evident that it is a species closely allied to the preceding.

17. LASEGUEA JÆGERI, nob.: *Urechites Jægeri*, Müll. in Linn. xxx. p. 443. In Hayti: *non vidi*.

There is no indication whatever that this plant belongs to *Urechites*; on the contrary, it differs in its habit and inflorescence, in which respects it agrees well with *Laseguea*. Müller saw only an immature flower, and, what is more important, knew nothing of its fruit and seeds. Its branches are subscandent, cinereously purpurescent, glabrous, the branchlets slender, paler, terete, patently hirsute; leaves oblong-elliptic or broadly oblong, subcordate at the base, suddenly and shortly acuminate, membranaceous, pilose on both sides, paler beneath, with reticulate veins, $1\frac{3}{8}$–$3\frac{1}{4}$ in. long, $1\frac{3}{8}$–2 in. broad, on petioles (short, as stated in the final note) $1\frac{1}{2}$–2 lines long ($3\frac{1}{2}$–5 mm., not cm.); racemes lateral, longer than the leaves, hirsute, with long white hairs; peduncle many times longer than the petiole, laxly many-flowered; pedicels twice as long as the sepals, supported by linear-acute bracts $5\frac{3}{4}$–$8\frac{1}{2}$ lines long, 1–$1\frac{1}{4}$ line broad; sepals linear, acuminate, 7–$8\frac{1}{2}$ lines long; corolla immature, narrowed at its base for one fourth of its length, broader above, niveo-hirsute outside, with short segments; disk distinctly 5-lobulate, a little shorter than the ovaries. These characters strictly conform with *Laseguea*, not with *Urechites*.

The *Laseguea calycosa*, Griesb., = *Rhodocalyx calycosus* (suprà, p. 140).

HÆMADICTYON.

It has already been stated (p. 143) that the authors of the 'Genera Plantarum' have merged this genus in *Prestonia*, merely on account of the presence, in both cases, of certain faucial appendages in the corolla; and some of the reasons were then given (*loc. cit.*) for rejecting this union; others, equally potent, are here offered. The plants of *Hæmadictyon* may generally be recognized by their habit: their leaves are very often more diaphanous, of a peculiar hue, exhibiting beautifully coloured veins (whence the generic name); the dilated axils of the branches are quite bare of the many stipules present in *Prestonia*; the inflorescence, upon a long simple flexuose peduncle always bare at its base, rises laterally from the node, and is furnished above with several laxly alternate flowers upon longish pedicels, thus contrasting ostensibly with *Prestonia*, where the peduncle, always branching, rises out of a cluster of stipuloid scales, and bears numerous almost sessile flowers generally aggregated in capitate heads; the disk also consists of 5 free fleshy erect lobes (not combined into a cylindrical cup); the 2 follicles are always divaricately separate, long, narrow, and torulose (not combined into a long, stout, 2-celled capsule). Other minor differences exist, as the following amended diagnosis will show.

HÆMADICTYON, Lindl. (char. emend.): *Prestonia* (in parte) Benth. & Hook. (non aliorum). *Sepala* aut minora et lineari-acuminata, vel majora et acute ovata, membranacea, intus squamula acute lineari apice 3-dentata munita. *Corolla* hypocrateriformis; *tubus* latiuscule cylindricus, fauce subconstrictus, et ibi *annulo* integro signatus, remotiuscule sub ore segmentis alternis, *appendicibus* 5 anguste linearibus bidenticulatis apice exsertis instructus; *segmenta* obtuse inæquilatera et deltoidea, tubo subbreviora, dextrorsum convoluta. *Stamina* 5, e pilis retrorsis in cristulas totidem, medio tubi inserta, apice vix exserta, in conum subcohærentia; *filamenta* brevia, retrorsum ciliata; *antheræ* lineari-acuminatæ, imo divergenter biaristatæ. *Discus* e lobis 5, erectis, obtuse oblongis, intus canaliculatis, carnosis constans; *ovaria* 2, ovata, disco æquilonga; *stylus* tenuis; *clavuncula* incrassata, imo indusiata; *stigmata* 2, parva, ovata, terminalia. *Folliculi* 2, longi, teretes, subtorulosi, plus minusve divergentes. *Semina* plurima, oblonga, dorso costata, ventre *raphe* longitudinali signata. *Embryo* in *albumine*; *cotyledonibus* 2, oblongis, foliaceis; *radicula* tenuiter tereti supera his breviore.

Suffrutices *Americæ meridionalis scandentes*; rami *cum axillis remotis nude dilatatis*; folia *oblonga, opposita, sæpe subtranslucentia et eleganter venosa, petiolata*; inflorescentia *laterali, simpliciter longe pedunculata*; flores *laxe alterni, tenuiter pedicellati et bracteolati*.

1. HÆMADICTYON VENOSUM, Lindl. Trans. Hort. Soc. vi. p. 71: *Hæmadictyon nutans*, A. DC. Prodr. viii. p. 426: *Echites nutans*, Anderson, Bot. Mag. li. tab. 2473; Griseb. Fl. Br. W. Ind. p. 413: *Echites sanguinolenta*, Juss., Tussac. Fl. Ant. i. tab. 11; A. DC. *l. c.* p. 413. In Amer. merid. et Antillis: *v. s. in herb. Mus. Brit.* Amer. merid. (Shakespear, sub *Tabernæmontana axillaris*).

A climbing species with smooth branches; leaves oblong-ovate, acute at the base, narrowing upwards into an acute reflected point, submembranaceous or chartaceous, subtranslucent, very glabrous, with about 9 pairs of reddish fine nerves arcuately conjoined, with reticulated veins, margins scarcely revolute, pale-green above, yellowish-opake beneath, with slightly prominulent midrib and nerves, 4–10 in. long, 1½–2¼ in. broad, on slender petioles 2–4 lines long conjoined by a transverse ridge across the node; racemes solitary and lateral at each axil, 2½ in. long, on a peduncle bare at the base for 6 lines, bearing above several alternate flowers on pedicels 3 lines long, based by small bracteoles; sepals spathulate-lanceolate, 4 lines long, with an inner linear-pointed, denticulate scale; corolla greenish-yellow, its tube 7–8 lines long, having a narrow ring in the mouth, and below it 5 subulate appendages a little exserted; segments ovate, obtusely inequilateral, crispate and subreflexed, 4 lines long; disk half-cleft into 5 lobes, a little shorter than the 2 ovaries.

2. HÆMADICTYON EXSERTUM, A. DC. *l. c.* p. 426; Schlecht. Linn. xxvi. 661. In Venezuela, ad Caracas: *non vidi*.

A climbing species, with slender pubescent branches; leaves elliptic-oblong, acute at both ends, thinly chartaceous, intense green above, pallid green beneath, scarcely pubescent, 2–4¼ in. long, 1½–1¾ in. broad, on petioles 2–4 lines long; raceme lateral, longer than the leaves, on a peduncle bare at the base, bearing above 5–8 approximate alternate flowers, on pedicels 6–9 lines long, supported by bracteoles one fourth their length; sepals acuminate-lanceolate, revolute and ciliate on the margins, 2¼ lines long, with an inner ovoid scale equally broad; corolla glabrous, its tube 7 lines long, slightly constricted in the middle, its appendages semi-exserted; segments 2½ lines long, 1¼ line broad; stamens inserted on a pilose ring in the middle of the tube; anthers cohering, somewhat exserted; disk of 5 short lobes, longer than the fusiform ovaries.

3. HÆMADICTYON MARGINATUM, Benth. Hook. Journ. Bot. iii. p. 250; A. DC. *l.c.* p. 426. In Guiana Brit. Pirara (Schomb. 713) : *non vidi.*

A glabrous climbing plant, near *H. venosum*, with oblong leaves, acute at both ends, coriaceous, smooth above, with recurved thickened margins, 2–3 in. long; raceme longer than the leaves, on a peduncle bare at its base, bearing above several flowers on pedicels minutely bracteolate; calyx and corolla exactly as *H. venosum.*

4. HÆMADICTYON CAYENNENSE, A. DC. *l. c.* p. 427. In Cayenne: *non vidi.*

A climbing plant, with slender scabridulous branches; leaves elliptic, obtuse at the base, cuspidately acuminate, membranaceous, glabrous above, with distant nerves and veins, subscabridulous beneath, 2–2½ in. long, 1¼–1½ in. broad, on petioles 5 lines long; raceme elongated, glabrous, the bare portion of the peduncle as long as the leaves, bearing above many flowers on twisted pedicels 6–7 lines long, minutely bracteolate; sepals lanceolate, acuminate, glabrous, 2 lines long, with an inner ovate denticulate scale; tube of corolla 6–7 lines long, glabrous, cylindrical, a little wider above, with a callous ring in the mouth, and beneath it 5 linear included appendages; segments oblong, obtuse, crispate, shorter than the tube; anthers a little exserted; disk of 5 ovate obtuse lobes, subconnate at their base.

5. HÆMADICTYON GAUDICHAUDII, A. DC. (non Müll.) *l. c.* p. 426: *Echites suberosa*, Vell. Fl. Flum. p. 111, Icon. iii. tab. 34. In Brasilia: *v. v. et sicc. in herb. meo* (no. 1585), circa Rio de Janeiro; *v. s. in herb. Mus. Brit.* prov. Saõ Paulo, Santo Amaro (Bowie & Cunningham).

A climbing species, with slender terete flexuose branches marked by prominent lenticels, with dilated axils 9 in. apart, marked by a transverse somewhat vaginant ridge; leaves oblong, narrowed below the middle, roundish or subobtuse at the base, shortly acuminate and callously mucronate at the summit, margins sinuously undulate, chartaceous, very glabrous, bright green above, sulcate on the midrib, with about 7 pairs of fine divaricate nerves arcuately conjoined, pale yellowish beneath, opake, with prominent midrib, nerves, and finely reticulated veins, 4–6½ in. long, 1¼–2½ in. broad, on slender channelled petioles 3–4 lines long; raceme solitary and lateral at the nodes, 7 in. long, on a slender peduncle bare for half its length, bearing upwards 16–20 alternate or geminate flowers, on slender patent pedicels 4–5 lines long, supported by minute recurved bracteoles; sepals acutely oblong, with parallel nerves, imbricate, with an inner broad, roundish, denticulate scale, puberulous outside, 3 lines long, 1½ line broad; tube of corolla cylindrical, pale yellow, glabrous, 8 lines long, with a thin annular ring in the mouth, and beneath it 5 linear appendages half-exserted; segments rhomboidally inequilateral, acute at the sinister angle, 3 lines long, 2 lines broad, dextrorsely convolute; stamens seated on a pilose ring a little above the middle of the tube; filaments compressed, ciliate, reaching the mouth; anthers linear-oblong, acuminate, partially cohering and wholly exserted, 2 lines long, each with 2 subdivaricating basal prongs; disk of 5 free, oblong, obtuse, erect lobes, as long as the 2 acutely oblong ovaries; follicles, according to Velloz, 2, free, slender, torulose, slightly arcuate, 5–10 in. long, 2 lines broad at the distentions, glabrous; seeds 6 lines long, 1½ line broad, with an apical coma 9 lines long.

Velloz says the plant is called *Cipó carneiro* (fleshy climber) on account of the thick fleshy rugose stem, which is also lactescent; he found it at Santa Cruz, in the province of Rio de Janeiro.

6. HÆMADICTYON BRACTEOSUM, Müll. Fl. Bras. xxvi. p. 168. Prope Rio de Janeiro (Riedel): *v. v. et sicc. in herb. meo* (no. 3270), ad Morro Flamengo.

This is a slender twining species, with densely hirtellous branches, near 1 line thick, its axils 4–5 in. apart; leaves oblong-ovate, roundish at the base, where they are often subplicate, suddenly constricted at the apex into an acumen, thinly chartaceous, with subundulate margins, of a dark-olive hue, with 5–6 pairs of divergent, arcuately conjoined nerves and laxly reticulate veins, paler and subferruginous-opake beneath, the nerves prominulent, 3⅝–4¾ in. long, 1¾–2¼ in. broad, on petioles 5–7 lines long; racemes solitary at the nodes, 2½–3¼ in. long, shortly hirtellous, densely flowered on a peduncle bare at its base for the length of near 1 in., bearing above 10–20 flowers on very slender approximate pedicels 9 lines long, supported by a very membranaceous spathulately linear-acuminate bract 6 lines long, 1 line broad; sepals oblong-ovate, acute, submembranaceous, reticulately veined, subpuberulous, each with an inner deltoid 4-denticulate scale; corolla glabrous; tube broadly cylindrical, 9 lines long, with a crenulate annular ring in its mouth, and below it 5 linear semi-exserted appendages; segments rhomboidally inequilateral, expanding, 5 lines long, 3 lines broad; the usual stamens, inserted in the middle of the tube, nearly reaching the mouth; disk of 5 lobes, scarcely longer than the 2 glabrous ovaries.

7. HÆMADICTYON DENTICULATUM, nob.: *Echites denticulata*, Vell. Fl. Flum. p. 110, Icon. iii. tab. 30; A. DC. *l. c.* p. 455: *Hæmadictyon macroneurum* (in parte), Müll. *l. c.* p. 169. Prov. Rio de Janeiro (Velloz) in sylvis maritimis: *v. s. in herb. Mus. Brit.* Itagoahy (Bowie & Cunningham).

A climbing glabrous species, well represented by Velloz, and very distinct from *H. macroneurum*, Müll. Its branches are flexuose, striate, pale, glabrous, with axils 4–4¼ in. apart; leaves elliptic-oblong, acute at the base, suddenly constricted towards the summit into a very narrow acute acumen, dark green above, opake, somewhat translucent, with dark red midrib, nerves and very reticulate veins, obsoletely puberulous, yellowish and opake beneath, 3–4 in. long, 1½–2 in. broad, on subpubescent channelled petioles 3 lines long; raceme solitary and lateral at the nodes, 3½ in. long, on a slender peduncle bare for half its length, bearing above several alternate flowers on divergent puberulous pedicels 4 lines long, supported by acute bracteoles 1½ line long; sepals acutely oblong, puberulous, 1¼–3 lines long, each with a rather large, acute, broad inner scale; tube of corolla cylindrical, 6 lines long; segments inequilateral, acute, 2 lines long; stamens inserted in the middle of the tube; anthers slender, with acuminate summits, semi-exserted, biaristate at the base; appendages semi-exserted beyond the annular ring.

8. HÆMADICTYON OVATUM, nob.: *Hæmadictyon Gaudichaudii*, Müll. in parte (non A. DC.), Flor. Bras. XXVI. p. 168, tab. 50. fig. 5 (flos et semen). Circa Rio de Janeiro: *v. v.* in Monte Corcovado, *et sicc. in herb. meo* (no. 1567 et 4628).

A plant very distinct from De Candolle's species (*Gaudichaudii*), having oval leaves with a short very sudden acumen and long deflexed racemes; the branches are glabrous, pallidly terete, subflexuose, striolate, verrucosely lenticellate, dilated at the axils, which are 4½–6½ in. apart, with a crenulate transverse ring of many stipuloid fleshy glands; leaves ovate or oblong-ovate, rounded and often obsoletely cordate at the base, suddenly and shortly acuminate or retuse at the apex, chartaceous, with scarcely revolute margins, green and glabrous above, with about 6 pairs of slender semi-immersed nerves arcuately conjoined, yellowish opake beneath, subscabrid, somewhat hispidulous on the prominulent midrib and nerves, 3¼–5 in. long, 2–3 in. broad, on patent subpuberulous petioles 3 lines long; racemes lateral and solitary at the nodes, 4–5 in. long, on a rather slender subdeflexed peduncle, bare at its base for a length of 1½–2¼ in., subangular, subverrucose, subglabrous, subpuberulous, somewhat flexuose above and bearing many alternate flowers on slender patent or reflexed pedicels 1½ line apart, 4 lines long, supported by linear acute bracteoles ¼ line long; sepals oblong, acute, 2½ lines long, 2 lines broad, with an inner acute 3-denticulate scale; corolla salver-shaped; tube 6 lines long, with a faucial annular ring and 5 linear semi-exserted appendages arising from below the mouth; segments oblong, inequilateral, expanded, 3 lines long; disk, ovaries, style, clavuncle, and stigmata as in the generic character; follicles 2, immature, 4½–6 in. long, very strangulately torulose.

A drawing of this species, showing its floral and carpological structure, is given in Plate XXXIV.

9. HÆMADICTYON ASPERUM, Müll. *l. c.* p. 169. In Brasilia, prov. Rio de Janeiro et Bahia: *v. s. in herb. Mus. Brit.* Bahia (Lockhart).

A species having subangular branches, at first clothed with spreading long rigid hairs, afterwards scabrid; axils 5 in. apart; leaves oblong-ovate, roundish and plicately recurved at the base, obtusely subacute at the summit, with a fine mucronate point, margins very revolute, rigidly coriaceous, dark olive-green above, opake, scabridulous and sulcate along the fine arching nerves and reticulate veins, palish glaucous-green beneath, opake, scabridulous upon the prominent midrib, nerves, and veins, 2¾–6 in. long 1½–2¾ in. broad, on petioles 2¼–4 lines long; raceme solitary and lateral at the nodes, 1¼ in. long, on a fuscous reflexed peduncle bearing several alternate flowers on pedicels rather approximate and 2 lines long, supported by acutely ovate bracteoles 1 line long;

sepals acute, 3 lines long, rigidly puberulous; tube of corolla scarcely swelling above, 12 lines long; segments 6 lines long.

10. HÆMADICTYON TOMENTELLUM, Benth. Bot. Sulph. p. 126. In Guayaquil (Hartweg 670): *non vidi*.

A slender species, near the preceding, with glabrous or obsoletely glauco-tomentellous branches; leaves ovate-oblong, cordate at the base, shortly acuminate, glabrous or minutely hirtellous above, nerves scarcely visible, densely glauco-tomentose beneath, (size not given); raceme solitary and lateral at the nodes, shorter than the leaves, on a peduncle scarcely longer than the petioles, angular, minutely hirtellous, bearing several subaggregate flowers on pedicels shorter than the calyx; sepals lanceolate-acuminate, unequal, 5–6 lines long, with a broad short inner scale; tube of corolla cylindrical, 1 in. long, constricted above, with an annular ring in the mouth, the appendages extending a little beyond it; segments large, expanded; stamens seated in the middle of the tube, on slender filaments; anthers acuminate, scarcely exserted, with 2 long basal prongs; follicles 2, tomentellous, 4–6 in. long; seeds oblong, triquetrous, with a copious longer coma.

11. HÆMADICTYON PALLIDUM, A. DC. *l. c.* p. 428: *Echites annularis?*, Pavon MSS. (non Linn.). In Peruvia: *non vidi*.

A glabrous species, of which little is known. Its leaves are ovate-oblong, cordate at the base, acute, pallid, opake, 3 in. long, 1½ in. broad, on petioles 5 lines long; raceme shorter than the leaves; peduncle 1½ in. long, bearing several flowers on pedicels 4 lines long, supported by acute bracteoles 3 lines long; sepals oblong-obovate, subvelutinous, about 6 lines long, with an acutely ovate inner scale; tube of corolla yellow, cylindrical, 14 lines long, narrower at the throat, with segments 9 lines long; stamens seated in the upper portion of the tube; anthers hirtous behind, sagittate at the base, the appendages below the throat 2 lines long, pilose; disk of 5 obtuse lobes half as long as the ovaries.

12. HÆMADICTYON CALYCINUM, Lindl. (sec. Benth.): *Hæmadictyon Gaudichaudii*, Müll. in parte (non A. DC.) *l. c.* p. 168. In Brasilia, Rio Negro: *v. s. in herb. meo*, Barra do Rio Negro (Spruce 1882).

A handsome and peculiar species, very distinct from *H. Gaudichaudii*, which Müller probably did not see. It is a climbing plant, its branches being slender, pale, glabrous, angularly sulcate, verruculous, with dilated axils 9 in. apart, having a prominent crenulate ridge across the nodes; the leaves are elliptic-oblong, obtuse at the base, with a shortish, subreflexed, acute acumen, chartaceous, glabrous, green above, with about 10 pairs of fine prominulent divaricating nerves arcuately conjoined, pale yellow beneath, with prominent reddish midrib, nerves, and reticulate veins, 5–5¾ in. long, 2¼–2½ in. broad, on corrugated petioles 3 lines long; raceme solitary and lateral at the nodes, 3–3½ in. long; peduncle bare at the base for 1¼ in., bearing above about 10 alternate lax flowers on subreflexed slender pedicels 6–8 lines long, minutely bracteolate, all very glabrous; sepals acutely oblong, subacuminate, 5 lines long, 2 lines broad, submembranaceous, rugulous at the base, with a broad reddish pluridenticulate inner scale; corolla and other parts as usual.

13. HÆMADICTYON ACUTIFOLIUM, Benth. MSS.; Müll. *l. c.* p. 167. In Amazonas: *v. s. in herb. meo*, Barra do Rio Negro (Spruce 1002).

A climbing species, with extremely slender, terete, obsoletely puberulous twining branches, with axils 5-6 in. apart; leaves lanceolate-elliptic, subobtuse or acute at the base, gradually acuminate, chartaceous, glabrous, fuscous green above, somewhat shining, with about 8 pairs of semi-immersed nerves, ferruginous beneath, opake, with scarcely prominulent nerves and fine transversely reticulate veins, $2\frac{3}{4}$-$3\frac{1}{4}$ in. long, $9\frac{1}{2}$-15 lines broad, on slender channelled petioles $2\frac{1}{2}$-3 lines long; raceme solitary and lateral at the nodes, patent, 3-4 in. long, on a slender peduncle bare for half its length, bearing above about 10 flowers on rather distant, alternate or often geminate, very patent, slender pedicels 6 lines long, supported by small acute bracteoles; sepals ovate-acuminate, reflexed at the summit, $1\frac{1}{2}$ line long, each with an inner rounded scale; tube of corolla cylindrical, a little swollen above the middle, 7 lines long, with a broadish crenulate ring in the mouth and below it 5 linear short included appendages; segments dolabriform, 3 lines long; stamens inserted in the middle of the tube; anthers with acuminate summits extending beyond the mouth, with 2 long subdivergent basal prongs; disk of 5 oblong-obtuse lobes, connate at the base, concealing 2 ovate ovaries.

Müller's variety *latifolia*, from Minas and Cuyaba, is probably a distinct species, and must not be confounded with *Prestonia latifolia*.

14. HÆMADICTYON CALIGINOSUM, nob.: scandens, ramulis tenuibus, teretibus: foliis ellipticis, imo acutis, apice breviter acuminatis, integris, submembranaceis, glabris, supra nitidis, caliginoso-viridibus, subcorrugulatis, nervis tenuibus, subimmersis, subtus pallide ferrugineis, opacis, costa nervisque rubellis prominulis, venis reticulatis immersis; petiolis tenuibus, canaliculatis, limbo 12plo brevioribus; racemo laterali, reflexo, folium paullo excedente; pedunculo subflexuoso, longo; floribus alternis; pedicellis patentibus, imo bracteola parvula munitis; sepalis subparvis, lanceolatis, apice reflexis, cum squamula basali bidentata; corolla tubulosa, glabra; tubo cylindrico, imo paullulo latiore, fauce linea transversa vix prominula signato; segmentis tubo triplo brevioribus, rotunde dolabriformibus, angulo sinistro acutatis, dextrorsum convolutis; staminibus supra medium tubi, e lineis retrorsum pilosis ortis; antheris in conum cohærentibus, acuminatis, imo biaristatis; disco e lobis 5 oblongis, intus canaliculatis, imo connatis, ovariis 2 æquilongo; stylo tenuissimo; clavuncula incrassata, 5-sulcata, imo in membranam peltatam expansa; stigmatibus 2, minutis, terminalibus. In Peruvia: *v. s. in herb. Mus. Brit.* Tarapota (Spruce 4924).

A species near *H. acutifolium.* The axils of the branchlets are 1-2 in. apart; leaves $3\frac{3}{4}$-4 in. long, $1\frac{1}{2}$-$1\frac{3}{4}$ in. broad, on petioles $3\frac{1}{4}$-4 lines long; racemes 4 in. long; flowers 1-2 lines apart; pedicels patent or subreflexed, 4-5 lines long; sepals scarcely a line long; tube of corolla 7 lines long; segments $2\frac{1}{2}$ lines long; the 5 very short appendages are affixed lower than usual, and are hidden by the anthers.

15. HÆMADICTYON MEMBRANACEUM, Müll. *l. c.* p. 167. In Brasilia, ad Taipú, prov. Parahiba? (Schott 5389): *non vidi.*

A species with subangular reddish branches, clothed with subhirtellous hairs bulbous at the base, and with remote axils; leaves ovate or oblong-ovate, acute at the base, acuminate, thinly membranaceous, very translucent, very glabrous, darkish, marked by a rather broad midrib and 6–8 pairs of semi-immersed nerves, with laxly reticulate veins, 6–8 in. long, 2–3½ in. broad, subdecurrent on petioles 2½–7¼ lines long; raceme solitary at the nodes, one third the length of the leaves, on a puberulous peduncle bearing alternate or geminate flowers on slender pedicels, supported by much shorter bracteoles; sepals ovate-lanceolate, acuminate, greenish, membranaceous, 7¼ lines long.

The immature flower was useless for examination; but the plant is placed near *H. acutifolia* by Müller.

16. HÆMADICTYON SCHIZADENIUM, Müll. in Linn. xxx. p. 431. In Mexico, ad Papantla: *non vidi*.

Its branches are subangular and scabrid; leaves oblong-ovate or oblong-elliptic, rounded and subcordate at the base, shortly acuminate, rigidly membranaceous, margins revolute, yellowish green above, glabrous, beneath punctulate-scabrid, with conspicuously reticulate nerves and veins, 4¾–6 in. long, 1¾ in. broad, on petioles 2¾–3¾ lines long; raceme at the nodes half as long as the leaves, on a flexuose peduncle bare for 1 in., bearing above many approximately geminate flowers on pedicels as long as or longer than the calyx; sepals ovate or oblong-ovate, acute, glabrous, punctulate-scabrid, 6¾ lines long, 2¼ lines broad, with an inner acutely ovate denticulate scale; corolla 1 in. long, its tube glabrous, 8 lines long, segments 4 lines long; stamens inserted above the middle of the tube, on a retrorsely pilose ring; anthers dorsally hispid; the appendages scarcely exserted beyond the callous ring in the mouth of the tube; disk of 5 erect oblong laciniate lobes, connately cup-shaped at the base, and longer than the 2 ovaries.

17. HÆMADICTYON TRIFIDUM, Pöpp. Nov. Gen. iii. p. 67, tab. 275. In Peruvia, prov. Maynas, ad Yurimaguas: *non vidi*.

A climbing species, having a round stem 2 in. thick, with many twisted terete or angular, striate, fistulous, glabrous branches 2 lines thick, with axils 6–8 in. apart leaves elliptic-ovate, acute at the base, with a short sudden acumen, coriaceous, glabrous, green above, with 6 pairs of fine divergently arcuate nerves, yellowish-green beneath, with a carinate midrib, prominent reddish nerves and reticulate veins, 6 in. long, 3¼ in. broad, on stout channelled petioles 4 lines long, conjoined across the node by a prominent crenulate ridge; the younger leaves are smaller, the older ones 12 in. long and 10 in. broad; panicle solitary and lateral at the nodes, 6 in. long, on an elongated slender peduncle 4 in. long, trifid at its apex, each branch bearing 12–20 subapproximate flowers on alternate pedicels 3 lines long, supported by acute bracteoles 1 line long; sepals ovate-lanceolate, acute, coriaceous, puberulous at the base, 5 lines long, each with an inner oblong scale; corolla hypocrateriform; its tube cylindrical, 7 lines long, a little swollen in the middle, with an annular ring in the mouth, and beneath it 5 shortish linear included appendages; segments obliquely ovoid, 3 lines long; stamens inserted in the middle of the tube, included; anthers acuminate, biaristate at the base; disk of 5 ovate lobes, nearly as long as the 2 ovate ovaries.

18. HÆMADICTYON PAPILLOSUM, Müll. in Linn. xxx. p. 432. In Nova Granada (Triana 157): *non vidi*.

Its branches are slender, fuscous, papillosely scabridulous; leaves oblong-ovate, narrower below the middle, obtuse or subcordate at the base, subobtuse and mucronate at the apex, chartaceous, glabrous, fuscous green above, somewhat shining, with arcuate nerves and reticulate veins, beneath yellowish-green, 3–4¾ in. long, ¾–1 in. broad, on petioles 2–3 lines long; corymbs large, solitary at the nodes, much longer than the leaves, on a peduncle twice or thrice cleft from near its base, hirtellous, bearing many smallish flowers on pedicels 7–16 lines long; sepals acuminately ovate, recurved at the apex, 2–2¼ lines long, each with an inner deltoid crenulate scale; tube of corolla glabrous, cylindrical, broader at the base, constricted in the middle, again widening at its 5-plicate mouth, which bears within 5 small ovate appendages; segments obliquely obovate, ciliate on the margins, a little shorter than the tube; stamens seated on a pilose ring in the constriction of the tube; anthers glabrous, 1¾–2¼ lines long, their summits exserted.

19. HÆMADICTYON MACRONEURUM, Müll. Fl. Bras. xxvi. p. 169 (excl. syn. Vell.). In Amazonas, ad Rio Japurá (Martius 3029): *non vidi*.

A species very distinct from *Echites megalagrion* of Velloz, to which Müller refers it. It has glabrous branches; leaves elliptic or oblong-ovate, acute at the base, with a short acumen, rigidly subcoriaceous, fuscously palish above, very glabrous, sulcate on the strong midrib and nerves, fuscous-yellowish beneath, with stout prominent midrib, nerves, and reticulate veins, 5¼ in. long, 3⅓–4 in. broad, on petioles 3½–5¼ lines long; panicle upon a peduncle 1¼ in. long, bifid above, and densely flowered on alternate or geminate very approximate pedicels as long as the sepals, with 3 basal bracts of equal length; sepals oblong-ovate, acutely acuminate, membranaceous, glabrous, 5¾ lines long, each with an inner ovate truncate denticulate scale; corolla 1⅝ in. long; its tube 1 in. long, broadly cylindrical, reddish, its mouth furnished with an elevated spotted ring; segments scarlet, puberulous outside; stamens seated below the mouth on a retrorsely pilose ring; anthers glabrous, shortly exserted, the appendages extending beyond them; disk urceolate, with 5 short lobes as long as the 2 ovaries.

20. HÆMADICTYON AMAZONICUM, Benth. MSS.; Müll. *l. c.* p. 166. In Amazonas, Rio Trombetas (Spruce 239): *non vidi*.

A climbing species, with slender, pubescent, verruculous, fuscous-red branches, having remote axils; leaves elliptic-ovate, subobtuse at the base, shortly and acutely acuminate, rigidly membranaceous, fuscous, concolorous, shortly puberulous or glabrescent, with 5–6 pairs of nerves and reticulate veins, 4¾ in. long, 2¼ in. broad, on petioles 3¼ lines long; raceme at each node nearly as long as the leaves, on a rather long peduncle, bearing above few flowers on puberulous pedicels, supported by small ovate-lanceolate bracteoles; sepals ovate-acuminate, 3¾ lines long, with 4–6 inner subbifid scales; tube of corolla shortly hirtellous, 6¼ lines long, with a plicate callous ring in the mouth, and the usual semi-exserted appendages; segments obliquely inequilateral, 4 lines long; anthers slightly exserted; disk half-cleft into 5 lobes around the 2 hairy ovaries.

Species exclusæ :—

H. suberectum, G. Don, Dict. iv. p. 83 . . . =	*Chariomma surrecta*.
H. grandiflorum, A. DC. Prodr. viii. p. 426 . .	*Odontadenia grandiflora*.
H. circinalis, G. Don, Dict. iv. p. 83	*Anechites circinalis*.
H. molle, A. DC. *l. c.* p. 427	*Prestonia mollis*.
H. parviflorum, Benth. Pl. Hartw.	*Temnadenia parviflora*.
H. megalagrion, Müll. Fl. Bras. xxvi. p. 170 .	*Prestonia megalagrion*.
H. Reidelii, Müll. *l. c.* p. 170	*Temnadenia Reidelii*.
H. annulare, A. DC. *l. c.* p. 428	*Temnadenia annularis*.
H. glandulosum, A. DC. *l. c.* p. 427	*Echites glandulosa*.
H. glabratum, A. DC. *l. c.* p. 427	*Prestonia glabrata*, H. B. K.
H. Mexicana, A. DC. *l. c.* p. 428	*Mitozus Mexicanus*.
H. suberectum, G. Don, Dict. iv. p. 83 . . .	*Urechites suberecta*.

CYCLADENIA.

This interesting genus was established about 1850 by Mr. Bentham in his ' Plantæ Hartwegianæ ' (no. 1834), upon a solitary species from California. Its stems, probably herbaceous, only a few inches high, rise out of a perennial thickish rhizome, as in *Homaladenia* ; the ovate very obtuse leaves, less than 1 in. long, are smooth and fleshy ; the inflorescence axillary and laxly racemose, the peduncle bears about 6 flowers on bracteolate pedicels 6 lines long ; sepals unequal, narrow, 3 lines long, without internal scales ; corolla hypocrateriform, resembling that of *Vinca rosea*, of a purplish colour, campanulate in the upper part of the tube, which is furnished within, at the middle, with a pilose ring, and 5 distinct scales placed above the insertion of the stamens, as in *Hæmadictyon*, the mouth being quite bare ; the segments broad, gibbously ovate, are half the length of the tube, with a sinistrorse convolution ; the included stamens have very short filaments ; the anthers cohering in a cone by their agglutination to the clavuncle, are very acuminate above and biaristate at the base ; the disk annular, entire, shorter than the 2 free ovaries, which have amphitropous ovules ; style simple ; clavuncle incrassate, with a broad peltate basal membrane ; stigmata small and terminal ; fruit unknown.

C. humilis is a very pretty glabrous plant which I have not seen, has the habit of *Villarsia pumila*, and has no affinity with *Vinca*, as its stamens show. The form of the corolla, the presence of suprastaminal appendages, and the structure of the stamens, indicate its affinity towards *Hæmadictyon*.

The *Cycladenia Harrisonii*, Lem., is *Odontadenia Harrisii* (*suprà*, p. 128).

HETEROTHRIX.

A genus established by Müller in 1860, upon a single Brazilian species, well figured and described by him. It was repudiated by Bentham and Hooker in the ' Genera Plantarum,' ii. p. 724, who referred it to *Echites*, a genus, in their estimation, consisting of a very heterogeneous group of plants ; but it cannot be reconciled with that genus when the latter is restricted within its legitimate limits. One of the features, almost peculiar to it, is the double coma of its seeds, which suggested its generic name. The characters of *Heterothrix* may be thus summarized:—

HETEROTHRIX, Müller: *Echites*, in parte, auct. *Sepala* subparva, lanceolato-ovata, subæqualia, intus squamulis paucis minutis, acutis subalternis munita. *Corolla* mediocris, hypocrateriformis; *tubus* cylindricus, medio subconstrictus, et ibi staminigerus, fauce glaber et haud plicatus ; *segmenta* dolabriformia, dextrorsum convoluta. *Stamina*, in constrictione tubi inserta, inclusa ; *filamenta* brevia, lata, rigida, extus glabra, intus pilosula ; *antheræ* anguste oblongæ, apice membrana obtusa terminatæ, imo brevissime et obtuse bilobæ. *Discus* suburceolatus, fere ad basin in lobos 5 obtusos imo connatos fissus. *Ovaria* 2, distincta, obtuse ovoidea, disco fere æquilonga ; *stylus* gracilis ; *clavuncula* incrassata, conice pentagona, imo indusiata ; *stigmata* 2, parva, obtusa, terminalia. *Folliculi* 2, teretes, subulatim tenues, vix torulosi, erecti ; *semina* plurima, oblonga, apice truncata, subcompressa, costatim striata ; *coma* apicalis, duplo longior, e pilis numerosis rigidiusculis, in seriebus 2 dispositis, quorum exteriores quintuplo breviores.

Frutex *Brasiliensis*, *subhumilis*; *ramosus*; rami *validi*, *breves*; folia *opposita*, *rotundo-ovata*, *imo subcordata*, *apice emarginata*, *rigidiuscula*, *brevissime petiolata*; cyma *lateralis*, *pedunculata*, *apice capitato-densiflora*; flores breviter pedicellati.

1. HETEROTHRIX PYCNANTHA, Müll. Fl. Br. xxvi. p. 133, tab. 40: *Echites pycnantha*, Steudel, Nomenc. p. 540; A. DC. Prodr. viii. p. 469; Benth. & Hook. Gen. ii. p. 724: *Echites densiflora*, Pohl, Steudelm. Bot. Zeit. 1841, p. 56 (non Bl.). In Brasilia, prov. Minas Geräes, ad Serra do Pinheiro: non vidi.

A low bushy tree, 3–4 feet high, with very stout rigid branches, and branchlets 3½ lines thick, costate-striate, pubescent, with axils 1¼ in. apart; leaves orbicular or ovate, shortly cordate at the base, emarginate and mucronulate at the summit, rigidly chartaceous, fuscous and densely pubescent above, with about 12 pairs of subdivergent nerves, with others intermediate, all anastomosing and conjoined near the margin, sericeo-tomentous beneath, 3¼ in. long, 2¼ in. broad, on petioles (the depth of the sinus) 1 line long; the upper leaves smaller; the peduncle erect, lateral at the nodes, bare at its base for 1¼ in., supports a globular head of flowers 2 in. in diameter, on closely approximate pedicels 1¼ line long; sepals somewhat acuminate, 2 lines long, ½ line broad; corolla salver-shaped, in all 1 in. long; tube cylindrical, 8 lines long, shortly constricted in the middle; segments broadly dolabriform, with dextrorse convolution, 4 lines long, 3 lines broad; the filaments, seated in the constriction of the tube, are ¼ line long; the anthers 2½ lines long, cohering in a cone; the slender style 4 lines long; follicles 2, terete, 3¼ in. long, 1¼ line thick; the seeds 2 lines long, ¾ line broad; coma croceorufescent, erect, consisting of dense hairs, the inner series 5 lines long, the outer series 1 line long.

2. HETEROTHRIX VAN HEURCKII, Müll. in Pl. nov. Van Heurck. p. 164: *Mandevilla* sp., Benth. & Hook. Gen. Plant. ii. p. 727: non vidi.

I have not seen the detailed description of this species; but it would seem to differ from the foregoing in little else than that the more slender nerves and transversely parallel veins are more numerous and closer.

The authors of the 'Genera Plantarum' (*l. c. suprà*) refer these plants to *Mandevilla*; but this opinion cannot be accepted, because the plants differ widely in nearly every respect.

DESCRIPTION OF THE PLATES.

PLATE I.

A. Fruit of *Hancornia speciosa*. Fig. 1, a ripe fruit. Fig. 2, a longitudinal section of the same, showing the seeds imbedded in a whitish soft flesh exuding a milky juice, without any apparent dissepiment or placenta. Fig. 3, a seed, shown on the ventral and dorsal sides, and on the edge; the testa, which is corrugated, adheres to the flesh by a small peltate hilum. Fig. 4, the nucleus is white, oval, compressed, with a small hollow below the apex, shown in front and on the edge: *all natural size*. Fig. 5, the same: *magnified*. Fig. 6, the embryo, seen on its face and on its edge: *equally magnified*.

B. *Ambellania cucumerina*. Fig. 1, a portion of a branch, showing its leaf and axillary raceme. Fig. 2, a flower in æstivation. Fig. 3, the corolla of the same. Fig. 4, the same cut open: *all natural size*. Fig. 5, the same, *magnified*, showing the five hairy lines in the mouth, alternate with the segments, and the position of the stamens. Fig. 6, a stamen, seen before and behind, *magnified*. Fig. 7, ovary, style, clavuncle, and stigmata: *natural size*. Fig. 8, the same, *three times magnified*. Fig. 9, the ovoid pentagonal fruit. Fig. 10, a transverse section of the same, showing many seeds attached to the thick fleshy dissepiment. Fig. 11, a seed peltately attached, seen before and behind: *natural size*. Fig. 12, the same, seen on its ventral face and on its edge, showing the position of the hilum and its raphe. Fig. 13, a longitudinal section of the same, showing the position of the embryo. Fig. 14, the embryo: *all equally magnified*.

C. *Ceratites amœna*. Fig. 1, a portion of a branch, showing a leaf and the axillary raceme, *natural size*. Fig. 2, the raceme, *magnified*. Fig. 3, a flower of the same. Fig. 4, the same, showing the horn-like appendages of the corolla: *more magnified*. Fig. 5, the calyx, ovary, style, clavuncle, and stigmata. Fig. 6, the corolla cut open, showing the position of the stamens: *both equally magnified*. Fig. 7, a stamen, seen before and behind. Fig. 8, the disk, ovaries, style, clavuncle, and stigmata: *both more magnified*.

D. *Pomphidea Swartziana*. Fig. 1, portion of the plant, with a leaf and raceme. Fig. 2, a flower: *both natural size*. Fig. 3, the five unequal sepals. Fig. 4, the inner pluridentate scale at the base of each sepal. Fig. 5, the pustulate corolla cut open, showing its dextrorse æstivation and the position of the stamens: *all magnified*. Fig. 6, the pustulate stamens, shown in different positions, *more magnified*. Fig. 7, the disk. Fig. 8, the ovary and style. Fig. 9, a cross section of the 2-celled ovary, the summit of the style seen from above, showing the enclosed stigmata. Fig. 10, the two stigmata in the hollow of the style: *all magnified*.

DESCRIPTION OF THE PLATES.

PLATE II.

Cupirana Aubletiana. Fig. 1, a portion of a branch, showing a leaf and its congested solitary flowers. Fig. 2, a flower with its basal bract. Fig. 3, the pedicel and tubular calyx. Fig. 4, the inner calyx. Fig. 5, the corolla. Fig. 6, the same cut open, showing the sinistrorse convolution of the segments and the position of the stamens. Fig. 7, a segment of the corolla, seen on the inner and outer sides. Fig. 8, a stamen: *all natural size.* Fig. 9, a stamen seen before and behind, *magnified.* Fig. 10, a pollen grain, *highly magnified.* Fig. 11, the disk, ovary, style, clavuncle, and stigmata, *natural size.* Fig. 12, the disk and enclosed ovary, *magnified.* Fig. 13, a transverse section of the 2-celled ovary. Fig. 14, the style, clavuncle, and stigmata: *magnified.* Fig. 15, the fruit, copied from Aublet (not reversed), supported by the lacerated calyx and pedicel, *natural size.*

PLATE III.

A. *Aspidosperma Gomesianum.* Fig. 1, a portion of a branch, with its expanded terminal panicle. Fig. 2, a flower. Fig. 3, the corolla: *all natural size.* Fig. 5, the corolla, with sinistrorse convolution. Fig. 6, the same cut open, showing the position of the stamens. Fig. 7, a stamen. Fig. 8, calyx with the sepals thrown back, to show the ovaries and style: *all magnified.* Fig. 10, a follicle. Fig. 11, the same, seen on its edge in the act of dehiscence. Fig. 12, a longitudinal section of the same, showing each seed suspended from the summit by a slender funicle attached peltately to the central hilum of the scutcheon of the winged seeds. Fig. 13, the eight parallel seeds, with the funicles of four averse from the half of the pericarp on one side, and the other four also averse from the opposite half. Fig. 14, a seed membranaceously winged round the scutcheon, with the central hilum attached to the funicle. Fig. 15, the nucleus extracted from the scutcheon. Fig. 16, a longitudinal section of the nucleus, showing the heterotropous embryo enclosed in the albumen.

B. *Thyroma sessiliflora.* Fig. 1, portion of the plant, with its axillary panicle in flower. Fig. 2, the same in fruit: *natural size.* Fig. 3, a flower and portion of the peduncle, *magnified.* Fig. 4, a flower, *more magnified.* Fig. 5, the calyx and style. Fig. 6, the corolla cut open, showing the sinistrorse convolution and the five scales opposite the segment and the position of the stamens. Fig. 7, a stamen, shown before and behind: *still more magnified.* Fig. 8, the tubular disk enclosing two ovaries. Fig. 9, the style, clavuncle, and stigmata: *much magnified.* Fig. 10, the very compressed flat follicle. Fig. 11, the same, seen on its edge, showing the marginal suture. Fig. 12, the same in the act of dehiscence, showing the four seeds in two series, both upper and lower, appended to the marginal replum by as many horizontal flat funicles attached to the central hilum of each scutcheon upon the face furthest from the pericarp. Fig. 13, a transverse section of the same. Fig. 15, the dexter seed of the lower row, with an inferior scutcheon, showing the horizontal funicle upon its inner face. Figs. 16 and 17, the sinister and dexter seeds of the upper row, with superior scutcheons, showing that in both cases their funicles, facing one another, are turned to the middle of the cell of the pericarp. Fig. 18, the embryo, as placed in the two last figures, seen on its face and on its edge: *all natural size.*

PLATE IV.

A. *Thevetia calophylla.* Fig. 1, portion of a branch. Fig. 2, the corolla cut open, showing the position of the stamens: *twice magnified.* Fig. 3, a stamen, *more magnified.* Fig. 4, a profile view of the stamen and its attachment to the corolla, with the faucial appendage. Fig. 5, the calyx, with the sepals thrown back to show the inner basal scales, the disk, ovaries, and style: *much magnified.* Fig. 6, the style, clavuncle, and stigmata, *more magnified.* Fig. 7, a transverse section of the 2-celled ovary, *much magnified*. Fig. 8, a fruit in a very young undeveloped state within the calyx and on the peduncle. Fig. 9, a transverse section of the same. Fig. 10, a ripe fruit of *Thevetia Ahouai* supported by the calyx and pedicel. Fig. 11, the osseous endocarp of the same, with the short apical longitudinal slit. Fig. 12, a side view of the same, showing the apical transverse open slit continued along the marginal edges. Fig. 13, half the same, made by a knife passed through the long slit and separating the two lamellar plates of the placenta, one of which is seen showing the bundle of nourishing vessels rising from the base and divided into two branches, the vessels penetrating and passing through the placenta to be lost in the seed of each cell. Fig. 14, the nut is divided by a short transverse dissepiment, from the middle of which, to the right and left, branch off two placentas nearly dividing it into two, a seed being peltately attached to each branch, thus making four pseudocells, each one-seeded. Fig. 15, one of the fleshy seeds, showing the peltate hilum of attachment. Fig. 16, the same, seen on its edge, showing the hilum. Fig. 17 shows the radiating bundles of spiral vessels about the hilum. Fig. 18, the exalbuminous embryo, with thick fleshy cotyledons and the oblique short superior radicle. Fig. 19, the same, shown on its edge : *all natural size*.

B. *Condylocarpum gracile*, a portion of a pendent branch, with its opposite axillary branching panicles. Fig. 1, a flower. Fig. 2, the same expanded : *both natural size*. Fig. 3, a flower in bud, *magnified*. Fig. 4, the corolla cut open, to show the peculiar form of the segments, their sinistrorse convolution, and the position of the stamens near the base of the tube. Fig. 5, a segment of the corolla : *more magnified*. Fig. 6, a stamen, *much magnified*. Fig. 7, the calyx with the sepals thrown back, showing its membranaceous margins dotted with many red spots, the two ovaries, very short style, capitate hairy clavuncle, and stigmata. Fig. 8, one of the segments of the lomentaceous follicles, which contains two superposed seeds. Fig. 9, another, which contains only a single seed. Fig. 10, transverse section of one of these segments, showing the broad margins filled with pith, its single cell divided nearly into two by a longitudinal septiform placenta, with a nucleus attached to its margin by a central hilum and coiled round it: *all natural size*. Fig. 11, a seed with its margins coiled inwards to embrace the placenta, showing the hilar point of its attachment. Fig. 12, the same with its margins flattened out. Fig. 13, the heterotropous embryo imbedded in thin albumen, showing the thin foliaceous oblong cotyledons, and the superior thin terete radicle, of one third their length : *all somewhat magnified*.

Plate V.

A. *Manothrix valida*, a portion of the plant in fruit. Fig. 1, the 2-celled capsule dehiscing along the dissepiment, each half splitting along the line of the axis at the suture, whose margins are inflexed and combined into a narrow cylindrical placenta bearing many hairy seeds. Fig. 2, a transverse section of the capsule, showing the divisible dissepiment, the inflexed margins of the seminiferous placentas. Fig. 3, a seed : *all natural size*. Fig. 4, a seed, seen on its dorsal side, where it is pilose above the middle with long soft hairs. Fig. 5, the same, showing its ventral face, marked by a central hilum, by which it is peltately affixed to the placenta. Fig. 6, the copious albumen extracted. Fig. 7, the heterotropous embryo : *all much magnified*. Fig. 8, portion of one of the remarkable hairs, seen under a microscope of great power, and marked by a dark capillary axis with many alternate horizontal lines, the intervening spaces ornamented by close spiral lines.

B. *Manothrix nodosa*, portion of a plant, showing its opposite leaves and nodose joints at the remote axils and its short axillary raceme. Fig. 1, a flower, *natural size*. Fig. 2, the corolla cut open, to show the dextrorse convolution and the position of the stamens, *a little magnified*. Fig. 3, the same, showing the tube of the corolla pubescent inside, *more magnified*. Fig. 4, stamens, shown in different positions, *still more magnified*. Fig. 5, the calyx, pedicel, and long slender style, the clavuncle and short terminal stigmata, *much magnified*.

PLATE VI.

A. *Peschiera fuchsiæfolia*. Fig. 1, portion of the plant in flower and in fruit. Fig. 2, the corolla in bud. Fig. 3, the same expanded.. Fig. 4, the corolla cut open, to show its sinistrorse convolution and the position of the stamens: *all natural size*. Fig. 5, the same, *magnified*. Fig. 6, a stamen, *much magnified*. Fig. 7, the calyx. Fig. 8, the same, with the sepals thrown back to show the inner basal scales, the ovaries without any disk, the style, clavuncle and terminal stigmata. Fig. 9, the two echinated follicles, one of them in the act of dehiscence, showing two rows of seeds suspended from each margin of the suture by long fleshy funicles. Fig. 10, seeds, shown in different positions, attached at the other end of the funicle to a central hilum on the ventral side, the dorsal side glabrous and pluricostate. Fig. 11, a seed deprived of the funicle, shown on its ventral concave side with the central hilum. Fig. 12, the same, seen at the apex. Fig. 13, a transverse section of the seed. Fig. 14, the heterotropous embryo imbedded in albumen. Fig. 15, the embryo extracted, showing its foliaceous cotyledons and superior terete radicle. Fig. 16, the same, shown on its edge : *natural size*.

B. *Bonafousia undulata*. Fig. 1, portion of the plant. Fig. 2, the corolla in bud. Fig. 3, the corolla with the segments expanded. Fig. 4, the same cut open, to show the introflexion of the segments in æstivation, when their tips descend into the mouth of the tube and embrace the summits of the stamens (one is shown expanded). Fig. 5, the calyx, the sepals being thrown back to show the dentate inner scales, the disk, the ovaries, style, clavuncle, and terminal stigmata : *all magnified*. Fig. 6, the two divaricated follicles on the thickened pedicel, showing the prominent arching lines on each side. Fig. 7, one of the follicles dehiscing, showing the seeds half-imbedded in their fleshy funicles, but not in pulp, as generally described. Fig. 8, a seed deprived of its funicle, seen on its dorsal face. Fig. 9, the same, shown on its ventral face, with its central peltate hilum : *all natural size*.

PLATE VII.

A. *Tabernæmontana citrifolia*, part of a plant. Fig. 1, a flower in bud. Fig. 2, the corolla in bud. Fig. 3, the calyx. Fig. 4, the corolla after expansion. Fig. 5, the same cut open, to show the introflexion of the segments into the mouth of the tube in æstivation, and the position of the stamens always partially exserted : *all natural size*. Fig. 6, one of the slender stamens, always of a pale blue or greenish colour, *magnified*. Fig. 7, the sepals, thrown back to show their inner scales, the disk, ovaries, style, clavuncle, and stigmata, *all magnified*. Fig. 8, the two divaricated follicles,˙one of them dehiscing, showing the position of the seeds half-immersed in fleshy funicles (after Plumier). Fig. 9, a seed, seen on its dorsal face, suspended by its fleshy funicle. Fig. 10, the same, viewed sideways. Fig. 11, the same, on the ventral face. Fig. 12, the seed detached, seen on its ventral face, showing the central hilum, from which it is suspended. Fig. 13, the same, shown on its dorsal face : *all natural size*.

B. *Tabernæmontana lanceolata*, a plant in flower and in fruit. Fig. 15, a flower in bud. Fig. 16, the corolla expanded. Fig. 17, the same, cut open to show the position of the half-exserted stamens : *all natural size*. Fig. 18, a stamen, *magnified*. Fig. 19, the calyx, with the sepals thrown back to show the inner scales, the disk, ovaries, clavuncle, and stigmata. Fig. 20, a seed suspended by its fleshy funicle. Fig. 21, the same deprived of the funicle, shown on its dorsal face. Fig. 22, the same, shown on its ventral face, with the central hilum : *all natural size*.

PLATE VIII.

A. *Taberna cymosa*, portion of a plant. Fig. 1, a flower. Fig. 2, a follicle (after Jacquin) : *both natural size*.

B. *Codonemma calycina*, a portion of the plant. Fig. 1, a portion of the inflorescence. Fig. 2, a flower in bud. Fig. 3, the corolla in bud. Fig. 4, the same, cut open to show the simply convolute segments in æstivation, and the position of the stamens. Fig. 5, a stamen: *magnified*. Fig. 6, the same, with the disk, ovaries, style, clavuncle, and stigmata, *natural size*. Fig. 7, the tubular calyx cut open, showing the four series of internal scales. As I have not seen the follicle, no figure of it can be given.

PLATE IX.

A. *Phrissocarpus rigidus*, portion of a plant. Fig. 1, a flower in bud, *natural size*. Fig. 2, the corolla cut open, showing the simple sinistrorse convolution of the segments and the position of the stamens, *magnified*. Fig. 3, a stamen, *more magnified*. Fig. 4, the calyx, with the sepals thrown back to show the inner scales, the disk, and ovaries. Fig. 5, the style, clavuncle, and stigmata : *magnified*. Fig. 6, one of the echinated follicles. Fig. 7, the same dehiscing, showing the seeds. Fig. 8, one of the seeds suspended by its fleshy funicle. Fig. 9, the same with the funicle removed, showing on its ventral face the central hilum, where it is attached to the funicle. Fig. 10, the same, seen on its dorsal face : *all natural size*.

B. *Anacampta congesta*, a portion of a plant in flower. Fig. 1, a flower in bud, *natural size*. Fig. 2, the corolla in bud. Fig. 3, the same cut open, showing the segments introflexed as in *Bonafousia*, and the position of the stamens : *magnified*. Fig. 4, a stamen, *more magnified*. Fig. 5, the calyx, with the sepals thrown back to show the laciniulated scales, the disk, ovaries, style, clavuncle, and stigmata, *all magnified*. Fig 6, the two divaricate immature follicles. Fig. 7, immature seeds half-imbedded in fleshy funicles : *both natural size*.

PLATE X.

A. *Rhigospira quadrangularis*, portion of a plant. Fig. 1, the inflorescence. Fig. 2, a flower : *both natural size*. Fig. 3, the corolla in bud, showing the pyramidal form of the erect segments in æstivation. Fig. 4, the same cut open when expanded, showing their simple sinistrorse convolution and the nearly basal position of the stamens : *both magnified*. Fig. 5, the calyx, disk, very short style, clavuncle, and stigmata, *natural size*. Fig. 6, the same, *magnified*. Fig. 7, a stamen, *much magnified*.

B. *Stemmadenia insignis*, portion of a plant in flower. Fig. 1, the calyx, with its bract, pedicel, and its five unequal sepals, the two exterior shorter. Fig. 2, the same, with the sepals thrown back to show the coronal ring of very numerous inner scales, divided disk, ovaries, style, clavuncle, and stigmata : *both natural size*. Fig. 3, the same parts, *magnified*. Fig. 4, the corolla cut open, showing the position of the stamens, *natural size*. Fig. 5, a stamen, *magnified*.

PLATE XI.

A. *Merizadenia amplifolia*, portion of a plant in flower. Fig. 1, a flower in bud. Fig. 2, the calyx and style. Fig. 3, the corolla, with its segments retroflexed when expanded : *all natural size*. Fig. 4, the corolla in bud, the tube spirally twisted. Fig. 5, the corolla cut open, showing the inflexion of two of its segments in æstivation, the others expanded, and the position of the stamens. Fig. 6, the calyx, with the sepals thrown back to show the inner scales, divided disk, ovaries, and style : *all magnified*. Fig. 7, a stamen, *more magnified*. Fig. 8, the two follicles, one of them half cut away to show the placentary expansions of the sutural margins. Fig. 9, a seed suspended by its fleshy funicle, as seen on that side. Fig. 10, the same, shown on the dorsal face. Fig. 11, the same with the funicle removed, showing it pluricostate on the dorsal face. Fig. 12, the same, shown on the ventral face with the central hilum, where it is attached to the funicle : *all natural size*.

B. *Anartia recurva*, a portion of a plant, showing its heterophyllous opposite leaves and its axillary inflorescence. Fig. 1, a flower in bud. Fig. 2, the corolla, with the segments expanded: *both natural size*. Fig. 3, the corolla in bud. Fig. 4, the corolla cut open, to show the manner of the inflexion of the segments when in bud, their expansion afterwards, and their *dextrorse* convolution and the position of the stamens. Fig. 5, the pedicel and calyx, with the sepals thrown back to show the inner scales, the disk, ovaries, style, clavuncle, and stigmata: *all magnified*. Fig. 6, a stamen, *more magnified*.

PLATE XII.

A. *Geissospermum Solandri*, a portion of a plant in flower, showing its *alternate* leaves and terminal inflorescence. Fig. 1, one of its minute flowers, *natural size*. Fig. 2, the same, *five times magnified*. Fig. 3, the corolla, cut open to show the *dextrorse* simple convolution of its segments and the position of the stamens. Fig. 4, the urceolate disk with ciliolate margin, concealing two globose pilose ovaries: *both equally magnified*. Fig. 5, an anther, *more magnified*. Fig. 6, the two follicles of *Geissospermum Vellosii*, one of them dehiscing, showing five seeds in each row suspended from the sutural margins by fleshy funicles. Fig. 7, a transverse section of a follicle, to show the mode of placentation and attachment of the seeds. Fig. 8, a suspended seed, seen on its funicular side. Fig. 9, the same, viewed from the opposite face. Fig. 10, a seed detached from the funicle on its ventral side, showing the central hilum by which it is attached to the funicle. Fig. 11, the heterotropous embryo enclosed in copious albumen. Fig. 12, the embryo extracted: *all natural size*.

B. *Robbia cestroides*. Fig. 1, part of the plant, with its axillary inflorescence. Fig. 2, a flower: *natural size*. Fig. 3, the corolla in bud, *four times magnified*. Fig. 4, the same expanded. Fig. 5, the same cut open, showing the dextrorse simple convolution of the segments, and the position of the stamens. Fig. 6, the stamens cohering in a cone. Fig. 7, the pedicel, the calyx, with the sepals thrown back to show the inner scales, the disk, ovaries, style, clavuncle, and stigmata: *all equally magnified*. Fig. 8, a stamen seen before and behind. Fig. 9, the style, clavuncle, and stigmata: *both more magnified*. Portion of a plant of *Robbia gossipina*, showing the glands on the axils of the nerves and the two follicles, one of them beginning to open. Fig. 10, a seed, shown on its dorsal face, covered with long white cottony hairs. Fig. 11, the same, seen on its ventral face, where it is sparsely pubescent, channelled on its ventral face, with an oblong central hilum. Fig. 12, the albumen extracted. Fig. 13, longitudinal section of the same, with the enclosed heterotropous embryo. Fig. 14, the embryo extracted, with a superior radicle: *all natural size*.

PLATE XIII.

A. *Malouetia glandulifera*, portion of a plant, showing the porous glands in the axils of the nerves, its inflorescence, and its follicles. Fig. 1, a flower in bud. Fig. 2, the corolla cut open, showing the five acute scales in its mouth, the tube with five conspicuous nerves. Fig. 3, one of the anthers more than half exserted. Fig. 4, the five anthers cohering in a cone: *all natural size*. Fig. 5, a stamen, *magnified*. Fig. 6, calyx, with the sepals thrown back to show the alternate basal scales, the 5-lobed disk, the ovaries, the style, clavuncle, and stigmata, *magnified*. Fig. 7, a seed, shown on its ventral and dorsal faces, *natural size*. Fig. 8, the same, *magnified*. Fig. 9, the embryoniferous albumen, extracted. Fig. 10, the embryo removed: *both equally magnified*.

B. *Thyrsanthus bracteatus*, a portion of the plant. Fig. 1, the panicle. Fig. 2, a flower: *both natural size*. Fig. 3, a flower. Fig. 4, the corolla cut open, showing the position of the stamens: *both mag-*

nified. Fig. 5, a stamen, *more magnified.* Fig. 6, the sepals, thrown back to show the inner scales, the lobes of the disk and the ovaries: *much magnified.* Fig. 7, the two divergent follicles, a portion of one being removed, showing the placenta and seeds. Fig. 8, a seed in its convoluted form. Fig. 9, the same, flattened, showing on its ventral face the hilar point of attachment; the same is also shown on its back and edge. Fig. 10, a transverse section of a seed, to show its convolution round the placenta: *all somewhat magnified.*

PLATE XIV.

A. *Elytropus pubescens,* a portion of a plant. Fig. 1, a flower just opening, *natural size.* Fig. 2, the corolla, cut open to show its dextrorse convolution and the position of the stamens, *magnified.* Fig. 3, a stamen shown before and behind, *more magnified.* Fig. 4, the sepals, thrown back to show the two scales at the base of each, the 5-lobed disk, the ovaries, style, clavuncle, and stigmata, *much magnified.* Fig. 5, the two pilose follicles. Fig. 6, a transverse section of the same, to show the manner of placentation: *more magnified.* Fig. 7, one of many seeds attached to the placenta by a central hilum, *natural size.* Fig. 8, a seed, shown in three positions, *magnified.*

B. *Eriadenia obovata,* a portion of a plant in flower and fruit. Fig. 1, a flower in bud. Fig. 2, the corolla cut open, to show the peculiar form of the segments, which are introflexed in æstivation, the scales in the mouth of the tube, and the position of the stamens: *natural size.* Fig. 3, a stamen, in different positions, *magnified.* Fig. 4, the calyx, with the sepals thrown back, showing each with three acute basal scales, the disk, style, clavuncle, and stigmata, *somewhat magnified.* Fig. 5, the same parts, shown separately. Fig. 6, one of the lobes of the disk, shown outside: *magnified.* Fig. 7, the ovaries, style, and clavuncle. Fig. 8, the two subtorose follicles. Fig. 9, a seed: *natural size.* Fig. 10, the same, *magnified,* showing it to be linear oblong, compressed, rostrate, covered all over with long rigid hairs spreading in all directions.

PLATE XV.

A. *Rhabdadenia paludosa,* a portion of a plant in flower. Fig. 1, the corolla cut open, showing the dextrorse convolution of its short segments, and the position of its stamens. Fig. 2, the calyx. Fig. 3, the same, with the sepals thrown back to show the minute basal scales, the disk, ovaries, style, and clavuncle: *all natural size.* Fig. 4, the same parts, *somewhat magnified.* Fig. 5, the rest of the style, clavuncle, and hairy stigmata, *also magnified.* Fig. 6, a stamen, *much magnified.* Fig. 7, the two erect follicles. Fig. 8, one of the seeds, narrowly rostrate at the apex, where it is feathered with numerous long silky hairs, which must not be mistaken for a coma; the longitudinal raphe, proceeding from a central hilum, terminates below the rostrum in a short funicle. Fig. 9, the same with the hairs removed, to show the form of the rostrum. Fig. 10, the nucleus, consisting of a heterotropous embryo imbedded in albumen. Fig. 11, the embryo extracted, with a terete superior radicle much longer than the two short oblong cotyledons: *all natural size.*

B. *Chariomma surrecta,* portion of a plant in flower. Fig. 1, the corolla in bud. Fig. 2, the same cut open, to show the sinistrorse convolution of its large very acute segments and the position of its stamens furnished with long spirally-twisted apical appendages. Fig. 3, the calyx on its pedicel. Fig. 4, the same with the sepals thrown back, to show the absence of inner scales, the 5-lobed disk, the style, and clavuncle: *all natural size.* Fig. 5, the same parts, *magnified.* Fig. 6, portion of the style, clavuncle, and stigmata, *more magnified.* Fig. 7, a stamen with its very long torsile apical appendage, *three times magnified.*

DESCRIPTION OF THE PLATES.

PLATE XVI.

Odontadenia grandiflora, a portion of a plant in flower, from Hayes's specimen. Fig. 1, the lower ventricose part of the corolla, opened to show the insertion of the stamens included in it. Fig. 2, stamens with the anthers cohering in a cone: *both natural size*. Fig. 3, a stamen, seen in front, the filament inserted in a tuft of hairs, *much magnified*. Fig. 4, the same, on the dorsal side, where it is pilose. Fig. 5, the unequal sepals thrown back to show the broad inner scales, the 5-cleft disk, and the ovaries. Fig. 6, the two ovaries surrounded by the disk, the style, clavuncle, and stigmata. Fig. 7, the follicle, from Smith's specimen. Fig. 8, a transverse section of the same, to show the mode of placentation. Fig. 9, portion of the submembranaceous placenta, seen on the side facing the pericarp, studded with the cicatrices on which the seeds are imbricately seated. Fig. 10, one of the terete erect seeds. Fig. 11, a longitudinal section of the same seed, showing the anatropous seed enclosed in it. Fig. 12, the embryo embedded in albumen. Fig. 13, the embryo extracted, with the short basal radicle: *all natural size*.

PLATE XVII.

Macrosiphonia prostrata, a plant in flower and in fruit. Fig. 1, the corolla cut open, showing the position of the cohering stamens. Fig. 2, a stamen detached: *both natural size*. Fig. 3, the same, seen in front and sideways, *magnified*. Fig. 4, the calyx, with the lanceolate sepals thrown back to show the row of many minute inner scales, the disk of five erect lobes surrounding the much longer ovaries, the very elongated slender style, the clavuncle extricated from the cohering anthers, and the stigmata. Fig. 5, the two subtorose, suberect follicles. Fig. 6, a seed, seen before and behind. Fig. 7, the nucleus. Fig. 8, the anatropous embryo extracted from the corneous albumen of the nucleus: *all natural size*.

PLATE XVIII.

Stipecoma pulchra, a portion of the plant, showing its opposite deeply peltate leaves, and its opposite axillary panicles on a stout recurved peduncle, charged at its base with large leaf-like bracts, and branching above, with somewhat distant branchlets, each with several large foliaceous imbricated petiolate bracts, the upper ones having in their axils a single flower on a pedicel, bibracteolate, all densely tomentose. Fig. 1, a flower on its bibracteolate pedicel, the corolla in bud. Fig. 2, the corolla expanded. Fig. 3, the same cut open, to show the dextrorse contortion of the segments and the position of the stamens. Fig. 4, the calyx, with the sepals thrown back to show the few minute basal scales, the 5-cleft disk, the ovaries, style, and clavuncle: *all natural size*. Fig. 5, a stamen. Fig. 6, the style, clavuncle, and stigmata: *both magnified*. Fig. 7, the disk and ovaries, *more magnified*.

PLATE XIX.

Stipecoma ovata, portion of a plant in fruit. Fig. 1, the two erect follicles conjoined at the apex, one of them gaping open, dehiscing along the ventral suture, and showing in the centre the tubular submembranaceous placenta, charged inside with numerous imbricate seeds. Fig. 2, a transverse section of the follicle beginning to dehisce, with the placenta separating at the keel from the sutural margins. Fig. 3, a transverse section of the placenta, showing the keel separated from the said margins, free from the pericarp on the dorsal side: *all natural size*. Fig. 4, a portion of the submembranaceous placenta, viewed from the inside, showing the many slender parallel ribs, resolved at distant intervals into a small cone-shaped appendage open at the bottom and concealing the funicle of a seed attached at its apex, where it is continuous with the joint of the rib, *magnified*. Fig. 5, a seed with a long superior slender rostrum terminated by a fleshy ring, which surrounds the micropyle and bears a coma of many long elastic hairs; on one side of the seed is the longitudinal raphe proceeding from the basal chalaza, and terminating at the summit in the short funicle above mentioned, by which it is suspended. Fig. 6, the same deprived of its coma and showing the same parts. Fig. 7, the embryo enclosed in the albumen. Fig. 8, the embryo extracted, with the terete superior radicle and foliaceous cotyledons: *all natural size*.

PLATE XX.

A. *Rhodocalyx crassifolius*, portion of a plant in flower. Fig. 1, the calyx. Fig. 2, the same parallel-nerved, with the sepals thrown back, to show the basal scales, disk, ovaries, style, and clavuncle. Fig. 3, the corolla cut open, showing the shape and simple dextrorse convolution of the segments and the position of the stamens: *all natural size*. Fig. 4, a stamen, *magnified*. Fig. 5, a follicle of *Rhodocalyx rotundifolium*. Fig. 6, a seed suspended by a long slender funicle and an apical coma. Fig. 7, the same deprived of the coma and funicle, shown on the dorsal face. Fig. 8, a transverse section of the same, showing it channelled on the ventral face, with the longitudinal raphe and the enclosed embryo: *all natural size*.

B. *Prestonia tomentosa*, portion of a plant in flower. Fig. 1, the pedicellate calyx with its bracteole. Fig. 2, the corolla, in bud. Fig. 3, the same, cut open to show the faucial ring and row of five acute appendages in its mouth, the simple segments dextrorsely convoluted, and the insertion of the stamens on a broad pilose ring. Fig. 4, the five stamens cohering in a cone. Fig. 5, a single one detached: *all natural size*. Fig. 6, a stamen, *magnified*. Fig. 7, the crenulate faucial ring. Fig. 8, the row of appendages in the mouth of the tube. Fig. 9, the calyx, with the sepals thrown back, showing the scales, disk, style, and clavuncle. Fig. 10, the 2-celled capsule. Fig. 11, a transverse section of the same, showing the double dissepiment and the inflexed seminiferous placentas. Fig. 12, the capsule, beginning to open along the septicidal dissepiment, and the seeds beginning to escape. Fig. 13, a seed, with its apical coma, shown on its dorsal face. Fig. 14, the same, on its ventral face: *all natural size*.

PLATE XXI.

A. *Rhaptocarpus odoriferus*, portion of a plant in flower and fruit. Fig. 1, a flower with its bract. Fig. 2, the corolla in bud. Fig. 3, the same, cut open, showing the form and simple dextrorse convolution of its segments, and the position of the stamens: *all natural size*. Fig. 4, a stamen, *magnified*. Fig. 5, the calyx, with the sepals thrown back, to show the multilaciniate inner scale, the disk, ovary, style, clavuncle, and stigmata, *magnified*. Fig. 6, the lower half of the capsule inverted, and the other half erect. Fig. 7, a transverse section of the same, showing the septicidal dissepiment and mode of placentation. Fig. 8, a seed: *all natural size*.

B. *Aptotheca corylifolia*, portion of a plant in flower and fruit. Fig. 1, the calyx. Fig. 2, the corolla, in bud. Fig. 3, the corolla, cut open, showing the simple sinistrorse convolution of the segments, the faucial ring, and the basal insertion of the stamens: *all magnified*. Fig. 4, a stamen, *more magnified*. Fig. 5, the calyx, with the sepals thrown back, showing the simple inner scales, the disk, and ovary, *magnified six times*. Fig. 6, a capsule beginning to open at its apex. Fig. 7, a transverse section of the same, showing the septicidal dissepiment and the manner of its placentation. Fig. 8, a seed: *all natural size*.

DESCRIPTION OF THE PLATES.

PLATE XXII.

Dipladenia illustris, a plant in flower and fruit, the stem arising from a tuberose root. Fig. 1, the calyx and pedicel of a flower. Fig. 2, the sepals, thrown back to show their inner scales, one of the two opposite lobes of the disk nearly as large as the two ovaries: *both natural size*. Fig. 3, the same, *magnified*. Fig. 4, the same, with the addition of the style and clavuncle. Fig. 5, the corolla cut open, showing its large segments with dextrorse convolution, and the position of the stamens: *both natural size*. Fig. 6, a stamen, seen before and behind, *magnified*. Fig. 7, the two ovaries and two lobes of the disk, seen from above, showing their relative positions, *magnified*. Fig. 8, the two follicles. Fig. 9, a seed: *both natural size*.

PLATE XXIII.

Micradenia crassinoda, portion of a plant in flower. Fig. 1, the calyx and pedicel. Fig. 2, the corolla in bud. Fig. 3, the corolla expanded, cut open to show the simple dextrorse convolution of its segments and the position of its stamens. Fig. 4, a stamen: *all natural size*. Fig. 5, a stamen, *magnified*. Fig. 6, the sepals, thrown back to show the disk, style, and clavuncle, *natural size*. Fig. 7, the same parts, showing the two inner bifid scales within each sepal (the two smaller opposite lobes of the disk alternate with the two pointed ovaries), the style, clavuncle, and stigmata, *magnified*. Fig. 8, the two follicles. Fig. 9, a comose seed: *both natural size*.

PLATE XXIV.

A. *Homaladenia tenuifolia*, one of several slender erect stems, all issuing from a napiform root, in flower and fruit. Fig. 1, a flower in bud. Fig. 2, the same expanded: *both natural size*. Fig. 3, the calyx. Fig. 4, the corolla in bud. Fig. 5, the same, cut open to show the simple dextrorse convolution of its segments and the position of the pilose ring, on which the stamens are inserted. Fig. 6, the cone of cohering anthers. Fig. 7, a single anther. Fig. 8, the calyx, with the sepals thrown back to show the small 2-lobed disk, the two ovaries, style, and clavuncle: *all natural size*. Fig. 9, the lobes of the disk alternate with the two ovaries, *magnified*. Fig. 10, the two ovaries and two lobes of the disk, to show their relative positions, *more magnified*. Fig. 11, the two follicles. Fig. 12, a seed crowned by a double coma. Fig. 13, the albumen extracted. Fig. 14, the embryo: *all natural size*.

B. *Prestoniopsis pubescens*, portion of a plant in flower. Fig. 1, a flower in bud. Fig. 2, the calyx. Fig. 3, the corolla in bud: *all natural size*. Fig. 4, the calyx, *magnified*. Fig. 5, the corolla in bud. Fig. 6, the same, cut open to show the simple dextrorse convolution of the segments and the position of the stamens inserted near the base of the tube. Fig. 7, a stamen: *all equally magnified*. Fig. 8, a stamen, *much magnified*. Fig. 9, the calyx, with the segments thrown back to show one of the lobes of the disk, half as long as the two alternate ovaries, the short style, and clavuncle, *natural size*. Fig. 10, the style, clavuncle, and stigmata, *magnified*.

PLATE XXV.

Amblyanthera Claussenii, portion of a plant, with its lateral raceme, the flowers half concealed by its large imbricated foliaceous bracts. Fig. 1, a flower in bud, with its basal bract much longer than the calyx. Fig. 2, the calyx. Fig. 3, the corolla in bud. Fig. 4, the same, cut open to show the simple sinistrorse convolution of the segments and the position of the stamens. Fig. 5, the stamens, with the anthers cohering in a cone. Fig. 6, a stamen separated: *all natural size*. Fig. 7, a stamen, shown on its inner face. Fig. 8, the same, on its outer face. Fig. 9, the same, on its edge. Fig. 10, the filament: *all magnified*. Fig. 11, the calyx, with the sepals thrown back to show the inner scales, the 5-lobed disk, and the ovaries. Fig. 12, the style, the clavuncle, and stigmata: *both magnified*. Fig. 13, the two follicles of *Amblyanthera hispida* agglutinated at the apex. Fig. 14, a seed with its apical coma, seen on its ventral face. Fig. 15, the same deprived of its coma, shown on the dorsal face. Fig. 16, a transverse section of the same. Fig. 17, the albumen extracted. Fig. 18, the embryo removed from it: *all natural size*.

PLATE XXVI.

Anisolobus oblongus, portion of a plant in flower. Fig. 1, the calyx. Fig. 2, its unequal imbricated sepals. Fig. 3, a diagram of their mode of imbrication. Fig. 4, the corolla in bud. Fig. 5, the same expanded, showing the folded segments with dextrorse convolution. Fig. 6, the same cut open, showing the mode of their inflexion in the bud. Fig. 7, the corolla cut open, to show the position of the stamens cohering in a cone. Fig. 8, a stamen separated: *all natural size*. Fig. 9, a stamen, seen before and behind, *magnified*. Fig. 10, the two divergent follicles of *Anisolobus hebecarpus*, copied from Müller. Fig. 11, a seed rostrate at the apex, with a long apical coma: *both natural size*.

PLATE XXVII.

A. *Angadenia Sprucei*, portion of a plant in flower. Fig. 1, the calyx. Fig. 2 shows the quincuncial imbrication of the sepals. Fig. 3, the corolla in bud. Fig. 4, the same expanded. Fig. 5, the same cut open, showing the simple dextrorse convolution of the segments. Fig. 6, a stamen: *all natural size*. Fig. 7, a stamen, seen on its inner face. Fig. 8, the same, on its outer face. Fig. 9, the filament: *all magnified*. Fig. 10, the calyx, with its sepals thrown back to show the disk, style, and clavuncle, *natural size*. Fig. 11, the tubular disk, denticulate on its margin, nearly concealing the two ovaries, *much magnified*.

B. *Angadenia pruinosa*, portion of a plant in fruit. Fig. 1, a section of the follicle, replete with seeds. Fig. 2, a seed with its erect coma: *both natural size*.

PLATE XXVIII.

Perictenia stipellaris, a branch in flower, showing the peculiar row of stipules at each node. Fig. 1, a flower in bud. Fig. 2, the corolla in bud. Fig. 3, the same, cut open to show the singular manner of introflexion of its long linear segments with sinistrorse convolution, and the position of the stamens near the base of the tube. Fig. 4, the same with the segments expanded. Fig. 5, a stamen: *all natural size*. Fig. 6, a stamen, seen before and behind, *magnified*. Fig. 7, the calyx, pedicel, and basal bracts, the style and clavuncle, *somewhat magnified*. Fig. 8, the same with the sepals thrown back, to show the inner scales, the 5-cleft disk, the ovaries, short style, and clavuncle, *more magnified*. Fig. 9, a diagram to show the quincuncial imbrication of the sepals.

PLATE XXIX.

Echites convolvulacea, portion of a plant in flower, together with a drawing of the follicles. Fig. 1, the calyx. Fig. 2, the corolla in bud. Fig. 3, the same with the border expanded. Fig. 4, the same cut open, showing the sinistrorse convolution of the segments and the position of the stamens. Fig. 5, a stamen: *all natural size*. Fig. 6, a stamen, seen before and behind, *magnified*. Fig. 7, the calyx, with the sepals thrown back to show the inner scales, the disk, ovaries, style, and clavuncle, *natural size*. Fig. 8, the same parts, *magnified*. Fig. 9, the two follicles. Fig. 10, a seed with its apical coma: *both natural size*.

PLATE XXX.

Temnadenia Lobbiana, portion of a plant in flower and immature fruit. Fig. 1, a flower in bud. Fig. 2, the corolla opened, to show the form and simply dextrorse convolution of the segments and the position of the stamens. Fig. 3, a stamen: *all natural size*. Fig. 4, a stamen, shown in three positions, *magnified*. Fig. 5, a grain of pollen, *exceedingly magnified*. Fig. 6, the calyx, with the sepals thrown back to show the inner scales, the 5-lobed disk, the ovaries, style, and clavuncle, *natural size*. Fig. 7, the same parts, *magnified*. Fig. 8, the summit of the style, clavuncle, and stigmata, *also magnified*. Fig. 9, a seed of *Temnadenia violacea*, rostrate at the apex, with its apical coma, *natural size*. Fig. 10, the same, shown on its dorsal face. Fig. 11, the same, seen on its ventral face. Fig. 12, a side view of the same. Fig. 13, a transverse section of the same: *all magnified*.

PLATE XXXI.

Mitozus exilis, a portion of a plant in flower and fruit. Fig. 1, the calyx and pedicel. Fig. 2, the corolla, cut open to show the form and simply dextrorse convolution of the segments and the position of the stamens. Fig. 3, a stamen: *all natural size*. Fig. 4, the same, shown on its inside. Fig. 5, the same with the filament removed. Fig. 6, the same, seen outside. Fig. 7, the filament: *all much magnified*. Fig. 8, the calyx, with the sepals thrown back to show the denticulated inner scale, the disk, ovaries, and style, *magnified*. Fig. 9, the two follicles conjoined at the apex. Fig. 10, a seed with its apical coma: *both natural size*.

PLATE XXXII.

Secondatia densifolia, portion of a plant in flower, from Gardner's specimen. Fig. 1, the short panicle. Fig. 2, a flower expanded: *both natural size*. Fig. 3, the corolla expanded. Fig. 4, the same, cut open, showing the simple dextrorse convolution of the segments, the tube ventricose in the middle, pubescent in the contracted mouth, the position of the stamens in the lower constriction of the tube. Fig. 5, one of the anthers detached. Fig. 6, the filament. Fig. 7, the calyx, with the sepals thrown back to show the urceolate disk half-cleft into five lobes, the style, and clavuncle: *all magnified on the same scale*. Fig. 8, the follicle, from a specimen of Martius in the Brit. Museum. Fig. 9, a seed. Fig. 10, the albumen. Fig. 11, the embryo extracted: *all natural size*.

PLATE XXXIII.

A. *Mesechites myrtifolia*, portion of a plant in flower and fruit. Fig. 1, the calyx. Fig. 2, the corolla in bud. Fig. 3, the same, cut open to show the simple dextrorse convolution of the segments and the position of the stamens: *all natural size*. Fig. 4, the calyx with the sepals thrown back, showing the inner scales, the five free lobes of the disk, and the ovaries, *magnified*. Fig. 5, the two parallel torose follicles, *natural size*.

B. *Anechites circinalis*, portion of a plant in flower. Fig. 1, a flower, *natural size*. Fig. 2, the corolla in bud. Fig. 3, the same expanding. Fig. 4, the same, cut open, showing the simple dextrorse convolution of the segments and the position of the half-exserted stamens. Fig. 5, the calyx. Fig. 6, the same, with the sepals thrown back to show the inner scales, the five free lobes of the disk, and the ovaries: *all equally magnified*. Fig. 7, an anther. Fig. 8, its filament: *both more magnified*.

PLATE XXXIV.

Hæmadictyon ovatum, portion of a plant in flower and fruit. Fig. 1, a flower in bud. Fig. 2, the corolla expanding: *both natural size*. Fig. 3, the same expanded, showing the exserted appendages and the partially exserted stamens. Fig. 4, the same, cut open, showing the crenulate ring in the mouth, the position of the appendages and of the cohering stamens, the filaments inserted in five tufts of hairs, and the ten longitudinal nervures of the tube. Fig. 5, the buccal ring. Fig. 6, the five appendages. Fig. 7, the filaments of the stamens seated in the tufts of hairs: *all magnified*. Fig. 8, the cohering stamens. Fig. 9, a stamen separated: *both natural size*. Fig. 10, the same, *much magnified*. Fig. 11, the calyx, with the sepals thrown back to show the inner scales, the disk of five free lobes, the ovaries, style, clavuncle, and stigmata, *magnified*. Fig. 12, one of the two follicles grown to its full size. Fig. 13, a seed: *both natural size*.

PLATE XXXV.

A. *Laseguea latiuscula*, portion of a plant in flower, showing its lateral very imbricated inflorescence and its fruit. Fig. 1, a flower in bud, with its basal bract much longer than the pedicel and calyx. Fig. 2, the pedicel and calyx. Fig. 3, the corolla expanded: *all natural size*. Fig. 4, the corolla, cut open, showing the simple dextrorse convolution of its segments and the position of the stamens, *magnified*. Fig. 5, an anther. Fig. 6, its filament: *both more magnified*. Fig. 7, the calyx, with the sepals thrown back to show the inner scales, the 5-lobed disk, the ovaries, style, clavuncle, and stigmata, *magnified as in fig. 4*. Fig. 8, the two erect follicles. Fig. 9, a seed with its apical coma: *both natural size*.

B. *Forsteronia refracta*, portion of a plant in flower and fruit. Fig. 1, one of its minute flowers, *natural size*. Fig. 2, the same in bud, *much magnified*. Fig. 3, the same with the corolla expanded, showing the exserted cone of anthers. Fig. 4, a stamen, seen on its inner face, with its inflexed apex. Fig. 5, the same, shown on its edge. Fig. 6, the same, on its outer face. Fig. 7, the calyx, with the sepals thrown back to show the 5-lobed disk, the ovaries, style, clavuncle, and stigmata: *all equally magnified*. Fig. 8, one of the two torose follicles, 10 inches long, with many long strangulations. Fig. 9, a seed with its apical coma: *both natural size*.

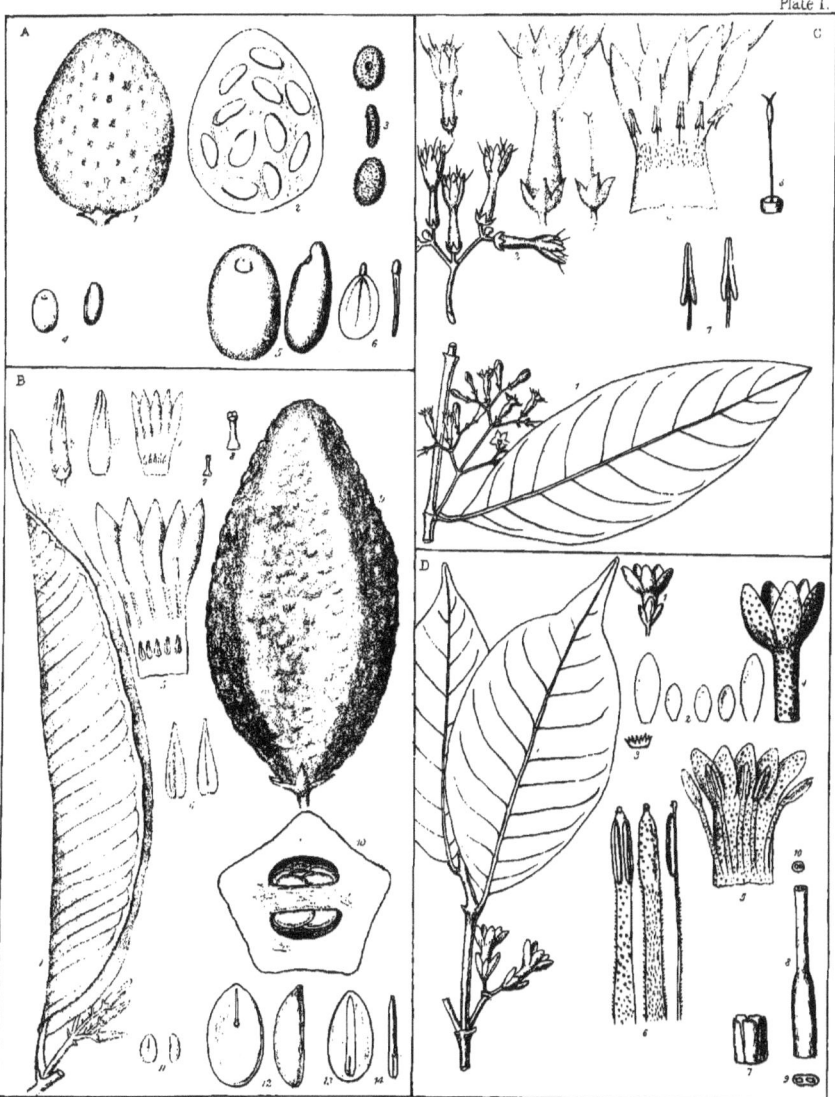

A HANCORNIA SPECIOSA.
B. AMBELLANIA CUCUMERINA.
C CERATITES AMÆNA
D POMPHIDEA SWARTZIANA

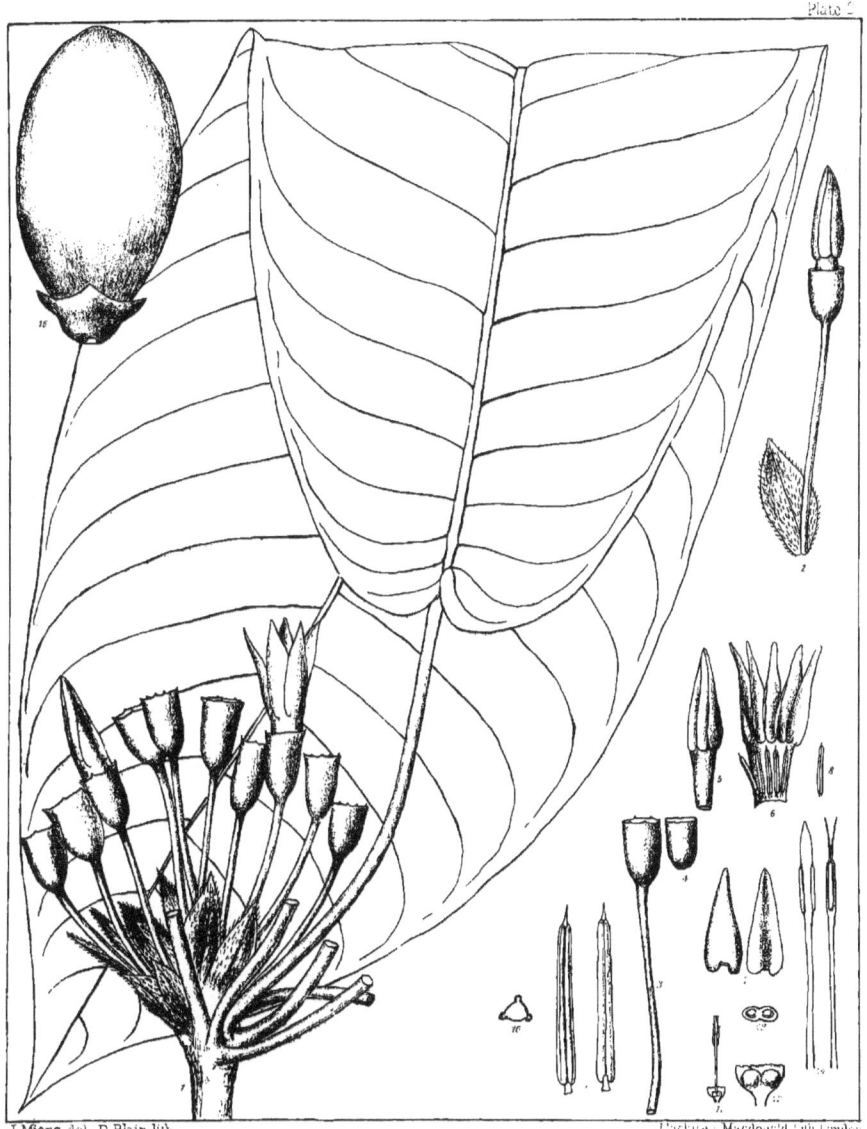

CUPIRANA AUBLETIANA.

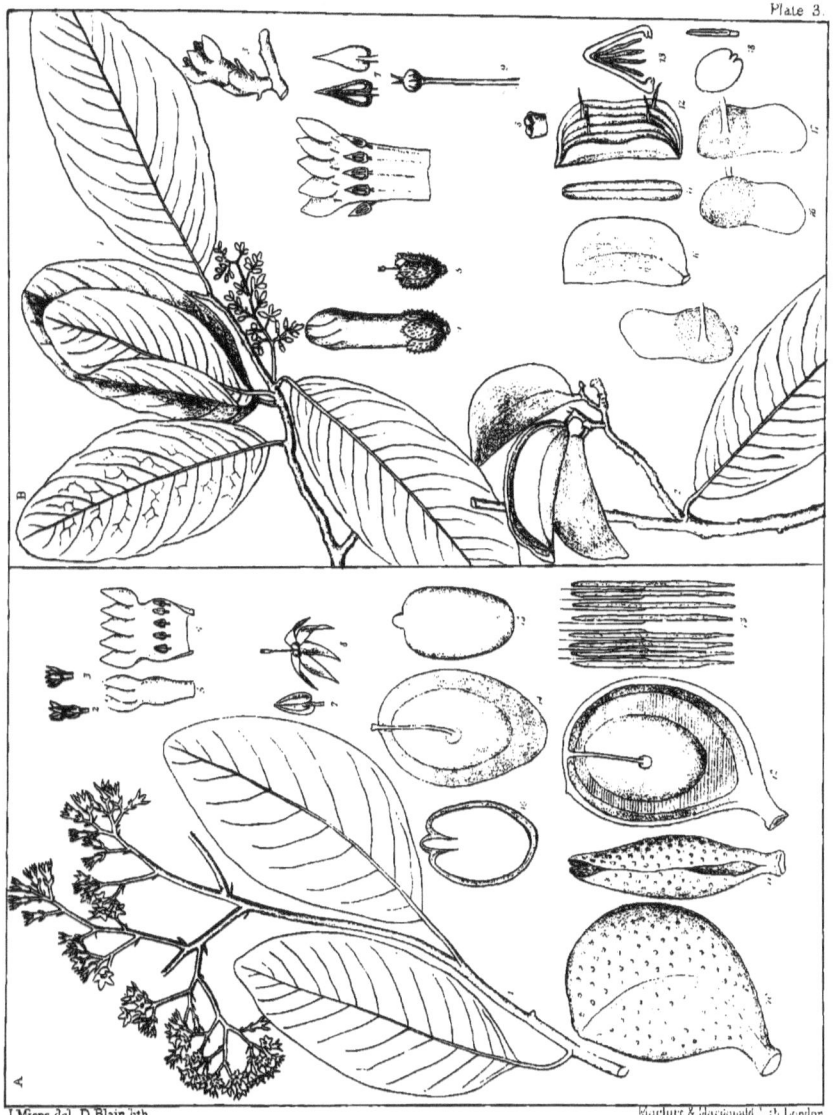

Plate 3.

Plate 4

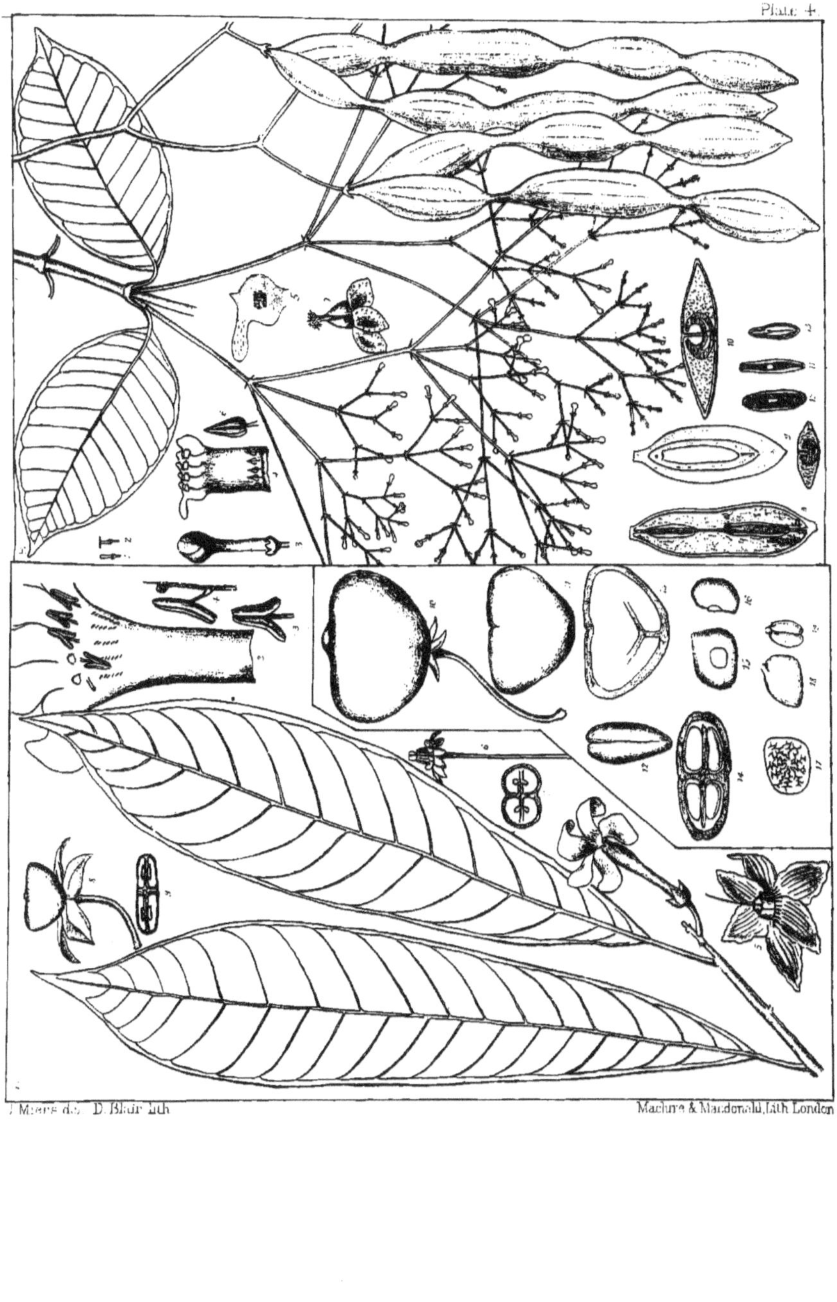

CONDYLOCARPON GRACILE.

T. AHOUAI.

THEVETIA CALOPHYLLA.

T Miers del. D. Blair lith.   Maclure & Macdonald, lith London.

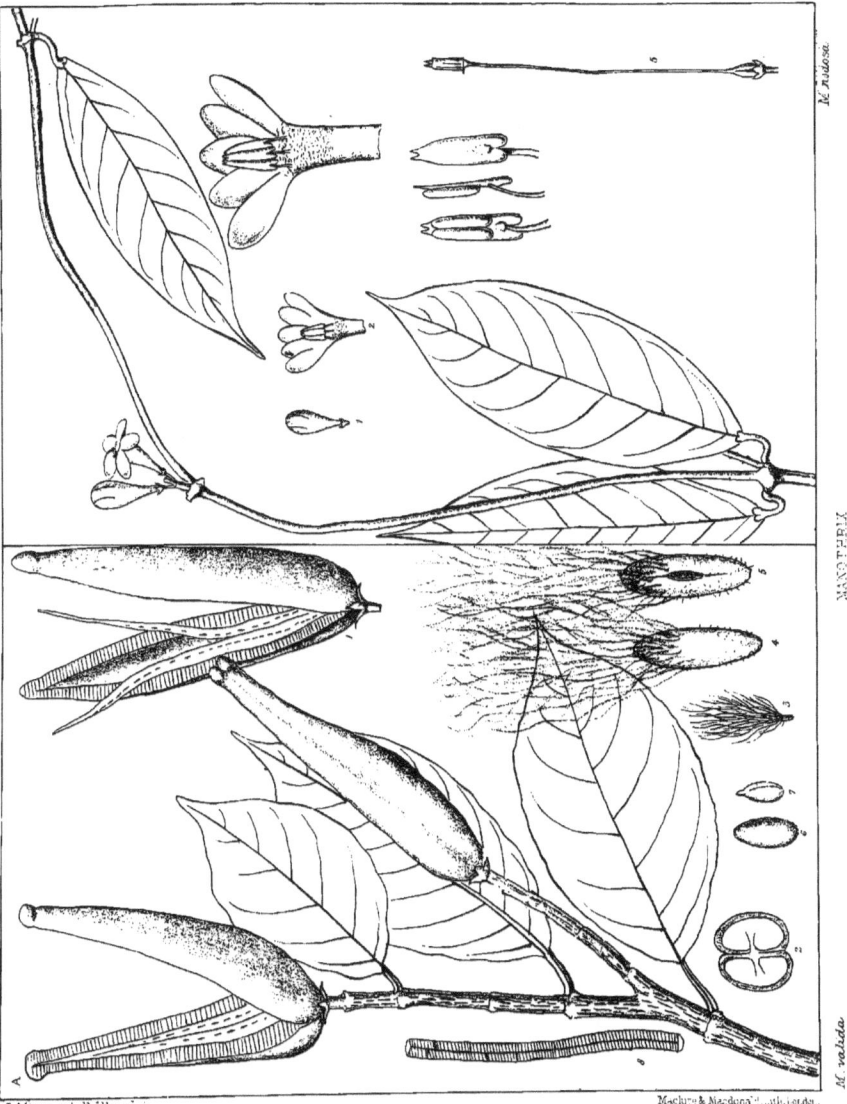

Plate 5.

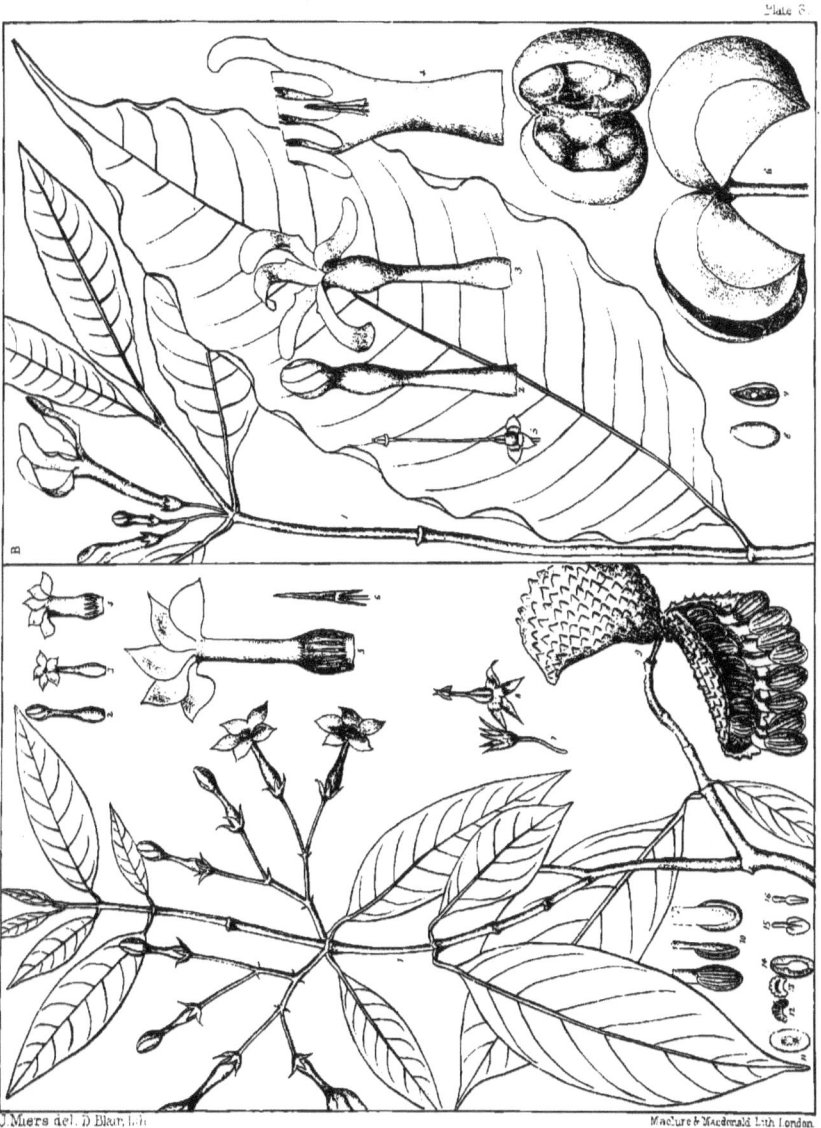

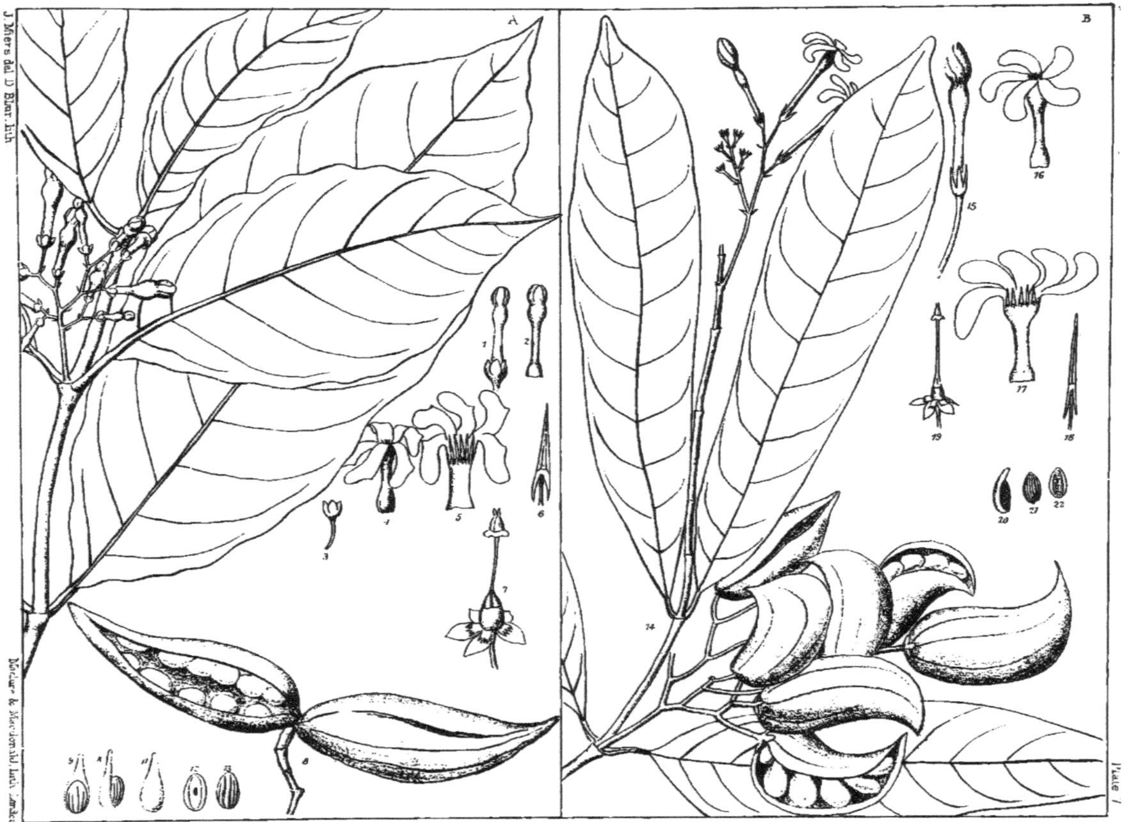

Plate 7

T. lanceolata

TABERNAEMONTANA

T. cordata

J. Miers del D Blair lith

Maclure & Macdonald, lith London

Plate 8.

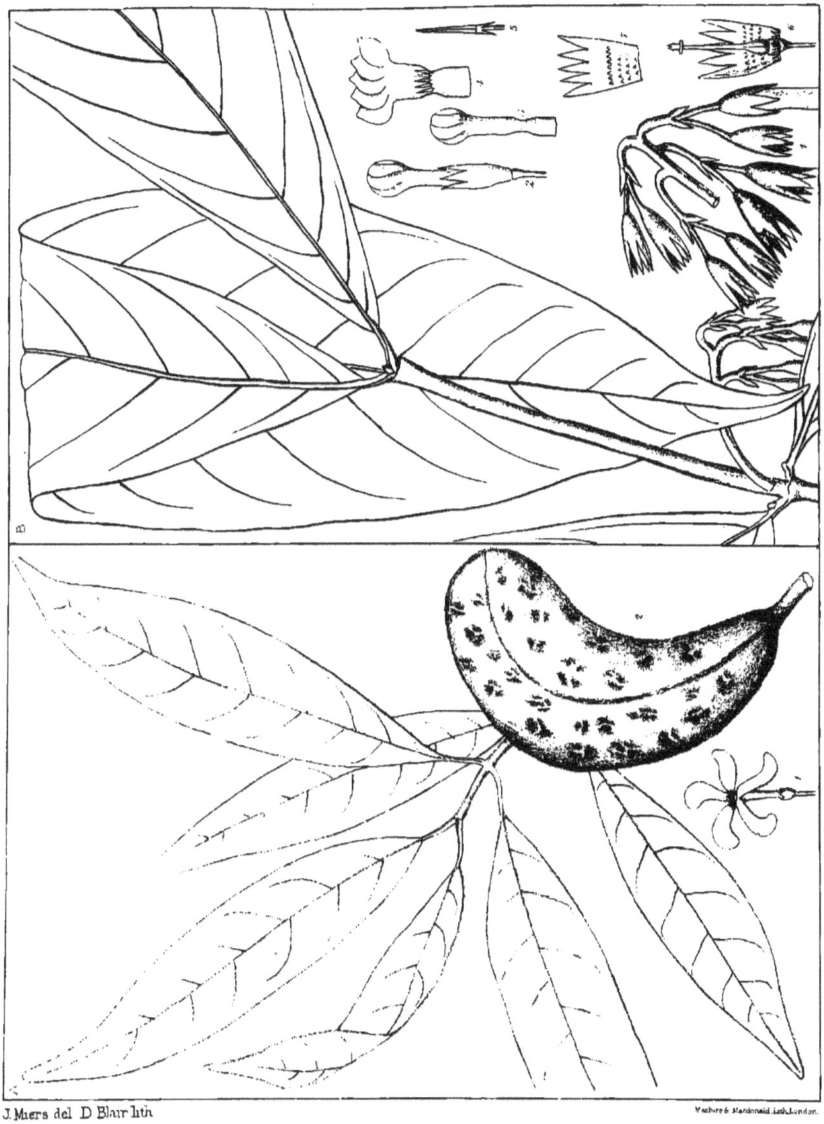

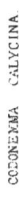

CODONEMMA CALYCINA.

TABERNA CYMOSA.

J. Miers del. D. Blair lith.

Mackie & Macdonald lith. London.

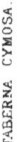

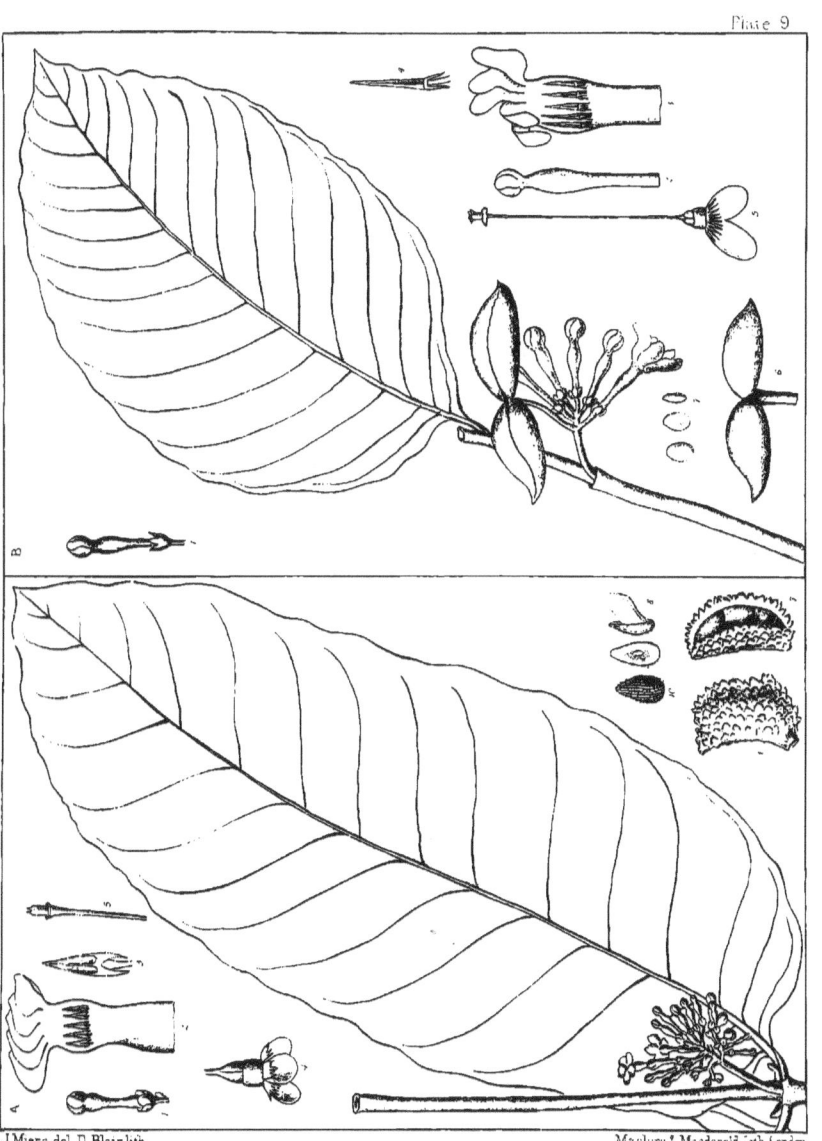

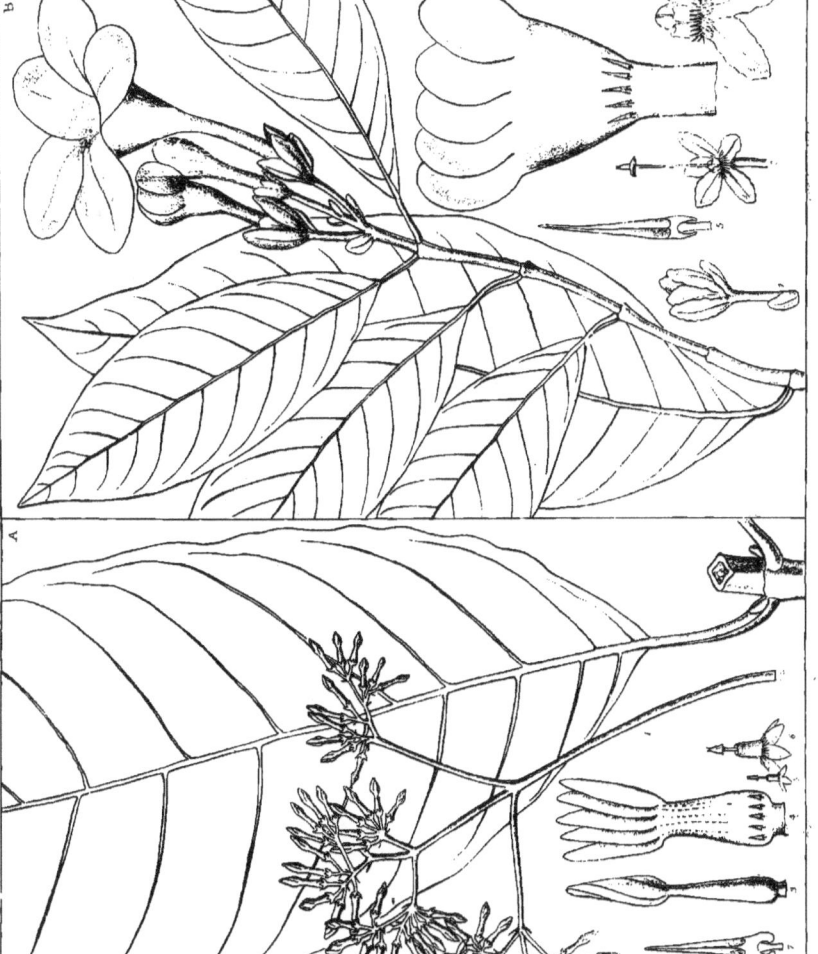

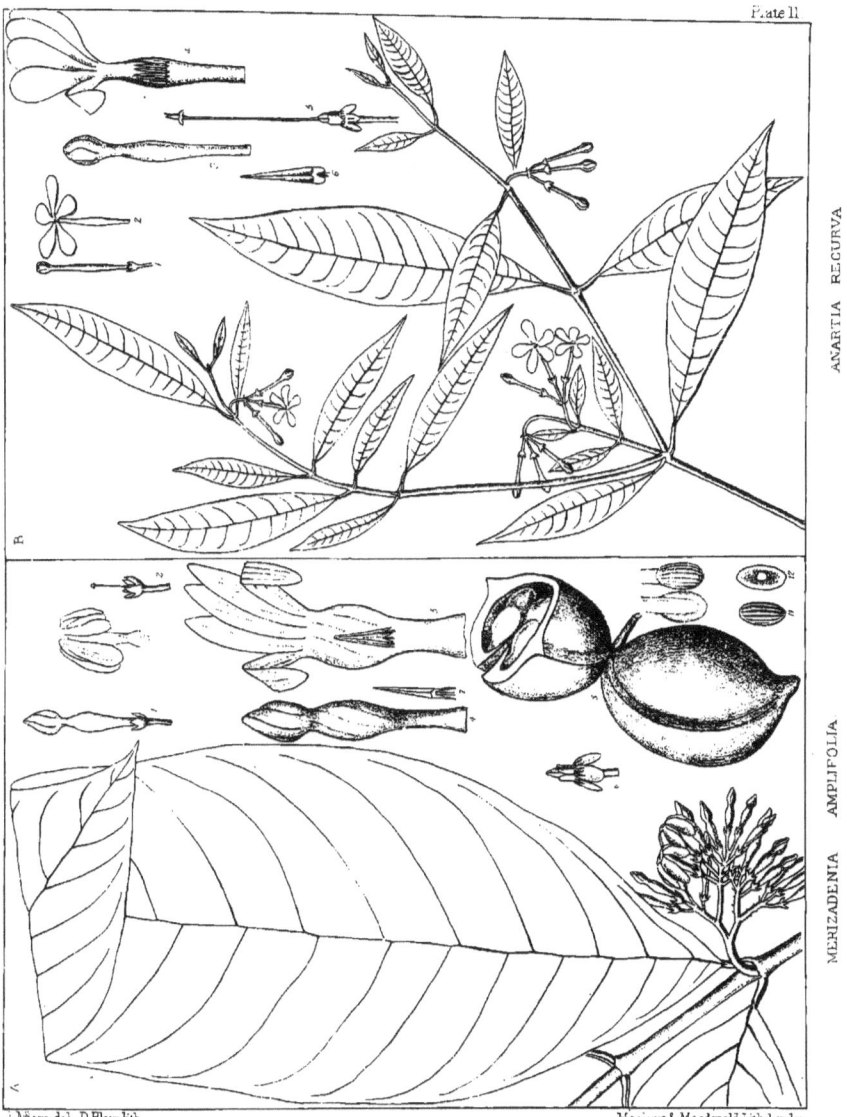

Plate II

ANARTIA RECURVA

MERIZADENIA AMPLIFOLIA

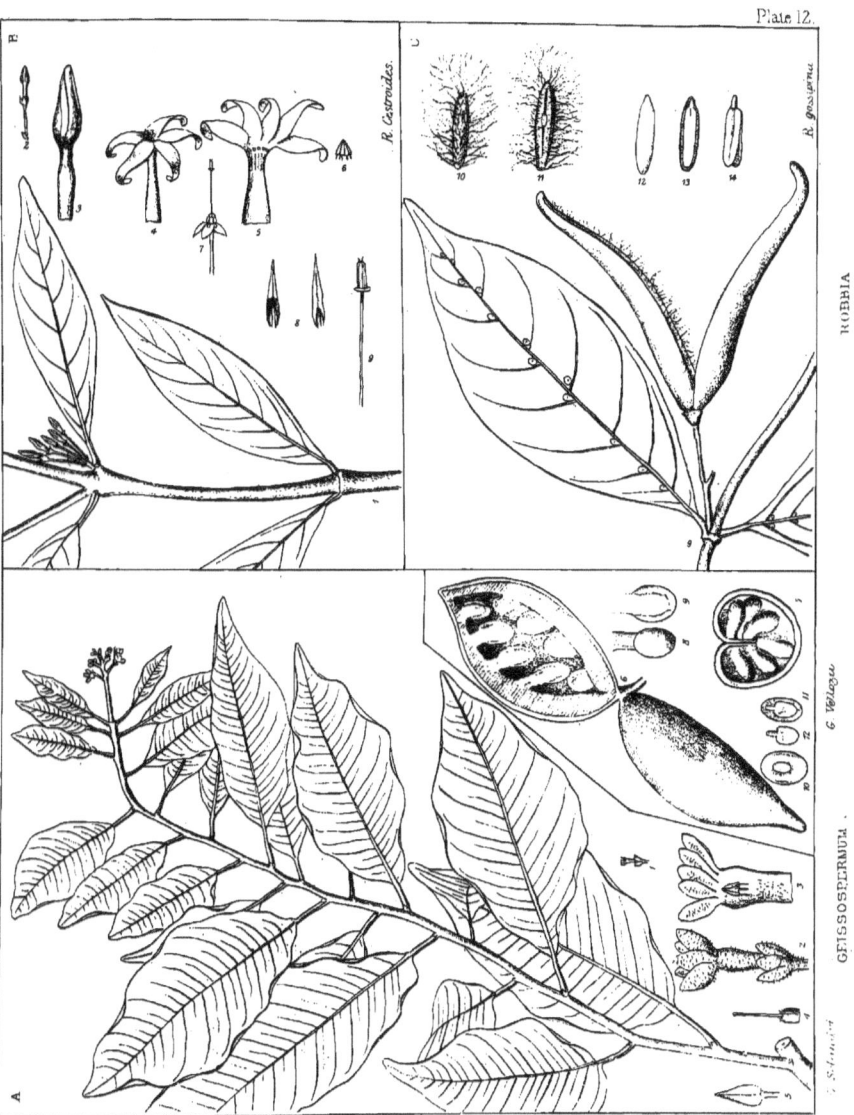

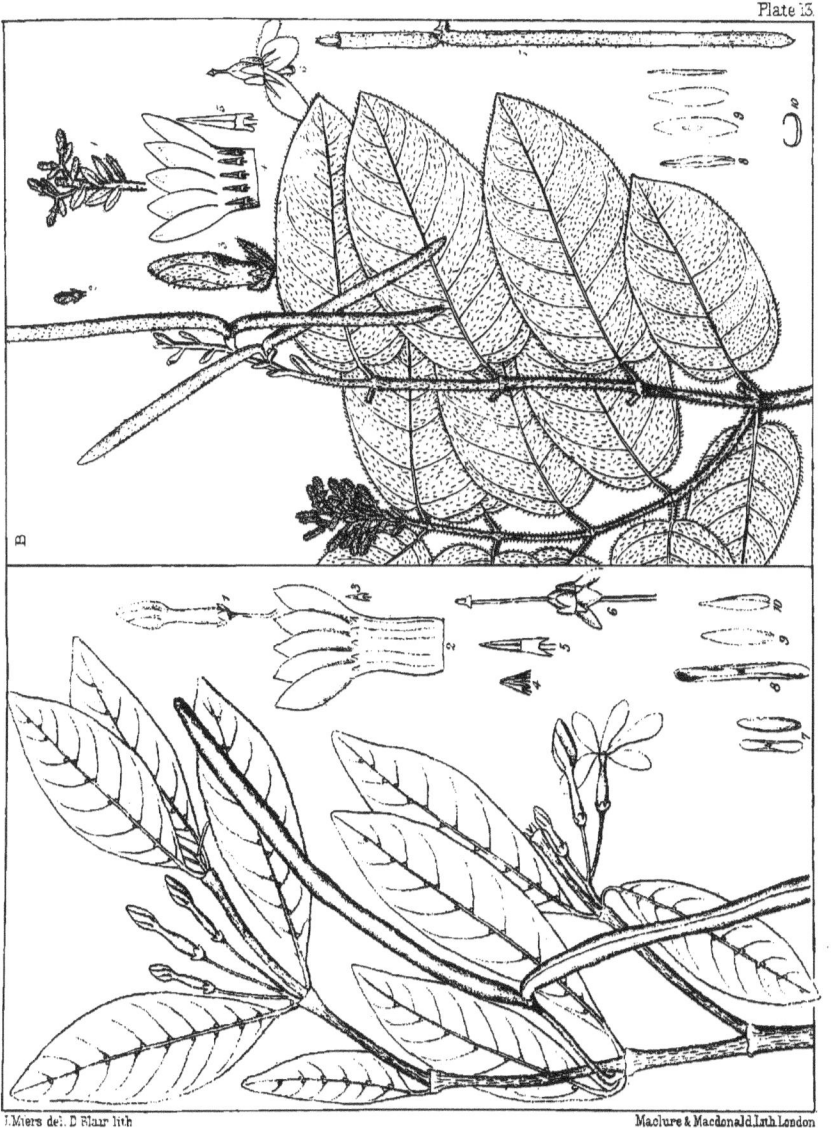

Plate 13.

MALOUETIA GLANDULIFERA.   THYRSANTHUS BRACTEATUS

J. Miers del. D. Blair lith.   Maclure & Macdonald Lith. London

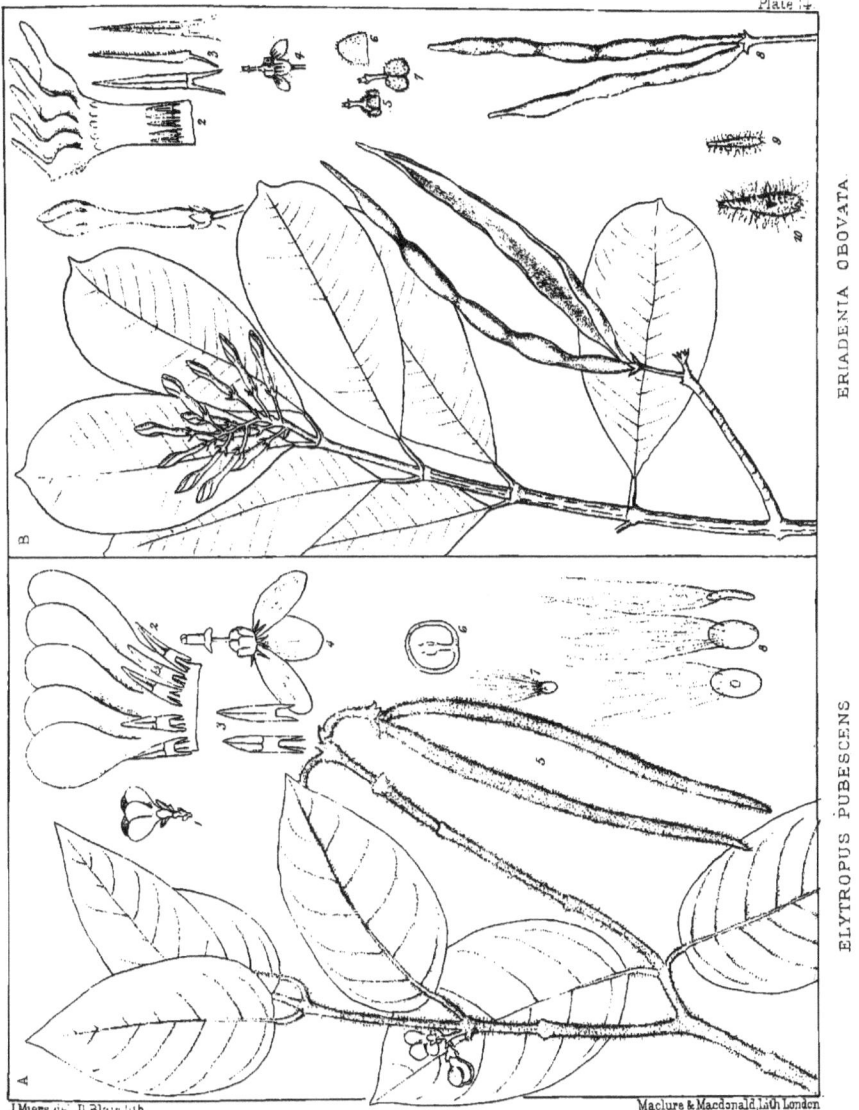

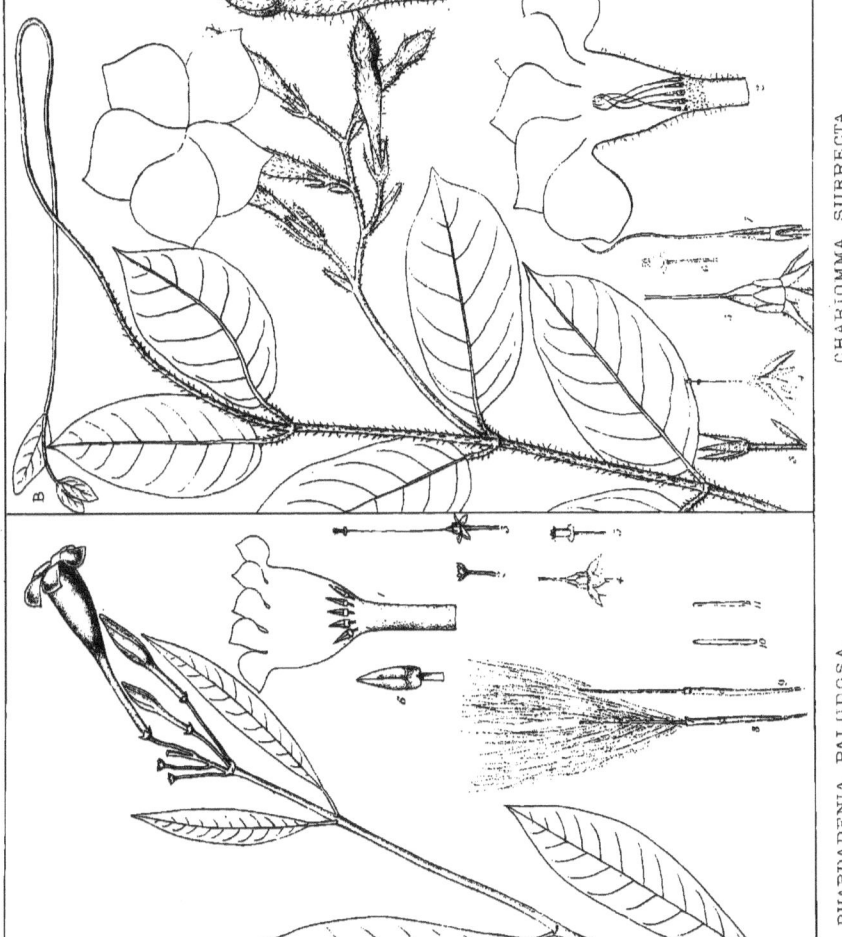

RHABDADENIA PALUDOSA.   CHARIOMMA SURRECTA.

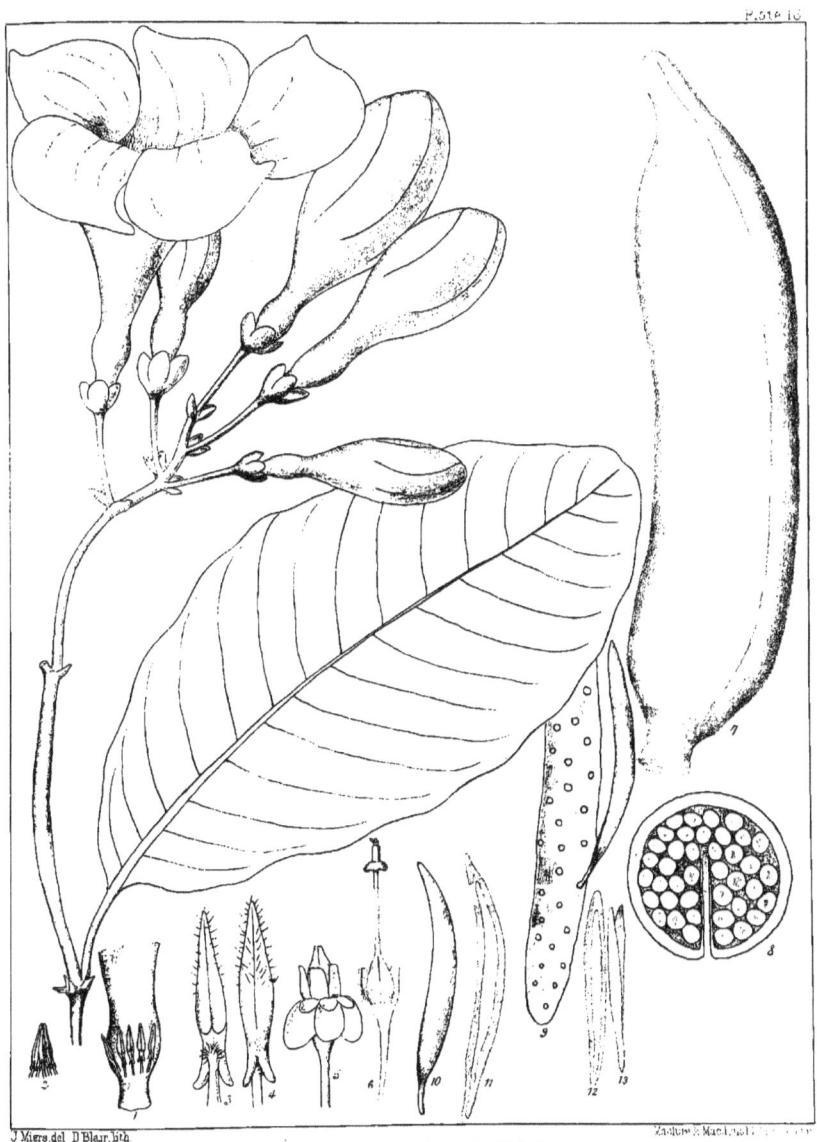

ODONTADENIA GRANDIFLORA

Plate 17

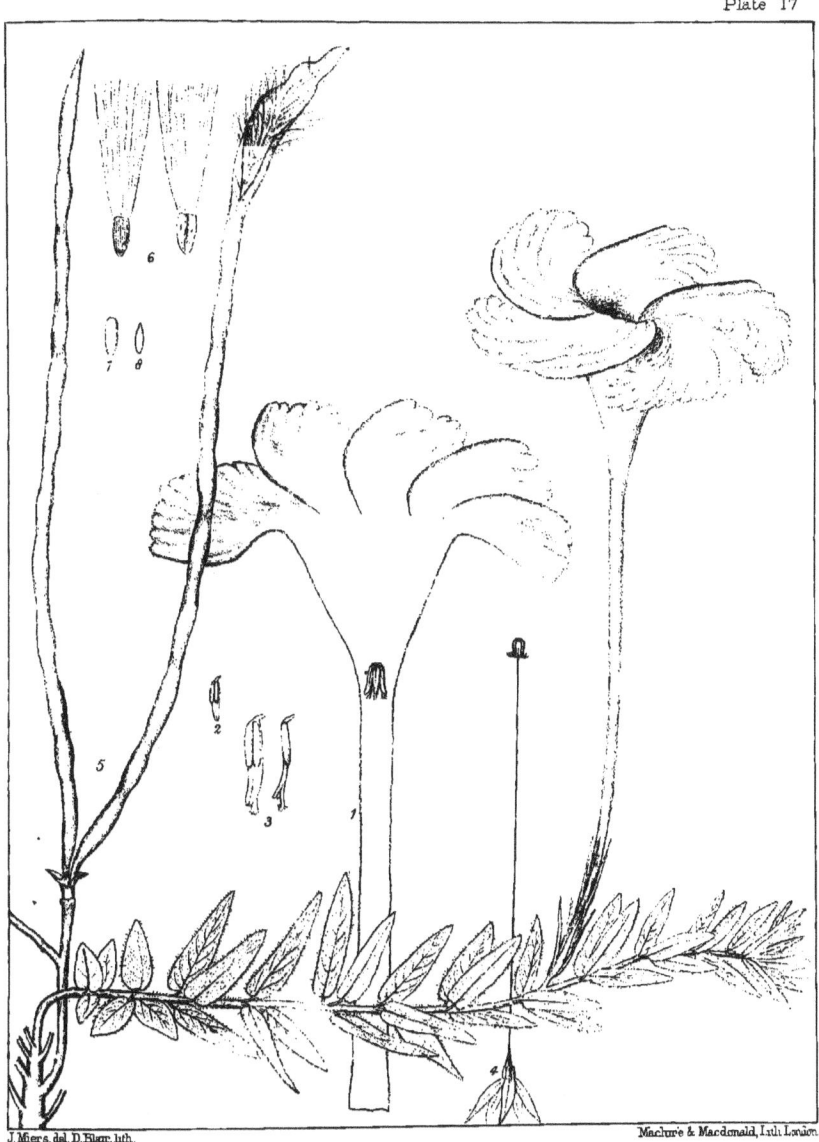

MACROSIPHONIA PROSTRATA.

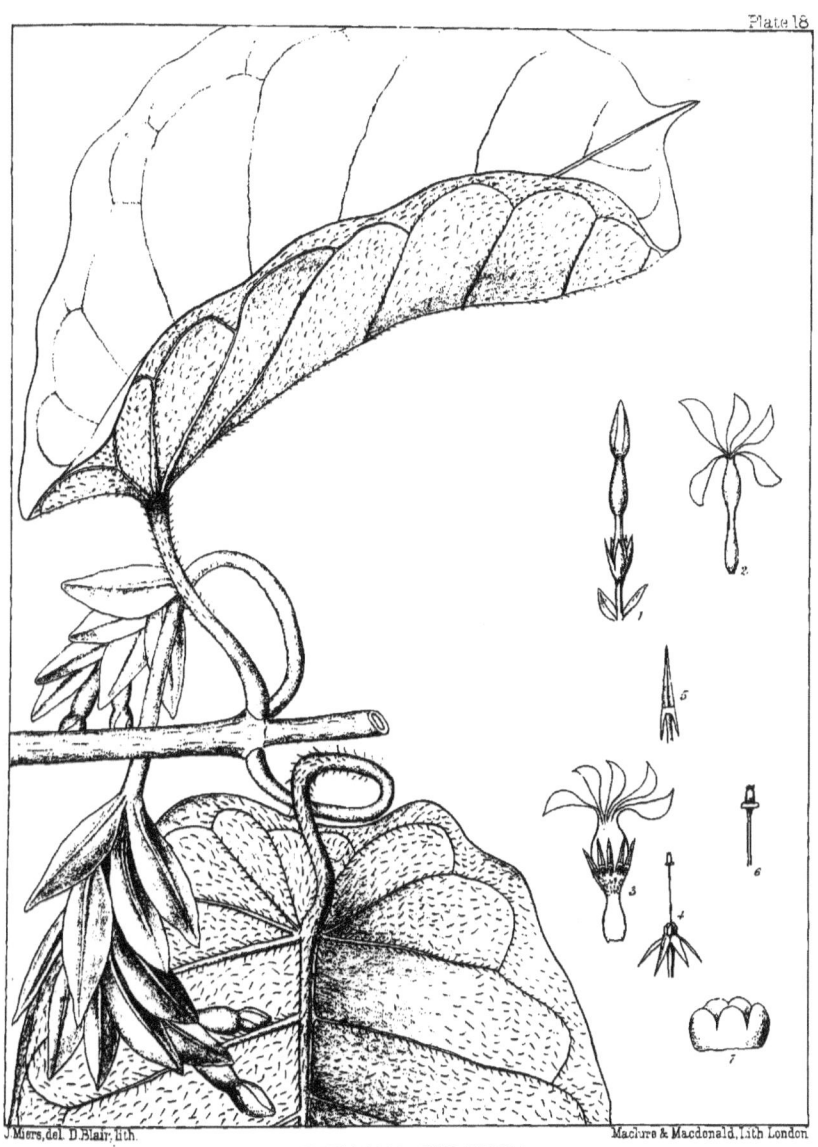

STIPECOMA PULCHRA

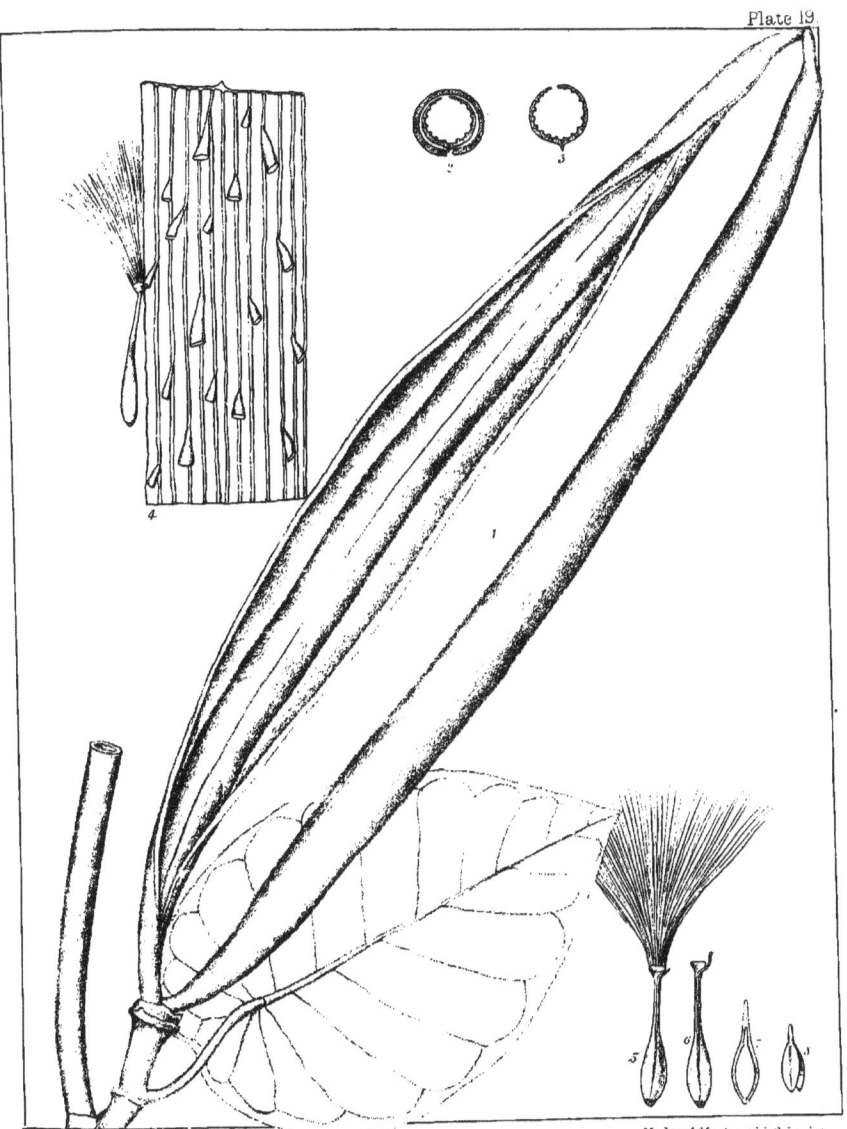

STIPECOMA OVATA.

RHODOCALYX

PRESTONIA TOMENTOSA

R. CRASSIFOLIUS
R. ROTUNDIFOLIUS

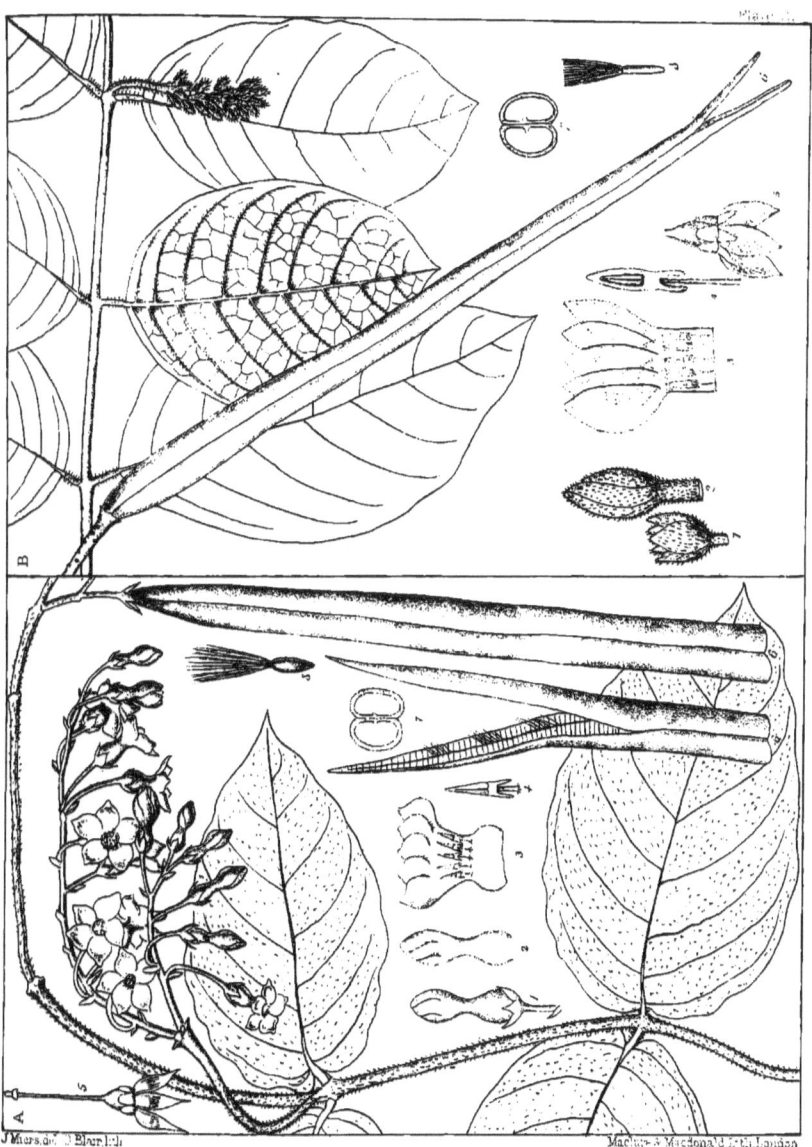

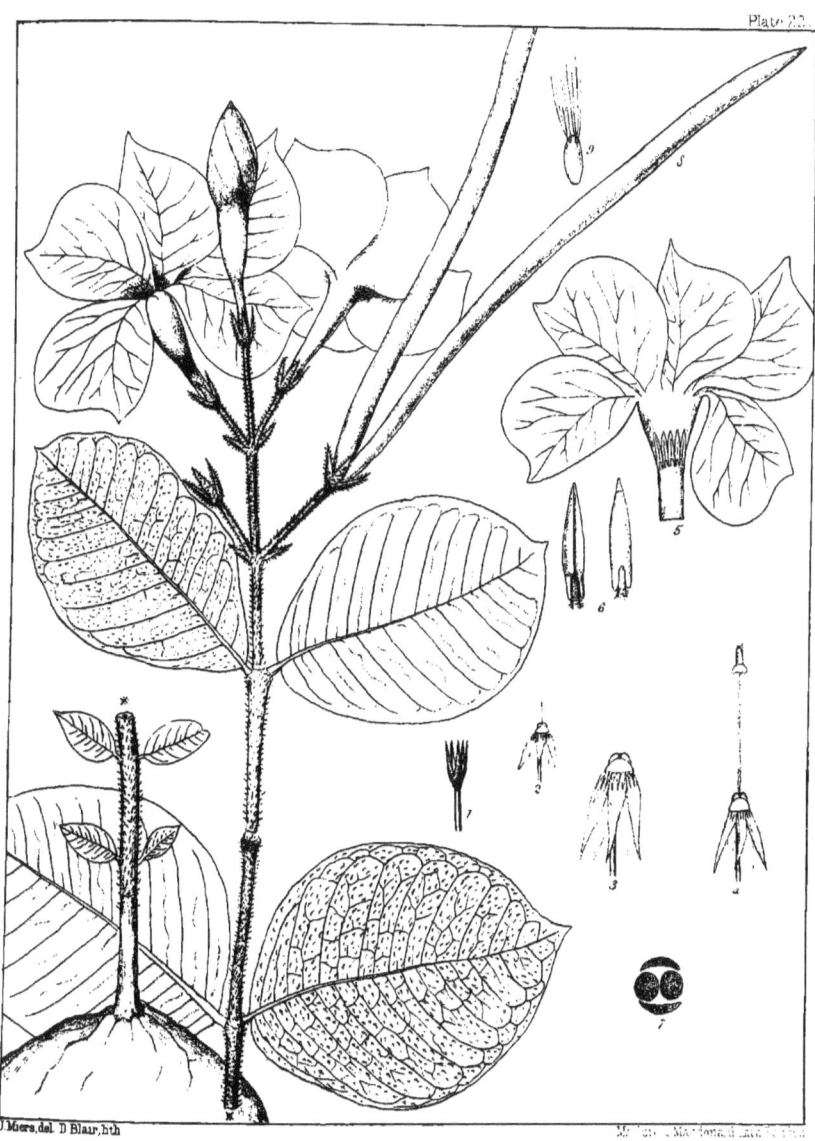

DIPLADENIA ILLUSTRIS

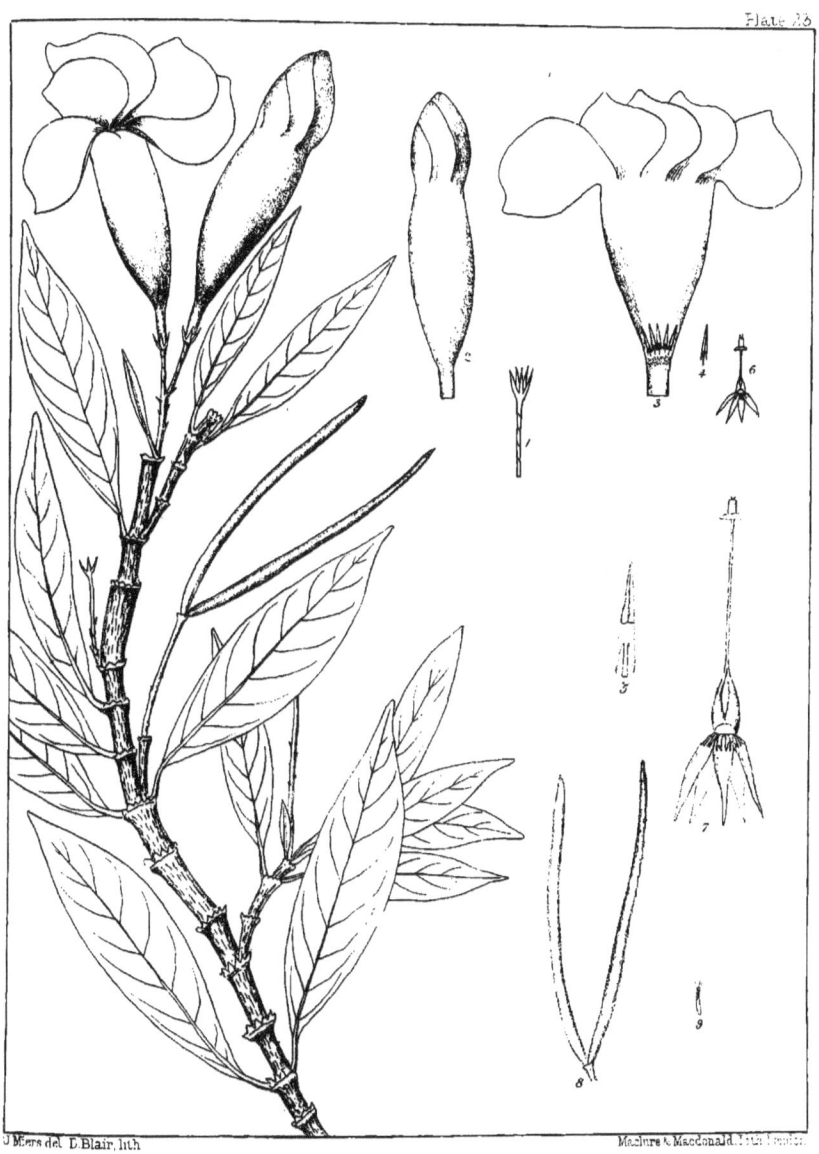

MICRADENIA CRASSINODA

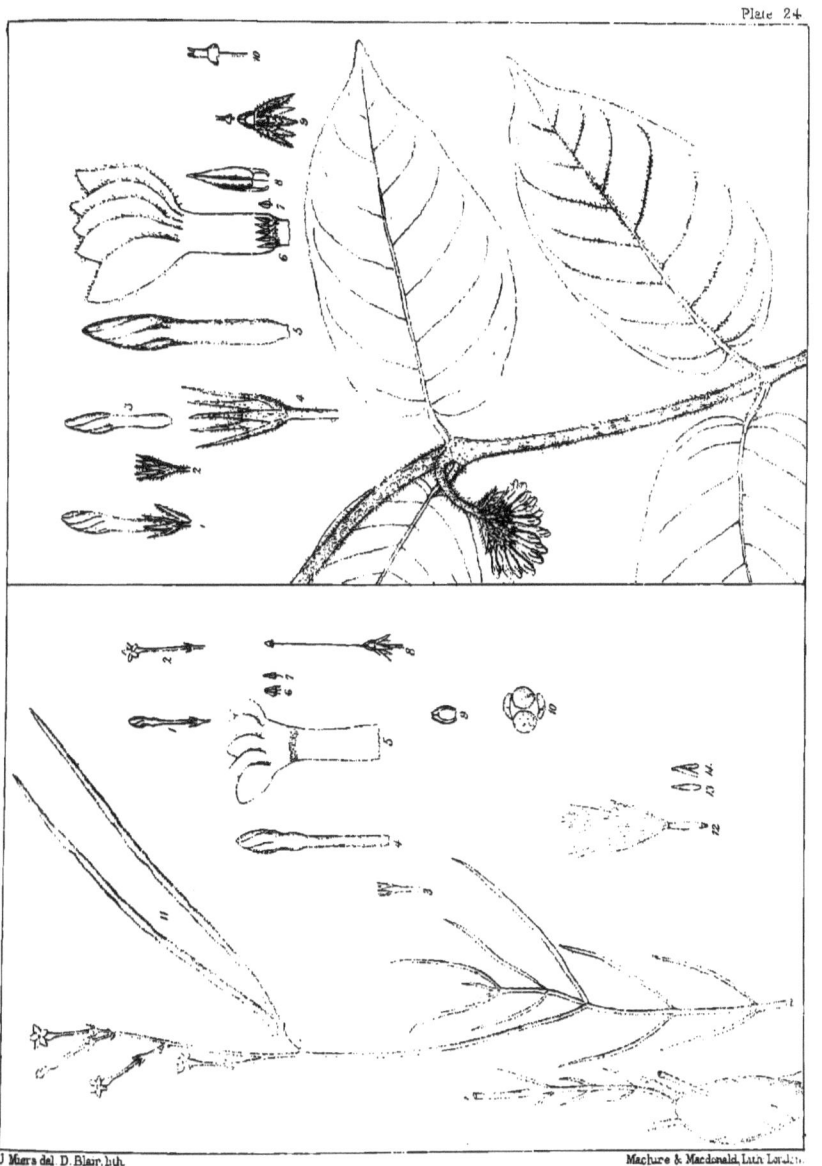

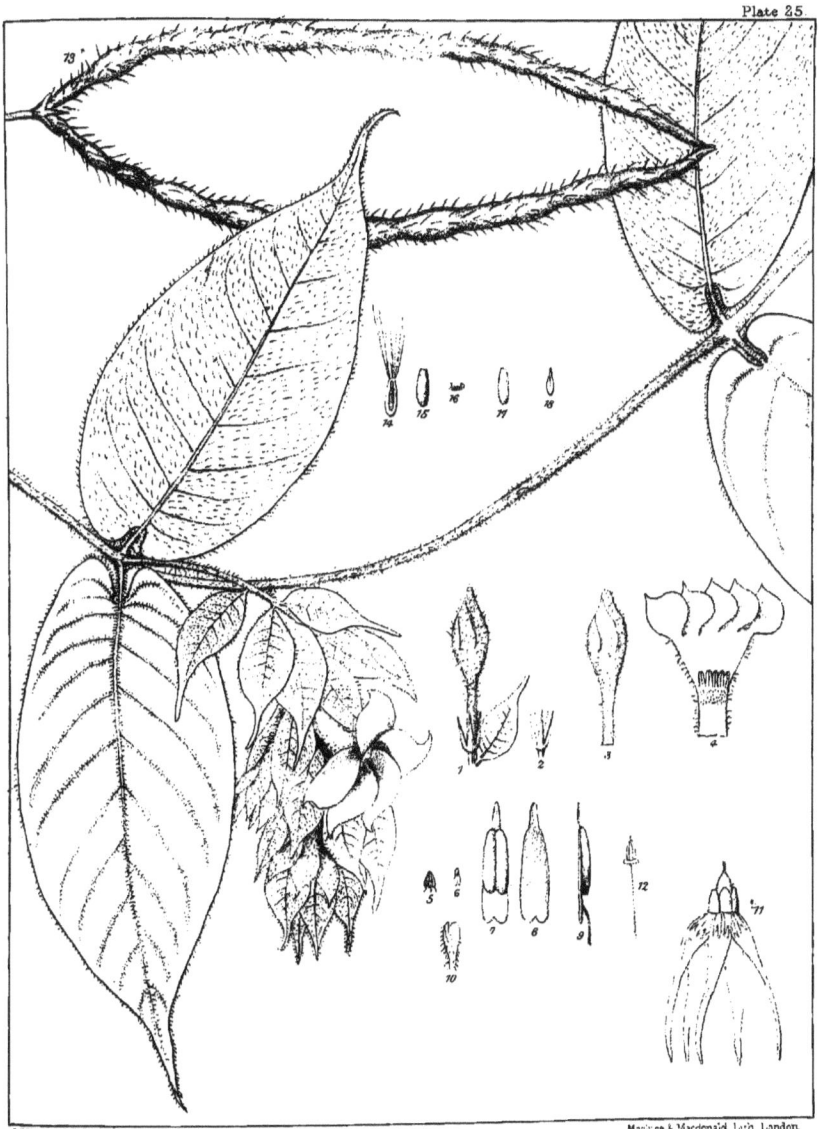

AMBLYANTHERA CLAUSSENII.

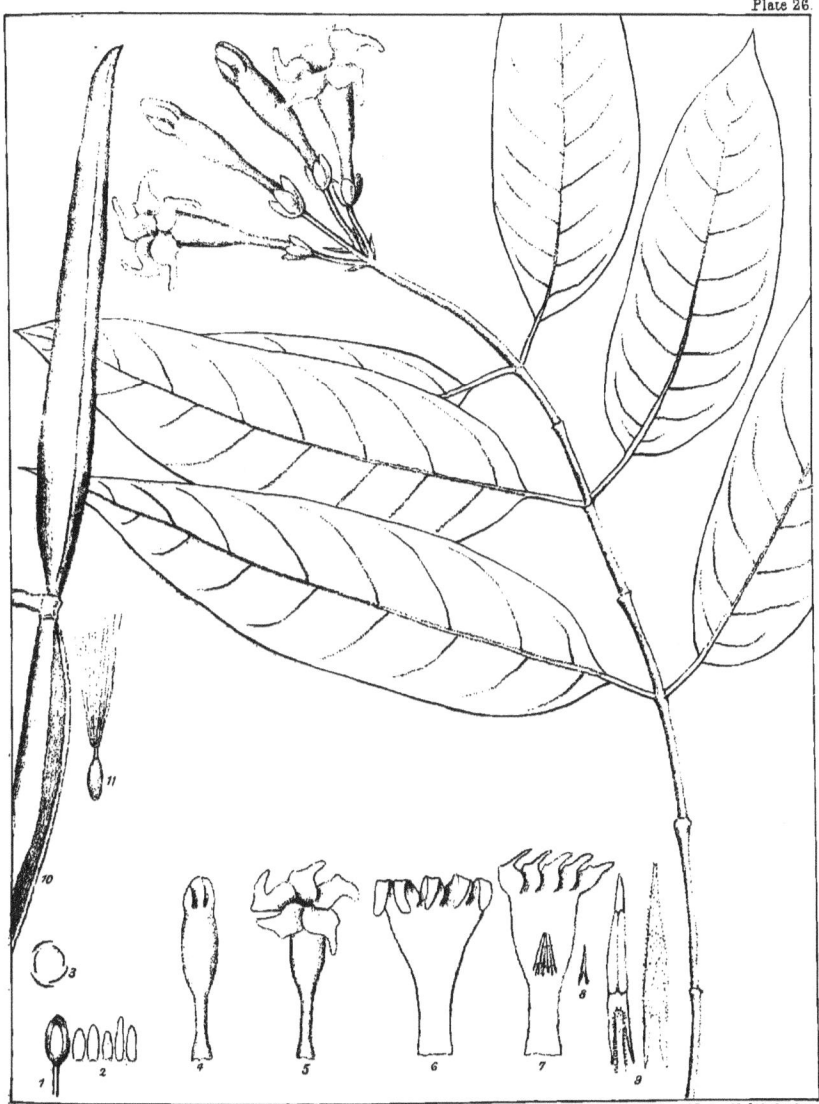

ANISOLOBUS OBLONGUS.

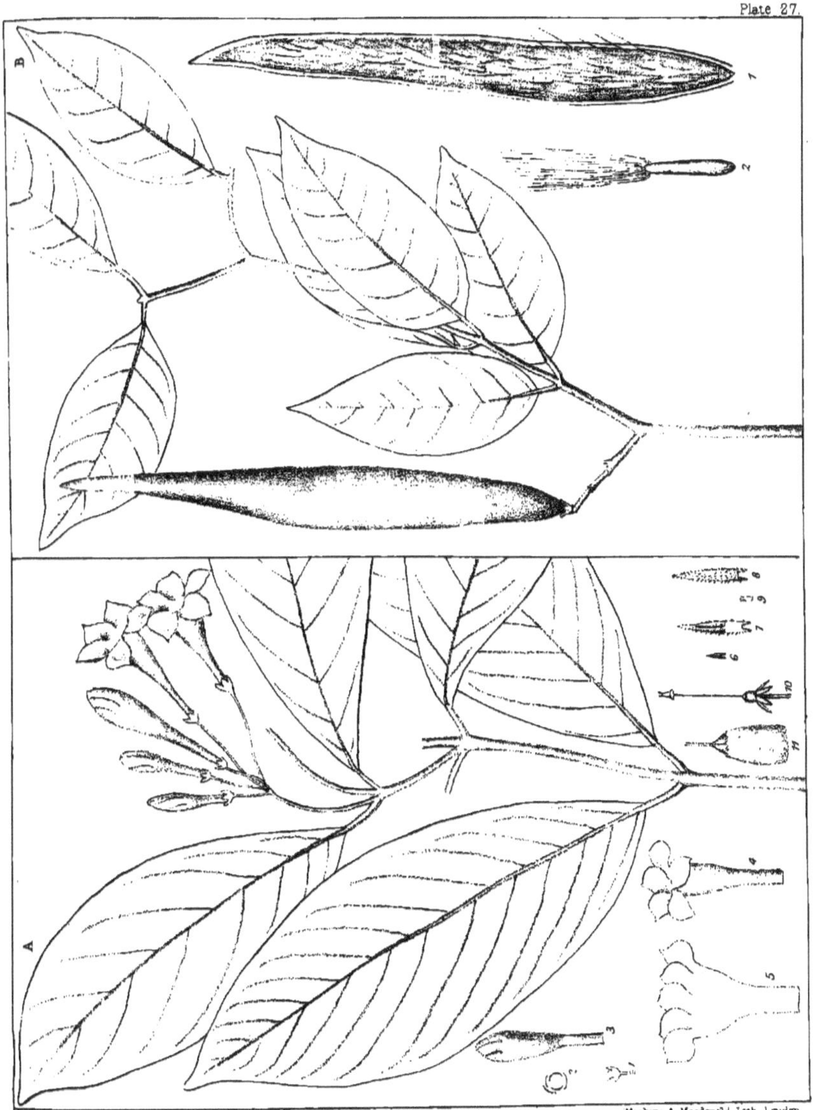

Plate 27.

ANGADENIA PRUINOSA.

ANGADENIA SPRUCEI.

J. Miers, del. D. Blair, Lith.   Maclure & Macdonald, Lith. London

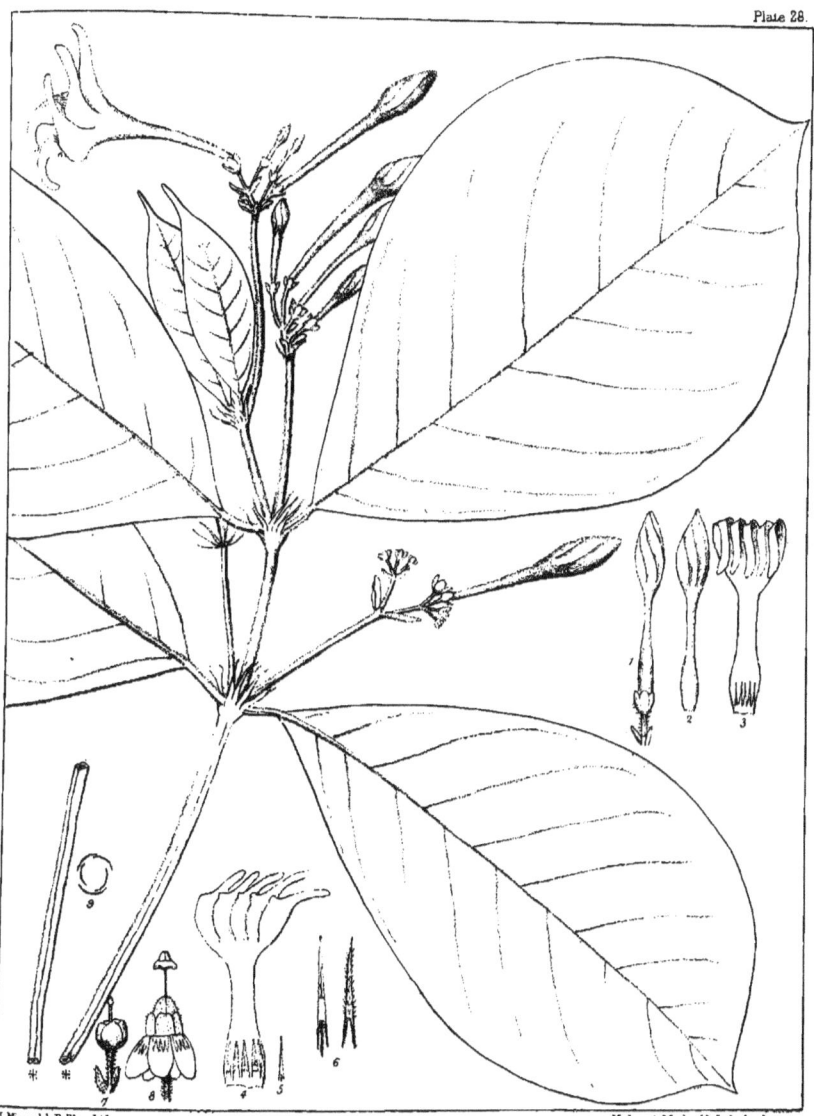

PERICTENIA STIPELLARIS.

Plate 29

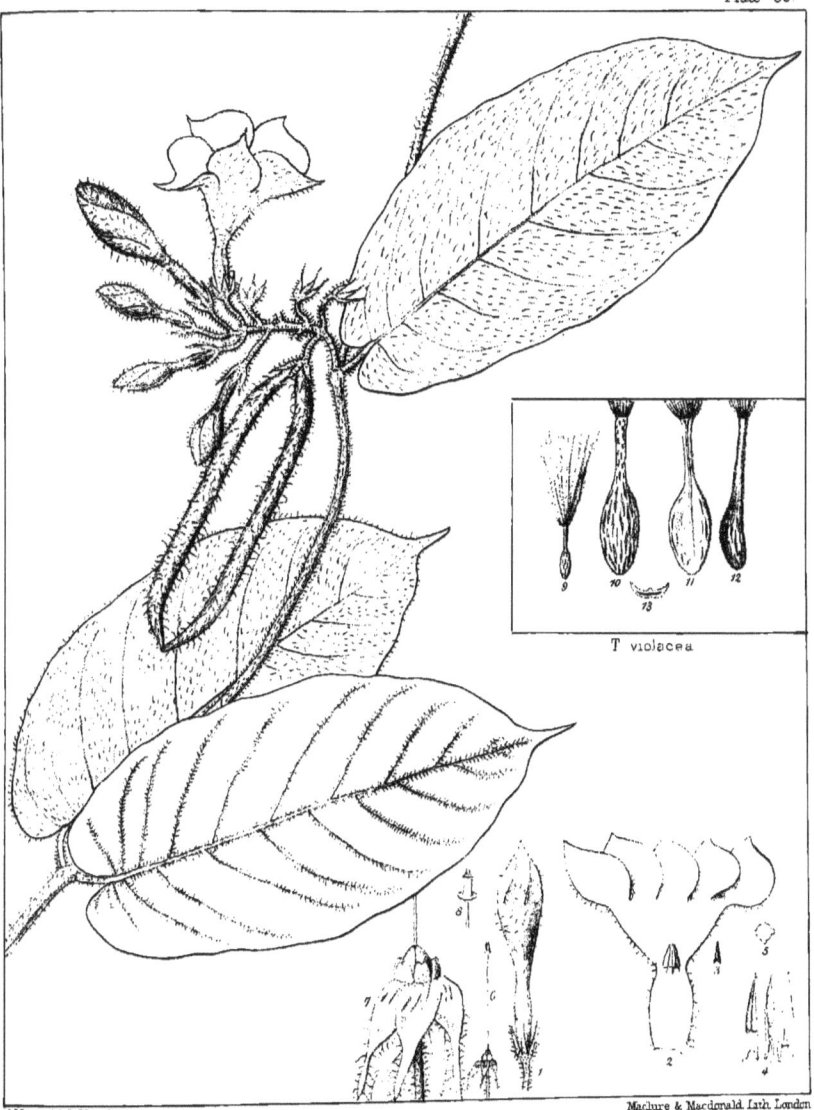

TEMNADENIA LOBBIANA

MITOZUS EXILIS.

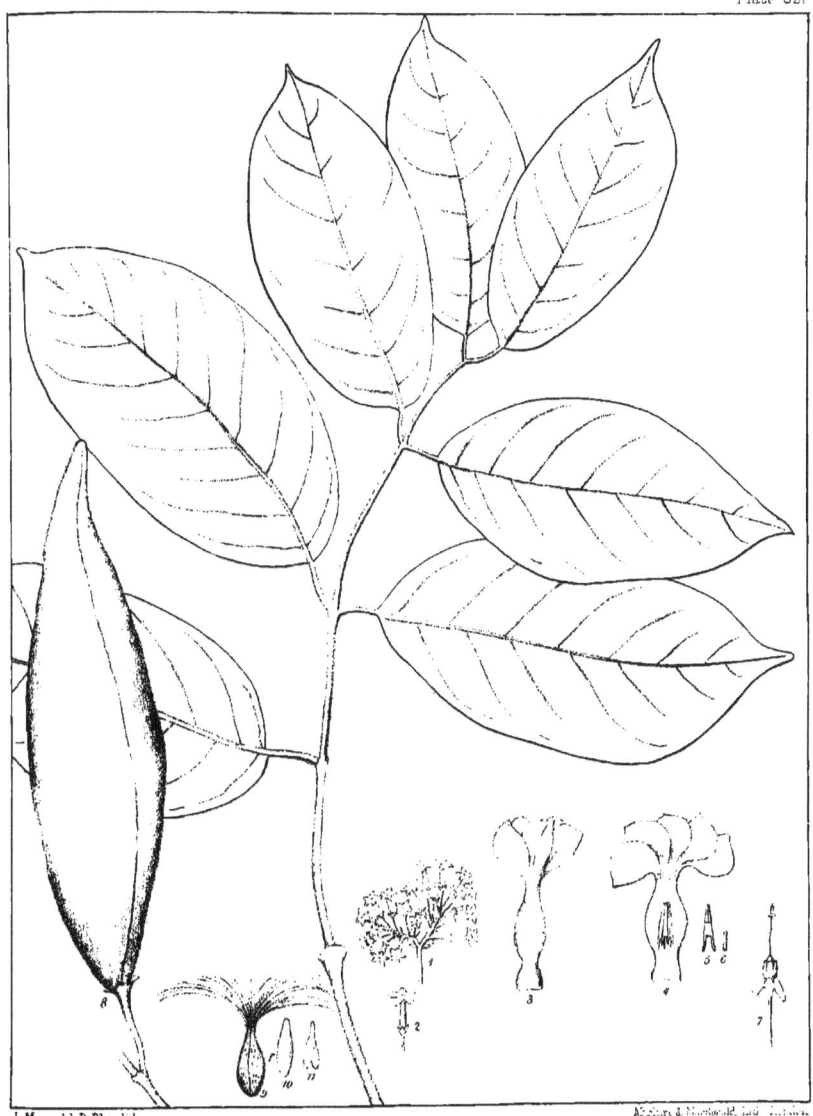

SECONDATIA DENSIFLORA.

Plate 33.

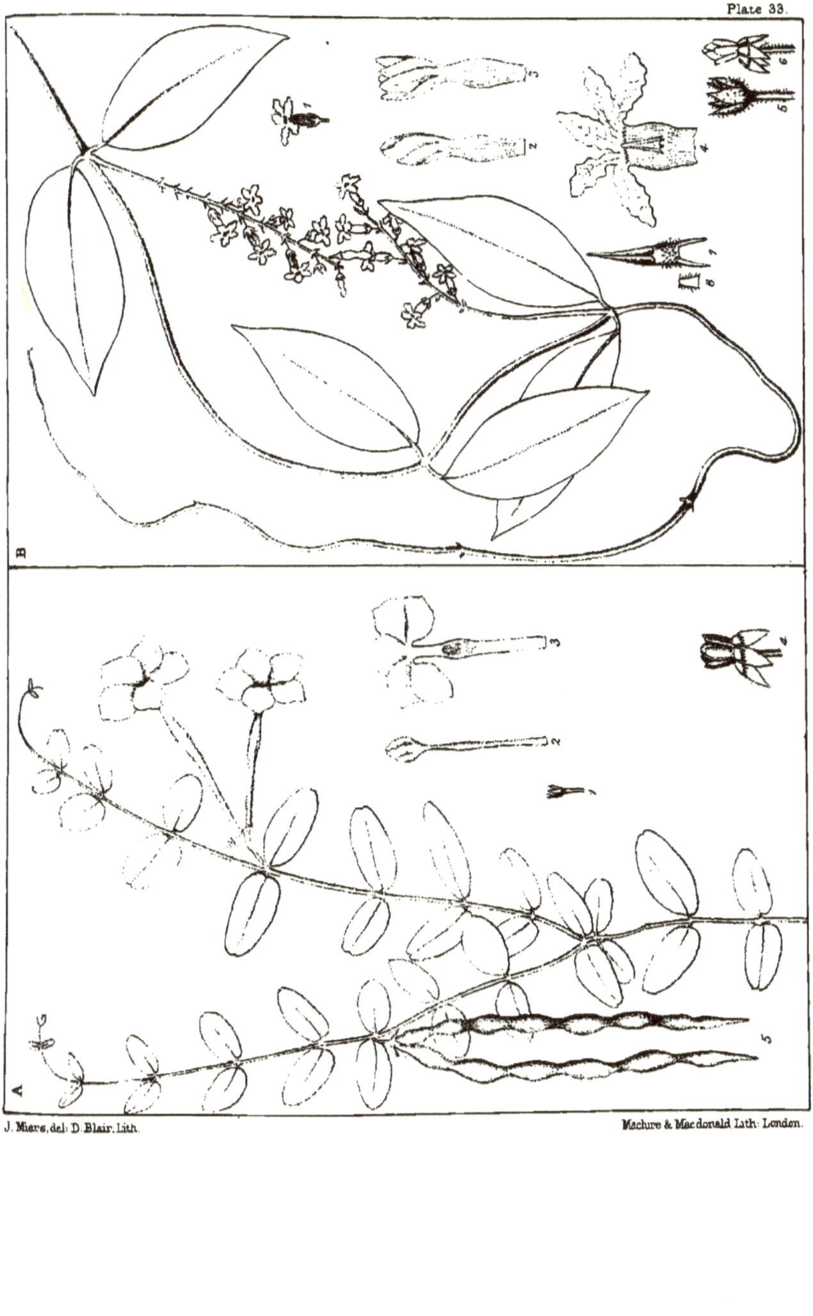

MESECHITES MYRTIFOLIA.

ANECHITES CIRCINALIS.

J. Miers, del: D. Blair, Lith. Machure & Macdonald Lith: London.

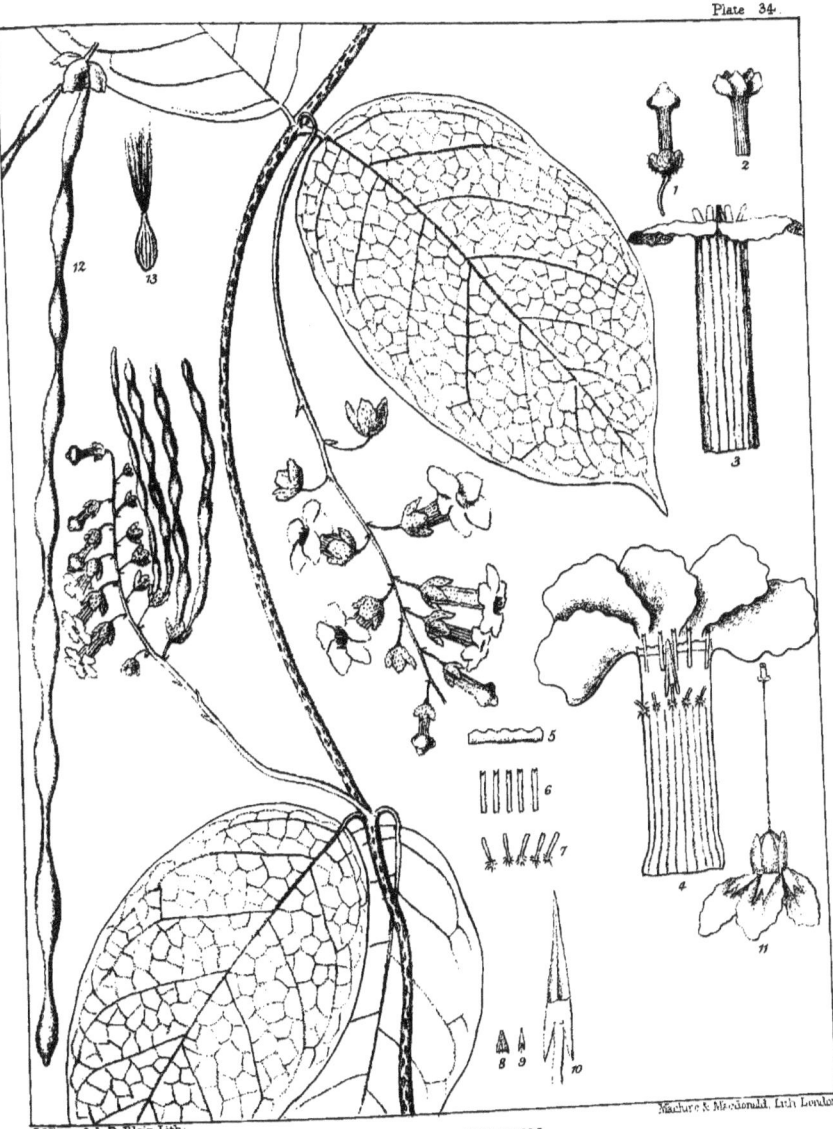

HÆMADICTYON OVATUM.

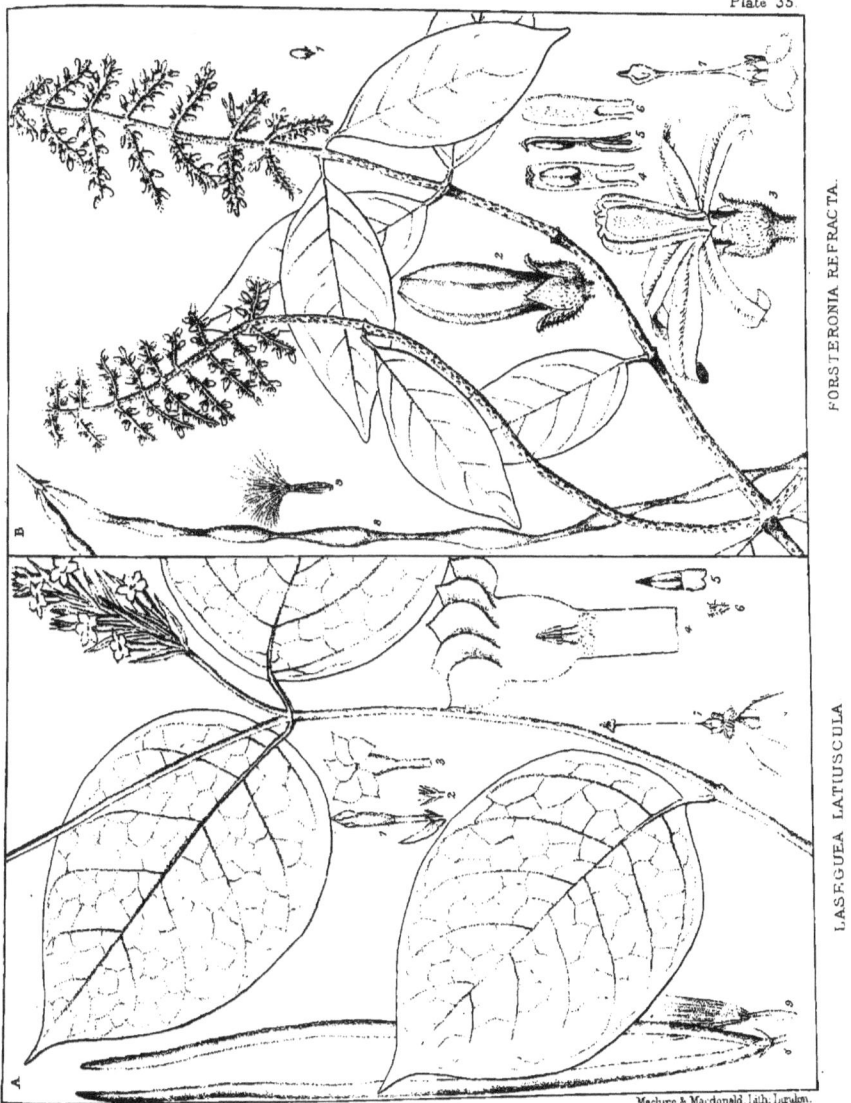

INDEX.

[The Synonyms are in *italics*.]

	Page
AMBELLANIA	6, 13
cucumerina, Pl. 1 B	13
laxa	13
Ambellania macrophylla, Müll.	14, 68
quadrangularis, Müll.	14, 68
AMBLYANTHERA	10, 184
Bridgesii, *Müll.*	189
ciliata, *Müll.*	188
Claussenii, nob., Pl. 25	187
Fendleri, *Müll.*	190
Fluminensis, *Müll.*	186
hirsuta, nob.	185
hispida, *Müll.*, Pl. 25	187
Moritziana, *Müll.*	189
ovata, nob.	188
Schlimii, *Müll.*	189
Spruceana, *Müll.*	190
Amblyanthera Andina, Müll.	204
Andrieuxii, Müll.	206, 235
Bogotensis, Müll.	82
brachyloba, Müll.	203
campestris, Müll.	121
citrifolia, Müll.	200
congesta, Müll.	200
convolvulacea, Müll.	195
crassifolia, Müll.	139
Cuiabensis, Müll.	223
Fluminensis, Müll. (in parte)	185
,, var. *Clausseni*, Müll.	187
foliosa, Müll.	253
funiformis, Müll.	210
,, var. *pedunculata*, Müll.	218
,, var. *microphylla*, Müll.	218
Guianensis, Müll.	235
Karwinskii, Müll.	206

	Page
Amblyanthera madida, Müll.	121
Mexicana, Müll.	205
microcalyx, var. *trichantha*, Müll.	203
Oaxacana, Müll.	234
palustris, Müll.	213
,, var. *Almadensis*, Müll.	179
pandurata, Müll.	182
Prieurii, Müll.	182
tomentosa, Müll.	213
torosa, Müll.	229
tubiflora, Müll.	206
versicolor, Müll.	221
,, var. *intermedia*, Müll.	222
,, var. *olivacea*, Müll.	221
ANACAMPTA	8, 31, 64
acutissima, nob.	66
angulata, nob.	65
congesta, nob., Pl. 9 B	65
hirtula, nob.	67
longifolia, nob.	66
submollis, nob.	67
ANARTIA	8, 32, 79
Bogotensis, nob.	82
flavescens, nob.	82
flavicans, nob.	82
glabrata, nob.	81
Meyeri, nob.	80
recurva, nob., Pl. 11 B	80
Wulfschlægelii, nob.	81
ANECHITES	10, 236
agglutinata, nob.	236
asperuginis, nob.	237
circinalis, nob., Pl. 33 B	236
lappulacea, nob.	237
revoluta, nob.	238

INDEX

	Page
ANECHITES	
Thomasiana, nob.	237
ANGADENIA	10, 173
Almadensis, nob.	179
Amazonica, nob.	175
Berterii, nob.	180
cognata, nob.	176
coriacea, nob.	177
Cubensis, nob.	182
Cururu, nob.	175
elegans, nob.	178
elliptica, nob.	180
geminata, nob.	178
grandifolia, nob.	175
Havanensis, nob.	181
hypoglauca, nob.	173
latifolia, nob.	176
Lindeniana, nob.	180
majuscula, nob.	174
nitida, nob.	177
pandurata, nob.	182
Pöppigii, nob.	179
Prieurii, nob.	182
pruinosa, nob., Pl. 27 B	177
reticulata, nob.	179
Sagræi, nob.	181
Sprucei, nob., Pl. 27 A	176
sylvestris, nob.	174
Valenzuelana, nob.	181
ANISOLOBUS	10, 168
distinctus, nob.	169
Fockei, *Miquel*	172
hebecarpus, *Müll.*	170
Hostmanni, *Miq.*	172
oblongus, nob., Pl. 26	169
Perottetii, *A. DC.*	169
Pohlianus, nob.	171
psidiifolius, nob.	172
pulcherrimus, nob.	171
puncticulosus, *Miq.*	172
rubidulus, nob.	173
Salzmanni, *A.DC.*	169
Stadelmeyeri, *Müll.*	170
Zuccarinianus, nob.	171
Anisolobus Amazonicus, Müll.	175
" var. *latifolius*, Müll.	176
cognatus, Müll.	176
cururu, Müll.	175
" var. *grandifolius*, Müll.	175
gracilipes, Müll.	220

	Page
Anisolobus hebecarpus, var. *erectus*, Müll.	171
" var. *scandens*, Müll.	171
Kappleri, Miq.	175
Sprucei, Müll.	176
Aptotheca	9, 150
corylifolia, nob., Pl. 21 B	150
Apocynum Acouci, Aubl.	98
apiculatum, Lam.	98
cordatum, Miller	122
nervosum, Miller	122
obliquum, Miller	193
scandens, Plum.	113
scandens neriifolium, Plum.	114
umbellatum, Aubl.	98
ASPIDOSPERMA	7, 21
Gomezianum, *A. DC.*, Pl. 3 A	22
Aspidosperma bicolor, Müll.	25
decipiens, Müll.	25
Lhotzkianum, Müll.	25
nitidum, Müll.	24
parvifolium, Müll.	25
polyneurum, Müll.	24
ramiflorum, Müll.	85
Reidelii, Müll.	26
Sellowii, Müll.	24
sessiliflorum, Müll.	23
ASPIDOSPERMEÆ (tribe)	7
Bignonia obovata, Hook. & Arn.	75
BONAFOUSIA	8, 48
attenuata, nob.	51
Guyanensis, nob.	51
latiflora, nob.	50
obliqua, nob.	49
oblongifolia, nob.	50
olivacea, nob.	52
Perottetii, nob.	51
polyneura, nob.	53
rariflora, nob.	53
rupicola, nob.	52
undulata, *A. DC.*, Pl. 6 B	48
CAMERARIA	7, 27
Cameraria Guianensis, Aubl.	87
lutea, Lam.	87
tamaquarina, Aubl.	87
CERATITES	6, 17
amœna, Pl. 1 C	18
Cestrum nervosum, Miller	56

INDEX.

	Page
CHARIOMMA	8, 110
Domingensis, nob.	112
flava, nob.	113
mucronulata, nob.	112
nobilis, nob.	113
scandens, nob.	114
surrecta, nob., Pl. 15 B	111
verticillata, nob.	113
CODONEMMA	8, 31, 72
calycinum, nob., Pl. 8 B	73
macrocalyx, nob.	73
CONDYLOCARPON	7, 28
gracile, nob., Pl. 4 B	28
Coupoui	16
aquatica, Aubl.	16
CUPIRANA	6, 15
Aublctiana, nob., Pl. 2	16
Martiniana, nob.	17
CYCLADENIA	19, 263
humilis, Benth.	263
Cycladenia Harrisonii, Lem.	128, 263
DIPLADENIA	9, 153
alexicaca, A. DC.	156
androssæmifolia, A. DC.	156
Gardneriana, A. DC.	155
gentianoides, A. DC.	157
illustris, A. DC., Pl. 22	153
linearis, Müll.	157
longiloba, A. DC.	157
rosa-campestris, Lem.	156
sancta, A. DC.	154
saponaria, A. DC.	157
scabra, Müll.	155
epigeliæflora, Müll.	157
velutina, A. DC.	154
venulosa, Müll.	156
Dipladenia acuminata, Hook.	162
atroviolacea, A. DC.	159
coccinea, Müll.	141
crassinoda, Müll.	158
„ Lindl.	159
Fendleri, Müll.	168
flava, Hook.	113
fragrans, A. DC.	162
gentianoides, var., Müll.	154
Harrisii, Purdie	128
Harrisonii, Müll.	128
illustris, var. glabra, Müll.	155, 156
linariæfolia, A. DC.	164

	Page
Dipladenia Martiniana, Müll.	161
„ var. glabra, Müll.	159
„ var. pubescens, Müll.	156
Moricandiana, Müll.	162
nobilis, Lem.	113
pastorum, A. DC.	164
peduncularis, A. DC.	165
polymorpha, var. brevifolia, Müll.	165
„ var. peduncularis, Müll.	165
„ var. puberula, Müll.	165
„ var. tenuifolia, Müll.	164
pulchella, A. DC.	157
Riedelii, Müll.	160
Sellowii, Müll.	161
epigeliæflora, var. longiloba, Müll.	157
tenuifolia, A. DC.	164
„ var. puberula, A. DC.	165
urophylla, Hook.	161
vincæflora, Van Houtte	165
xanthostoma, Müll.	157, 212
ECHITEÆ (class)	8
ECHITES	10, 191
acuminata, R. & P.	197
acutiloba, A. DC.	198
albiflora, nob.	204
andina, nob.	204
Andrieuxii, nob.	206
brachyloba, nob.	203
chlorantha, Schlecht.	196
citrifolia, H. B. K.	200
congesta, H. B. K.	200
convolvulacea, A. DC., Pl. 29	195
disadena, Miq.	204
glandulosa, R. & P.	196
hirsuta, R. & P.	198
hirtiflora, A. DC.	200
Japonensis, Stadelm.	205
Karwinskii, nob.	206
lanata, Mart. & Gal.	207
laxa, R. & P.	197
linearis, Vell.	207
litorea, H. B. K.	199
longiflora, nob.	194
lutea, Vell.	194
Manscana, A. DC.	201
membranacea, A. DC.	196
Mexicana, nob.	205
microcalyx, A. DC.	203
montana, H. B. K.	199

2 o

ECHITES
obliqua, nob. 193
ovata, R. Browne 192
pallida, nob. 195
riparia, H. B. K. 199
subsagittata, R. & P. 198
subsessilis, A. DC. 199
Surinamensis, Miq. 203
trifida, Jacq. (non Müll. nec Griseb.) 202
tubiflora, Mart. & Gal. 206
tubulosa, Benth. 202
umbellata, Jacq. 193
Vauthieri, A. DC. 201
venenosa, Stadelm. 205
Veraguensis, Seem. 203
Echites adglutinata, Griseb. (non Jacq.) 236
„ Jacq. 236
Almadensis, Stadelm. 179
Amazonica, Stadelm. 175
angustifolia, Benth. (non Poir.) 231
„ Poir. 230
annularis, Linn. 216
„ Pavon (non Linn.) 259
antennacea, A. DC. 251
arborea, Vell. 89
asperuginis, Sw. 237
atro-purpurea, Lindl. 159
atro-violacea, Stadelm. 159
augusta, Vell. 130
barbata, Desv. 123
(Urechites) barbata, Griseb. 123
Berterii, A. DC. 180
bicolor, Miq. 251
bicornis, Spruce 175
biflora, Jacq. 121
bifurcata, Pöpp. 178
bignoniæflora, Schlecht. 77
Blanchetii, A. DC. 220
Bogotense, H. B. K. 82
brachystachya, Benth. 222
bracteata, H. B. K. 239
„ Vell. 102
brevipes, Benth. 224
Brownei, Griseb. 232
calycosa, Rich. 140
campestris, Vell. 121
Chilensis, A. DC. 115
„ Müll. 115
ciliata, Stadelm. 188
cinicifuga, Moc. & Sess. 228

Echites cinerea, Rich. 141
circinalis, A. DC., var. Thomasiana 237
„ Griseb. (non Sw.) 236
„ „ var. adglutinata 237
„ Müll. (non Sw.) 238
„ Sw. (non Müll.) 236
Claussenii, A. DC. 187
coalita, Müll. (non Vell.) 153, 201
„ Vell. 152
coccinea, Hook. 141
„ var. ovata, Hook. 141
cognata, Stadelm. 176
cordata, A. DC. 212
coriacea, Benth. 177
corymbosa, Jacq. 97
crassifolia, Spruce 139
crassinoda, Gardn. 158
crassipes, Rich. 140
Cubensis, Griseb. 182
Cururu, Mart. 175
„ var. grandifolia, Stadelm. 175
Cuyabensis, A. DC. 223
densevenulosa, Stadelm. 170
denticulata, Vell. 257
dichotoma, H. B. K. 233
didyma, Vell. 152
difformis, Walth. 99
discolor, Moritz 224
Domingensis, Sw. 112
Ehrenbergii, Schlecht. 121
elegans, Benth. 178
emarginata, Vell. 250
erecta, Vell. 249
ferruginea, A. Rich. 227
floribunda, Sw. 243
Fluminensis, A. DC. 185
fragrans, Stadelm. 162
Franciscea, Hook. (non Lindl.), var. pallidiflora 211
„ Lindl. (non Hook.) 212
funiformis, Vell. 219
geminata, R. & Sch. 178
glaucescens, Mart. & Gal. 214
gracilipes, Stadelm. 220
gracilis, H. B. K. 240
grandiflora, Hook. & Arn. 130
„ var. minor, Hook. 131
„ Mey. 127
„ Stadelm. (non Mey.) 174
Guanabarica, Cæsar. 218
Guarantica, St.-Hil. 129

INDEX.

	Page
Echites Guayaquilensis, Benth.	233
Guianensis, A. DC.	235
kebecorpa, Benth.	170
heterophylla, Gmel.	112
„ Miq. (non Gmel.)	116
hirsuta, Hook. (non Vell.)	209
„ Vell.	185
hirtella, Benth. (non H. B. K.)	234
„ H. B. K.	234
Hookeri, A. DC.	141
hypoglauca, Stadelm.	173
hypoleuca, Benth.	140
illustris, Vell.	153
insignis, Spreng.	127
jasminiflora, M. & Gal.	235
Javitensis, Benth. (non H. B. K.)	190
„ H. B. K.	239
lanuginosa, M. & Gal.	139
lappulacea, Lam.	237
„ var. asperuginis, A. DC.	237
lasiocarpa, A. DC.	209
leptoloba, Stadelm.	211
leptophylla, A. DC.	221
linearifolia, Ham.	230
„ Stadelm. (non Ham.)	221
longiflora, Desf.	130
lucida, R. & Sch.	123
macrantha, R. & Sch.	127
macrocalyx, Müll.	136
macrocarpa, Rich.	108
macrophylla, H. B. K.	240
macrostoma, Benth.	123
madida, Vell.	121
Martiana, Stadelm.	161
Martii, Müll.	152
Maximiliana, Stadelm.	212
megagros, Vell.	149
Meyeriana, R. & Sch.	127
microphylla, A. DC. (non Stadelm.)	218
„ Stadelm.	219
mollissima, H. B. K.	240
multifolia, nob.	131
myrtifolia, R. & Sch.	232
nitida, Vahl	177
nutans, And.	255
Oaxacana, A. DC.	234
odorifera, Vell.	151
ovalifolia, Poir.	248
paludosa, H. B. K.	241
„ Vahl (non H. B. K.)	119

	Page
Echites (Laubertia) paludosa, Griseb.	122
palustris, Salzm.	213
pandurata, A. DC.	182
pastorum, Stadelm.	164
Pavonii, A. DC.	198
peduncularis, Stadelm.	165
peltigera, Stadelm.	133
peltata, Müll. (non Vell.)	134
„ „ (in parte)	135
„ Vell.	134
petræa, St. Hil.	131
pilosa, Vell.	106
pinifolia, St. Hil.	131
plicata, A. DC.	134
Pohliana, Stadelm.	171
Prieurii, A. DC.	182
psidiifolia, Mart.	172
ptarmica, Müll. (non Pöpp.)	115
„ Pöpp.	115
puberula, Mich.	99
pubescens, Hook. & Arn.	114
„ Willd. (non Hook. & Arn.)	186
pulchella, Gardn.	157
pulcherrima, Pohl	171
puncticulosa, Rich.	172
pycnantha, Steud.	264
quinquangularis, Jacq.	217
repens, A. DC. (non Jacq.)	230
„ Jacq.	229
revoluta, A. DC.	238
rosacampestris, Hügel	156
rosea, A. DC.	232
rugosa, Benth.	222
sancta, Stadelm.	154
Sagræi, A. DC.	180
sanguinolenta, Juss.	255
secundiflora, A. DC.	210
semidigyna, Berg	213
sessilis, Vell.	104
speciosa, H. B. K.	241
spectabilis, Steud.	116
spicata, Jacq.	95
spigeliæflora, Stadelm.	157
splendens, Hook.	163
stellaris, Lindl.	210
stipellaris, Spruce	183
suaveolens, A. DC.	184
„ M. & Gal.	139
subcarnosa, Benth.	231
suberecta, Griseb. (non Jacq.)	120

INDEX.

Echites suberecta, Linn., Jacq. 125
„ Sw. (non Jacq.) 111
suberosa, Vell. 256
subsagittata, Griseb. (non R. & P.) 203
subspicata, Vahl 252
sulphurea, Vell. 201
sylvestris, A. DC. 174
symphytocarpa, Mey. 222
tenuicaulis, Stadelm. 221
tenuifolia, Mikan 164
thyrsoidea, Vell. 247
tomentosa, Vahl 213
„ var. laticordata, A. DC. 213
torosa, Jacq. 229
„ var. Brownei, A. DC. 232
torquata, Cas. 103
torulosa, Lam. (in parte) 232
„ Linn. 229
trifida, Griseb. (non Jacq.) 202
tropaeolifolia, A. DC. 133
umbellata, var. longiflora, Griseb. 194
Valenzuelana, Rich. 181
varia, Müll. 208
„ var. purpurea, Müll. 212
„ var. rosea, Müll. 210
„ var. sulphurea, Müll. 211
Velame, St.-Hil. 129
Velloziana, A. DC. 102
velutina, Stadelm. 154
verrucosa, R. & Sch. 175
versicolor, Stadelm. 221
violacea, Müll. (non Vell.) 212
„ Vell. (non Müll.) 208
virescens, St.-Hil. 130
„ Stadelm (non St.-Hil.) 130
xanthostoma, Stadelm. 212
Zuccariniana, Stadelm. 171
ELYTROPUS 8, 114
Chilensis, Müll. 115
heterophyllus, nob. 116
ptarmica, nob. 115
pubescens, nob., Pl. 14 A 114
spectabilis, nob. 116
Elytropus Chilensis, Müll. (in parte) 114, 116
ERIADENIA 8, 117
obovata, nob., Pl. 14 B 117
EXOTHOSTEMON 10, 238
bracteatum, G. Don 239
contortum, nob. 241
gracile, G. Don 240

EXOTHOSTEMON
Javitense, G. Don 239
macrophyllum, G. Don 240
mollissimum, G. Don 240
paludosum, G. Don 241
sericeum, nob. 241
speciosum, G. Don 241

FORSTERONIA 10, 242
acutifolia, Müll. 246
australis, Müll. 246
divaricata, nob. 247
floribunda, Meyer 243
minutiflora, Müll. 244
montana, Müll. 245
obtusiloba, Müll. 246
ovalifolia, nob. 248
Pavonii, A. DC. 243
protensa, nob. 246
refracta, Müll., Pl. 35 B 244
Riedelii, Müll. 245
rotundiuscula, nob. 248
Sellowii, Müll. 245
thyrsoides, Müll. 247
Forsteronia Acouci, A. DC. 98
acutifolia, var. pubescens, Müll. 246
adenobasis, Müll. 96
affinis, Müll. 101
Benthamiana, Müll. 95
bracteata, Müll. 102
Brasiliensis, A. DC. 103
corylifolia, Griseb. 150
corymbosa, Mey. (non A. DC.) 98
„ A. DC. 97
difformis, A. DC. 99
diospyrifolia, Müll. 96
embelioides, Müll. 106
floribunda, Müll. (non Mey.) 105
Gardneri, Müll. 96
glabrescens, Müll. 102
Guyanensis, Müll. 97
lancifolia, Müll. (in parte) 98
laurifolia, A. DC. 94
linearis, Müll. 207
Luschnatii, Müll. 106
macrophylla, Müll. 96
multinervia, A. DC. 103
pilosa, Müll. 106
pubescens, A. DC. 101
rufa, Müll. 104

INDEX. 285

	Page
Forsteronia Schomburgkii, A. DC.	94, 98
,, var. *umbellata*	98
spicata, Mey.	95
GEISSOSPERMUM	8, 31, 83
læve, *nob.*	84
Martianum, *nob.*	84
ramiflorum, *Mart.*	85
sericeum, *Benth. & Hook.*	86
Solandri, *nob.*	85
Vellosii, *Allem.*, Pl. 12 A	83
Habsburghia comans, Mart.	110
HÆMADICTYON	10, 254
acutifolium, *Benth.*	260
Amazonicum, *Benth.*	262
asperum, *Müll.*	258
bracteosum, *Müll.*	257
caliginosum, *nob.*	260
calycinum, *Lindl.*	259
Cayennense, *A. DC.*	256
denticulatum, *nob.*	257
exsertum, *A. DC.*	255
Gaudichaudii, *A. DC.*	256
macronourum, *Müll.*	262
marginatum, *Benth.*	256
membranaceum, *Müll.*	260
ovatum, *nob.*, Pl. 34	258
pallidum, *A. DC.*	259
papillosum, *Müll.*	261
Schizadenium, *Müll.*	261
tomentellum, *Benth.*	259
trifidum, *Pöpp.*	261
venosum, *Lindl.*	255
Hæmadictyon annulare, A. DC.	216
circinalis, G. Don	236
contortum, M. & Gal.	241
Gaudichaudii, Müll. (in parte)	258
,, ,, ,, ,,	259
glabratum, A. DC.	145
glandulosum, A. DC.	196
grandiflorum, A. DC.	127
macroneurum, Müll. (in parte)	257
megalagrion, Müll.	149
molle, A. DC.	148
nutans, A. DC.	255
parviflorum, Benth.	215
Riedelii, Müll.	216
solanifolium, Müll.	214
suberectum, G. Don	111

	Page
HANCORNIA	8, 12
Gardneri, *nob.*	12
pubescens, *Nees & Mart.*	12
speciosa, *Gomez*, Pl. 1 A	12
Hancornia floribunda, Pöpp.	13, 15
laxa, A. DC.	13
macrophylla, Spruce	68
HAPLOPHYTUM	10, 228
cimicifugum, *A. DC.*	228
HETEROTHRIX	10, 263
pycnantha, *Müll.*	264
Van Heurckii, *Müll.*	264
Hippocratea neurocarpa, Griseb.	23
HOMALADENIA	9, 164
brevifolia, *nob.*	165
linariæfolia, *nob.*	164
pastorum, *nob.*	164
peduncularia, *nob.*	165
puberula, *nob.*	165
tenuifolia, *nob.*, Pl. 24 A	164
vincæflora, *nob.*	165
LACMELLIA	6, 14
edulis, *Karst.*	14
lucida, *nob.*	14
LASEGUEA	10, 248
antennacea, *nob.*	251
bicolor, *nob.*	251
emarginata, *A. DC.*	250
erecta, *Müll.* (in parte)	249
folioca, *nob.*	253
glabra, *A. DC.*	250
Guilleminiana, *A. DC.*	249
Hookeri, *Müll.*	253
Jægeri, *nob.*	254
latiuscula, *nob.*, Pl. 35 A	251
leptocarpa, *nob.*	254
obliquinervia, *A. DC.*	250
Pentlandiana, *A. DC.*	253
pubiflora, *nob.*	253
subspicata, *nob.*	252
venustula, *nob.*	252
villosa, *nob.*	250
Laseguea acutifolia, A. DC.	249
calycosa, Griseb.	140
erecta, var. *Guilleminiana*, Müll.	249
Guilleminiana, var. *obliquinervia*, Müll.	250
LAUBERTIA	8, 124
Boissieri, *A. DC.*	124
Laubertia Urechites, Griseb.	125

INDEX.

MACOUBEA 6, 11
   Guianensis, *Aubl.* 11
MACROSIPHONIA 9, 129
   Guaranitica, *Müll.* 129
   longiflora, *Müll.* 130
   Martii, *Müll.* 130
   pinifolia, *nob.* 131
   prostrata, *nob.*, Pl. 17 131
   Velame, *Müll.* 129
   verticillata, *Müll.* 131
   virescens, *Müll.* 130
Macrosiphonia hypoleuca, Müll. 140
   suaveolens, M. & Gal. 139
   verticillata, var. *pinifolia*, Müll. ... 131
MALOUETIA 8, 86
   amplexicaulis, *Müll.* 91
   arborea, *nob.* 89
   Cubana, *A. DC.* 92
   furfuracea, *Spruce* 91
   glandulifera, *nob.*, Pl. 13 A 90
   gracilis, *A. DC.* 87
   Guianensis, *nob.* 87
   jasminoides, *nob.* 92
   lactiflua, *nob.* 88
   lanceolata, *Müll.* 88
   Martii, *Müll.* 90
   nitida, *Spruce* 91
   obtusifolia, *A.DC.* 88
   odorata, *nob.* 87
   Panamensis, *Müll.* 93
   riparia, *A. DC.* 91
   Schomburgkii, *Müll.* 88
   tamaquarina, *A. DC.* 87
   Tarumensis, *Benth.* 87
   tetrastachya, *nob.* 92
   virescens, *Spruce* 90
Malouetia cestroides, Müll. 90
   sessilis, Müll. 104
   tamaquarina, var. *minor* 87
    „ var. *Brasiliensis*, A. DC. 88
    „   „ Müll. 90
MANDEVILLA 10, 184
   suaveolens, *Lindl.* 184
Mandevilla subcarnosa, Benth. & Hook. .. 231
   Van Heurckii, Benth. & Hook. 264
MANOTHRIX 7, 28
   nodosa, *nob.*, Pl. 5 B 30
   valida, *nob.*, Pl. 5 A 29
MERIZADENIA 8, 31, 78
   amplifolia, *nob.*, Pl. 11 A 79

MERIZADENIA
   arcuata, *nob.* 79
   Sananho, *nob.* 78
MESECHITES 10, 229
   Andrieuxii, *nob.* 235
   angustata, *nob.* 231
   angustifolia, *nob.* 230
   Brownei, *nob.* 232
   dichotoma, *nob.* 233
   Guayaquilensis, *nob.* 233
   Guianensis, *nob.* 235
   hastata, *nob.* 233
   hirtella, *nob.* 234
   hirtellula, *nob.* 234
   jasminiflora, *nob.* 235
   lanceolata, *nob.* 230
   linearifolia, *nob.* 230
   myrtifolia, *Müll.*, Pl. 33 A 232
   Oaxacana, *nob.* 234
   repens, *nob.* 229
   rosea, *nob.* 232
   subcarnosa, *nob.* 231
   torulosa, *nob.* 229
Mesechites brevipes, Müll. 224
   Japurensis, Müll. 205
   sulphurea, Müll. 201
   trifida, Müll. (in parte) 202
MICRADENIA 9, 158
   acuminata, *nob.* 162
   atroviolacea, *nob.* 159
    „ var. *ovata*, nob. 159
   crassinoda, *A. DC.*, Pl. 23 158
   fragrans, *nob.* 162
   hirsutula, *nob.* 160
   Martiana, *A. DC.* 161
   Moricandiana, *A. DC.* 162
   nodulosa, *nob.* 159
   Riedelii, *nob.* 160
   Sellowii, *nob.* 161
   splendens, *A. DC.* 163
   urophylla, *nob.* 161
MITOZUS 10, 217
   Blanchetii, *nob.* 220
   brachystachyus, *nob.* 222
   brevipes, *nob.* 224
   concinnus, *nob.* 223
   Cuyabensis, *nob.* 223
   discolor, *nob.* 224
   exilis, *nob.*, Pl. 31 218
   funiformis, *nob.* 219

INDEX. 287

MITOZUS
 gracilipes, *nob*. 220
 Guanabaricus, *nob*. 218
 Jamaicensis, *nob*. 225
 leptophyllus, *nob*. 221
 Mexicanus, *nob*. 225
 microphyllus, *nob*. 219
 rugosus, *nob*. 222
 scabridulus, *nob*. 224
 symphytocarpus, *nob*. 223
 tenellus, *nob*. 220
 tenuicaulis, *nob*. 221
 versicolor, *nob*. 221

Neriandra angustifolia, A. DC. 109
 hancorniæfolia, A. DC. 109
 Havanensis, Müll. 110
 Martiana, Müll. 110
 suberecta, A. DC. 111
Nerium lanceolatum, Plum. 230
 Oleander, Lun. (in parte) 113
 sarmentosum (2), P. Browne 111
  " (4), P. Browne 232
 caule volubili, Plum. 237

ODONTADENIA 8, 126
 formosa, *nob*. 127
 grandiflora, *nob*., Pl. 16 127
 Harrisii, *nob*. 128
 speciosa, *Benth*. 126
Odontadenia, sp., Benth. 176
 angustifolia, A. DC. 220
 cordata, A. DC. 177
 coriacea, Müll. 177
 geminata, Müll. (in parte) 178
 grandiflora, Miq. 127
 hypoglauca, Müll. 173
  " Müll. (in parte) 174
 lucida, Müll. 123
 nitida, Müll. 177
 Pöppigii, Müll. 179
 speciosa, Griseb. (non Benth.) 128
  " Müll. (non Benth.) 127
 sylvestris, Müll. 174
  " " (in parte) 177
Odontostigma Galeottiana, Rich. 76

Parsonsia bracteata, Hook. & Arn. 253
 floribunda, R. Br. 243
 leptocarpa, Hook. & Arn. 254

Parsonsia spicata, R. Br. 95
PERICTENIA 10, 182
 stipellaris, *nob*., Pl. 28 183
Periploca (*Nerium*) *oblongo-cordata*, Plum. ... 193
 scandens, Miller 122
PESCHIERA 8, 31, 32
 acuminata, *nob*. 43
 affinis, *nob*. 40
 albidiflora, *nob*. 39
 australis, *nob*. 46
 blanda, *nob*. 44
 breviflora, *nob*. 45
 Catharinensis, *nob*. 41
 concinna, *nob*. 44
 cuspidata, *nob*. 37
 diversifolia, Miq. 39
 echinata, *A. DC*. 33
 fallax, *nob*. 40
 florida, *nob*. 41
 fuchsiæfolia, *nob*., Pl. 6 A 34
 Gaudichaudii, *nob*. 40
 gracillima, *nob*. 41
 granulosa, *nob*. 37
 heterophylla, *nob*. 38
 Hilariana, *nob*. 41
 hystrix, *A. DC*. 33
 læta, *nob*. 35
 lingulata, *nob*. 42
 Linkii, *nob*. 47
 litoralis, *nob*. 45
 lorifera, *nob*. 47
 Lundii, *nob*. 36
 multiflora, *Spruce* 45
 muricata, *A. DC*. 34
 ochracea, *nob*. 42
 præclara, *nob*. 47
 psychotriæfolia, *nob*. 42
 puberiflora, *nob*. 43
 Salzmanni, *nob*. 40
 Solandri, *nob*. 46
 solanifolia, *nob*. 46
 Spixiana, *nob*. 36
 stenoloba, *nob*. 38
 tenuiflora, *Pöpp*. 38
 umbrosa, *nob*. 44
Peschiera albiflora, Miq. 204
 latiflora, Benth. 50
 muricata, Benth. (non A. DC.) 72
PHRISSOCARPUS 8, 31, 71
 rigidus, *nob*., Pl. 9 A 72

	Page
PLUMERIA	7, 26
POMPHIDEA	6, 18
Swartziana, *nob.*, Pl. 1 D	19
PRESTONIA	9, 143
Bahiensis, *Müll.*	147
calycina, *Müll.*	146
Cearensis, *nob.*	148
glabrata, *H. B. K.*	145
hirsuta, *Müll.*	147
ipomeifolia, *A. DC.*	145
læta, *nob.*	149
lanata, *Müll.*	147
latifolia, *Benth.*	145
lutescens, *Müll.*	147
megalagrion, *nob.*	149
mollis, *H. B. K.*	148
Seemanni, *nob.*	146
Surinamensis, *Müll.*	147
tomentosa, *R. Br.*, Pl. 20 B	144
Prestonia annularis, G. Don	216
hirsuta, Spreng.	198
Mexicana, A. DC.	225
Peruviana, Spreng.	196
quinquangularis, Spreng.	217
sericea, M. & Gal.	241
tomentosa, Seem. (non R. Br.)	146
PRESTONIOPSIS	9, 166
Fendleri, *nob.*	168
hirsuta, *nob.*	167
pubescens, *Müll.*, Pl. 24 B	166
venosa, *nob.*	167
RHABDADENIA	8, 118
barbata, *nob.*	123
biflora, *Müll.*	121
campestris, *nob.*	121
cordata, *nob.*	122
laxiflora, *nob.*	120
lucida, *nob.*	123
macrostoma, *Müll.*	123
madida, *nob.*	121
nervosa, *nob.*	122
paludosa, *nob.*, Pl. 15 A	119
Pohlii, *Müll.*	119
Rhabdadenia Berterii, Müll.	180
Cubensis, Müll.	181
Ehrenbergii, Müll.	121
Lindeniana, Müll.	180
„ var. *angustifolia*, Müll.	180
Sagræi, Müll.	180

	Page
Rhabdadenia Wrightiana, Müll.	181
RHAPTOCARPUS	9, 151
apiculatus, *nob.*	153
coalitus, *nob.*	152
didymus, *nob.*	152
Martii, *nob.*	152
odoriferus, *nob.*, Pl. 21 A	151
RHODOCALYX	9, 138
calycosus, *nob.*	140
cinereus, *nob.*	141
coccineus, *nob.*	141
crassifolius, *nob.*, Pl. 20 A	139
crassipes, *nob.*	140
cuneifolius, *nob.*	142
hypoleucus, *nob.*	140
lanuginosus, *nob.*	139
ovatus, *nob.*	141
rotundifolius, *Müll.*	138
suaveolens, *nob.*	139
Tweedianus, *nob.*	142
RHYGOSPIRA	8, 31, 67
paucifolia, *nob.*	69
quadrangularis, *nob.*, Pl. 10 A	68
reticulata, *nob.*	69
sinuosa, *nob.*	70
Sprucei, *nob.*	70
ternstrœmiacea, *nob.*	71
venulosa, *nob.*	68
ROBBIA	8, 107
cestroides, *A. DC.*, Pl. 12 B	107
gossipina, *nob.*, Pl. 12 B	108
macrocarpa, *nob.*	108
ROBBIEÆ (tribe)	8
SECONDATIA	10, 225
densiflora, *A. DC.*, Pl. 32	226
ferruginea, *nob.*	227
floribunda, *A. DC.*	227
foliosa, *A. DC.*	227
Peruviana, *Pöpp.*	228
Schlimiana, *Müll.*	227
Secondatia arborea, Müll.	89
difformis, Bth. & Hook.	99
SKYTANTHUS	8, 109
acutus, *Meyer*	109
hancornizefolius, *nob.*	109
Havanensis, *nob.*	110
Martianus, *nob.*	110
Skytalanthus acutus, Schauer	109
STEMMADENIA	8, 31, 74

INDEX.

	Page
STEMMADENIA	
bella, *nob.*	77
bignoniæflora, *nob.*	77
Galeottiana, *nob.*	76
glabra, *Benth.*	74
grandiflora, *nob.*	75
insignis, *nob.*, Pl. 10 B.	76
mollis, *Benth.*	75
pubescens, *Benth*,	75
Stemmadenia Guatemalensis, Müll.	93
STIFFCOMA	9, 132
macrocalyx, *nob.*	136
mucronata, *nob.*	135
ovata, *nob.*, Pl. 19	137
parabolica, *nob.*	137
peltata, *nob.*	134
peltigera, *Müll.*	133
plicata, *nob.*	134
pulchra, *nob.*, Pl. 18	135
speciosa, *nob.*	136
STREMPELIOPSIS	7, 26
Cubensis, *Benth. & Hook.*	26
TABERNA	8, 31, 61
cymosa, *nob.*, Pl. 8 A	62
discolor, *nob.*	62
disparifolia, *nob.*	63
disticha, *nob.*	64
laurina, *nob.*	63
Pöppigii, *nob.*	63
Riedelii, *nob.*	64
TABERNÆMONTANA	8, 53
Acapulcensis, *nob.*	57
alba, *Miller*	56
amygdalæfolia, *Jacq.*	56
Berterii, *A. DC.*	58
citrifolia, *Plum.*, Pl. 7 A	54
lanceolata, *Linn.*, Pl. 7 B	55
laurifolia, *Linn.*	57
neriifolia, *Vahl*	55
occidentalis, *nob.*	58
utilis, *Arn.*	58
Tabernæmontana acuminata, Müll.	43
acutissima, Müll.	66
affinis, Müll.	40
amygdaliæfolia, Seem (non Jacq.)	57
angulata, Mart.	65
arcuata, R. & P.	79
australis, Müll.	46
Benthaminina, Müll.	45

	Page
Tabernæmontana Benthaminina (*bis*), Müll.	73
bracteolaris, Müll.	33
calycina, Spruce	73
Catharinensis, Müll.	41
cestroides, Nees & Mart.	107
collina, Gardn.	34
congesta, Benth.	65
cymosa, Soland (non Jacq.)	46
„ Mart. (non Jacq.)	84
echinata, Aubl.	33
„ Vell. (non Aubl.)	33
fallax, Müll.	40
fasciculata, Poir.	100
flavescens, R. & Sch.	82
flavicans, R. & Sch.	82
„ Müll. (non R. & Sch.)	50
frutescens, Sloane	54
„ P. Brown (non Sloane)	57
fuchsiæfolia, A. DC.	34
Gaudichaudii, A. DC.	40
glabrata, Mart.	81
gracilis, Benth.	87
„ Müll. (non Benth.)	41
grandiflora, Jacq.	75
Guyanensis, Müll.	51
heterophylla, Vahl	38
„ Benth. (non Vahl)	39
Hilariana, Müll.	41
hirtula, Mart.	67
hystrix, Steud.	33
jasminoides, H. B. K.	92
lactiflua, Benth.	88
læta, A. DC.	35
„ Mart. (non A. DC.)	35
„ var. puberiflora, Müll.	41
lævigata, Mart.	82
lævis, Vell.	84
laurifolia, Ker (non Linn.)	63
„ Schott (non Ker nec Linn.)	76
Linkii, A. DC.	47
litoralis, H.B.K.	45
longifolia, Benth.	66
Lundii, A. DC.	36
macrocalyx (odontadenia), Müll.	73
macrophylla, Poir.	79, 96
„ Müll. (non Poir.)	72
Meyeri, G. Don	80
multiflora, R. & Sch.	47
muricata, Müll. (non R. & Sch.)	42
muricata, R. & Sch.	34

2 P

INDEX.

	Page
Tabernæmontana oblongifolia, A. DC.	50
ochracea, Spruce	42
odorata, Vahl.	87
olivacea, Müll.	52
parviflora, Poir.	100
paucifolia, Spruce	69
Perrottetii, A. DC.	51
populifolia, Poir.	99
psychotriæfolia, H. B. K.	42
Rauwolfia, A. DC.	40
recurva, Sagot	80
reticulata, A. DC.	69
riparia, H. B. K.	91
rubro-striolata, Müll.	65
rupicola, Benth.	52
" var. *Sprucei*, Müll.	53
" var. *oblongifolia*, Müll.	53
Salzmanni, A. DC.	40
Sananho, R. & P.	78
sessilis, Vell.	104
solanifolia, A. DC.	46
Spixiana, Mart.	36
Sprucei, Müll.	70
stenoloba, Müll.	38
subcordata, Linn.	193
submollis, Mart.	67
tenuiflora, Müll.	38
ternstræmiacea, Müll.	71
tetrastachya, H. B. K.	92
umbrosa, H. B. K.	44
undulata, Meyer (non Vahl)	80
" Vahl (non Mey.)	48
Wulfschlagelii, Griseb.	81
TABERNÆMONTANEÆ (tribe)	8, 31
TEMNADENIA	10, 207
annularis, nob.	216
bicrura, nob.	208
cordata, nob.	212
corrugulata, nob.	215
Franciscea, nob.	212
glaucescens, nob.	214
lasiocarpa, nob.	210
leptoloba, nob.	211
Lobbiana, nob., Pl. 30	209
pallidiflora, nob.	211
palustris, nob.	213
parviflora, nob.	215
quinquangularis, nob.	217
Riedelii, nob.	216
secundiflora, nob.	211

	Page
TEMNADENIA	
semidigyna, nob.	213
solanifolia, nob.	214
stellaris, nob.	210
tenuicula, nob.	216
tomentosa, nob.	213
violacea, nob., Pl. 30	208
xanthostoma, nob.	212
THENARDIA	10, 242
floribunda, H. B. K.	242
suaveolens, M. & Gal.	242
Thenardia corymbosa, Benth.	98
laurifolia, Benth.	94
umbellata, Spreng.	98
THEVETIA	6, 20
ahouai, A. DC., Pl. 4 A	20
calophylla, nob., Pl. 4 A	20
cornuta, Müll.	21
plumeriæfolia, Benth.	20
THYRSOMA	9, 22
bicolor, nob.	25
decipiens, nob.	23
Llotschyana, nob.	25
nitida, nob.	24
parvifolia, nob.	25
polyneura, nob.	24
Riedelii, nob.	26
Sellowii, nob.	24
sessiliflora, nob., Pl. 3 B	23
THYRSANTHUS	8, 93
Acouci, nob.	96
adenobasis, nob.	96
affinis, nob.	101
Aubletianus, nob.	98
Benthamianus, nob.	95
bracteatus, nob., Pl. 13 B	102
Brasiliensis, nob.	103
corymbiferus, nob.	98
corymbosus, nob.	97
crebriflorus, nob.	105
difformis, nob.	99
diospyrifolius, nob.	96
embelioides, A. DC.	106
fasciculatus, nob.	100
Gardneri, A. DC.	96
glabrescens, nob.	102
gracilis, Benth.	99
Guyanensis, nob.	97
laurifolius, nob.	94
Luschnatii, nob.	106

INDEX.

	Page
THYRSANTHUS	
macrophyllus, *nob.*	96
meridionalis, *nob.*	106
multinervius, *nob.*	103
myrianthus, *nob.*	105
parviflorus, *nob.*	100
pilosus, *A. DC.*	106
placidus, *nob.*	101
populifolius, *nob.*	99
pubescens, *nob.*	101
pyriformis, *nob.*	100
rufus, *nob.*	104
Schomburgkii, *Benth.*	94
sessilis, *nob.*	104
spicatus, *nob.*	95
Thyrsanthus corylifolius, Griseb.	150
sericeus, Sagot	86
URECHITES	8, 124
Andrieuxii, *Müll.*	125
Karwinskii, *Müll.*	125

	Page
URECHITES	
suberecta, *Müll.*	125
Urechites barbata, Müll.	123
Jægeri, Müll.	254
Jamaicensis, Griseb.	112
neriandra, Griseb.	111
Vallesia Vellozii, Ried.	83
Vinca sternutatoria, Pöpp.	115
Wheeleria alternifolia, Soland.	85
oppositifolia, Soland.	103
ZSCHOKKEA	6, 15
arborescens, *Müll.*	15
floribunda, *Müll.*	15
gracilis, *Müll.*	15
Guianensis, *Müll.*	15
microcarpa, *Müll.*	15
monosperma, *Müll.*	15
ramosissima, *Müll.*	15

PRINTED BY TAYLOR AND FRANCIS, RED LION COURT, FLEET STREET.

www.ingramcontent.com/pod-product-compliance
Lightning Source LLC
Chambersburg PA
CBHW020233240426
43672CB00006B/511